Antipodean Early Modern

Antipodean Early Modern

European Art in Australian Collections, c. 1200–1600

Edited by
Anne Dunlop

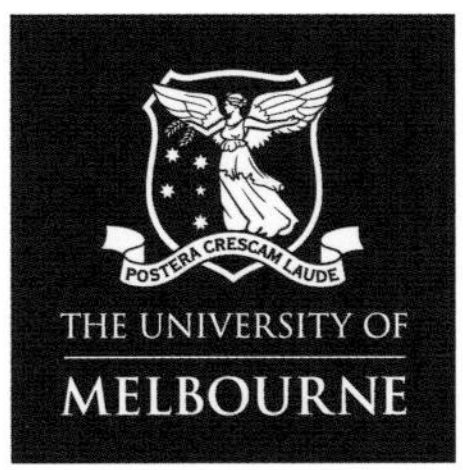

Amsterdam University Press

The publication of this book was made possible with the support of the University Collections of the University of Melbourne.

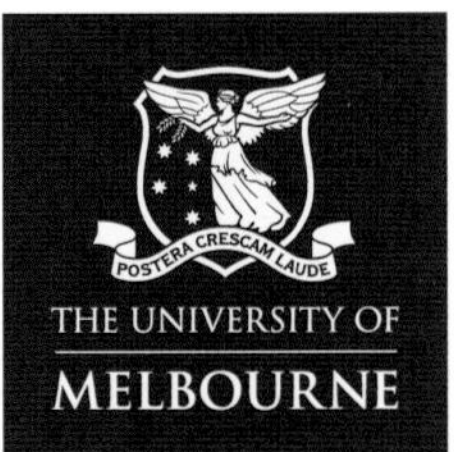

Cover illustration, Front: Nuremberg, The Altvater costume of 1492, in *Schembart Buch* (*The Book of the Nuremberg Shrovetide Carnival*). Folio 32v, *c.*1540. Paper, 32.8cm × 21cm. Kerry Stokes Collection, Perth. Accession number LIB.2006.088. Image courtesy of the Kerry Stokes Collection.

Back: Gerard David et al. Virgin and Child and Landscape from the *Rothschild Prayer Book*. Folio 197v, *c.*1505. Tempera on parchment, 22.8cm × 16cm. Kerry Stokes Collection, Perth. Image courtesy of the Kerry Stokes Collection, Perth.

Cover design: Coördesign, Leiden
Lay-out: Konvertus / Newgen

Amsterdam University Press English-language titles are distributed in the US and Canada by the University of Chicago Press.

ISBN   978 94 6298 520 9
e-ISBN   978 90 4853 623 8
DOI   10.5117/9789462985209
NUR   685

Contents

List of Figures

Kate Challis

Dagmar Eichberger

Elaine Shaw

Bernard Muir

Jan Fox

Hilary Maddocks

Miya Tokumitsu

Callum Reid

Ursula Betka

Charles Zika

Acknowledgments

This book grew from a series of lectures presented in conjunction with the exhibition *An Illumination: The Rothschild Prayer Book and Other Works from the Kerry Stokes Collection, c. 1280–1685*, held at the Ian Potter Art Museum of the University of Melbourne in 2015. I am grateful to the many people who have made the exhibition and the present book possible, Kerry Stokes first among them. Philip Kent, former University Librarian at Melbourne, supported both projects from beginning to end and in too many ways to count. Shane Carmody put together the lecture series and public programing, and he and Philip first proposed this book. Kelly Gellatly and her staff at the Potter presented a beautiful and rewarding show. My colleagues in Art History and Curatorship have answered questions and provided references and information on collections that were new to me. Erica Gaffney at Amsterdam University Press is the kind of editor and collaborator that every academic writer would like to have. The research assistant for this project, Louise Box, deserves very special thanks for her professionalism, organization, and intelligent support to the writers at every stage of the process.

It is a pleasure that my first official task as the fourth Herald Chair of Fine Arts at the University of Melbourne is to edit a book that attests to the legacy of the two previous Herald Chairs, Margaret M. Manion and Jaynie Anderson. Margaret was the curator for *An Illumination*, and her influence as a teacher and scholar will be clear in many of the essays that follow. Jaynie's work on Italian Renaissance art is also well represented. Together they have made the study of early European art a central strength at Melbourne and beyond. I am grateful to both for their gracious and warm help.

1. Legacies of early European art in Australian collections

Anne Dunlop

Dunlop, Anne (ed.), *Antipodean Early Modern. European Art in Australian Collections, c. 1200–1600*, Amsterdam University Press, 2018

DOI: 10.5117/9789462985209/CH01

Abstract

Australia has rich collections of medieval and early-modern European art. Although not always well known outside the country, they are the legacy of a strong tradition of private and public collecting and bequests. This essay is intended as an introduction to this history, from the Felton Bequest of the early twentieth century, to the recent acquisitions of the Kerry Stokes Collection. It also introduces the legacy of art history around the Herald Chair of Fine Arts at the University of Melbourne, as well as the major themes and subjects of the rest of the book.

Keywords: Art Collecting, Australia; Kerry Stokes Collection; Felton Bequest; Medieval art; Renaissance art; Herald Chair of Fine Arts

The objects discussed in this book are likely to surprise many people. Most of them were featured in an exhibition called *An Illumination: the Rothschild Prayer Book and Other Works from the Kerry Stokes Collection, c.1280–1685*, held at the University of Melbourne in late 2015. The sixty-one objects exhibited ranged from manuscripts to stained glass and panel paintings, and were drawn from one of the great private collections of European medieval art: the Kerry Stokes Collection of Perth, Western Australia. Many of the essays here began as public lectures associated with the exhibition, while others developed in response to the objects presented and their links to other artworks in local and national collections.

At the centre of the exhibition was one of the most extraordinary European manuscripts that has come down to us. The *Rothschild* *Prayer Book* runs to 254 folios and was written and illuminated by the most important Netherlandish artists of the early sixteenth century; individual leaves were done by Gerard David among others (Figure 1.1). The manuscript has been linked to the immediate circle of Margaret of Austria, daughter and sister of Holy Roman Emperors, Regent of the Netherlands, and an important patron of art in general and of manuscripts in particular. But its exact patronage and date of production are uncertain. It is one of a cluster of beautiful and lavish manuscript books created for the highest court circles of sixteenth-century Europe.[1]

Until fairly recently, the Kerry Stokes Collection was not widely known beyond Australia. In 2014, however, when the collector acquired the

---

1   Manion, *An Illumination*.

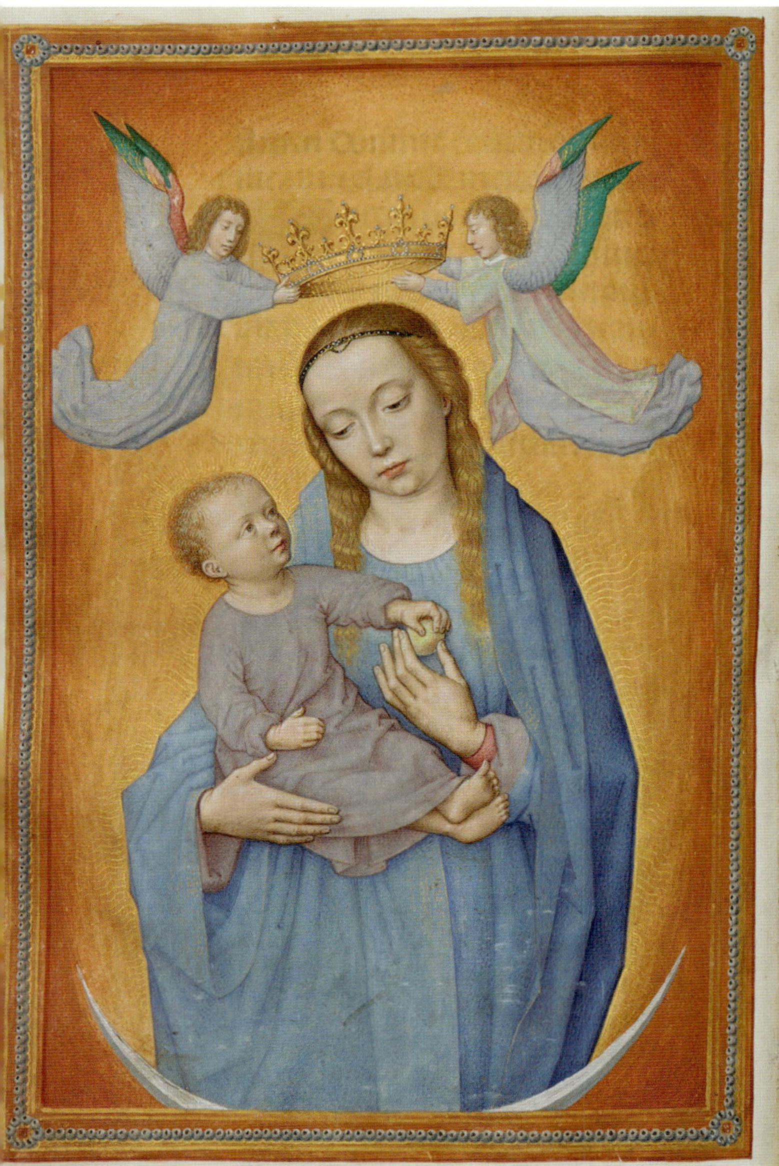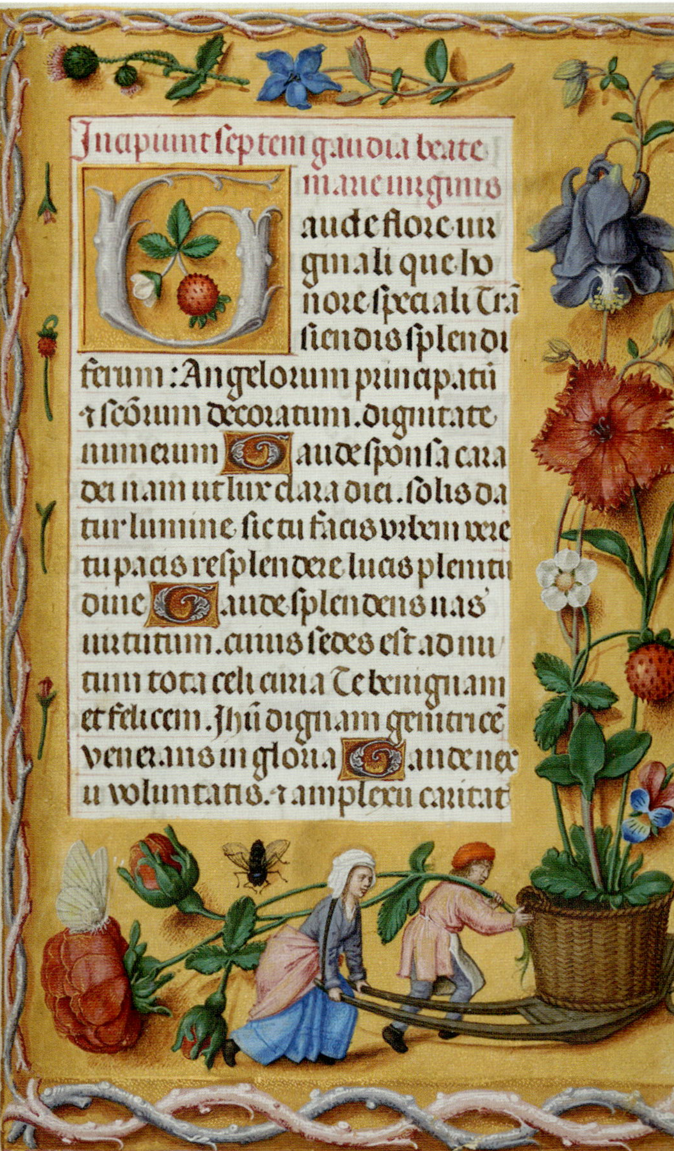

Figure 1.1: Gerard David et al. Virgin and Child and Landscape from the *Rothschild Prayer Book*. Folios 197v–198r, *c.*1505. Tempera on parchment, each folio 22.8cm × 16cm. Kerry Stokes Collection, Perth.

Prayer Book for more than 13.5 million US dollars, it made international news. The sale price set a new record for a manuscript at auction, and it was widely covered in the art press and beyond.[2] Many of the news reports suggest bemusement, not only at the cost, but that European art of any sort should be found in Australia in the first place, let alone in Perth, sometimes said to be the most remote capital city on the planet.

Yet the *Prayer Book* is only one of the many important medieval and early-modern European art objects in the Stokes Collection and elsewhere in Australia. To take a single case, the National Gallery of Victoria in Melbourne ('NGV') houses portraits by Rembrandt and El Greco (Figure 1.2), a bust of Cardinal Richelieu

▼ Figure 1.2: El Greco. *Portrait of a Cardinal. c.*1600. Oil on canvas, 57cm × 46.0cm. National Gallery of Victoria, Melbourne. Felton Bequest 1950, 2253–4.

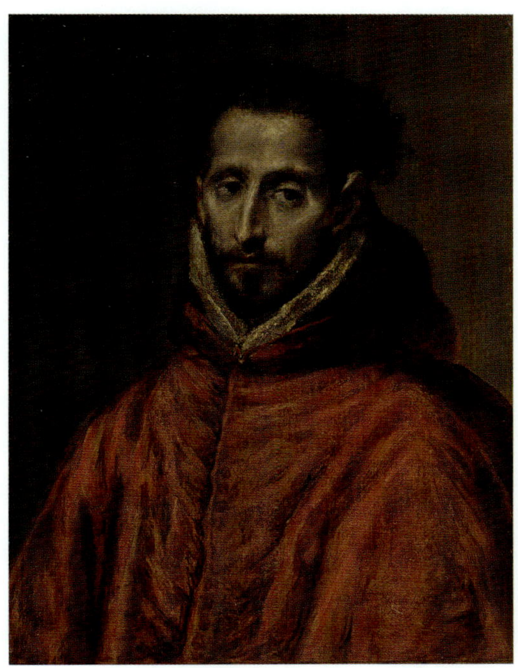

by Bernini, and history paintings by Tiepolo, Titian, and Veronese; it has an early Paolo Uccello, Renaissance maiolica and gilded glass reliquaries from fourteenth-century Italy; medieval French and Spanish sculpture, a tiny *Man of Sorrows* by Memling (Figure 1.3) and enormous Flemish polyptych altarpieces.[3] These and other national collections in Australia have encouraged a rich public interest in art and an important tradition of writing and research on early European art and culture. It is the goal of this book to make this artistic legacy and these holdings better known, beginning with the Stokes Collection itself, as well as to showcase the tradition of art-historical scholarship and the range of current research and inquiry in this country. The hope is to encourage further work on these extraordinary collections, as much still remains to be explored.[4]

The historical richness of Australia's public collections is largely due to a series of important private patrons and bequests. In repeatedly allowing generous loans from his collection to public museums and institutions, Kerry Stokes follows a notable line of private collectors and donors. The city of Melbourne and the state of Victoria are particularly rich, largely because of a man called Alfred Felton (1831–1904), who bequeathed his enormous fortune to found a philanthropic trust there.[5] Felton

2   See for instance: Vogel, 'Renaissance Prayer Book is Set for Auction' and 'Christie's Old Master Week achieves $68 million in New York'.

3   See Gott and Benson, *Painting and Sculpture Before 1800* and Hoff, *European Paintings before 1800* for an introduction to the NGV collections; and Wilson, *Italian Maiolica* for the maiolica holdings.

4   Kisler, *Angels & Aristocrats*, has written a fundamental study and survey of European art in New Zealand public collections. Partly because of much greater number and types of objects, there is as yet no similar overview of Australian holdings.

5   John Poynton, 'Alfred Felton and the Art of Making Bequests,' and Alison Inglis, 'Alfred Felton as a Collector of Art,' in Grimwade and Vaughan, *Great Philanthropists on Trial*, pp. 36 and 37–56; Hoff, *European Paintings before 1800.* For

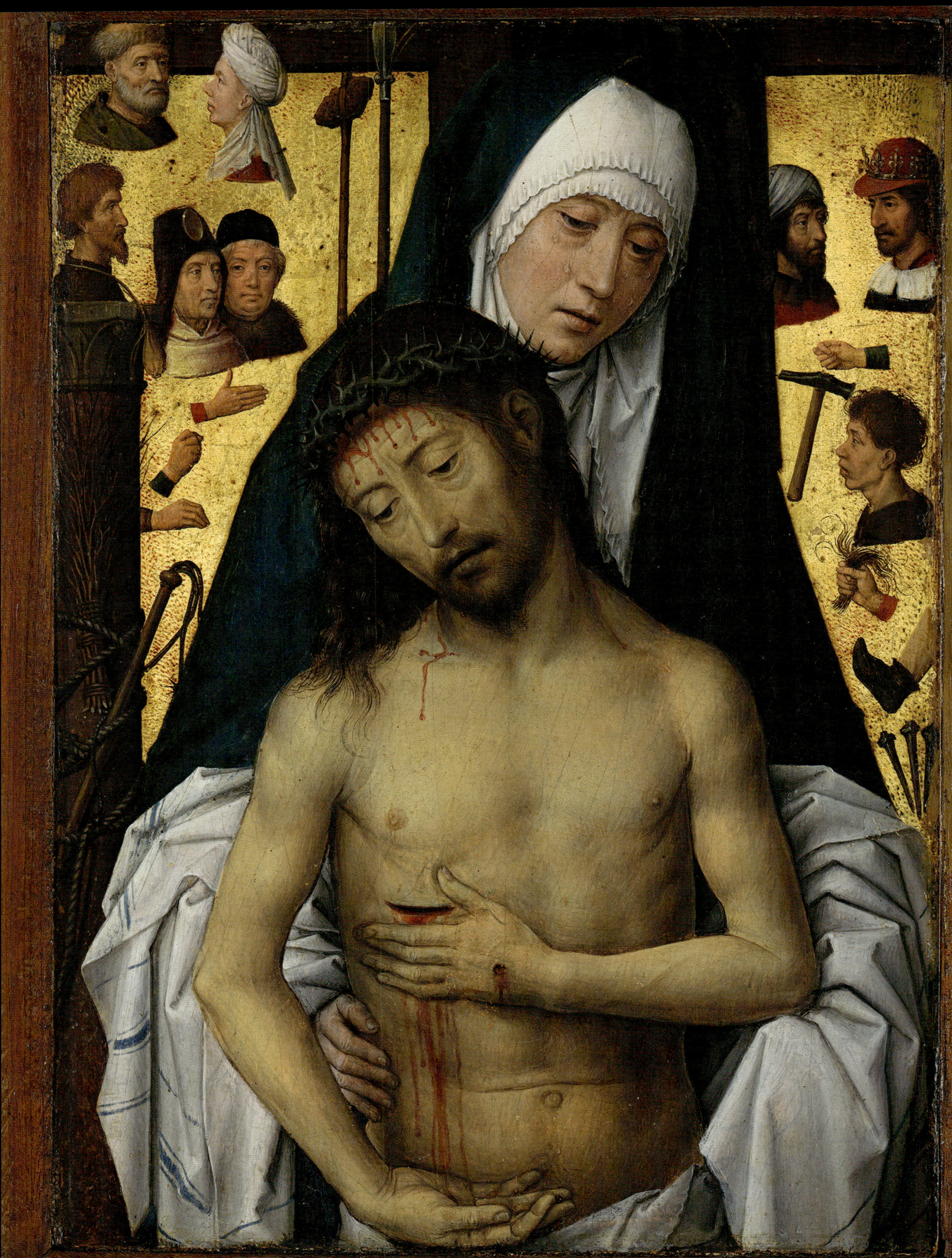

was born in England, but in 1851 a gold rush began in Victoria, and Felton was one of the many thousands who shipped out from all over the world hoping to strike it rich in the Australian goldfields. He would instead make a fortune in business, and he began to collect art. The initial *net* funding for the Felton bequest was almost 400 000 pounds, with half of it earmarked for the city's art gallery, which had been founded in 1861. Felton's own art collection was also given to the institution. Less than twenty years after Felton's death, the NGV was spending more on acquisitions than even London's National Gallery. To date, the Felton Bequest has been used to buy more than 15 000 works of art with some of the greatest artists of Renaissance and Baroque Europe well represented (Figure 1.4).

Other museums in Victoria and across Australia have also benefited from private donors and patrons, with the relatively portable manuscripts, prints, and rare books particularly well represented. The State Library of Victoria houses both medieval European manuscripts and a significant incunabula collection. It holds one of only three existing complete copies of the first printing of Euclid's *Elementa* (1482), for instance, acquired as part of the collection of the engineer Robert Carl Sticht.[6] The University of Melbourne has prints and drawings by Albrecht Dürer, Jacques Callot, Diana Mantuana and Marcantonio Raimondi, among many others, formed around the gift of Dr. John Orde Poyton in 1959 (Figure 1.5).[7] The

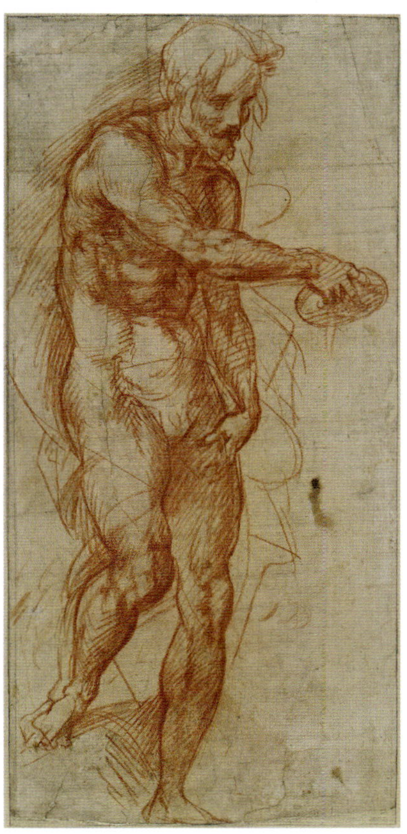

Figure 1.4: Andrea del Sarto. *Figure Study for a Saint John the Baptist. c.*1517. Red chalk on paper, approximately 38.5cm × 18.8cm. National Gallery of Victoria, Melbourne, Felton Bequest 1936, 351–4.

politician and collector Richard Crouch (1868–1949) left a collection of European manuscripts and incunabula to the Art Gallery of Ballarat, west of Melbourne.[8] Nationally, the Art Gallery of South Australia in Adelaide holds Old Master works from Tudor portraits to Ruisdael landscapes; there are bequest works by Sano di Pietro, Titian, and Ter Brugghen in the Art Gallery of New South Wales, and the list could

manuscripts acquired though the Felton bequest: Manion, *The Felton Illuminated Manuscripts in the National Gallery of Victoria.* The essays in Grimwade and Vaughan are a good introduction to private bequests to Australian collections; and although the interest here is on European holdings, a similar point can be made for other fields in Australia, including Chinese and Indigenous Australian works.

6   Lowe, 'The Robert Carl Sticht Collection: A Forgotten Legacy'.

7   Stone and Jaehrling, *Print Matters at the Baillieu.*

8   These and twenty-seven manuscripts in the State Library have been digitized and can be accessed online. See also Manion and Vines, *Medieval and Renaissance Illuminated Manuscripts in Australian Collections*; and Manion, Vines, and de Hamel, *Medieval and Renaissance Manuscripts in New Zealand Collections.*

Figure 1.3: Hans Memling. *Man of Sorrows in the Arms of the Virgin. c.*1475–9. Oil on panel, 27.4cm × 19.9cm. National Gallery of Victoria, Melbourne. Felton Bequest, 1924, 1335–3.

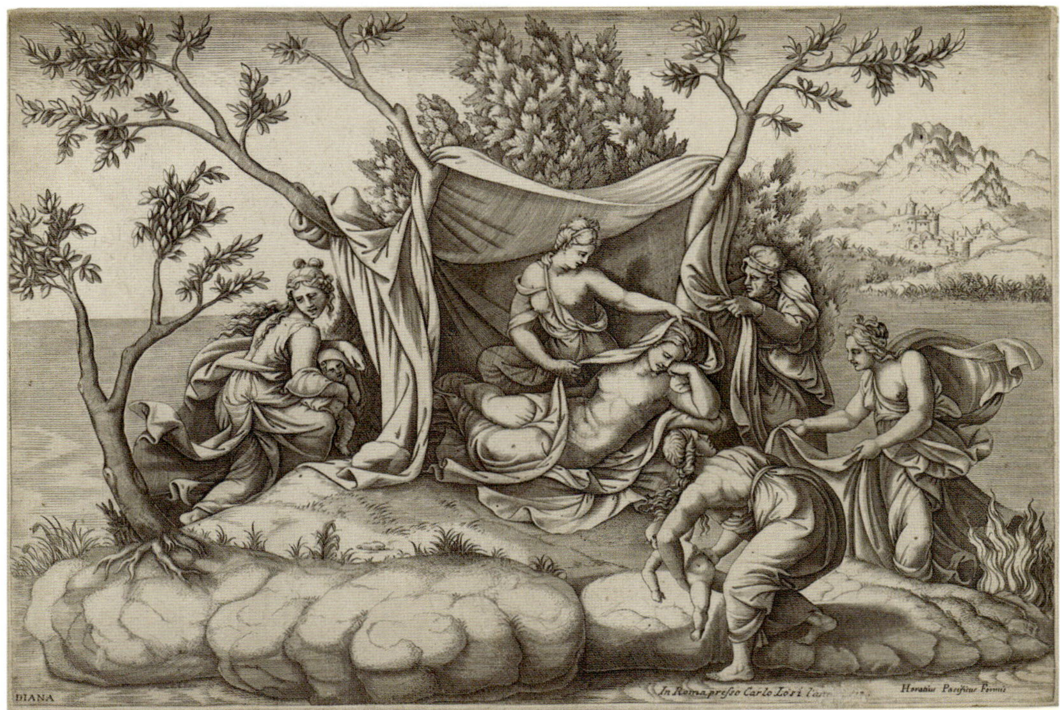

Figure 1.5: Diana Mantuana after Giulio Romano. *Latona Giving Birth to Apollo and Diana on the Island of Delos*, c.1570. Engraving, 25.4cm × 38.2cm. Baillieu Library Print Collection, University of Melbourne. Gift of Dr. J. Orde Poyton 1958.

be easily extended to collections in Perth, Brisbane, Canberra, and elsewhere.[9]

The essays here pick up on the range and richness of these European art collections, with the Stokes Collection at the centre of them. They are also however, a record of a legacy of art-historical scholarship and collaboration that spans many years. When the Stokes Collection successfully acquired the *Rothschild Prayer Book*, one of the first people to hear the news was Professor Margaret M. Manion, Emeritus of the University of Melbourne and Herald Professor of Fine Art there from 1979

until 1995. Manion has been working on European manuscript and book culture for many decades, and she has known and worked with Kerry Stokes for almost two. She was the force behind *An Illumination*; she wrote the introduction to the *Prayer Book* manuscript in the beautiful catalogue of the exhibition, and, with her colleague Charles Zika, she co-authored a study of some of the most important manuscripts in the Stokes Collection.[10] Manion's international career has brought her into contact with objects and specialists around the world; yet if many of the authors in this book are affiliated in some way with the University of Melbourne, it is not only because of the city

9   For an introduction to some of the bequests in these collections: Christopher Menz, 'The Elder and Morgan Thomas Bequests at the Art Gallery of South Australia,' and Edward Capon, 'The James Fairfax Collection', both in Grimwade and Vaughan, *Great Philanthropists on Trial*, pp. 113–125 and 126–135.

10   Manion, *An Illumination*; Manion and Zika, *Celebrating Word and Image 1250–1600: Illuminated Manuscripts from the Kerry Stokes Collection*.

and university's rich collections. Together with Joseph Burke and Jaynie Anderson, her predecessor and successor as Herald Chair of Fine Arts, Manion and her colleagues at Melbourne have fostered and trained generations of eminent medieval and early-modern European art historians and manuscript specialists. Thus the essays here attest to this tradition of scholarship on European art and culture, and to intellectual friendships, both local and international, that have grown over many years.

The studies that follow are also intended to suggest some of the themes, problems, and questions in early modern art history as it is currently practiced in Australia and elsewhere. This is a further reason for this book, and a major difference from the catalogue work. As will become apparent, the authors represent a range of approaches and research methods. They hold different and even contradictory views on many issues, beginning with the original circumstances of the *Rothschild Prayer Book* commission. The first essays, by Kay Sutton and Kate Challis, focus on that book: the circles of patrons and artists that surrounded its creation, its extraordinary imagery, and its later history as a particularly important kind of cultural capital. Together they outline what we know, and what we would like to know, about the manuscript. The next essay, by Dagmar Eichberger, moves to the larger court context of collecting and reception in which such luxury objects were created. Eichberger takes up the case of Margaret of Austria, sometimes put forward as the original patron of the *Prayer Book*, and her relative Margaret of York, Duchess of Burgundy, in order to explore how female collectors both participated in the market for books and manuscripts and were represented within it.

The *Rothschild Prayer Book* was made more than half a century after the advent of movable type printing, and as a Book of Hours

illuminated by hand, it came at the end of a long development in manuscript culture. The next essays open onto this moment of transition from manuscript to print, including the materials and technologies involved in the shift. Exploring two early thirteenth-century manuscripts now in the State Library of Victoria, Libby Melzer reveals how parchment can provide clues to the rise of large-scale book production in medieval Europe. The first book, an *Epistles of Saint Paul,* emerges as the product of a small-scale monastic scriptorium with materials linked to the local agricultural cycles; the second, a *Leviticus*, was instead a product of the streamlined and urban mass market coming into being around the court and university in Paris. In the following essay, Margaret M. Manion looks at the early forms of the Book of Hours by focusing on two manuscripts from the years on either side of 1300, the *Liège Psalter Hours* and the *Aspremont-Kieveraing Psalter-Hours* in the State Library of Victoria and the National Gallery of Victoria respectively. Manion considers what endured, and what changed, over the long life of the Book of Hours form.

The following chapters turn to a series of important single case studies. Most are drawn from fifteenth- and sixteenth-century France and the essays are ordered roughly by chronology. Elaine Shaw's essay picks up the theme of urban versus other production centres discussed in Melzer's paper, but at a later moment of development, moving into the 1470s. Shaw's focus is on manuscript production beyond Paris, and she uses the elegant Breviary made for a high-ranking ecclesiastic, Prior François Robert, Canon of Bourges, to explore some of the challenges and innovations that emerged in smaller art centres. Bernard Muir looks at the changes in format and organization in Books of Hours that came in the transition from handwork to print. He discusses two sixteenth-century examples made in France, both now in Victorian collections, to show how the border decorations of these printed works were adapted, borrowed, and circulated from one publisher to another and one edition to the next, even over several decades. Jan Fox examines the intriguing 1472 case of an early printing house, the Sorbonne Press at the University of Paris, issuing a manuscript presentation copy of the *Satires* by the Roman writer Juvenal alongside the printed edition. The manuscript copy was presented to the new Royal Chancellor, Pierre Doriole, and includes an unusual image of him at the beginning of the book. Fox explores this image as a homage and appeal to the Chancellor from the scholarly promotors of the Press. In the last essay in this section, Hilary Maddocks examines a Book of Hours printed by the Paris-based publisher Thielman Kerver in 1522. The book had elaborate metalcut illustrations and borders, but the copy in the Stokes Collection also includes hand-painted initials and scenes. Maddocks discusses the designers and artists who worked on the book, and she traces the role of decoration, both manual and mechanical, in the market for printed books, including in Kerver's own successful publishing ventures. Together the essays in this section reveal the small and interconnected worlds of early publishing and production both in Paris and beyond it, and some of the ways that the advent of printing changed both the form and the content of even long-standing genres and types.

The final essays move to the larger world of objects and rituals in which early books were consumed and collected. Miya Tokumitsu's essay centres on a small bronze casket with classicising decoration and the arms of the Piccolomini family of Renaissance Siena; two men of the family became Popes Pius II and Pius III. Tokumitsu discusses the role of such miniature luxury objects in early collections, and in the studies and private spaces where books were – more or less ostentatiously – consulted and read. She also shows how, for all its illustrious provenance, the casket and objects like it were assembled in a kind of mix-and-match of standardized elements, very much like the manuscripts and incunabula that would have surrounded it.

In the next essay, Callum Reid examines another chest with classicizing decoration, a *cassone*, or wedding chest, made in Italy in the later 1500s. Reid argues that it can be linked to the Valenti family of Umbria and he traces the place of such lavish chests in both Renaissance family rituals and the later history of taste. One theme that emerges here is the importance of artworks produced to mark weddings, funerals, and other milestones in families and clans, and it is central to the next chapter, by Ursula Betka. Where Tokumitsu and Reid examine objects from domestic space, Betka looks at a public commission, a Catalonian altarpiece of the *Dormition of the Virgin*, made in the early fifteenth century, connected to the circle of the artist Mateu Ortoneda. Drawing on close reading of the imagery and on contemporary sources on liturgy and devotion, Betka argues that the panel should be linked to the Viscounts of Cabrera of Blanes, and she explores how it gave shape to their hopes and fears, earthly and otherwise.

The last two chapters in the book return to northern Europe and the Netherlands, where the *Rothschild Prayer Book* was produced. Larry Silver's essay picks up on the theme of families and lineage: he examines a *Crucifixion* by Peter Brueghel the Younger, done however, as Silver suggests, very much on the model of works by the artist's father, Peter Brueghel the Elder, one of the most sought-after artists of the mid-1500s. Even decades later, the son was adapting his father's works for new contexts and ends, and Silver examines the adaptations and citations that made up this long and successful practice.

In the concluding paper, Charles Zika analyzes one of the most wonderful works in the Stokes Collection, one of the so-called *Schembart* books that served as records of Nuremberg's Carnival celebrations from the first occurrence in 1349 until they were permanently banned in 1539. The Stokes *Schembart* was made about 1540, and is one of the earliest surviving examples; in seventy-five beautiful, elaborate, and colourful images, the book records the lavish and fantastical costumes, players, parades, and floats that marked the Nuremberg ritual. As Zika reveals, however, the *Stokes Schembart* is also a record of a small and tense world, where every mock battle might have a very real political or factional fight behind it. As such it seems like an upside-down version of the serene and well-ordered world created by the illuminations of the *Rothschild Prayer Book*. Together, they are ideal objects to begin and end the studies of this book.

About the author

Anne Dunlop holds the Herald Chair of Fine Arts at the University of Melbourne. Her most recent books are *Andrea del Castagno and the Limits of Painting* (2015), and the co-edited volume *The Matter of Art: Materials, Practices, Cultural Logics, c. 1250–1750* (2014). anne.dunlop@unimelb.edu.au

Works cited

'Christie's Old Master Week achieves $68 million in New York; Rothschild Prayer Book sells for $13,606,000', accessed 19 July 2017 at http://artdaily.com/news/67851/ Christie-s-Old-Masters-Week-achieves-68-million-in-New-York.

Ted Gott, Laurie Benson, and contributors, *Painting and Sculpture Before 1800 in the International Collections of the National Gallery of Victoria* (Melbourne: National Gallery of Victoria, 2003).

Andrew Grimwade and Gerard Vaughan, eds., *Great Philanthropists on Trial: The Art of the Bequest* (Melbourne: Miegunyah Press, National Gallery of Victoria, and the Felton Bequests' Committee, 2006).

Ursula Hoff, *European Paintings before 1800 in the National Gallery of Victoria*, 4th edition (Melbourne: National Gallery of Victoria, 1995).

Mary Kisler, *Angels & Aristocrats: Early European Art in New Zealand Public Collections* (Auckland: Auckland Art Gallery Toi o Tamaki and Godwit, 2010).

Heather Lowe, 'The Robert Carl Sticht Collection: A Forgotten Legacy,' *Art Bulletin of Victoria: NGV Annual Journal*, 38 (1997) pp. 13–24.

Margaret M. Manion, ed., *An Illumination: The Rothschild Prayer Book and other works from the Kerry Stokes Collection c.1280–1685* (West Perth: Australian Capital Equity, 2015).

Margaret M. Manion, *The Felton Illuminated Manuscripts in the National Gallery of Victoria* (Melbourne: Macmillan Art Publishing and the National Gallery of Victoria, 2005).

Margaret M. Manion and Vera F. Vines, *Medieval and Renaissance Illuminated Manuscripts in Australian Collections* (Melbourne, London, New York: Thames and Hudson, 1984).

Margaret M. Manion, Vera F. Vines, and Christopher de Hamel, *Medieval and Renaissance Manuscripts in New Zealand Collections* (Melbourne, London, New York: Thames and Hudson, 1989).

Margaret M. Manion and Charles Zika, *Celebrating Word and Image 1250–1600: Illuminated Manuscripts from the Kerry Stokes Collection* (West Perth: Australian Capital Equity, 2013).

Kerriane Stone and Stephanie Jaehrling, *Print Matters at the Baillieu* (Melbourne: Cussonia Press, 2011).

Carol Vogel, 'Renaissance Prayer Book is Set for Auction', www.thenewyorktimes.com, 31 October 2013, accessed 19 July 2017 at http://www.nytimes.com/2013/11/01/arts/design/renaissance-prayer-book-is-set-for-auction.html?_r=0.

Timothy Wilson with Amanda Dunsmore, and Marika Strohschnieder, *Italian Maiolica in the Collection of the National Gallery of Victoria* (Melbourne: Council of Trustees of the National Gallery of Victoria, 2015).

2. Heaven and earth: the worlds of the *Rothschild Prayer Book*

Kay Sutton

Dunlop, Anne (ed.), *Antipodean Early Modern. European Art in Australian Collections, c. 1200–1600*, Amsterdam University Press, 2018

DOI: 10.5117/9789462985209/CH02

Abstract
This introduction to the *Rothschild Prayer Book* – an illuminated manuscript that is one of the finest products of the Flemish Renaissance – discusses the function of the book beyond its devotional use and seeks to place it in the context of its production, drawing attention to distinctive Flemish architecture, contemporary liturgical practices and the luxury accessories of the Habsburg court included in the sacred scenes of the miniatures. The role of the principal artists responsible for the miniatures – Gerard Horenbout, Alexander Bening, his renowned son Simon Bening, and Gerard David, primarily known for his panel-paintings – is discussed along with the division of their labour within the *Prayer Book* and the nature of artistic collaboration. Little is known of the manuscript's provenance before *c.*1870 when it entered the collection of Anselm von Rothschild, but here possible identities are offered for the original patron and an early owner.

Keywords: Simon Bening; Alexander Bening; Gerard David; *Rothschild Prayer Book*; Gerard Horenbout; Flemish illumination

The *Rothschild Prayer Book* is a fabulous manuscript. Made for an unknown patron in the early years of the sixteenth century by a group of the most notable Flemish painters, it is essentially a very luxurious example of a Book of Hours, the most popular form of prayer book from the fourteenth to the sixteenth centuries. Although such books emulated elements of the liturgy performed by priests and members of religious orders, Books of Hours were not primarily intended for use in church: they were for private prayer. The component texts could vary, although there were standard inclusions. The central and most important devotion was the Office or Hours of the Blessed Virgin Mary. Made up of hymns, psalms and prayers to be said at the eight canonical divisions of the day, this was the text that gave the book its name.

The illumination of the pages with the opening of prime, the first daylight hour, in the Office of the Virgin in the *Rothschild Prayer Book* is a great demonstration of both the narrative richness and the opulent technique (Figure 2.1). Scenes from the Life of the Virgin, mostly from the Infancy of Christ, were the most common subjects to illustrate this Office, yet this opening is far from a routine treatment. The central miniature has the Virgin and angels venerating the newly delivered Christ Child, but the story extends into the borders showing the events immediately before and

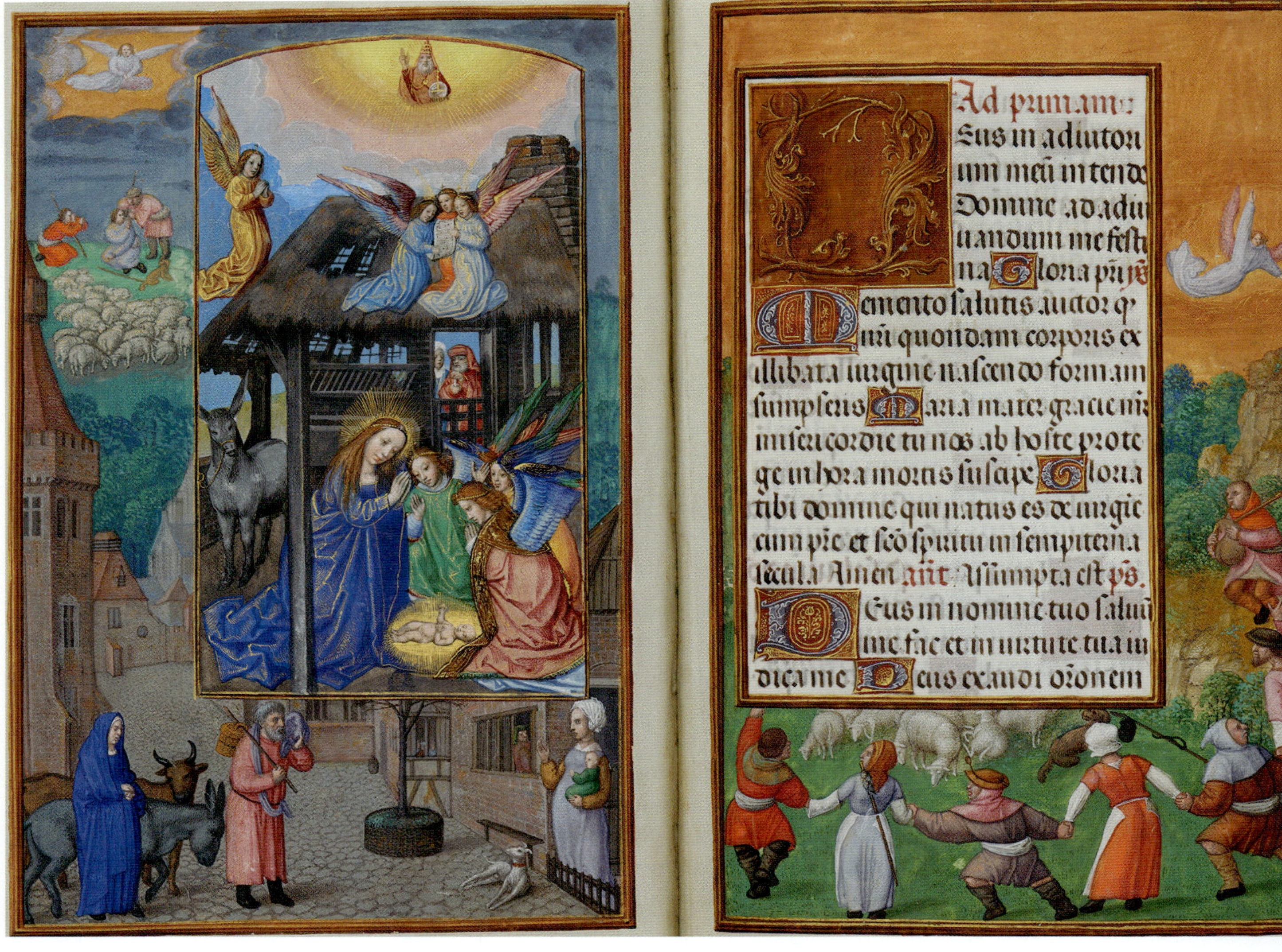

Figure 2.1: Ghent and Bruges, Nativity from *Rothschild Prayer Book (Book of Hours, Use of Rome)*. Folios 108v and 109, *c.*1505–1510. Parchment, 22.8cm × 16cm. Kerry Stokes Collection, Perth. LIB.2014.017.

after the Nativity. The lower border shows Joseph and the Virgin being turned away from the inn, while the landscape that continues up to the top left contains the angel announcing the miraculous birth to the shepherds 'watching their flocks by night'. The shepherds are so delighted at the news that they go off to celebrate with music and dance on the facing page. This lively anecdotal treatment features in the central scene too: the figures visible in the stable doorway seem to be Joseph who has brought the innkeeper's wife to pay her respects, and to see what a mistake she has made; the ass shows his interest by his cocked ear. The execution too is exceptionally fine: although it is barely discernible, the backs of the sheep in the top-left border are touched with gold – their fleeces catch the miraculous light from heaven.

To the devout Christian, the devotions in Books of Hours were a channel for direct communication with the Virgin Mary. One could make a personal plea for well-being and spiritual salvation without depending upon a priest or going to church. The books and their prayers could be integrated into one's personal and private life. This is demonstrated in both historical record and contemporary image. One of the most dramatic, and perhaps surprising, recorded incidents concerns Thomas Cromwell, chief minister to Henry VIII from 1532 to 1540, who is

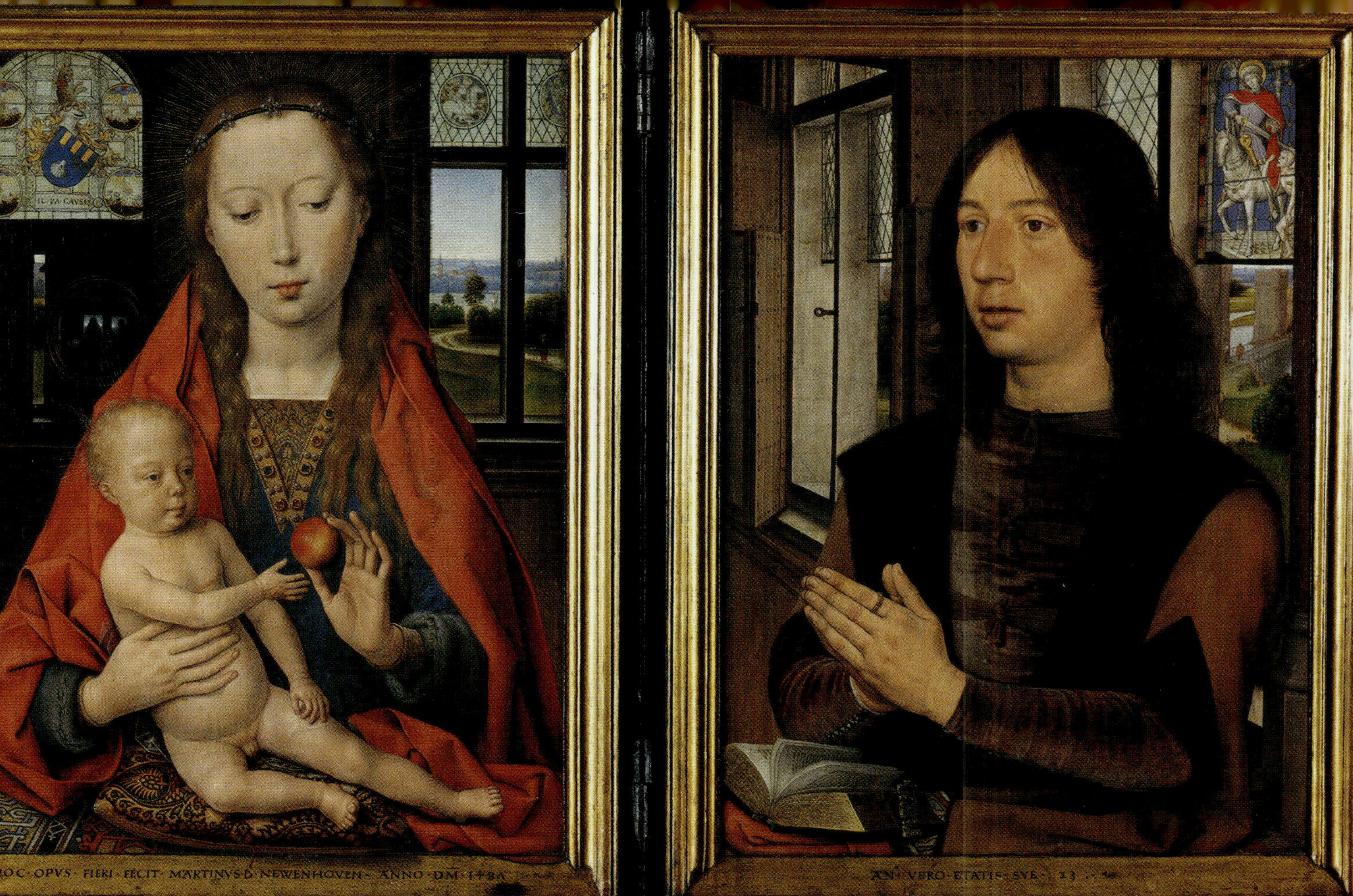

Figure 2.2: Hans Memling, *Madonna and Child with Maarten van Nieuwenhove*, diptych, 1487. Oil on panel, 33.5cm × 44.7cm. Memlingmuseum, Bruges.

renowned as a prime mover in the English Reformation and for his role in the dissolution of the English monasteries. In 1529, when he was still in Cardinal Wolsey's service, rightly fearful of the Cardinal's downfall, and thereby his own ruin, Cromwell was observed at the window of Wolsey's Great Chamber with his Hours, simultaneously weeping and praying to the Virgin.[1]

To move from an English example to Flanders, where the *Rothschild Prayer Book* was made, the diptych painted by Hans Memling for the Bruges citizen Maarten van Nieuwenhove (Bruges, Memlingmuseum) is one of many visual renderings of a prayer book being used in a secular domestic setting (Figure 2.2). In the right-hand panel Maarten is shown at prayer, his book in front of him, in a room identifiable as his own by the presence of his coat of arms and his patron saint, Martin of Tours, in the stained glass windows. The room continues on the left wing of the diptych where the Virgin offers an apple to the Christ Child. The implication must be that as a result of Maarten's devotions they have appeared before him as a vision.

In the fifteenth century, the County of Flanders was one of the lands ruled by the Dukes of Burgundy. When the last Valois duke, Charles the Bold, died in 1477, he was succeeded by his daughter Mary of Burgundy, wife of the Habsburg Archduke of Austria, Maximilian, later Holy Roman Emperor. The opening miniature in *Mary of Burgundy's Hours* (Vienna, ONB, Ms. 1857) shows the

---

1   Richard S. Sylvester, *The Life and Death of Cardinal Wolsey*, p. 104.

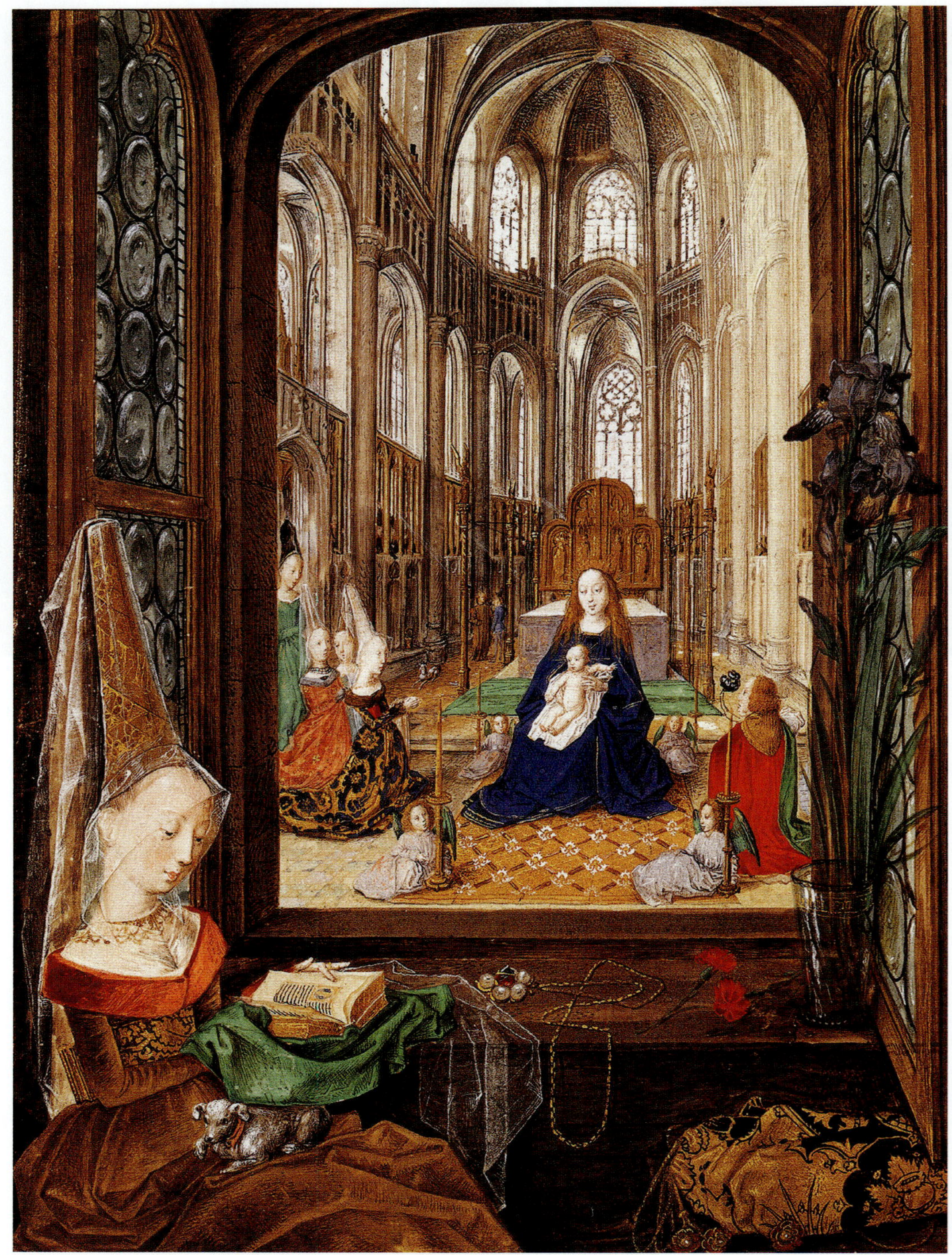

Figure 2.3: Maximilian and Mary of Burgundy before the Virgin / Mary of Burgundy Reading her Devotions from the *Hours of Mary of Burgundy*. Folio 14v, *c.*1470–75. Tempera on parchment, 22.5cm × 16.3cm. Österreichische Nationalbibliothek, Vienna. Ms. 1857.

duchess at her devotions, with her manuscript to hand (Figure 2.3). Visible through the window of her room is a church interior where the Virgin and Child sit before the altar. We can be certain that this is intended as a vision, for this miniature faces a text reporting the appearance of the Virgin and Child granted to Thomas à Becket. The portraits of Maarten and Mary express the idea that the sitter's prayers to the Virgin, aided by their prayer books, have brought her, however ethereally, into their world, offering reassurance of her accessibility and attention and her readiness to give support in their quest for forgiveness and aid.

It was the Virgin's role as a tender-hearted mother that made her a suitable intercessor: she could be expected to be at once sympathetic and to have the ear of her son. But she was not alone in being well suited to this role. The community of saints could also intercede on one's behalf because, on the one hand, they too had been human and could share mortal concerns, but, on the other, once sanctified they were immediately admitted into heaven and the presence of God. This was in contrast to the majority of humankind, which was expected to spend time between death and the Last Judgment suffering in purgatory. The miniature opening the Hours of the Trinity in the *Rothschild Prayer Book* shows God the Father, the Son and the Holy Ghost, with ranks of angels and saints in adoration (Figure 2.4).

Saints were a channel between heaven and earth, one that was particularly effective if associated with a physical relic, usually a body part, in or near an altar; impressive collections of relics were put together by medieval and Renaissance princes. The golden reliquary made for Duke Charles the Bold, father of Mary of Burgundy, shows the prince presented by his patron saint, St George, and holding a rock crystal container with the finger of St Lambert. Charles presented this reliquary to the church

of St Lambert in Liège. Whereas the saints in the Trinity miniature are shown in a celestial context, here Saint George is transposed and shown as a patron companion in the same realm as a man, recommending him and promoting his cause. The final section of the *Rothschild Prayer Book* would have enabled its owner to enlist similar saintly support, for it is a long sequence of prayers addressed to individual saints, each portrayed in a facing miniature. Many are shown in half-length, close-up, near enough for direct conversation and entreaty. They seem deliberately comforting images: little reference is made to the saints' martyrdoms and torture. Even Catherine's customary wheel is absent; just the hilt is shown of the sword of her execution (Figure 2.5), and Stephen has calmly gathered up the stones that killed him, apart from the two lodged discreetly at his hairline (Figure 2.6).

This sense of accessibility and an ability to relate to the saints was aided by showing the heavenly environment they inhabited to be much like the world of the owner of the book. Expressing the supernatural in terms of the corporeal was eminently well served by the realism and naturalism characteristic of northern Renaissance painting. One could readily identify with these intercessors, and be reassured of their help: they were recognisably human, and unlike the glory of heaven in the Trinity, they were shown in familiar worldly settings. The worlds of those praying and those prayed to were integrated: the buildings represented in the Suffrages, the prayers directed at individual saints, generally provide no more than added interest and detail to a landscape setting, but whether religious or secular, they are immediately recognisable as Flemish. The stepped gables, dormer windows in the steep roofs, the mixture of brick with white stone string-courses, all place the saints in familiar local territory.

The saints themselves are similarly treated. If appropriate their status is identified in contemporary terms. Stephen, the first Christian

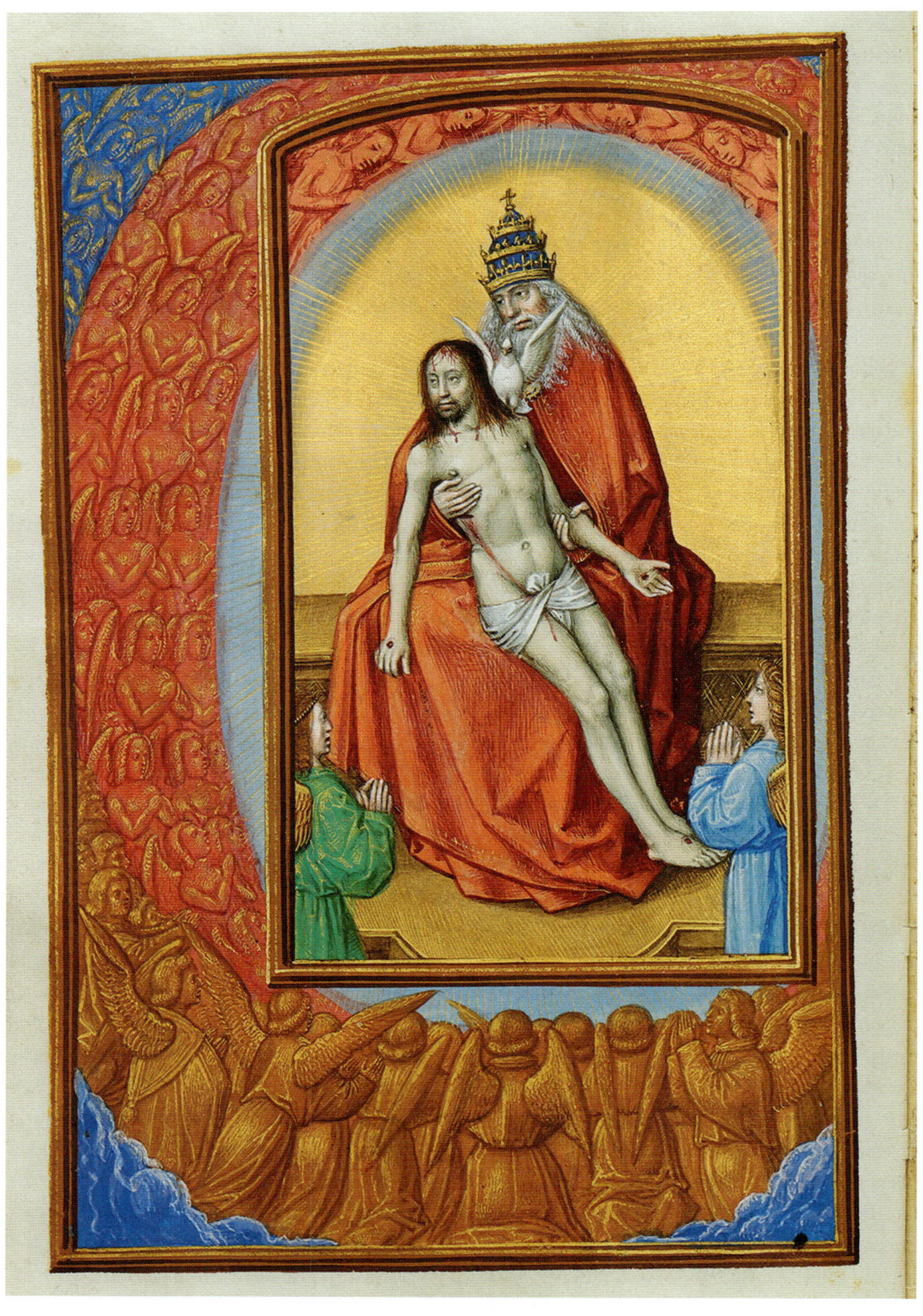

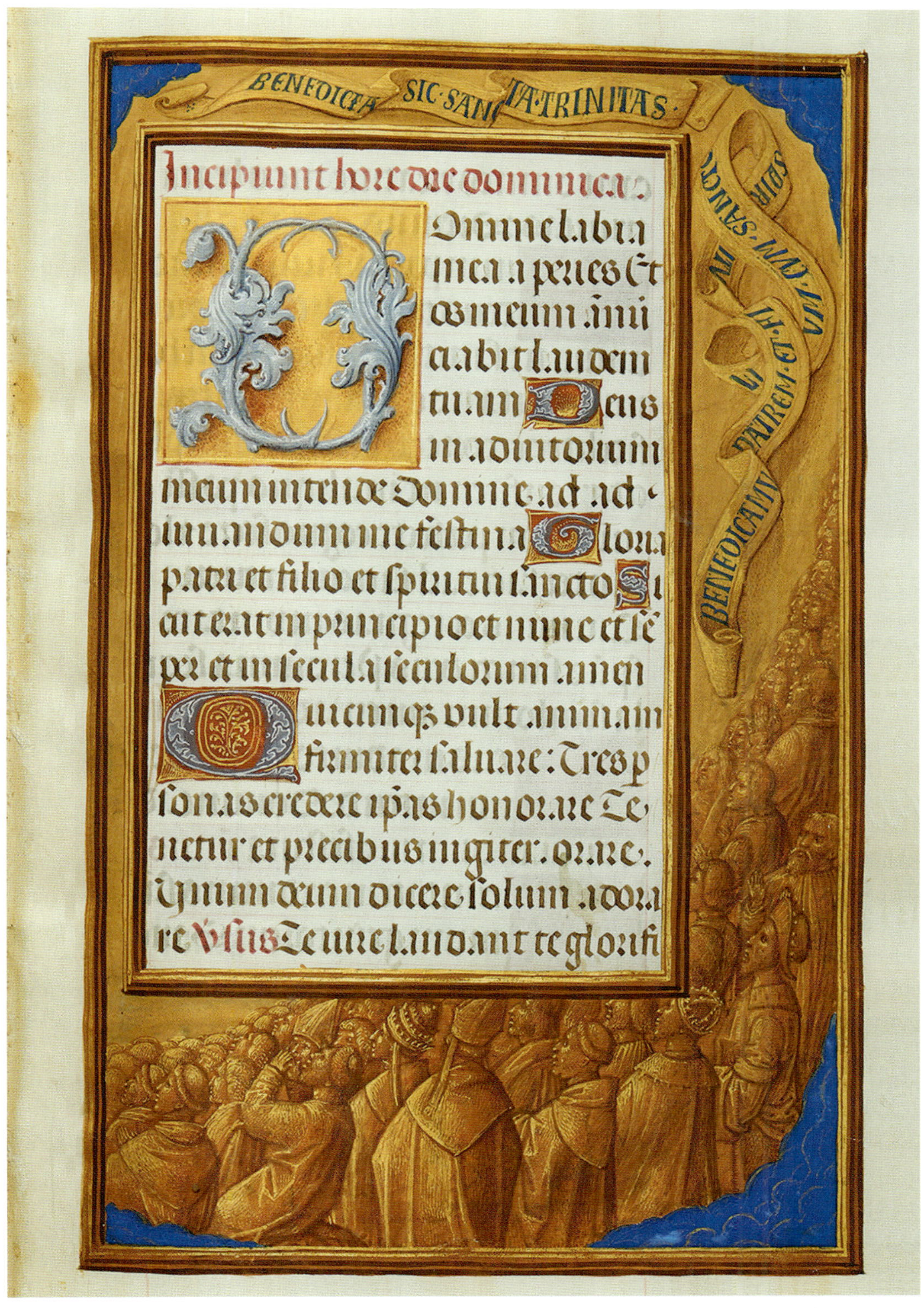

Figure 2.4: Hours of the Holy Trinity for Sunday from the *Rothschild Prayer Book*. Folios 10v-11, c.1505-1510. Parchment, 22.8cm × 16cm. Kerry Stokes Collection, Perth.

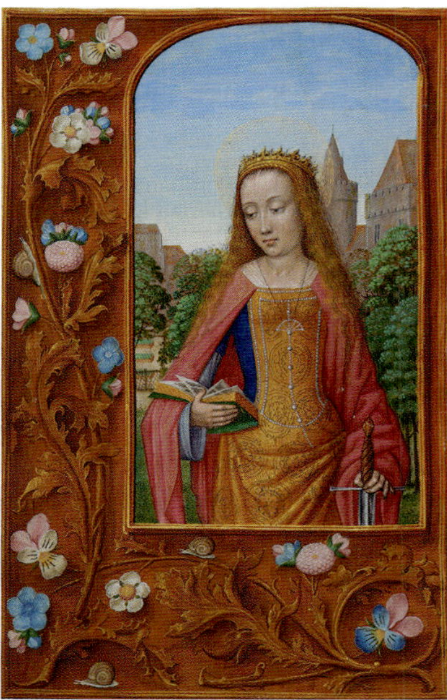

Figure 2.5: Saint Catherine from the *Rothschild Prayer Book*. Folio 228v, *c*.1505–1510. Parchment, 22.8cm × 16cm. Kerry Stokes Collection, Perth.

martyr, was described as a deacon in the Acts of the Apostles, so he is shown in a splendid contemporary vestment – a dalmatic made of Italian cloth of gold (Figure 2.6). The royal status of Saints Catherine and Helena is not only shown by their crowns but by their open-sided gowns, the court garments of French and Flemish princesses (Figure 2.5). Even the prayer books in their hands look much as the Rothschild Prayer Book is likely to have looked when newly bound. The golden edges of its pages still have the same gauffered diagonal pattern seen on the books that the saints hold. It may no longer preserve its original binding but it seems likely that it would have had a protective textile chemise like that hanging from Catherine's volume. Maybe the binding that the chemise concealed was of brocade and was ornamented with gold corner-pieces

and clasps like the book held by St Vincent (Figure 2.7).[2]

The portrayal of contemporary details in the religious scenes, locating them in the world of the user of the manuscript, served to encourage a sense of rapport and easy communication. Yet perhaps it is misguided to think about a manuscript as exceptional as the *Rothschild Prayer Book* in these practical devotional terms, a bit like considering a Bugatti as a good means of getting to work. Neither object is about being functional – that was just one aspect of their purpose: show, status and technical excellence were of equal importance. By the time this manuscript was made, printed Books of Hours were being produced in large numbers, and, to continue the automobile analogy, these printed editions, readily available and affordable, were the equivalent of the Model T Ford – although in this case there was a choice of colour other than black.[3]

One of the selling points of a printed Hours was the profusion of illustration and decoration it might have – once the woodblocks or plates had been cut, multiple copies or slight variants could be easily produced. This was in radical contrast to illuminated manuscripts where each was a unique work reliant on individual endeavour. A reasonably smart fifteenth-century manuscript Book of Hours is likely to have between fourteen and eighteen large miniatures; the *Rothschild Prayer Book* originally had seventy – of which sixty-seven survive.[4] To judge from the

2   This is very similar to the binding the *Prayer Book* has now. Although this is not the original binding and the silver-gilt decorations are German and of the second-half of the sixteenth-century (so some 50 years later than the manuscript) they may well emulate the manuscript's original form.

3   For examples of printed hours where some copies were supplied with the black and white cuts painted see Tenschert and Nettekoven, *Horae B.V.M.*

4   Irregularities in the structure of the manuscript and in the programme of illustration show that it lacks four

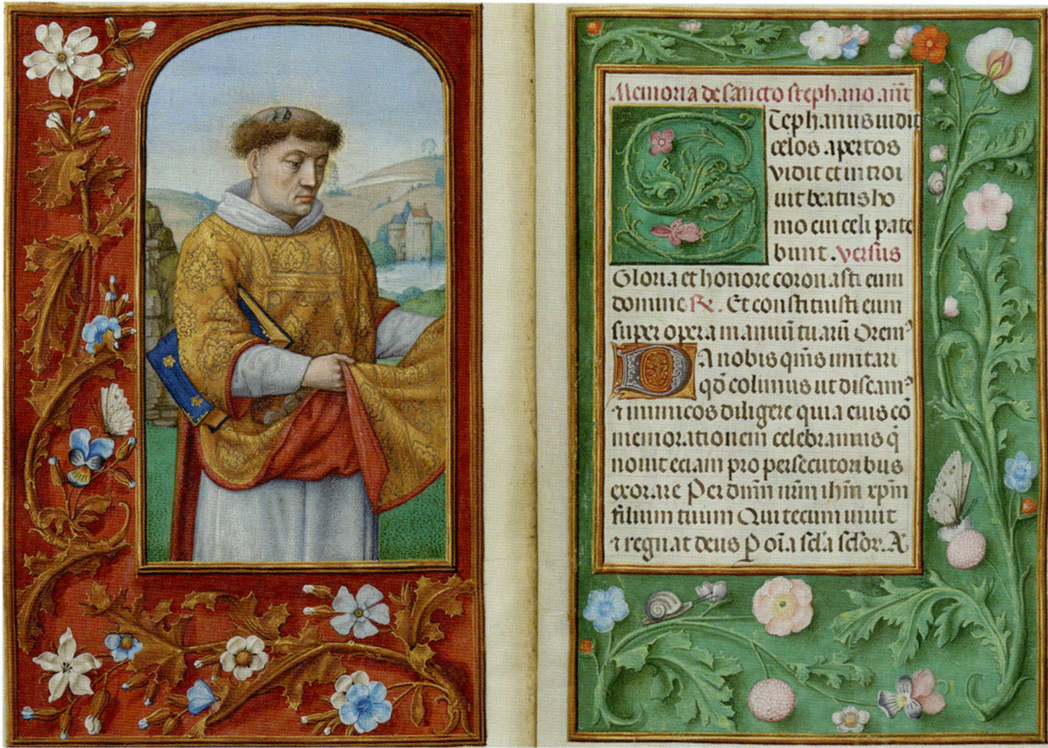

Figure 2.6: Saint Stephen from the *Rothschild Prayer Book*. Folios 218v–219, *c.*1505–1510. Parchment, 22.8cm × 16cm. Kerry Stokes Collection, Perth.

number of extant manuscript Hours datable to the sixteenth century, the availability of printed versions had caused a falling off in the production of routine illuminated manuscript copies: a high proportion of the sixteenth-century manuscript Hours known to us are top quality, luxury volumes. They were made for the richest patrons of their time, owners who can be identified by the presence of their coats of arms and inclusions entirely specific to them. To some degree at least, these Hours can be considered

leaves: two before folio 51, and one each before folios 144 and 244. Three of the missing leaves would have had full-page miniatures to open the Short Hours of the Sacrament and the prayers *O intemerata* and *Ave sanctissima maria mater dei regina celi.*

bespoke volumes. Among the rich and noble, unique, high quality Books of Hours maintained their prestige.

Of all such manuscripts that have come onto the market in the last century, none has been finer or achieved a higher price than the *Rothschild Prayer Book*. With its extensive illustration and decoration by the most respected Flemish artists of the day, the manuscript was undoubtedly as highly valued and as costly a volume originally as it is now. Yet, surprisingly, it is one of a group of spectacularly luxurious manuscripts produced around 1490–1520 for an international clientele and for members of the Habsburg court in the southern Low Countries. These manuscripts are closely related in style and splendour but they are far from identical – and the *Rothschild Prayer*

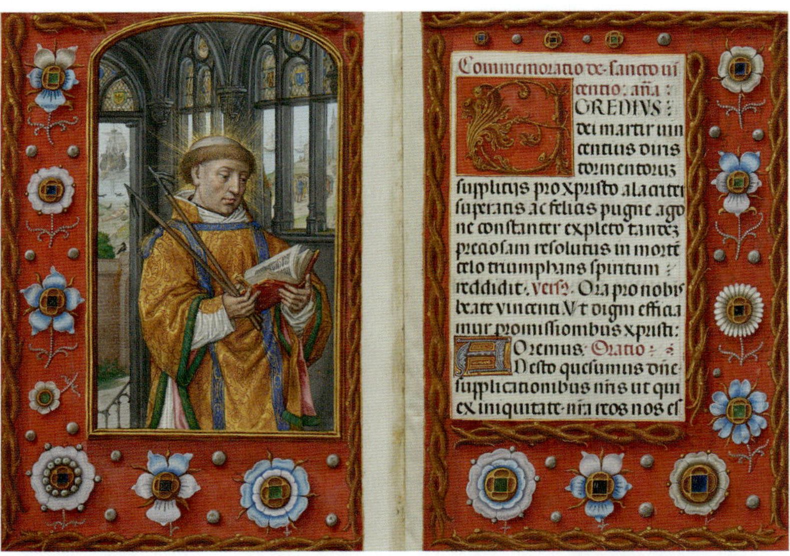

Figure 2.7: Saint Vincent from the *Rothschild Prayer Book*. Folios 238v–239, *c.*1505–1510. Parchment, 22.8cm × 16cm. Kerry Stokes Collection, Perth.

Book is arguably the most beautiful and immediately affecting. As a group they are unique. There are occasional deluxe French, German or Italian Books of Hours of a similar date but, as far as one can tell from the surviving manuscripts, there was no comparable output, no other coherent production from a group of artists working at a similar level of sumptuousness. It seems that these Flemish illuminators had cornered the international market in luxury prayer books.[5]

Already in the fifteenth century the diplomatic alliances and marriages made by the Burgundian dukes, along with the importance of Flemish cities – particularly Bruges – as centres of international trade and finance, had established an enthusiasm for Flemish painting among the princes and merchants of Europe. The intermarriages between royal houses are particularly relevant to understanding the

international exposure and appreciation of Flemish art. To take Mary of Burgundy as an example, her grandmother was Portuguese, Mary herself married Maximilian, a Habsburg Archduke of Austria who later became Emperor, and his mother was Portuguese as well. Mary and Maximilian had two children, Philip the Fair and Margaret of Austria, who, to secure alliances, both made Spanish marriages. This was the princely context in which the extravagant group of manuscripts including the *Rothschild Prayer Book* was made, and it is unsurprising that some of the books seem to have been made with Iberian owners in mind. Several are written in the rounded script associated with Spain, Portugal or Italy. What is surprising is that for most of these manuscripts there is no evidence that they were planned with a specific southern owner in mind, even if they very soon ended up with one. This is the case for instance with a breviary in the Morgan Library. The coat of arms on the *prie-dieu* in the frontispiece identifies the kneeling queen pictured

5   The manuscripts attributed to the so-called 1520s Hours Workshop are somewhat later in date and seem to have been produced for a solely French clientele.

as Eleanor of Portugal, consort of John II, but her face and the coat of arms are repainted, suggesting that the book was originally made for someone else.[6] In another breviary from the group, now in the British Library, an inscription added to an opening border records the presentation of the manuscript to Isabella of Castile in 1497 by Francisco de Rojas. He was the ambassador sent to the Low Countries to negotiate the marriages between the children of Maximilian and Mary of Burgundy and the children of Isabella and Ferdinand of Aragon, the Catholic Monarchs.[7] Two other splendid and complex breviaries, painted by the same group of illuminators, also ended up with illustrious southern European owners although the circumstances of their creation and commissioning likewise remain mysterious.[8]

Equal obscurity surrounds the origin and intention for the *Rothschild Prayer Book* but, even though no immediate patron seems identifiable, it was certainly made in and destined for a courtly context. This context is reflected in details of its illumination, particularly in the decorative borders that surround the miniatures. The fifteenth-century Burgundian court was renowned for its lavishness and this is reflected in the illumination. The frame around the scene of the Mass of the Dead is one of the most opulent borders, painted as though sumptuous silks lined the page itself (Figure 2.8). It shows a velvet cloth of gold with loops of silver-gilt – the costliest and showiest of textiles, likely made in Italy in the final third of the fifteenth century.

Such fabrics were fabulously expensive. Ostentatious display was a vital component of medieval and renaissance statecraft, used to enhance the status and power of a sovereign, and imported textiles played their part. In 1473, when Charles the Bold went to Trier to negotiate with the emperor Frederick III, it has been calculated that the silks he bought to outfit his retinue cost the equivalent of the annual salary of 555 master masons.[9] Charles also took along and displayed a wealth of silver and gold plate, tapestries and a vast collection of relics and reliquaries. It made the desired impression: the Emperor and German princes were reported to be disconcerted, being unused to such luxury.

Other costly accoutrements also decorate the borders of the *Prayer Book*. There is a profusion of precious jewels and enamelled goldsmiths' work. The collar worn by Margaret of York, wife of Charles the Bold, in her portrait in the Louvre features enamelled flowers and pendant pearls like those that pattern many of the Prayer Books' illusionistic margins (Figures 2.9 and 2.10).[10] Courtly events as well as accessories are portrayed: the varied scenes and activities shown in other borders include a tournament set in front of a building very reminiscent of the Burgundian dukes' castle in Ghent.

But it was not exclusively the lives and context of noble courtiers that were shown. The calendar miniatures unrolled the passage of the year through the activities of labour as well as leisure. And the final earthly fate of all, no matter their rank, was spelled out emphatically in the burial scene, once again set in a characteristically Flemish town (Figure 2.9). This scene served as a dramatic reminder to the reader to use the book for its religious purpose, for it opens the Office of the Dead, which was not simply part of the funeral services: priests were encouraged to recite

---

6   New York, The Morgan Library Ms. M.52, see Kren and McKendrick, *Illuminating the Renaissance*, No. 91, pp. 321–4.

7   London, BL, Add. Ms 18851: see Kren and McKendrick, *Illuminating the Renaissance*, No. 100, pp, 347–51. See also the essay by Eichberger in this volume and figures 3.5 and 3.8.

8   Antwerp, Museum Mayer van der Bergh, inv. no 426 and Venice, Bibl. Naz. Marciana, Ms. Lat. I, 99 (2138): see Kren and McKendrick, *Illuminating the Renaissance*, Nos. 92 and 126, pp. 324–9 and 420–4.

9   Marti, *Charles le Téméraire*, p. 270.

10   Marti, *Charles le Téméraire*, Cat. No. 6, p. 177 and pl. 20.

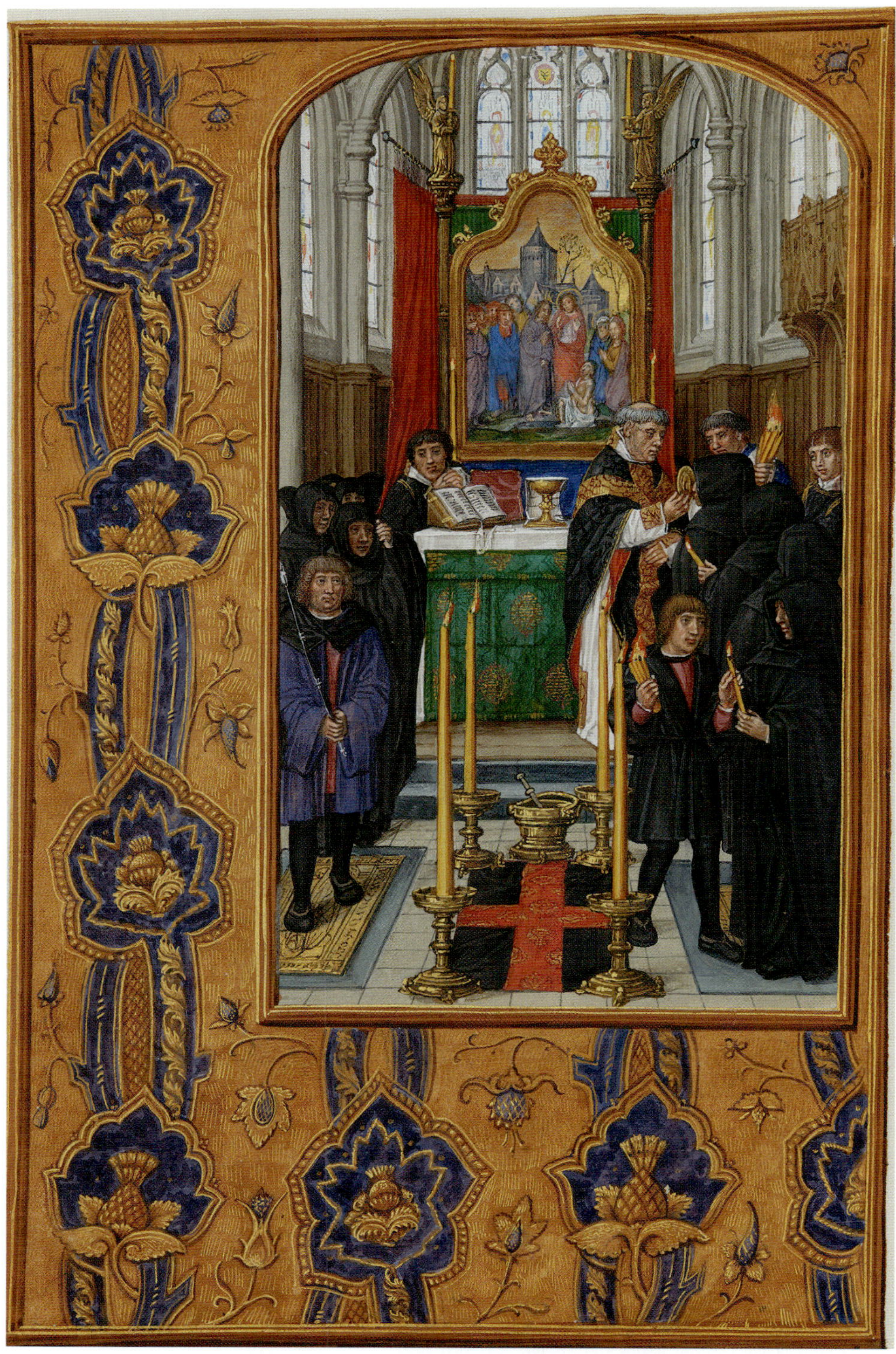

Figure 2.8: Memorial Mass of the Dead from the *Rothschild Prayer Book*. Folio 28v, c.1505–1510. Parchment, 22.8cm × 16cm. Kerry Stokes Collection, Perth.

it daily, and the laity to pray it as often as possible. Along with paid memorial masses, this was the best means of shortening the time a deceased beloved would spend suffering in purgatory.

The group of manuscripts to which the *Prayer Book* belongs showcased the very best that Flemish illuminators could provide. The variety in type of image and style of painting serves to make them Renaissance picture galleries as much as devotional books: these manuscripts were themselves objects of display and luxury just like the fabrics and jewels they depict. As Francisco de Rojas' inscription in the *Isabella Breviary* makes explicit, they were also clearly used as gifts that flattered both giver and recipient. Yet there is no evidence that any of them were destined for a specific owner when they were produced. The *Rothschild Prayer Book* is no exception for there is no provable provenance for the manuscript before 1868 when it entered the collection of Baron Anselm von Rothschild in Vienna. Any suggestion about the manuscript's genesis or earlier whereabouts is conjectural, and can only be based on details within the book or comparison with similar works.

Yet this group of closely related manuscripts were the most lavish and luxurious productions of the early sixteenth-century book trade in Flanders and it is clear that they required the efficient organisation and collaboration of a group of artists to bring them to completion. There were two principal illuminators of this group, Gerard Horenbout and Alexander Bening, both based in Ghent, and they appear to have been responsible for the overall programmes of illumination of the *Prayer Book*. Horenbout is now generally accepted as the author of the body of work once attributed to the so-called Master of James IV of Scotland, named from a portrait of the king in a book in Vienna (ONB, Ms. 1897).[11] His technique was

detailed and realistic: he described textures with great attention and beauty, and the compositions he devised were thoughtful evocations of events where unidealised figures were placed in convincing relationship to buildings or landscapes (Figure 2.9 and Figure 2.10). Horenbout is documented as a citizen of Ghent and in 1515 he entered the service of Margaret of Austria, the daughter of Emperor Maximilian and Mary of Burgundy. He left Ghent for England sometime in the 1520s and was recorded in the accounts of the household of Henry VIII between 1528 and 1531. His only surviving documented work is a rather anomalous one: the *Hours of Bona Sforza* (London, BL, Add. Ms. 34294). This, refreshingly, is a manuscript with a well-documented early history.[12] It was begun in Milan in 1490 for the Sforza duchess by the illuminator and priest Giovanni Pietro Birago. Before the manuscript was finished, Birago reported that a friar from a local convent had stolen parts of it. The friar went to prison but the missing sections of the work were not recovered. What remained was inherited by Margaret of Austria and she took it with her when she returned to the Low Countries in 1506 to act as Governor of the Netherlands on behalf of her nephew, the future Emperor Charles V. Between 1517 and 1521, Margaret had the stolen sections replaced, and Horenbout, by then appointed as her court painter, was paid for illuminations in 1520. Margaret had herself portrayed as a participant in several of the scenes: in the Presentation in the Temple she is one of the attendant women and her father Emperor Maximilian acts as Simeon.

The identification of the other principal illuminator of the *Rothschild Prayer Book* has followed a similar scholarly path to that of Horenbout – moving from anonymity to an artist recorded in documents. Initially he was

11   Kren and McKendrick, *Illuminating the Renaissance*, pp. 366–75 and 437–42.

12   Kren and McKendrick, *Illuminating the Renaissance*, no 129, pp. 428–31.

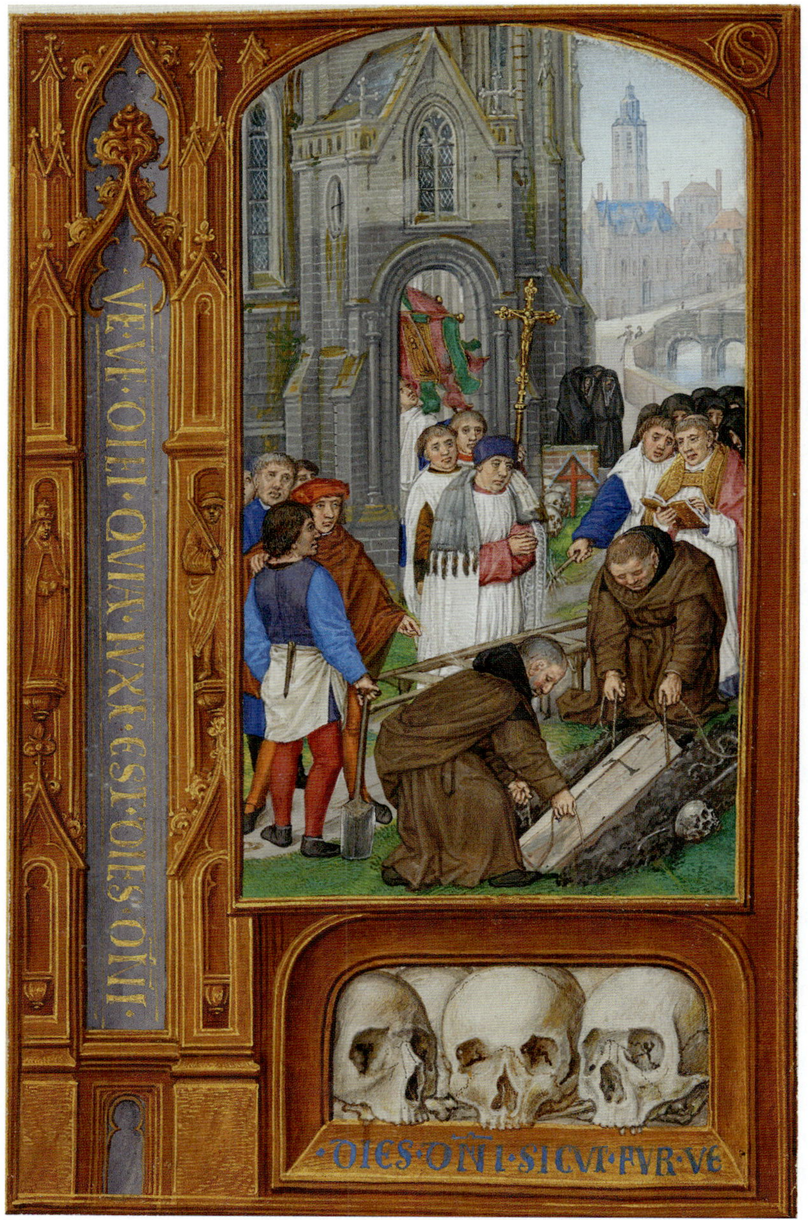

Figure 2.9: Burial in a Flemish Courtyard from the *Rothschild Prayer Book*. Folio 164v, *c.*1505–1510. Parchment, 22.8cm × 16cm. Kerry Stokes Collection, Perth.

known as the Master of the First Prayer Book of Maximilian, from his work in a prayer book for Emperor Maximilian I (Vienna, ONB, Ms. 1907), but he is now widely identified as the illuminator Alexander Bening who registered with the guild of St Luke in Ghent in 1469 and died in the city in 1519.[13] Bening's style and compositions were clearly dependent upon those of Ghent

13   Kren and McKendrick, *Illuminating the Renaissance*, pp.190–8; De Kesel, *The Hours of Queen Isabella*, pp. 41–4 et passim.

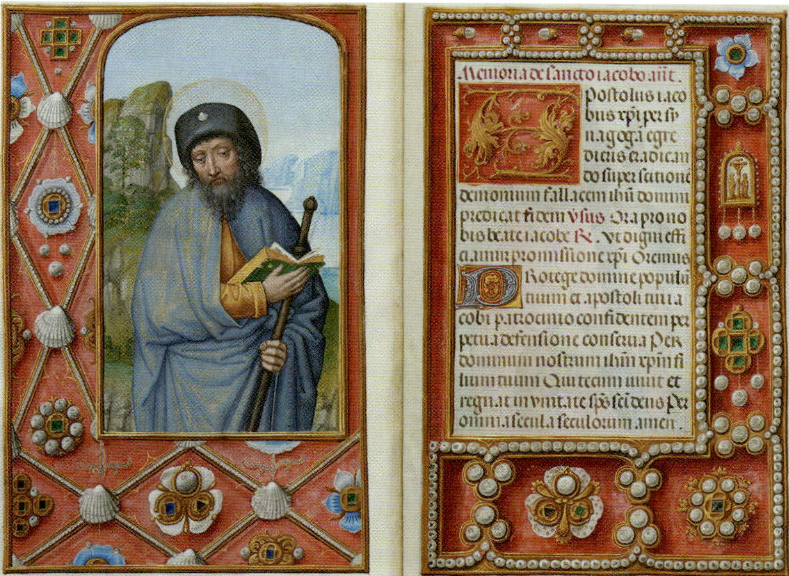

Figure 2.10: Saint James from the *Rothschild Prayer Book*. Folios 209v–210, *c*.1505–1510. Parchment, 22.8cm × 16cm. Kerry Stokes Collection, Perth.

illuminators of the 1470s and 1480s, and he worked in a less detailed technique than Horenbout: pigments were handled more broadly. Alexander Bening's characters are usually easily recognised: often the men have a greyish flesh tone, usually with wide cheekbones and rather pouty mouths (Figure 2.13).

On the basis of style it appears that Horenbout was to provide the illustration of the most prominent and important miniatures in the manuscript – including the opening miniatures for the Office of the Virgin and the remarkable opening of the Office of the Dead – while Alexander Bening and his workshop were to paint or provide the patterns, and perhaps even underdrawing, for many others. However, three other distinctive artists played a less extensive but still significant role. The Master of the Prayer Books of around 1500 – not yet rescued from anonymity or even provided with a snappier pseudonym – provided just six miniatures, including the miniature of the Nativity (Figure 2.1).[14] Alexander Bening's son, Simon – who went on to become the most celebrated illuminator in Europe – painted a third or so of the images of saints in the Suffrages, usually on designs previously used by his father (Figure 2.10).[15] The third major participant, the renowned Bruges painter Gerard David, made the most minimal but also the most emotionally engaging contribution (Figure 2.11). David was famed for his panel paintings and only a small number of illuminations, dispersed among a few manuscripts, have ever been attributed to him.[16] Quite often, as in the *Prayer Book*, he supplied only faces or figures to miniatures painted by others. It seems as though

14   Kren and McKendrick, *Illuminating the Renaissance*, pp. 394–405; De Kesel, *The Hours of Queen Isabella*, pp. 53–4.
15   Kren and McKendrick, *Illuminating the Renaissance*, pp. 447–71.
16   Kren and Ainsworth, 'Illuminators and Painters', pp. 39–41.

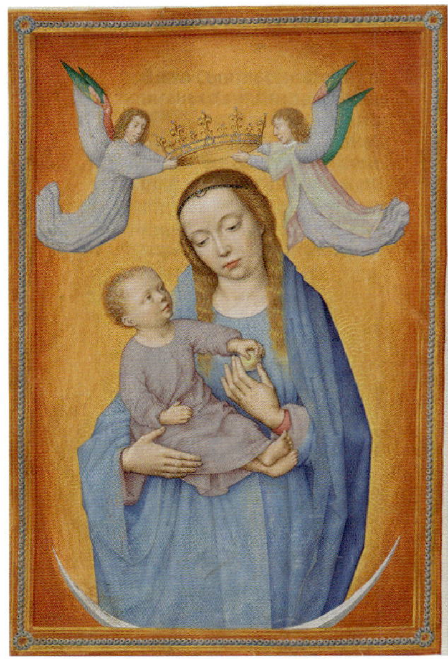

Figure 2.11: Virgin and Child from the *Rothschild Prayer Book*. Folio 197v, *c.*1505–1510. Parchment, 22.8cm × 16cm. Kerry Stokes Collection, Perth.

David's participation added a special gloss. In the Virgin and Child the rather awkward angels are recognisably in the style of Alexander Bening while the young mother and her infant son are painted with David's unsurpassed delicacy and charm. But it is as much the sense of their relationship and feelings – the Christ Child's trust and the Virgin's apprehension – that makes this such a beautiful and moving image.

It made sense to employ a group of artists for such extravagant labour-intensive projects: it would be the only way to bring the work to an acceptably speedy conclusion. Providing a manuscript, such as the Prayer Book, with seventy or more highly finished miniatures, each with complicated illuminated surrounds and facing complementary borders, was a daunting prospect, an undertaking that an individual artist would be unlikely to bring to completion swiftly enough to satisfy either the wishes of a client or his own cash-flow requirements. It is almost impossible to know how long such a manuscript project might have taken. Even when there seems some indication – such as Horenbout's being paid for the sixteen miniatures in the *Hours of Bona Sforza* over a two-year period – the circumstances surrounding the work are unknown. As court painter, Horenbout is likely to have been working on many other projects at the same time; between 1515, when he was appointed by Margaret of Austria, and the early 1520s when he moved to England, he painted pictures, including portraits, designed a window and even collaborated with nuns on making a little embroidered garden – a three-dimensional artefact with fabric flowers and plants. Perhaps he also produced ephemeral decorations for court celebrations.

One effective way for an artist to speed up the process of production was to rely on a model or pattern-book exemplar and to reuse a successful design from one manuscript to another. The documentary evidence for this practice shows how highly artists valued collections of such patterns: they were bequeathed, traded, borrowed or rented, even stolen. Gerard David went to prison for failing to return patterns he had commandeered from another artist who had reneged on an agreement.[17] Illumination in the *Rothschild Prayer Book* reusing long-established, successful designs includes the cycle of calendar scenes, which was repeated in at least seven manuscripts and seems to have been devised by Horenbout. Patterns particularly associated with the work of Alexander Bening lie behind many of the borders with figurative inclusions and many of the miniatures with saints. The illustrations of the Mass of St Gregory in both the *Maximilian* and *Rothschild Prayer Books* are a good example. In this instance Alexander Bening seems to have painted the miniatures as well as supplying the design, but this is far from universally the

17   Kren and Ainsworth, 'Illuminators and Painters', p. 47.

case: more than one artist may have contributed to a single miniature, and there are obvious instances where Simon Bening and Horenbout painted on designs or patterns associated with Alexander Bening's earlier output.[18]

This intermingling of work raises questions about how such collaboration was organised. It is clear that by the end of the fifteenth-century members of the book trade – booksellers, binders and scribes – took on the role of merchants and co-ordinated different crafts and artists. This was not always an easy task. In 1492–3, a particularly bad year in Antwerp, Simon the illuminator was fined for trying to stab a fellow illuminator; Damian the bookbinder was convicted for coming to blows with yet another illuminator; and Gheraert Leeu, a printer, was murdered by a 'slight stab' to the head by the punch-maker Hendrick van Symmen.[19] Sometimes historians postulate the idea of workshops of illuminators where several worked in a reasonably unified style, but differences in detail and technique lead to miniatures getting attributed to 'assistants' or 'followers'. But there is no documentary evidence to support the idea of large workshops. Horenbout for example is known to have hired only one journeyman, in 1498, and to have taken on a single apprentice illuminator, in 1502.[20] It is thought that later he trained his daughter and son, who were illuminators by the time they moved to England with him in the 1520s. Even Willem Vrelant, the enormously successful and influential Bruges illuminator, is only known

to have registered four apprentices during the thirty-year span of his career.[21] Two of them were female and it is probable that the other two were his children. After Vrelant's death in 1484 his wife and daughter continued his business for some years. It seems that such small-scale family workshops may have been the customary situation. Simon Bening is thought to have trained with his father Alexander and to have inherited a body of patterns from him that he used throughout his long career.

Perhaps therefore one should think of the pages of the *Prayer Book* to be illuminated by being distributed among the artists, sometimes moving from one to another, with different tasks allocated to each; once the desired work on a leaf was finished, whether drawing only, background painting or border, it was passed on for the next contribution. Instances are known where pages travelled surprising distances. The most stunning example of a long-distance collaboration involved Simon Bening. In 1530, when he was thought 'the principal painter of this art in all of Europe', Bening painted part of an enormous and elaborate genealogical tree for the Infante Dom Fernando of Portugal.[22] The manuscript was designed to demonstrate the line of descent through the kings and queens of Spain and Portugal to culminate in Manuel I, Dom Fernando's father. This was a manuscript with a political agenda – the Portuguese king had ambitions to rule the whole of the Iberian peninsula. Antonio da Holanda devised and drew the genealogy in Lisbon and the leaves were sent to Bruges for Simon Bening to paint. The Portuguese

18   Examples of designs painted by Alexander in the *Breviary of Eleanor of Portugal* that are raised to an entirely higher level in miniatures painted by Horenbout in the *Rothschild Prayer Book* include St Stephen (Figure 2.7) and St Vincent (Figure 2.8).
19   van der Stock, 'Flemish Illuminated Manuscripts', pp. 117–22.
20   Heyder, 'Corporate Design made in Ghent/Bruges?', p. 183.

21   Bousmanne, *Item à Guillaume Wyelant aussi enlumineur*; Kren and McKendrick, *Illuminating the Renaissance*, pp. 117–9.
22   de Góis, *Crónica do Felicissimo Rei D. Manuel*, Vol. 2 p. 56 (for Bening as the leading painter of Europe); and for London, BL, Add. Ms 12531; Kren and McKendrick, *Illuminating the Renaissance*, No.147, pp. 460–3.

diplomat in Antwerp who had organised the work described the price he had paid as 'a great deal of money'. In other instances it was the artists rather than the manuscripts that did the travelling. Antonio da Holanda had trained in the Netherlands before settling in Portugal in the service of the crown. Horenbout continued to live in Ghent after his appointment as court painter to Margaret of Austria; every time he was needed at court he travelled the 150 miles to Mechelen.

Aside from the logistical difficulties of production, projects as expensive in materials, skill and time as the *Rothschild Prayer Book* and its fellows raises the question of who financed these undertakings. Clearly there was no problem in financing the speculative production of a modest Book of Hours, nor even a special commission for a patron able to make interim payments to keep the wolves from the craftsmen's door. But who was behind the manufacture of the *Prayer Book* and the other manuscripts of this group? Was there some capitalist entrepreneur behind their production, or could it have been the scribes and illuminators themselves? Is it significant that no similarly extravagant collaborative manuscripts seem to be datable after Alexander Bening's death? Or was it some prince or prince's agent? One possibility, perhaps, is that they could have been made for Margaret of Austria. Her mother and grandmother were both great patrons of illuminated manuscripts and she amassed an extensive library herself including fourteen manuscript Books of Hours.[23] Margaret had appointed Horenbout to her own court and had him complete the *Sforza Hours*, it is thought as a gift for her nephew the Emperor Charles V. Might this group of extravagant and splendid books have been made for her to present to her peers or those she wished to impress and

influence? The international gifts she made of music manuscripts compiled under the direction of the musician, merchant, diplomat and spy Petrus Alamire are well known; but those volumes, with illumination incorporating the coats of arms and emblems of the intended owners, were clearly illuminated specifically with them in mind.[24] This is not the case with the *Rothschild Prayer Book*.

Some aspects of the *Prayer Book's* content and illumination, however, could be clues to an intended owner or at least a class of recipient. The most original and, I think, impressive demonstrations of Horenbout's ability and the intellectual rigour that he brought to illumination are the miniatures he painted to illustrate the Masses for the Days of the Week (Figure 2.8 and Figure 2.12). These subjects are a rare inclusion and they called for an innovative treatment. Horenbout came up with a stunning sequence, providing an image not of the subject of the votive mass but a precise record of a moment during that mass. They are among the most remarkable and successful of Flemish illuminations, almost like snapshots of contemporary liturgy with the figures convincingly integrated in their settings and in relationship one to another. The celebrants and their assistants wear the appropriate colour and style of vestment, altars are correctly furnished and the settings and actions are informatively detailed. In the miniature of the memorial Mass of the Dead the pall lies in front of the altar with candles at its corners rather than over a coffin as it would for a funeral Mass, and a particular, rather recondite action is shown – a survival from early Christian practice where the priest offered the paten to be kissed before communion. This was uniquely retained for the Mass of the Dead. Even the altarpiece is

23   Debae, *La Librairie de Marguerite d'Autriche*.

24   McKendrick, Lowden and Doyle, *Royal Manuscripts: The Genius of Illumination*, No. 153, pp. 422–3.

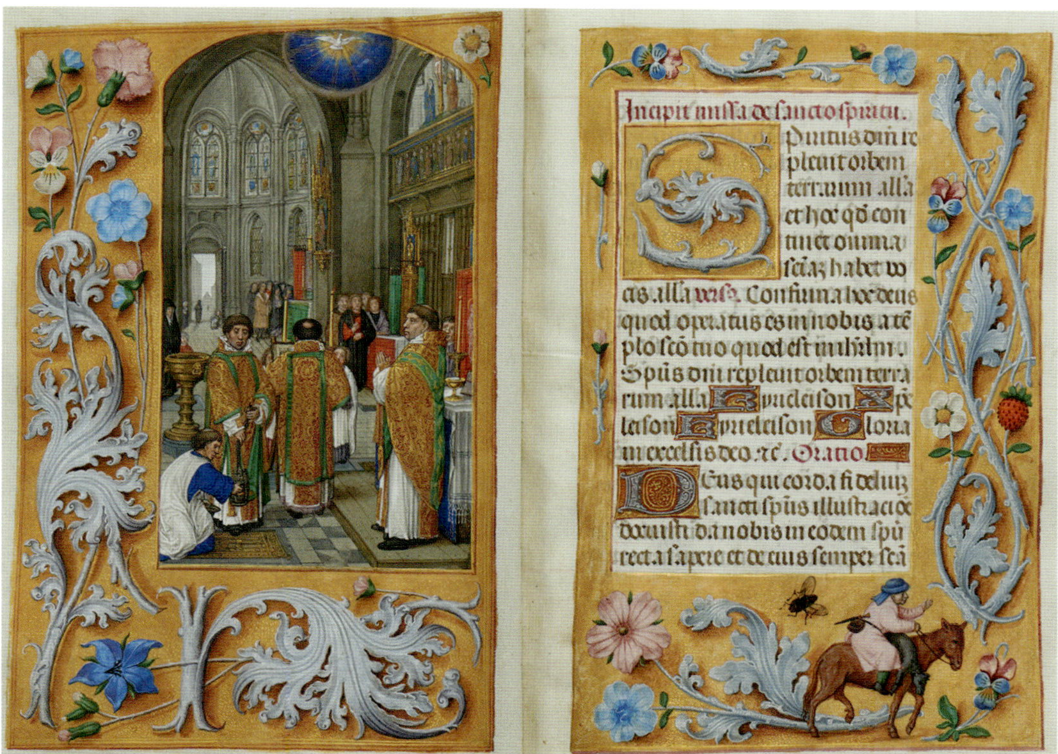

Figure 2.12: Mass of the Holy Spirit from the *Rothschild Prayer Book*. Folios 37v–38, *c.*1505–1510. Parchment, 22.8cm x 16cm. Kerry Stokes Collection, Perth.

fitting: showing the Raising of Lazarus, it was a reassurance of the redemption and promise of everlasting life ensured by Christ's sacrifice of his body and blood. The miniature for the Mass of the Holy Spirit (Figure 2.12) is remarkable for the evocative and convincing recession that extends the scene into the street beyond and for the telling details showing the partial polychromy of the sculpture on the pillars and rood screen. The scene depicts the deacon giving the Gospel reading from an evangeliary. When the reading is over he will hand the book to the priest to be blessed, and the young acolyte is shown preparing the censer in readiness.

The inclusion, the detail, and the accuracy of these seven miniatures prompt the idea that

the manuscript may have been commissioned with an ecclesiastic owner in mind. One decorative detail, the acorn jewel, appears in several borders and seems particular to the *Prayer Book* (Figure 2.13). Could this be an identifying emblem? One family that had an oak tree with acorns on its coat of arms was the della Rovere of Italy, the family of Pope Sixtus IV (r. 1471–1484) and his descendants; acorns were incorporated into decorations and displays put on by family members. At one feast, for example, the extravagant confections provided by the pope's nephew included ten trays with sailing ships of spun sugar filled with silver acorns and roses.[25] The most eminent della Rovere at

25   Reed, *The Edible Monument*, p. 104.

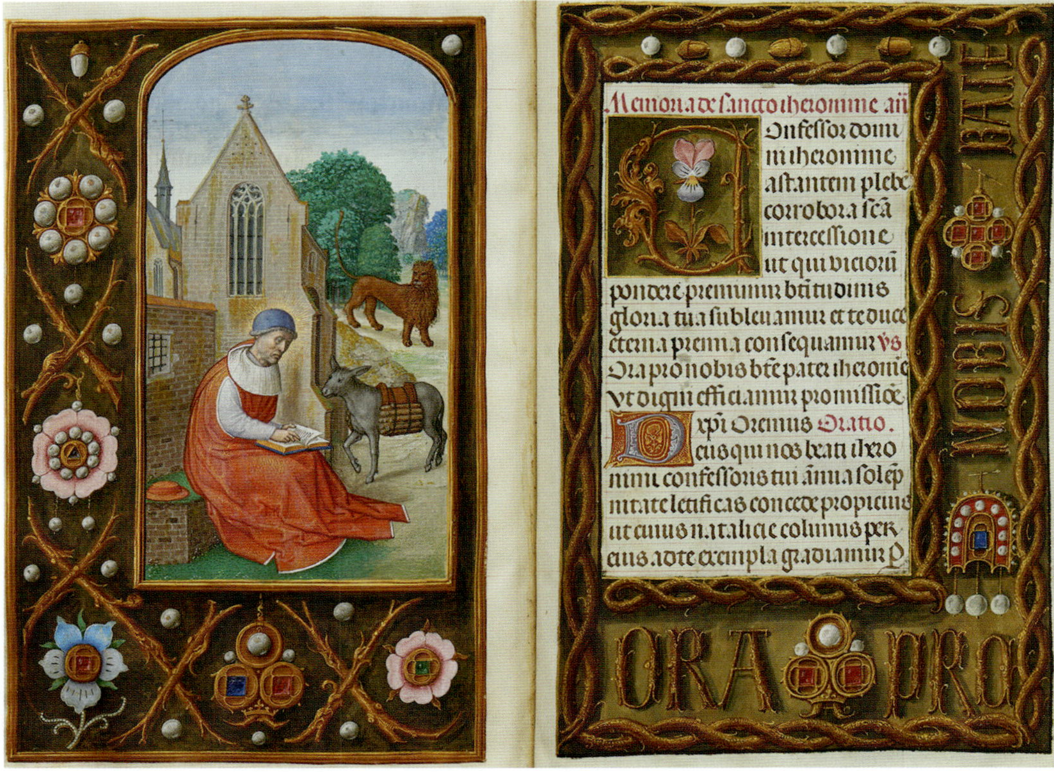

Figure 2.13: Saint Jerome from the *Rothschild Prayer Book*. Folios 221v and 222, *c.*1505–1510. Parchment, 22.8cm × 16cm. Kerry Stokes Collection, Perth.

the time the *Prayer Book* was being made, most likely around 1505, was Pope Julius II, the patron of Michelangelo, who reigned between 1503 and 1513. Perhaps someone had him or one of his cardinal nephews in mind when the manuscript was being painted, but hedged their bets by not making precise heraldic references.

This is of course conjectural and it is impossible to reach a conclusion without further evidence of the commissioner or indication of an intended owner. On balance it seems that the *Prayer Book* was produced speculatively to some degree, made at the cost of someone confident that the need or desire for a suitably lavish and impressive manuscript would soon arise. Yet one section of the manuscript is particularly tantalising in regard to early

ownership, and seems to offer some clues that, even if the *Prayer Book* was not initially made with a churchman in mind, it was later seen as suitable for one. The final four Suffrages of the manuscript are an addition, a discrete group of pages written by a scribe whose distinctive style is not found in the rest of the book. The miniatures, two by Horenbout and two by Simon Bening, appear to be later than their work elsewhere in the *Prayer Book*. The recessed coloured panels that frame Horenbout's St Benedict make a border completely unlike any other around his work, and the spectacular diptych framing of Simon Bening's Vision of St Bernard is even more innovative and remarkable (Figure 2.14). Both seem an advance on the very varied but well-established types of border

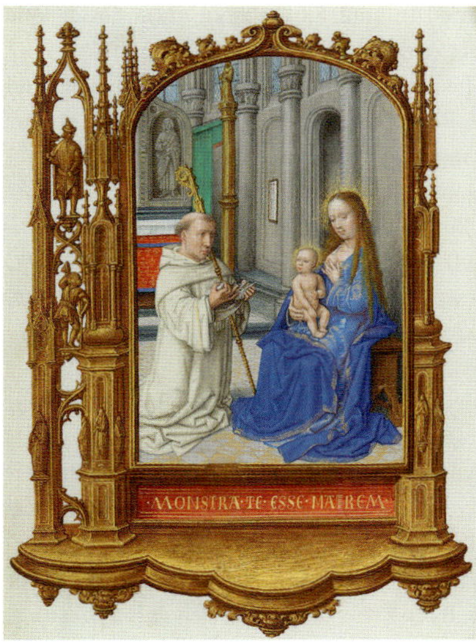

Figure 2.14: Vision of Saint Bernard of Clairvaux from the *Rothschild Prayer Book*. Folio 245v, *c.*1505–1510. Parchment, 22.8cm × 16cm. Kerry Stokes Collection, Perth.

used throughout the rest of the volume, and it seems likely that this addition was made to suit the book for a new owner. Each saint represents a religious order: Dominican, Franciscan, Cistercian and Benedictine. It is possible perhaps that the owner or destined recipient was a cleric; these added elements augment the ecclesiastical focus seen in the miniatures of the Masses.

These thoughts prompt a final speculation. The script of this added section is closely similar, and perhaps by the same hand, as that of a later Book of Hours illuminated by Simon Bening for a known patron: Cardinal Albrecht of Brandenburg, Elector of Mainz.[26] Perhaps most widely known for being behind the sale of indulgences that prompted Martin Luther to nail his ninety-five theses to the door of the church in Wittenberg, the cardinal was a great patron of the arts and he had two, or

possibly three, manuscripts illuminated by Simon Bening for his own use.[27] Perhaps the *Rothschild Prayer Book* was his introduction to Simon Bening's art. From 1520 to 1528 Albrecht had an agent who purchased works of art for him in the Low Countries, and he could have acquired the book for the cardinal; or, alternatively, it might have been among the inducements given by Margaret of Austria and Archduke Charles in 1519 when they were seeking the cardinal's support for the election of Charles as Holy Roman Emperor. The gilt corner-pieces and bosses currently on the binding are Nuremburg work and have the coat of arms of the Wittelsbach family; if they have always been with the book they show that it must have already reached Germany in the sixteenth century.

The circumstances of the creation and early ownership of the *Prayer Book* may remain in obscurity, but now for the first time the manuscript itself does not. Entering the Stokes Collection is the beginning of a new chapter for the *Prayer Book* and rather the conclusion of one for me. *The Rothschild Prayer Book* first came onto my desk at Christie's in 1999 when the goods seized by the Nazis from Alphonse von Rothschild's palace in Vienna were finally restituted to his heirs. I had the task of researching, cataloguing, and marketing the manuscript.[28] We had no clear idea of what the *Prayer Book* might be worth, for we had sold nothing comparable before; only the auction would establish its value. Pre-sale we insured it for 2 million pounds sterling and this meant that when the book needed to travel, I went with it. There was occasional paranoia but our travels passed without mishap and were, on occasion, entertaining. In 1999, on my way to

---

26   Sold at Sotheby's, London June 19 2001, lot 36.

27   Kren and Ainsworth, *Illuminating the Renaissance*, Nos. 145 and 146, pp. 456–460.

28   Christie's, London, 8 July 1999, lot 102.

take the *Prayer Book* for exhibition in New York the customs officer at Heathrow called me into the back room and insisted that I unpack the manuscript for examination. I complied but then asked if there was something the matter with the export papers. I was told, 'no, we just wanted to see what a book worth two million pounds looked like'. It would turn out to be a book worth more than eight million, and when the manuscript returned to Christie's for sale fifteen years later there was no question of my hand-carrying it anywhere.

It has been a great good fortune to have worked with such an exceptional book: having the chance to introduce such a great manuscript to collectors, curators, scholars and the interested was always a joy, often instructive and even moving. I shall never forget turning the pages for a very elderly and learned bibliophile. He remained head bowed and silent throughout. It was after a good lunch and I wondered if he had dozed off. But at the end when I closed the book there was a pause and then he raised distinctly moist eyes, saying, 'this is beyond question the most beautiful book I've ever seen'.

About the author

Kay Sutton is Director and Senior Specialist for Medieval and Renaissance Manuscripts at Christie's London. ksutton@christies.com

Works cited

Bernard Bousmanne, *Item à Guillaume Wyelant aussi enlumineur: Willem Vrelant: un aspect de l'enluminure dans les Pays-Bas méridionaux sous le mécénat des ducs de Bourgogne Philippe le Bon et Charles le Téméraire* (Brussels and Turnhout: Bibliothèque royale de Belgique and Brepols, 1997).

Christie's, 'The Collection of Barons Nathaniel and Albert von Rothschild. Sale 6179.' 8 July 1999 (London: Christie's, 1999).

Marguerite Debae, *La Librairie de Marguerite d'Autriche* (Brussels: Bibliothèque royale Albert I, 1987).

Lieve De Kesel, *The Hours of Queen Isabella the Catholic, the Cleveland Museum of Art/Ohio Leonard C. Hanna Jr. Fund 1963. 256, Commentary volume to the facsimile* (Munich: Güterslohe 2013).

Damião de Góis, *Crónica do Felicissimo Rei D. Manuel*, 4 vols (Coimbra: Coimbra University Press, 1955).

Joris Corin Heyder, 'Corporate Design made in Ghent/Bruges? On the Extensive Reuse of Patterns in Late Medieval Flemish Illuminated Manuscripts', in *The Use of Models in Medieval Book Painting*, ed. by Monika E. Müller (Newcastle upon Tyne: Cambridge Scholars Publishing, 2014), pp. 167–201.

Thomas Kren and Maryan W. Ainsworth, 'Illuminators and Painters: Artistic Exchanges and Interrelationships', in *Illuminating the Renaissance, The Triumph of Flemish Manuscript Painting in Europe,* ed. by Thomas Kren and Scot McKendrick. (Los Angeles: J. Paul Getty Museum, 2003), pp. 39–41.

Thomas Kren and Scot McKendrick, eds., *Illuminating the Renaissance, The Triumph of Flemish Manuscript Painting in Europe* (Los Angeles: J. Paul Getty Museum, 2003).

Susan Marti, *Charles le Téméraire (1433–1477), Faste et déclin de la cour de Bourgogne* (Brussels: Fonds Mercator, 2008).

Scot McKendrick, John Lowden, and Kathleen Doyle, eds., *Royal Manuscripts: The Genius of Illumination* (London: British Library, 2011).

Marcia Reed, *The Edible Monument: The Art of Food for Banquets* (Los Angeles: Getty Trust Publications, 2015).

Sotheby's, *Western Manuscripts and Miniatures, June 19, 2001* (London: Sotheby's, 2001).

Jan van der Stock, 'Flemish Illuminated Manuscripts: Assessing Archival Evidence', in *Flemish Manuscript Painting in Context: Recent Research*, ed. by Elizabeth Morrison and Thomas Kren (Los Angeles: J. Paul Getty Museum 2006), pp. 117–22.

Richard S. Sylvester, ed., *The Life and Death of Cardinal Wolsey* by George Cavendish, Early English Text Society, No. 243 (London: Oxford University Press, 1959).

Heribert Tenschert and Ina Nettekoven, *Horae B.V.M.: 158 Stundenbuchdrucke der Sammlung Bibermühle, 1490–1550* (Ramsen, Switzerland: Antiquariat Bibermühle, 2003).

3. The *Rothschild Prayer Book* as political, social and economic agent through the ages

Kate Challis

Dunlop, Anne (ed.), *Antipodean Early Modern. European Art in Australian Collections, c. 1200–1600*, Amsterdam University Press, 2018

DOI: 10.5117/9789462985209/CH03

Abstract

Deluxe illuminated manuscripts such as the *Rothschild Prayer Book* – produced in the early modern era – were rarely used for their intended purpose as religious books to aid private devotion. Instead, they acted as potent political, social and economic agents during both the early sixteenth century and the Third Reich: a way to curry favour, an investment piece, and also more recently a symbol of wealth, power and culture used as a tool for negotiation and one of reparation.

Keywords: Art repatriation; Manuscript production; Diplomatic gifts; Anschluss; Führermuseum

In my final year as an undergraduate, I travelled to Vienna to examine a number of early sixteenth-century Flemish illuminated manuscripts in the collection of the Austrian National Library. One of the numbers I carefully wrote on the request form was Cod ser n 2844. As the librarian presented the closed book to me, its sumptuous crimson velvet binding with silver-gilt coat of arms, catches and clasps signaled that it was something extraordinary; but little did I know that it would become a central part of both my undergraduate and doctoral dissertations.[1] Nor did I know that within a few years it would no longer call the National Library home and would find itself in a place that at the time of its birth, Europeans did not even know existed.

Famed for the sheer quantity and quality of its illustrations capturing charming details of early sixteenth-century life, the *Rothschild Prayer Book* has also gained notoriety over the past century for its monetary value. In 1906 it was already highly prized at 150,000 crowns, making it the most valuable of all the manuscripts in the collection of Baron Nathaniel Rothschild.[2] Twice in the last two decades, it has broken records for the highest amount ever paid for an illuminated manuscript: in 1999 for $13.3m USD and in 2014 for $13.6m USD.[3] It has

---

1   Challis, 'Marginalised Jewels' and Challis, 'Things of Inestimable Value'.

2   de Hamel, *The Rothschilds and their Collections of Illuminated Manuscripts*, p. 10.

3   Vogel, 'At $90 Million, Rothschild Sale Exceeds Goals' and Christie's, 'THE ROTHSCHILD PRAYERBOOK'.

also kept extraordinary company, being associated with important historical individuals including the formidable Margaret of Austria, Regent of the Netherlands (r. 1506–1530); three generations of the cultured Viennese branch of the Rothschild banking family; members of Adolf Hitler's inner circle; and more recently self-made Australian billionaire, philanthropist and collector Kerry Stokes.

So it is not surprising that there is an intense appetite to know more about this extraordinary object. Over the last century, however, research on the *Rothschild Prayer Book* and other manuscripts made in the southern Netherlands at the beginning of the sixteenth century has primarily focused on issues of identity: that of the artist and that of the original owner or owners.[4] While these questions are undoubtedly interesting, they reflect our modern concerns and those of the contemporary art market. Although there is no known documentary evidence regarding how the *Rothschild Prayer Book* came into being, or for whom it was made, it is often assumed that works of such opulence relied on a patron as originator. Scholars continue to ask the same questions in the hope that documentation will be discovered to reveal its commissioner and owner, yet asking different questions will allow new answers to arise. In the discussion that follows, I would like to change the lens through which we view these works, and to look instead at the book's potent social role at two transformative moments in European history. The first is the moment of its creation, in the decades prior to the Reformation when deluxe devotional manuscripts including the *Rothschild Prayer Book* were part of the culture of gift-giving and diplomatic exchange at the European courts. The second is four hundred years later during the social, economic and political upending of Europe during and after World War II, when the book was a potent symbol of Nazi claims to cultural ascendency.

Devotional manuscripts as mediators of power at the European courts

The *Rothschild Prayer Book* is a Book of Hours, a devotional text that was so common that it has been dubbed 'the medieval best seller'; they were produced in greater numbers than the Bible.[5] By the 1510s, when the *Rothschild Prayer Book* was made, Books of Hours had been in existence for over two hundred years. Thousands still exist in libraries, galleries and private collections around the world. With its sixty-seven full-page miniatures and meticulously illustrated borders, the *Rothschild Prayer Book* is one of the peaks of the genre, but it comes near the end of its development. The success of the printing press from the mid-fifteenth century did not immediately put an end to handwritten illuminated codices.[6] Rather than being competitors, they complemented each other by satisfying different market segments. It can be argued that the printing press pushed illuminated books into a high-end deluxe niche for an audience that differed enormously from those who consumed the affordable printed texts in black and white with their flat, comparatively crude, two-dimensional imagery.

4   See for example Brinkmann, *Die Flämische Buchmalerei*; Winkler, *Die Flämische Buchmalerei des XV. und XVI Jahrhunderts*; Kren, *Renaissance Painting in Manuscripts*. Thoss, *Flämische Buchmalerei*. Smeyers and Van der Stock, *Flemish Illuminated Manuscripts, 1475–1550;* Kren and McKendrick, *Illuminating the Renaissance*; and Krieger, *Gerard Horenbout und der Meister Jakobs IV. von Schottland.*

5   Wieck, *The Book of Hours in Medieval Art and Life*, p. 27.

6   By 1490, printing presses existed in over 200 cities across Europe. In Venice alone, there were some 233 presses between 1469–1500. See Pettegree, *The Book in the Renaissance.*

The *Prayer Book* is a notable example, yet within a few decades of its production, the Reformation greatly reduced the demand for private devotional texts.

Given the pristine condition of the *Rothschild Prayer Book* and many other sixteenth-century manuscripts today, it is unlikely that these books were actually much used as devotional or liturgical texts. It is tempting, but too simplistic, to state that they were status symbols: most of these books, including the *Rothschild Prayer Book*, bear no marks of ownership. To understand why such a luxurious and costly manuscript was made, we must turn to the book itself, and examine the context of similar manuscripts to explore the role of deluxe devotional manuscripts in the rapidly shifting economic and political world of pre-Reformation Europe.

The *Rothschild Prayer Book* is an extraordinarily complex and comprehensive devotional book with a tantalizing juxtaposition of standard and unique elements in its texts and decoration.[7] Over the centuries that Books of Hours were popular, standard subjects were developed to accompany the texts and much of the illustrative cycle of the *Rothschild Prayer Book* follows this tradition: together these create a type of medieval storyboard. Few people who owned these books (if they used them at all) would have understood Latin, let alone fluently. Images instead acted as mnemonic devices, prompting the reader to recall corresponding texts that could then be recited by heart. Evoking the emotion of the worshipper was vital to private devotion and the images aided this.

Yet the text itself is far more exhaustive than other Books of Hours and incorporates a number of unusual components: there are Hours and Masses for each day of the week totaling an additional seventy-eigth pages, and four additional devotions.[8] As the *Prayer Book* contained texts for which there were no pre-existing illustrative programmes, new subjects had to be devised. Often the illuminator chose logical subjects such as an image of the Holy Trinity illustrating the Hours of the Holy Trinity (folio 10v), or a glorious vision of All Saints (folio 41v) accompanying the Hours of All Saints. While these are beautifully executed miniatures, the choice of subject is conventional. More noteworthy are the miniatures to accompany the Masses for each day of the week. This was an unusual inclusion, and as there was no established visual tradition, the artist depicted a compilation of rituals performed during the celebration of the Mass: Prayers at the Foot of the Altar (folio 16v), Lighting Candles at the Offertory (folio 28v), Preparation of the Thurible (Figure 2.12), Raising of the Paten (folio 46v), Elevation of the Host (folio 55v), Prayer in Consecration (folio 65v) (Figure 6.14) and the Kiss of Peace (folio 75v).

The appearance of the Hours and Masses for each day of the week with detailed depiction of liturgical rituals might suggest that the book was intended for a cleric. As tantalising, and perhaps even accurate, as this argument may be, the nobility and gentry attended Mass daily and would also have been well acquainted with the intricacies of its rituals. Even breviaries, highly complex liturgical texts used by the clergy, were also owned by members of the aristocracy.[9] The mere appearance of the images of the Mass is not enough to conclude

---

8   These four additional devotions are: *Gaude flora uirginali* (a prayer to the Seven Joys of the Virgin), *O bone ihesu O piissime ihesu* ('a Prayer to the Praise of the Holy Name'), *Ave maris stella dei mater alma* ('Hymn to St Bernard'), and the Athanasian Creed.

9   Two examples among others: the *Breviary of Isabella of Castile* (BL, Add MS 18851) and the *Breviary of Eleanor of Portugal* (NY, Pierpont Morgan Library, MS M 52).

7   See the essays in this volume by Manion and Maddocks for the standard inclusions in Books of Hours.

that the manuscript was destined for a cleric. When we look beyond the manuscript itself to its peers, we shall see the absence of signs of ownership is a rule, not the exception.

The *Rothschild Prayer Book* may be grouped with no fewer than nineteen similar manuscripts made by the same group of Flemish illuminators for the same milieu of consumers in the first decades of the sixteenth century.[10] Each manuscript was a deluxe product with superb high quality full-page illuminations and exquisite borders, yet they combined both standard and unique texts and images. Nowhere is this better illustrated than in the questionably titled but magnificent *Hours of Joanna I of Castile* (BL, Add MS 35313). Like the *Rothschild Prayer Book* it has no overt signs of ownership, no coats of arms or crests.[11] Containing 55 full-page miniatures with an abundance of border illustrations, this manuscript is just as luxurious as the *Rothschild Prayer Book*. It combines texts typically found in Books of Hours with a few popular prayers less

commonly included.[12] What gives this manuscript its individuality are its stunning, fully-illuminated, double page openings juxtaposing Old and New Testament scenes; even the *Rothschild Prayer Book* begins a new section of text with just one image on the verso.

The makers of these books seduced their clientele with spectacular illusionism, charming detail and gorgeous colour, setting their scenes in contemporary Flanders. Interiors feature wooden floorboards, thatched roofs and fireplaces while landscapes exemplify the beauty and gentleness of the Flemish countryside. Meticulous *trompe l'oeil* borders are strewn with flowers and jewellery (Figures 3.1 and 3.2), composed of wooden altarpieces (see Figure 3.4), or depict charming scenes from the Bible or everyday life. Such features were a specialty of the illuminators active in the southern Netherlands during the late fifteenth and early sixteenth centuries, and were part of what could be considered a Flemish 'brand' of illumination. Another aspect of this brand was the constant repetition of compositional patterns. Appropriating and modifying images enabled the artists to produce at a faster rate, as they did not have to invent new compositions for each manuscript: many manuscripts share images for both miniatures and border illustrations.[13] For example, the Virgins in the Annunciation in the *Rothschild Prayer Book* (folio 84v) and the *Hours of Joanna of Castile*

10   These include the *Sforza Hours* (BL, Add MS 34294), the *Grimani Breviary* (Venice, Bibl. Marciana Ms lat. XI), the *Spinola Hours* (LA, J. Paul Getty Museum, Ludwig IX 18), the Croy Hours (Vienna, ÖNB, Cod. 1858), the *Hours of James IV of Scotland and Margaret Tudor* (Vienna, ÖNB, Cod. 1897), the *Breviary of Isabella of Castile*, the *Mayer van den Bergh Breviary* (Antwerp, Mus. Mayer van den Bergh, MS off 285), the *Hours of Isabella of Castile* (Cleveland, Museum of Art, MS 63256), the *Breviary of Eleanor of Portugal*, the *Soane Hours* (London, Sir John Soane's Museum, MS 4), a three volume Psalter Hours in the Vatican (Biblioteca Apostolica Vaticiana, Vat lat 3770–3768), as well as London, BL, Add MS 35313 and Add MS 35314; Munich, Bayerische Staatsbibliothek Clm 28345 and Clm 28346; Oxford, Bodleian Library, MS Douce 112 and MS Douce 256; Vienna, ÖNB, Cod see n 2625 and Cod see n 13238. See also Challis, 'Things of Inestimable Value'.

11   Scholars have argued that due to the lavishness of the manuscript it must have been made for a monarch or a very high ranking aristocrat. Furthermore, the presence of several Spanish saints indicates that it was intended for a member of the Spanish royal family. Joanna of Castile is the primary candidate as in 1496 she married Philip the Handsome, Mary of Burgundy and Holy Roman Emperor, Maximilian I's son and heir. García-Tejedor, Libro de Horas de Juana I des Castilla.

12   Two prayers in honour of the Virgin: *Gaude dei genitrix virgo immaculata* ('Rejoice o Immaculate Virgin) and *Ave sanctissima Maria mater dei* ('Hail Mary Mother of God').

13   For example, the *Rothschild Prayer Book's* Nativity and border narrative of Mary and Joseph being turned away from an Inn (folio 108v-109) can be seen in the Croy Hours (folio 55). The fantastic bas-de-page of the Beasts Fighting and the Man (folio 212) and woman pushing the wheelbarrow with the over-sized flowers (folio 198) appear in the *Hours of Albrecht of Brandenburg* (folio 250v). For more on the use of models see: Challis, 'Things of Inestimable Value', and Heyder, 'Corporate Design Made in Ghent/Bruges?'.

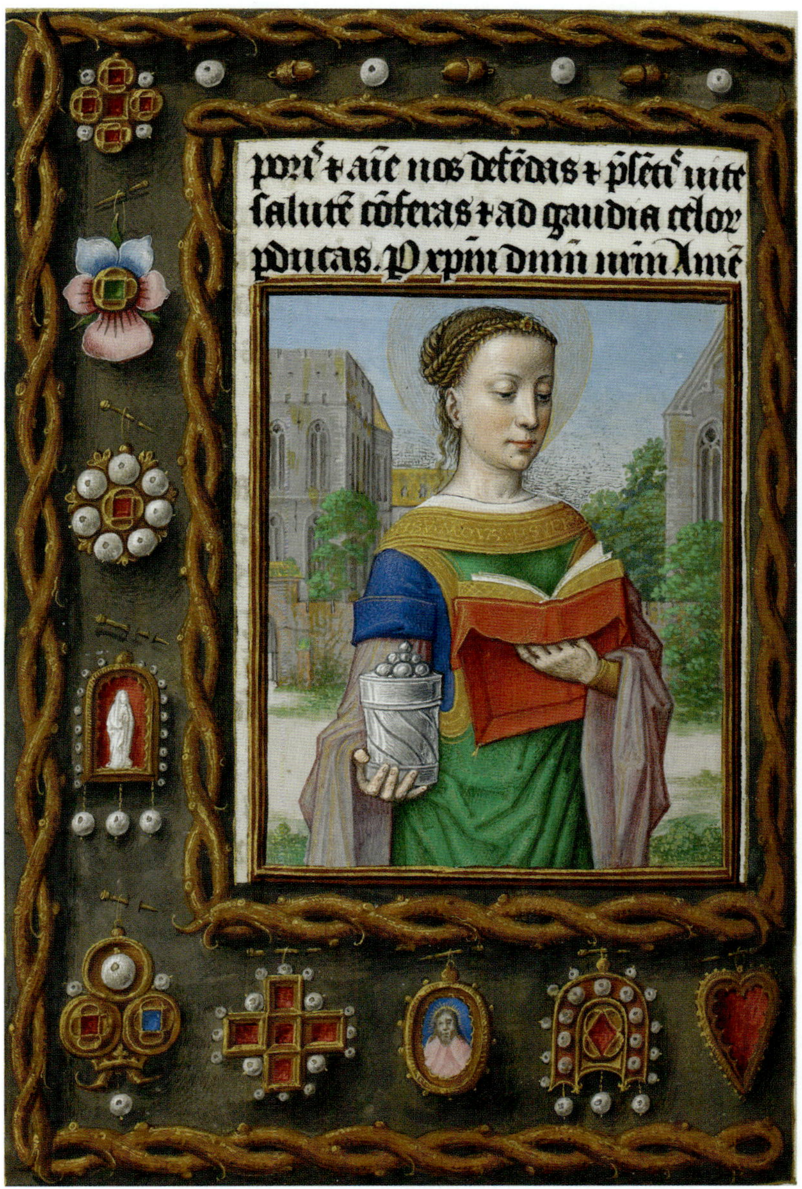

Figure 3.1: Southern Netherlands (Ghent?), Mary Magdalen from the *Hours of Joanna of Castile*. Folio 231v, *c*.1500. Parchment, 23.5cm × 16.5cm. The British Library, London. Add MS 35313.

(folio 56v) are identical with the exception of a few minor details such as the colour of the angels' and the Virgin's robes. The same compositional patterns were also used in the Coronation of the Virgin, the Visitation, the Nativity, the Crucifixion, the Death of the Virgin, King David in Penance as well as certain saints such as Joanna's Mary Magdalen (Figure 3.1) and the Rothschild's St Helena (Figure 3.2).[14]

14   The Coronation of the Virgin (Joanna folio 120, Rothschild folio 134v); the Visitation (Joanna folio 76v, Rothschild

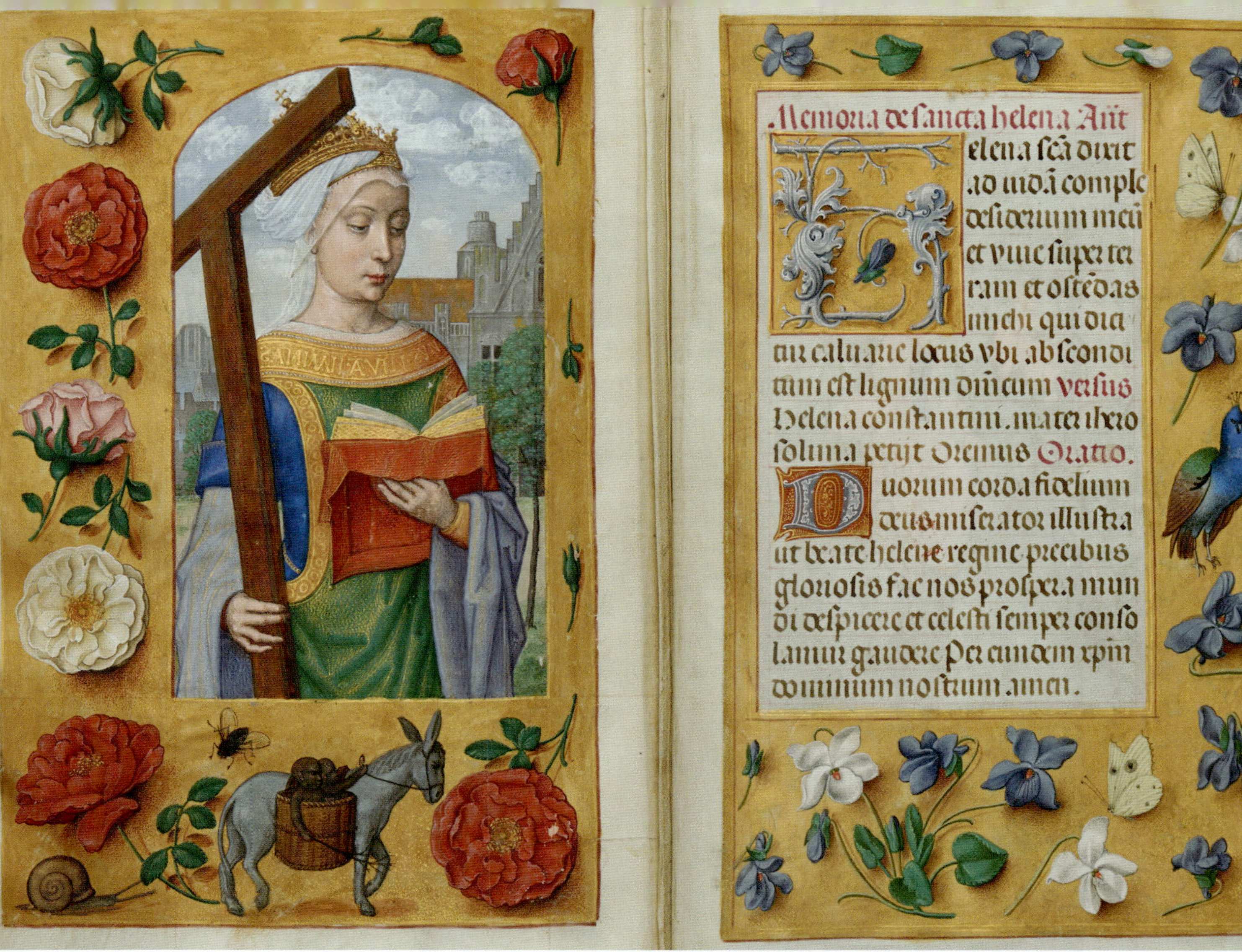

Figure 3.2: St Helena from the *Rothschild Prayer Book*. Folios 233v–234, *c*.1505–1510. Parchment, 22.8cm × 16cm. Kerry Stokes Collection, Perth.

Certain patterns were very popular, such as the Death Bed scene, the Visitation, the Coronation of the Virgin and St George and the Dragon (Figure 3.3 and Figure 3.4).[15] While these

folio 99v), the Nativity (Joanna folio 89v, Rothschild folio 108v), the Crucifixion (Joanna folio 29v, Rothschild folio 59v), the Death of the Virgin (Joanna f.119v, Rothschild folio 130v), King David in Penance (Joanna folio 135, Rothschild folio 147v), as well as certain saints such as Joanna's Mary Magdalen (folio 231v) and the Rothschild's St Helena (folio 233v)

15   St George: Book of Hours (Cambridge, Fitzwilliam Museum, MS 1058–1975, folio 173); the *Hours of Joanna I of Castile* (folio 223v); the *Rothschild Hours* (folio 220v); the *Grimani Breviary* (folio 538v); and the *Hortulus Animae* (Vienna, ÖNb, Cod Bibl. Pal. Vindob. 2706, folio 250v). The Death Bed: Vatican Hours (vat. lat. 3768 folio 3v); the

compositions are all based on the same model they were never precisely the same. The illuminators changed details, colours, clothing, landscape and the borders to ensure each product nevertheless remained unique.

Despite these duplications, it is unlikely that the owners knew that variations of the images inside their books existed elsewhere. Yet it complicates the common assumption that books of such quality and with such an abundance of text and images must have been made for specific individuals. In fact, only five codices

Spinola Hours (folio 184v), the *Grimani Breviary* (folio 449v); Cod ser n 2625 in Vienna (folio 118v).

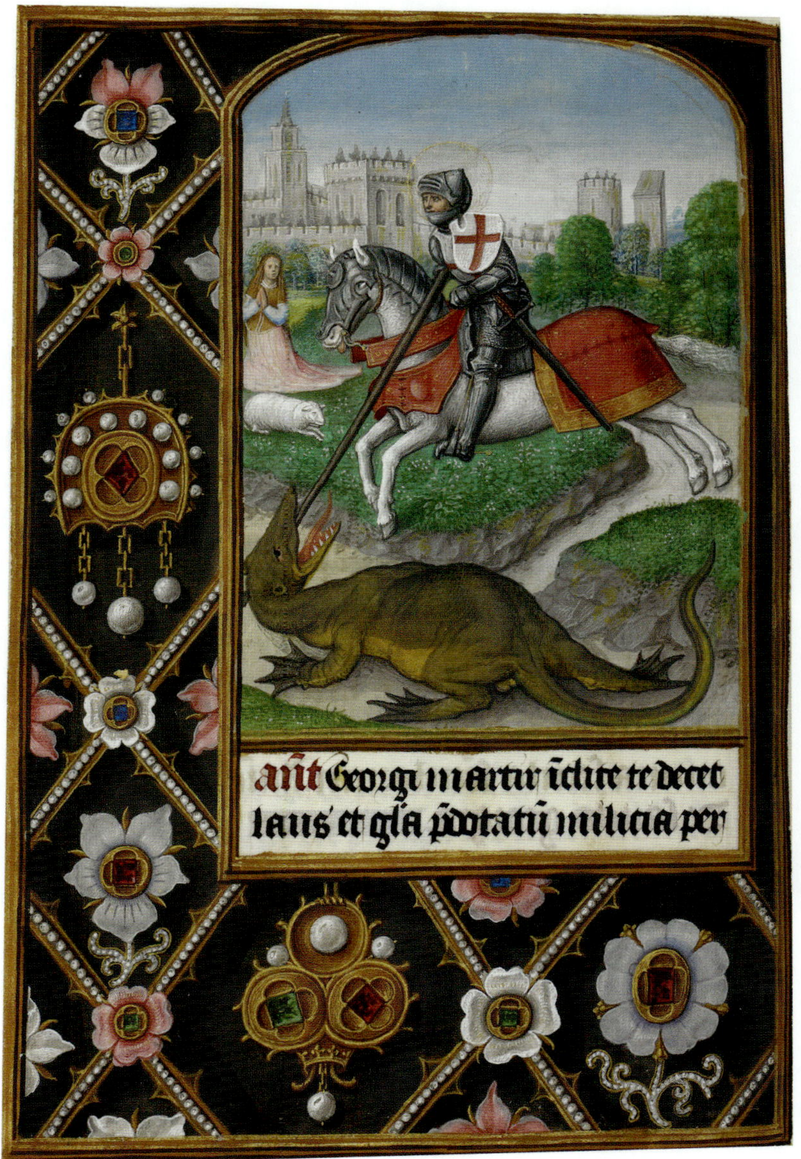

Figure 3.3: Southern Netherlancs (Ghent?), St George from the *Hours of Joanna of Castile*. Folio 223v, *c.*1500. Parchment, 23.5cm × 16.5cm. The British Library, London. Add MS 35313.

in the circle of nineteen around the *Rothschild Prayer Book* possess clear references to owners. In the case of three manuscripts, they were customised for a specific person after or nearing their completion. This was done by inserting a separate folio with the coats-of-arms or a portrait, as seen in the *Breviary of Eleanor of Portugal* (folio 1v), the *Hours of Isabella of Castile* (folio 1v) and the opulent *Breviary of Isabella of Castile* (BL, Add MS 18851). Folio 436v of the latter displays the coats of arms of both Queen Isabella and her husband, Ferdinand, as well as those of the Spanish Infante and Infanta and their Burgundian spouses (Figure 3.5).

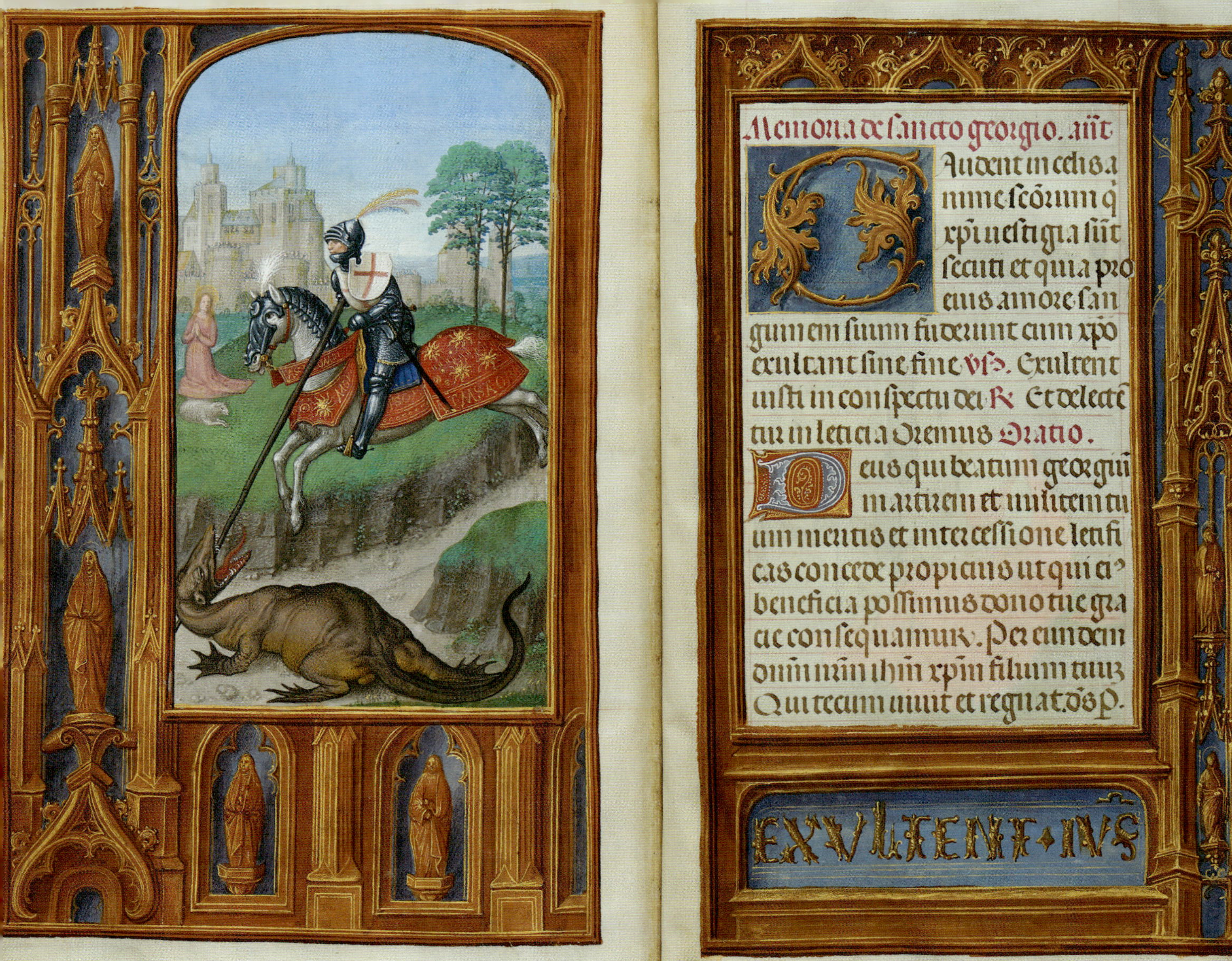

Figure 3.4: St George from the *Rothschild Prayer Book*. Folios 220v–221, c.1505–1510. Parchment, 22.8cm × 16cm, Kerry Stokes Collection, Perth.

This folio has been 'tipped in' or inserted independently of the rest of the gatherings and demonstrates that this was a later addition and not part of the original decorative programme.

Only in two manuscripts were marks of ownership an integral part of the decoration. One is the *Hours of James IV of Scotland and Margaret Tudor* (ÖNB, Cod 1897), in which their monograms, portraits, coats of arms, initials and mottoes demonstrate that this book was designed specifically for the Scottish king and queen (Figure 3.6).[16] The second is the *Sforza Hours*

(BL, Add MS 34294). It is a cautionary case. The book was unfinished when the original commissioner, Bona of Savoy, Duchess of Milan, died in 1503. When Margaret of Austria inherited it, she commissioned Gerard Horenbout, one of her court artists, to complete it, which

16   A magnificent portrait on folio 24v shows the Scottish monarch kneeling in prayer before an altar displaying

his coat of arms and accompanied by his patron saint St James the Greater, leaving no doubt to the identity of the original owner. Margaret Tudor (as depicted in Figure 3.6) is portrayed in a full-page miniature kneeling in front of an altar and a *prie-dieu*, both displaying the coat of arms of the Queen (folio 243v). James' motto (folio 14v), the couple's monogram composed of pearls (folio 183v) and the more 'hidden symbolism' of the thistle and marguerite are also integrated into the decorative programme.

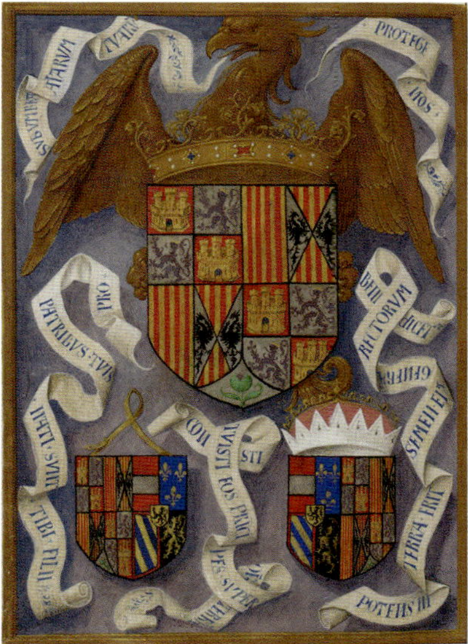

Figure 3.5: Bruges, *Breviary of Queen Isabella of Castile*. Folio 436v, *c.*1497. Parchment, 23cm × 16cm. The British Library, London. Add MS 18851.

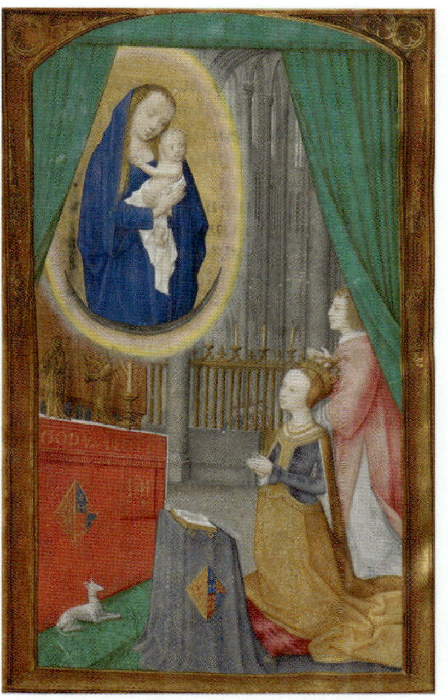

Figure 3.6: Ghent, Margaret Tudor in Prayer from the *Hours of James IV of Scotland*. Folio 243v, *c.*1500–1599. Parchment, 20cm × 14cm. Österreichische Nationalbibliothek, Vienna, Cod. 1897.

was done between 1517–1521.[17] Horenbout included portraits of both Margaret and her nephew, Charles. He is shown on a medallion on the *bas-de-page* of folio 213 surrounded by the letters K (Karolus) and I (Imperator) referring to his new appointment as Holy Roman Emperor. Margaret appears in the guise of St Elizabeth in the Visitation (Figure 3.7). The image has been seen as a 'subtle reference to Margaret's role as surrogate mother to Charles V'.[18] Significantly, after its completion Margaret gave the book to her nephew who was residing in Spain at the time.

This culture of gift giving was a vital part of courtly etiquette in the medieval and early modern period. Jewellery, silverware and paintings were frequently given, received and exchanged among the members of the court. European courts bustled with advisors, tutors, councilors, clerics, ambassadors and administrators. These people were potential

commissioners, donors and recipients of a wide variety of bespoke luxury goods including illuminated manuscripts. Illuminated manuscripts like the *Rothschild Prayer Book* can also, therefore, be seen as potent political, social and economic agents, capable of enhancing or even mediating power as gifts. When Margaret of Austria gave the *Sforza Hours* to her nephew, Charles was Holy Roman Emperor, but he is depicted as a Burgundian noble wearing the Order of the Golden Fleece and not in his imperial robes. Dagmar Eichberger has convincingly argued that this was done to remind Charles of his Burgundian heritage and his responsibilities to these territories.[19] The *Breviary of Isabella of Castile* was also a gift. A dedicatory inscription in the border of folio 437 reveals that it

17   Evans, *The Sforza Hours*.
18   Eichberger, 'The Culture of Gifts', p. 291.

19   Eichberger, 'The Culture of Gifts', p. 290.

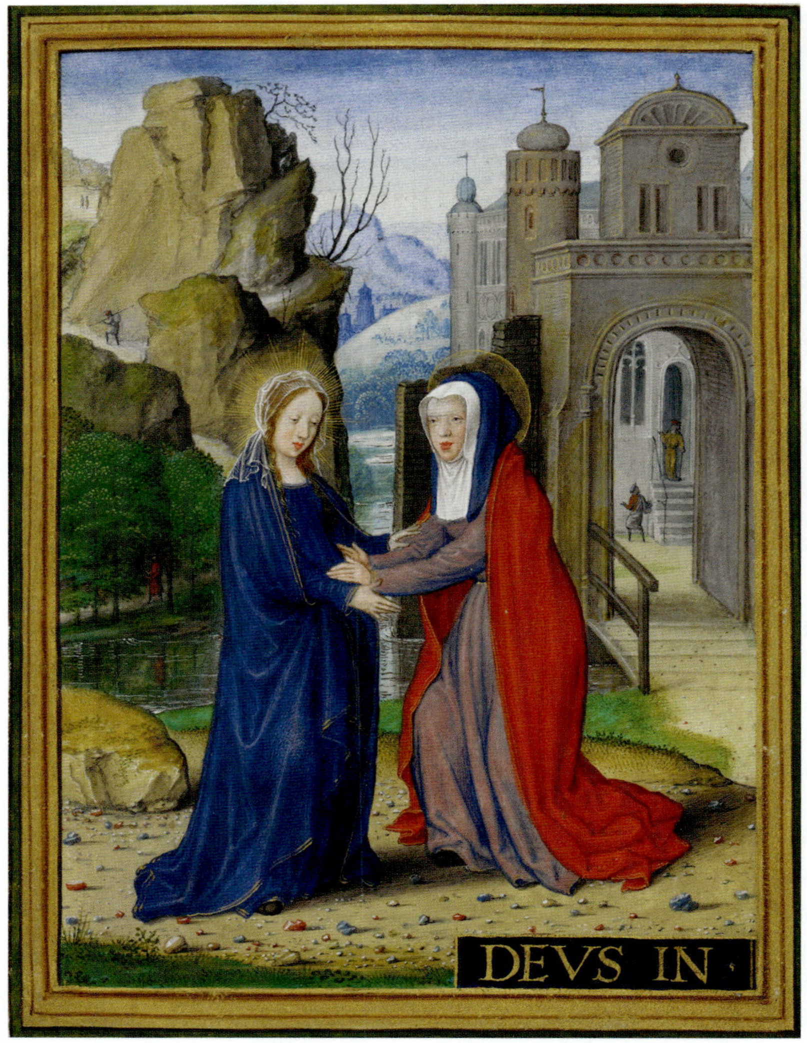

Figure 3.7: Giovanni Birago and Gerard Horenbout, Visitation from *The Sforza Hours*. Folio 61, *c*.1490 and 1517–1521. Parchment, 13.1cm × 9.3cm. London, British Library, Add. MS. 34294.

was given to the Spanish queen by Francisco de Rojas, one of her most trusted advisors and ambassadors (Figure 3.8).[20] He had been a frequent traveller to the Netherlands from

1492 and commissioned altarpieces from Jan Gossart (Rome, Galleria Dora Pamphilj) and Hans Memling (Cincinnati, Estate of Fred Ziv) both of which bear his portrait and coat of arms. The most significant negotiation of his long and successful career was the politically astute Spanish-Burgundian double marriage that eventually led to the Spanish Habsburg Empire. Rojas personally signed the marriage contract on behalf of the Spanish monarchs

20 Like the Sforza Hours, the Isabella Breviary was made in two phases. Most likely de Rojas obtained an incomplete manuscript and had it finished with the double marriage in mind. See Backhouse, *The Isabella Breviary*, p. 54 and Brinkmann, *Die Flämische Buchmalerei*, p. 133.

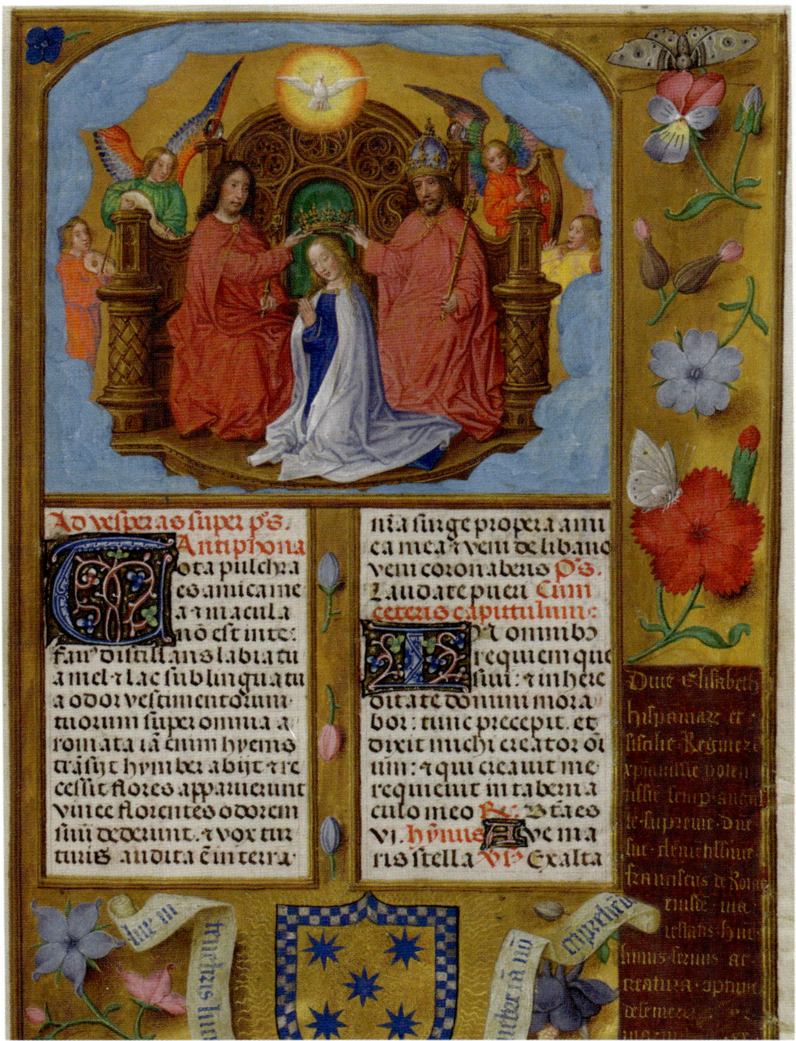

Figure 3.8: Bruges, *Breviary of Queen Isabella of Castile*. Folio 437, *c.*1497. Parchment, 23cm × 16cm. The British Library, London. Add MS 18851.

and a dedication in the *Breviary* is strategically placed opposite the folio bearing the coats of arms of the monarchs and both wedded couples. It is likely the gift was presented to the queen and king to mark this momentous occasion and as a constant reminder of who was responsible. The *Breviary of Eleanor of Portugal* and the *Hours of Isabella of Castille*, with their tipped in portrait folios, were also very likely diplomatic gifts from aspirants

earning or cementing favour at court or abroad.[21] With births, deaths and marriages bringing about rapidly shifting allegiances, retaining and strengthening alliances and sources of support were a perennial preoccupation.

21   For the *Hours of Isabella of Castile*, Cardinal Francisco Jimenez de Cisneros has been suggested as the commissioner. He was an important cleric and member of Isabella and Ferdinand's court. This is however unlikely as there is no documentation of him travelling to the north around

Manuscripts such as the *Rothschild Prayer Book* can thus be seen as valuable vehicles to signify and transmit power in ways specific to the nobility and members of the court. These manuscripts were not just given as diplomatic gifts, they were also often inscribed with personal dedications and even endorsements and letters of reference.[22] A compelling and moving example is the dedication towards the end of the *Hours of James IV of Scotland and Margaret Tudor*, written in old English in the border of the manuscript, in the hand of the Scottish Queen: *Madame I pray your grace / Remember on me when ye / loke upon this boke / Your loving syster / Margaret*. Following the death of her husband in 1513, Margaret gave this stunning manuscript to her sister Mary Tudor, upon Mary's marriage to Louis XII of France.[23] The date of the gift is critical as it reveals the intent behind the gesture. Once widowed, Margaret was appointed Regent of Scotland, but her position was tenuous as she was at war with her brother, Henry VIII. Furthermore, the Duke of Albany, their closest male relative and third in line to the throne, was attempting to supplant her. Books of Hours were often given as wedding presents and it is possible that Margaret gave her sister her exquisite devotional book as a means to pledge alliance and ask for support. The portraits in the book showing Margaret as Queen of Scotland were powerful reminders of her claims as Regent of the territories. However, Mary's own power was short lived. She was widowed only three months after her marriage to the French king, and secretly wed Charles Brandon, 1st Duke of Suffolk, only two months later. As this marriage occurred without the

consent of Henry VIII, it was considered an act of treason and the Privy Council urged that Brandon be imprisoned or executed. Henry however relented and they were eventually pardoned.[24] If Mary received the book at this time, it could also have served as a more personal gift of kinship and love between two siblings, both former monarchs who had married against the wishes of the king and whose status was uncertain.

The Croy Hours is another example of this phenomenon, bearing not one, but three inscriptions referring to members of Margaret of Austria's court in Mechelen.[25] The first appears on the front paste down: *en voz bonnes prières se recommande Celluy qui vostre bonne grace demande. De Lalaing* ('He who asks for your good favour recommends himself to your good prayers. De Lalaing').[26] It can be attributed to Antoine de Lalaing, Count of Hoogstraten (1480–1540). Marrying Elisabeth van Culemborg, first lady in waiting to Margaret of Austria, he was appointed Councillor and Chamberlain in 1510 to the ten year old Charles and became a member of the Great Council of Mechelen. In 1516 he was elected a Knight of the Order of Golden Fleece and in 1530 he was acting Governor to the Netherlands as Margaret of Austria's health was failing. Antoine de Lalaing and Margaret of Austria seem to have been extremely close from at least 1506 when Antoine was sent to Savoy to convince her to accept the role of Regent of the Netherlands. During her reign, Margaret bestowed more gifts on him than anyone else, including a number of illuminated manuscripts.[27] The identities of the 'Croy' and 'Charles' mentioned in the other two inscriptions are uncertain, however. They

---

1495–1500 when the manuscript was made. For the *Breviary of Eleanor of Portugal*, Emperor Maximilian I and his daughter Margaret of Austria have been suggested as possible patrons.

22 Eichberger, 'The Culture of Gifts', p. 290.

23 Unterkircher, *Das Gebetbuch Jakobs IV*, p. 16.

24 Perry, *The Sisters of Henry VIII*.

25 Mazal and Thoss, *Das Buch der Drolerien*, p. 30.

26 Translations by the author unless otherwise noted.

27 Eicherger, 'The Culture of Gifts', p. 292.

seem to be commendations, a means to show the owner's connections, from highly placed persons, conceivably even Charles V.[28] Yet they reveal valuable social and political connections, and they demonstrate the importance, even for high-ranking members of the aristocracy, to constantly strengthen their alliances.

These manuscripts had a further important function: to generate wealth. Such books were occasionally used as vehicles for speculative investment. For instance, in another Flemish manuscript, the *Grimani Breviary*, the coat-of-arms of Antonio Siciliano, chamberlain to the Duke of Milan, appears in an unassuming position. Given the extensive size and nature of the breviary, it is unlikely that Siciliano was the end user or even the original patron of the manuscript. More probably he commissioned or bought it in 1514 when he visited Margaret of

Austria at her court in Mechelen; and we know that Cardinal Grimani then purchased the breviary from Siciliano for 500 ducats.[29] To put this into perspective, Leonardo da Vinci valued his *Virgin of the Rocks* at a hundred ducats in the same year, and he earned between 50–100 ducats in each of his most productive years.[30] It is probable that Siciliano was engaging in speculative commercial activities: he purchased the manuscript for resale and added his coat of arms in an obscure position like a manufacturer might add a brand to a product today. How common this practice was is unknown, as is the frequency of such transactions: was Siciliano behaving opportunistically, or did he know that there was an established market?

These three factors – the existence of commercial speculation, the use of such books as gifts to secure influence, and the relative absence of clear marks of ownership – clearly contradict the traditional hypothesis of a rich patron commissioning such books for his or her own use. A better question is: who else was in the position to initiate the production of a group of manuscripts like those around the *Rothschild Prayer Book*?

Margaret of Austria has already appeared as a figure who can be connected to many of the manuscripts around the *Prayer Book*. But did

28   The second inscription (folio 156v) states: *affin que je soye de vous recommandé aceste bonne dame cest mis sy en escript votre vray bon mestre Charles* ('In order that I may be recommended by you to this good lady, your truly good Master has put his inscription here. Charles'). The third dedication is on folio 164: *Tant auen ce monde vivray/parent et amy vous seray CROY.* ('So long as I am alive in this world you will be my relation and friend. CROY'). There are two possible men named Croy (uncle and nephew), who might be identified as the writer. The first, Guillaume II de Croÿ (1458–1521) was Count of Chièvres and an integral part of the administration and political culture in the Low Countries and Spain at the beginning of the 16th century. His authority in the court is evinced in his politically astute decision to move the nine-year-old Charles away from the influence of his aunt Margaret of Austria to his residence in Beaumont, Hainaut. Among his many titles and roles he was chief tutor and First Chamberlain to Charles V; in 1519 he became a Knight of the Order of the Golden Fleece. Guillaume III de Croÿ (1498–1521), a cleric, was Guillaume II's nephew. At the young age of seventeen he was made bishop of Cambrai; and in his first year as Holy Roman Emperor Charles made him archbishop of Toledo, considered the wealthiest in the Empire after the see of Rome. Scholars have debated the identity of the Charles mentioned in the inscription, suggesting it is either Charles de Lalaing (1466–1525), the brother of Antoine mentioned above, or else Charles I de Croy

(1455–1527), a high-ranking member of the court of Maximilian I and godfather and tutor to the young Charles. It might however be Charles, Holy Roman Emperor, given the close connection between Croÿ and Charles V and association between Antoine de Lalaing and Margaret of Austria. The manuscript entered the Österreichische Nationalbibliothek as part of the library of Prince Eugen von Savoyen (d. 1736), a direct descendent of Charles V. Prince Eugene's great-grandmother was Catalina Micaela, granddaughter of Charles V.

29   The Venetian connoisseur Marcantonio Michiel (c.1486–1552) recorded that the breviary was in Cardinal Grimani's house in 1521 and that Grimani had purchased the manuscript from Antonio Siciliano for 500 ducats. See Grote and Ferrari, *Breviarium Grimani*, p. 9.

30   Evans, *The Sforza Hours*, p. 9.

she commission it? Regent of the Netherlands from 1506 to 1514 and then from 1519 until her death in 1530, Margaret was one of the most powerful women in Europe. As the only elected female of the powerful Franche-Comté Assembly and Privy Council, she negotiated war activities as well as economic and peace treaties.[31] At her court in Mechelen, she raised a generation of rulers: queens of France, Denmark, Hungary and Portugal, as well as two Holy Roman Emperors. Margaret also understood the importance of diplomacy and alliance. In 1483, at the age of three, she was moved to the French court to be raised as the future wife of Charles VIII. Eight years later the marriage treaty was annulled when her husband-to-be married Anne, Duchess of Brittany. Margaret was kept at the French court for a further two years, stripped of her title and position. Despite being married to the Spanish *Infante* in 1496, her fortunes did not change and she found herself widowed within six months. Her subsequent marriage to Philibert II, Duke of Savoy, was also shortlived. At the age of twenty-four, she was once again a widow and she returned to the Netherlands. A turning point came when her brother, Philip the Fair (1482–1506) suddenly died, and their father Maximilian appointed Margaret Regent of the Netherlands and guardian of her four nieces and two nephews. Over the next two decades, Margaret's reputation as an astute politician and collector of art and books spread across Europe and she was visited by the likes of Erasmus and Albrecht Dürer.

In her time Margaret was recognised as the most important patron in the north and among the most influential figures in continental Europe, yet she has only recently emerged among modern scholars as a central figure of the sixteenth century.[32] There is now a tendency to attribute most art objects of value made in the north to her patronage, including the *Rothschild Prayer Book*. Yet Margaret was surrounded by courtiers, tutors, advisors, senior bureaucrats and clerics such as Antoine de Lalaing and others.[33] Ambassadors, diplomats and courtiers such as Francesco de Rojas and Antonio Siciliano came from all over Europe for political and economic negotiations. Every one of these figures had the means, status, aspirations and desire to own, commission or gift one of these deluxe manuscripts. They had the motive to build political alliances for themselves and their masters, as well as mobility and the means to initiate the production of these deluxe manuscripts for economic gain, political advantage and social enhancement.

The *Prayer Book* and the Third Reich

From these beginnings, the *Rothschild Prayer Book* then disappears completely from view. Despite its social, political and economic value, its numerous keepers ensured it was safe but out of sight for almost 350 years. It reappeared only in 1872, as part of the collection of Baron Anselm von Rothschild of Vienna (1803–74), who had purchased it some time in the preceding four years.[34] This began another period in which the book became a potent social, political and economic symbol in the politics of Europe.

---

31 Eichberger (forthcoming publication), pp. 10–12.
32 Debae, La Librairie, and Eichberger, 'The Culture of Gifts'.

33 See footnote 27 above for Guillaume II de Croÿ, Guillaume II de Croÿ, Charles de Lalaing and Charles de Croÿ. Another such figure was Jean II Carondelet, Archbishop of Palermo. Influential at the courts of both Charles and Margaret, he accompanied the seventeen-year-old Charles to Spain when he moved there to claim the Crowns of Aragon and Castile. See Eichberger, 'The Culture of Gifts', pp. 16–17.
34 de Hamel, *The Rothschilds and their Collections of Illuminated Manuscripts*, p. 9.

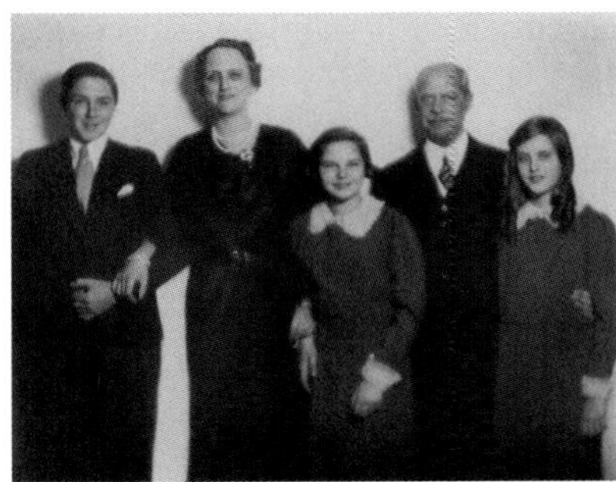

Figure 3.9: *Photograph of the Rothschild family.* Left to right: Albert de Rothschild, Baroness Clarice de Rothschild, Bettina de Rothschild, Alphonse de Rothschild, and Gwendoline de Rothschild. Taken on the 25th wedding anniversary of Clarice and Alphonse Rothschild on November 20, 1937. Museum of Fine Arts, Boston.

By 1938 the *Rothschild Prayer Book* had been passed down through three generations to Anselm's grandson, Alfonse (1878–1942).[35] On 12 March in that year, Austria was annexed by the Third Reich. Alfonse and his wife were in England. Within days their residence at 16–18 Theresesianumgasse was plundered and the *Prayer Book* was among the stunning collection of art, books and musical and scientific instruments 'confiscated' by the *Sicherheitsdienst des Reichführers* – the SS. It then disappears again until 5 January 1942, when the codex was recorded in the National Library in Vienna. These were the facts known until now.

The *Rothschild Prayer Book* was among the thousands of art objects seized by the Nazis following the invasion of Austria. Looting of artworks by the Gestapo and by Nazi Party members was significant enough that on 18 June 1938,

only a month after the Nazis' arrival in Vienna, a decree was issued that all artworks seized in Austria were to be under Hitler's personal jurisdiction. Hitler well understood the symbolic potency of art, and he conceived an ambitious plan to overhaul Linz, his hometown, by constructing there a new 'European Centre for Culture'. This was to include 'the greatest museum in the world', to be called the *Führermuseum*, as well as a theatre, concert hall, opera house, cinema, university, planetarium, and a library of a quarter of a million volumes.[36] It also included an Adolf Hitler Hotel, a parade ground, community hall, Nazi headquarters and a mausoleum for Hitler's parents. In 1940, the architect Hermann Giesler was instructed to design extensive plans for these buildings, and also the necessary infrastructure, including a new railway station, boulevards and bridges.[37] The *Führermuseum* lay at the very centre of the plan, and was to house 'only the best of all periods from the pre-historic to the nineteenth century and recent times'.[38]

On 21 June 1939, Hitler personally appointed Hans Posse, Director of the Gemäldegalerie Alte Meister in Dresden, to build the collection for the *Führermuseum*. It was stipulated that: 'all Party and State services are ordered to assist [him] in fulfilment of his mission'.[39] In the following months, Posse travelled to Vienna to inspect the works held at what was called the 'Central Depot at Wien 1, Neue Burg,' that is, the Kunsthistorisches Museum, where the confiscated items were stored. By October Posse had finalised his list of works for the Linz Museum, and sent it to Hitler's private secretary, Martin Bormann, for Hitler's approval. Of the 324 works Posse had chosen, 182 had been seized

---

35   Anselm's son Nathaniel Mayer inherited the *Rothschild Prayer Book* in 1874. In 1906, the year after Nathaniel's own death, the book appears in an inventory. As Nathaniel did not have any heirs, his bother Salomon or Saloman's son Alphonse Mayer von Rothschild (1874–1942) inherited the *Rothschild Prayer Book* along with an immense collection of other manuscripts and art.

36   Fest, *The Face of the Third Reich*, p. 97 and p. 543 n. 19.

37   Spotts, *Hitler and the Power of Aesthetics*, pp. 374–76.

38   Spotts, *Hitler and the Power of Aesthetics*, p. 187.

39   Edsel and Witter, *The Monuments Men*, p. 15.

from the Rothschild family, including works by Hans Holbein the Elder, van Dyck, Rembrandt, Franz Hals, and Tintoretto.

The *Rothschild Prayer Book* is noteworthy for its absence. Indeed, this manuscript was never destined for the *Führermuseum*; and there is no evidence that Hitler knew of the existence of the *Prayer Book* and actively pursued it for his collection. Much has been made of the *Führermuseum*, but equally significant to the Linz redevelopment was the *Führerbibliotek*. The scale of Hitler's ambitions for this library became apparent in May 1945, when the Allied Forces liberating Austria discovered more than half a million volumes in a monastery at Tanzenberg. These had been stolen from Jewish collectors, as well as from book dealers and publishers all over Europe and Russia; and they were destined to be the heart of the *Führerbibliothek*.[40] The *Rothschild Prayer Book* was not however among the books at Tanzenberg, since in 1945 the manuscript had been in the collection of the Austrian National Library for over three years.

How it came to be there is a fascinating part of its history, involving complex and delicate negotiations between powerful political figures. It demonstrates yet again the agency of this book as a potent tool to fuel ambition and aspiration. Four days after the annexation of Austria, the Gestapo arrested the Director of the Austrian National Library, Josef Bick, at his desk. He was then sent to Dachau on trumped-up charges that he had given valuable manuscripts from the national collection to Pope Pius XII. Paul Heigl, an ardent National Socialist since 1933, was immediately instated as Bick's successor. Heigl aggressively pursued books for the collection and under his leadership the National Library became the depository for the confiscated libraries of

many prominent Jewish scholars and collectors including Moriz von Kuffner, Oskar Ladner, Viktor von Ephrussi, Stefan Auspitz, Rudolf Gutmann, and Alphonse Rothschild.[41] In June 1941 Heigl began an intense campaign to secure seven illuminated Rothschild manuscripts, including the prized *Rothschild Prayer Book*, by appealing directly to Hitler's secretary Martin Bormann. In his letter of 6 June, he wrote:

> Given that the Führer will be imminently making a decision about the allocation of the manuscripts originated from Rothschild ownership, may I be permitted to suggest in the interests of the National Library that the listed manuscripts are transferred to the largest institute in Austria [...] to support my request, may I stress as I have already repeatedly stressed to Dr Hans Posse, that since 1938 the National Library has been identifying all valuable doubles in its holdings for the collection of the great library in Linz, and we are doing so with great joy as the future cultural centre is in the hometown of the Führer.[42]

On the same day Heigl also composed a letter to Hans Posse asking that the Rothschild manuscripts be kept in Vienna and transferred to the National Library. What followed was a few months of agreeable correspondence between the two men; Posse asserted that he would support the claim as much as he could.[43] This culminated on 8 October 1941 when Posse confirmed that the codices including the *Rothschild*

40   Adunka, *Der Raub der Bücher*.

41   Adunka, 'The Nazi looting'.

42   *Da de Fuehrer in allernächster Zeit eine Entscheidung über die Zuweisung der auf dem Rothschild'schen Besitz stammenden Handschriten treffen wird, gestatte ich mir, Sie im Interesse der Nationalbibliothek zu bitten, die Überlassung der anliegend aufgeführten Handschriften an diese größte Institut of Ostmark befürworten zu wollen.* 6 June 1941. Vienna, ÖNB, H. 305/1941.

43   5 July 1941. Vienna, ÖNB, H. 305/1941 and 7 July 1941. Vienna, ÖNB, H. 305/1941.

Prayer Book should go to the National Library rather than to Linz. He accepted Heigl's offer that any precious duplicates in the holdings of the library be 'handed over for the purpose of the Führer's Library in Linz'.[44] Without delay, on 17 October 1941 Heigl wrote to Leopold Rupprecht, Director of the Kunsthistorisches Museum, requesting that the manuscripts be transferred to the National Library.[45] On 5 January of the following year they officially entered the collection. Thus the *Rothschild Prayer Book* had been stored in the Kunsthistorisches Museum – along with the other works of art looted from Alphonse Rothschild's Thereseianumgasse residence – until it was transferred to the library three years later. Nor was it ever moved to the Altaussee salt mines, as is sometimes claimed: Hitler ordered the art works destined to grace the walls of the *Führermuseum* to be moved to the Altaussee salt mines, and only in 1943. By this time the *Rothschild Prayer Book* was securely housed in the National Library in Vienna, where it would spend the duration of the war.

Even after the war, the *Rothschild Prayer Book* continued to be a potent symbol of power and a tool of negotiation. It became, for decades, a symbol of shame. In 1946, the Allies delegated the Austrian government to handle the restitution of property. Institutions were required to complete a 'Notification of Confiscated Property' document. On 14 November 1946, the National Library declared a 'few thousand printed books in other locations, presumably German libraries, and seven manuscripts in the holdings of the National Library' that had belonged to Alphonse Rothschild on 13 March 1938.[46] The former Director, Josef Bick had survived the war and was reinstated. Within a fortnight of the form being lodged, a letter from Alphonse

Rothschild's executor arrived in Vienna asking that an inventory of the books and manuscripts which had belonged to his client be sent to him. Bick responded immediately, confirming that the manuscripts had been transferred to the Library on 5 January 1942 on Hitler's orders. He promised to do 'everything in my power as Director of the National Library to ensure that the books be given back to the rightful heir'.[47] The manuscripts were among the 344 items taken from Alphonse and 919 from his brother Louis Rothschild. Bick followed this letter with another to the *Bundesdenkmalamt* (Federal Moments Office) stating that Baron Karl Wilczek, the appointee of the Rothschild Family, had proposed that the *Rothschild Prayer Book* be presented as a gift and the *Cornaro Missal*, another seized book, be given to the Library as a long term loan, on condition that the *Bundesdenkmalamt* support the application by the heirs to export the rest of the illuminated manuscripts and books.[48] In 1947, the *Bundesdenkmalamt* conceded that this was 'the optimal solution' and on 3 February Bick and the Rothschild lawyer and executor signed an agreement stating that AR3390 (the Nazi inventory number given to the *Rothschild Prayer Book*) was 'assigned to the Library as a gift from the family'.[49] The *Prayer Book* was sacrificed to enable the other items to be liberated following their Nazi confiscation.

This was not the end of the matter. In May 1947, Dr Wilhelm Roniger wrote to Bick introducing himself as the court commissioner in the probate matter for Alphonse Rothschild. He requested an inventory of the Rothschild possessions and their estimated value. Again the response was swift: the 3,800 printed codices were estimated at 40,000 Swiss francs and illuminated manuscripts at a value of 900,000

44   8 October 1941. Vienna, ÖNB, H. 305/1941

45   17 October 1941. Vienna, ÖNB, H. 305/1941

46   14 November 1946. Vienna, ÖNB, H. 1072/1946

47   16 December 1946. Vienna, ÖNB, H. 1072/1946

48   18 December 1946. Vienna, ÖNB, H. 1072/1946

49   3 February 1947. Vienna, ÖNB, H. 8/1947

Swiss francs. Bick stressed that the 'possession of these books has been legally registered and the negotiation has been handed over to the owner's lawyer'.[50] In the spring of 1947, Alphonse's widow, Clarice, by then residing in New York, visited the salt mines in Austria where looted artworks had been hidden. She discovered crates containing art belonging to her husband and his brother, Louis. They had even been meticulously catalogued and labelled as AR and LR by the Nazis. In the following year, however, she was notified by the *Finanzalandesdirektion* (Central Office of Finance) that the exportation of the collection was against the *Denkmalschutz* law of 23 September 1923, which prohibited the export of culturally significant works.[51] The argument was made despite the unlawful and unethical manner in which the works had been obtained. Eventually a deal was brokered whereby the most significant works, some 250 pieces, were 'donated' to Austrian government in exchange for the right to export the remainder.[52]

It took another half century for change to come. In 1998, two canvases by Egon Schiele from the Leopold Museum (on loan to the Museum of Modern Art in New York) were impounded by the New York County District Attorney. The works had been taken from the Jewish art collector Fritz Grünbaum and his wife Elizabeth, both killed in concentration camps. The case shone an international spotlight on the injustices committed after the war and Austria's dubious handling of restitution. In 1998, a 'Return of Works of Arts Act' was passed and a commission created to oversee the return of art objects acquired by institutions between 1938 and 1945. With great publicity, the 224 items belonging to the Rothschild family were among the first collections to be handed back. Bettina Looram Rothschild, Clarice and Alphonse's daughter and heir, decided to sell everything that same year.

The auction broke records for the largest single owner sale and the *Rothschild Prayer Book* became famous for fetching a staggering $13.3m USD, a record price for an illuminated manuscript. More significantly, it became a symbol of Austria's national penance, as well as an emblem of the continued injustices committed after the war. This is part of the manuscript's history and its significance, as much as its beauty and its value: it has been a way to curry favour, an investment piece, a symbol of wealth, power and culture, a tool for negotiation and reparation.

About the author

Kate Challis wrote her thesis on early sixteenth century Flemish illuminated manuscripts including the *Rothschild Prayer Book*. She contributed to *An Illumination: The Rothschild Prayer Book and Other Works from the Kerry Stokes Collection c.1280–1685* (2015). She runs her own interior design studio and is active as an art historian. kate@katechallis.com

Works cited

Unpublished sources

Österreichische Nationalbibliothek, Vienna (ÖNB): H. 305/ 1941, H. 1072/1946, H. 8/1947.

Published Sources

Eveynn Adunka, *Der Raub der Bücher. Plünderung in der NS-Zeit und Restitution nach 1945. Über Verschwinden und Vernichten von Bibliotheken in der NS-Zeit und ihre Restitution nach 1945* (Vienna: Czernin, 2002).

---

50   4 June 1947. Vienna, ÖNB, H. 8/1947
51   7 December 1948. Vienna, ÖNB, H. 8/1947
52   Kauffman, 'The Rothschild affair'.

Eveynn Adunka, 'The Nazi looting of books in Austria and their partial restitution', *Lootedart.com The Central Registry of Information on Looted Cultural Property 1993–1945*, accessed 16 July, 2017 at http://www.lootedart.com/MFVALY48822.

Janet Backhouse, *The Isabella Breviary* (London: British Library, 1993).

Bodo Brinkmann, *Die Flämische Buchmalerei am Ende des Burgunderreichs. Der Meister des Dresdener Gebetbuchs und die Miniaturisten seiner Zeit* (Turnhout: Brepols, 1997).

Kate Challis, 'Marginalised Jewels. The Depiction of Jewelry in the Borders of Flemish Devotional Manuscripts' in *The Art of the Book. Its Place in Medieval Worship*, ed. Bernard Muir and Margaret M. Manion (Exeter: Exeter University Press, 1998), pp. 253–89.

Kate Challis, 'Things of Inestimable Value. Deluxe Manuscript Production and the Marketing of Devotion in Late Southern Netherlandish Illumination', PhD dissertation, The University of Melbourne, 2002.

Christie's, 'THE ROTHSCHILD PRAYERBOOK, a Book of Hours, use of Rome, in Latin, ILLUMINATED MANUSCRIPT ON VELLUM', *www.christies.com*, accessed 16 July 2017 at http://www.christies.com/lotfinder/books-manuscripts/the-rothschild-prayerbook-a-book-of-hours-5766082-details.aspx.

Marguerite Debae, *La Librairie de Marguerite d'Autriche. Essai de reconstruction d'après l'inventaire de 1523–1524* (Louvain and Paris: Editions Peeters, 1997).

Robert Edsel and Brett Witter, *The Monuments Men: Allied Heroes, Nazi Thieves, and the Greatest Treasure Hunt in History* (New York: Center Street, 2009).

Dagmar Eichberger, 'The Court in Mechelen. A Hub of Political, Diplomatic and Cultural Activities' (forthcoming).

Dagmar Eichberger, 'The Culture of Gifts. A Courtly Phenomenon from a Female Perspective' in *Women of distinction. Margaret of York / Margaret of Austria*, ed. by Dagmar Eichberger (Turnhout: Brepols, 2005), pp. 287–295.

Mark Evans, *The Sforza Hours*, (London: British Library, 1992).

Joachim Fest, *The Face of the Third Reich* (New York: Penguin Books, 1979).

Carlos Miranda García-Tejedor, *Libro de Horas de Juana I de Castilla* [with] *The Book of Hours of Joanna of Castile*, 2 vols (Barcelona: M. Moleiro, 2005).

Andreas Grote and Giorgio Ferrari, *Breviarium Grimani; Faksimileausgabe der Miniaturen und Kommentar* (Berlin: Gebr. Mann, *c.*1973).

Christopher de Hamel, *The Rothschilds and their Collections of Illuminated Manuscripts* (London: British Library, 2005).

Joris Corin Heyder, 'Corporate Design Made in Ghent/Bruges? On the Extensive Rescue of Patterns in late Medieval Flemish Illuminated Manuscripts' in *The Use of Models in Medieval Book Painting*, ed.by Monika Müller (Newcastle upon Tyne: Cambridge Scholars Publishing, 2014), pp. 167–201.

Jason Edward Kaufman, 'The Rothschild Affair: A Test of Austria's Conscience', *The Wall Street Journal*, 6 July 1999, accessed 25 April 2017 at http://www.wsj.com/articles/SB931225858127090793.

Thomas Kren, ed., *Renaissance Painting in Manuscripts. Treasures from the British Library* (New York: Hudson Hill Press, 1983).

Thomas Kren and Scot McKendrick, *Illuminating the Renaissance: The Triumph of Flemish Manuscript Painting in Europe* (Los Angeles: Getty Publications, 2003).

Michaela Krieger, *Gerard Horenbout und der Meister Jakobs IV. von Schottland* (Vienna and Cologne: Boehlau Verlag, 2012).

Otto Mazal and Dagmar Thoss, *Das Buch der Drolerien: Croy-Gebetbuch* (Lucerne: Faksimile Verlag Luzern, 1993).

Maria Perry, *The Sisters of Henry VIII: The Tumultuous Lives of Margaret of Scotland and Mary of France* (Boston: Capo Press, 1998).

Andrew Pettegree, *The Book in the Renaissance* (New Haven: Yale University Press, 2010).

Maurits Smeyersand Jan Van der Stock, eds., *Flemish Illuminated Manuscripts, 1475–1550* (Ghent: Guidon Press, New York: Abrams, 1996)

Frederic Spotts, *Hitler and the Power of Aesthetics* (Woodstock and New York: The Overlook Press, 2009).

DagmarThoss,*FlämischeBuchmalerei.Handschriftenschätze aus dem Burgunderdreich* (Vienna; Österreichische Nationalbibliothek, 1987).

Franz Unterkircher, *Das Gebetbuch Jakobs IV. von Schottland und seiner Gemählin Margaret Tudor, Codex Vindobonensis 1897 des Österreichischen Nationalbibliothek* (Graz: Adeva, 1987).

Carol Vogel, 'At $90 Million, Rothschild Sale Exceeds Goals', *The New York Times*, July 9, 1999, accessed 16 July 2017 at http://www.nytimes.com/1999/07/09/world/at-90-million-rothschild-sale-exceeds-goals.html.

Rogier Wieck, *The Book of Hours in Medieval Art and Life* (London: Sotheby's Publications, 1988).

Friedrich Winkler, *Die Flämische Buchmalerei des XV. und XVI Jahrhunderts*, (Leipzig and Berlin: Seemann, 1925).

4. 'Women who read are dangerous': illuminated manuscripts and female book collections in the early Renaissance

Dagmar Eichberger

Dunlop, Anne (ed.), *Antipodean Early Modern. European Art in Australian Collections, c. 1200–1600*, Amsterdam University Press, 2018

DOI: 10.5117/9789462985209/CH04

Abstract

This paper looks at what Renaissance women were supposed to read according to the educational manuals of their time, and what we know about their de facto reading habits. The noblewomen Margaret of York and Margaret of Austria represent two poles within the spectrum of possibilities – one focusing in particular on beautifully illuminated spiritual treatises, the other aiming at an encyclopedic library with a wide range of literary genres. The bedroom and the study are singled out as the most private spaces to which a woman could withdraw from her daily chores. Here she could enjoy reading and writing, praying and meditating.

Keywords: Women; Books; Education; Devotion; Margaret of York; Margaret of Austria

In recent years, the number of publications, conferences, and exhibitions on women as patrons of the arts and as collectors of manuscripts has grown immensely.[1] When dealing with women as patrons, many facets have to be taken into account such as marital status, financial means, and political role within the family network. In the Renaissance, only a very small number of noble women actively built up a proper collection of artefacts, such as the Marchioness Isabella d'Este, the Archduchess Margaret of Austria and the dowager Duchess Mary of Hungary. Many more women, however, owned a small set of manuscripts and printed

---

An earlier version of this article was presented at the J. Paul Getty Museum in Los Angeles in October 2010 ('A tale of two Margarets. Women and their Manuscripts c.1500'). I am grateful to Thomas Kren for having given me the opportunity to explore this topic on this occasion. I am equally thankful to Philip Kent and the University of Melbourne for having invited me to Australia to develop the subject further.

1 The title of this essay is based on a 'coffee table' book entitled *Women who read are dangerous*, by Stefan Bollmann (New York: Abbeville Press Publishers, 2016). This book assembles numerous paintings of glamorous women who read a book or contemplate a text. The images, mostly from the nineteenth and twentieth centuries, predominantly show examples of modern women either devouring books, or taking on a sphinx-like character. For women as patrons of the arts and collectors of manuscripts see: Chevalier, *Patronnes et mécènnes en France à la Renaissance*; Legaré, *Livres et lectures des Femmes entre Moyen-Âge et Renaissance*; Brown and Legaré, *Les femmes, la culture et les arts en Europe entre Moyen Âge et Renaissance*.

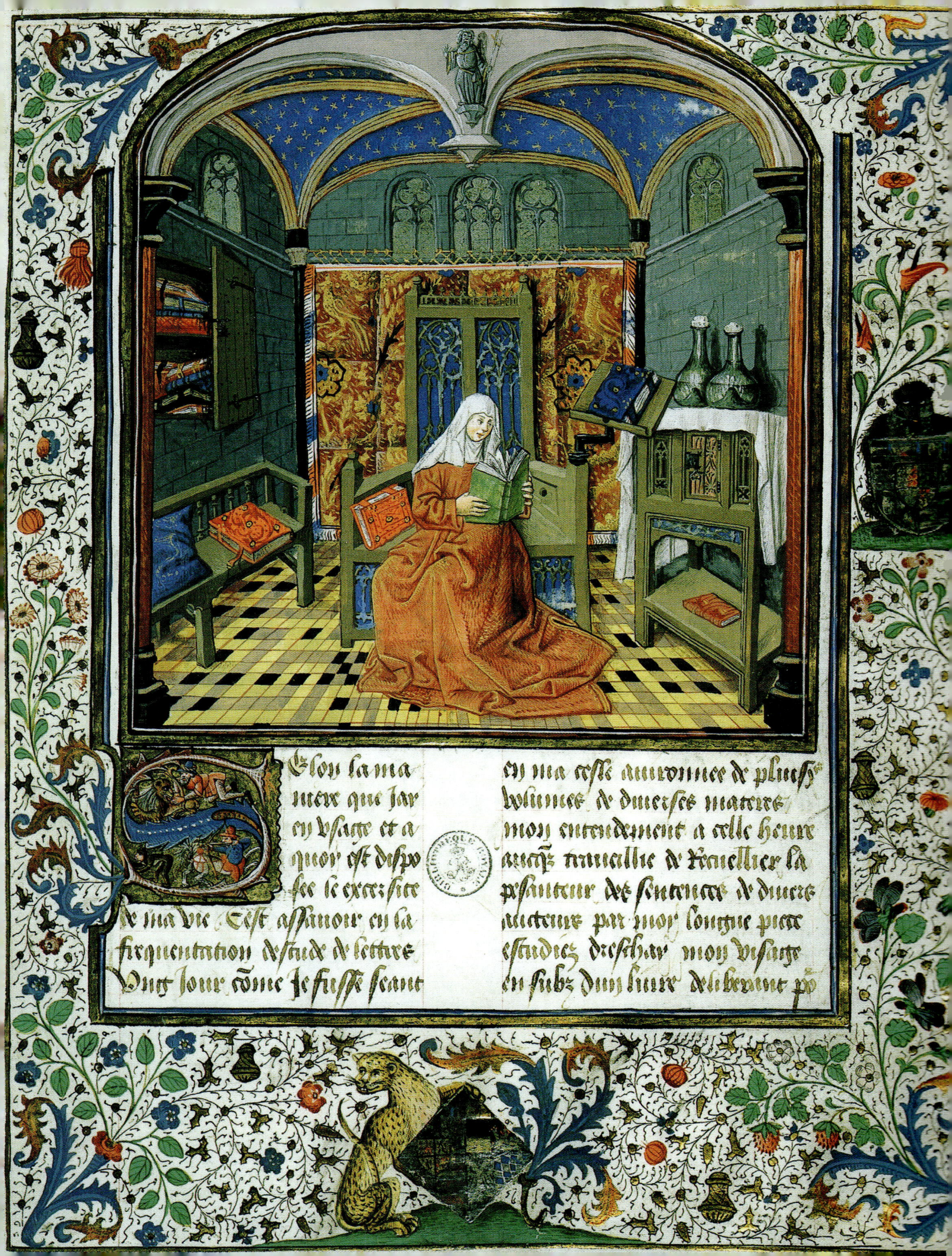
Selon la ma
niere que j'ay
en usage et a
quoy est dispo
see le exercite
assavoir en la
frequentation destude de lettre
ung jour comme je fusse seant
en ma teste auronnee de plus
volumes de diuerses matires
mon entendement a celle heure
auoit trauaillie de reueiller la
pesanteur de sentence de diuers
auteur par moy longue piece
estudiez dresshay mon visage
en subz dun liure deliberer po

books. Lavishly decorated manuscripts were passed on from one generation to the other: from mother to daughter, from godmother to godchild, from aunt to niece and so forth. In addition to inheritance, books could be received as gifts or were acquired on the open market.

This may be one of the reasons why in the Renaissance there was an ever-growing number of illustrations in which women hold a book in their hands, whether they are female saints or the Virgin Mary.[2] In other cases, one can encounter the portrait of a patron or the image of a female author, such as Christine de Pizan (1364-c.1429). In a late fifteenth-century edition of her book *Le Livre de la Cité des Dames* ('The Book of the City of Ladies') she is portrayed in her majestic study (Figure 4.1), holding up a large manuscript covered in green cloth; additional volumes are placed on benches and in cupboards.[3] Such visual evidence suggests that by 1460–1470 reading was considered a suitable occupation for well-educated women.[4] But what do we know about the reading habits of these women? Which types of books were women advised or discouraged to read?

In the first part of this paper, the theoretical framework for this question will be discussed, and then two women will be examined in more detail as case studies: Margaret of York and Margaret of Austria, whose interest in illuminated manuscripts and books is well documented, and who can thus serve as touchstones for the wider practice. Both were members of the Burgundian court, either by marriage or by birth, and both were in close touch with the most avant-garde centres of manuscript illumination in the fifteenth and sixteenth centuries, namely Ghent, Bruges, and Valenciennes. The *Rothschild Prayer Book*

in the Stokes Collection is a good example of a Flemish manuscript of outstanding quality. Most of the artists who produced illuminations for this volume worked for the Burgundian high nobility.[5] Gerard Horenbout is one of the artists who has been associated with the *Rothschild Prayer Book*; he was Margaret of Austria's court illuminator.[6]

The dangers of reading novels and romances

The question of what women should read was of crucial significance in the fifteenth and sixteenth centuries and is reflected in many texts on family life and education. The Spanish humanist Juan Luis Vives (1493–1540) is one of several authors who commented on the education of women and warned against the dangers of reading the wrong books, especially those focussing on love and war.[7] In 1523, Vives wrote an educational manual for Queen Catherine of Aragon, in which he provided clear guidelines for young girls, married women, and widows. He sharply criticizes adolescent women who spent their leisure time reading light literature, such as romances and adventure stories. In Book 1, Chapter 5, entitled 'Which writers are to be read and which are not to be read', Vives condemns this practice in the following words:

> For such girls it would have been preferable not only that they had never learned literature, but that they lost their eyes, so that they could

2   Sandro Boticelli, *Madonna del Libro*, 1480–1481, tempera on wood, Milan, Museo Poldi Pezzoli.

3   See Eichberger, *Women of Distinction*, cat. 77.

4   Eichberger, 'Frauenbibliotheken', pp. 241–64.

5   See: Manion, *An Illumination*, p. 24.

6   The unusual set of illustrations which focus more than usual on the performance of the mass and contain many liturgical scenes, in my opinion suggests that the manuscript was commissioned with a high-ranking cleric in mind. See chapters 2 and 3 for further discussion.

7   Vives, *De institutione feminae*; see also: Jacobi, 'Juan Luis Vives', Jacobi, *Mädchen und Frauenbildung*, Chap. 1: 'Ehrbarkeit und Frömmigkeit', pp. 17–106.

Figure 4.1: Christine de Pizan in her Study from *Le livre de la Cité des Dames*. Folio 3, 1460-1470. Parchment, 37.2cm × 26.5cm. Bibliothèque Royale de Belgique, Brussels, MS 9235–37.

not read, and their ears so that they could not hear. [...] This kind of girl is a disgrace not only to Christians but would be an object of shame and hatred even to the pagans. Wherefore I am all the more astonished that devout preachers, although often inveighing in tragic tones against petty matters, do not decry this practice in their every sermon. I marvel that wise fathers permit this to their daughters, husbands concede it to their wives, and public morals and institutions ignore the fact that women become addicted to vice through reading.[8]

While Vives can be described as a hardliner, the Spaniard was not alone in claiming that women with bad reading habits were worse off than women with no education at all. According to such educational texts, secular novels had no benefit whatsoever. They mostly dealt with romantic love and were believed to lead women into idleness and corruption. Yet as far as we can gauge from the contents of specific libraries and from the reading habits of contemporary women, Vives was probably fighting a wide-spread practice.

The benefits of reading good books

In Book 1, Chapter 4, Vives provides the following advice to mothers with young daughters:

> When she is taught to read, let her peruse books that impart instruction in morals, when she learns to write, do not have her imitate idle verses or vain and frivolous ditties, but rather some grave saying or a wise and holy sentiment from the holy Scriptures or the writings of the philosophers, which should be copied

out many times so that they will remain firmly fixed in the memory.[9]

In the primer that Queen Anne of Brittany (1477–1514) commissioned for her daughter Claude of France (1498–1524), the young princess is recommended to Saint Anne by Saint Claude, her patron saint, while Anne teaches her daughter Mary how to read by learning prayers by heart.[10] On folio 2r, the book starts with the alphabet and continues with the prayer *Pater Noster* ('Our Father'). The line of text at the top of the page invokes another well-known prayer: *Ave Maria gratia plena, Dominus tecum* ('Hail Mary, full of grace, the Lord is with thee'). The devout motto of the Queen herself underlines the pious attitude prevailing in this educational manual: *Penson en dieu* ('Let us think of God'); The principal image on Folio 1v is dedicated to Saint Claude, and shows Saint Anne taking Mary and Claude under her wings.[11] Saint Anne and Anne of Brittany follow the same goal by caring for the proper upbringing of their daughters.

There are earlier writers who comment on the education of young women in a similar vein to Vives, albeit not quite as forcefully. In her educational handbook *Le Trésor de la Cité des Dames* (1405), Christine de Pizan recommends the following:

> When a daughter grows older, she will learn to read according to the instructions of her mother. She will first get to know the Book of Hours and the prayers said during Mass. Later on she will be given devotional books and such texts to read that will teach her good manners.

8   Vives, *The Education of a Christian Woman*, Book 1, Chap, 5, p. 74.

9   Vives, *The Education of a Christian Woman*, Book 1, Chap, 5, p. 71.
10   Anonymous French, Primer, 1508, Cambridge, The Fitzwilliam Museum, ms. 159, fol. 14.
11   Anonymous French, Primer, 1508, Cambridge, The Fitzwilliam Museum, ms. 159, fol. 1r-2v.

[The mother] will, however, not tolerate any vain, extravagant or immoral writings in the vicinity of her daughter, as the teachings that she received at a very young age will accompany her throughout life.[12]

It is remarkable that Books of Hours are listed as one of the first types of books to be given to young girls. Christine de Pizan's comment mirrors the popularity of this private devotional book in the late Middle Ages and points to its multifunctional use. A mid-fifteenth century French Book of Hours in the Stokes Collection is a typical example of its kind – one that was made specifically for a female recipient.[13] The devotional portrait of a kneeling widow appears twice, once next to Saint Margaret (Figure 4.2) and once to the right of the Crucifixion with Mary and Saint John (Figure 4.3).

When Anne de Beaujeu (1461–1521), sister of the French king Charles VIII, drafted an educational manual for her daughter Suzanne in 1503, she also gave advice as to what the young girl should read:

Make sure never to be idle, and especially keep your mind occupied by performing good deeds, such as contemplating whole-heartedly and with deep devotion the holy and worthy

Passion of our sweet Saviour Jesus, by giving him thanks and praising him affectionately.

…In order to lead a better spiritual life and to practice your devotions appropriately, I advise you to read the booklet by the nobleman of Saint-Louis, namely Saint Peter of Luxemburg, the *Somme le roi*, the *Horologe de Sapience*, and other books with saints' lives, also the sayings of philosophers and ancient sages. Their ideas should serve you as guiding principles and as a model; this is a very respectable occupation and also a pleasant pastime.[14]

Anne de Beaujeu and Juan Luis Vives both consider idleness as a particularly dangerous state of mind that could become the gateway for vice and corruption.

By 1500, many noblewomen had turned into active patrons and collectors of books and were courted by authors and illuminators alike. Louise of Savoy (1476–1531), Anne of Brittany (1477–1514), Margaret of York (1446–1503), and Margaret of Austria (1480–1530) were among the most active female patrons of their time. These women commissioned illuminated manuscripts themselves and were offered books as gifts by relatives, courtiers, and diplomats. Many contemporary authors knew of their passion for books and offered their services to these women as potential clients or end-users.[15]

12   Translation by the author from Christine de Pizan, *Der Schatz der Stadt der Frauen*, p. 92: 'Wenn die Tochter älter ist, wird sie auf Wunsch der Mutter lesen lernen und zunächst mit dem Stunden- und dem Messgebet vertraut gemacht werden. Später wird sie Andachtsbücher und solche Schriften zur Lektüre erhalten, aus denen sie gute Sitten erlernen kann. Doch wird die Fürstin keine eitlen, extravaganten oder unmoralischen Schriften in der Nähe ihrer Tochter dulden, denn von den Lehren und der Erziehung, die das Kind in seiner frühesten Jugend erhält, zehrt es im allgemeinen sein ganzes Leben lang.'

13   French, *Book of Hours*, c.1440, Kerry Stokes Collection, LIB.2013.224, fol. 157: St. Margaret and the Dragon with a female donor; see: Manion, *An Illumination*, cat. 13, pp. 62–67.

14   Translation by the author from Anne de France, *Enseignement*, pp. 40–41: Et pour mieux vous savoir vivre et conduire en dévotion, je vous conseille que lisiez le livre du prud'homme de Saint-Louis, celui de saint Pierre de Luxembourg, les Sommes le roi, l'Horologe de Sapience, ou autres livres de Vies des saints, aussi les Dits des ancien philosophes et sages. Lesquelles doctrines vous doivent être comme droite règle et exemple, et c'est très honnête occupation et plaisante passe-temps'.

15   Legaré, 'La librairye de Madame', pp. 206–219; Fontaine, 'Olivier de la Marche and Jean Lemaire de Belges', pp. 220–229; Eichberger, 'Manoeuvering between competing courts'.

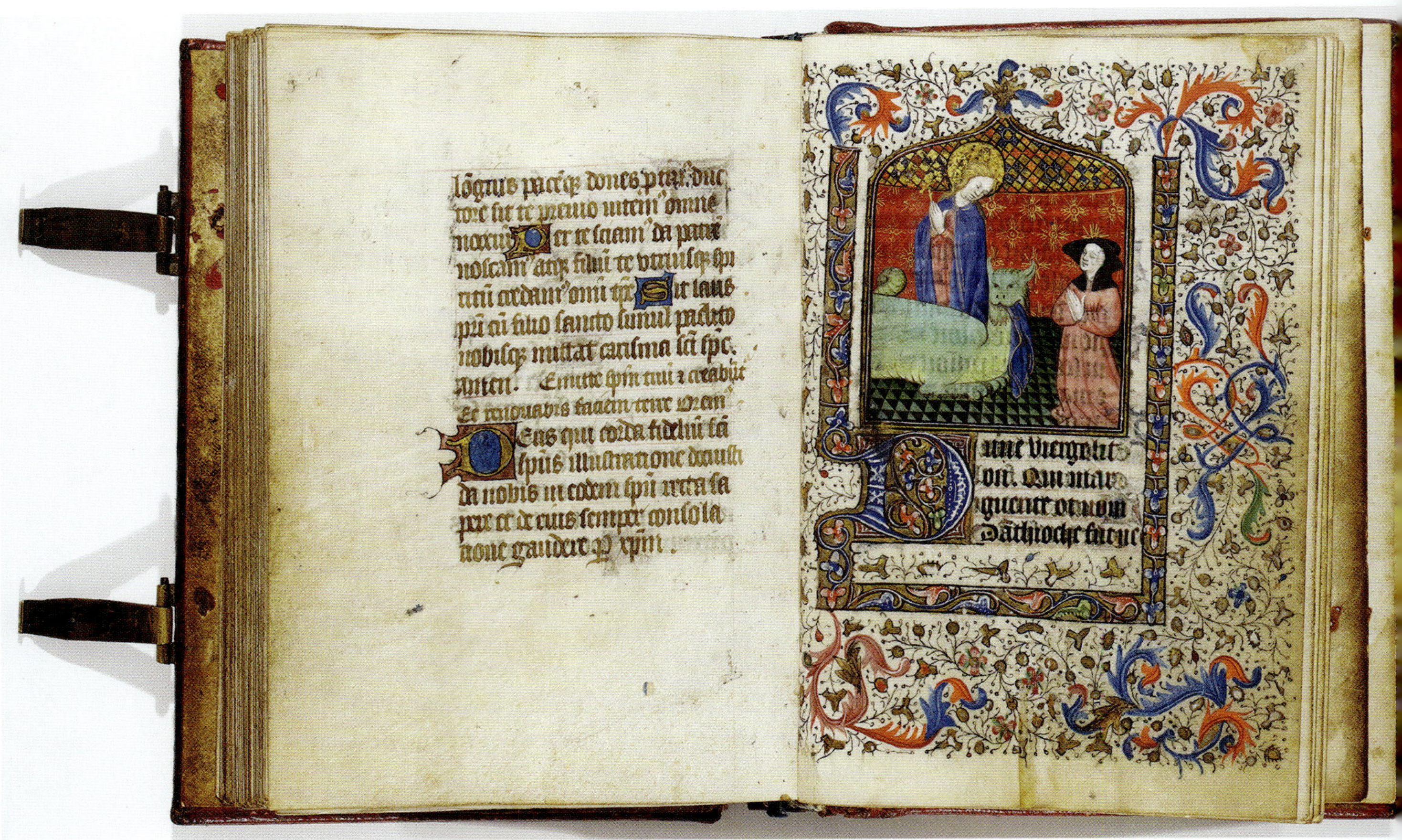

Figure 4.2: Paris or Rheims, St. Margaret and the Dragon with a female donor from *Book of Hours, Use of Rheims*. Folios 156v–157, *c*.1440. Parchment, 18cm × 12.5cm. Kerry Stokes Collection, Perth. LIB.2013.224.

A general trend in manuscript illumination emerges parallel to this development: the depiction of female saints with an open book in their hands. This is particularly noticeable in the *Rothschild Prayer Book* and applies to Saint Mary Magdalene (Figure 3.1), Saint Catherine of Alexandria, Saint Barbara (Figure 4.4), and Saint Helena (Figure 3.2).[16]
These idealized beauties all hold an open manuscript with a colourful leather cover in their hands and modestly cast their eyes onto the text. In the Annunciation scene of the *Rothschild Prayer Book*, the Virgin Mary is also kneeling in front of an open book (folio 84v), thus featuring as a woman interested in devotional reading – the scene takes place in a church interior. Even more striking is a small devotional painting by the Italian artist Vincenzo Foppa (*c*.1427–*c*.1515), in which the Virgin supports the standing Christ Child with her left hand, while she holds up a book in her right hand with utmost concentration, expressing her desire to continue reading (Figure 4.5).[17] All these examples demonstrate that many women cherished their manuscripts and that it was considered appropriate to read devotional or morally uplifting texts.

Illuminated manuscripts are intimate objects, especially if they are small in size. Such books were a popular vehicle for transmitting ideas on religion, family matters, and politics. Book illustrations can contain subtle messages that have to be discovered and understood by a sensitive reader. It is the combination of text

16   *Rothschild Prayer Book*, folio 226v: St Anne and Virgin and Child; folio 227v: St Mary Magdalene, folio 228v: St Catherine of Alexandria, folio 229v: St Barbara, folio 233v: St Helena.

17   Vincenzo Foppa, *Madonna del Libro*, 1475, tempera on wood, Milan, Pinacoteca del Castello Sforzesco.

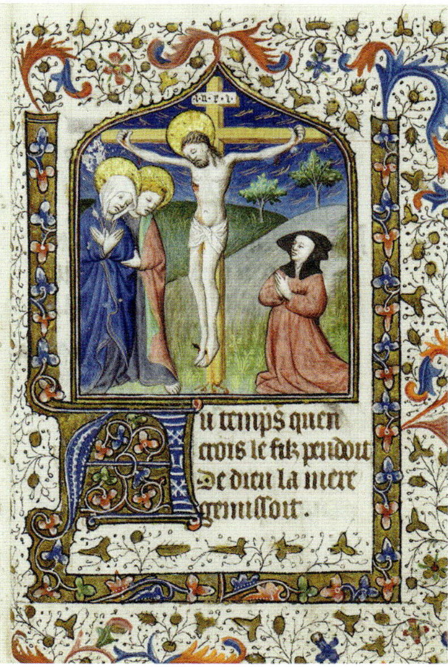

Figure 4.3: Crucifixion with Mary, Saint John and a female donor from *Book of Hours, Use of Rheims*. Folio 161, *c.*1440. Kerry Stokes Collection, Perth.

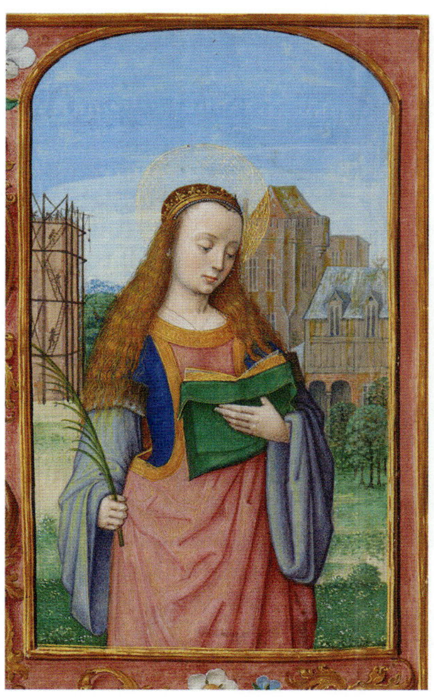

Figure 4.4: St. Barbara from the *Rothschild Prayer Book*. Folio 229v, *c.*1505–1510. Parchment, 22.8cm × 16cm. Kerry Stokes Collection, Perth.

and image within a book offers a wealth of information, more than we generally find in other visual media, such as tapestries, paintings, or sculptures. This aspect is best illustrated by one of the most famous Flemish miniatures, a page from the Vienna Book of Hours of Mary of Burgundy.[18] In the opening miniature to the section called the 'Hours of the Cross', the personal accoutrements of a lady are spread out inside a window frame: a jewellery box, a perfume bottle, a damask cushion with a precious rosary and, last but not least, a devotional book with gold clasps and a dark velvet cover. The absent owner has marked the page depicting the Crucifixion of Christ by a register bookmark. The

scene in the landscape outside the window shows an earlier moment of the same Passion account: the Nailing of Christ to the Cross. Although the owner of the manuscript is absent from this miniature, the act of meditating on the Passion of Christ takes centre stage. The illuminated manuscript is portrayed as an aid used by a noble woman to engage in her spiritual exercises.

Two noblewomen, two libraries: Margaret of York and Margaret of Austria

The second part of this paper concentrates on the collections of printed books and illuminated manuscripts once owned by Margaret of York (1446–1503) and Margaret of Austria

18   Vienna Master of Mary of Burgundy, *Books of Hours*, Vienna, ÖNB, Cod. Vind. 1857, fol. 43v: Opening page of the Hours of the Cross with the *Nailing to the Cross*; see: König, *Das Stundenbuch der Maria von Burgund*; Kren, *Illuminating the Renaissance*, cat. 19, pp. 137–141 (Thomas Kren) and pp. 122–123.

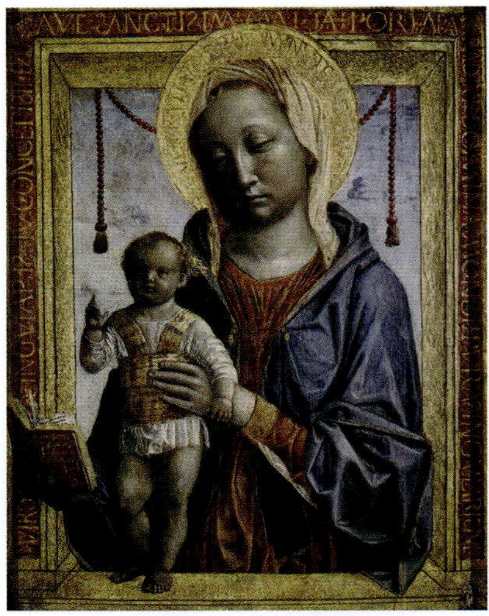

Figure 4.5: Vincenzo Foppa, *Virgin and Child (Madonna del Libro)*. *c.*1460–68, Tempera on wood, 37.5cm × 29.6cm. Pinacoteca del Castello Sforzesco, Milan.

(1480–1530), thus showing two different examples of female patronage. Duchess Margaret of York, the sister of King Edward of England, was thirty-four years older than the young princess from the house of Habsburg. Margaret of York was Margaret of Austria's godmother; being the third wife of Duke Charles the Bold, she was also her step-grandmother.[19] After the death of the duke in 1477, Margaret of York's political influence increased as she had to support her twenty-year old step-daughter Mary of Burgundy (1457–1482), heir to the Burgundian Empire. Not long after Mary's marriage to Maximilian I (1459–1519), Margaret of York moved to the city of Mechelen, a cosmopolitan town that formed part of her dowry lands.[20] Margaret of York conducted most of her business from her princely residence. Time and again in moments of political unrest, her mansion functioned as a safe haven for Margaret of Austria and for the children of Maximilian and his wife Joanna of Castile (1479–1555). Her principal residence and that of the widowed Archduchess Margaret of Austria faced one another on the main street called *Keizerstraat* ('Emperor's Avenue').

Among the few portraits that exist of Margaret of York, the likeness in the Louvre is the most interesting one, as it shows the twenty-two year old princess as the demure bride of Duke Charles the Bold.[21] She is dressed in Burgundian fashion, wears a necklace with their initials C and M, and a pin with the letter B for *Bourgogne* ('Burgundy'). As pretty as the young princess is presented to be, the image nevertheless remains a fairly formal image, produced with a particular purpose in mind. This portrait of Margaret of York seems to aim at meeting the expectations of her bridegroom; she is depicted as young, healthy, beautiful and devout; and her choice of clothing and her jewellery signals her willingness to accommodate her husband's family and to the customs of her new home.

How much more can we learn about Margaret of York from her illuminated manuscripts and her printed books! In two of her manuscripts, Margaret is depicted as the recipient of a finished book. David Aubert, a scribe at the Burgundian court, presents the duchess with a French translation of Boethius's treatise *De consolatione philosophiae*.[22] In the opening miniature, she is accompanied by five ladies-in-waiting and meets the copyist in the courtyard

19   Blockmans, 'Margaret of York', pp. 42–47; Weightman, *Margaret of York*; Kren, *Margaret of York*.
20   Prevenier, 'Mechelen circa 1500', pp. 30–41; Stabel and Marnef, *Urban Identities*.

21   Netherlandish, *Margaret of York*, oil on wood, 20.5 x 12cm, Paris, Louvre, see: Eichberger, *Women of Distinction*, p. 68, cat. 1 (Paul Matthews); see also: Matthews, 'Apparel, Status, Fashion', pp. 146–153.
22   Flemish, Boethius, *De consolatione philosophiae, 1476*, Jena, Thüringer Universitäts und Landesbibliothek, Ms. El., fol. 85: David Aubert presents his translation to Margaret of York; see: Eichberger, *Women of Distinction*, cat. 79, p. 241 (Dagmar Eichberger).

of a noble residence. On Raoul Lefèvre's engraved frontispiece for the *Recuyell of the Historyes of Troye*, William Caxton, a printer and Governor of the English Nation in Bruges, hands over his translation of the *History of the Trojan War* to her.[23] (Figure 4.6). Margaret is again depicted in the company of a large number of ladies-in-waiting. She forms the centre of attention in a stately hall with precious tableware on display. The prologue tells us that Margaret of York initiated the translation of the popular historical work into English. The book was printed with moveable type and accompanied by an engraving – quite a novelty in the realm of courtly collections.

Despite the fact that Margaret of Austria's library was more than fifteen times larger than Margaret of York's personal collection of manuscripts, there is not a single illumination in which her younger relative is portrayed in a similar position, as patron of a scribe or translator. While Margaret of Austria commissioned several books in translations, it is mostly her coat of arms and her motto that signal ownership. Nevertheless, Margaret of Austria features frequently in miniatures, but in another context or for different reasons.

In a fine portrait by the French court painter Jean Hey, one can see Margaret of Austria as an eleven-year-old princess.[24] During those years, she was raised in Amboise, at the court of the future King Charles VIII. As Charles' designated bride she wears a large pendant with a fleur-de-lis and additional ornaments that

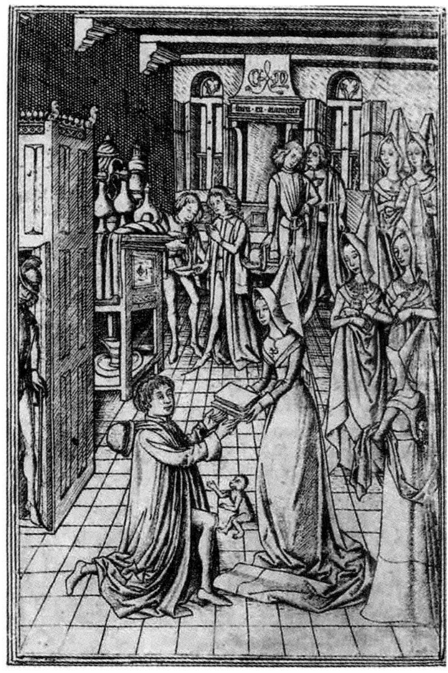

Figure 4.6: Raoul Lefèvre, Caxton presenting the book to Margaret of York from *Recueil des histoires de Troie. English*. Leaf [1][A]1, 1473–1474. Engraving, Huntington Library, San Marino, California.

point to the union of two individuals and two dynasties. Margaret, who was generally called the 'young queen' (*le petite reine*), exudes pride and self-confidence – quite a difference to the presence of the English princess Margaret in the Paris portrait. Two years later, however, Margaret was repudiated by the dauphin and – to her chagrin – she was sent back to the Netherlands. Charles had found a better match in Anne of Brittany, the sole heir to the neighbouring Duchy of Brittany.

This offence remained a recurrent theme in several of the manuscripts that focus on her biography. Margaret is the main character in the Italian humanist Michele Riccio's *Changement de Fortune en toute Prosperité*[25] and in Jean

23   *Recuyell of the Historyes of Troye*, London, Royal College of Physicians, D 139/11: the frontispiece is unbound and held by the Huntington Library, San Marino; see: Eichberger, *Women of Distinction*, p. 242–43, cat. 80 (Harry Schnitker).

24   Jean Hey (called Master of Moulins), *Margaret of Austria c.1490*, oil on wood, Metropolitan Museum of Art, Robert Lehman Collection, 1975. Eichberger, 'A Renaissance Princess'.

25   Michele Riccio, *Changement de Fortune en toute prospérité*, 1507–1509, Wien, ÖNB, Cod. 2625, folios 2v-3r, 1493: Fortuna pulls the French crown off Margaret of Austria's head; Debae, *La Bibliothèque*, cat. [52], pp. 509–12.

Lemaire de Belges' *Couronne Margaritique*.[26] Riccio dwells extensively on the strokes of fate that hit Margaret of Austria during the first twenty-five years of her life. In this richly illuminated manuscript she is variously depicted as wife of the Spanish prince (folio 18v), as wife of Philibert II of Savoy (folio 21r) and as Queen of France (folio 2v–3r). The only double spread in the entire manuscript is reserved for an image of the winged personification of Fortune on a wheel who pulls the French crown off Margaret's head. The young woman sits under a baldachin, carries sceptre and globe and wears a blue dress covered with fleur-de-lis ornaments. This illumination was made more than ten years after Margaret of Austria was forced to leave the French court and expresses the public humiliation that Margaret and her family experienced when she was toppled from power. Michele Riccio's text starts off with an excursus on four virtues which the author deems appropriate for a woman such as Margaret of Austria, the recipient of this manuscript. Text and image point to her moral qualities as can for instance be seen from the personifications of Strength (folio 10r), Prudence (folio 11r), Justice (folio 13v) and Temperance (folio 15v).[27]

While Margaret of York's collection of books – approximately twenty-five in all – consisted of contemporary Flemish manuscripts, Margaret of Austria was more eclectic in her approach. She gathered a much wider variety of codices from Italy, Spain, central France, Savoy, Germany, and last but not least, from Flanders. Some of these were old manuscripts, books that had

been passed on from generation to generation; others were new books written especially for her such as Riccio's text. By 1530, Margaret owned about 380 books, manuscripts and genealogies – a library of considerable proportions, especially for an early sixteenth century woman.[28]

The breakdown of Margaret's library is revealing in several respects. First of all, devotional or religious books only constitute about twenty-five per cent of the collection. Anne-Marie Legaré revealed that this category took up 83.5 percent in the case of Margaret of York.[29] Margaret of Austria kept more than fifty romances and fiction books in her collection, housed at Mechelen, in contradiction to what Juan Luis Vives had recommended. She also owned a small number of song and dance books. There were many types of books that one would not expect in a woman's library, categories that Vives strongly advised against, such as books on warfare and hunting, philosophical texts, and classical literature.[30] The section that could be grouped as educational treatises for princes (thirteen volumes) provides a further clue to understanding the particular composition and purpose of the Mechelen library. This was not an ordinary library for a high-ranking noble woman; this was a library for the Governess General of the Burgundian Netherlands, a woman with political power and clout, a reference library not just for Margaret of Austria herself, but also for her male courtiers and political advisors. As she was also the aunt and foster mother of the imperial children of her brother Philip the Fair, King of Castille (Eleanor, born 1498, Charles, born 1500, Isabel, born 1501, Ferdinand, born 1503, and Mary, born 1505), there had to be a good spread of texts that could serve as instructional literature for

---

26   Jean Lemaire de Belges, *La Couronne Margaritique, 1504–1505*, Vienna, Österreichische Nationalbibliothek, cod. 3441, see: Debae, *La Bibliothèque*, cat. [374]; Fontaine, 'Olivier de la Marche and Jean Lemaire de Belges', pp. 224–28 and cat. 85; Blattes-Vial, 'Le manuscrit de la Couronne margaritique', pp. 83–126.

27   Eichberger, 'Margaret of Austria. A Princess with Ambition and Political Insight', pp. 48–55, ill. 13–17.

28   Debae, *La Bibliotèque*.

29   Legaré, 'La librairye de Madame', p. 207.

30   Eichberger, 'Frauenbibliotheken'.

them. Four of these children were raised in Mechelen to become kings and queens on the chessboard of European politics. In 1518, Ferdinand I would travel from Spain to Mechelen to prepare himself for his new role as governor of the Austrian Habsburg lands.

A space for female devotion: the bedroom and study

Devotional books generally played a particularly important role in the lives of noblewomen and usually outnumbered secular books. Juan Luis Vives comments on how married women should set aside time for their devotions:

> The virtuous woman, when she is free of domestic cares, will choose for herself – daily, if possible, but if not on feast days – a secluded part of the home, away from the noise and bustling. There, laying aside for a while the worries of the house and recollecting her thoughts, she will meditate on the contempt of these worldly things, since they are frivolous and unstable, insubstantial and quick to perish. [...] Then with the help of some divine reading she will raise herself to the thought and contemplation of divine things. Finally, having confessed her sins to God, she will suppliantly beg for pardon and peace from him and will pray first for herself. Then, having found more favour with God, she will pray for her husband, her children, and, finally, her whole household, so that the Lord Jesus will inspire a better mind in all of them.[31]

Vives refers to 'a secluded part of the home' without specifying if he has a bedroom, a study, or an oratory in mind. Leandro Bassano's portrait

of a pious widow visualizes the notion of a 'virtuous woman' (Figure 4.7). The elderly lady portrayed in this unusual painting kneels in a darkened room while performing her prayers with the help of her rosary beads; a small manuscript with two golden clasps – perhaps a Book of Hours – is lying on the stool in front of her. In a window-like opening, a religious scene takes place that depicts either the Nativity of Christ or Saint Anne giving birth to the Virgin Mary. This scene, which must have been of particular significance to the female sitter, appears like a mental image in the background of the scene. The widow is not looking directly onto the scene, but seems to be gazing into the distance.

In the case of Margaret of Austria, the private study next to her bedroom was a most intimate space in which she kept a small selection of books.[32] Of the eight books listed in her inventory as being kept in this space, four were intended for devotional practice: three illuminated Books of Hours and a tome with extracts from the gospels. We also learn that Margaret kept an ivory box with silver bookmarks in her study, given to her by an abbess. It seems as if Margaret of Austria kept some of her best Books of Hours in her private apartments – the entries mention finely bound codices that were lavishly decorated (*bien historiés et enlumynée*). There is reason to believe that in her case piety was combined with connoisseurship or art appreciation. In her bedroom Margaret of Austria kept many devotional paintings by leading artists such as Jan van Eyck, Jan Gossaert, Marco d'Oggiono, Jan Mostaert and others. The descriptions in her inventory contain differentiated value judgements that pay tribute to the artistic quality of the object. [33]

31 Vives, *The Education of a Christian Woman*, p. 263.

32 Eichberger, *Leben mit Kunst – Wirken durch Kunst*, pp. 109–12, p. 195, pp. 372–88.

33 Eichberger, 'Stilpluralismus und Internationalität', pp. 272–77; see also de Kesel, 'New perspectives on devotional manuscripts', pp. 89–113.

Margaret of Austria is one of the few early modern women who had a bedroom and a private study at her disposal. In Mechelen, she thus adopted a custom that high-ranking men had established in the course of the late fourteenth and fifteenth centuries.[34] In his third book of *I Libri della famiglia* (1434), Leon Battista Alberti presents a *pater familias* who employs his study to conceal his most precious belongings from curious eyes:

> I show her [i.e. his young wife] all my material goods and explain their significance to her. As to the books and the writings of my ancestors, I have always preferred to keep them locked away, so that my wife cannot read them, and cannot even see them. I do not carry these books with me in the sleeve of my dress, but orderly put them up in my study, as if it was something sacred and venerable. I never permitted my wife to enter this space, neither by herself nor in my company; quite on the contrary, I told her to hand over any of my books immediately, should she accidentally come across one of them.[35]

Margaret of Austria used both her study and her bedchamber for devotional exercises. In her study she kept a desk and a chair to facilitate reading and writing; in her bedroom, she had installed an altar-like structure fitted with a baldachin, an antependium and a cushion to kneel on. The altar decoration was made from costly

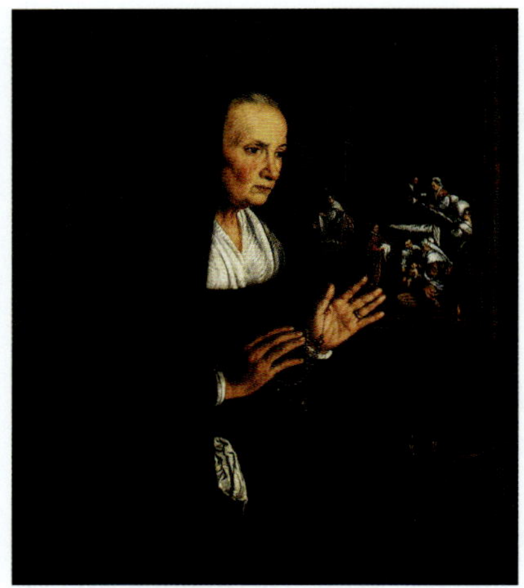

Figure 4.7: Leandro Bassano, *Portrait of a Widowed Woman in Prayer*, first half of the seventeenth century. Oil on canvas, 105cm × 89cm. Private Collection.

textiles such as richly patterned gold brocade, blue velvet, yellow damask, and green silk. The dossal of the baldachin was embroidered with the letter M for Marguerite. This structure is a clear indication that Margaret practiced her devotions in the seclusion of her bedroom.

Several of her finest devotional manuscripts were in fact inherited from her step-grandmother, Margaret of York. One of these manuscripts was a book by Margaret of York's almoner Nicolas Finet, entitled *Blessed are the merciful*, a quotation taken from the Sermon on the Mount.[36] This book was intended to guide the young duchess towards an active and charitable life. The manuscript was executed while her husband Charles the Bold was still alive and was decorated with the initials of both husband and wife and with their combined coats of arms. In the main miniature on folio 1r, two registers with eight individual compartments display the seven acts of mercy (Figure 4.8). On

---

34 Already at the beginning of the fifteenth century, Christine de Pizan described the private study of the French king Charles V (1338–1380) in her book *Livres des fais et bonnes meurs du sage Roy Charles V* as follows: 'Après son dormir estoit un espace avec ses plus privez en esbatement de choses agréables, visitant joyaulx ou autres richeces.' ('Following from his bedroom, there was a space for diversion with most private and pleasant things, to behold jewels and other riches'); cited after Bergvelt and others, *Verzamelen*, p. 7, footnote 10. For a further discussion of such studies, see the essay by Miya Tokumitsu in the present volume.

35 Alberti, *Vom Hauswesen*, p. 284.

36 Nicolas Finet, *Benois seront les misericordieux*, 1468–1477, Brussels, Bibliothèque Royale de Belgique, ms. 9296; Debae, La Bibliothèque, pp. 266–68.

the lower right, Margaret of York is kneeling in her prayer tent accompanied by her personal patron St Margaret with the dragon. The duchess is looking up from her book and is envisioning the *Seven Acts of Mercy*. In six of the seven scenes, she herself plays a central role: feeding the poor and offering drink to the thirsty, giving clothes and shelter to those in need, visiting the imprisoned and caring for the sick.

One of the most expressive illuminations from Margaret of York's collection is the frontispiece of a manuscript entitled, *The Dialogue between the Duchess of Burgundy and Jesus Christ*.[37] The boldly coloured miniature shows Margaret of York kneeling on the floor of her stately bedroom (Figure 4.9). She has raised her hands as if attempting to touch the body of the resurrected Christ who stands in front of her holding the banner of his victory in his hand. Christ appears in front of the duchess in a composition very similar to a usual *Noli me tangere* scene when Christ meets Mary Magdalene after his resurrection.[38] This is perhaps the most intimate scene of all the devotional portraits we known of Margaret of York, one that perfectly meets Vives' expectations ('away from the noise and bustling'). The miniature suggests that Margaret mediates on the life of Christ in her private bedroom, where the canopy of the bed carries the initials of Charles and Margaret.

Outstanding manuscripts for exceptional women

In the Burgundian Netherlands of the late fifteenth century, the best illuminators were vying for the attention of the great patrons, always inventing new pictorial schemes to cause astonishment and wonder. Margaret of York and Margaret of Austria, both bibliophiles in their own right, formed part of a wider Burgundian family network. The third person to be mentioned in their context is Mary of Burgundy (1457–1482), step-daughter of Margaret of York and the mother of Margaret of Austria, who also owned a number of outstanding manuscripts.

The opening page of the *Vienna Hours of Mary of Burgundy* can be described as one of the most audacious experiments of its time. On folio 14 verso, the Burgundian princess who once owned the manuscript is portrayed in the foreground, sitting in front of an open window.[39] There has been some debate regarding her identity. While several scholars have argued that this is a portrait of Margaret of York, Thomas Kren identified the princess as Mary of Burgundy. The young woman wears a fine dress and an elaborate headpiece; she is adorned with precious jewellery and keeps a lapdog with a red collar on her knees. She is immersed in reading a devotional book – her eyes are firmly fixed onto the pages of the open book, resting on the window sill. The three prayers that immediately follow this opening miniature are all dedicated to the Virgin Mary. And indeed, the Virgin Mary with her Child appears in the middle ground of the miniature; she is seated in front of an altar inside a Gothic church. Mary is much smaller in size than the beautiful princess at the open window. Is the illuminator suggesting that we are looking at a mental image of the young princess? The composition of this scene is comparable to Leandro Bassano's portrait of a pious window discussed earlier, albeit much earlier in date. The spatial

37   Nicolas Finet, *Le dialogue de la duchesse de Bourgogne à Jesus Christ*, after 1468, London, BL, Add. Ms. 7970, folio 1v.

38   Pearson, 'Gendered Subject, Gendered Spectator', pp. 47–66.

39   Vienna Master of Mary of Burgundy, *Book of Hours of Mary of Burgundy*, c.1475, Vienna, Österreichische Nationalbibliothek, ms. 1857, folio 14v: A young princess reading a devotional book; see fn. 18. Refer to Figure 2.3.

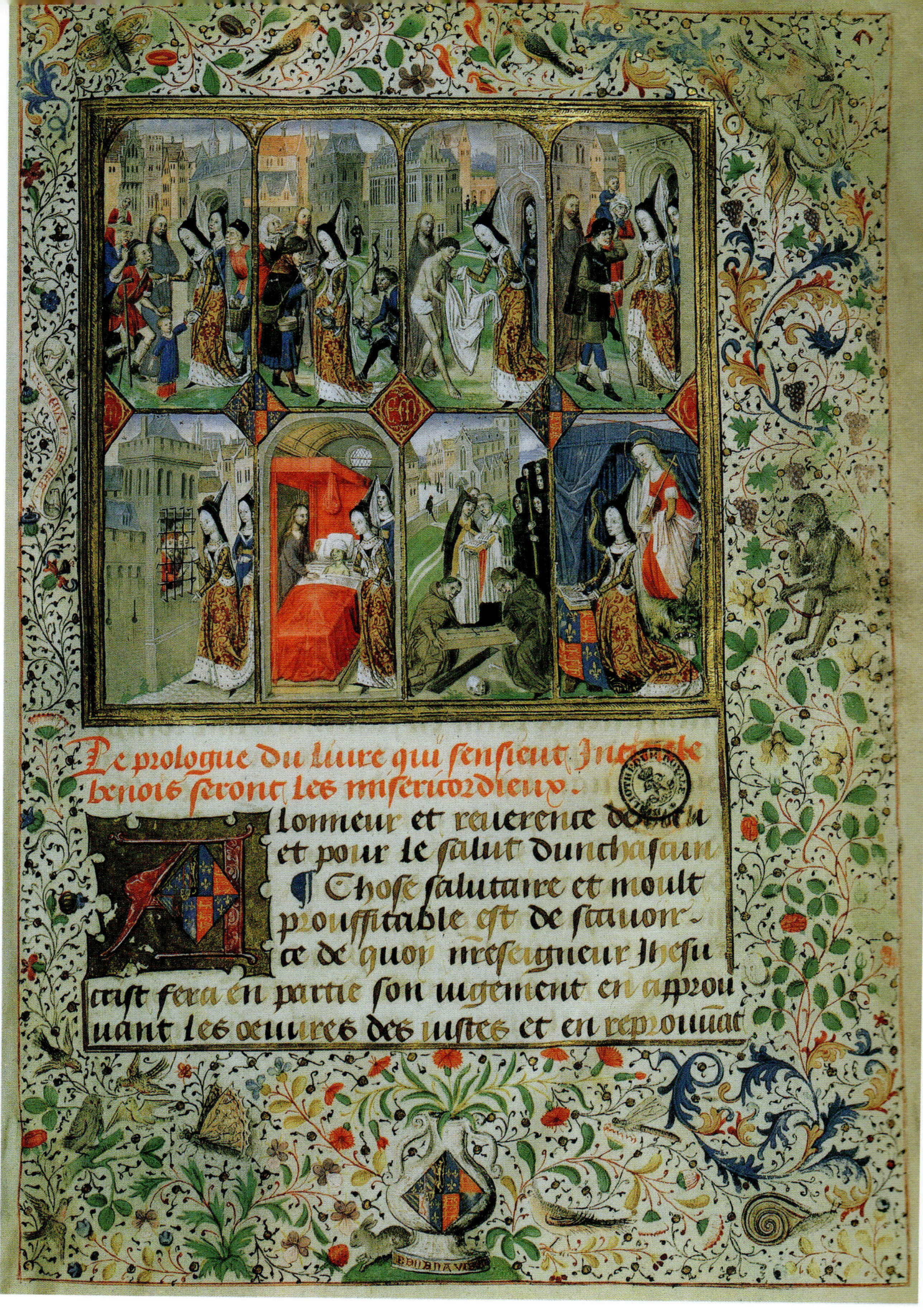

Figure 4.8: Nicolas Finet, Margaret of York and the Seven Acts of Mercy from *Benois seront les misericordieux*. Folio 1, 1468–1477. Parchment, 37.2cm × 26.5cm. Bibliothèque Royale de Belgique, Brussels. MS 9296.

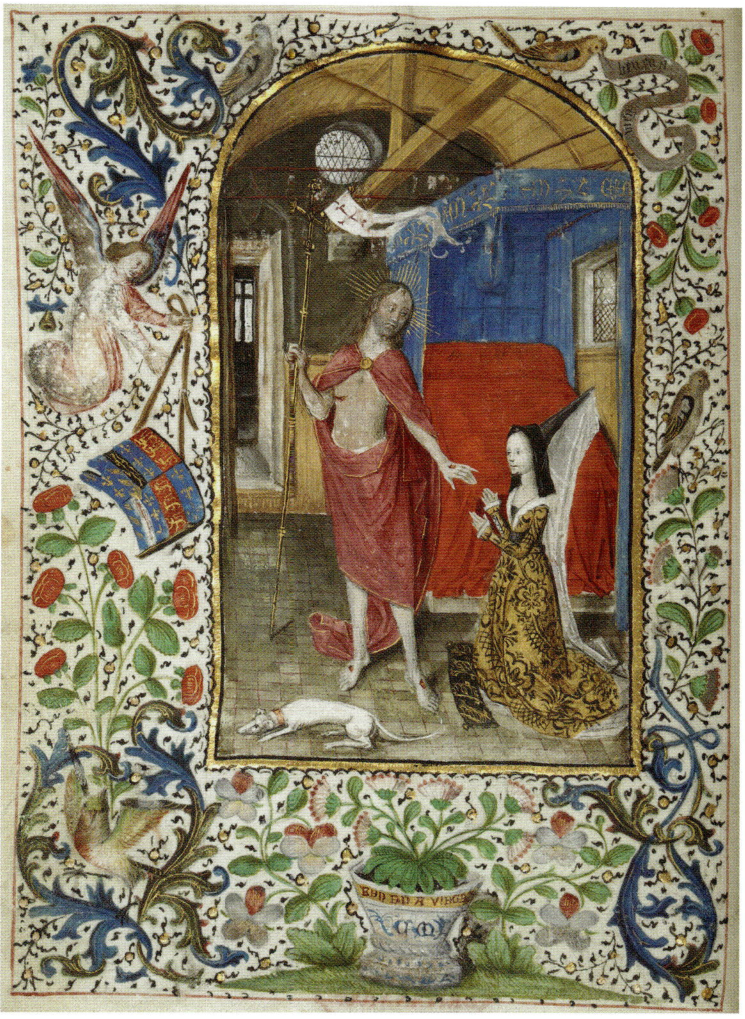

Figure 4.9: Nicolas Finet, *Christ appears to Margaret of York* from *Le dialogue de la duchesse de Bourgogne à Jesus Christ*. Folio 1v, after 1468. Parchment, 20.4cm × 13.8cm. British Library, London. Add. Ms. 7970.

illusionism employed in this miniature is in many ways more convincing. The notion of looking from the window of a private oratory directly onto the main altar of a large church existed both in Bruges (Our Lady's Church) and Mechelen (St Peter); however the private space was not positioned in the central axis of the church.

A small Book of Hours, now in Berlin, once belonged to Mary of Burgundy and her husband Maximilian I.[40] This precious manuscript was illuminated in about 1481–82 by an artist called the Berlin Master of Mary of Burgundy. Fol. 220v marks the beginning of the Office of the Dead and the opening miniature seems to contain a visual reference to the death of Mary of Burgundy in a hunting accident on 27 March

40 König, *Das Berliner Stundenbuch der Maria von Burgund.*

1482. In this miniature, a hunting party consisting of two men and a young woman is attacked by the 'Three Living and the Three Dead'. This theme has a long tradition in illuminated manuscripts and frequently served as a reminder that death can strike anytime and anywhere.[41] A handwritten dedication on folio 13r: *a vous lealle margot, vostre maximilian Leal* ('for you, faithful Margaret, from your loyal Maximilian'), indicates that Maximilian bequeathed this very personal manuscript to his only daughter, Margaret of Austria.[42] It is quite likely that this occurred in 1483, the year in which the three-year-old girl had to leave her country of birth in order to be educated at the French court as bride of the future king, Charles VIII. This arrangement had been negotiated in the Peace of Arras (1482) in order to put an end to the battle between the French and the Habsburg parties over the Burgundian territories. As mentioned earlier, 'the young queen' was sent back to the Netherlands in 1493, a humiliation that Margaret would never forget.

A woodcut in a book from the former Cistercian priory of Muizen (now in Mechelen) reflects Margaret's ill-feelings towards the French.[43] The coloured print shows Saint Margaret as a vigilant shepherdess, guarding her sheep against two predators that appear at the outskirts of a forest. The shape and colour of the saint's dress, the coat of arms (Austria) and the daisies on the margins (*marguerites* in French) leave no doubt that the image of the saint is a crypto-portrait of Margaret of Austria, the Regent of the Netherlands. Margaret's 'flock'

lives in a prosperous country in which corn grows abundantly. Since the beginning of the fifteenth century, the wolf and the lion were well-known symbols employed in French manuscripts to express the political struggle for supremacy.[44] Margaret is known as an astute and politically active woman who used manuscripts, books and prints to argue her case.

Illuminated manuscripts served many different purposes; they were passed on within a family and could serve as diplomatic gifts. In 1511, Emperor Maximilian I commissioned a large illuminated choir book from Petrus Alamire (*c.*1470–1536), a famous German composer, copyist and singer.[45] After the emperor's death in 1519, the manuscript passed, like the Book of Hours, from Maximilian to his daughter Margaret. The illuminated manuscript was rebound and probably used in her court chapel. Choir books were large manuscripts and were frequently used in communal services. The opening miniature (folio 1v) shows Maximilian's grandson Charles – Margaret's nephew – with sceptre and sword in his hands, seated on a throne underneath a baldachin surmounted by an oversized double-headed imperial eagle (Figure 4.10). Archduke Charles, the future Emperor Charles V, is depicted as the rightful heir to the Habsburg Empire, a vast territory that Maximilian had forged through his marriage with Mary of Burgundy. Charles is accompanied by his siblings: Ferdinand and Mary, Isabel, Eleanor, and Catherine. In the foreground, the representatives of the church

---

41   Anzelewsky and others, 'Das berühmteste Bild', pp. 29–37.

42   Steenbock, 'Zur Überlieferungsgeschichte des Stundenbuchs', pp. 155–64.

43   Woodcut, late 15th century, Tournai, Bib. Sem.de Tournai, cod. 12, folio 10v; Lebigue and Vanwijnsberghe, 'Marguerite d'Autriche, Marguerite d'Antioche ', cat. LM 9, pp. 117–121; Eichberger, 'Instrumentalising Art', pp. 571–84.

44   This may be a subtle reference to the well-known image of the lion (=John the Fearless) attacking the wolf (=Louis of Orleans) that serves as a frontispiece in several copies of Jean Petit's *La Justification de Jean sans Peur*, for instance the copy in Vienna, ÖNB, ms. 2657, folio 1v.

45   Netherlandish, *Choir book of Margaret of* Austria, folio 1v, Mechelen, Stadsachief, no inventory number; Schreurs, *De Schatkamer van Alamire*, pp. 69–71; Meconi, 'Pierre de la Rue', pp. 78–109.

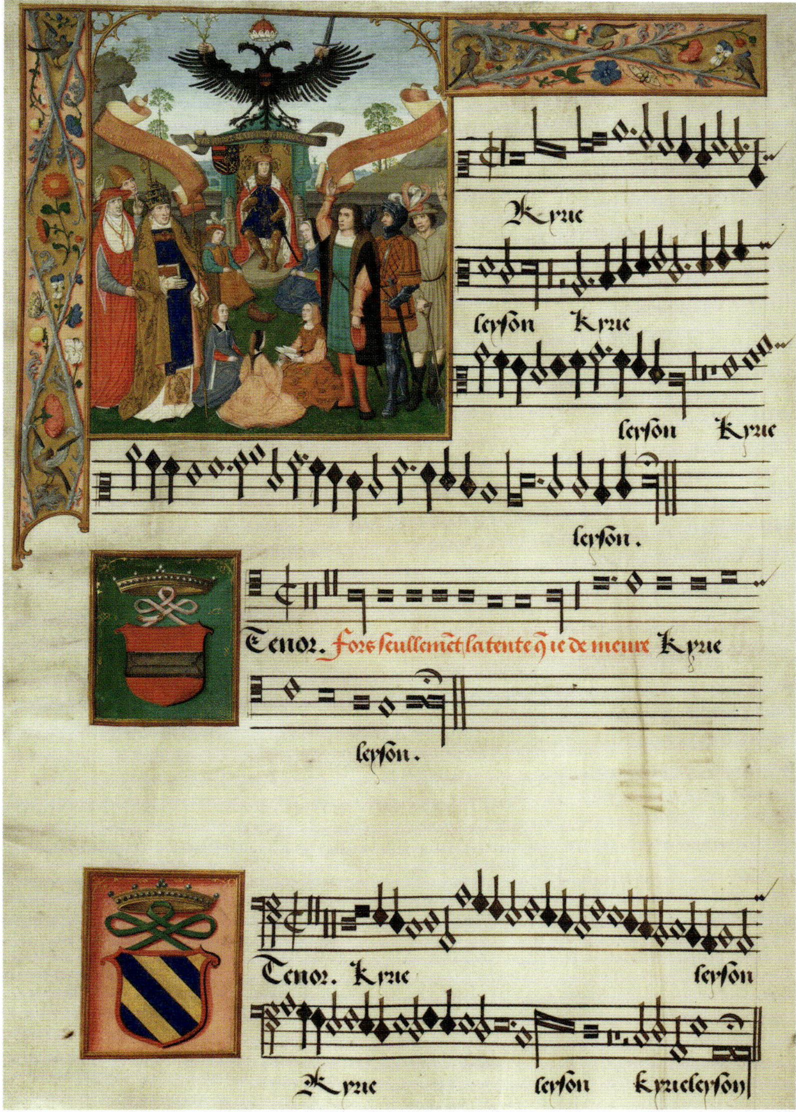

Figure 4.10: Netherlandish, Archduke Charles enthroned from *Koorboek van Margareta van Oostenrijk* (Choir book of Margaret of Austria). Folio 1v, *c.*1515. Parchment, 65cm × 43.8cm. City Archives Mechelen, Mechelen.

and three social classes pay homage to Prince Charles and acknowledge his position of authority.

Margaret of Austria served her family as Regent of the Netherlands from 1507 to 1515 and again from 1519 up to her death in 1530.[46] In 1515, she was temporarily replaced by her nephew, Archduke Charles, who having come of age was given a more prominent role within the family hierarchy by Maximilian I. Perhaps in an attempt to come to terms with her unavoidable discharge, Margaret commissioned an illuminated *chansonnier* of large dimensions that contained her portrait in courtly attire as well

46   Eichberger, 'Margaret of Austria', pp. 52–55.

as her coats of arms.[47] The manuscript consists mainly of secular songs in French, Flemish, and Latin as well as a few motets. On the opening pages, Margaret is kneeling in prayer, with an open book in front of her (folio 2r); in this miniature, she turns to a representation of the Virgin Mary as Queen of Heaven (folio 1v) and utters the words *memento mei* ('remember me'), almost as if appealing to the Virgin for help. These two images appropriately accompany the sacred motet: *Ave sanctissima Maria, mater dei, regina coeli, porta paradise, domina mundi...* ('Hail most holy Mary, mother of God, queen of heaven, gate to paradise, mistress of the world...'). As the musicologist Honey Meconi has argued, it was most unusual to have a portrait of that size and quality inserted into a songbook.[48] Margaret soon however regained her position of power, and in 1519 she was appointed Regent and Governess General of the Burgundian Netherlands yet again. In the following years she made a strong effort to leave her mark as an avid collector and patron of the arts. She commissioned many works of art; paintings, sculptures, illuminated manuscripts, tapestries and other objects. Her portraits frequently stress her role as the representative of the Emperor, as is for instance the case in a terracotta medallion by Conrat Meit.[49]

For a long time, Margaret of Austria was seen as a minor patron of illuminated manuscripts, because her interest in manuscripts differed from that of her bibliophile relative. This view has, however, gradually changed thanks to Honey Meconi and others.[50] The so-called *Sforza Hours* is one of the best examples for judging Margaret of Austria's discerning taste, her connoisseurship, and her creative mind.[51] This northern Italian Book of Hours had once belonged to Bona Sforza and had remained a fragment when Margaret of Austria inherited it.[52] Approximately ten years after her return to the Netherlands, she commissioned a scribe to complete the missing texts and asked her court illuminator, Gerard Horenbout (1465–1541), to supply the additional illuminations in the latest Flemish style.[53] Margaret intended to give this fine manuscript as a gift to her nephew Charles on the occasion of his coronation as King of the Romans. Horenbout produced several miniatures of the highest quality in which he skilfully combines Flemish pictorial traditions with Italian features. In the Sforza Hours Italian and Flemish miniatures are placed next to one another; the Milanese artist Giovann Pietro Birago (active 1471–1513) and the Ghent illuminator Gerard Horenbout are treated as equals. The manuscript is full of subtle references to Margaret of Austria and her nephew Charles, who grew up at her court in Mechelen. In the *Visitation* scene, Margaret of Austria appears in the guise of Saint Elizabeth who meets the pregnant Virgin Mary outside the city gate. In this miniature, Margaret is portrayed as a mature woman who is physically close to Mary and Christ. Such a highly

---

47   Brussels, Bibliothèque Royale de Belgique, ms. 228.

48   Meconi, 'Margaret of Austria', pp. 11–36.

49   Conrat Meit, *Margaret of Austria*, painted terracotta, inscription: MARGARITA CESAVM AVSTRIE VNICA FILI- AET AMITA 1528 (roughly, 'Margaret, the only daughter and aunt of the Austrian Emperor'), Vienna, Kunsthistorisches Museum

50   Eichberger, 'The culture of gifts', pp. 287–95.

51   Giovanni Birago and Gerard Horenbout, *The Sforza Hours*, London, British Library, Add. MS. 34294; see: Evans, The Sforza Hours.

52   When Margaret's first husband, Philibert II of Savoy, died in 1504, she was allowed to take with her a small number of books from the Savoy library, including among others the 'Sforza Hours'. Evans, *The Sforza Hours*, p. 24–28.

53   Duverger, 'Gerard Horenbault', pp. 81–90.

personalized miniature would not have been produced without the consent of the patron who wanted to be represented in the most favourable light.

Conclusions

This essay has argued that it is important to make a distinction between the educational principles that were laid down in instructive manual and the realities of everyday life. Judging from the books that have survived and analysing the inventories of private collections, one can conclude that women cherished a wide variety of books, including romance and historic books. The more assertive female reader did not limit herself to devotional books or saints' lives as recommended by Vives and others.

Margaret of York and Margaret of Austria were two remarkable patrons and collectors of manuscripts. Close family ties and a long-standing tradition of collecting illuminated manuscripts guaranteed that bibliophile traditions continued. Undoubtedly, both women left their mark as discerning book collectors and patrons – each in her own way. The surviving manuscripts often tell more about these women and their preferences than written documents. Margaret of York acquired most of her precious manuscripts while she was Charles's spouse; Margaret of Austria built up her library after becoming Regent and Governess General of the Netherlands.

The expression 'women who read are dangerous' does not correspond to the enthusiasm for books that many high-ranking women displayed in the late Middle Ages and the early Renaissance. This dictum only holds truth for those who are afraid of education and erudition, those who fear an independent mind.

About the author

Dagmar Eichberger is Professor of Art History at the Institut für Europäische Kunstgeschichte of the Universität Heidelberg. Her most recent books are the co-edited volumes *The Artist between Court and City, 1300–1600* (2017), and *Religion, the Supernatural and Visual Culture in Early Modern Europe* (2015). d.eichberger@zegk.uni-heidelberg.de

Works cited

Leon Battista Alberti, *Vom Hauswesen (Della Famiglia)*, transl. by Walther Kraus (Munich: Deutscher Taschenbuchverlag, 1986).

Fedja Anzelewsky, Bodo Brinkmann and Eberhard König, 'Das berühmteste Bild: Die Begegnung der drei Lebenden und der drei Toten', in *Das Berliner Stundenbuch der Maria von Burgund und Kaiser Maximilians. Handschrift 78 B 12 im Kupferstichkabinett der Staatlichen Museen zu Berlin Preußischer Kulturbesitz*, ed. by Eberhard König (Berlin: Nicolai, 1998), pp. 29–37.

Ellinoor Bergvelt, ed., *Verzamelen, van rariteitenkabinet tot kunstmuseum* (Heerlen: Open Universiteit, 1993).

Françoise Blattes-Vial, 'Le manuscrit de la *Couronne margaritique* de Jean Lemaire de Belges offert par Marguerite d'Autriche à Philippe le Beau en 1505. La rhétorique et l'image au service d'une princesse assimilée à la paix', *Le Moyen Age*, 121 (2015), pp. 83–126.

Wim Blockmans, 'Margaret of York. The subtle influence of a Duchess', in *Women of Distinction. Margaret of York and Margaret of Austria*, ed. by Dagmar Eichberger (Leuven: Davidsfonds, 2005), pp. 42–47.

Stefan Bollmann, ed., *Women who read are dangerous* (London: Merrell, 2008).

Cynthia J. Brown and Anne-Marie Legaré, eds., *Les femmes, la culture et les arts en Europe entre Moyen Âge et Renaissance* (Turnhout: Brepols, 2016).

Kathleen Wilson Chevalier, ed., *Patronnes et mécènnes en France à la Renaissance* (Sainte-Etienne: Université de Saint-Etienne, 2007).

Anne de France, *Enseignement à sa fille suivis de l'Histoire du siege de Brest*, ed. by Tatiana Clavier and Eliane Viennot (Saint-Étienne: Publications de l'Université de Saint-Ètienne, 2006).

Christine de Pizan, *Der Schatz der Stadt der Frauen. Weibliche Lebensklugheit in der Welt des Spätmittelalters*, ed.

and intro. by Claudia Opitz, trans. by Claudia Probst (Freiburg: Herder, 1996).

Marguerite Debae, *La Bibliothèque de Marguerite d'Autriche. Essai de reconstitution d'après l'inventaire de 1523–24* (Leuven and Paris: Peeters, 1995).

Lieve De Kesel, 'New perspectives on devotional manuscripts associated with Margaret of Austria and her relations: The Role of the Prayer Book Master', in *Les femmes, la culture et les arts en Europe entre Moyen Âge et Renaissance*, ed. by Cynthia J. Brown and Anne-Marie Legaré (Turnhout: Brepols, 2016), pp. 89–113.

Jozef Duverger, 'Gerard Horenbault (1465–1530), hofschilder van Margareta van Oostenrijk', *Kunst: Maandblad voor oude en jonge kunst*, 4 (1930), pp. 81–90.

Dagmar Eichberger, 'A Renaissance Princess named Margaret. Fashioning a Public Image in a Courtly Society', *Melbourne Art Journal*, 5 (2001), pp. 4–24.

Dagmar Eichberger, 'Frauenbibliotheken des 16. Jahrhunderts zwischen Ideal und Wirklichkeit', in *Die lesende Frau*, ed. by Gabriela Signori (Wiesbaden: Harrassowitz, 2009), pp. 241–64.

Dagmar Eichberger, 'Instrumentalising Art for Political Ends. Margaret of Austria, regente et gouvernante des pais bas de l'empereur', in *Femmes de pouvoir, femmes politiques durant les derniers siècles du Moyen Âge et au cours de la première Renaissance*, ed. by Éric Bousmar et al. (Brussels: De Boeck, 2011), pp. 571–84.

Dagmar Eichberger, *Leben mit Kunst – Wirken durch Kunst. Sammelwesen und Hofkunst unter Margarete von Österreich, Regentin der Niederlande* (Turnhout and London: Brepols, 2002).

Dagmar Eichberger, 'Manoeuvring between Competing Courts: Jean Lemaire de Belges (1473–1515), Historiographer and Connoisseur', in *Imagery and Ingenuity in Early Modern Europe: Essays in Honor of Jeffrey Chipps Smith*, ed. by Catharine Ingersoll et al. (Turnhout: Brepols, forthcoming, 2017).

Dagmar Eichberger, 'Margaret of Austria. A Princess with Ambition and Political Insight', in *Women of Distinction. Margaret of York and Margaret of Austria*, ed. by Dagmar Eichberger (Leuven: Davidfonds, 2005), pp. 48–55.

Dagmar Eichberger, 'Stilpluralismus und Internationalität am Hofe Margarete von Österreichs (1506–1530)' in *Wege zur Renaissance*, ed. by Norbert Nußbaum et al. (Cologne: SH-Verlag, 2003), pp. 260–83.

Dagmar Eichberger, 'The Culture of Gifts. A Courtly Phenomenon from a female perspective', in *Women of Distinction. Margaret of York and Margaret of Austria*, ed. by Dagmar Eichberger (Leuven: Davidfonds, 2005), pp. 287–95.

Dagmar Eichberger, ed., *Women of Distinction. Margaret of York and Margaret of Austria* (Leuven: Davidfonds, 2005).

Mark Evans, ed., *The Sforza Hours Ad. MS 34294 of the British Library*, 5 vols (Lucerne: Faksimile Verlag, 1995).

Marie Madeleine Fontaine, 'Olivier de la Marche and Jean Lemaire de Belges. The Author and his Female Patron', in *Women of Distinction. Margaret of York and Margaret of Austria*, ed. by Dagmar Eichberger (Leuven: Davidfonds, 2005), pp. 220–229.

Juliane Jacobi, 'Juan Luis Vives' *De institutione feminae Christianae*. Eine humanistische Schrift zur Mädchenerziehung für Europa', in: Themenportal „Europäische Geschichte – Geschlechtergeschichte" (2011), accessed 26 June 2016 at http://www.europa.clio-online.de/site/lang__de/ItemID__495/mid__11428/40208214/default.aspx.

Juliane Jacobi, *Mädchen- und Frauenbildung in Europa von 1500 bis zur Gegenwart* (Cologne: Campus, 2013).

Eberhard König, ed., *Das Berliner Stundenbuch der Maria von Burgund und Kaiser Maximilians. Handschrift 78 B 12 im Kupferstichkabinett der Staatlichen Museen zu Berlin Preußischer Kulturbesitz* (Berlin: Nicolai, 1998).

Thomas Kren and Scot McKendrick eds., *Illuminating the Renaissance. The Triumph of Flemish Manuscript Painting in Europe* (Los Angeles: The J. Paul Getty Museum, 2003).

Thomas Kren, ed., *Margaret of York, Simon Marmion, and the Visions of Tondal* (Malibu: The J. P. Getty Museum, 1992).

J.-B. Lebigue and Dominique Vanwijnsberghe, 'Marguerite d'Autriche, Marguerite d'Antioche. Une gravure énigmatique', in *Séminaire de Tournai, Histoire, Bâtiments, Collections*, ed. by Monique Maillard-Luypaert (Leuven: Peeters, 2008), pp. 117–21.

Anne-Marie Legaré, '"La librairye de Madame". Two Princesses and their libraries', in *Women of Distinction. Margaret of York and Margaret of Austria*, ed. by Dagmar Eichberger (Leuven: Davidfonds, 2005), pp. 206–219.

Anne-Marie Legaré, ed., *Livres et lectures des Femmes entre Moyen-Âge et Renaissance* (Turnhout: Brepols, 2007).

Margaret M. Manion, ed., *An illumination. The Rothschild Prayer Book and other works from the Kerry Stokes Collection, c.1280–1685*, (West Perth: Australian Capital Equity, 2015).

Paul Matthews, 'Apparel, Status, Fashion. Woman's clothing and Jewellery', in *Women of Distinction. Margaret of York and Margaret of Austria*, ed. by Dagmar Eichberger (Leuven: Davidfonds, 2005), pp. 146–53.

Honey Meconi, 'Margaret of Austria, Visual Representation, and Brussels, Royal Library, Ms. 228', *Journal of the Alamire Foundation*, 2 (2010), pp. 11–36.

Honey Meconi, 'Pierre de la Rue (*c.*1452–1518), Missa Alleluia, Mechelen, Stadsarchief, Ms. s.s.', in *Meerstemmigheid in beeld. Zeven meesterwerken uit het atelier van Petrus Alamire*, ed. by David J. Burn et al. (Leuven: Davidfonds, 2015), pp. 78–109.

Andrea Pearson, 'Gendered Subject, Gendered Spectator: Mary Magdalen in the Gaze of Margaret of York', *Gesta*, 44 (2005), pp. 47–66.

Walter Prevenier, 'Mechelen circa 1500. A cosmopolitan biotope for social elites and non-conformists,' in *Women of Distinction. Margaret of York and Margaret of Austria*, ed. by Dagmar Eichberger (Leuven: Davidfonds, 2005), pp. 30–41.

Eugen Schreurs, ed., *De Schatkamer van Alamire. Muziek en miniature uit Keizer Karels tijd (1500–1535)* (Leuven: Davidsfonds, 1999), 69–71.

Peter Stabel, ed., *Urban identities in the late-medieval and early modern city. Mechelen in the 15th and 16th centuries* (forthcoming, 2018).

Frauke Steenbock, 'Zur Überlieferungsgeschichte des Stundenbuchs der Maria von Burgund und Kaiser Maximilians', in *Das Berliner Stundenbuch der Maria von Burgund und Kaiser Maximilians. Handschrift 78 B 12 im Kupferstichkabinett der Staatlichen Museen zu Berlin Preußischer Kulturbesitz*, ed. by Eberhard König (Berlin: Nicolai, 1998), pp. 155–64.

Juan Luis Vives, *De institutione feminae christianae*, ed. and trans. by Charles E. Fantazzi (Leiden: Brill, 1996 and 1998).

Juan Luis Vives, *The Education of a Christian Woman: a sixteenth-century Manual*, ed. and trans. by Charles Fantazzi (Chicago and London: CUP, 2000).

Christine Weightman, *Margaret of York, Duchess of Burgundy, 1446–1503* (Gloucester: Sutton, 1989).

5. Medieval parchment: two glossed Bible books in context

Libby Melzer

Dunlop, Anne (ed.), *Antipodean Early Modern. European Art in Australian Collections, c. 1200–1600*, Amsterdam University Press, 2018

DOI: 10.5117/9789462985209/CH05

Abstract

This paper explores the history and role of parchment in understanding the circumstances of production of two glossed books of the Bible in the State Library of Victoria. These two manuscripts – an Italian copy of the *Epistles of St Paul* from around 1200, which was almost certainly monastically produced; and a copy of *Leviticus* produced in the first quarter of the thirteenth century in Paris, then a major centre for commercial book production – have very different patterns of how the skins of their parchment have been used. This difference is mirrored in developments in their complex page layout – an important characteristic of this genre of book.

Keywords: Parchment; Bible; Glossed book; Leviticus; Epistles of St. Paul; Medieval art

This essay focuses on two manuscripts in the collection of the State Library of Victoria in relation to both their layout and the use of parchment, showing how both these elements can be used to place the manuscripts in context. The manuscripts are both glossed Bible books, and were probably produced around a quarter of a century apart in two different regions and under quite different circumstances. The first is a copy of the *Epistles of Saint Paul* accompanied by the *Glossa ordinaria*. It was produced in central Italy, and has been dated to *c.*1200.[1] The second is a copy of the Book of *Leviticus* accompanied by a gloss from the commentaries of Rabanus Maurus. It was produced in the first quarter of the thirteenth century, a product of what was arguably the most well-organised centre for commercial book production in the Middle Ages – the Paris book trade at its height.

Neither the *Leviticus* nor the *Glossed Epistles of St Paul* is a deluxe manuscript. They have very little decoration and no gold at all, but they are interesting for several reasons. The first is that they are representations of a particular genre in the evolution of the most important book in Europe in the Middle Ages, the Bible, and at two different stages of that evolution. The second is that their simplicity conceals complexity. They are tools – adaptable, uniquely designed for their purpose, and able to be used in multiple ways. These manuscripts demonstrate two stages in the changing layout of glossed books in response to the greater demand brought about by the rise of

---

1   Manion et al, *Description and Analysis*, pp. 4–6

church schools and the shift from monastic to commercial book production. These stages are echoed in the use of parchment which shows a distinct difference in the availability of animal skins and evidence of different farming systems. When analysing the parchment of manuscripts, we can determine the type and number of animals used, their age and health; we can also identify regional differences in production techniques, and the relative skill and expertise of the parchment-maker. By examining the material elements of these two books, we gain insight into the circumstances in which books were produced around the turn of the thirteenth century, and the priorities of the people who used them.

What is parchment?

Parchment or vellum was the most significant medieval writing support in Western Europe, all but replacing papyrus from around the fourth century CE and itself superceded by paper from the middle of the Renaissance.[2] Its ascent was inseparably connected with the dissemination of early Christian texts, and the increase in status of their dominant format, the codex book. In its simplest form, parchment is an animal skin that has been treated with lime, scraped, and dried under tension. As an animal skin processed by hand, parchment retains many of the features of the animal from which it is taken, as well as the marks of the parchment-maker's tools. Its attributes are affected by the priorities and resources of the culture of its production, and the purpose and status of its intended manuscript.

The significance of parchment to the medieval book cannot be overstated. It was parchment that provided the foundation that allowed the medieval book to achieve the complexity and beauty of its greatest attainment, which was not equalled by books made from either papyrus or paper. Parchment provided the strength and flexibility required for complex book structures, a surface that could hold the fine lines required to permit the elegant and legible scripts, and a foundation that was strong and flexible enough to support the many layers of gesso, bole, gilding, and tempera of the illuminations of the later Middle Ages and Renaissance.

The rise of parchment as the material of the medieval codex, rather than the papyrus scroll favoured by classical Antiquity, had several driving forces. Neither the codex format nor parchment was an invention of the Middle Ages. The first written record of parchment is in Pliny the Elder's *Natural History*, which famously credits the invention to Pergamon and associates it with the rivalry between the library there and the great library at Alexandria, sometime in the second century BCE.[3] This rivalry was supposed to have prompted an embargo on the export of papyrus to Pergamon from Alexandria, a major port city through which most of the papyrus trade must have passed.[4] This almost certainly apocryphal account more probably relates to the period when parchment was introduced to Rome, rather than its invention, since forms of parchment had been used in Western Asia for thousands of years. Pliny cites his source as Marcus Terentius Varro (116–27 BCE), whose

2   Johnson, 'The Role of Parchment', pp. 84–8 and Reed, *Ancient Skins*, pp. 115–6.

3   Henderson, pp. 140–1, citing Pliny the Elder, *Natural History*, Book 13: 'subsequently, also according to Varro, when owing to the rivalry between King Ptolemy and King Eumenes about their libraries Ptolemy suppressed the export of paper [papyrus], parchment was invented at Pergamum; and afterwards the employment of the material on which the immortality of human beings depends spread indiscriminately'.

4   Johnson, 'The Role of Parchment', pp. 22–51.

account describes the period when Pergamon was politically aligned with Rome before being finally incorporated into the Roman Empire in 133 BCE. During this time Egypt was invaded, and Alexandria was several times under siege, undoubtedly disrupting all forms of trade including that of papyrus.

The Romans did embrace parchment to a small extent, both in scroll format for rough drafts of texts, and as single gathering codices used as notebooks. These were a more convenient version of the wax tablet, and relied on the ability of parchment to be wiped clear of ink and re-written. By the time Martial was writing in the first century CE, the parchment codex had some acceptance as a format for less expensive texts for the middle classes, though neither the form nor the material replaced the papyrus scroll as the definitive and authoritative format for the Roman book.[5]

By contrast, the earliest Christian texts from the first and second centuries were almost exclusively written in codex form.[6] These texts initially took the form of single gatherings of papyrus, but by the third century they had transitioned almost completely to the parchment codex, which became the accepted format for the book for the next millennium. There were many reasons for this change in the format and material of the book – economic, sociological, cultural, and religious – but one chief advantage of parchment over papyrus was that its production could be decentralised. The production in papyrus was limited by the availability of the *Cyperus papyrus* plant only grown in commercial quantities in the Delta regions of the Nile Valley, and further restricted by a highly regulated market.[7] In contrast, all

that was required to produce parchment was water, a small selection of tools, and two byproducts of agriculture: lime and animal skins. The decentralised production created diversity in the finished product, making parchment an interesting and informative element in the study of books.

Glossed books in the history of the Bible

The Bible, as we commonly understand it today, is a series of 'books' within a single volume in a relatively set order – definitive, searchable, and consistent, with chapter numbers within the text and often running titles at the top of the page. But this format largely arose out of the church schools of the University of Paris in the twelfth and thirteenth centuries.[8] *Pandects* (single volumes containing the books of both the Old and New Testaments), were not unknown in the early Middle Ages, but they were not the common form for the transmission of the early Bible. Reasons for this include, significantly, that the materials and time required to produce a complete Bible were great, and the resulting text cumbersome. For example, possibly the oldest complete Latin Vulgate Bible, the *Codex Amiatinus*, written in Northumbria around 800, perhaps as a gift for the Pope, measures 50cm x 34cm, contains 1030 leaves (2060 pages) and weighs over 34kg.[9] During the Carolingian period it was the prestige associated with deluxe one- and two-volume Bibles that gave them their status as important gifts presented to churches and monasteries. Thus for most of the early history of the Bible, books were produced individually or in groups

---

5   Roberts and Skeat, *The Birth of the Codex*, pp. 24–9.
6   Roberts and Skeat, *The Birth of the Codex*, p. 42 and Lewis, *Papyrus in Classical Antiquity*, pp. 90–4.
7   Lewis, *Papyrus in Classical Antiquity*, p. 4.

8   de Hamel, *The Book: A History of the Bible*, pp. 114–20.
9   Florence Biblioteca Medicea-Laurenziana, cod. Amiatino 1; de Hamel, *The Book: A History of the Bible*, pp. 32–4.

of associated texts such as the Gospels, or the Pentateuch. Groups of books were produced for individual libraries which formed sets that functioned as a reference Bible, relatively complete by modern standards.

Along with the Bible itself, of great importance to medieval understanding were the commentaries on biblical texts by Church Fathers such as Jerome, Augustine, Cassiodorus, Gregory the Great, Isidore of Seville, and the Venerable Bede, along with later writers such as Rabanus Maurus (d. *c.*855) and Claudius of Turin (d. *c.*830). These commentaries were produced in great numbers, and provided authority and orthodoxy in the interpretation of scripture. The commentaries were compiled and extended, and they commented in turn on the works of earlier authors; eventually they attained the status of lesser biblical texts in their own right.

It was common medieval practice to annotate books, correcting the text, clarifying terminology, and referencing other texts, a process known as 'glossing'. Biblical texts in particular were frequently glossed, annotated directly with notes from separate commentaries, either in the margins or between the lines.[10] These glosses came to serve as important study aids by forming a link between the biblical texts in one book and the commentaries in another. From the early twelfth century, the glosses began to be standardised. Standard extracts from the commentaries that were written alongside the biblical texts in what came to be known as glossed books.

The biblical text was immersed within the words of the authors of these commentaries, and various techniques were used to differentiate the biblical text from the commentary itself, including early speech marks called *diplé* and contrasting coloured inks. Sometimes however there was no attempt to distinguish the biblical text from the gloss, which gave the commentaries a quasi-biblical status in their own right. These systems for understanding biblical texts led to the development of complex systems of text layout within glossed Bible books. The commentary had to be closely associated with, but easily distinguishable from, the biblical text. The usual format was for the biblical text to occupy a central column in a large script, with the interlinear and marginal glosses fitted around the edges and between the lines. The downside of this format was that some sections of the texts attracted more gloss than others, leading to a very inconsistent page layout. During the thirteenth century, this issue was resolved by using an adaptive system of page layout where the columns were allowed to merge and divide in order to allow text and gloss to track together.[11]

The two glossed Bible books in the State Library of Victoria represent different phases in the development of this format. Both the *Epistles* and *Leviticus* are of a similar size, measuring 320mm by 205mm and 310mm by 220mm respectively in their current formats. Each contains a central column of biblical text in a large script, with both marginal and interlinear glosses. Many later glosses in multiple hands show that they were actively used as scholarly books. Both books are constructed of gatherings of eight parchment leaves, but in most other aspects they are dissimilar, and these divergences provide information about the different circumstances of their production.

---

10   Marginal notes are referred to as marginal glosses, and those between the lines as interlinear glosses.

11   de Hamel, *Glossed Books*, pp. 14–28.

Figure 5.1: Central Italy, Page layout with a historiated initial of St Paul from *St Paul, Epistles, Vulgate Bible [Glossed Epistles of St. Paul]* with the *Glossa ordinaria* by Anselm of Laon. Folios 85v, *c.*1200. Parchment, 32cm × 20.5cm. State Library of Victoria. RARESF 096 B47E.

Contingit uno mundum mihi mortuus est et ego mundo. In Christo Jesu neque circumcisio

aliquid valet. neque praeputium sed nova

creatura. et quicumque hanc regulam

secuti fuerint pax super illos. misericordia Israel

Israel dei. De cetero nemo mihi molestus

sit. ego enim stigmata domini nostri

Jesu. in corpore meo porto. Gratia domini

nostri Jesu Christi cum spiritu vestro fratres amen.

Ephesii Asiani. Hi praeputium confirmati in fide, firmiter steterant in fide, bonis operibus...

Bene dictus...

P
Paulus apostolus Jesu Christi per voluntatem dei sanctis

omnibus qui sunt

Ephesi. et fidelibus in Christo.

Gratia vobis et pax a deo patre

nostro. et domino Jesu Christo. Benedic-

tus deus et pater domini nostri Jesu

Christi. qui benedixit nos in omni...

Epistles – background and execution

The State Library of Victoria *Epistles* was produced in central Italy in the early thirteenth century.[12] The script is late Caroline, in a dark brown ink with a paler ink for the gloss, the interlinear gloss in particular. Individual Epistles commence with four-line decorated initials in yellow on blue grounds with white vine in-fills picked in red and green. One initial is historiated with a portrait of St Paul (Figure 5.1), and several others have small beasts. Individual glosses begin with alternating red and blue initials, sometimes with simple contrasting flourishes, and very occasionally larger and more exuberant examples. The biblical text occupies a central column measuring 205mm by 74mm, with eighteen lines of text per page, blind ruled with the text written on every second line. The marginal gloss has independent ruling lines, with between five and six lines of gloss to each line of biblical text. There is pricking at the outer margins, and it lacks the headings or chapter marks which became a standard feature of Bibles from the thirteenth century.

Ker has identified four distinct stages in the development of the layout of glossed Bible books:

1. Independent ruling for the text and gloss with both commencing above the top line
2. Alternate-line ruling for text and gloss with both commencing above the top line
3. Alternate-line ruling, with the gloss commencing above and text below the top line
4. Alternate-line ruling, with text and gloss below the top line[13]

The *Glossed Epistles of St Paul* falls in the earliest of these four categories, but de Hamel noted that even though the change in layout occurred in different texts at roughly the same time, editions of the *Psalter* and *Epistles of St Paul* accompanied by earlier glosses were late to adopt the updated format. This explains the incongruity between the older format of the text with the proposed date of the manuscript based on the style of decoration.[14]

The *Epistles* is constructed of nineteen gatherings, mostly of eight leaves. The parchment is similar to many Italian manuscripts – smooth and white on the flesh side, the side of the skin which faces in towards the animal, with a distinct grain layer, the remains of the skin epidermis which incorporates the hair follicles. In the case of the *Glossed Epistles*, there is a significant quantity of hair fragments and follicular remains (Figure 5.2 a, b, c, d).

Gatherings were constructed from animals of different ages and different species. Samples of the parchment analysed by the University of York revealed that both sheep and goats were used, while mapping of anatomical features indicates that two, four, and eight folios were formed from a single skin at different points in the text block.[15] The range of sizes of the skins indicates that animals ranging from close to newborn to fully mature were used (Figure 5.3). The complete manuscript comprises the skins of approximately thirty-five animals. Of these, nineteen were most likely kids or lambs close to newborn; at least six animals were greater than two months of age, but less than full grown (around 10.5kg), and approximately ten were mature animals. Thus the bulk of the manuscript is composed of very young animals and fully mature animals, with a few in between.

The diversity of the skins and their arrangement within the text suggest the product of local agriculture, rather than a commoditised

---

12   Manion et al, *Description and Analysis*, pp. 4–7.
13   Ker, 'From "Above Top Line"', pp. 13–14.
14   Manion et al, *Description and Analysis*, p. 7.
15   For method of analysis of species see Buckley, 'Species Identification'.

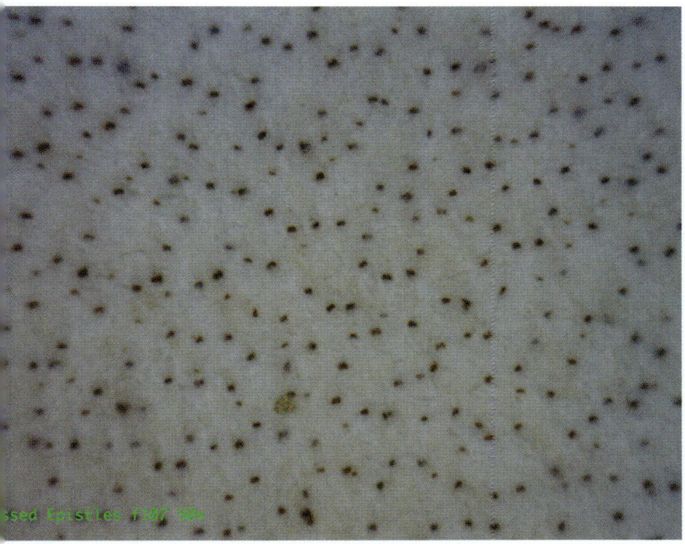

re 5.2a: 50x magnification from *Glossed Epistles of St. Paul* with the *Glossa
inaria by Anselm of Laon. Folio 107, *c.*1200. Parchment 32cm × 20.5cm.
e Library of Victoria. RARESF 096 B47E.

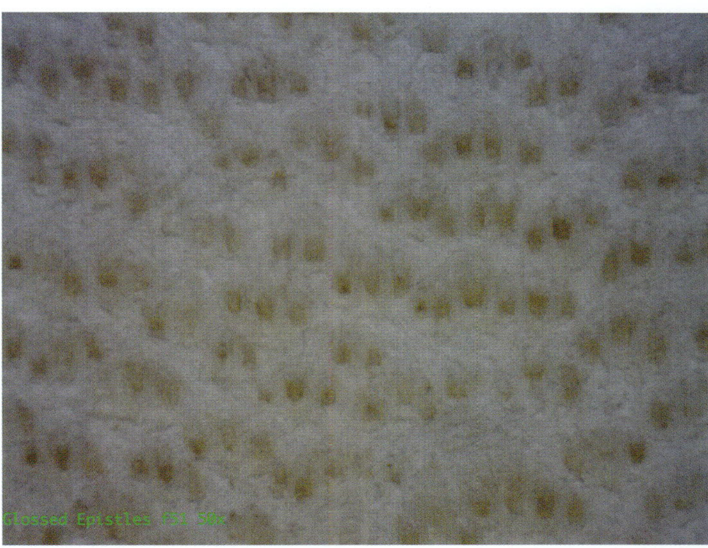

Figure 5.2b: 50x magnification from *Glossed Epistles of St.
Paul* with the *Glossa ordinaria* by Anselm of Laon. Folio
51, *c.*1200. Parchment 32cm × 20.5cm. State Library of
Victoria. RARESF 096 B47E.

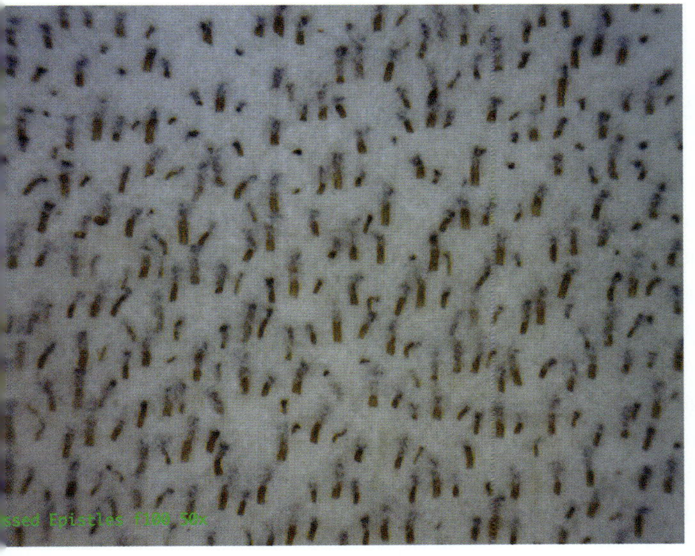

ure 5.2c: 50x magnification from *Glossed Epistles of St. Paul* with the *Glossa
inaria by Anselm of Laon. Folio 100v, *c.*1200. Parchment 32cm × 20.5cm.
e Library of Victoria. RARESF 096 B47E.

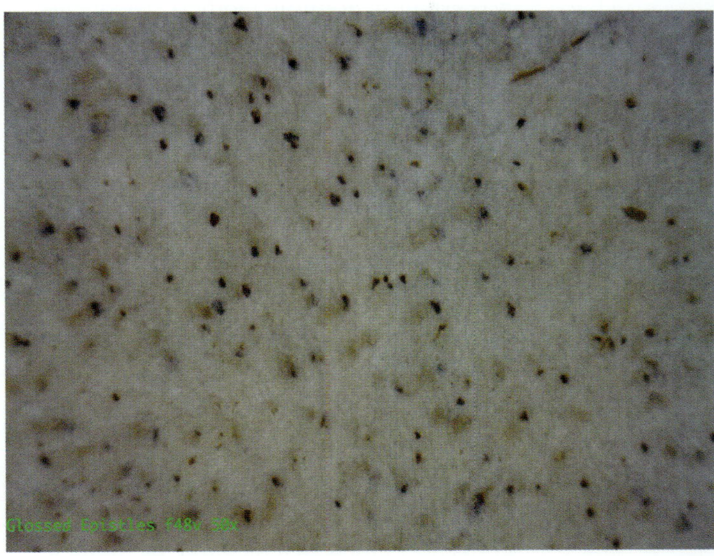

Figure 5.2d: 50x magnification from *Glossed Epistles of St.
Paul* with the *Glossa ordinaria* by Anselm of Laon. Folio
48v, *c.*1200. Parchment 32cm × 20.5cm. State Library of
Victoria. RARESF 096 B47E.

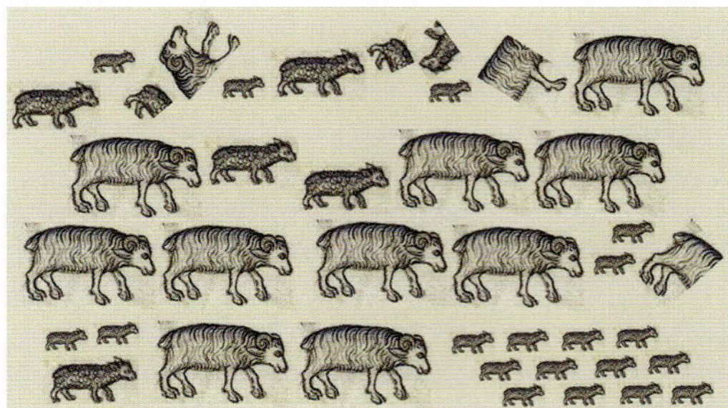

Figure 5.3: Relative sizes and sequence of skins in *Glossed Epistles of St. Paul* with the *Glossa ordinaria* by Anselm of Laon. *c.*1200.

material. If we accept this assumption, then we have what may represent a sample of the animals extracted from the local herds where the manuscript was produced. Based on the skins, the ages at which the animals were slaughtered suggests a mixed-use herd with a focus on dairy, hence the slaughter of the very young animals which was done once milk production was established in the mothers. The inclusion of skins of fully mature animals, without obvious indications of disease or injury, suggests that some animals were retained until they were fully grown for the production of meat, since animals yielded the most meat immediately after reaching maturity while making the least drain on other resources. The manuscript also includes a selection of medium-sized animals, slaughtered for any number of reasons between these two agriculturally significant milestones, including perhaps for the celebration of a feast day or as may have been necessitated when animals were sick or injured. Further, there is evidence of either less skilled or delayed processing of the skins in the form of pigmented blood vessels, which indicate that the blood was allowed to pool and stain the skin – a sign of less systematic processes of production than is found in the *Leviticus*, as we shall see.

If we make another assumption, that the manuscript was produced in roughly the order in which it is read – a reasonable assumption because of the probably monastic production of the manuscript, supported by the make-up and ordering of the skins – an interesting picture emerges of what might having been happening in the annual cycle at the scriptorium where it was produced. The first three sections are composed of mixed groups of skins, with small full skins of a young animals mixed with many fragments of larger ones, suggesting a limited availability of skins at this time. This is followed by two clusters of gatherings. The first comes from single skins of large animals suggesting the milestone of the slaughter of animals for meat; the second cluster of the final three gatherings is composed solely of skins of recently-born animals, suggesting the milestone of the slaughter of animals to support diary production. These differences appear to correspond to seasonal variances in the annual cycle of the harvesting and availability of skins.

The *Leviticus*

In contrast to the *Epistles*, the *Leviticus* was produced in Paris in the early thirteenth century as a product of the highly organised and specialised systems of book production that flourished there at that time.[16] In Paris there were significant opportunities for the patronage of luxury books through the presence of the royal court and wealthy Church officials. The University of Paris, founded in the twelfth century, required significant quantities of consistent utilitarian texts, particularly Bibles and glossed books of the Bible, to support its students and academics. The on-going and long-term demand for a broad spectrum of books,

16   Manion et al, *Description and Analysis*.

combined with a critical population mass, saw the organisation of the book trade and the development of highly discrete specialisations within manuscript manufacture where few had existed previously. This is evident in the considered use of high and consistent quality materials and methods in the *Leviticus*.

The text of the *Leviticus* is executed in a dark opaque black ink which is largely consistent throughout. The Biblical text commences with a three-line pen-flourished puzzle initial in red and blue, and chapters open with one-line, pen-flourished initials in alternating red and blue with contrasting flourishes. The gloss has alternating red and blue paraphs without flourishes, reflecting the respective hierarchy of the two texts. This text includes running titles in alternating red and blue letters which became the standard for Bibles from this time onward (Figure 5.4a and 5.4b).

The layout of the *Leviticus* has at its foundation a similar three-column layout to the *Epistles*, but with important modifications to make it adaptable to the variable amount of gloss associated with different sections of the biblical text. In the *Leviticus*, both the biblical text and the gloss are written on the same set of rulings. The small marginal gloss is on every line, while the larger biblical text occupies every second line. Both the text and the gloss commence below the top line, placing this manuscript in the final of the four stages identified by Ker.[17] The width and number of the columns are adapted to the relationship between the two texts with the columns merging and dividing to ensure that the gloss tracks with the text and that the full text space is used.[18]

The significance of the script type was noted by de Hamel. While the biblical text remained large, the gloss became increasingly compact and abbreviated, allowing more text to be included in smaller spaces.[19] The measurements taken of the gloss of the *Leviticus* indicate that the approximate width of a vertical stroke is 0.7mm across, with the height of a lower case 'm' being approximately 2.5mm. This compact script, now called gothic book hand, was an innovation that permitted the development of the single-volume Paris Bibles in the thirteenth century – one of the great achievements of the Paris book trade.[20]

Though the *Leviticus* is (on first inspection) a plain book, without decoration or embellishment, it is an elegant exercise in pragmatism and functionality. The materials and execution of the manuscript show a considered and informed use of resources. The text block is constructed from one hundred and one leaves in twelve gatherings of eight leaves, with a thirteenth gathering of five leaves. The parchment is fine and uniform throughout, ranging from 0.15–0.25mm in thickness.[21] The surfaces are consistently pounced to a fine nap so that the flesh and hair sides are largely indistinguishable (Figure 5.5a and 5.5b).

Dark hair follicles are occasionally evident at the axillae or base of the tail of the skin. Analysis carried out by the University of York identified the animals used in this manuscript as cattle, and the size of the skins allowed them to be identified as very young calves. The axillae, identified by the comparative thinness and flexibility of the skin, are consistently located at the lower front edge margin,

---

17   Ker, 'From "Above Top Line"', pp. 13–14.

18   This system of ruling was identified by de Hamel as developed for the glossed books of Peter Lombard. See de Hamel, *Glossed Books*, p. 26.

19   de Hamel, *Glossed Books*, p. 37.

20   Kauffman, *Biblical Imagery*, pp. 149; de Hamel, *The Book*, p. 119.

21   Average thickness (derived by dividing the thickness of the textblock by the number of pages) is 0.22mm.

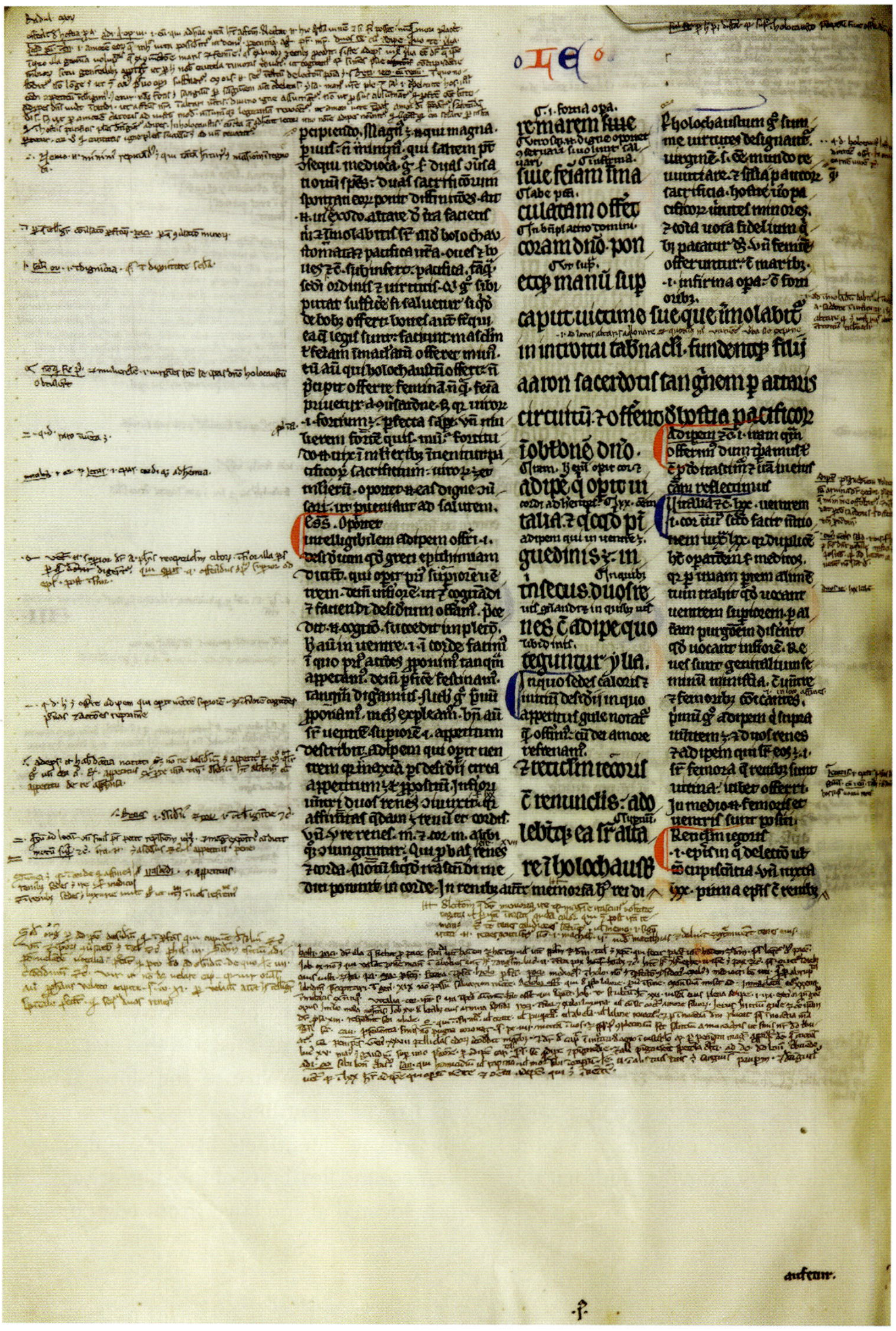

Figure 5.4a: Paris, *Leviticus, Vulgate Bible,* with commentary of Rabanus Maurus. Folio 8v, first quarter of the thirteenth century. Parchment, 31.5cm × 25.5cm. State Library of Victoria. RARES 096 B47L.

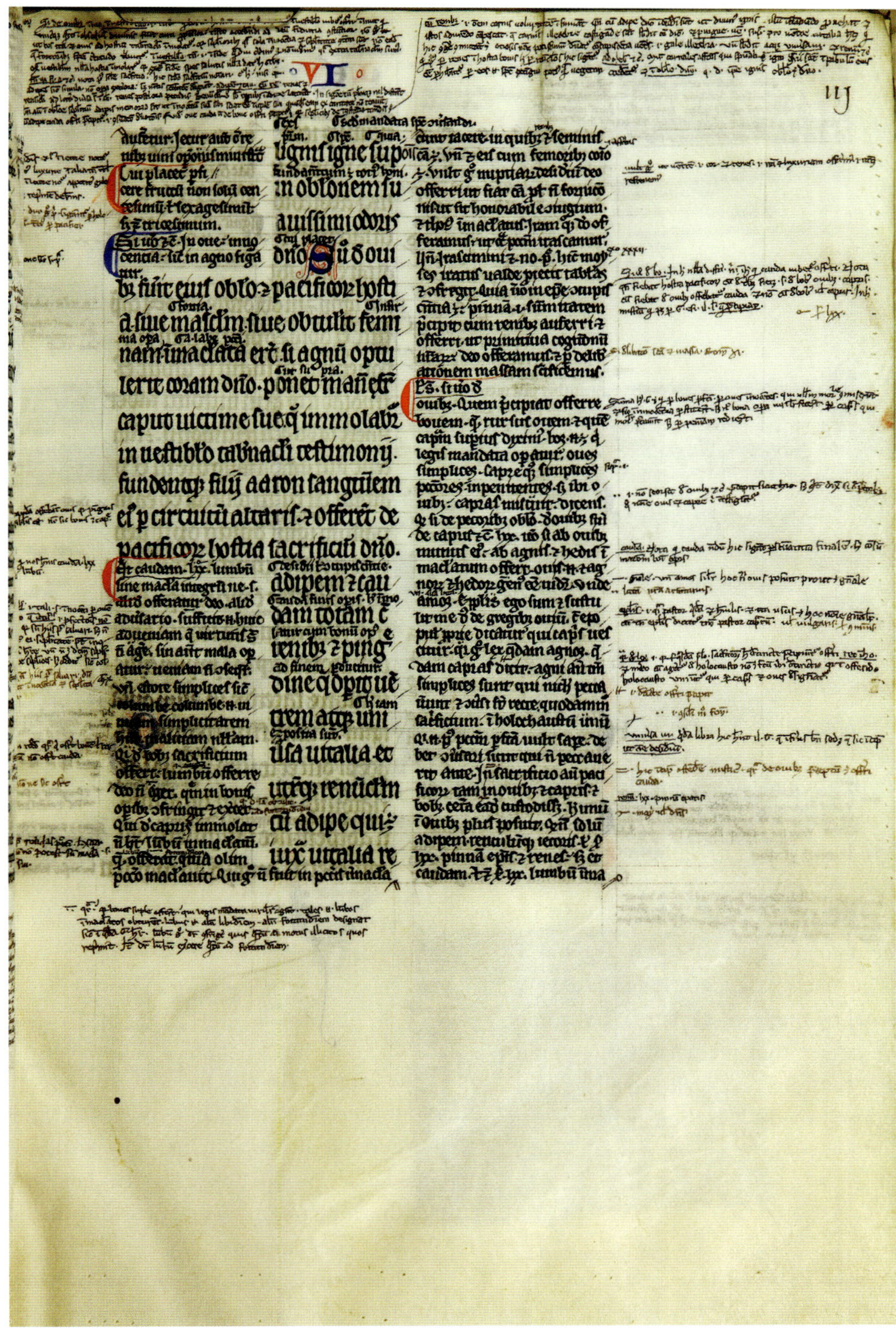

Figure 5.4b: *Leviticus, Vulgate Bible,* with the commentary of Rabanus Maurus. Folio 9, first quarter of the thirteenth century. Parchment, 31.5cm × 25.5cm. State Library of Victoria. RARES 096 B47L.

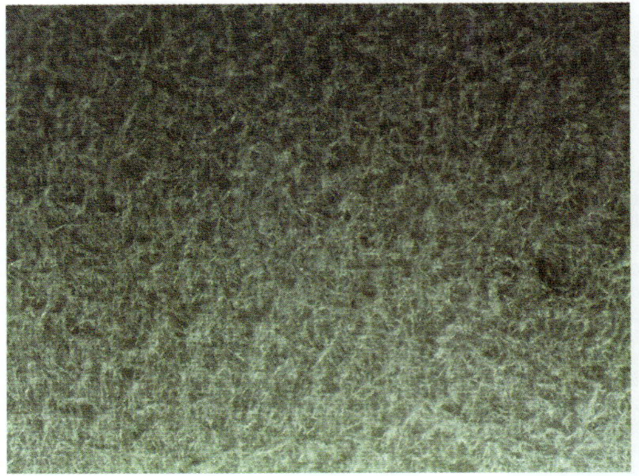

Figure 5.5a: Parchment surface showing velvet-like nap at 50x magnification in *Leviticus, Vulgate Bible*, with commentary of Rabanus Maurus. State Library of Victoria. RARES 096 B47L.

Figure 5.5b: Parchment surface showing velvet-like nap at 50x magnification as observed in *Leviticus, Vulgate Bible*, with commentary of Rabanus Maurus, first quarter of the thirteenth century. Parchment, 31.5cm × 25.5cm. State Library of Victoria. RARES 096 B47L.

indicating that the skins were all worked in the same manner. In total the skins of twenty-five calves of uniform size and age were used in the construction of the text block. An additional one quarter skin is included in the final gathering which has been shortened to accommodate the length of the text (Figure 5.6). A few folios have irregular edges, indicating that the skins were only minimally trimmed; from this the full skin size can be extrapolated to be approximately 450mm x 630mm. The size of the skin suggests a very small animal by modern standards, but some estimates suggest that medieval cattle could have been between 40–60% smaller than many modern breeds.[22] So the *Leviticus* skins most likely represent a calf at several weeks

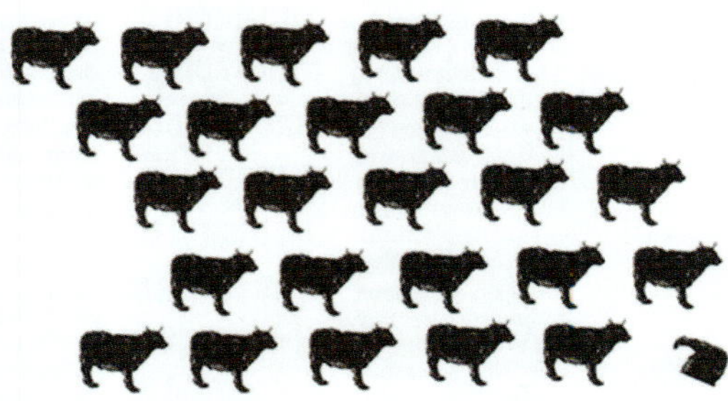

Figure 5.6: Relative sizes and sequences of skins in *Leviticus, Vulgate Bible*, with commentary of Rabanus Maurus, first quarter of the thirteenth century.

old. The large-scale slaughter of animals at this young age is evidence of a substantial and well-ordered industry which almost certainly included diary production, as well as contributing skins for parchment and providing meat for Parisian consumption.

Parchment was not an inexpensive material in the Middle Ages so the retention of wide margins which were then commonly used for annotations suggests a calculated use of resources in the production of a manuscript

22   Based on bone fragments found at archaeological sites, Gibson proposes a live weight range for British Medieval cattle of 379lbs to 771lbs (172kg to 350kg). By comparison, Dairy Australia sets goal weights for Holstein-Friesians at between 550kg to 650kg at maturity, and 400kg to 480kg for Jersey cattle. Gibson, 'The Size and Weight', p.166 and Morton et al, *The InCalf book*, p. 46.

for academic work. Given that a serious scholar would be more likely to pay for a well-organised text with wide margins of high quality parchment for annotation than for superfluous decoration, the scholarly value of this text is evident and endorsed by the copious later glossing.

The two glossed Bible books in the collection of State Library of Victoria represent different stages of the evolution of an important genre in the progression of the format of the Bible. Both are practical scholarly texts with evidence of usage through the inclusion of many later annotations in multiple hands. Yet the variety in their materials and layout provides insight into the different circumstances of their manufacture and use. While the *Epistles* gives us a closer appreciation of the cycle of agriculture at the monastery of its production, with evidence of mixed-use farming, the *Leviticus* manifests all the systematic processes of commercial agriculture and manuscript production developed to meet a specific and highly developed market – scholarly texts required by the church schools of the University of Paris. Use. These differences are evident when comparing Figures 5.3 and 5.6. Similarly, the page layout of the *Epistles* is an earlier and simplified system supporting the copying of a text from start to finish, as would be expected of smaller scale monastic production, while the complicated page layouts of the *Leviticus* would only be possible with the exact replication of sophisticated exemplars. The changes in the materials and format of these manuscripts mirror the larger societal changes of the period with both farming and scriptoriums moving from smaller local and monastic production to larger and more commercial manufacture.

About the author

Libby Melzer is the Senior Conservator of Paper and Parchment at the Grimwade Centre for Cultural Materials Conservation, University of Melbourne. eamelzer@unimelb.edu.au

Works cited

Michael Buckley, Matthew Collins et al., 'Species Identification by Analysis of Bone Collagen Using Matrix-Assisted Laser Desorption/Ionisation Time-of-Flight Mass Spectrometry', *Rapid Communications in Mass Spectrometry*, 23 (2009), pp. 3843–54.

A.J.S. Gibson, 'The Size and Weight of Cattle and Sheep in Early Modern Scotland', *The Agricultural History Review*, 36, 2 (1988), pp. 162–71.

Christopher de Hamel, *Glossed Books of the Bible and the Origins of the Paris Booktrade* (Woodbridge: D.S. Brewer, 1984).

Christopher de Hamel, *The Book: A History of the Bible* (London: Phaidon Press, 2001).

Richard Ronald Johnson, 'The Role of Parchment in Greco-Roman Antiquity', unpublished PhD Thesis, University of California, Los Angeles, 1968.

C.M. Kauffmann, *Biblical Imagery in Medieval England 700–1550* (London: Harvey Miller, 2003).

N.R. Ker, 'From "Above Top Line" to "Below Top Line": A Change in Scribal Practice', *Celtica*, 5 (1960), pp. 13–17.

Naphtali Lewis, *Papyrus in Classical Antiquity* (Oxford: Oxford University Press, 1974).

Margaret M. Manion, Shane Carmody, Bernard Muir, Toby Burrows, and Hugh Hudson, *Description and Analysis of Raresf 096 B47e* (Melbourne: State Library of Victoria, 2013).

John Morton, Mike Larcombe, and Steve Little, eds., *The InCalf book for dairy farmers*, (Dairy Australia, 2003), accessed 16 July 2017 at http://www.dairyaustralia.com.au/Animal-management/Fertility/InCalf-book-and-other-tools/The-InCalf-book.aspx.

Pliny the Elder, *Natural History, Books 12–16*, ed. by Jeffrey Henderson (Cambridge: Harvard University Press, 1968).

C.H. Roberts and C.T. Skeat, *The Birth of the Codex* (Oxford: Oxford University Press, 1983).

Ronald Reed, *Ancient Skins, Parchments and Leathers* (London: Seminar Press, 1972).

6. Beginnings and endings: the shaping of the Book of Hours

Margaret M. Manion

Dunlop, Anne (ed.), *Antipodean Early Modern. European Art in Australian Collections, c. 1200–1600*, Amsterdam University Press, 2018

DOI: 10.5117/9789462985209/CH06

Abstract

This paper focuses on the relationship between the *Rothschild Prayer Book* and the Book of Hours, the most popular and best known prayer book of the medieval period, especially in France, Italy and the Netherlands. The paper discusses how the origins of the *Rothschild Prayer Book* are based on a liturgical format which persisted in a variety of ways throughout the life of the Book of Hours. They may be discerned quite clearly in the *Rothschild Prayer Book* (which represents one of the latest stages of the illuminated prayer book).

Keywords: *Rothschild Prayer Book*; Book of Hours; Medieval; France; Italy; Netherlands

The acquisition in January 2014 by Kerry Stokes AC of the splendid Netherlandish manuscript familiarly known as the *Rothschild Prayer Book* has had a number of positive consequences for medieval manuscript studies in Australia. As well as its great beauty and excellent state of preservation, the *Rothschild Prayer Book* represents the peak of development of one of the most popular types of Western medieval illuminated manuscripts: the Book of Hours. This personal prayer book takes its name from the traditional 'canonical hours' of prayer – Matins, Lauds, Prime, Terce, Sext, None, Vespers, and Compline. Throughout its history the Christian Church has used this system – which goes back to ancient Roman times – to describe the schedule of one of its main forms of public worship: the Divine Office. The service involves the solemn chanting of select Psalms at the canonical hours for each of the feasts of the year. Short verses or antiphons accompany these psalms, and sung responsories highlight the relevant readings, usually taken from the Scriptures or the Fathers of the Church. These are read at Matins, the longest hour of the Office. Hymns relating to the theme of the feast are also part of the service.

Originally, these texts were contained in a number of separate books, but from the eleventh century on, they were also sometimes compiled in one comprehensive liturgical book called the Breviary. By the time the *Rothschild Prayer Book* was made – probably in Bruges and Ghent in the first decade of the sixteenth century – extracts from certain Breviary Offices, along with a number of other personal devotions, had been incorporated in a prayer book known as the Book of Hours. This book was designed, for the most part, for the less formal needs of the laity, and was often illustrated by splendid paintings.

Not only has the arrival of the *Rothschild Prayer Book* in Australia been accompanied by the acquisition of a considerable number of other fine Books of Hours for the Stokes Collection, but the generous support of Kerry Stokes in this field, together with the scholarly investigations of a fresh generation of academics, has helped to focus attention anew on a number of medieval manuscripts which have long been in Australian public collections and which invite comment and discussion in the light of more recent research, both in Australia and internationally. This paper draws attention to two manuscripts in Australian collections that provide distinctive documentation of the beginnings of the Book of Hours. It also highlights certain formal characteristics that have remained constant throughout this genre's long history, showing how these characteristics have contributed in various ways to the effective relationship of text and image in the last phase of the handmade Book of Hours as represented in the *Rothschild Prayer Book* and its contemporaries.

The early manuscripts discussed here are two transitional Psalter-Hours. The first, now in the State Library of Victoria, Melbourne, was produced in the diocese of Liège in the 1270s (MS RARES 096 R66). It is called here the *SLV Psalter-Hours*. The other, the *Aspremont-Kievraing Psalter-Hours*, dates from around 1300 and is in two volumes. The Psalter section is in the Bodleian Library, Oxford (MS Douce 118). The second volume, which contains the Office for Christmas and four Marian Offices, is in the National Gallery of Victoria, Melbourne (MS Felton 1254–3). While both these prayer books represent the transition from the Psalter to the Book of Hours, they nevertheless differ markedly from each other in several respects, especially in their reflection of the individual interests and needs of particular types of patrons and owners.[1]

From Psalter to Psalter-Hours

Up until the mid-thirteenth century the literate laity throughout Europe used the Psalter – the biblical Book of the Psalms – as their chief devotional prayer book. Clearly, devotees varied in the number of Psalms selected for regular recitation: the saintly French King Louis IX, for example, is said (exceptionally) to have recited all 150 Psalms daily. The usual language of the Psalter was Latin, which must have been reasonably familiar to the literate medieval Christian, since it was used for such diverse activities as participation in the Mass, as well as business transactions of a purely secular nature. Children were also taught to read from the Psalter, and Psalter manuscripts, especially those made for the families of wealthy patrons, often attracted elaborate decoration and illustration. In many cases, these ornamental features would also have contributed to a general understanding of the text.

Many early medieval Psalters also contained particular texts, which, over the years, had received a discrete devotional emphasis in the Breviary, in addition to their formal liturgical place in the Divine Office. These included the Canticles – a series of chants or songs taken from the Old and New Testaments – the Office or Vigils of the Dead, the Litany of the Saints, the Seven Penitential Psalms, and the Little Office of the Virgin. Since the first half of the twelfth century, it had become customary in some Benedictine and Cistercian communities to recite the Little Office of the Virgin as an additional act of devotion.[2] It is the inclusion of this Office that gave the name 'Psalter-Hours' to the transitional prayer book of the early twelfth century, and later to the fully developed personal manual known as the Book of Hours.

---

1   For the Book of Hours, see Wieck, *Time Sanctified*; and Morgan and Stocks, 'The Personal Prayer Book', pp. 119–193.

2   Morgan and Stocks, 'The Personal Prayer Book', p. 122.

Psalter-Hours containing these additional devotional components were reasonably plentiful throughout England, France, and parts of the Netherlands in the twelfth and early thirteenth centuries. The diocese of Liège, however, was particularly well placed, both geographically and socially, to make a distinctive contribution to the way in which lay devotions and supportive literature were developed at this time. As part of the archdiocese of Cologne, Liège shared in the political and cultural dominance of the Holy Roman Empire. Moreover, a large number of the Liège clergy were attached to distinguished religious institutions of which the ruler was often a German with imperial interests. This resulted in the religious life of the laity being especially influenced by the formal liturgy of the Church.

One notable consequence of the religious nature of Liège was the increase in devotional prayers in honour of Mary in the form of abbreviated Offices. These prayers became popular with the laity as well as with clergy and religious, and it is often difficult to determine whether in the first instance they were written for clerics or lay persons. By the second half of the thirteenth century, however, Liège had declined in political imperial power and become more closely aligned with the Flemish and French gothic cultures rising to the west.

Judith Oliver has provided a thorough study of medieval Liège Psalter-Hours and their relationship to the spiritual culture of the period in a catalogue of forty-one known manuscripts, which date from *c*.1250 to *c*.1330. It is drawn on here.[3] She also draws attention to the fact that

the artistic culture of 'Liège', which was famous for its metal work from the twelfth century on, is often called 'Mosan', from the valley of the Meuse River. Oliver uses the name 'Mosan' interchangeably with 'Liège', and this is followed here.

Oliver persuasively identifies the illuminator of the *SLV Psalter-Hours* as belonging to a team of gothic-influenced artists who moved from Hainault to Liège and were active in production there in the 1270s.[4] The leader of this group was responsible for the Psalter-Hours which is now in the Bibliothèque nationale de France (lat. MS. 1077), and, as Oliver demonstrates, the chief artist of the *SLV Psalter-Hours* worked closely with him, incorporating several specific Liège features into the contents and design of the Melbourne prayer book. These include a 'Lambertian Calendar and table' (problematically attributed to the twelfth-century patron saint of the diocese, St Lambert), and a poem in French in honour of the Passion '*Un faisselet de myre est mes amis a moi*' ('A bundle of myrrh is my well-beloved unto me') which is positioned immediately before the beginning of the Psalter text proper.[5] In the *SLV Psalter-Hours*, a series of six Canticles follows the Psalter, opening with the confessional theme of Isaiah, 12:1–6, *Confitebor tibi*. Saints in the Litany of this manuscript also include a number that were particularly honoured in the Liège diocese, and a full version of the Breviary Office of the Nativity of the Virgin is presented as the *Cursus* or principal Marian Office in place of the Little Office, presumably because the Liège Cathedral was dedicated to this feast. Devotional texts in the *SLV Psalter-Hours* also

---

3   See Oliver, *Gothic Manuscript Illumination in the Diocese of Liège*, especially I, pp. 144, 155–59; and for the *SLV Psalter-Hours*, II, pp. 273–74, Catalogue Entry No 25; See also Oliver, 'Devotional Images and Pious Practices in a Psalter from Liège', pp. 24–29; and 'Psalter-Hours Use of Liège', pp. 140–41.

4   Oliver, *Gothic Manuscript Illumination in Liège*, I, pp. 148–158.

5   For the Lambertian Calendar and table see Oliver, *Gothic Manuscript Illumination in Liège*, I, pp. 32–34.

include the Office of the Dead for the Use of Liège. In keeping with most complete Mosan Psalters, the final text associated with the Psalter proper in the *SLV Psalter-Hours* is a prayer in Latin called the *Aves* or Psalter of the Virgin. It bears the title *Salutationes* and opens with the words *Ave porta paradysi.* This prayer was popular at first with the Cistercians who transformed the 150 Psalms into a series of four-line paraphrases in praise of the Virgin. Later, the Dominicans divided this into three crowns or garlands, which is the pattern adopted by the Melbourne *Aves.*[6] Three abbreviated Offices of the Virgin, also a characteristic Liège feature, conclude the contents of the manuscript, adding, as it were, a Breviary Office section to the Psalter elements: the Hours of the Purification (folios 190–199v); the Hours of the Annunciation (folios 199v-206v); and the Hours of the Assumption (folios 206v-215).

Illustration of the *SLV Psalter-Hours*

The Psalter attracted illustration from very early times. In some cases, its opening word or phrase was accompanied by images, which played on the literal meaning of the words, one of the most famous examples of this being the ninth-century *Utrecht Psalter* and its derivatives. The first Psalm which begins with the words 'Beatus Vir' ('Blessed is the man') was regularly introduced by a portrait of King David who was venerated as the author of all the Psalms (although this was impossible since their composition was spread over several centuries). This literal approach persisted in the illumination of the Psalm openings, which introduced the weekly divisions of the Psalter in the Divine Office. From the eleventh century

on, especially in France and England, deluxe Psalters were often prefaced by a pictorial cycle, which might contain scenes from the life of David, or more expansively, from both the Old and New Testaments. These cycles thus extended the information provided by the Psalter text, and often covered the whole story of Christian redemption from Judaic prophecy to the incarnation, death and resurrection of Christ.

In keeping with contemporary Mosan Psalters, the illustration of the *SLV Psalter-Hours* draws on parts of these programs, although not always systematically. Three full pages of miniatures preface its Psalter text. The first two pages are devoted to scenes of Mary and the Infancy of Christ: the *Annunciation* and the *Nativity of Christ* (folio 17v); and the *Adoration of the Magi* and the *Presentation of Christ in the Temple* (folio 18v). The third page depicts the end of Christ's mission on earth and the birth of the Church in scenes of the Ascension and Pentecost (Figure 6.1).

At the same time, this folio explicitly announces the beginning of the Psalter itself, with a large historiated initial 'B' that introduces the first word of Psalm 1, written in red below. It also draws attention to the full text of the opening Psalm which is opposite. One of the particular features of Mosan Psalters is that they highlight the text of Psalm 2 as well as Psalm 1. This is skilfully carried out here by the representation of King David at the base of folio 20 (Figure 6.2), which refers to him as author in the context of both Psalms 1 and 2. A graceful figure of an archer wielding a bow and taking aim at a bird above, in the right hand margin of the same page, is the first marginal image in this group of Liège Psalters.

The illumination in the *SLV Psalter-Hours* is plentiful, but, apart from these three full-page illustrations, it is confined either to small-scale

6   Oliver, *Gothic Manuscript Illumination in Liège*, I, p. 40.

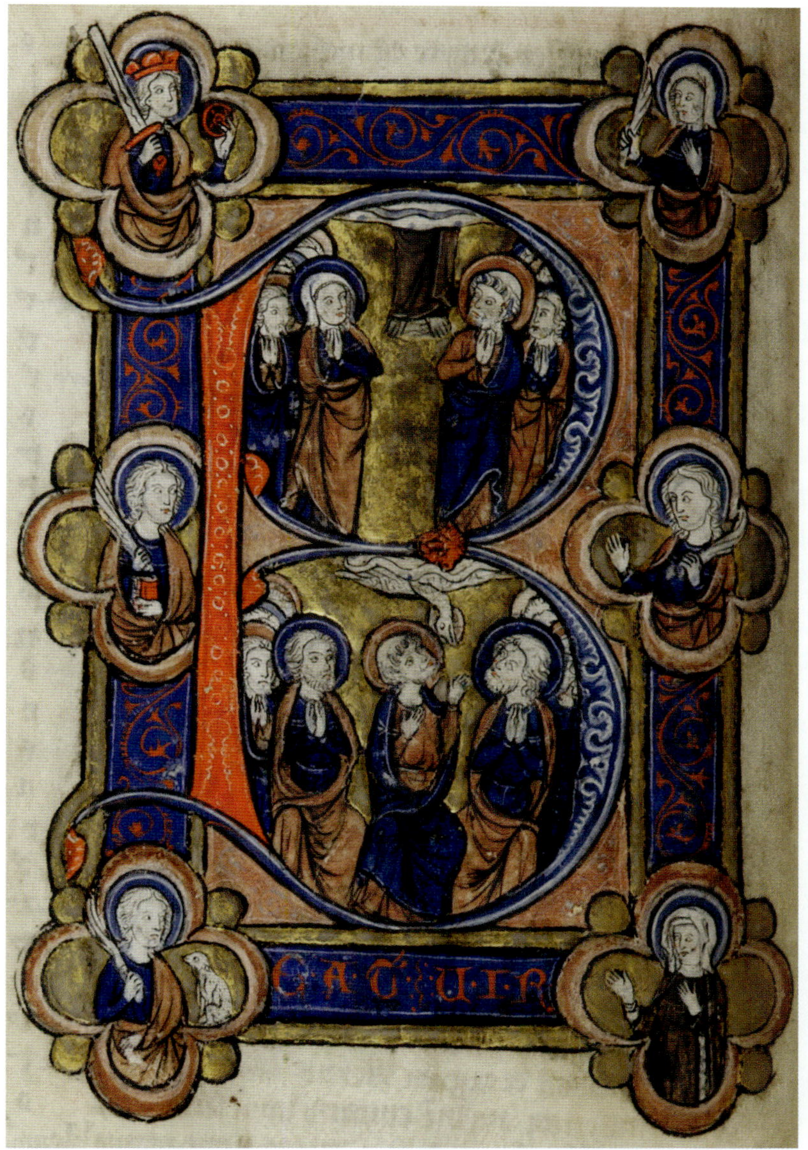

Figure 6.1: Liège, Historiated initial 'B' for Psalm 1 in Ascension and Pentecost and Psalter, *The Liège Psalter-Hours [Psalter-Hours, Use of Liège, in Latin and French]*. Folio 19v, *c.*1270–1279. Parchment, 17cm × 12cm. State Library of Victoria, Melbourne. MS RARES 096 R66.

miniatures or equally small historiated initials.[7] Each of the pages with large miniatures (folios 17v and 18v), and with the large historiated initial 'B' (Figure 6.1), is flanked by six roundels with images of the saints, most of whom are

7   The whole of the *SLV Psalter-Hours* is reproduced digitally in the Catalogue of Medieval manuscripts in the State Library of Victoria. All images are presented in high resolution and are freely available. This entry is also accompanied by a commentary incorporating up-to-date research.

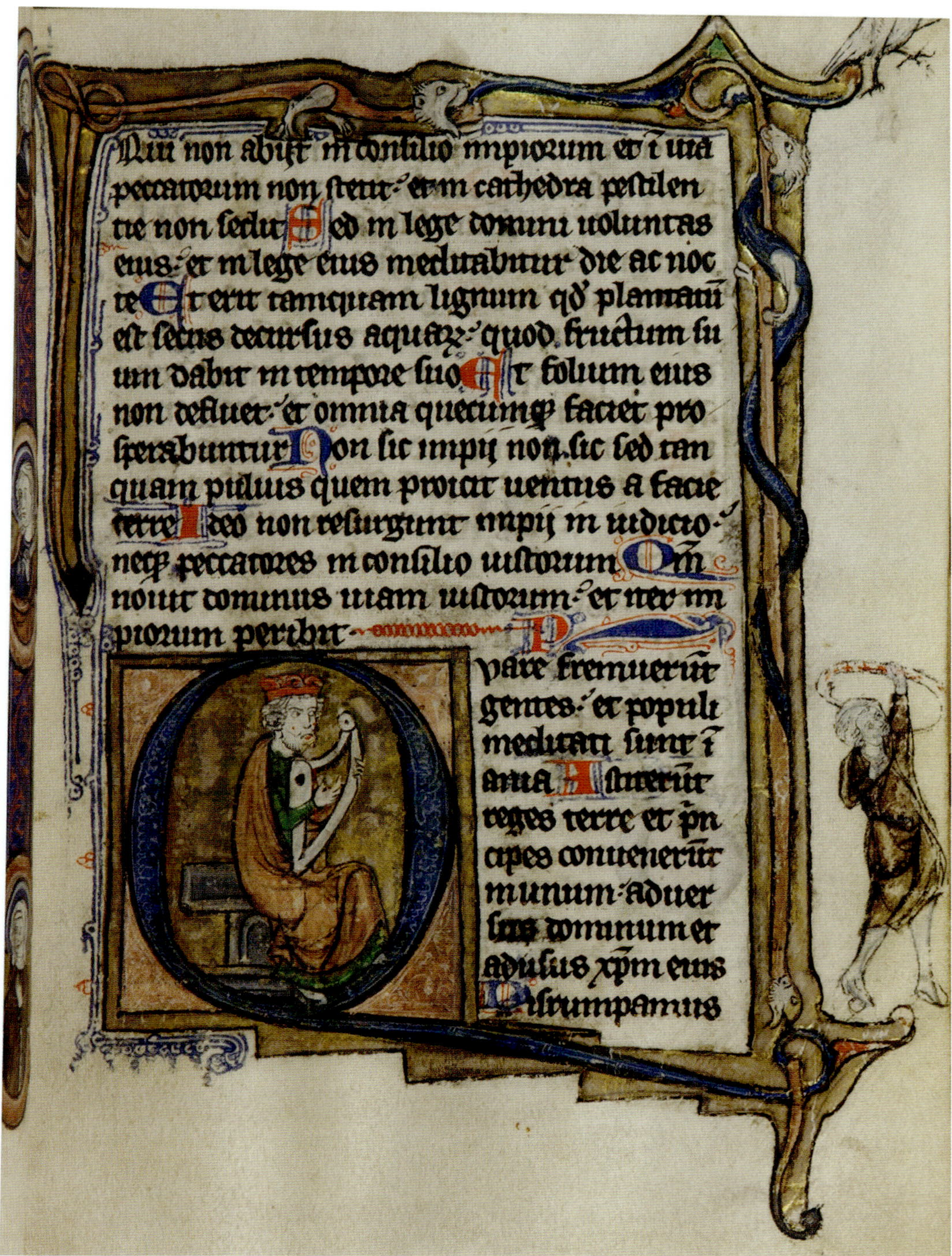

Figure 6.2: David Playing the Harp from *The Liège Psalter-Hours* Psalm 2, folio 20, *c.*1270–1279. Parchment, 17cm × 12cm. State Library of Victoria, Melbourne. MS RARES 096 R66.

identifiable from their attributes as apostles, deacons, bishops, and martyrs (both men and women) of the early Church.

The Calendar in the *SLV Psalter-Hours* is also illustrated. A Calendar was a regular feature in liturgical manuscripts from very early times. It provided an essential guide to the changing dates of certain feasts in the Church's Temporal cycle, as well as to the distinctions in the Sanctoral between saints venerated locally and those honoured by the Universal Church. Although there was not the same need for a Calendar in a personal prayer book, nevertheless its presence was obviously desired by lay as well as clerical patrons, and it is rarely absent from the contents of a personal Psalter or Psalter-Hours. From the twelfth century on, a series of small images of the signs of the zodiac and the activities or labours of each month is frequently added to the written contents of the Calendar, to communicate a sense of the passing of the seasons. The Calendar pages of the *SLV Psalter-Hours* contain twenty-four medallions of the labours of the months and the signs of the zodiac. Each medallion is composed of a diamond shape set on a quadrilobe (Figure 6.3). For the most part, the monthly activities depicted follow a pattern characteristic of Mosan Calendars, with five months indicating certain regional distinctions: 'tree pruning in February, the fiddler in May, fruit or flower gathering in June, carrying a hog in November, and slaughtering an ox in December.'[8] There is also a reversal of two traditional themes in order to reflect more seasonal times for the vintage, which is shown in September, and for sowing, which appears in October.[9]

The illustrative program of the Psalter proper in the State Library manuscript closely follows a complex Mosan model with only a small number of importations and modifications drawn from the simpler French version. Several of the historiated initials which mark the week day divisions following Psalms 1 and 2 (i.e. Psalms 26, 38, 51, 52, 68, 80, 97, 101 and 109) are based on scriptural exegeses in which Old Testament events are interpreted in the light of the New. Psalm 38, for example, is illustrated with the *Flight into Egypt* (folio 45), as the antitype of the Old Testament's account of David's flight from Saul (1 Samuel 18–19).[10] On the other hand, the illustration for Psalm 26 '*Dominus illuminatio mea et salus mea*' ('The Lord is my light and my salvation') conflates the French and Mosan traditions by depicting Christ healing a blind King David (folio 35).[11] The French version typically interprets the words of the Psalm literally with David pointing to his eyes before the Lord, the source of divine light (Figure 6.4).

As was customary, the Hours of the main Office of the Virgin – here that of her Nativity – are introduced at Matins by a historiated initial of the Virgin and Child enthroned (folio 130). The other Hours of this Office, from Lauds to Compline (folios 139v, 144v, 150, 152v, 154v, 157, 160), are illustrated by a Passion cycle. Its conclusion at Compline, with the depiction of the arrival of the three Maries at Christ's empty tomb (folio 160), indicates the fulfilment of the promise of the Resurrection. The initial illustrating the Office of the Dead, which shows the faithful in the Bosom of Abraham (folio 162v), is also expressive of Christian hope.

---

8   Oliver, *Gothic Manuscript Illumination in Liège*, I, p. 32.

9   Oliver, *Gothic Manuscript Illumination in Liège*, I, p. 32

10   Oliver, *Gothic Manuscript Illumination in Liège*, I, pp. 66–67.

11   Oliver, *Gothic Manuscript Illumination in Liège*, I, p. 65, n. 23.

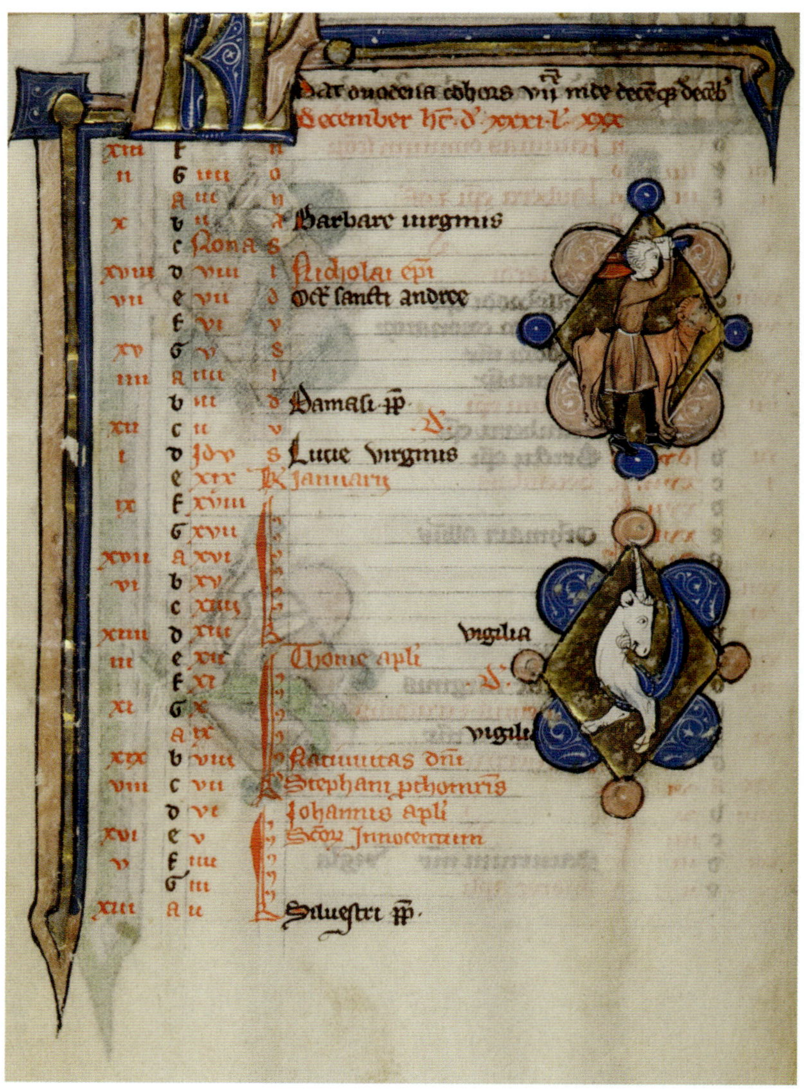

Figure 6.3: Man killing an ox, Calendar, December, Capricorn from *The Liège Psalter-Hours*, folio 15v, c.1270–1279.
Parchment, 17cm × 12cm. State Library of Victoria, Melbourne. MS RARES 096 R66.

The Psalter of the Virgin, or the *Aves*, is illustrated by an initial which shows the priest Theophilus before the Virgin and refers to his deliverance by Mary from the contract which he had made with the devil. This popular theme illustrates the *Aves* in thirteen of the forty-one Mosan Psalters in Oliver's catalogue. It comes from the equally popular text of the *Miracles of the Virgin*, edited in the early thirteenth century by the Benedictine monk Gautier de Coincy (d. 1236). An initial based on the theme of the particular Office marks the beginning of each of the three abbreviated Marian Offices or Hours that follow: the *Presentation in the Temple* (folio 190); the *Annunciation* (folio 199v) and the *Coronation of the Virgin* (for the Hours of the Assumption, folio 206v).

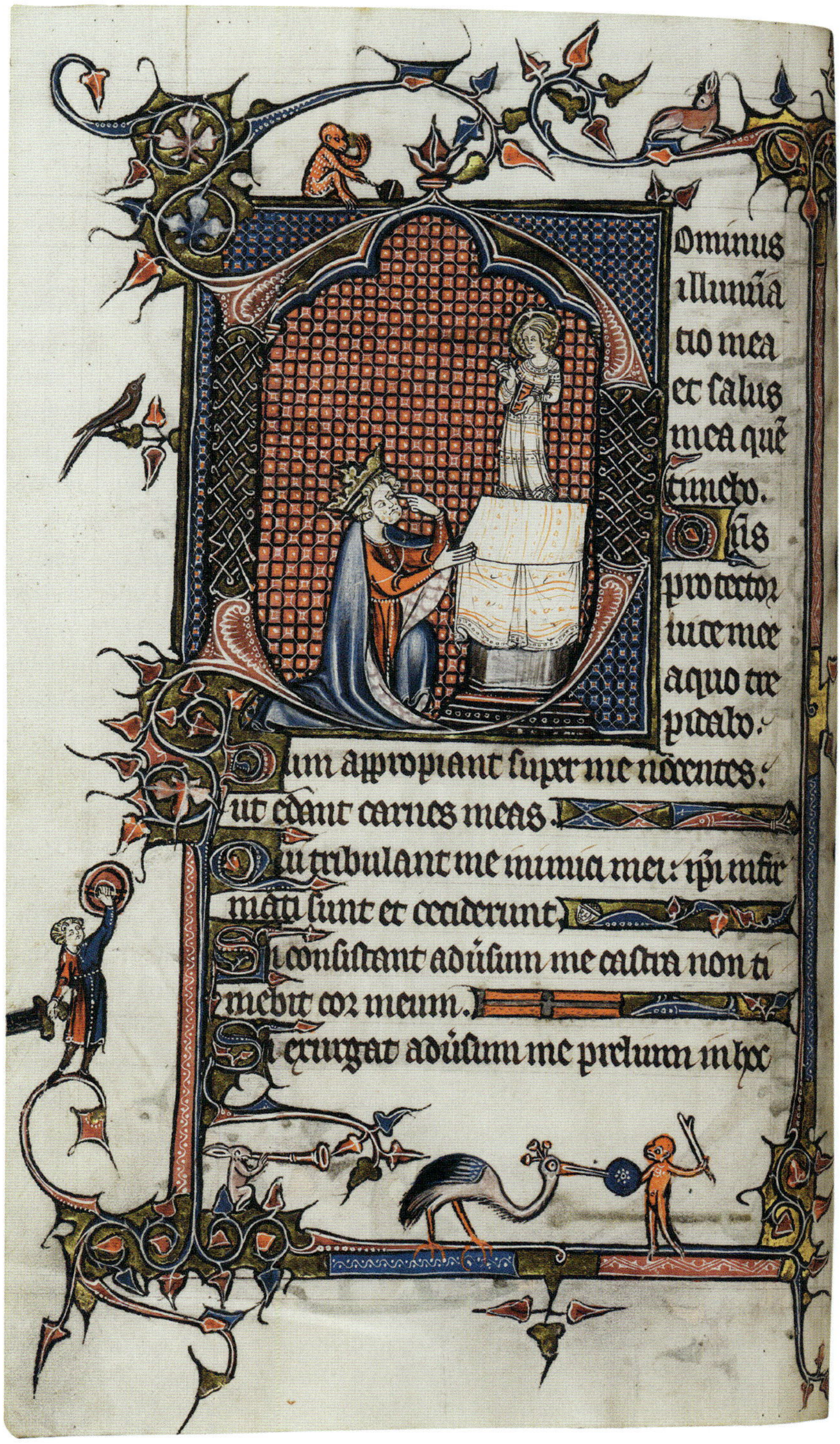

Figure 6.4: Lorraine, King David points to his eye from *The Aspremont-Kievraing Psalter-Hours*, volume 1, folio 31v, *c.*1290–1302. Parchment, 21.5cm × 15cm. Bodleian Library, Oxford. Douce MS 118, vol. 1.

A small number of the group of Liège Psalter-Hours, though not the Melbourne example, also contain prayers to be said at Mass. These mostly relate to prayers of confession and penitence, together with devotions in honour of the Eucharist, indicating that the books were probably taken to Mass.[12]

Oliver characterises the *SLV Psalter-Hours* as 'textually elaborate' and 'amply illustrated'. She concludes that the owner must have been 'a person of considerable means and one who presumably devoted a substantial portion of the day to private religious exercises'.[13] Such a description would aptly fit one of the Beguines, many of whom lived in Liège.[14] These were devout women, unmarried or widowed, who spent their lives in prayer and good works, but who did not follow a monastic way of life. Instead, their spirituality was directed by one of the friars, often a Franciscan or Dominican, rather than a monk. Like many other Mosan Psalter-Hours, however, the contents of the *SLV Psalter-Hours* provide no explicit indication of original or early ownership. References in the prayers are in the masculine; but this, as Oliver points out, may simply mean that the book was bought ready-made and gender distinctions were not required by the purchaser.[15] The manuscript is clearly the product of competent and skilled illuminators, probably working in the experienced workshop environment of the Master of BnF MS lat. 1077. While respectful of Liège traditions in Psalter production, this workshop also contributed to the development of the French gothic style in Liège. Already

figures and compositional elements in the *SLV Psalter-Hours* express a new liveliness and naturalism.

The *Aspremont-Kievraing Psalter-Hours*: France, the Lorraine

In the later years of the thirteenth century and the early part of the fourteenth (*c.*1280–1330) developments in the production of illuminated liturgical books such as Breviaries, Pontificals and Psalter-Hours were more evident in parts of Gothic France, such as Paris, Metz and Verdun, than in Liège. Although the *Aspremont-Kievraing Psalter-Hours* combines a Psalter with Offices from the Breviary, it offers a striking contrast to the Liège *SLV Psalter-Hours*. This prayer book in two volumes was probably produced in Verdun or Metz around 1300, and done for a noble French couple, the knight Joffroy d'Aspremont and his wife Isabelle de Kievraing.[16] By contrast to the anonymity favoured by Liège manuscripts, numerous coats of arms in the margins and line-endings, and on the clothes of the patrons, identify the couple as the first owners of the manuscript. Joffroy is documented as having taken part in a popular tournament at Chauvency in 1285. This memorable event was organised by Louis, Count of Chiny, the uncle of Isabelle de Kievraing. Joffroy's coat of arms and his elegant

---

12   Oliver, *Gothic Manuscript Illumination in Liège*, I, pp. 35–38.

13   Oliver, 'Psalter-Hours Use of Liège' p. 141.

14   See Oliver, *Gothic Manuscript Illumination in Liège*, I, pp 112–119.

15   Oliver, *Gothic Manuscript Illumination in Liège* I, p. 117.

16   For comprehensive studies of the *Aspremont-Kievraing Psalter-Hours* see Avril, *L'Art au Temps*, No. 217, p. 319; Morgan, 'Gendered Devotions and Social Rituals', pp. 5–24; Stones, *Gothic Manuscripts 1260–1320*, Vol.1, pp. 60–75; Manion, 'The Aspremont Kievraing Hours', pp. 100–203. The most detailed study of the arms, lineage and connections of these patrons is by Davenport, 'Manuscripts illuminated for Renaud of Bar, Bishop of Metz (1303–1316)'.

appearance at Chauvency were described by the contemporary poet Jacques Bretel:

Joffroy d'Aspremont came first/ He had neither cape nor mantle
He was all covered in fine silk/ So rich that I marvelled greatly
It was vermilion silk/With a silver cross on it
He looked like an angel/Who had come from paradise
To go to the tournament.[17]

Originally, both Joffroy's arms (*gules a cross argent*: a silver or white cross on red) and those of Isabelle (*or chief bendy of six argent and gules*: gold and diagonal silver bars on red arms) were painted throughout the two volumes of this prayer book, but a later owner of volume two had them overpainted in a muddy orange colour. They are however still discernible beneath the later paint.

In this two-volume manuscript, the Calendar, Psalter, Canticles and Litany of the Saints appear in volume one, while five Breviary Offices are presented in volume two: Christmas, the Purification, the Annunciation, the Assumption, and the Nativity of the Virgin. The Christmas Office is a distinctive if not unique addition to the Offices customarily included in Psalter-Hours, and the provision of a generous number of Breviary Offices clearly raised problems for their layout and illustration. Both the beginning of the Psalter volume (Psalm 1, folio 7, Figure 6.5) and the opening Office for Christmas (The Presentation of Mary in the Temple) in volume two (Figure 6.6), have large matching frontispieces, with decorative side panels of thirteen lines each introducing their respective texts. The illustrations marking the eight divisions of

the Psalter in the Oxford volume also follow a traditional French pattern (Figure 6.4).

So, too, does the illumination of the texts for the Canticles and the Litany of the Saints in this first volume (folios 163, 178v). While, however, the first illustration for each Office in volume two announces its particular Marian theme, there is no discernible illustrative system applied after this to the sequence of Hours which appear in each Office. Instead, improvisation becomes increasingly evident as both script and illumination unfold. It would seem that both scribe(s) and illuminator(s) were confronted with the difficulty of adapting a detailed illustrative program to a Breviary format which was usually illustrated more sparingly. Often in Breviary illustration only the opening hour of an Office received illumination, whereas all ten Hours of each of the five *Aspremont-Kievraing* Offices are illustrated. Scenes from the infancy of Christ are repeated (Figure 6.7 and Figure 6.8), and one or both of the patrons appear several times as the subject of the introductory initial for a particular Hour, usually with their coats-of-arms proudly displayed (Figure 6.9).

It was not only the patrons who were pleased to leave signs of their personal involvement in the production of this prayer book. A figure in the upper margin of folio 110 in volume one holds a scroll which states '*Nicolaus me fecit qui illuminat librum*' (Nicolas made me who illuminated [this] book); and on folio 134 in volume two, a figure holds a scroll with the words, '*Je prie que le dieu me fasse merci*' ('I pray that the Lord have mercy on me'). Given that the use of French seems to be confined in the rest of this volume to explanatory rubrics and the remains of a direction to the illuminator on folio 29, this prayer may come from one of the scribes or illuminators.

The abundance and variety of marginal imagery in both volumes of the *Aspremont- Kievraing Psalter-Hours* are also striking. While

---

17   For the poem, see Delbouille, *Jacques* (verses here 3231–3240). See also the modern verse translation by Henriot-Walzer, *Le Tournoi de Chauvency*.

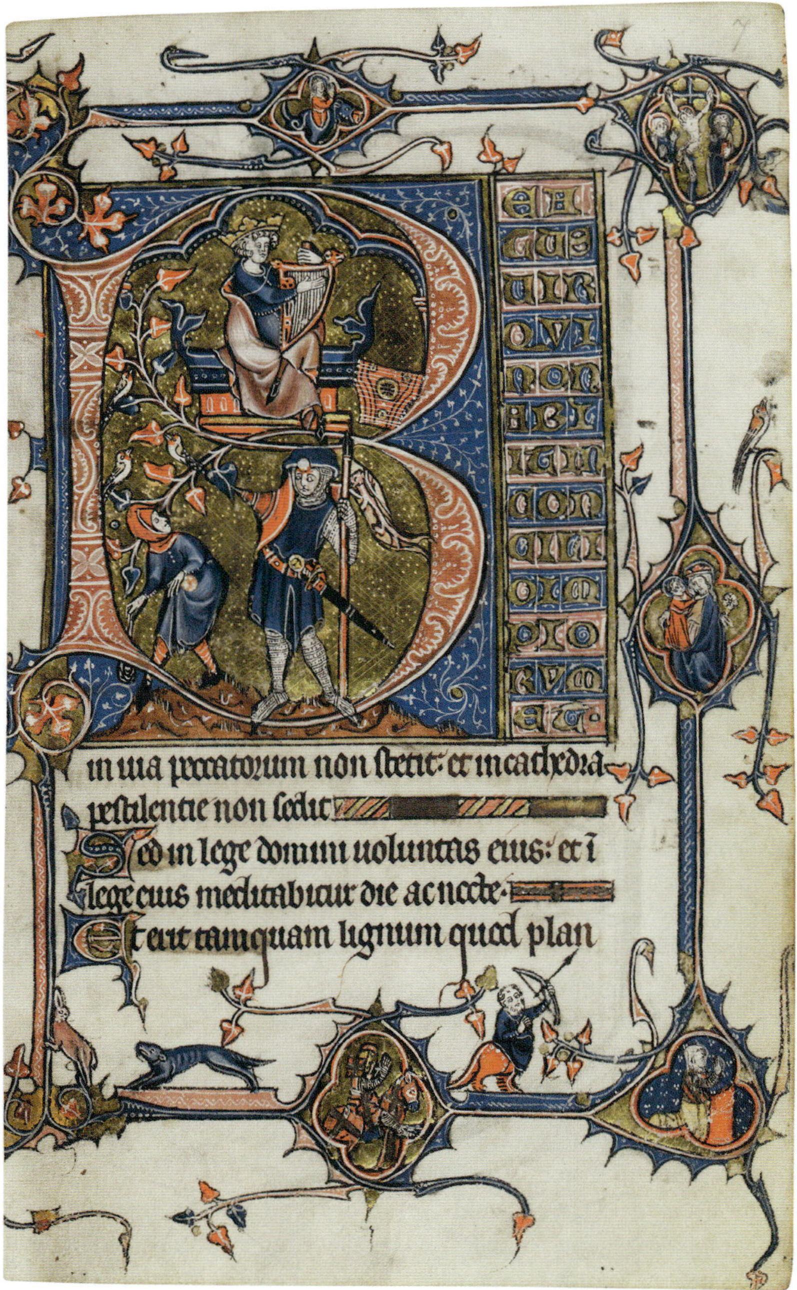

Figure 6.5: David with harp and Goliath from *The Aspremont-Kievraing Psalter-Hours*, Initial 'B', volume 1, folio. 7, *c*.1290–1302. Parchment, 21.5cm × 15cm. Bodleian Library, Oxford. Douce MS 118, vol. 1.

some of this material refers explicitly to the patrons, other images reflect more general interests with subjects drawn from sources such as proverbs or bestiary tales. The image

in the *bas-de-page of* folio 123, volume two (Figure 6.10) for example, refers to the popular account of how to tame a lion: one ties up the wild beast and beats a dog in front of it! Clearly

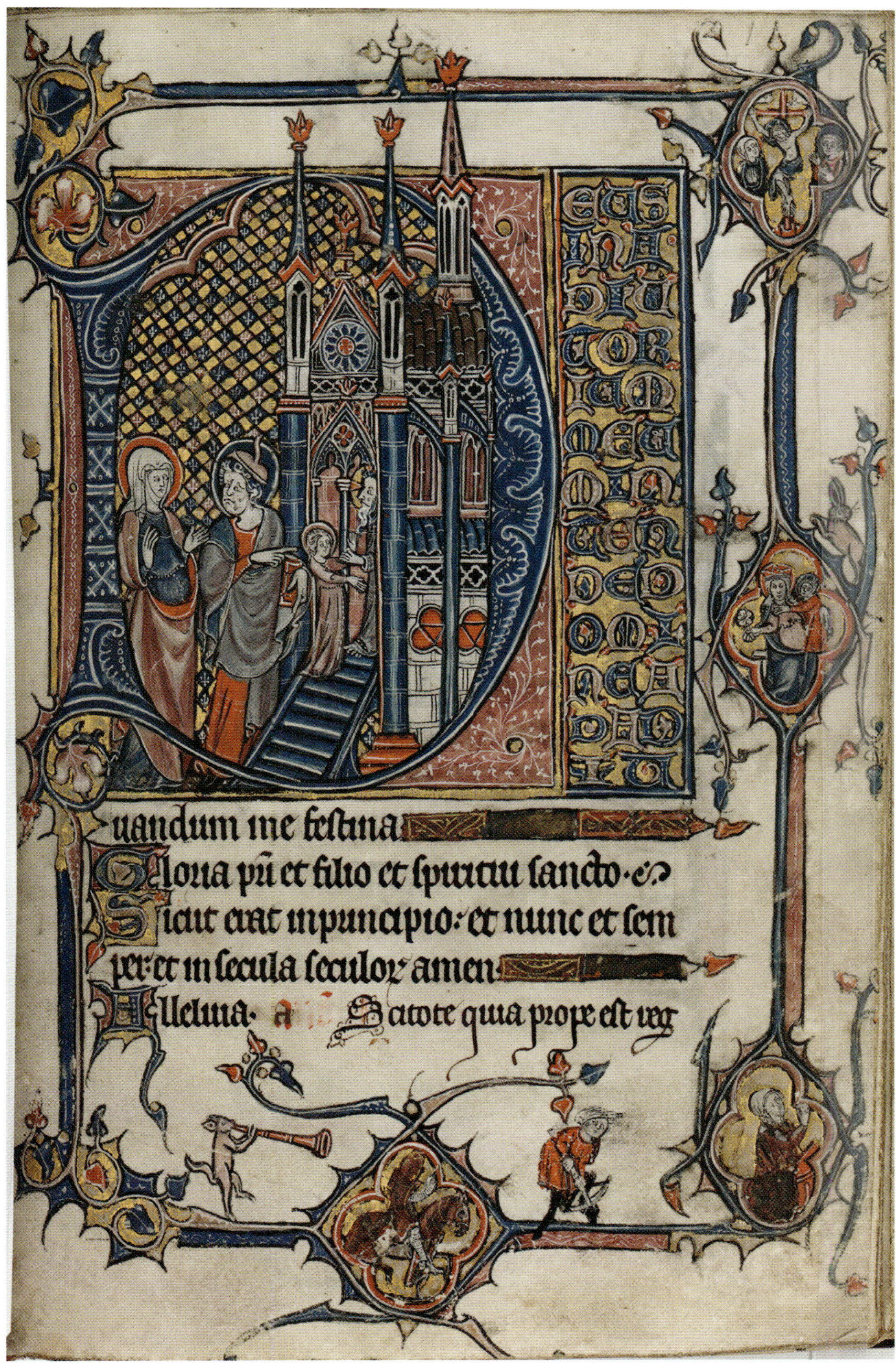

Figure 6.6: Presentation of the Child Mary in the Temple from the *Aspremont Offices of the Virgin*. Volume 2, folio 1, *c.*1290–1302. Parchment, 21.5cm × 15cm. National Gallery of Victoria, Melbourne. MS Felton 1254–3.

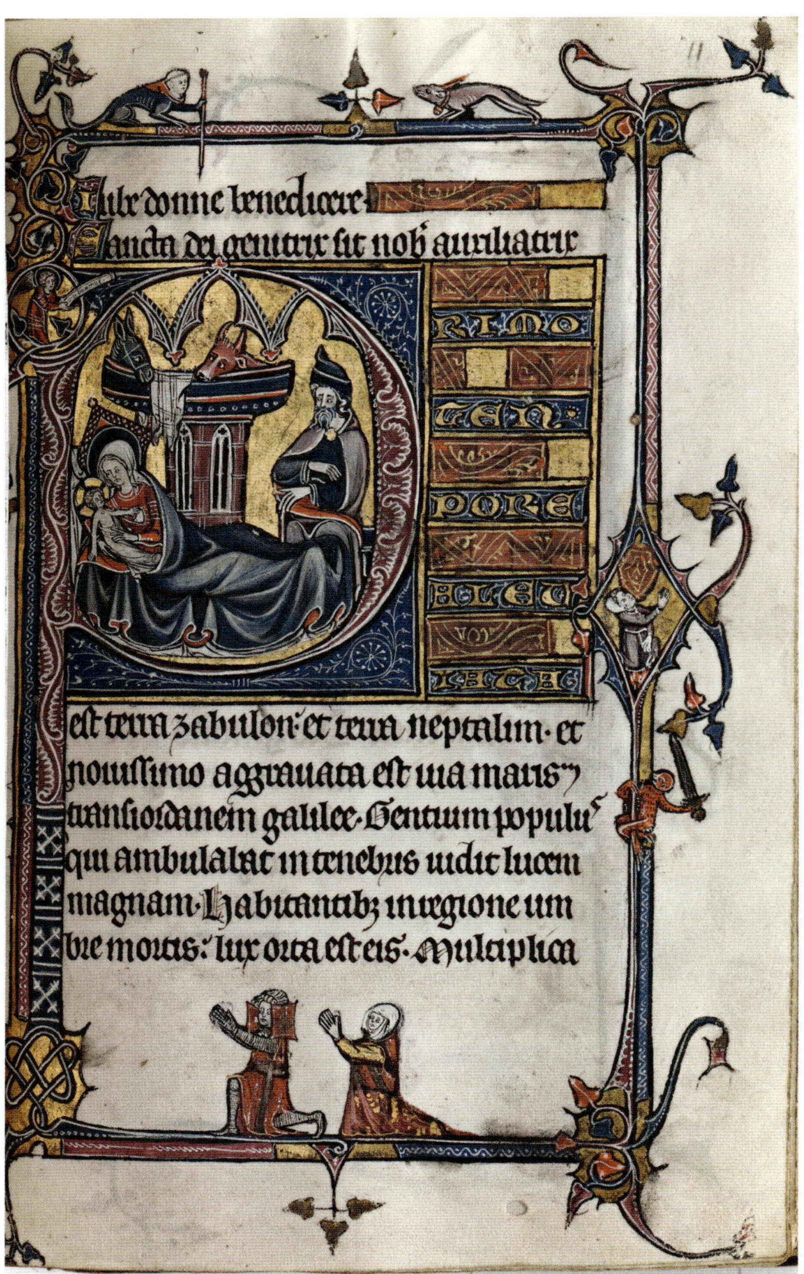

Figure 6.7: Nativity of Christ from the *Aspremont Offices of the Virgin*. Volume 2, folio 11, *c.*1290–1302. Parchment, 21.5cm × 15cm. National Gallery of Victoria, Melbourne. MS Felton 1254–3. Image courtesy of the National Gallery of Victoria.

many of these marginalia have little or nothing to do with the textual contents of the prayer book, and the numerous allusions to jousting and tournaments (Figure 6.11) further refer to secular interests of the patrons.

The style of the *Aspremont-Kievraing Psalter-Hours* has been related to a group of artists working not only in Verdun and Metz, where members of the prestigious de Bar family numbered among their clients, but also to

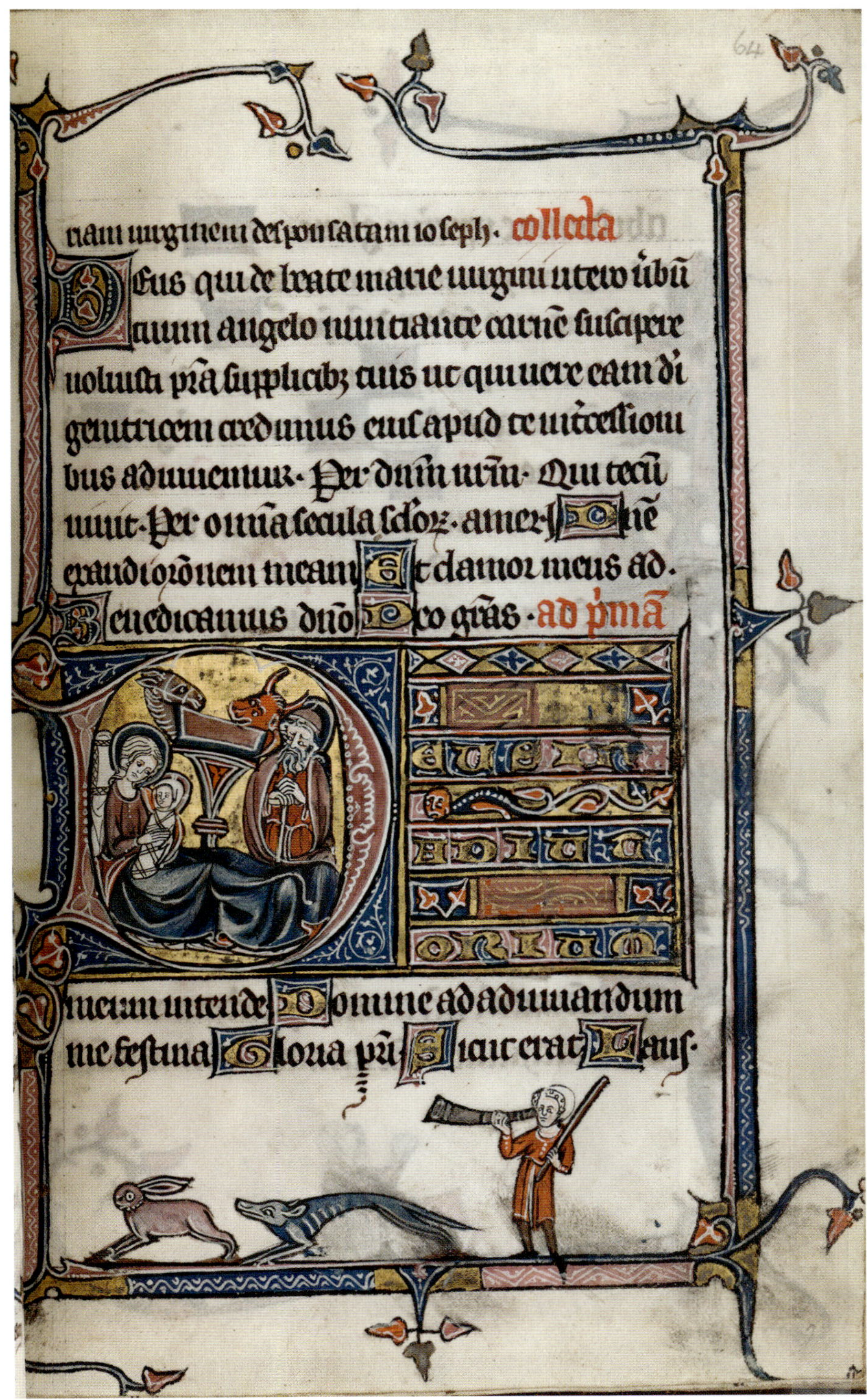

Figure 6.8: Nativity of Christ from the *Aspremont Offices of the Virgin*. Volume 2, folio 64, *c.*1290–1302. Parchment, 21.5cm × 15cm. National Gallery of Victoria, Melbourne. MS Felton 1254–3.

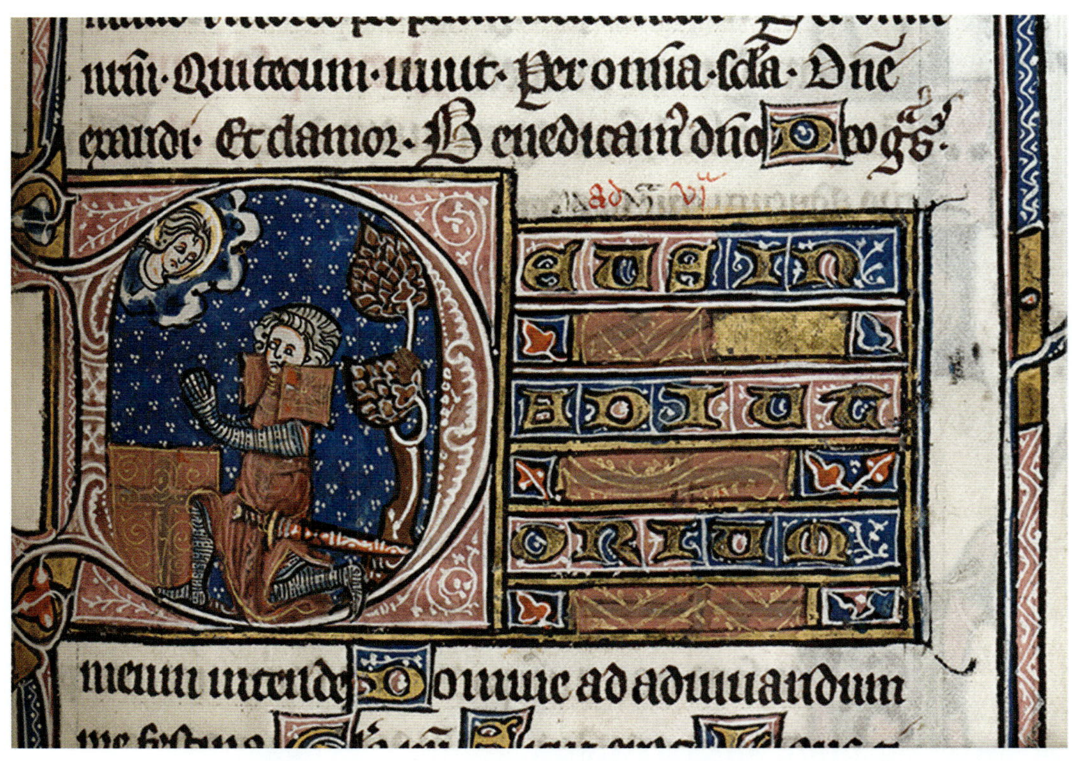

Figure 6.9: Joffroy d'Aspremont at prayer, Initial 'D' from the *Aspremont Offices of the Virgin*. Volume 2, folio 66, *c*.1290–1302. Parchment, 21.5cm × 15cm. National Gallery of Victoria, Melbourne. MS Felton 1254–3.

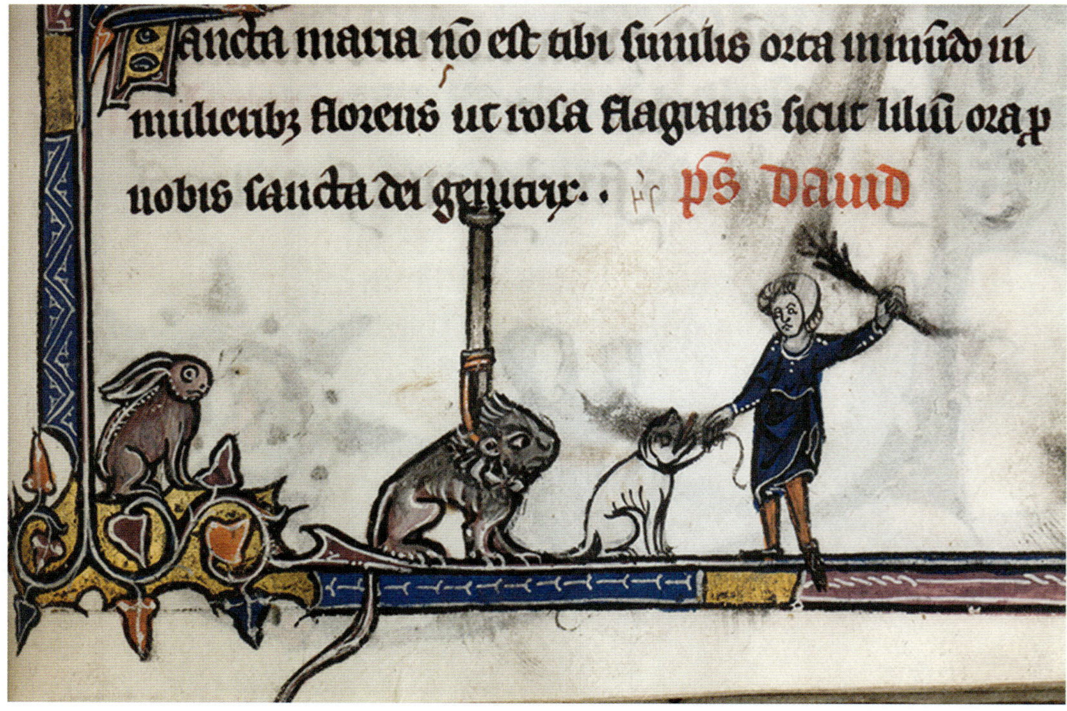

Figure 6.10: How to tame a lion, *bas-de-page* from the *Aspremont Offices of the Virgin*. Volume 2, folio 123, *c*.1290–1302. Parchment, 21.5cm × 15cm. National Gallery of Victoria, Melbourne. MS Felton 1254–3.

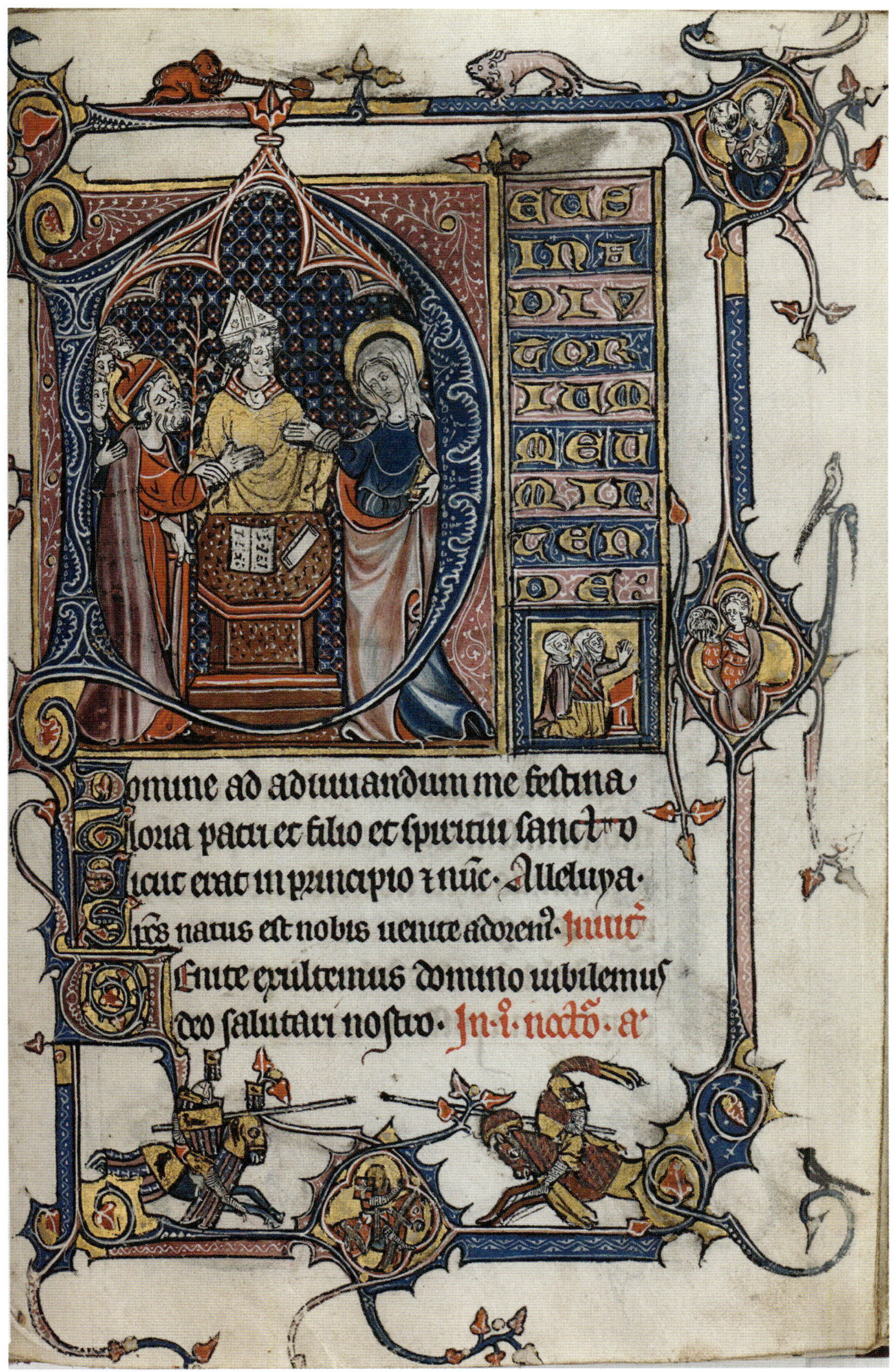

Figure 6.11: Jousting knights, *bas-de-page* from the *Aspremont Offices of the Virgin*. Volume 2, folio 7, *c.*1290–1302. Parchment, 21.5cm × 15cm. National Gallery of Victoria, Melbourne. MS Felton 1254-3.

illuminators in Amiens and Reims.[18] In this context, the idea of a lay prayer book which, on the one hand, reflects considerable freedom in its range of visual subject matter, and, on the other, maintains – albeit with some difficulty – the basic liturgical format of the Breviary, indicates the vitality and flexibility of the canonical hours as a framework for Christian prayer at a time of considerable change.

The *Rothschild Prayer Book* and the Book of Hours

Other scholars have contributed in this publication to particular aspects of the *Rothschild Prayer Book*. My observations here are confined to the ways in which this Netherlandish book witnesses to the last flowering of the hand-crafted Book of Hours, and how it perpetuates in its structure and contents a number of the basic elements that originated in the Psalter-Hours of the late thirteenth and early fourteenth centuries.

As we have seen, the Church Calendar, which was an important aspect of liturgical manuscripts, was already present in the early *SLV Psalter-Hours* and the *Aspremont-Kievraing Psalter-Hours*. It became a regular part of the Book of Hours in the fourteenth and fifteenth centuries, usually retaining the simple schematic format of the signs of the zodiac and the labours of the months characteristic of earlier periods. Occasionally, they present a full-scale celebration of the seasons with the people portrayed being part of the changing landscapes and environmental contrasts, as in the Calendar of the *Très Riches Heures* of Jean de Berry which was begun and probably largely designed by the Brothers Limbourg around 1410. In the Calendar

pages of the *Rothschild Prayer Book* and related Netherlandish manuscripts, the diagrammatic character of liturgical and early Psalter Calendars is transformed into lively agricultural, landscape and genre scenes. In the *Rothschild Calendar* these are rendered along the base of the page, with wooden sculptures referring to the feasts of major saints for each month presented in the vertical margins. Thus the representation of the rhythmic movement of time and place in the Calendar pages draws on both ancient and new ways of presenting the passage of time and place for the enjoyment and contemplation of the beholder (Figure 6.12).

Apart from the Calendar, the layout of the illuminated pages in the *Rothschild Prayer Book* is consistent throughout. A full-page miniature on the left or verso introduces each subject or theme. This image is matched on the right with a page of text preceded by an explanatory Latin title or rubric written in red, together with one or more decorated initials which are in harmony with the overall ensemble of the double-page opening (Figure 6.13). Decorative borders are a key part of the illuminated design of these double-page openings, where naturalistic features often mingle with the illusionistic, and strewn flowers and colourful foliage give the impression of lying on the surface of the page (Figure 6.13). Such border decoration is in disciplined contrast to the exuberant marginalia that abounds in the *Aspremont-Kievraing Psalter-Hours*.

Most of the devotions in the *Rothschild Prayer Book* are presented as short Offices or Hours, a format which, as mentioned above, is based on the Breviary Office. Clearly recognisable in both the texts and illustrative programs of the Hours or Offices of the *Rothschild Prayer Book* is the continuing concern to communicate age-old Christian beliefs and revered devotions relating to the Passion, Cross, and Resurrection of Christ, and the abiding presence of the Holy Spirit. Mary presides over this

---

18   See Avril, *L'Art au Temps* No. 217, p. 319; Stones, *Gothic Manuscripts 1260–1320*, especially p. 70.

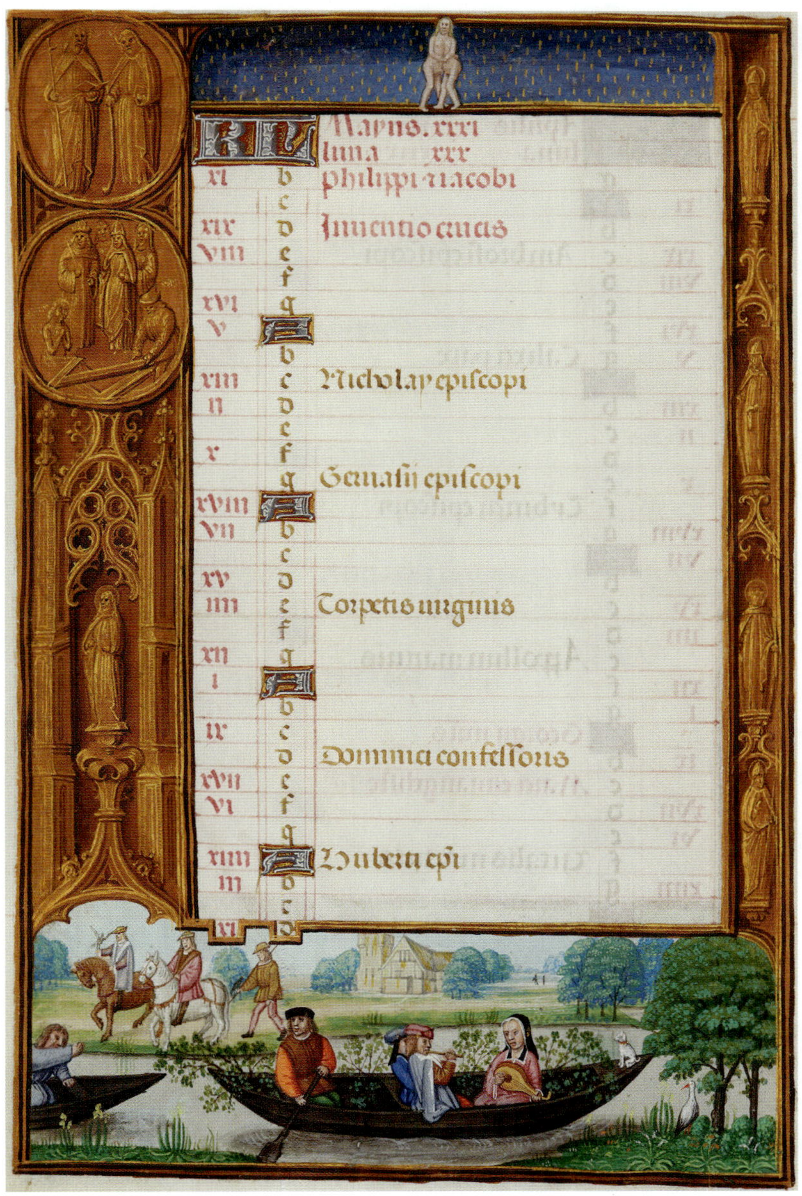

Figure 6.12: Calendar, May, boating and hawking, Gemini, from the *Rothschild Prayer Book*. Folio 3v, *c.*1505–1510. Parchment, 22.8cm × 16cm. Kerry Stokes Collection, Perth. LIB.2014.017.

incarnational world in her Hours and in such exquisite paintings as the Virgin and Child by the Bruges panel painter Gerard David (folio 197v, illustrated in Chapter 1, Figure 1.1).

The significance of the Mass and the Eucharist for the observant Christian was already emphasised visually in some of the Mosan Psalters, and it is clear that sometimes these prayers were recited by their owners in church. In the *Rothschild Prayer Book*, texts for both the Mass and corresponding Hours for each day of the week appear alongside

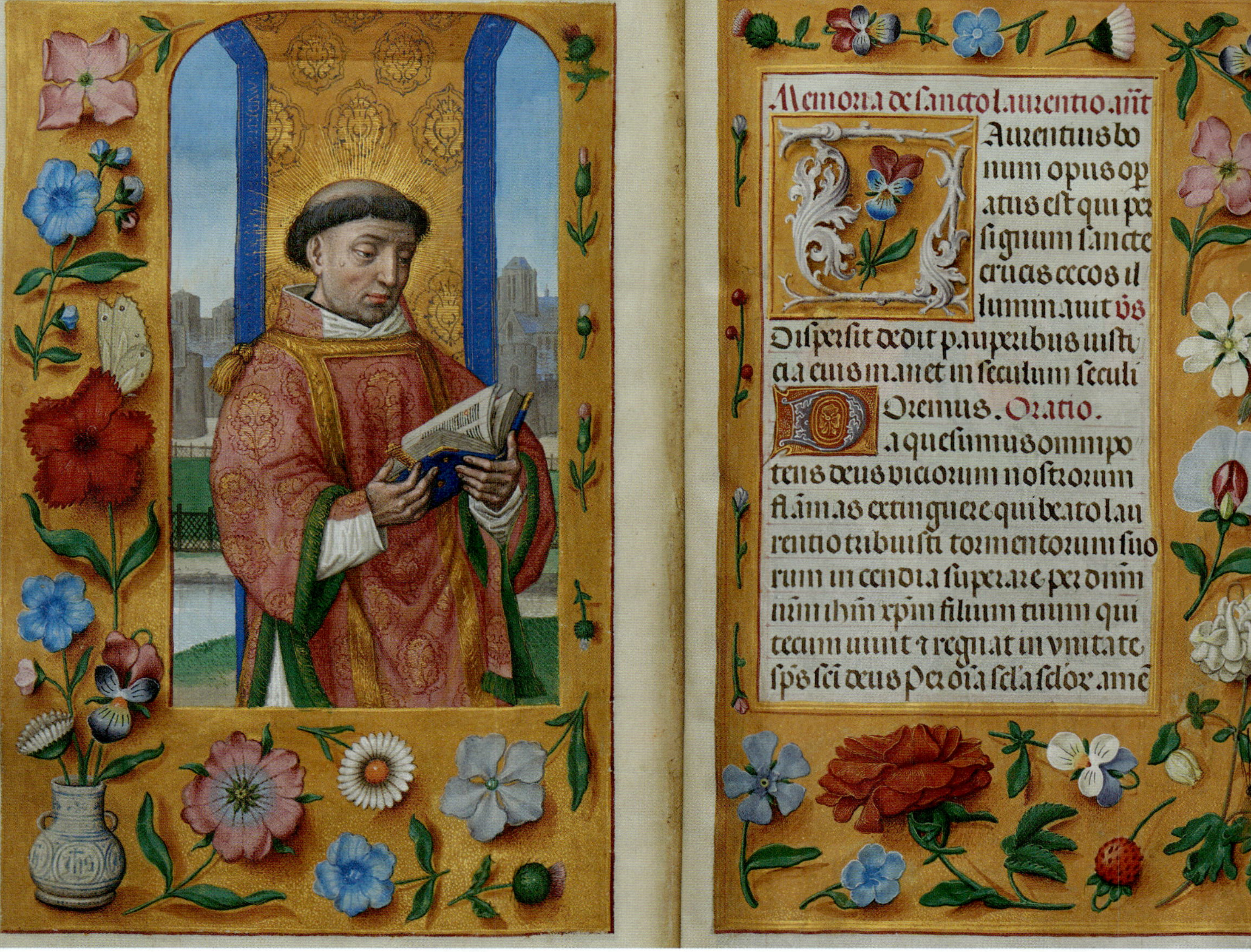

Figure 6.13: St Lawrence, Suffrage from the *Rothschild Prayer Book*. Folios 219v–220, *c.*1505–1510. Parchment, 22.8cm × 16cm. Kerry Stokes Collection, Perth.

one another. This particular combination already occurs in some fifteenth-century Books of Hours. Less usual is the focus in the *Rothschild Prayer Book* on specific parts of the Eucharistic celebration. The Consecration, for instance, appears in the miniature for Friday's Mass, rather than the particular Christian theme being honoured – here the Holy Cross (Figure 6.14). The viewer is thus explicitly invited to participate in the Eucharistic service as well as in the continuing prayer of the canonical Hours.

Finally, one of the most impressive visual expressions of popular devotion in the *Rothschild Prayer Book* is the rendering of the

saints as part of an annual commemorative cycle. By contrast to the small number of saints framed in the roundels of the *SLV Psalter-Hours*, the Rothschild cycle contains some thirty-seven images, usually of single figures shown against appropriate ornamental or naturalistic backgrounds. Intercessory images of the saints called suffrages or *memoriae* may be traced back to the custom of commemorating or petitioning certain saints at Lauds in the Divine Office. The prayers which accompany these images are composed of short antiphons, versicles and responsories, which affirm their liturgical origins. At the same time, the treatment of

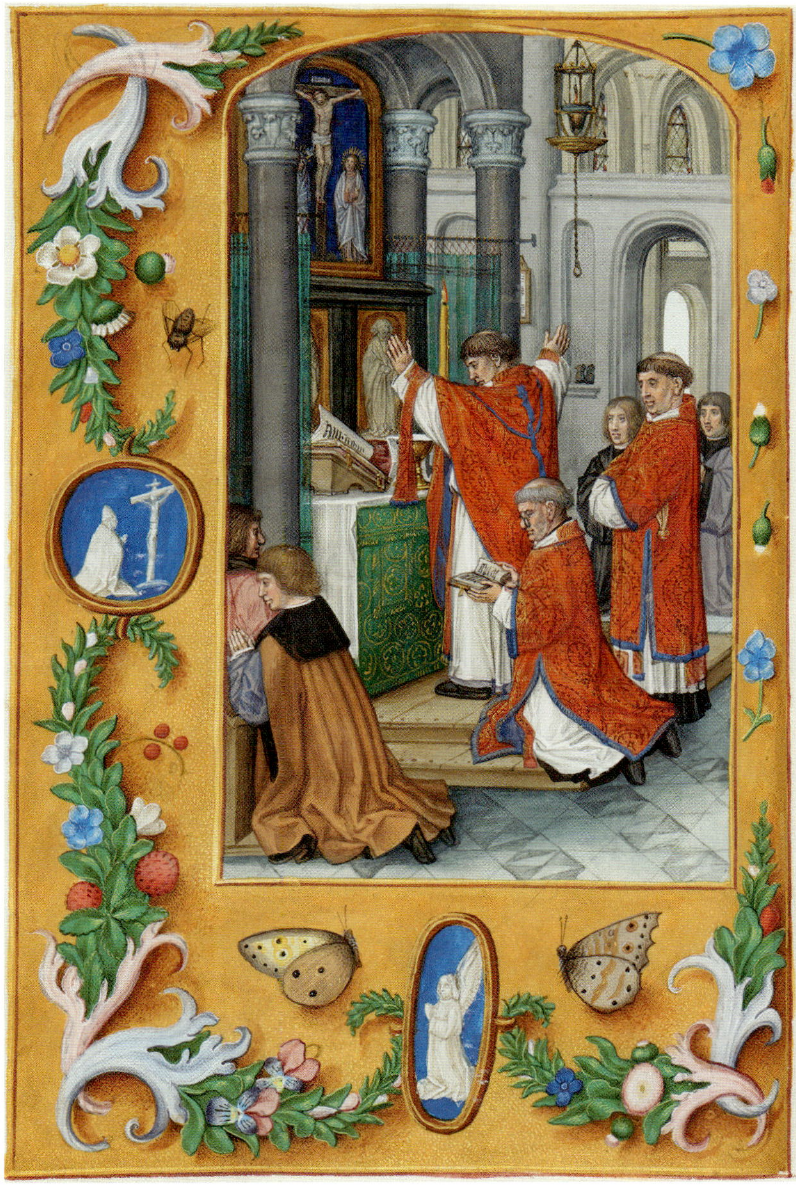

Figure 6.14: Prayer of Consecration, Mass of the Holy Cross for Friday from the *Rothschild Prayer Book*. Folio 65v, *c.*1505–1510. Parchment, 22.8cm × 16cm. Kerry Stokes Collection, Perth.

these figures, their settings and framing borders are examples of Flemish painting of the highest order. As such they are a powerful reminder that Netherlandish art of this period flourished both in the illuminated book and in panel painting. In particular, the images of the saints in the *Rothschild Prayer Book*, many of whom bear attributes which relate to martyrdom (St Catherine of Alexandria, see Chapter 2, Figure 2.5), invite the viewer to enter a world where suffering and death have been overcome and the instruments of torture are transformed by a vision of beauty and serenity. Such images are a combination of long-held traditions and the more recent achievements of Flemish artists. Nor were these achievements confined to the distinguished oeuvre of one or more highly competent and collaborative workshops active in the southern Netherlands in the early sixteenth century. The initial appeal of such manuscripts was surely due to the artists' familiarity with the devotional and social milieu of their clientele. Paradoxically, these values were to be dramatically disturbed in a few short years with the onset of the Reformation in Europe and England and the advent of the printed book. Such a basic shift invites pause for reflection on how the arts at times may achieve a rare insight into the beauty and fragility of the human condition. At a more pragmatic level, similar objectives and themes are presented in the two early Psalter-Hours discussed here. This highlights the tenuous origins of a particular visual tradition, the nature of its flowering, and its subsequent disappearance.

About the author

Margaret M. Manion is Emeritus Professor of Art History at the University of Melbourne, where she was the Second Herald Chair of Fine Arts. Her many works on European manuscripts include the exhibition and catalogue *An Illumination: The Rothschild Prayer Book and Other Works from the Kerry Stokes Collection c.1280–1685* (2015). m.manion@unimelb.edu.au

Works cited

François Avril, *L'Art au Temps des Rois Maudits Philippe le Bel et ses fils, 1285–1328* (Paris: Réunion des Musées Nationaux, 1998).

Sharon Kay Davenport, 'Manuscripts illuminated for Renaud of Bar, Bishop of Metz (1303–1316)', PhD. dissertation, Courtauld Institute of Art, University of London, 1984.

Maurice Delbouille, ed., *Jacques Bretel, Le Tournoi de Chauvency* (Paris: Droz, 1932).

Dominique Henriot-Walzer, trans., *Le Tournoi de Chauvency, Jacques Bretel 1285*, (Dampicourt: Editions de La Joyeuserie, 2002).

Margaret M. Manion, 'The Aspremont Kievraing Hours,' in *The Felton Illuminated Manuscripts in the National Gallery of Victoria*, ed. by Margaret M. Manion (Melbourne: Macmillan Art Publishing and the National Gallery of Victoria, 2005), pp. 100–203.

Nigel J. Morgan, 'Gendered Devotions and Social Rituals: The Aspremont Psalter-Hours and the Image of the Patron in Late Thirteenth and Early Fourteenth-Century France', *Melbourne Art Journal*, 6 (2003), pp. 5–24.

Nigel J. Morgan and Bronwyn Stocks, 'The Personal Prayer Book and the Book of Hours' in *The Medieval Imagination. Illuminated Manuscripts from Cambridge, Australia and New Zealand*, ed. by Bronwyn Stocks and Nigel Morgan, (South Yarra: Macmillan Art Publishing, 2008).

Judith H. Oliver, 'Devotional Images and Pious Practices in a Psalter from Liège', *The La Trobe Journal*, No. 51, 52 (1993), pp. 24–29.

Judith H. Oliver, *Gothic Manuscript Illumination in the Diocese of Liège (c.1250–c.1330)*, 2 vols. (Leuven: Peeters, 1988).

Judith H. Oliver, 'Psalter-Hours Use of Liège', in *The Medieval Imagination. Illuminated Manuscripts from Cambridge, Australia and New Zealand*, ed. by Bronwyn Stocks and Nigel Morgan, (South Yarra: Macmillan Art Publishing, 2008), pp. 140–41.

Alison Stones, *Gothic Manuscripts 1260–1320*, 2 vols (London and Turnhout: Miller 2014).

Roger S. Wieck, *Time Sanctified. The Book of Hours in Medieval Art and Life*, (New York: G. Braziller in association with the Walters Art Gallery, Baltimore, 1988).

7. An associate of the Jouvenel Master and the Breviary of Prior François Robert

Elaine Shaw

Dunlop, Anne (ed.), *Antipodean Early Modern. European Art in Australian Collections, c. 1200–1600*, Amsterdam University Press, 2018

DOI: 10.5117/9789462985209/CH07

Abstract

Prior François Robert's incomplete Breviary would originally have been produced as a single volume. Today, however, it has only the texts for the feasts of the Temporal Cycle. When or how the Calendar, the Sanctoral and a complete Psalter were separated from the Temporal section cannot be determined. This study examines the manuscript's liturgical format and its relationship to the Jouvenel style and the manner in which its illustrations compare with selected images in early fifteenth-century Breviaries and Books of Hours. It highlights the stylistic developments of manuscript production in regional France, particularly Bourges.

Keywords: Breviaries; Books of Hours; Jouvenel Group of artists; Jouvenel style; Prior François Robert; Bourges

The focus of this essay is a relatively small Breviary, made in northern France around 1460–1470. It bears an inscription on folio 1 identifying the owner as François Robert, Prior of the College of Canons of St-Cyr at Issoudun in the Diocese of Bourges, in the province of Berry (*Ex libris magistri francisci Robert prioris sancti Circi Exolduni*), as well as thirteen coats-of-arms belonging to Robert.[1] The manuscript (hereafter called *Prior Robert's Breviary*) is attributed to an associate of the Jouvenel Master, named for his illumination of a *Mare Historiarum* made in 1448–9 for Guillaume Jouvenel des Ursins, Chancellor of France.[2] This manuscript (Figure 7.1) has an impressive illustrative cycle developed over several years by a group of illuminators working in a relatively unified style.The Jouvenel Master ran a large workshop for patrons living in Brittany, the Loire Valley, and Berry.[3] His style, as defined by Eberhard König, includes figures with 'long noses, high and rather solemn earnest

---

1   For a full catalogue description see Manion, 'Liturgical Manuscripts', Cat. no. 3, pp. 38–41. See also: Manion and Zika, *Celebrating Word and Image 1250–1600*, Cat. no. 4, pp. 24–29; Sotheby's, *Western Manuscripts*, London, 6 July, 2006; Faye and Bond, *Supplement to the Census of Medieval and Renaissance Manuscripts*.

2   A collection of historical texts written by Giovanni Colonna (*c.*1298–1343). He was a Dominican friar in Rome and ended his history of the world in 1250.

3   Plummer, *The Last Flowering*, pp. 32–36 and Seidel, 'Un livre d'heures Berruyer du XVᵉ Siècle', pp. 2–24. See also Avril, 'Le groupe Jouvenel', pp. 109–20; Avril, 'Les Heures de Jeanne de France: un chef d'œuvre du Maître de Jouvenel' pp. 20–21.

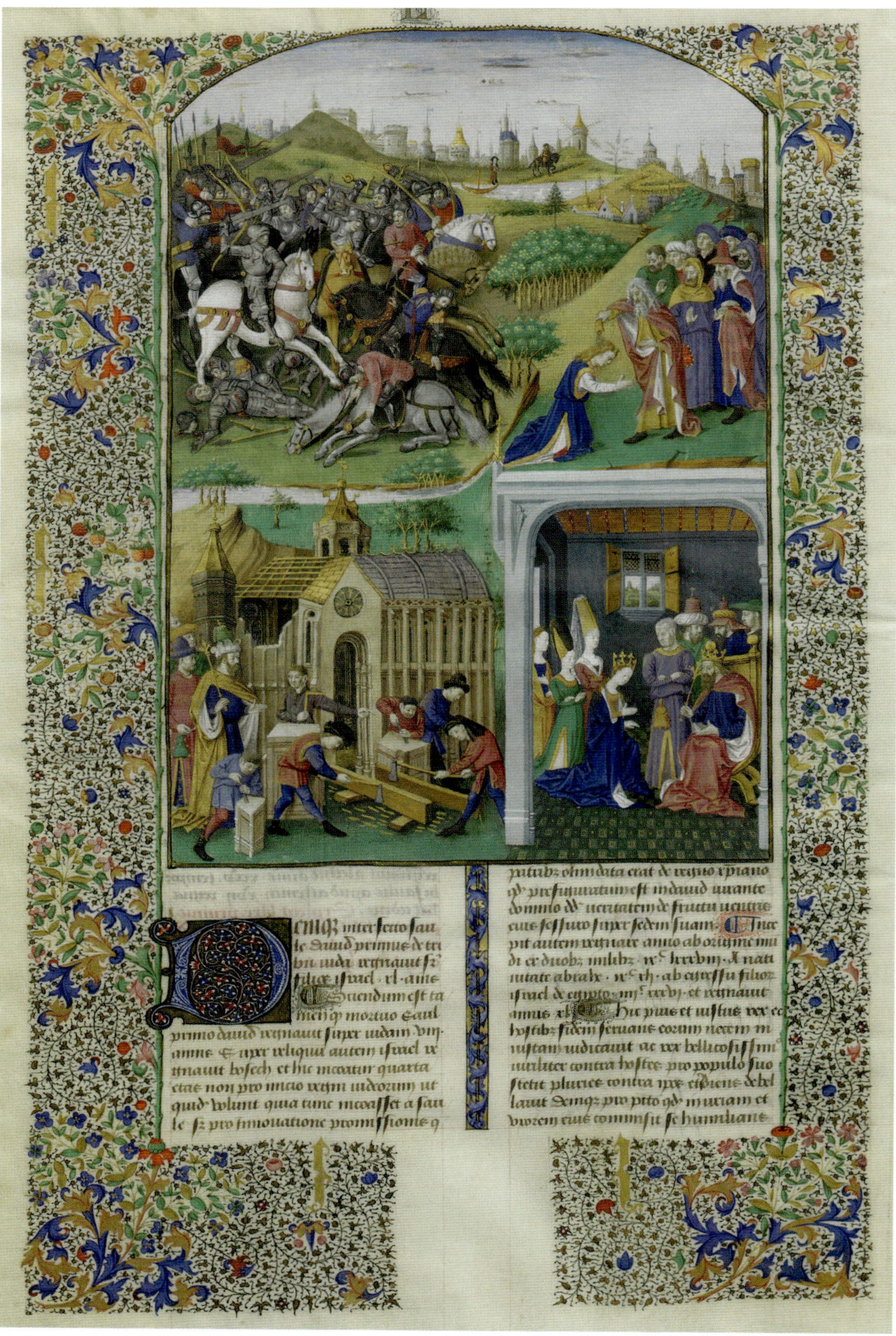

Figure 7.1: Jouvenel Master, Queen of the Sabines and Solomon (Book II) from *Mare historiarum*. Folio 46v, 1448–9. Manuscript. Bibliothèque Nationale de France, Paris. MS lat. 4915.

faces, a delight in profiles, and ...very distinctive pale green and gold and blue leaves in the borders'.[4] What follows here will situate *Prior Robert's Breviary* within stylistic developments in illuminated manuscript production in regional France; though linked to developments at the courts and in Paris, this regional production was distinctive and needs to be studied in its own right. It will also explore the visual imagery, including how the illumination both followed the traditions of Breviary illustration and adapted it for the prior's personal use.

Art historians have always been aware of the extraordinary vitality of the art of book illumination in France in the first two decades of the fifteenth century. Paris has always been recognized as the centre of this production, but new approaches to the study of this period have shown the important role of other patronage centres. The large exhibition held at the Musée du Louvre in 2004, and related exhibitions at Dijon, Bourges and Chantilly, focussed on the art of the capital and its links with distinguished ducal courts, and highlighted Paris as the principle European centre for the production of luxury goods at this time.[5] Prominent among these luxury goods was the illuminated book, with unprecedented developments in Parisian illumination brought about by the emergence of a new generation of younger artists, including artists employed by Jean de Berry at the court of Bourges, such as Jacquemart d'Hesdin and the gifted Limbourg Brothers.[6] The duke and his artists spent considerable time in the capital, thus ensuring a robust artistic association between the art of Paris and the art of the court at Bourges.

Among the leading artist-illuminators of this generation were the *Cité des Dames* Master, the Boucicaut Master, the Mazarine Master – whose work has only recently been distinguished from that of the Boucicaut Master – the Egerton Master, the Master of the Breviary of Jean sans Peur, and the Bedford Master. Recent studies have shown that these artists not only significantly advanced the art of illumination in the capital, but also interacted with the Limbourg Brothers employed by Jean de Berry at the court of Bourges.[7]

The work of this new generation of artists is distinguished by a richer and more varied palette of clear, bright colours, and by a renewed interest in the depiction of space which indicated fresh contacts with Italian artists. The Master of the Brussels Initials, for example – so named after his work in a splendid Book of Hours made for Jean, Duc de Berry (KBR, MS 11060–61), called the Brussels Hours – testifies to the presence of Italian illuminators in Paris at this time. Trained in the atelier of Niccolò da Bologna, this master spent some eight years in Paris from around

---

4   See König, *Französische Buchmalerei um 1450*, pp. 189–91, p. 254.

5   Taburet-Delahaye, ed., *Paris 1400: Les arts sous Charles VI*; Nash, *Between Florence and Flanders*.

6   Avril, 'Grands et petit maîtres vers 1400–1415', pp. 276–77.

7   For the Bedford Master, see Rouse and Rouse, *Manuscripts and their Makers*, 11, pp. 73–74 and 1, p. 299, 403 n. 90; König, *The Bedford Hours*, pp. 36–37. See also Hofmann, 'Haincelin de Hagenau et l'acanthe a Paris', pp. 99–109, and Stirnemann and Rabel, 'The *Très Riches Heures*' pp. 534–538. For a recent study of the Boucicaut Master and a complete reproduction of the miniatures in the Book of Hours for which he was named by Millard Meiss, see Chatelet, *L'Âge d'or du manuscrit à peintures en France*; and Bartz and König, *Der Boucicaut-Meister*. For the seminal work on the Boucicaut Master see Meiss, *French Painting in the Time of Jean de Berry: The Boucicaut Master*. For the Mazarine Master see Villela-Petit, 'Grandes Heures de Jean de Berry', Cat. no. 175–176, pp. 284–285; and Villela-Petit 'Devises de Charles VI' pp. 80–92. For the *Cité des Dames* Master see Meiss, *French Painting in the Time of Jean de Berry: The Limbourgs and Their Contemporaries*, pp. 283–287; König, *Boccaccio, Decameron*; Kobayashi, 'La dernière étape de l'enluminure des Œuvres de Christine de Pizan'. For the Egerton Master see Schilling, 'The Master of the Egerton', pp. 272–282.

1400, and carried out prestigious commissions for Charles le Noble, King of Navarre, and possibly for the Dauphin, Louis de Guyenne, as well as for Jean de Berry and members of his court. He is credited with introducing several Italian motifs to Parisian illumination, such as brightly coloured acanthus leaves, innovative landscapes that sometimes 'invaded' the borders, and imaginative architectural settings, some of which were derived from Italian frescoes.[8]

Millard Meiss's work on early fifteenth-century French illumination advanced our knowledge of many of these artists and the innovative nature of their illumination. For the most part, however, Meiss presented them from the perspective of the patronage of Jean de Berry, whom he persuasively characterized as the most discerning and passionate art collector of the period. He thus interpreted artistic developments in both Paris and at the court of Berry as very much dominated by this one man's patronage. Indeed, Meiss' comprehensive three-volume study of the period goes by the name *French Painting in the Time of Jean de Berry*.[9] Meiss also tended to emphasize the distinction between the artistic context of the ducal court and the Parisian workshops. Certain artists favoured by the duke – Jacquemart

d'Hesdin, the Pseudo-Jacquemart, the sculptor André Beauneveu, who also occasionally turned to illumination, and, above all, the Limbourg Brothers– tended to be viewed as working in the comparative seclusion of Bourges. More recent writers, such Richard and Mary Rouse, for example, have expanded Meiss's categorizations and provided a new wealth of documentation on the careers and activites of Parisian illuminators.[10] Other art historians have studied individual master illuminators, including those listed above, and the interests of the patrons for whom they worked. In particular, the Bedford, Mazarine and Boucicaut Masters have emerged alongside the Limbourg Brothers not only as innovative artists in their own time but also as forerunners of key developments in the field of both panel painting and illumination which are associated with the work of later painters that include Jan van Eyck and Jean Fouquet.[11] It is now clear that the death of the Limbourg Brothers and the Jean de Berry, possibly in the plague of 1416, did not mean that high-powered artistic stimulus no longer existed beyond the capital. Artistic patronage remained as robust as ever but much of it was relocated to regional towns in the Loire Valley and Berry. Between 200 and 2010, at least four manuscripts from this region surfaced from private or unused collections; included in this group is *Prior Robert's Breviary*. All four manuscripts not only incorporate the work of the Jouvenel Master but reflect his association at an early period with the art of Tours and Angers, and with the workshop of

---

8   The identity of the Master of the Brussels Initials is unknown. Originally he was thought to be Zanobi (Zebo) da Firenze based on a signature in the *Hours of Charles the Noble* (Cleveland, Museum of Art, MS 64.40). Meiss did not accept the reading of the signature and named him instead the 'Master of the Brussels Initials': Meiss, *French Painting in the Time of Jean de Berry: The Late Fourteenth Century and the Patronage of the Duke*, I, pp. 229–41; Calkins, 'The Brussels Hours Re-evaluated', pp. 3–26, and 'An Italian in Paris' pp. 223–32. See also Villela-Petit, 'Grandes Heures de Jean de Berry', pp. 104–109.

9   These works are: *French Painting in the Time of Jean de Berry: The Late Fourteenth Century and the Patronage of the Duke*, I; *French Painting in the Time of Jean de Berry The Boucicaut Master*, II; *French Painting in the Time of Jean de Berry The Limbourgs and their Contemporaries*, III.

10   Rouse and Rouse, *Manuscripts and their Makers*.
11   See Bloem, 'Changing Workshop Policies' pp. 111–136; and Herman, 'Fouquet and the Absent Frame', pp. 51–71. For a study of the Rohan Masters as members of the group of artists who 'paved the way' for Jan Van Eyck and their artistic association with Jean Fouquet and Limbourg Brothers see, Panayotova, 'The Rohan Masters: Collaboration and Experimentation in the *Hours of Isabella Stuart*'.

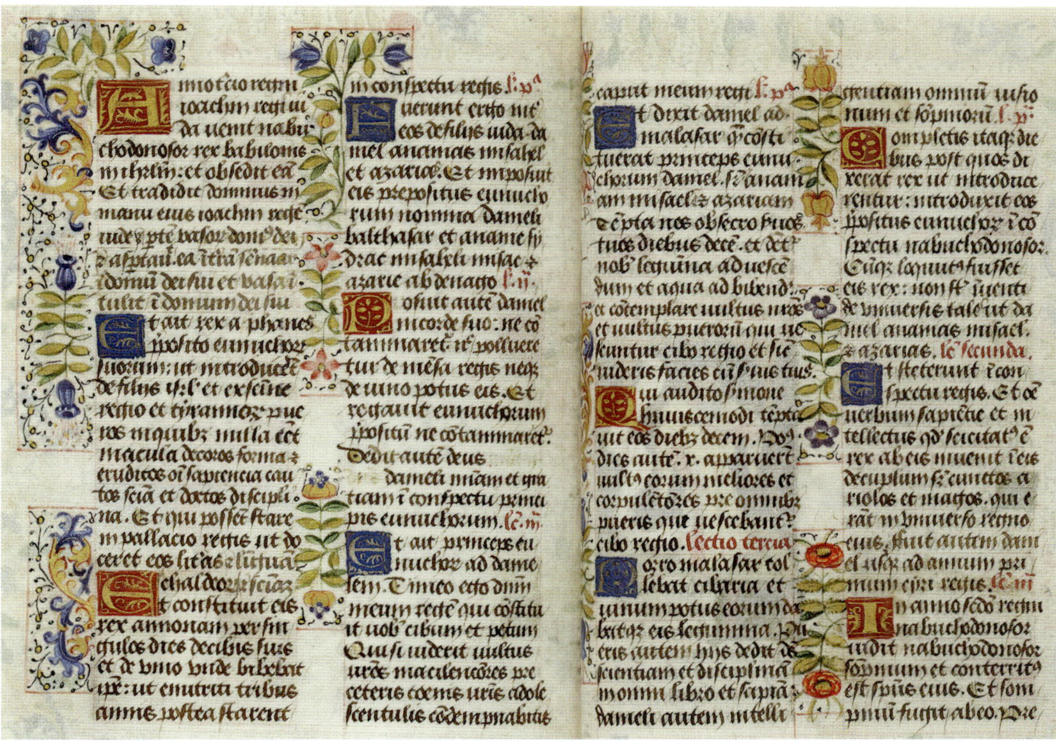

Figure 7.2: Associate of the Jouvenel Master, Partial Border from the *Breviary of Prior François Robert*. Folios 217v and 218, *c*.1460–1470. Parchment, 16.4cm × 11cm. Kerry Stokes Collection, Perth, LIB.2006.092.

Jean Fouquet.[12] One of the stylistic similarities between *Prior Robert's Breviary* and the Jouvenel manuscripts is the treatment of the figures and faces in the miniatures. Another characteristic aspect is the borders in which pale green and gold acanthus leaves feature throughout, and occasional red and blue flowers replace traditional Parisian ivy-leaf bar borders. This recurs in two books illustrated by the Jouvenel Master and associates: a Book of Hours, made in Bourges *c*.1455 (Bibliothèque municipale, Saint-Étienne, MS ANC A119), and

the *Hours of Jeanne de France* (Paris, BnF N.a.l, 3244), possibly made in Angers. The decorative vocabulary of *Prior Robert's Breviary* and that of the *Hours of Jeanne de France* is particularly close. Both manuscripts include heraldic arms in their borders and are ornamented with animals, hybrids, and figures both fantastic, and human. The borders of *Prior Robert's Breviary* feature scenes like a woman holding a baby in her raised arms, a peacock, and a man riding a hybrid woman and lion; while the queen's Book of Hours feature shepherds, a naked lady, apes dressed as soldiers, and the *genette*, the animal Jeanne chose as her emblem.[13] Yet the *mise-en-page* of *Prior Robert's Breviary* is different in

12   The other manuscripts are: The *Heures de Jeanne de France* (Paris, BnF, N.a.l. 3244; Book of Hours, Use of Bourges (Saint-Étienne, Bibliothèque municipale, MS ANC A119); Book of Hours, Use of Rome (Madrid, Bibliothèque nationale d'Espagne, vitr. 25–3). On these see Gras, 'The Master of Jeanne de France, duchesse de Bourbon' p. 165; and Seidel, 'Un livre d'heures Berruyer du XVᵉ Siècle', pp. 2–24 and 26–45.

13   See Avril, 'Reproduction des miniatures des Heures de Jeanne de France', pp. 29–65. See also Gras, 'The Master of Jeanne de France, duchesse de Bourbon, pp. 145–169 and

several ways. For example, the partial borders throughout the book consist of tiny sprays of red and blue flowers, and acanthus leaves extend from the red or blue two-line initials and replace the more customary continuous vertical or horizontal borders (Figure 7.2).

Of these four manuscripts, Prior Robert's book is the only Breviary. Both the liturgical format of this book and its relationship to the Jouvenel style invite attention. The Breviary is a book that contains the Divine Office. This text was based on the recitation of the Psalter at the canonical hours of the day – Matins, Lauds, Prime, Terce, Sext, None, Vespers and Compline. It varied throughout the week and throughout the year. The prayers and readings accompanying the psalms harmonized with the changing feasts of the Church Calendar and its dual cycle: the Temporal, with the seasonal feasts such as Advent, Christmas, Lent, Easter, Ascension and Pentecost; and the Sanctoral with the Feasts of the Saints. The prayers for the daily performance of the Divine Office were initially contained in a variety of large and imposing separate books: the Psalter, Martyrology, Hymnal, Antiphonal, various Lectionaries (biblical, hagiographic, and homiletic); and a collection of prayers read by the presiding religious or cleric.[14] In the course of the eleventh and twelfth centuries, however, this material was compiled into a single book called the Breviary.[15]

In his pioneering study of Breviary manuscripts in the public libraries of France, Victor Leroquais distinguished two basic types: a book of imposing dimensions, with very long lessons or readings, intended for public and

solemn performance of the Office in the choir of a monastery, cathedral, or major church; and a shorter version, usually with shorter lessons or readings, designed for private recitation, perhaps in one's room or while travelling.[16] The small size of *Prior Robert's Breviary* (164mm x 110mm), suggests that it was made for his personal use, either for private devotion or to follow the service silently in church. The manuscript originally would have contained a Calendar, the Sanctoral, and a complete Psalter. Today, it has only the texts for the feasts of the Temporal Cycle. Folios 1 – 6 contain prefatory rubrics which may have been added as a type of 'Calendar' or as an index.

Breviaries also reflected the distinction between the form of the Office performed by ancient monastic orders, such as the Benedictines, and that celebrated by the diocesan clergy and more recent types of religious congregations, like the mendicant friars. For example, the monastic Benedictine Office had twelve lessons or readings at Matins on Sundays and feast days, while the secular office had only nine. Liturgical uses reflected the customs and feasts of particular regions and religious orders. The basic structure of most of these derived from the Roman rite. The use of certain religious orders, however, was not confined to books for its members; but might also feature in those made for lay people associated with the order. This was sometimes the case in French royal and aristocratic households, for example, where the chaplain belonged to a particular religious order.

Breviaries might be bound in one or two volumes. A fully-illustrated Breviary would have been rather bulky and thus for the sake of portability they were often produced as a winter volume (Advent to Lent) and a summer volume (Easter through the rest of the liturgical year). Some Breviaries began as a single volume but

'Les Heures de Madrid: un exceptionnel manuscript inspiré by Jean Fouquet et le Maître de Jouvenel', pp. 2–73.

14   Leroquais, *Les Bréviaires manuscrits des bibliothèques publiques de France*, 2, cliv, lii. See also Calkins, *Illuminated Books of the Middle Ages*, pp. 226–34.

15   Leroquais, *Les Bréviaires*, introduction, 1, liii.

16   Leroquais, *Les Bréviaires*, introduction, 1, l–cxxxiii.

were separated and bound as two volumes. In the Baillieu Library at the University of Melbourne, there is a small fourteenth-century Breviary containing the Psalter and Sanctoral; there is another fourteenth-century breviary in the Bodleian Library, Oxford, containing the Calendar and the Temporal. Both have the same stylistic characteristics and the final page of the Bodleian volume has an offset of the Psalm I initial and border as in the Baillieu volume, which indicates that they were originally produced as a single volume.[17] As far as we know, *Prior Robert's Breviary* was also originally produced as a single book. It cannot be determined, however, when or how the Calendar, Psalter and Sanctoral sections were parted from the Temporal section.

By the early fifteenth century conventions for the production of deluxe breviaries for royal and aristocratic patrons were also well established. The format and illustrative program of this genre were sufficiently flexible to allow for the presentation of different uses, as well as considerable variation in the number of feasts illustrated and their subject matter. There were also many different sources for the illustrations. These included compositions in other liturgical books such as Missals and Martyrologies, as well as the texts and illustrations of more popular genres such as Jean de Vignay's *Legende dorée*, a French translation of Jacobus de Voragine's *Legenda aurea*, or the personal prayer books called Books of Hours, which by this time were in widespread use.

For many years, art historians and others have been interested in the ways in which visual programs were devised for medieval books. And, although neither illuminators nor patrons or scholarly advisers have left much detailed or explicit evidence as to how this was done, through research on the books themselves, as well as on contemporary records and contracts, scholars have pieced together some of the different facets of this activity and the variety of methods and people involved.[18] The participants might have included all or some of the following: the commissioning patron or adviser; the *libraire* (described by Rouse and Rouse as 'part book-seller and part book-contractor'); the scribe and rubricator; and the chief illuminator or head of the relevant team or workshop.[19] In addition to the various narrative devices employed to illustrate texts, miniatures were anchored in the world of the contemporary reader by the consistent use of certain conventions relating to both the setting and costume of the protagonists. Despite the sophistication achieved by Parisian illuminators in the early years of the fifteenth century, and the contacts established with some of the foremost developments in Italy and Flanders in the realistic depiction of architectural and landscape settings, French illumination of this period maintained a highly conventional approach to the representation of historical and antique themes. While architectural details may reflect observation of contemporary buildings, the rendering of the buildings themselves, and the cities and towns in which they cluster, suggests an imaginative world whose occupants are either of diminutive size or else tower over the constructions. Once the viewer enters into a 'willing suspension of disbelief', however, architectural interior and exterior details, and the protagonists that exist in and around them, reveal an abundance of realistic references.

---

17   Morgan, 'The Book and Church Services: Liturgy and Ritual' pp. 70–71. See also Michael and Morgan, 'The Sarum Breviary in the Bodelian and Baillieu Libraries', pp. 30–37.

18   Alexander, *Medieval Illuminators and their Methods of Work*; and Rouse and Rouse, *Manuscripts and their Makers*, I and II.

19   See Alexander, *Medieval Illuminators*, p. 53; and Rouse and Rouse, *Manuscripts and their Makers*, I, p.14.

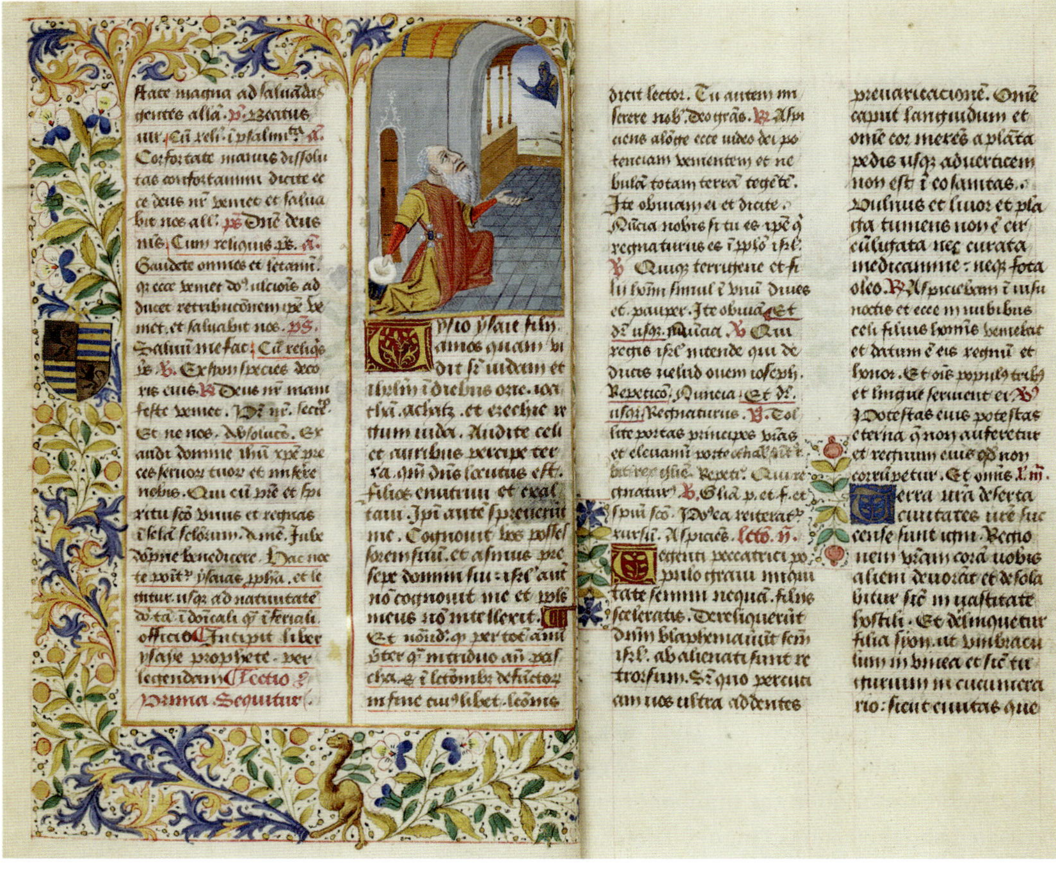

Figure 7.3: Associate of the Jouvenel Master, Isaiah speaking to God from the *Breviary of Prior François Robert*. Folios 7v–8, *c.*1460–1470. Parchment, 16.4cm × 11cm. Kerry Stokes Collection, Perth, LIB.2006.092.

Some of these characteristics feature in *Prior Robert's Breviary* and contribute to an understanding of the illustrative program as a whole. To demonstrate more precisely how the illustrations of Prior Robert's book reflect or depart from selected images in early fifteenth-century prayer books, the illumination will be discussed in accordance with the arrangement of the text, beginning with Advent, which heralds the coming of Christ, and concluding with two Books from the Old Testament. The first reading at Matins for the first Sunday of Advent is taken from the first chapter of the Prophet Isaiah. His vision of the coming of the Lord as the Messiah to Judah and of Jerusalem

has always been interpreted by the Church in terms of the coming of Christ in the Incarnation and his Second Coming at the end of time. These two themes permeate the season of Advent which leads up to the birth of Christ at Christmas. The illustration of the beginning of Advent in French deluxe Breviaries underwent considerable development in the early fifteenth century, but Isaiah usually featured in some way. For example, in the *Armagnac Breviary*, illuminated at the turn of the fifteenth century by the Luçon Master, a single figure of the Prophet accompanies the responsory to the reading at Matins which begins *'Aspiciens a longe'* ('Behold I see from afar off

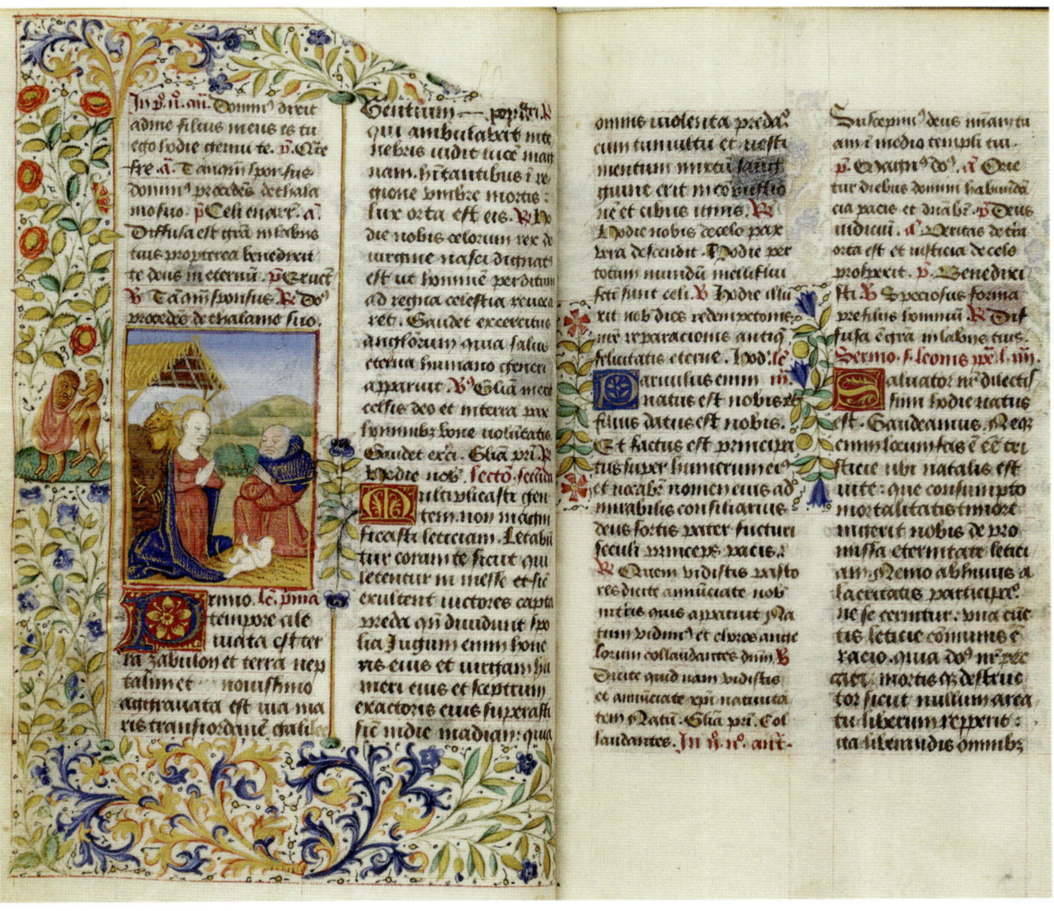

Figure 7.4: Associate of the Jouvenel Master, The Nativity from *Breviary of Prior François Robert*. Folios 31v–32, *c.*1460–1470. Parchment, 16.4cm × 11cm. Kerry Stokes Collection, Perth, LIB.2006.092.

the Lord coming in might').[20] The miniature in the *Salisbury Breviary* (BnF, MS lat. 17294) by the Bedford Master, shows that by the mid-1420s the theme of longing for the Messiah had given rise to a complex composition in which prophets and other figures from the Old Testament petitioned the Lord – represented as the Trinity – to come and rescue the human race.[21] Yet the illustration of Isaiah in *Prior Robert's Breviary* closely follows that of the earlier *Armagnac Breviary* iconography (Figure 7.3). Isaiah is portrayed as a single figure kneeling in a porch with his hat in his hand as he speaks to God in the sky above. It would appear that by the 1460–70s the simple theme was once again preferred to the earlier more complex composition.

20   See *Sotheby's Catalogue: Western Manuscripts and Miniatures* (London, 2007), cat. no. 57, pp. 130–143. See also de Hamel, *The Armagnac Breviary*.

21   For more information on the Salisbury Breviary see, Spencer, 'The Master of the Duke of Bedford', pp. 606–612. See also Pearce, 'Text and Image'.

The illustration of the Nativity is a further case (Figure 7.4). As was customary, the first reading for Christmas is taken from Isaiah 9:1-6. This passage includes the words 'For a child is born to us and a son is given to us', and it has long been associated in Christian worship with the birth of Christ. Beneath a thatched, partly damaged shelter, an ox and an ass gaze adoringly at the Holy Family. Their presence at the Nativity since early Christian times is based on Isaiah 1:3: 'The ox knows his owner, and the ass his master's crib: but Israel has not known me, and my people have not understood'. The iconography of this image combines the ancient tradition of the worshipping ox and ass with the more recent depiction of the Virgin and Joseph shown kneeling before the Christ Child. Representations of a kneeling Virgin in Nativity scenes were greatly influenced by St Bridget of Sweden's vision of the Nativity at Bethlehem, during her pilgrimage to the Holy Land in 1372.[22] Earlier Nativity images were influenced by the Byzantine tradition which shows Mary reclining, and Joseph seated apart pondering the mystery of Christ's birth.

Christmas and Epiphany, which is celebrated on January 6, are linked by a cluster of images relating to feasts that fall within their octaves. The Offices of a group of saints customarily appear here instead of in the Sanctoral. St. John the Evangelist is one of these although according to tradition he was the only apostle who was not martyred. He did, however, suffer the torture of being boiled in oil, a narrative related in the *Golden Legend*, when John arose unharmed from a barrel of boiling oil into which he had been thrown on the orders of the pagan Emperor Domitian.[23] In this illustration (Figure 7.5), a seemingly calm St. John is shown sitting in a barrel while one

man applies bellows to the fire and another prepares to ladle oil over the saint's head. In the background, a group of people watch from the town wall. A much simpler representation of St. John before the Latin Gate occurs in the *Armagnac Breviary*, where he is shown in a stony landscape, standing naked in a barrel, presumably of boiling oil although there is no fire; and in the *Belles Heures du Duc de Berry*, made in Paris, *c.*1405–1408/9, and illustrated by the Limbourg Brothers, where he appears as a majestic figure, fully clothed, with no reference to his torture.[24] In all three images, however, snakes sprout from a chalice held by the saint. These allude to another salvific tale in the *Golden Legend*, when St. John drank unharmed from a poisoned chalice offered by Aristodemus, the priest of the goddess Diana, to test the power of his God. [25]

After the Entombment for Holy Saturday, which is not represented in *Prior Robert's Breviary*, the pictorial narrative changes into a celebration of Christ's Resurrection which continues throughout Easter Week. The rather sprightly figure of the Saviour stepping from his tomb dominates the miniature for Easter Sunday (Figure 7.6). Around him the soldiers fall back in wonder while in the distance the ghost-like figures of the three Maries approach over the green Mount of Calvary in the early dawn. The first reading at Matins for the celebration of the Feast of the Ascension of Christ is taken from the beginning of the Acts of the Apostles (Acts 1:6–11) in which the writer explains how Christ is taken up into heaven after he has spent forty days appearing and speaking to the apostles about the kingdom of God. The miniature accompanying this text shows the 'rather large solemn faces' of the disciples

22   See Pearce, 'Text and Image', p. 9.

23   de Voragine, *The Golden Legend*, I, p. 53.

24   For more information see Husband, *The Art of Illumination*.

25   de Voragine, *The Golden Legend*, I, p. 51.

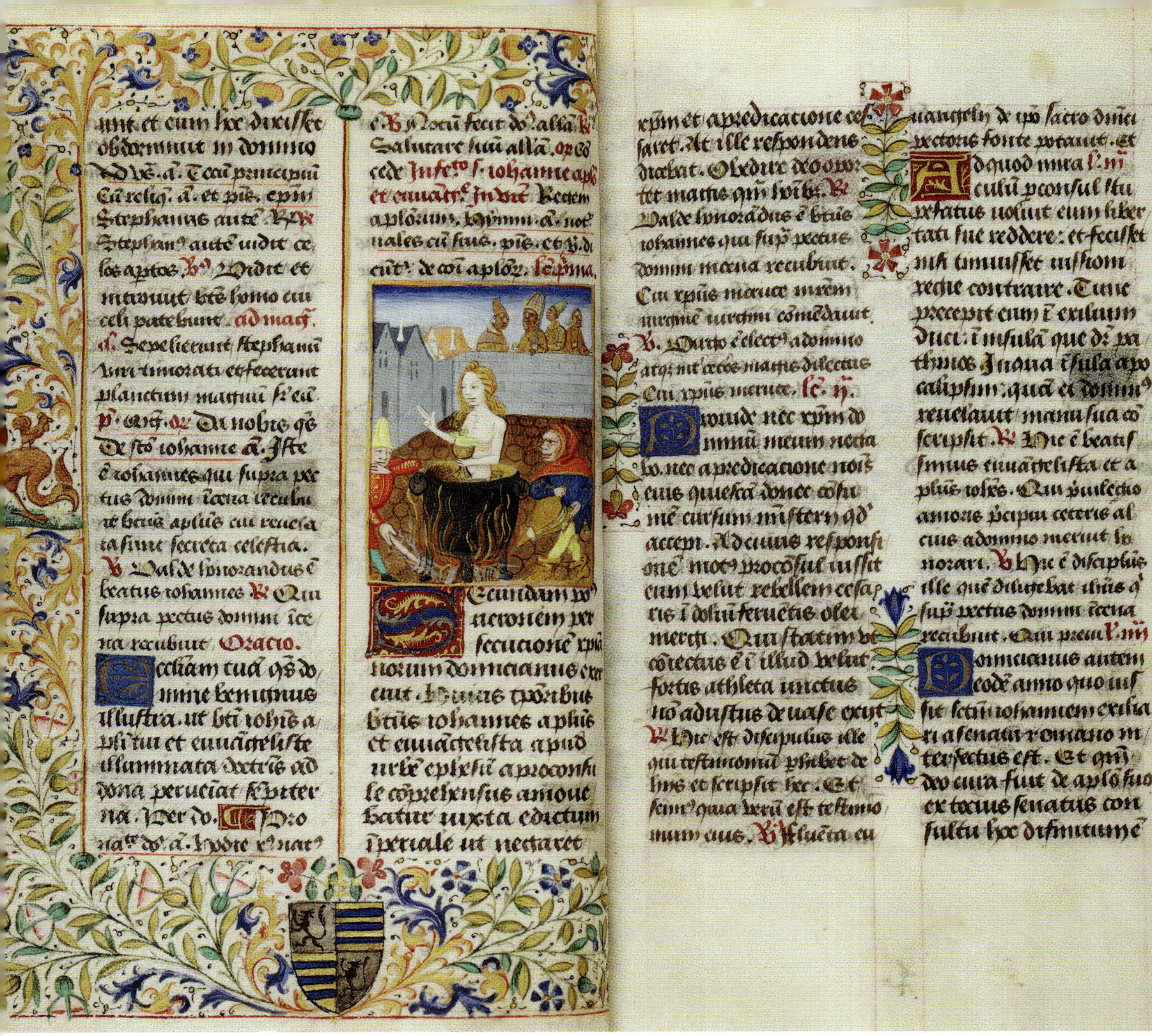

Figure 7.5: Associate of the Jouvenel Master, St John the Evangelist being boiled in oil from *Breviary of Prior François Robert*. Folios 36v–37, c.1460–1470. Parchment, 16.4cm × 11cm. Kerry Stokes Collection, Perth, LIB.2006.092.

looking up to Christ as he disappears into the heavens. Meyer Schapiro labelled this type of image of the Ascension 'the disappearing Christ'.[26] Such representations often show, as here, the impression of Christ's feet left on the Mount of Olives which was honoured as a sacred place by pilgrims.

In early medieval and Byzantine manuscripts illustrations of the Pentecost, which celebrates the descent of the Holy Spirit on the Apostles, Mary is often portrayed at the event as *Mater Ecclesiae* or Mother of the Church, surrounded by the twelve

26   See Schapiro, 'The Image of the Disappearing Christ' pp. 133–52. The first extant manuscript in England to portray a 'disappearing Christ' is the eleventh-century Missal of Robert of Jumièges of Canterbury. See also Deshman, 'Another Look at the Disappearing Christ', pp. 518–546.

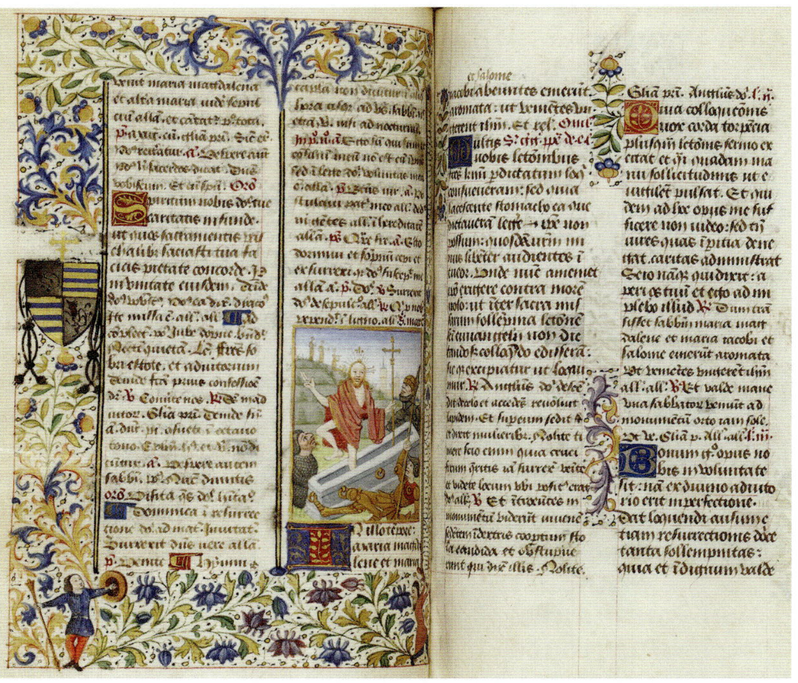

Figure 7.6: Associate of the Jouvenel Master, The Resurrection from *Breviary of Prior François Robert*. Folios 137v–138, *c*.1460–1470. Parchment, 16.4cm × 11cm. Kerry Stokes Collection, Perth, LIB.2006.092.

Apostles, the dove of the Holy Spirit, with golden tongues, symbolizing all the languages of the known world, falling on the assembled group. Such representations refer to a passage from the Acts of the Apostles (Acts 2:1-4), which relates how when the Christians were together in one place '... There appeared to them parted tongues as it were of fire, and it sat upon every one of them. And they were all filled with the Holy Ghost, and they began to speak with divers tongues, according as the Holy Ghost gave them to speak'.[27] By the mid- to late-fifteenth century, expanded compositions of the Pentecostal theme were relatively routine in French Books of Hours. The composition in Prior Robert's illustration has an extra element consisting of a host of figures represented by golden haloes (Figure 7.7). A

miniature from a Book of Hours illustrated by Jean Colombe in Bourges *c*.1475 also has a host of golden haloes, but with the addition of a haloed woman on either side of the Virgin.[28] A slight variation on both of these images occurs in the *Madrid Hours* made in Tours, *c*.1465–1470, where the composition has a large group of men (without haloes), and two haloed women on either side of the Virgin. These Pentecostal scenes refer to a passage in the Acts of the Apostles (Acts 1:13-15):

And when they were come in they went up to the upper room, where abode Peter and John, James and Andrew, Philip and Thomas, Bartholomew, Matthew, James of Apheus, and Simon Zelotes, and Jude the brother of James. All these were persevering with one mind in prayer with the

27   Challoner and Gibson, *The Holy Bible: translated from the Latin Vulgate*.

28   The miniature is from a Book of Hours sold at Christie's, 2 June, 1999, Lot 38.

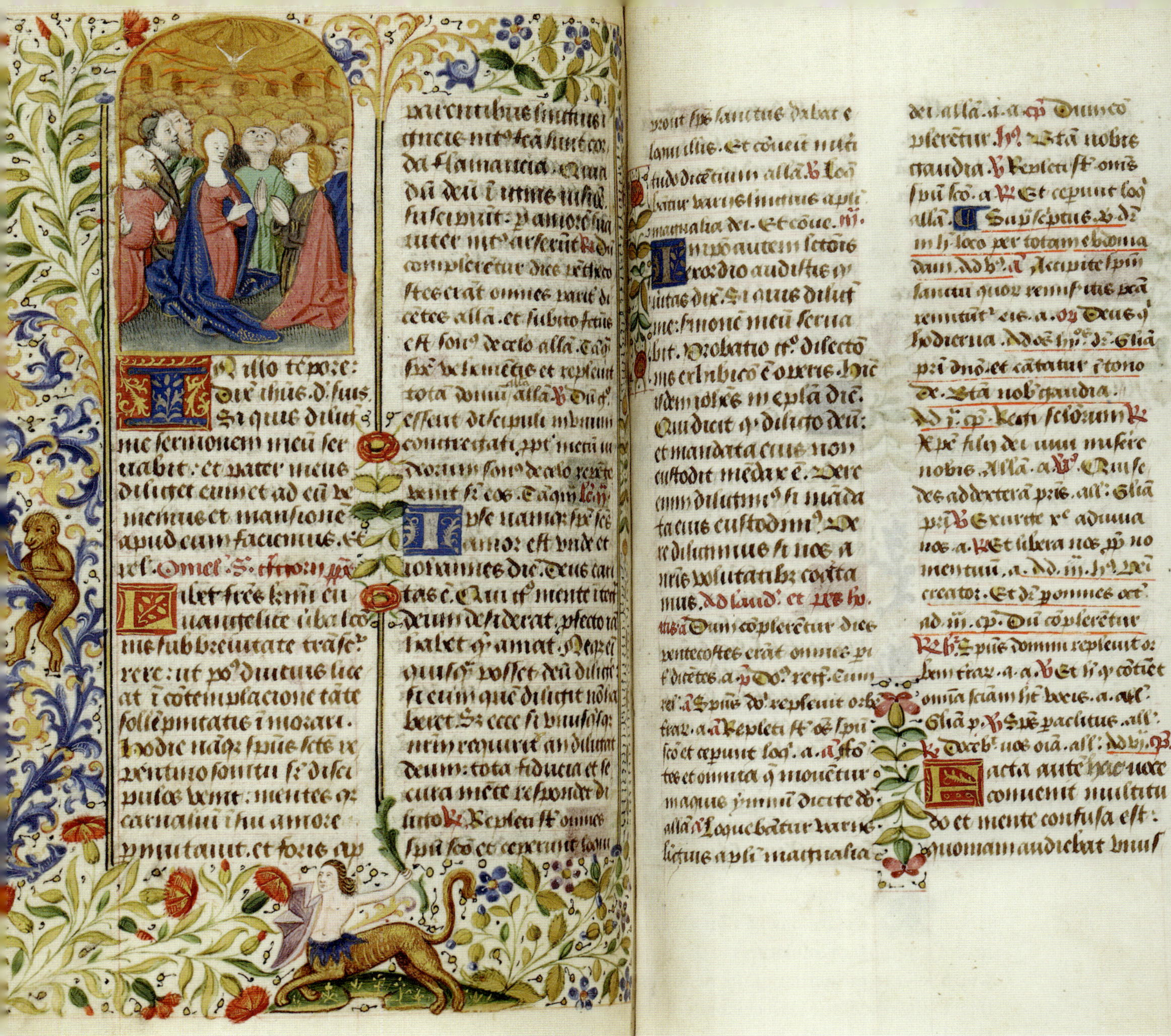

igure 7.7: Associate of the Jouvenel Master, The Pentecost from *Breviary of Prior François Robert*. Folios 174v–175, *c.*1460–1470. Parchment, 16.4cm × 11cm.
erry Stokes Collection, Perth, LIB.2006.092.

women and Mary the mother of Jesus and his brethren…Now the number of persons gathered together was about an hundred and twenty.[29]

The large number of golden haloes in *Prior Robert's Breviary* may have been due to the artist's knowledge of the *Madrid Hours*. Both people

and manuscripts were relatively mobile; thus it is not inconceivable that the illustrator of *Prior Robert's Breviary* and that of the *Madrid Hours* were aware of each other's works. Samuel Gras has noted that the Master of the Madrid Hours and members of the Jouvenel workshop worked in distant locations.[30] Moreover, the dating of

29   See Challoner and Gibson *The Holy Bible: translated from the Latin Vulgate*. Manion, *An Illumination*, p. 106.

30   Gras, 'The Master of Jeanne de France', p.159.

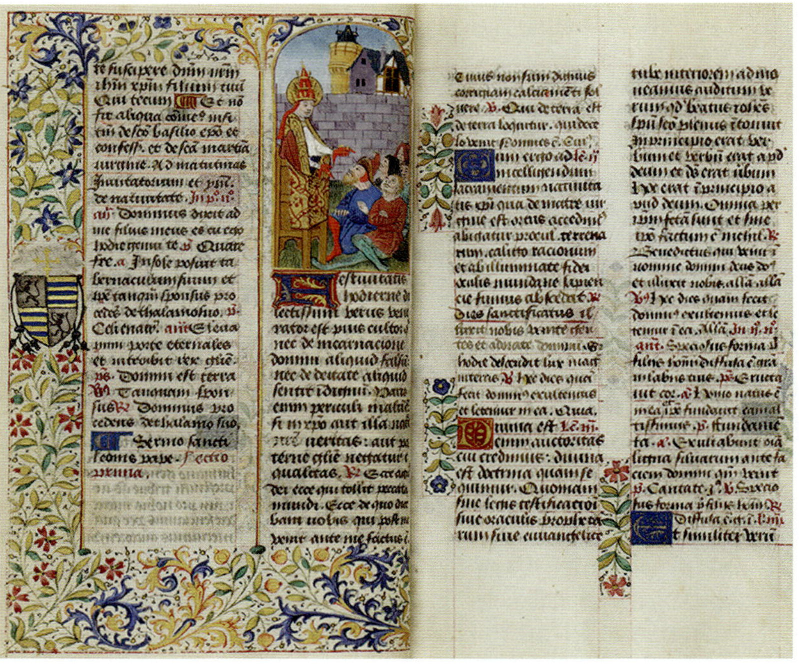

Figure 7.8: Associate of the Jouvenel Master, St. Leo the Great Preaching from *Breviary of Prior François Robert*. Folios 46v–47, *c.*1460–1470. Parchment, 16.4cm × 11cm. Kerry Stokes Collection, Perth, LIB.2006.092.

*c.*1460–1470 for the production of both manuscripts makes such a hypothesis feasible.

The illustration to the reading at Matins for January 1, the Octave day of Christmas, is the first of a number of miniatures in the Temporal which refer to the author of the reading rather than to the text of the feast celebrated. The text here is an extract from a sermon of the early pope, Saint Leo the Great. Instead of an illustration of the Circumcision, which is celebrated on this day, the introductory column miniature shows Saint Leo in full liturgical robes, standing in a pulpit outside a city wall as he addresses a group of lay men and women seated on the grass (Figure 7.8). He is usually shown either writing or dictating the text, or else, as here, proclaiming it to the assembled faithful. Such images not only fulfilled the need to relate the text but emphasized its authority, and they reflect an ancient tradition going back to the writers of classical literature.

In the Roman use, the readings at Matins for the Sundays and weekdays from Trinity Sunday until the beginning of Advent were taken from the Old Testament. The miniatures from the apocryphal Book of Tobias and the Book of Judith provide interesting examples of the distinctive treatment in *Prior Robert's Breviary* of different sections of the texts. The *Breviary of John the Fearless*, made in Paris, *c.*1412–1419, has a miniature introducing the Book of Tobias with the blind father Tobit welcoming his son Tobias and new daughter-in-law, Sara, together with the dog that accompanied them. This signals the happy ending to the story.[31] In *Prior Robert's Breviary* there

31   This manuscript is British Library Harley ms. 2897, fol. 252v. The Harley volume, combined with BL. Ms 35311, originally formed a single volume, illustrated by the Master of the Breviary of John the Fearless and others. Only Harley 2897 is fully digitized. For a full catalogue entry of both volumes, see Pearce, 'Text and Image'.

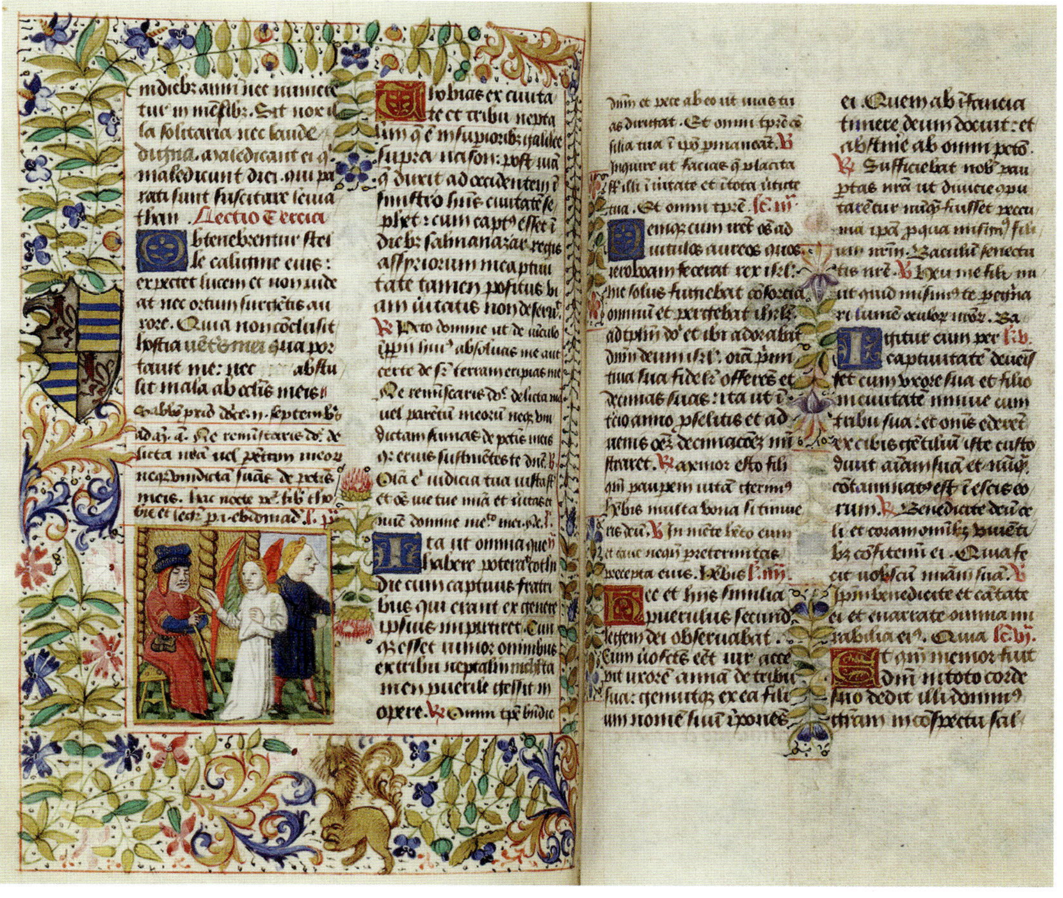

Figure 7.9: Associate of the Jouvenel Master, Tobias and the Angel from *Breviary of Prior François Robert*. Folios 204v–205, *c*.1460–1470. Parchment, 16.4cm × 11cm. Kerry Stokes Collection, Perth, LIB.2006.092.

is instead a depiction of the anxious parting of Tobias from Tobit, who sent him away from Ninevah with the words, 'May you have a good journey, and God be with you in your way, and his angel accompany you' (Book of Tobias 5: 21). Standing at Tobias's side is the archangel Raphael (Figure 7.9). The Book of Judith is usually illustrated with reference to Judith's decapitation of Holofernes. The miniature in *Prior Robert's Breviary* is dramatic in its presentation of this bloodthirsty theme (Figure 7.10). Judith is depicted holding a sword in one hand and the severed head of

Holofernes in the other. In the background, his headless body is visible through an open tent.

We do not know whether Prior Robert or the illuminator, or both, were involved in designing the Breviary's illustrative program. The visual imagery of *Prior Robert's Breviary* features many of the elements associated with the Jouvenel Master and associates, including the distinctive 'fouquetian' bright colours, throughout the manuscript and epitomized by the Judith and Holofernes miniature. There is, however, a certain *naiveté* in the presentation of the subject matter of the illustrations, which leaves it

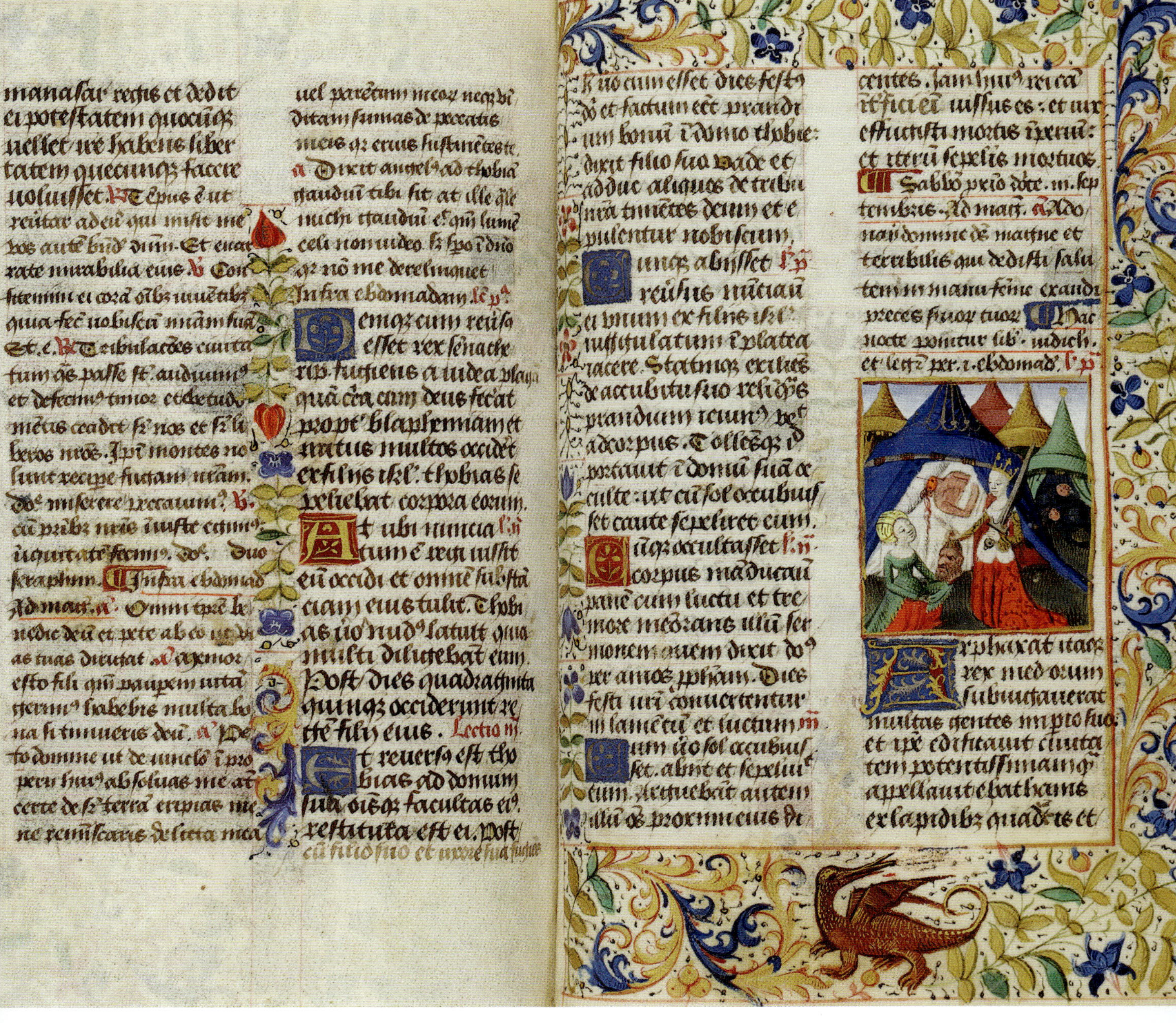

Figure 7.10: Associate of the Jouvenel Master, Judith and Holofernes from *Breviary of Prior François Robert*. Folios 205v–206, *c.*1460–1470. Parchment, 16.4cm × 11cm. Kerry Stokes Collection, Perth. LIB.2006.092.

open to a more in-depth comparative analysis with other works of the Jouvenel Group and of Jean Fouquet. Such a study would be greatly assisted by the recovery of the Breviary's lost Calendar (Sanctoral cycle) and Psalter. It is to be hoped that one day the missing sections of *Prior Robert's Breviary* will come to the notice of the public and perhaps reunited with the manuscript in the Kerry Stokes Collection.

About the author

Elaine Shaw has a PhD on the Patronage of Jean sans Peur, Duke of Burgundy, 1404–1419. She has been research assistant on several projects for Professor Emeritus Margaret M. Manion and is at present working on a book project on medieval Italian art history. eshaw@snac.unimelb.edu.au

Works cited

Jonathan Alexander, *Medieval Illuminators and their Methods of Work* (New Haven and London: Yale University Press, 1992).

François Avril, 'Grands et petit maîtres vers 1400–1415', in *Paris 1400. Les arts sous Charles VI*, ed. by Elisabeth Taburet-Delahaye (Paris: Réunion des musées nationaux, 2004), pp. 276–277.

François Avril, 'Le groupe Jouvenel', in *Les manuscrits à peintures en France 1440–1520*, ed. by François Avril and Nicole Reynaud (Paris: Flammarion, 1993), pp. 109–20.

François Avril, 'Les Heures de Jeanne de France: un chef d'œuvre du Maître de Jouvenel', *Art de l'enluminure*, 47 (Dec. 2013/Feb. 2014), pp. 4–28.

François Avril, 'Reproduction des miniatures des Heures de Jeanne de France', *Art de l'enluminure*, 47, (Dec. 2013/Feb. 2014), pp. 29–65.

Gabriele Bartz and Eberhard König, *Der Boucicaut-Meister: ein unbekanntes Studenbuch* (Ramsen, Switzerland: H. Tenschert 1999).

Miranda Bloem, 'Changing Workshop Policies: Passion Cycles by the Masters of Sweder van Culemborg', in *Usage of Models in Medieval Book Illumination*, ed. by Monika E. Müller (Newcastle upon Tyne: Cambridge Scholars Publishing, 2014), pp. 111–136.

Robert. G. Calkins, 'An Italian in Paris: the Master of the Brussels Initials and His Participation in the French Book Industry', *Gesta*, 20, 1 (1981), pp. 223–32.

Robert G. Calkins, *Illuminated Books of the Middle Ages* (London: Thames and Hudson, 1983), pp. 226–34.

Robert G. Calkins, 'The Brussels Hours Re-evaluated', *Scriptorium*, 24 (1970), pp. 3–26.

Robert Challoner and James Gibbons, *The Holy Bible: translated from the Latin Vulgate, diligently compared with the Hebrew, Greek and other editions in divers languages; The Old Testament first published by the English College at Douay, A.D. 1609, and the New Testament first published by the English College at Rheims, A.D. 1582: with annotations, references, and an historical and chronological index* (London: Baronius Press, 2007).

Albert Châtelet, *L'Âge d'or du manuscrit à peintures en France au temps de Charles VI et les Heures du Maréchal de Boucicaut* (Dijon: Editions Faton, Institut de France, 2000).

Christie's, *Books, Sale 6125, London, 2 June, 1999* (London: Christie's, 1999).

Robert Deshman, 'Another Look at the Disappearing Christ: Corporeal and Spiritual Vision of Early Medieval Images', *Art Bulletin*, 79, 3 (1997), pp. 518–546.

Christopher U. Faye and William H. Bond, *Supplement to the Census of Medieval and Renaissance Manuscripts in the United States and Canada* (New York: Bibliographical Society of America, 1962).

Samuel Gras, 'Les Heures de Madrid: un exceptionnel manuscrit inspiré par Jean Fouquet et le Maître de Jouvenel' *Art de l'enluminure*, 50 (Sept/Nov 2014), pp. 2–73.

Samuel Gras, 'The Master of Jeanne de France, duchesse de Bourbon: A Bridge Between Jean Fouquet and the Artists of the Jouvenel Group', in *Traditions on the Transmissions of Late Medieval Manuscript Illumination*, ed. by Christine Seidel and J. Corin Heyder (Frankfurt am Main: Peter Lang 2015), p. 145–169.

Christopher de Hamel, *The Armagnac Breviary* (Milan: Presse à Canard, 2006).

Nick Herman, 'Fouquet and the Absent Frame: Pictorial and Textual Relationships in the Hours of Etienne Chevalier', *Contrapposto* (2006), pp. 51–71.

Mara Hofmann, 'Haincelin de Hagenau et l'acanthe a Paris', in *Quand la Peinture était dans les Livres: Mélanges en l'honneur de François Avril*, ed. by M. Hofmann, E. König, and C. Zöhl (Berlin: Brepols Publishers, 2007), pp. 99–110.

Timothy Husband, *The Art of Illumination: The Limbourg Brothers and the Belles Heures of Jean de France, Duc de Berry* (New York: Metropolitan Museum of Art, 2008).

Noriko Kobayashi, 'La dernière étape de l'enluminure des Œuvres de Christine de Pizan', *Art de l'enluminure*, 18 (2006), pp. 2–41.

Eberhard König, *Boccaccio, Decameron: Alle 100 Miniaturun der Ersten Bilderhandschrift* (Stuttgart: Belser, 1989).

Eberhard König, *Französische Buchmalerei um 1450: Der Jouvenel-Maler de Genfer Boccaccio und Jean Fouquet* (Berlin: Gebr. Mann, 1982).

Eberhard König, *The Bedford Hours: The Making of a Medieval Masterpiece* (London: British Library, 2007).

Victor Leroquais, *Les Bréviaires manuscrits des bibliothèques publiques de France*, 5 vols (Paris: Protat Frères, 1934).

Margaret M. Manion, *An Illumination: The Rothschild Prayer Book and other works from the Kerry Stokes Collection c.1280–1685* (West Perth: Australian Capital Equity, 2015).

Margaret M. Manion and Charles Zika, *Celebrating Word and Image 1250–1600. Illuminated Manuscripts from the Kerry Stokes Collection* (West Perth: Australian Capital Equity, 2013).

Millard Meiss, *French Painting in the Time of Jean de Berry: The Late Fourteenth Century and the Patronage of the Duke*, 2 vols. (London: Phaidon, 1967).

Millard Meiss, *French Painting in the Time of Jean de Berry: The Boucicaut Master* (London: Phaidon, 1968).

Millard Meiss, Sharon Off Dunlap Smith, and Elizabeth Home Beatson, *French Painting in the Time of Jean de Berry: The Limbourgs and Their Contemporaries*, 2 vols (New York: Barziller, 1974).

M.A. Michael and Nigel Morgan, 'The Sarum Breviary in the Bodelian and Baillieu Libraries' *La Trobe Library Journal*, 51–52 (1993), pp. 30–37.

Nigel Morgan, 'The Book and Church Services: Liturgy and Ritual' in *The Medieval Imagination: Illuminated Manuscripts from Cambridge, Australia and New Zealand*, ed. by Bronwyn Stocks and Nigel Morgan (South Yarra: Macmillan Art Publications, 2008), pp. 70–71.

Susie Nash, *Between France and Flanders: Manuscript Illumination in Amiens in the Fifteenth Century* (London: British Library and Toronto: University of Toronto Press, 1999).

Stella Panayotova, 'The Rohan Masters: Collaboration and Experimentation in the *Hours of Isabella Stuart*' in *Manuscripta Illuminata: Approaches to Understanding Medieval and Renaissance Manuscripts*, ed. by C. Hourihane (Princeton: Princeton University Press and Penn State University Press, 2014), pp. 14–46.

Judith. M. Pearce, '"Text and Image" in the Salisbury Breviary (Paris, BNF ms lat 17294): The Decorative Cycle and its Paris Precursors', unpublished PhD thesis, Australian National University, Canberra, 1987.

John Plummer, *The Last Flowering: French Painting in Manuscripts 1420–1530* (New York: Pierpont Morgan Library and Oxford University Press, 1982).

Richard H. Rouse and Mary A. Rouse, *Manuscripts and their Makers: Commercial Book Producers in Medieval Paris 1200–1500* (Turnhout: Harvey Miller Publishers, 2000).

Meyer Schapiro, 'The Image of the Disappearing Christ. The Ascension in English art around the year 1000', *Gazette des Beaux-arts*, 6 (1943), pp. 133–52.

Rosy Schilling, 'The Master of the Egerton 1070 (Hours of René d'Anjou)', *Scriptorium*, 8 (1954), pp. 272–282.

Christine Seidel, 'Un livre d'heures Berruyer du XVe Siècle', *Art de l'enluminure*, 48 (2014), pp. 2–26.

Sotheby's, *Medieval and Renaissance Manuscripts London, 3 December, 2013* (London, Sotheby's, 2006).

Sotheby's, *Western Manuscripts, London, 6 July, 2006* (London: Sotheby's, 2006).

Eleanor P. Spencer, 'The Master of the Duke of Bedford: The Salisbury Breviary', *The Burlington Magazine*, 108, 765 (1966), pp. 606–612.

Patricia Stirnemann and Claudia Rabel, 'The *Très Riches Heures* and Two Artists Associated with the Bedford Workshop', *Burlington Magazine*, 147 (2005), pp. 534–538.

Elizabeth Taburet-Delahaye, ed., *Paris 1400: Les arts sous Charles VI* (Paris: de la Réunion des musées nationaux, 2004).

Inés Villela-Petit, 'Devises de Charles VI dans les *Heures Mazarine*, la personnalisation d'un manuscrit', *Scriptorium*, 55, 1 (2001), pp. 80–92.

Inés Villela-Petit, 'Grandes Heures de Jean de Berry', in *Paris 1400. Les arts sous Charles VI*, ed. by Elisabeth Taburet-Delahaye (Paris: de la Réunion des musées nationaux, 2004), pp. 104–109.

Jacobus de Voragine, *The Golden Legend: Readings on the Saints*, trans. by W. G. Ryan, (Princeton, N.J: Princeton University Press, 1995).

8. Chrysalis to butterfly: an aspect of the evolution of the Book of Hours from manuscript to print

Bernard J. Muir

Dunlop, Anne (ed.), *Antipodean Early Modern. European Art in Australian Collections, c. 1200–1600*, Amsterdam University Press, 2018

DOI: 10.5117/9789462985209/CH08

Abstract
This paper explores the continuities and innovations found in the Book of Hours during the early years of the Age of Print, with particular attention to the development of thematic border illustrations.

Keywords: Book of Hours; Incunables; Hardouyn Press; Border decoration

This essay is concerned with the innovations found in printed Books of Hours that mark them as a departure from the conventions of Hours recorded in manuscript form. This metamorphosis is alluded to here in the title, in reference to the emergence of a beautiful butterfly from a pupa; the latter morphs into the former, looks different, but is essentially the same. So too, many structural elements in manuscript Books of Hours are carried over into the age of print, but new elements are introduced which give printed Hours a revitalised and refreshing new look. This essay describes and discusses two hand-decorated, early sixteenth-century French Books of Hours held in the Baillieu Library of the University of Melbourne and the Art Gallery of Ballarat. These will be referred to throughout as the *Baillieu Hours* and the *Ballarat Hours*.[1] Both

are printed on vellum and then systematically and carefully illuminated, with metalcut border illustrations on the outer and bottom margins of their texts. Since these Books of Hours are hand-illuminated and on vellum it may be assumed that they were owned by people of some means, perhaps merchants or professionals. People of lesser means would have been able to acquire the same books, but these would have been printed on paper and not been hand-decorated at additional expense.

The observations here are specific, not generalised, since such a small sampling of a genre whose editions numbered in the hundreds, if not thousands, cannot be taken as necessarily representative. As will be demonstrated, however, the printed borders of these books are of particular interest since they are related to

---

1   The foundational studies of the medieval Book of Hours are: Leroquais, *Les livres d'heures manuscrits de la Bibliothèque nationale*; Harthan, *The Book of Hours*; Wieck, *Painted Prayers*; Wieck, *Time Sanctified*; and Duffy, *Marking the Hours*. See also: Smith, *Art, Identity and Devotion*, and Scott-Stokes, *Women's Books of Hours in Medieval England*. Wieck has more recently produced a succinct analysis of the origin and contents of Books of Hours, and observations on their use: 'Prayer for the People: The Book of Hours'.

metalcuts and woodblocks used by other contemporary printers and publishers; they are also the most unique or innovative features of these books, since the disposition of the full-page miniatures introducing the various canonical hours in them is for the most part conventional.[2] Illustrations were not legally protected in France until the 1520s; consequently, it is often difficult to determine whether metalcuts, woodblocks, and typefaces were owned, borrowed, or copied by those using them: as the printers and publishers resided cheek by jowl in the street opposite Notre Dame de Paris.

The *Baillieu Hours*

The Table of Contents at the end of the *Baillieu Hours* (folio m_{viii}) suggests that although preserved, it has suffered considerable loss at its beginning, since the first six items it lists are lacking (Figure 8.1a and 8.1b). It now opens with a much worn Annunciation miniature and the Hours of the Virgin (on folio a_i) – its covers had apparently been missing for a considerable period for the image to become so worn.[3]

The signature at the bottom of the page is 'a', which suggests that when the book was first compiled and printed, this was the opening page of the text. Preliminary matter in sixteenth-century books, however, was often either unnumbered or subject to a different numbering system. Moreover, it is not unknown for the preliminary matter to begin with an 'a' on its first quire and to have an identical letter used to identify the first quire of the text proper; indeed, that is a significant indication of the structural differentiation between the preliminary matter and the text. The *Baillieu Hours* also contains a Litany (folios f_i-f_v), the Vigils of the Dead, Suffrages to the Saints, the French *Chapelet* ('Rosary') and the Hours of the Conception of the Virgin. A folio, which was the first of the third quire and would have had the signature 'c', has been lost after the present folio b_{viii}; it would have contained the short texts for Prime from the Hours of the Cross and from the Hours of the Holy Spirit. The rubric for Terce for the Hours of the Virgin which begins on the present folio c_{ii} was also on the lost folio. The seventh folio in the 'l' quire is also missing, so that the opening of the prayer sequence for the French *Chapelet* is wanting after the present folio l_{vi}: the text continues on the present folio l_{viii}. That the borders on the left in the *Baillieu Hours* are painted confirms that there was originally a full-page miniature on the excised leaf, which was probably the reason why it was removed; whenever there is a painted full-page miniature in the *Baillieu Hours*, the metalcut borders on the facing page are also painted, providing each opening with an aesthetically pleasing and balanced appearance.

What has been identified as the only other existing copy of this Book of Hours is held in the Marian Library of the University of Dayton, Ohio, but it too is defective, unfortunately in the very places where information would have established beyond a doubt that it and the

---

2   See Harthan, *Book of Hours*, pp. 28–29 for a list of the subjects of the miniatures customarily associated with each Hour.

3   The Baillieu Library catalogue entry by Hilary Maddocks (UniM Bail SpC/RB 39A/16) notes that the book lacks its first three quires and the almanac for 1503–20; this information is derived from a comparison of the *Baillieu Hours* with another surviving book from the same publisher, although its printer remains unidentified (see below). More recently, Maddocks has stated that it was published in Paris by Anthoine Vérard around 1507–1508 (in Maddocks, 'A Book of Hours by Anthoine Vérard in the University of Melbourne Library', p. 15). In its present state, the *Baillieu Hours* lacks three folios, c1 (the conclusion of Prime for the Hours of the Virgin), c8 (the beginning of None for the same), and l7 (the beginning of the *Chapelet*). Folio c1 and folio c8 are conjugates and would have formed the outer sheet of the gathering, which suggests that they were either lost or excised when the book was unbound and awaiting rebinding.

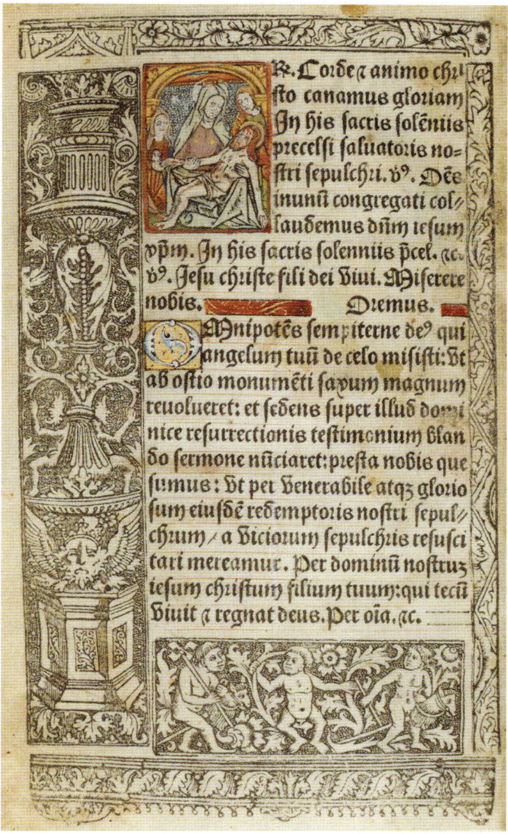

Figure 8.1a: Antoine Verard, Table of Contents from the *Baillieu Hours* (*Heures à l'usage de Rouen*). Folio m viii, not before late 1507. Vellum, 18cm. Rare Books Collection, University of Melbourne. G.F. Pendlebury Collection. UniM Bail SpC/RB 39A/16.

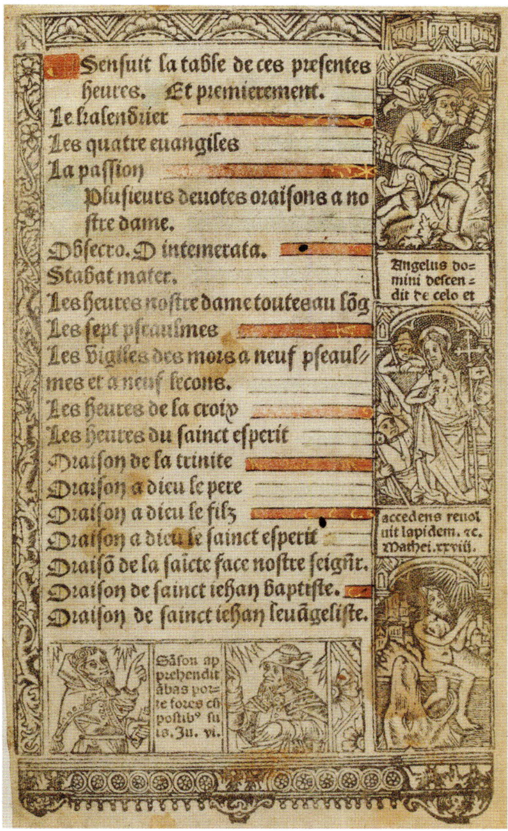

Figure 8.1b: Table of Contents from the *Baillieu Hours*. Folio m viii, not before late 1507. Vellum, 18cm. Rare Books Collection, University of Melbourne. UniM Bail SpC/RB 39A/16.

Baillieu Hours are siblings.[4] It lacks a Title Page, Colophon, Table of Contents, and a complete quire containing the Suffrages (prayers to the saints). Hilary Maddocks noted that the *Dayton Hours*' title page has the 'customary image of the Grail' of the publisher Vérard, and suggested that this was the publisher.[5] Vérard's device is, however, usually two eagles on a starred base,

supporting a red heart upon which are the three letters 'AVR' (or some version of this). The 'Grail' image was used by a number of publishers in the sixteenth century and it is not apparent why Vérard would have abandoned his customary mark for a more generic one; in any event, it is best not to refer to the Grail as his mark. When he does use the Grail at the beginning of an edition, he often has the 'eagle and heart' device elsewhere in the book, especially at its

4   Its shelf number is 'ML-F.B Catholic 1500?'; it is referred to as 'the *Dayton Hours*' subsequently here.

5   Maddocks, 'Book of Hours' p. 15, argues that these two books represent a previously unrecorded Vérard edition. The most comprehensive study of Vérard's publications is

by Winn, *Anthoine Vérard: Parisian Publisher, 1485–1512*. For a recent survey of the work of Vérard and other Parisian publishers and printers, see Reinburg, *French Books of Hours*.

end. In the *Dayton Hours* there is a prayer below the image of the Grail, *Benedictio dei patris cum angelis suis sit sup(er) me. Amen.* It is sometimes attributed to Vérard and appears in a number of his publications from 1500 onwards.[6]

A comparison of a folio from the *Dayton Hours* containing the text for None from the Hours of the Virgin reveals that its text and decoration are identical to the same double opening in the *Baillieu Hours* (folios d_iv-d_{ii}), which confirms that it was printed from the same plate. If the rest of the text proper corresponds exactly to that of the *Baillieu Hours*, this would confirm that they are indeed the same edition, as Maddocks concludes. The issues discussed below, however, demonstrate that there are some outstanding matters that need to be resolved before accepting this conclusion.[7]

In spite of the similarities between the *Baillieu Hours* and the *Dayton Hours*, there are several important discrepancies in their collation. The *Dayton Hours* has an almanac for the years 1503–1520 on the verso of its unnumbered title page, as is common in early printed Hours, but this is among the items absent in the *Baillieu Hours* in its present state. There is other textual evidence to indicate that the *Baillieu Hours* was originally intended to follow the Use of Rouen. There are characteristic responses in the Office of the Virgin and the Office of the Dead, and a number of saints honored locally are included in its Litany (folios f_iv-f_v).[8] Most significant, perhaps, are St Martial and St Ouen/Audoene (on folio f_{ii} and folio f_{iii} respectively); the latter was consecrated Bishop of Rouen in 641.[9] The 'RO' at the foot of the first folio indicates that the *Baillieu Hours* follows the *Usus Rothomagensis* ('Use of Rouen') and, indeed, there is a prayer to St Roman, the patron saint of Rouen, among the suffrages towards the end of the book.[10]

It is of considerable importance for this discussion that there is disagreement between the Table of Contents at the end of the *Baillieu Hours* and the actual sequence of the texts. The Suffrages or prayers on folios i_{iv}r-v to Saints Julian and Roman (Figure 8.2a and 8.2b) – which are unlike the other suffrages in the book in that they lack small miniatures depicting the saint – are positioned differently in the Table of Contents (m_8v). There they are listed *after* the prayer on folio k_v to St Anthony and *before* the prayer to St Anne on folio k_vv. There is no loss

---

6 There may be problems with this attribution, however, since a printed Book of Hours printed by Philippe Pigouchet for Simon Vostre on 16 September 1498 has the same prayer. It is also associated there with an image of the Grail according to the catalogue entry. It was sold by Christie's (Sale 2706, Lot 214, 9–10 April 2013).

7 I have not collated the books completely and in view of the discrepancies in their foliation I am reluctant to assert that they are siblings, especially given the further discrepancy between the Table of Contents and the actual disposition of the suffrages to Roman and Julian in the *Baillieu Hours* (discussed below). Jason Bourgeois of the Marian Library reports (in emailed private correspondence, 22/7/15) that the first quire in the *Dayton Hours* has 'RO' at the foot of the page, but lacks an identifying quire letter; it contains the Liturgical Calendar. The first folio of the second quire is numbered 'RO A', and begins with an excerpt from St John's Gospel. The first folio of the third quire is marked 'RO B' the text on it continues from 'RO A'. The remaining quires of the *Dayton Hours* are numbered a-l8. The *Baillieu Hours*, by comparison, has the collation a-m8, with pages c1, c8 and l7 missing (as noted above). Maddocks, 'Book of Hours', p. 24, No. 16, acknowledges that, 'it remains unclear as to exactly how the contents of the two copies differ.' Given that there were upwards of 2000 editions of printed Books of Hours published in Paris in the early sixteenth century, it is not unlikely that many were hybrids, with an earlier book being modified and used as the base text for a subsequent publication, as suggested below for the case of the *Baillieu Hours*.

8 Maddocks, 'Book of Hours', p. 17.

9 Other saints included in the Litany and usually found in books associated with Rouen are Sever, Austreberta, Hugh, Ursin, and Taurin.

10 Roman, who died *c.*640, was bishop of Rouen; for a brief biographical sketch see Farmer, *Oxford Dictionary of Saints*, p. 422. The letters 'RO' can also indicate that the Hours follow the Use of Rome: indeed, the *Ballarat Hours* uses this abbreviation for 'Rome'.

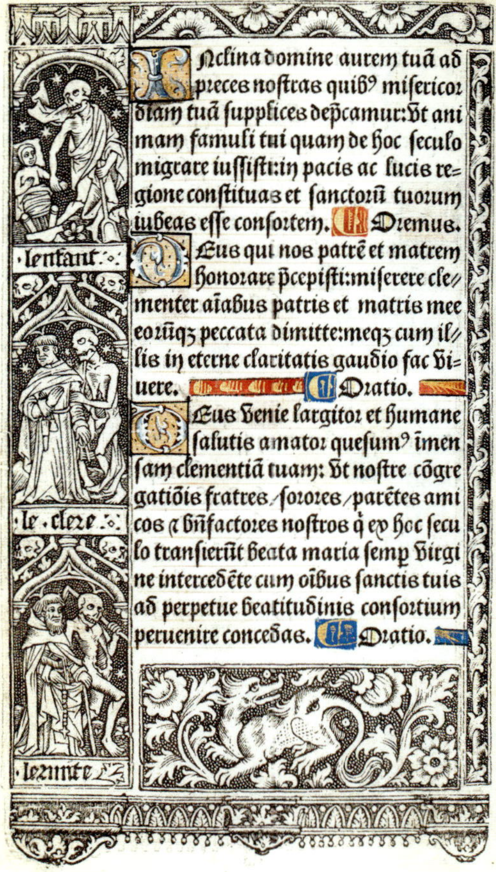

Figure 8.2a: Suffrages to Saints Julian and Roman from the *Baillieu Hours*. Folio iiv, not before late 1507. Vellum, 18cm. Rare Books Collection, University of Melbourne. UniM Bail SpC/RB 39A/16.

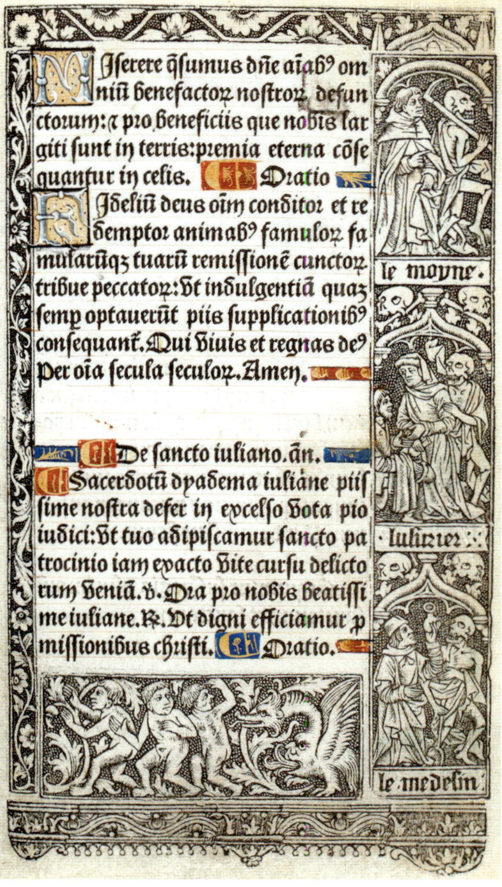

Figure 8.2b: Suffrages to Saints Julian and Roman from the *Baillieu Hours*. Folio iiv v, not before late 1507. Vellum, 18cm. Rare Books Collection, University of Melbourne. UniM Bail SpC/RB 39A/16.

of text at this point; the rubric for the prayer to St Anne is on the recto (of folio k$_v$) and the prayer itself begins at the top of the verso. That the prayer here was to Saint Roman, the patron saint of Rouen, may be significant in that the dislocation may have occurred when an existing Book of Hours was adapted for the Use of Rouen.[11] The *Dayton Hours* lacks this quire

and the Table of Contents, so it is impossible to know if it shared this inconsistency, something that would help to confirm its identity as a sibling of the *Baillieu Hours*.).

Table 8.1 compares the sequence of texts in the *Baillieu Hours* with the order in which they appear in its Table of Contents. The first thing to note, after the initial items not found in the *Baillieu Hours*, is that the Table of Contents indicates that the Hours of the Virgin are complete ('*toutes au lo(n)g*') and a discrete unit. The *Baillieu Hours*, however, represents the 'mixed' tradition

11   As noted above, it is unlike the other suffrages in lacking a miniature, as is the prayer to St Julian just before it on the recto.

Table 8.1: Comparison of the Text Sequence and Table of Contents in the *Baillieu Hours*.

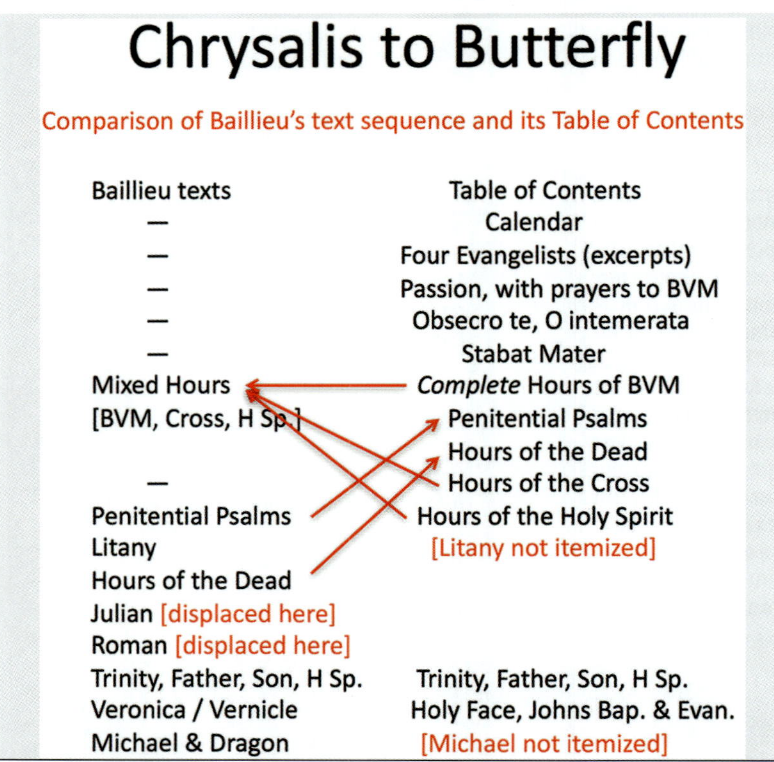

in that each of the various Hours is integrated rather than presented as a discrete unit.[12] In the Contents, the Hours of the Virgin are followed by the Penitential Psalms and then the Hours of the Dead. But in the text itself the penitential psalms come *after* the mixed Hours and before the Litany, which in turn is followed by the Hours of the Dead. Although the Litany is an essential

---

12   According to Harthan, *Book of Hours*, p. 17, the Hours of the Cross and the Hours of the Holy Spirit 'are both quite short, each Hour consisting of a hymn, antiphon and prayer but with no Psalms, lessons or responses. They usually come after the Hours of the Virgin, but sometimes appear in the midst of them, after Matins and Lauds, or they may alternate with them in what are known as "mixed Hours"'. The structure of the daily Hours in a Book of Hours mimics the structure of the *Opus Dei* as prescribed by St Benedict of Nursia (480–543 or 547) in his *Rule*, Chapters 8–19. A number of years ago, I argued that the fully developed Book of Hours of the fourteenth and fifteenth century can be seen 'in embryonic form' in an early eleventh-century book of private devotions, BL Cotton MSS Nero A.ii (ff. 3–13) and Galba A.xiv; see Muir, 'The Early Insular Prayer Book Tradition', p. 19. [On folios 105v-107v there is a series of short prayers (in Old English) to be said at the various 'Hours' of the day; it also has a Calendar, two Litanies, and the *Benedicite*, all constituents of fully developed Books of Hours. Of particular interest is a set of prayers in both Latin and Old English (ff. 110r-11v) for the Veneration of the Cross (*Adoratio Crucis*), consisting of a recitation of the *Penitential Psalms* integrated with the *Adoro te* petitions (attributed to Pope Gregory in the *Ballarat Hours*, mii, and in the *Baillieu Hours* lvr-v); this format seems to have been derived from the *Regularis Concordia*; see Symons, *The Monastic Agreement of the Monks and Nuns of the English Nation*, pp. 43–44.

feature of a Book of Hours, the Contents does not itemize it, but the omission of the Litany is not uncommon in printed Books of Hours. The two displaced suffrages to Julian and Roman follow next, and then the text and Contents align, but only briefly. After Veronica or the Vernicle – referred to as the 'Holy Face' in the Table of Contents – there are two prayers to Michael the Archangel, with a small miniature showing him defeating the Dragon. These texts are not mentioned in the Contents, which continues with suffrages to John the Baptist and John the Evangelist, Peter, Paul, James, and others (again agreeing with the text itself). The Table of Contents concludes with two further items following the suffrages: the Hours of the Conception and a prayer to the Holy Sepulchre. In the text proper, however, there are a number of items before the Hours of the Conception (which begin on folio m$_{iii}$). These additions include a set of prayers accompanied by a rubric indicating that Pope Boniface had granted an indulgence of two thousand years for their recitation, prayers attributed to St Gregory, and then the *Chapelet* (or Rosary) to the Virgin.[13]

The many disagreements between the Table of Contents and the text itself are enough to suggest that the Table of Contents in the *Baillieu Hours* may have been generic: that is, that it was used in more than one edition and was appended to this book even though it did not accurately reflect its contents and their proper sequence.[14] It may well be that the Hardouyn

publishers for instance also used generic descriptions on their title pages (see note 24). Indeed, the *Baillieu Hours* may not have lost any quires at all at its beginning – it may never have had them – so that the signature 'a' on its first folio denotes the actual original opening of the book. Given the dynamic nature of early sixteenth-century printing practices, such a proposal is not entirely unlikely, although it would be unusual.[15]

Turning to the decoration, the *Baillieu Hours* has borders that generally consist of fixed sets of devotional images, although a number of pages feature Renaissance-style secular images and motifs in their borders instead. The two major series of images repeated unsystematically throughout are either biblical or of the Dance of Death.[16] Pages of text facing a full-page miniature have painted borders (Figure 8.3a and 8.3b).

Here the miniature depicts Pentecost. The three metalcuts down the outer margin on the facing painted page depict biblical events with the theme of release or escape: Samson carrying off the gates of Gaza; Christ's Resurrection from the Dead; and Jonah being regurgitated by the whale. Many of the border metalcuts in the *Baillieu Hours* are similar or identical to those used by several other Parisian printers. Interestingly, its Dance of Death sets have

13   *Pape boniface a donne a to(us) ceulx qui diront deuotement ceste orayson q(ui) sensuit entre leleuation du corpus domini et le dernier agn(us) dei. deux mille ans de vrai pardon* (Pope Boniface has given 2000 years of pardon to all those who will devotely say this prayer which follows the Elevation of the Host and the final Agnus Dei). The pope here is apparently Boniface IX (1389–1404). As indicated above, the folio on which the *Chapelet* begins (lvii) has been excised.

14   Certainly, it was common for almanacs to be used in more than one edition and so to not always indicate exactly the year from which the book was first used.

15   That is, it may have been a bespoke book, made to order for a customer who perhaps did not require a calendar and the other items apparently 'missing' at its beginning. On the other hand, because the preliminary matter often had a discrete numbering system, it would have been easy for it to be separated from the book or misplaced during rebinding.

16   Thirteen sets of typological triads are used a total of ninety-two times, the least used set ('Elijah-Lazarus-Elisha') appearing twice and the two most common sets ten times ('Joseph-Christ Jonah' and 'Moses-Christ-Scouts & grapes'). The sixteen sets of Dance of Death triads are used forty-five times, ranging from two to four occurrences. When these illustrative sets were first used they would have been in a fixed order, but in time the border images came to be used randomly.

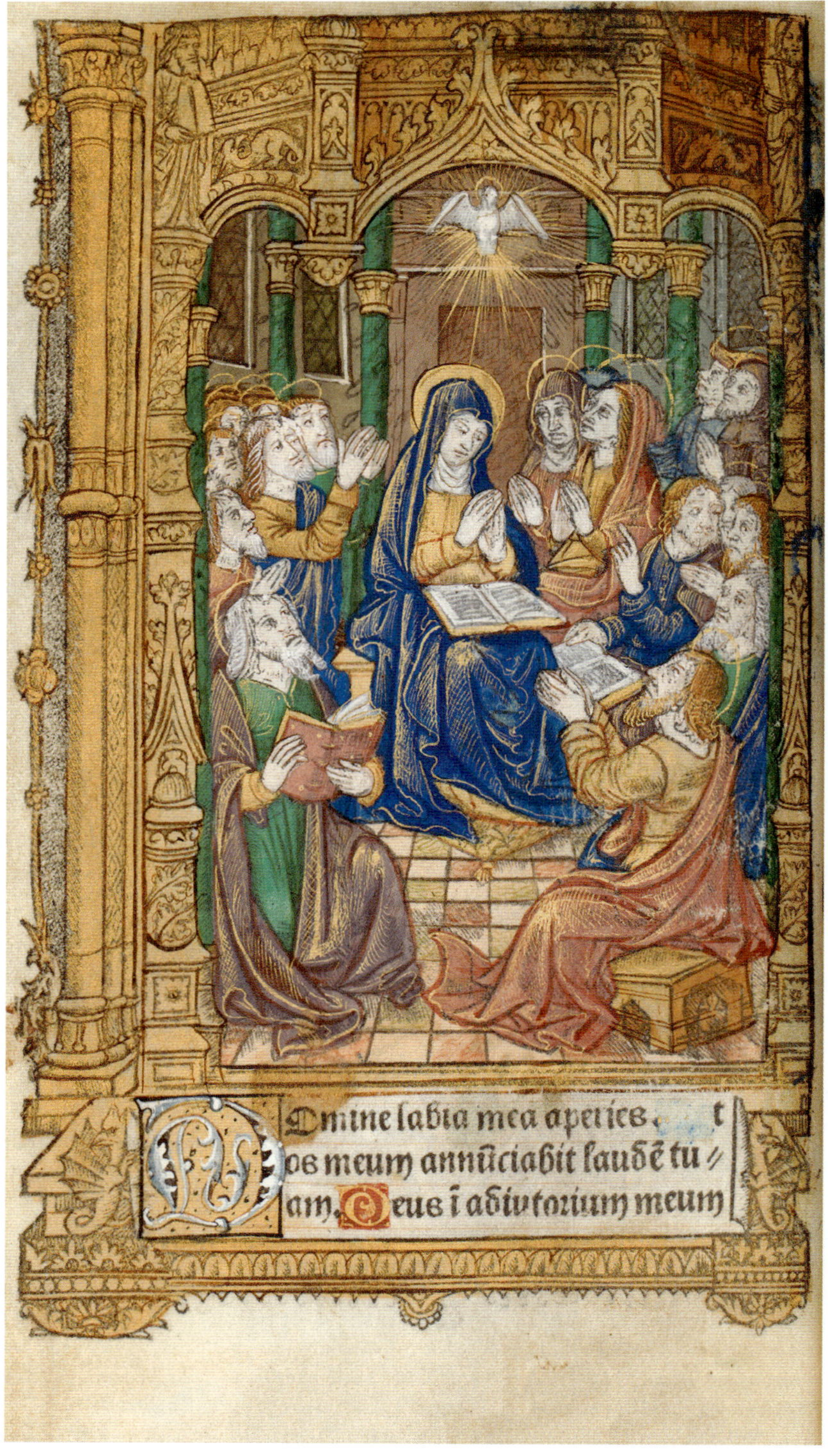

Figure 8.3a: Painted borders facing full-page miniature from the *Baillieu Hours*. Folio bvv, not before late 1507. Vellum, 18cm. Rare Books Collection, University of Melbourne. UniM Bail SpC/RB 39A/16.

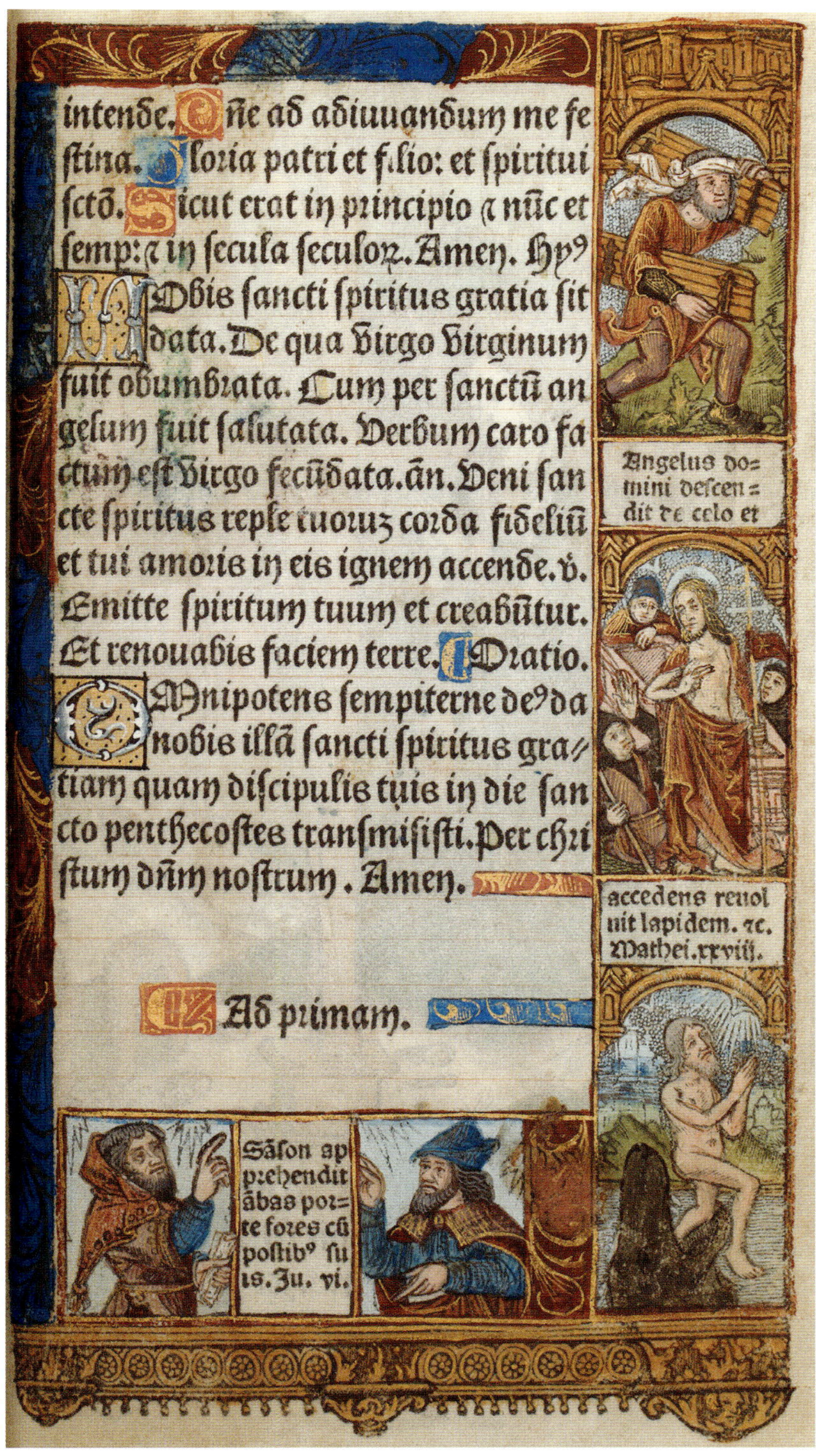

Figure 8.3b: Painted borders facing full-page miniature from the *Baillieu Hours*. Folio bvi, not before late 1507. Vellum, 18cm. Rare Books Collection, University of Melbourne. UniM Bail SpC/RB 39A/16.

Death positioned on the right, and thus resemble the woodcuts made by Guillaume Godard.[17] The biblical images are separated by quotations from the Bible, which include source references, such as 'Mathei iiii' or 'Gen iii', seen here (folios a$_{vi}$v-a$_{vii}$, Figure 8.4a and 8.4b).

The three images which appear in some borders are fixed sets, identical wherever they appear. For example, Esau sells his birthright to Jacob for a bowl of lentil stew; Christ is tempted in the desert by the devil; and Adam and Eve are tempted by a serpent with a female human head, which was common in fifteenth-century art. The text in two sections situated between the metalcuts in the outer margin identifies the middle image, the Temptation of Christ (Matthew 4). The text in the bottom margin between the two figures gesturing and looking upwards goes with the lower marginal image from Genesis 3, leaving the top image unidentified. The figures in the lower margin represent the Old Testament prophets from whose works the captions are derived.

There are thirteen sets of three biblical images used randomly ninety-two times throughout the book. Each of these sets has a common theme: they are derived from the fourteenth-century *Biblia Pauperum* ('Bible of the Poor') a well-known, popular woodblock book that used typological relationships between the Old and New Testaments for preaching and teaching. (Figure 8.5a and 8.5b).

Here the three metalcuts arranged vertically down the outer panel on the left depict Joseph being put in the well by his jealous brothers; Christ being laid in the tomb; and Jonah being thrown into the sea by sailors of Nineveh and about to be devoured by Leviathan. The exact

same series of images is arranged horizontally across the centre of the page in the *Biblia Pauperum* on the right (numbered 'g.').[18] Both the *Baillieu Hours* and the *Biblia Pauperum* feature identifying or source biblical passages and have depictions of Old Testament prophets and New Testament authors from whose writings the texts have been excerpted.

The illustrative tradition in which busts of Old Testament writers are placed at the bottom of a page in conjunction with the New Testament events that their writings foreshadow, goes back to the earliest surviving Christian illustrated gospel books. In the sixth-century Greek *Synope Gospels* (Figure 8.6) the busts atop the pillars filled with text at the bottom of the folio represent David and Isaiah, while the central scene depicts Christ healing two blind men (Matt. 20:29-34). Similarly, in the *Rossano Gospels,* also from the sixth century, there are often four Old Testament figures situated above columns of text containing their prophecies.

In the *Baillieu Hours* there are sixteen triads of images, used forty-five times in total, representing various social positions and grouped by sex (Figure 8.7a, 8.7b, 8.7c and 8.7d).

Different printers used varying numbers of triads. The printer Guillaume Godard generally

---

17   Maddocks, 'Book of Hours', pp.18–23, drawing on earlier research by Ina Nettekoven, Caroline Zohl, and Mary Beth Winn, provides a concise summary of the complex history of the metalcuts and woodcuts used by Vérard and other Parisian printers.

18   Labriola and Smeltz, *Bible of the Poor*, for g, see pp. 41, 126 and 171. Vérard developed a series of typological borders based on the *Biblia pauperum*, used as early as 1489. The *Bible Moralisée* worked in a similar way, using a less complex system of interpretation in which each Old Testament verse cited is interpreted to show its typological significance for New Testament events. For a readily available, extremely high quality example of this genre, see Guest, *Bible Moralisée: Codex Vindobonensis 2554.* Among fifteenth-century Books of Hours, the sumptuous *Rohan Hours* stands out in having captioned scenes from the *Bible Moralisée* in the outer margins of many of its pages, thus bringing the two genres together; Marcel Thomas notes that the inclusion of the *Bible Moralisée* material is 'totally unexpected' in a Book of Hours – see *The Rohan Master: A Book of Hours*, p. 21.

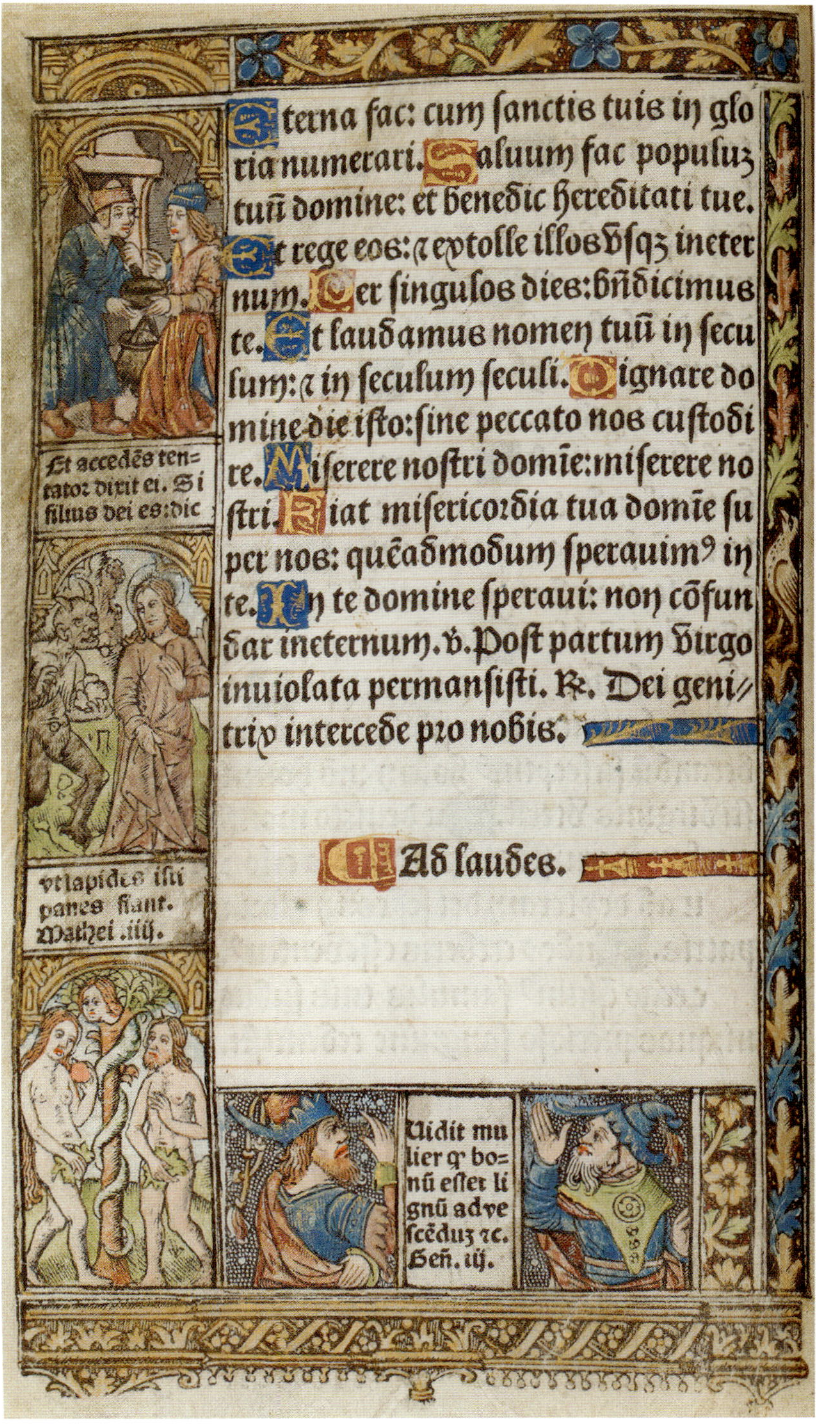

Figure 8.4a: Biblical images and quotations from the Bible with source references, such as 'Mathei iiii' or 'Gen iii', from the *Baillieu Hours*. Folio aviv, not before late 1507. Vellum, 18cm. Rare Books Collection, University of Melbourne. UniM Bail SpC/RB 39A/16.

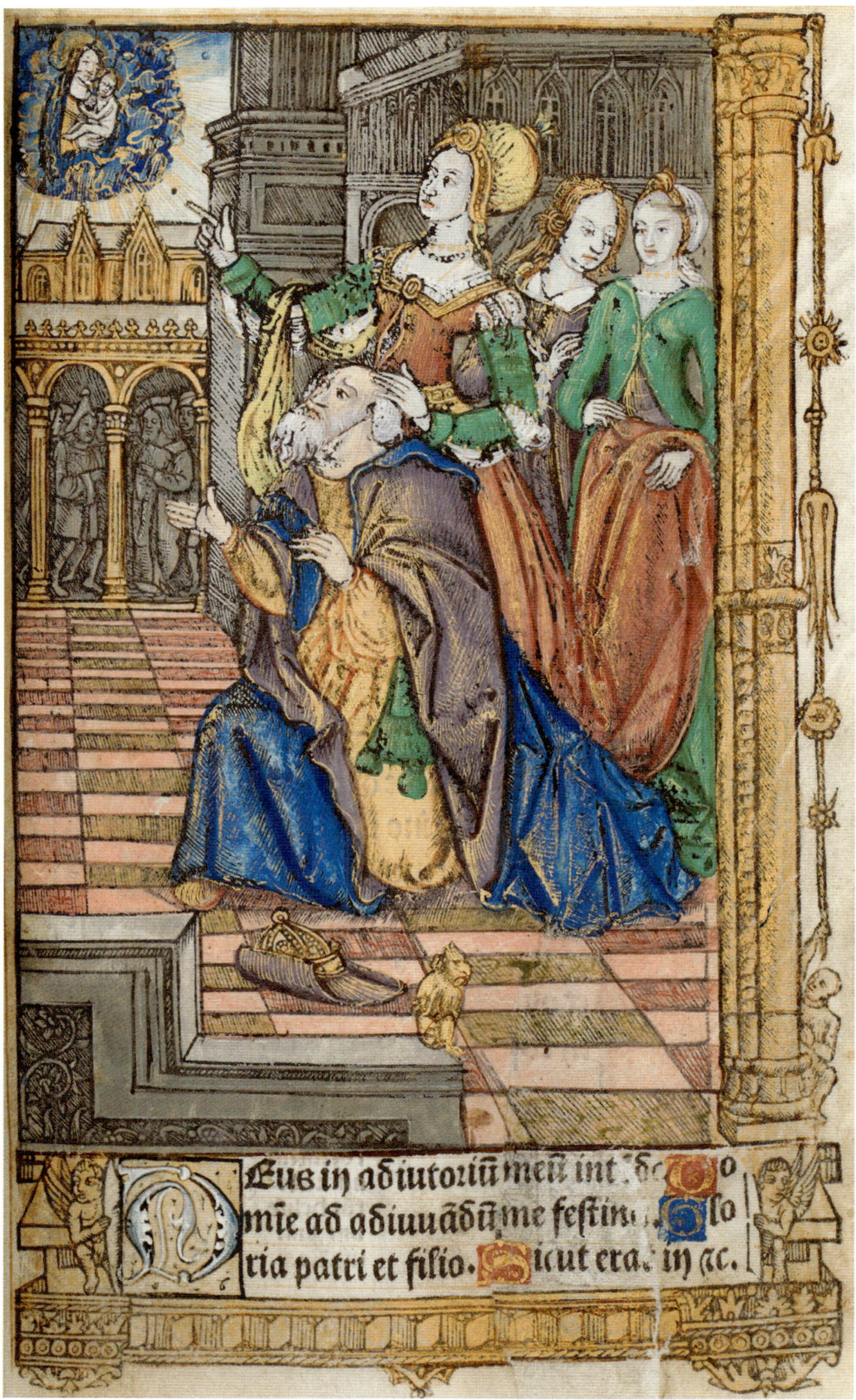

Figure 8.4b: Biblical images and quotations from the Bible with source references, such as 'Mathei iiii' or 'Gen iii', from the *Baillieu Hours*. Folio avii, not before late 1507. Vellum, 18cm. Rare Books Collection, University of Melbourne. UniM Bail SpC/RB 39A/16.

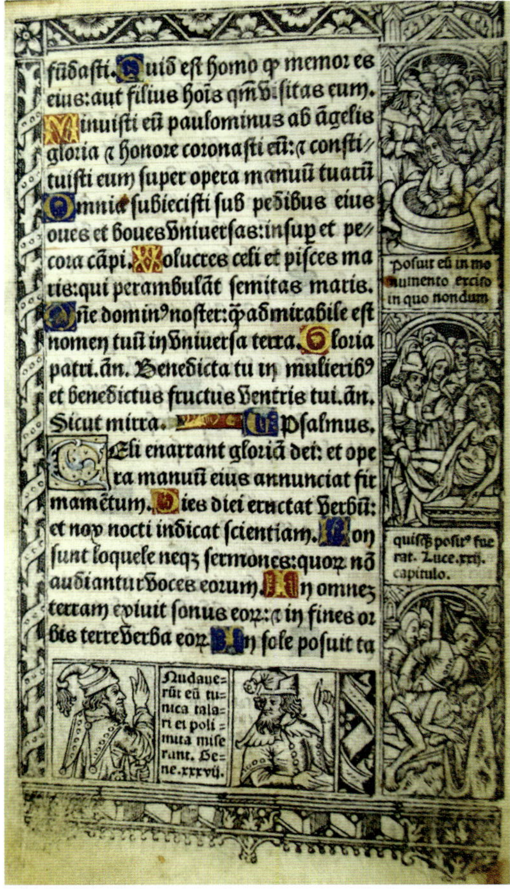

Figure 8.5a: *Baillieu Hours*. Folio 3, not before late 1507. Vellum, 18cm. Rare Books Collection, University of Melbourne. UniM Bail SpC/RB ⸆9A/16.

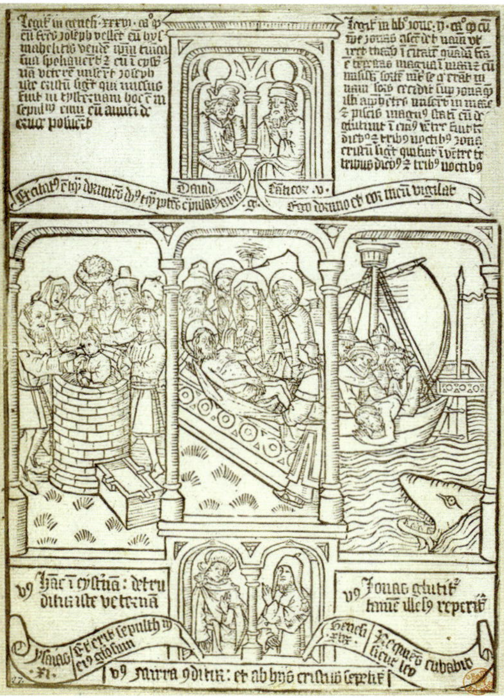

Figure 8.5b: *Biblia Pauperum* ('Bible of the Poor'). Page g, fourteenth-century. The British Library, London. BL Blockbook C.9.d.2.

The *Ballarat Hours*

used the same sixteen sets as those found in the Baillieu Hours, in exactly the same configurations of three characters.[19] Godard's images were woodblocks, not metalcuts; this is known because one of the blocks has survived. The resulting prints look slightly clumsy when compared to the sharp metalcut sets used for instance by the printer Simon Vostre.

The *Ballarat Hours* has a publication notice and so can be more readily dated and attributed. It was a gift from the Victorian parliamentarian Richard Crouch to the Gallery in 1944. It has a Title Page identifying it as an Hours of the Virgin following the use of Rome, illustrated with figures from Apocalypse and from Josephus' *Jewish Wars*, referred to as the *Destruction of Jerusalem* in the popular tradition, and with many other biblical figures.[20] There is

---

19　This may eventually prove significant in trying to determine the printer of the *Baillieu Hours*.

20　*Hore divine virginis Marie secundum usum Romanum cum alijs multis folio sequenti notatis: una cum figuris Apocalipsis et destructio Hierusalem et multis figuris Biblie insertis.* Many of these scenes of the Apocalypse can be identified, although some tentatively. There are different versions of John on Patmos, always on the recto of a folio (e.g. c1 and c2); otherwise, the Apocalypse images appear

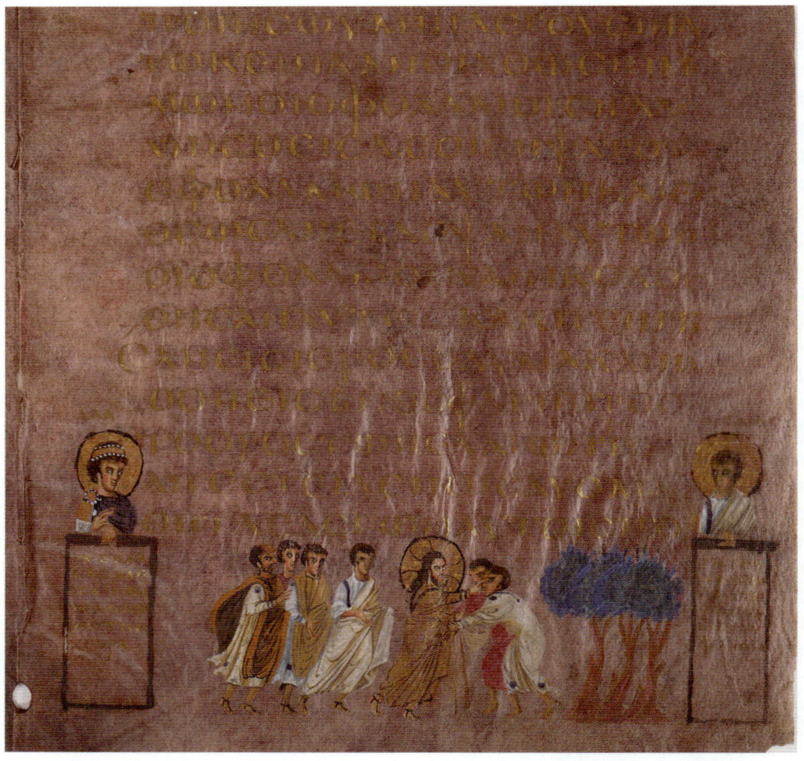

Figure 8.6: Greece, *Supplément grec 1286* ('The Synope Gospels'). Folio 29r, *c.*501–600, Parchment, 30cm × 25cm. Bibliothèque nationale de France, Paris, Department of Manuscripts. Supplément grec 1286 - bifeuillet 29/31.

also a shield intended for an owner's heraldic arms, but this has been left blank. The *Ballarat Hours* has an almanac (folio a$_{ii}$v) for the years 1518–1532. Its Colophon (folio m$_{viii}$) provides

on versos. Folio c1v (middle) shows the war in heaven, with angels fighting dragons; folio c2v shows an angel leading a risen person upwards. Folio d1v (top) has 6 (? not 7) candlesticks; (middle) depicts angels amidst clouds. Folio e3v shows riders on horses with lions' heads (it seems); (middle) depicts angels with trumpets. e6v (top) depicts a 'likeness' of God the Son in the clouds, surrounded by angels and holding a sickle (Apoc. 14:14,); (middle) shows an angel standing behind what looks like an altar, with a small crowd in the foreground. Folio g1v (top) shows mounted warriors, and (mid) shows three horsemen holding a bow, a sword, and scales (Apoc. 6:2-5). Folio g6v (top) depicts an angel holding a circular object (the great millstone of Apoc. 18:21?); (middle) shows Michael striking the serpent/dragon (Apoc. 12:7-9 or 20:1-3). These metalcuts are used a number of times throughout the book.

further information about the book's publication, attributing it to the Parisian printers and booksellers Gillet and Germain Hardouyn; it also provides a very basic list of contents.[21] The central image of Hercules rescuing Deianira from the centaur Nessus on the title page was Hardouyn's device. A more detailed Table of Contents on folio a$_{ii}$ concludes with the reassuring statement, *Omnia sunt summa accuratione impressa* ('all these are printed with the greatest accuracy').

21   The colophon tells us that Gillet's shop is located in the neighbourhood of Notre Dame bridge, in front of the church of St Denis in Carcare (Prison), at the sign of the rose, and that that of his brother Germain is located in front of the Palace at the sign of Blessed Margaret. The Hardouyns' motto (*Tout pour le mieux*, 'all for the best') does not occur in this book.

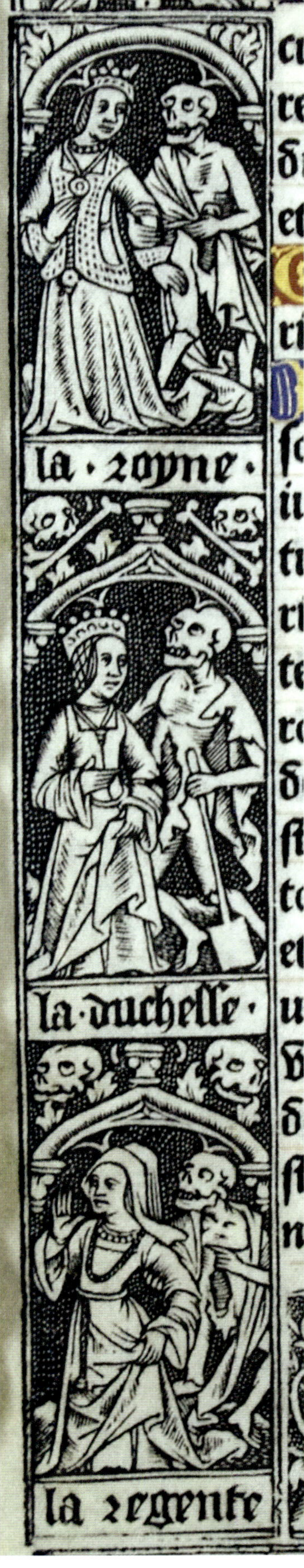

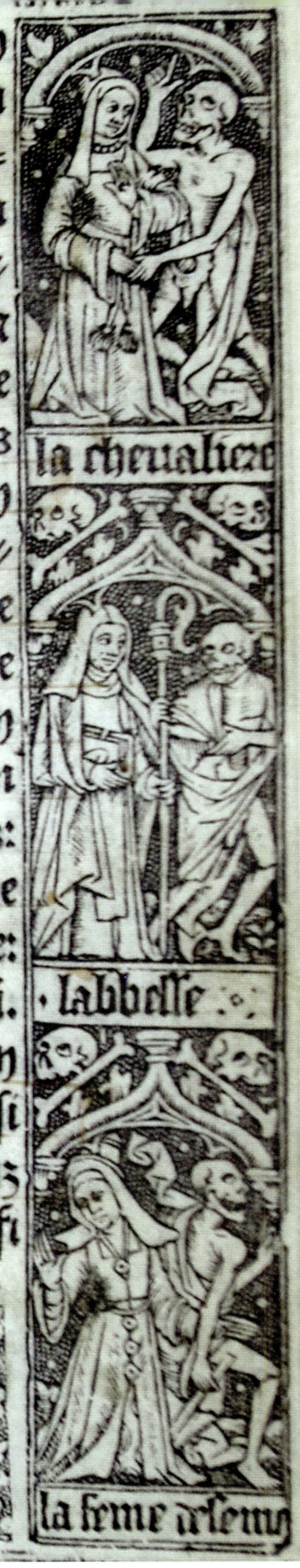

Figure 8.7a: *Baillieu Hours*. Folio 49v (detail), not before late 1507. Vellum, 18cm. Rare Books Collection, University of Melbourne. UniM Bail SpC/RB 39A/16.

Figure 8.7b: *Baillieu Hours*. Folio 60 (detail), not before late 1507. Vellum, 18cm. Rare Books Collection, University of Melbourne. UniM Bail SpC/RB 39A/16.

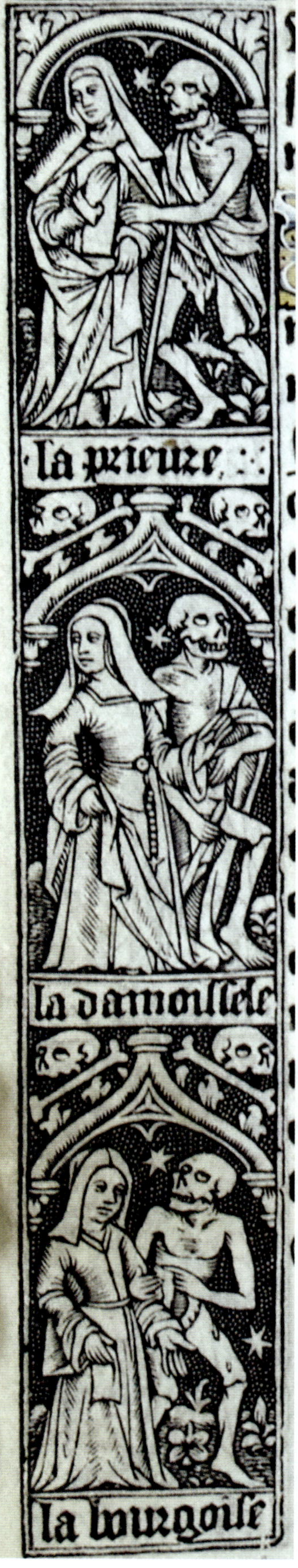

Figure 8.7c: *Baillieu Hours*. Folio 50v (detail), not before late 1507. Vellum, 18cm. Rare Books Collection, University of Melbourne. UniM Bail SpC/RB 39A/16.

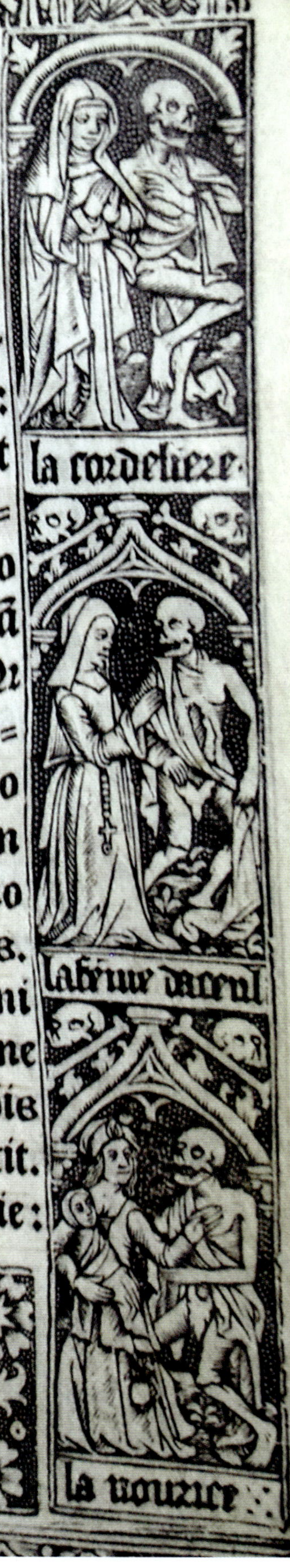

Figure 8.7d: *Baillieu Hours*. Folio 51 (detail), not before late 1507. Vellum, 18cm. Rare Books Collection, University of Melbourne. UniM Bail SpC/RB 39A/16.

The original series of *Destruction* metalcuts used in the *Ballarat Hours* was made for Hardouyn by Jean Pichore in 1505. A similar set was used at the same time by a competing publisher, Guillaume Godard, but these were copies of Hardouyn's, printed in reverse, probably to differentiate them from Hardouyn's originals.[22] The highly abbreviated captions describing these illustrations in fifteenth-century French are of considerable interest; they are transcribed in an appendix here.[23] The text is divided in two and placed between three smaller metalcut images in the outer margins (Figure 8.8), a *mise-en-page* that may be unique to this book.[24] The story of the *Destruction of*

Jerusalem was very popular throughout the Middle Ages and into the early modern period because it depicted the Emperor Vespasian, presented as a convert to Christianity, exacting revenge on the Jews for crucifying Christ by destroying Jerusalem and its temple.[25] Not only were series of illustrations of the *Destruction* common in Books of Hours, but they also had a separate existence as independent booklets or *bandes dessinées* of four or eight leaves, with full-page miniatures sometimes accompanying the smaller illustrations.[26] In the hours

22   One illustration contains the lamentation *'ve, ve, ve'* ('Woe, woe, woe'), which appears in Godard's work as *'ev, ev, ev'*, inadvertently revealing that the image was copied and printed in reverse by Godard; see Winn, *'La Destruction de Jérusalem, ter:* another "bande dessinée" pp. 213–37.

23   The captions are edited and translated here for the first time. I am indebted to Mary Beth Winn and to Véronique Duché for their assistance in deciphering them. A single illustration from this series (the second, depicting Pilate and the Council) occurs in the Gillet Hardouyn Book of Hours in the Kerry Stokes collection (LIB.2014.086, cviii), which is dated 8 March 1509, indicating that the *Destruction* series had by then been in use for some years; see Manion, *An Illumination*, No. 26 (it has an almanac for the years 1508–1520). It is interesting that the *Destruction of Jerusalem* images are mentioned on the title page ('… *avec les figures de la vie de l'homme et la destruction de hierusalem'*), since only one metalcut (of the full series of 21) appears in the book; this suggests that even the Title Page descriptions could also be generic and not refer specifically to the book as actually printed. The establishment of the original order of the illustrations is challenging because they appear in a variety of sequences in various Books of Hours and the captions accompanying them do not always describe the illustrations precisely or closely. Hillard proposes a logical sequence for the metalcuts ('Destruction de Jérusalem', pp. 315–16). Sometimes a single metalcut or woodblock image accompanies more than one caption, adding to the dilemma (in the *Ballarat Hours* the illustration of 'Pilate in Council' is used with two different captions).

24   In other Books of Hours and *bandes dessinées* the captions are formatted differently, often as three lines of text in prose beneath the illustrations, but sometimes also in verse set in double columns.

25   There is a detailed analysis of the development of the story of the destruction of Jerusalem and its illustrative tradition by Hillard, 'La Destruction de Jérusalem', pp. 302–40. She links its popularity at the end of the fifteenth century with the rise of anti-Jewish sentiment that resulted in the expulsion of Jews from France in 1498–1501. In the somewhat bizarre development of the story, the Emperor Vespasian, who is suffering from leprosy, is converted to Christianity and achieves almost saint-like status in the Church, as does the Jewish historian Josephus. His sacking of Jerusalem is interpreted as the triumph of Church over Synagogue, and the sacking of Jerusalem as an act of vengeance for the crucifixion of Christ by the Jews. For discussion of Vérard's playscript of *La Vengeance*, see Weigert, 'Anthoine Vérard's Illuminated Playscript', pp. 251–93. Winn, 'Another "bande dessinée"' p. 221, notes that Vespasian 'was revered as the ancestor to the French Kings', which may help explain why the *Destruction* was so popular in France.

26   See Hillard, 'Destruction de Jérusalem', pp. 326ff.; Winn also discusses these *bandes dessinées* and provides plates illustrating the integration of full-page miniatures into the 8-leaf version: Winn, '"La Destruction de Jerusalem", bis: a "bande dessinée" by Guillaume Godard', p. 9–41. The *Destruction* or *Vengeance* was very popular, in spite of, or perhaps *because of*, the gruesome events it depicts – killing and roasting a child, cutting open Jews in order to retrieve the treasures they had swallowed, the suicide of Archilaus, and Pilate's horrible death. Since the scenes of the *Destruction* are specifically unrelated to the texts they accompany, the violence they often depict seems gratuitous and perhaps reflects anti-Jewish attitudes prevalent throughout the Middle Ages: see Lipton, *Dark Mirror*. Both Hardouyn and Godard produced examples, but it seems likely that the idea originated with Hardouyn (see Winn, 'Another *"bande dessinée"*', pp. 221–22, for further discussion). Both Hardouyn and Godard include miniatures

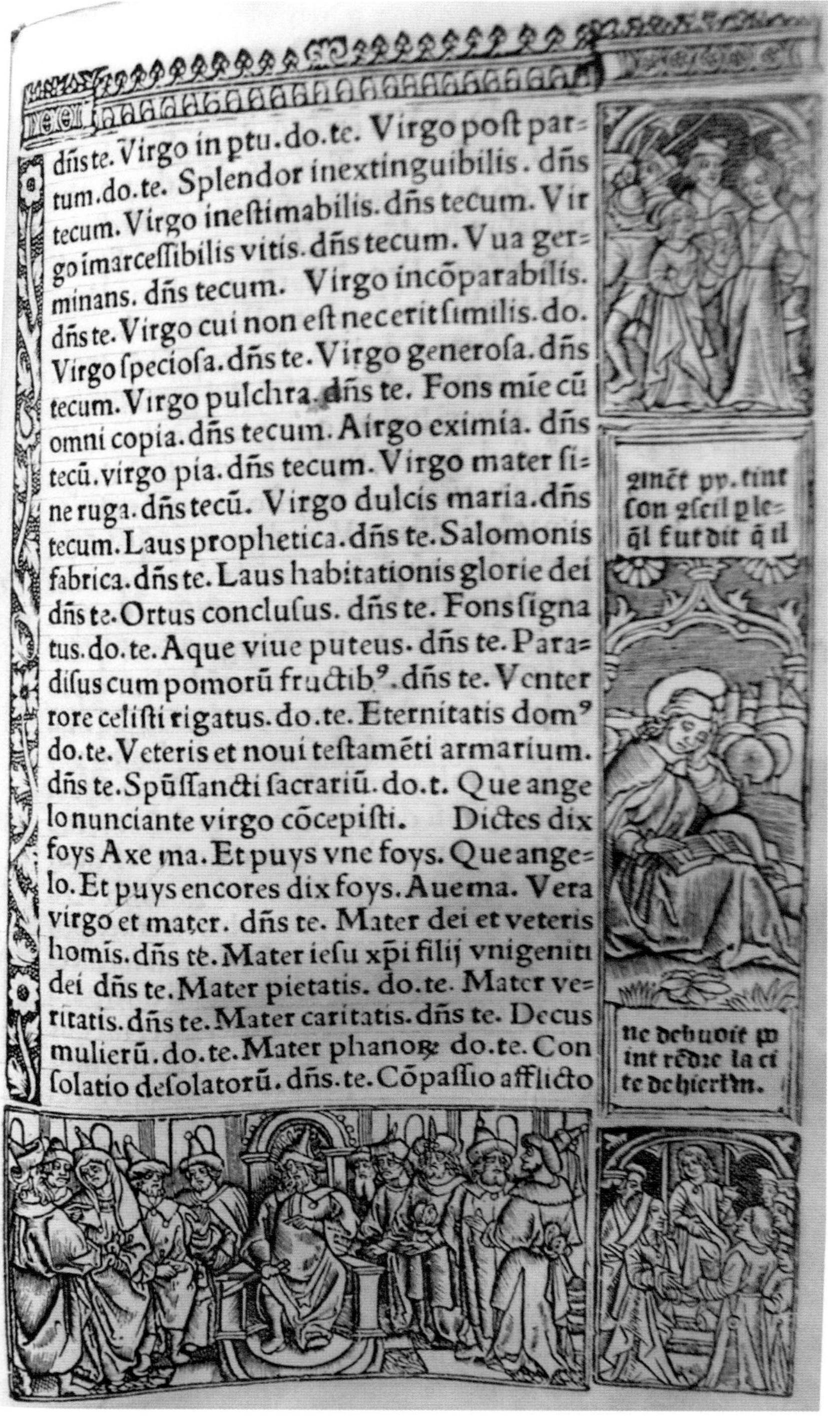

dñs te. Virgo in ptu. do. te. Virgo poſt par=
tum. do. te. Splendor inextinguibilis. dñs
tecum. Virgo ineſtimabilis. dñs tecum. Vir
go imarceſſibilis vitis. dñs tecum. Vua ger=
minans. dñs tecum. Virgo incōparabilis.
dñs te. Virgo cui non eſt necerit ſimilis. do.
Virgo ſpecioſa. dñs te. Virgo generoſa. dñs
tecum. Virgo pulchra. dñs te. Fons mie cū
omni copia. dñs tecum. Airgo eximia. dñs
tecū. virgo pia. dñs tecum. Virgo mater ſi=
ne ruga. dñs tecū. Virgo dulcis maria. dñs
tecum. Laus prophetica. dñs te. Salomonis
fabrica. dñs te. Laus habitationis glorie dei
dñs te. Ortus concluſus. dñs te. Fons ſigna
tus. do. te. Aque viue puteus. dñs te. Para=
diſus cum pomorū fructib?. dñs te. Venter
rore celiſti rigatus. do. te. Eternitatis dom?
do. te. Veteris et noui teſtaméti armarium.
dñs te. Spūſſancti ſacrariū. do. t. Que ange
lo nunciante virgo cōcepiſti.   Dictes dix
foys Axe ma. Et puys vne foys. Que ange=
lo. Et puys encores dix foys. Auema. Vera
virgo et mater. dñs te. Mater dei et veteris
homis. dñs tē. Mater ieſu xp̄i filij vnigeniti
dei dñs te. Mater pietatis. do. te. Mater ve=
ritatis. dñs te. Mater caritatis. dñs te. Decus
mulierū. do. te. Mater phanog do. te. Con
ſolatio deſolatorū. dñs. te. Cōpaſſio afflicto

Figure 8.8: Pilate with the Jewish Council (Destruction of Jerusalem) from Gillet and Germain Hardouyn, printers, *Book of Hours (Use of Rome)*. Page miii, 1518. Vellum, 19.4cm × 12.3cm × 4.8cm. Art Gallery of Ballarat. Accession no. 1944.34.

and *bandes dessinées* discussed by Winn the captions are much longer than they are in the *Ballarat Hours*, where they are truncated due to lack of space. These brief captions seem to have functioned essentially as mnemonics, just as the highly abbreviated rubrics did in Books of Hours and many liturgical manuscripts; it was assumed that viewers would know the story or text and only required a prompt to identify the illustrated scene properly. The subjects of the outer marginal metalcuts accompanying the *Destruction of Jerusalem* illustrations are often biblical or Christian and not related to the *Destruction* illustration; indeed, the rationale for associating these figures at all is unclear, as is often the case in these printed hours.

A second series of decorative border panels in the *Ballarat Hours* depicts the Dance of Death, a common artistic and literary motif throughout the Middle Ages that remained popular through the Renaissance and beyond. Quite appropriately, the Dance of Death images accompany the Vigils of the Dead, reminding the reader that death is the great leveller and will be suffered by rich and poor alike. The phrase *Omnia Mors (a)equat*, ('Death renders all equal'), sometimes accompanies his image in the Hours of the Dead, as in the Italian *Mirandola Hours*, from before 1499 (BL Add. MS 50002, folio 85).[27]

Unlike the *Baillieu Hours*, the *Ballarat Hours* is not 'mixed'. It is more traditional in presenting an integral Office of the Virgin, followed by other elements common to Books of Hours: the penitential psalms, a Litany, the Vigils of the Dead, the Hours of the Cross, the Hours of the Holy Spirit, the Office of the Conception of the Virgin, the Mass of the Virgin, more prayers to the Virgin, Suffrages to the Saints, and a variety of shorter prayers. The use of highly abbreviated rubrics, as noted above, reminds us that medieval and early-modern users of such books would have known the full texts from memory, having recited them repeatedly year after year; the rubrics thus serve primarily as mnemonics. The main illustration (at the bottom centre of the page) from the *Destruction of Jerusalem* is accompanied by biblical images in the outer border, which by their generic figural configurations are often difficult to identify (Figure 8.9); some, indeed, may not be biblical at all. The formulaic opening of the captions, such as 'Comment Pylate l'empereur et son fils Tytus...', suggest that they are either derived from or based upon chapter headings in a fifteenth-century French translation of the *Jewish Wars*. There is a manuscript of Josephus' works (BnF ms lat. 21013), made for the famous fifteenth-century bibliophile and patron Jean, Duc de Berry; its formulaic chapter headings generally begin, 'Comment...'. Although they do not correspond *verbatim* to those in the *Ballarat Hours*, they corroborate the assumption that such headings provided a template for its captions. In other printed hours, the *Destruction* captions are sometimes in verse in two columns or in a single block (as, for example, in a Godard Hours from *c*.1515).

In conclusion, the basic constituents of earlier manuscript Books of Hours largely remained the same in printed editions of the fifteenth and sixteenth century, and there

depicting the death of Uriah in these booklets, and Hardouyn also depicts David handing a letter to Uriah. This miniature of 'David Commissioning Uriah' generally precedes the penitential psalms in Books of Hours (as it does in the *Baillieu Hours* e3v and the *Ballarat Hours* folio 8); since Uriah the Hittite was killed during the siege of Rabbah [2 Samuel 11] after being sent to the front line by King David (so that he could have Bathsheba, whom he coveted), it must have seemed typologically appropriate to include this image in the group of metalcults depicting the *Destruction of Jerusalem*.

27   For this image, see Backhouse, *Books of Hours*, p. 62; the quotation is attributed to Claudius Claudianus (*c*.370–404), *De Raptu Proserpinae*, Bk. II, l. p. 302.

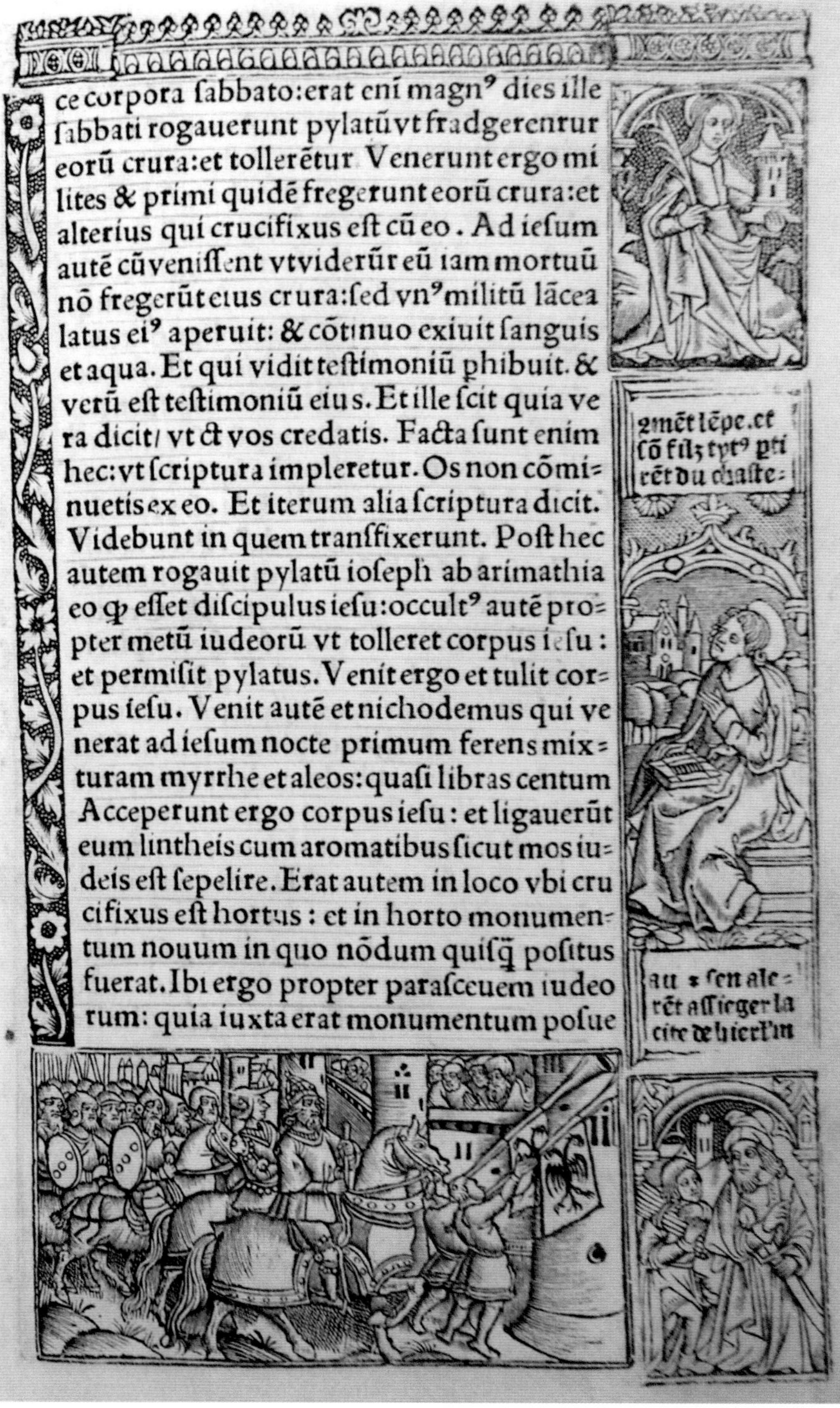

ce corpora sabbato:erat eni magn⁹ dies ille
sabbati rogauerunt pylatū vt frādgerentur
eorū crura:et tolleretur. Venerunt ergo mi
lites & primi quidē fregerunt eorū crura:et
alterius qui crucifixus est cū eo. Ad iesum
autē cū veniffent vtviderūr eū iam mortuū
nō fregerūt eius crura:fed vn⁹ militū lācea
latus ei⁹ aperuit:& cōtinuo exiuit fanguis
et aqua. Et qui vidit teftimoniū phibuit. &
verū est teftimoniū eiu s. Et ille fcit quia ve
ra dicit/ vt & vos credatis. Facta funt enim
hec:vt fcriptura impleretur. Os non cōmi=
nuetis ex eo. Et iterum alia fcriptura dicit.
Videbunt in quem transffixerunt. Post hec
autem rogauit pylatū ioseph ab arimathia
eo ⁊ effet difcipulus iesu:occult⁹ autē pro=
pter metū iudeorū vt tolleret corpus iesu:
et permifit pylatus. Venit ergo et tulit cor=
pus iesu. Venit autē et nichodemus qui ve
nerat ad iesum nocte primum ferens mix=
turam myrrhe et aleos:quafi libras centum
Acceperunt ergo corpus iesu:et ligauerūt
eum lintheis cum aromatibus ficut mos iu=
deis est fepelire. Erat autem in loco vbi cru
cifixus est hortus:et in horto monumen=
tum nouum in quo nōdum quifq positus
fuerat. Ibi ergo propter parafceuem iudeo
rum:quia iuxta erat monumentum posue

Figure 8.9: Gillet and Germain Hardouyn, printers. *Book of Hours*. Page biiii, 1518. Vellum, 19.4cm × 12.3cm × 4.8cm. Art Gallery of Ballarat. Accession no. 1944.34.

is considerable continuity in the illustrative program represented by their miniatures, yet new elements were introduced. In particular, the development and decoration of the borders in the printed books represent major innovations or transformations, with publishers routinely introducing structured series of thematic illustrations such as the Dance of Death, the *Destruction of Jerusalem,* the Apocalypse, or typological sets of biblical images derived from the *Biblia Pauperum.* The common practice among publishers and printers of borrowing metalcuts and woodblocks, or just plain copying, modifying, and reproducing them without permission, presents a range of challenges for researchers attempting to establish the relationship between individual versions of the same text, many of which, like the *Baillieu Hours,* are corrupt in places or lack clear Title Pages and Colophons that might have allowed their publishers and printers to be identified with certainty.

About the author

Bernard Muir is Emeritus Professor of English at the University of Melbourne. He founded the Bodleian Digital Texts Series at Oxford University in 2000, and is the editor of digital facsimiles of the 'Exeter Anthology' and 'Ms Junius 11'. He has also produced DVDs on medieval manuscript production and editions of classical and medieval Latin texts. bjem@uni-melb.edu.au

Appendix

Destruction of Jerusalem Captions in the *Ballarat Hours*

Comment Vaspasien qui estoit mesel envoya Gay son senachal en Hierusalem demander le tribut a Pylate ('How Vespasian, who had leprosy, sent Gay his seneschal to Jerusalem to demand tribute from Pilate')

Comment après que Pylate eust parlé [MS parler] a l'empereur manda son conseil lequel dist qu'ils estoient assés ('How after Pilate had spoken to the emperor he consulted his council and they said that they were [strong] enough')

Comment Gay amena la Véronique de Hierusalem pour donner santé a l'empereur adonc, etc. ('How Gay took the vernicle from Jerusalem to restore the health of the emperor and then..., etc')

Comment Pylate requist mercy a l'empereur. et parillement le roy Archileus lequel ne luy voulu pardon ('How Pilate asked the emperor for mercy, and similarly the king Archileus did not wish to pardon him [Pilate]')

Comment en Hierusalem menoyent grant ioye une voix vint sur la tour de Syon criant 've, ve, ve' ('How in Jerusalem during great festivity a voice came from the top of the Tower of Syon crying "Woe, Woe, Woe"') [*Jewish Wars*, 6.5.3]

Comment Vaspasien fist grant fosses autour de la cité et bailla. xxx. mille archirs pour affamer ('How Vespasian made great banks around the city and brought 30,000 archers to starve them') [*Jewish Wars*, 5.11.4]

Comment l'empereur et son fils Tytus partirent du chasteau et s'en alerent assieger la cité de Hierusalem ('How the emperor and his son Titus left the stronghold and went to besiege the city of Jerusalem')

Comment l'empereur demanda a Pylate purquoy il ne lui avoit envoyé le tribut, etc. ('How the emperor asked Pilate why he had not sent tribute to him')

Comment Pylate et les Juifz demenoient grant dueil a cause des signes a leur perte et confusion ('How Pilate and the Jews showed great sorrow because of the signs of their loss and confusion') [*Jewish Wars*, 6.5.3]

Comment Pylate fist sortir son armee et fut monstre beau miracle car entre. ii. iours n'eust point de nuit ('How Pilate sent out his army and there was a beautiful miracle, since between two days there was no night')

Comment Pylate fist enterer tous les Juifz que estoient mors pour la puenteur qui en sortoit, etc ('How Pilate had all the Jews who were dead buried because of the stench coming from them, etc') [*Jewish Wars*, 5.12.3]

Comment en Hierusalem avoit une raine convertie a la foy Jesuchrist fut constraincte tuer l'enfant de sa compaigne ('How in Jerusalem a queen converted to the Christian faith was forced to kill her companion's child') [*Jewish Wars*, 6.3.4]

Comment Pylate en passant par devant la maison de la rayne sentit le rost en envoya querir soudainement [*MS soude*], etc ('How Pilate while passing in front of the house of the queen smelled the roast and sent to ask for a piece') [*Jewish Wars*, 6.3.4]

Comment fut aporté devant Pylate ung cartier de l'enfant qui estoit roti [*MS rotir*] *pour son diner* ('How a quarter of a child who had been roasted was brought before Pilate for his dinner') [*Jewish Wars*, 6.3.4]

Comment avoit ung roy qui voyant [*MS voyer*] *que l'empereur l'avoit assiege* [*MS assieger*] *il se va tuer etc* ('How a king [Archilaus] who saw that the emperor was besieging him is going to kill himself')

Comment quant les Juifz ne sçavoient plus que menger tiroient le sang des mors pour menger ('How when the Jews when they no longer knew what to eat drew the blood of the dead to eat') [*Jewish Wars*, 5.10.4 and 6.7.3]

Comment ceulx de Hierusalem quant ils ne sçavoient plus que menger mengerent leur tresors ('How the inhabitants of Jerusalem, when they no longer knew what to eat, ate their treasures') [*Jewish Wars*, 5.10.1]

Comment Tytus donnoit en Hierusalem sus la mer trente Juifz pour ung denier ('How in Jerusalem across the sea Titus sold thirty Jews for one *denier*') [*Jewish Wars*, 4.11.5]

Après les Romains occirent les Juifs pour avoir leurs tresors qu'il[s] avoient mengé ('Afterwards, the Romans killed the Jews in order to have their treasures that they had eaten') [*Jewish Wars*, 5.13.4]

Comment Gay demanda a Pylate le tribut qu'il debvoit a Vaspasien lequel par mauvais conseil le refusa ('How Gay asked of Pilate the tribute that he owed Vespasian, which through bad counsel he refused him')

Comment on vouloit aller iusticier Pylate les dyables vindrent qui le confundirent en abis ('How they wanted to go to punish Pilate. The devils came who plunged him into the abyss')

Comment Pylate tint son conseil par lequel fut dit que il ne debvoit point rendre la cité de Hierusalem ('How Pilate consulted his advisers and they said that he should not surrender the city of Jerusalem')

Comment Gay raconta a l'empereur la fiere responce de Pylate, et incontinent manda son conseil et tout son ost pour aller en Hierusalem venger la mort nostre seigneur Jesuchrist, et montrer a Pylate qu'il luy devoit tribut. [second use of caption no. 2 above, Pilate and his Council.

Works cited

Janet Backhouse, *Books of Hours* (London: British Library, 1985).

Christie's, *The Collection of Arthur & Charlotte Vershbow, Sale 2706, 9–10 April 2013, New York, Rockefeller Center* (New York: Christie's, 2013).

Eamon Duffy, *Marking the Hours: English People and their Prayers 1240–1570* (New Haven: Yale University Press, 2006).

David Farmer, *Oxford Dictionary of Saints, 3rd edition* (Oxford: Oxford University Press, 1992).

Gerald B. Guest, *Bible Moralisée: Codex Vindobonensis 2554, Vienna, Österreichische Nationalbibliothek* (London: Harvey Miller, 1995).

John Harthan, *The Book of Hours, with a Historical Survey and Commentary* (New York: Crowell, 1977).

Denise Hillard, 'La Destruction de Jérusalem en bande dessinée' (Paris, vers 1515), *Bulletin du bibliophile*, 2 (1996), pp. 302–40.

Albert C. Labriola and John W. Smeltz, eds., *The Bible of the Poor [Biblia Pauperum]. A Facsimile and Edition of the British Library Blockbook C.9 d.2* (Pittsburgh: Duquesne University Press, 1991).

Victor Leroquais, *Les livres d'heures manuscrits de la Bibliothèque nationale*, 3 vols (Paris and Mâcon: Protat Frères, 1927–43).

Sara Lipton, *Dark Mirror: The Medieval Origins of Anti-Jewish Iconography* (New York: Metropolitan Books and Henry Holt and Company, 2014).

Hilary Maddocks, 'A Book of Hours by Anthoine Vérard in the University of Melbourne Library', *Collections*, 16 (June 2015), pp. 15–24.

Margaret M Manion, ed., *An Illumination: The Rothschild Prayer Book and other works from the Kerry Stokes Collection, c.1280–1685* (West Perth: Australian Capital Equity, 2015).

Bernard J. Muir, 'The Early Insular Prayer Book Tradition', in *The Art of the Book: Its Place in Medieval Worship*, ed. by Margaret M. Manion and Bernard J. Muir (Exeter: Exeter University Press, 1998, repr. 2006), pp. 9–19.

Virginia Reinburg, *French Books of Hours: Making an Archive of Prayer, c.1400–1600* (Cambridge: Cambridge University Press, 2012).

Charity Scott-Stokes, *Women's Books of Hours in Medieval England: Selected Texts Translated from Latin, Anglo-Norman French and Middle English* (Cambridge: Boydell and Brewer, 2006).

Kathryn A. Smith, *Art, Identity and Devotion: Three Women and Their Books of Hours* (London: British Library, 2003).

Thomas Symons ed., *The Monastic Agreement of the Monks and Nuns of the English Nation or Regularis Concordia* (London: Nelson, 1953).

Marcel Thomas, ed., *The Rohan Master: A Book of Hours. Bibliothèque Nationale, Paris, M.S. Latin 9471* (New York: George Braziller, 1973).

Laura Weigert, 'Anthoine Vérard's Illuminated Playscript of *La Vengeance Nostre Seigneur*: Marketing Plays and Creating the King's Image', in *the Social Life of Illumination*, ed. by Joyce Coleman et al. (Turnhout: Brepols, 2013), pp. 251–93.

Roger S. Wieck, *Painted Prayers: The Book of Hours in Medieval and Renaissance Art* (New York: George Braziller, 1997).

Roger S. Wieck, *Time Sanctified: The Book of Hours in Medieval Art and Life, 2nd edition* (New York: George Braziller, 2001).

Roger S. Wieck, 'Prayer for the People: The Book of Hours', in *The History of Prayer: The First to the Fifteenth Century*, ed. by Roy Hammerling (Leiden: Brill, 2008), pp. 389–416.

Mary Beth Winn, *Anthoine Vérard: Parisian Publisher, 1485–1512: Prologues, Poems and Presentations* (Geneva: Librarie Droz, 1997).

Mary Beth Winn, 'La Destruction de Jerusalem, bis: a "bande dessinée" by Guillaume Godard', *Bulletin du bibliophile*,1 (2008), pp. 9–41.

Mary Beth Winn, 'La Destruction de Jérusalem, ter: another "bande dessinée" by Gillet Hardouyn', *Bulletin du bibliophile*, 2 (2011), pp. 213–37.

9. The Sorbonne Press and the chancellor's manuscript

Jan Fox

Dunlop, Anne (ed.), *Antipodean Early Modern. European Art in Australian Collections, c. 1200–1600*, Amsterdam University Press, 2018

DOI: 10.5117/9789462985209/CH09

Abstract

This manuscript of Juvenal's *Satires* was prepared for presentation in 1472 to the new Chancellor of France, Pierre Doriole. It was commissioned by the Sorbonne Press, the first printing press in France, established in 1470 by two academic humanists, Guillaume Fichet and Johannes Heynlin. Enthusiastic for the new way of 'writing' – *'nova ars scribendi'* – they prepared copies of their printed books for presentation to important recipients, adding traditionally-structured illuminated frontispieces. This elegant copy of Juvenal's *Satires* is one of these, and is particularly interesting. It is a manuscript (not printed), its frontispiece is intriguingly like no other, and the circumstances of its presentation are mysterious. This essay addresses the unusual aspects of the manuscript.

Keywords: Sorbonne Press; Presentation; Manuscripts; Frontispiece; Juvenal *Satires*; Pierr Doriole

One of the very important medieval illuminated manuscripts in the Stokes Collection is an elegant copy of the *Satires* by the Roman author Juvenal. This manuscript was made in 1472 for presentation to the Chancellor of France, Pierre Doriole, and it is beautifully illuminated, with a large presentation frontispiece miniature (Figure 9.1) a historiated initial at the beginning of each of the satires, and partial borders of intertwined flowers and acanthus leaves throughout.[1] Such richness is reason enough to examine and value this manuscript, but it has, in addition, some particularly unusual elements.

Although a manuscript, it was made for the first printing press established in Paris, known as the Sorbonne Press; offered as a gift to one of the most powerful men in France, its large presentation miniature is unconventional and intriguing. This essay will consider the unusual aspects of the Juvenal manuscript in relation to its context, the Sorbonne Press, and to the late medieval practice of presentation manuscripts, and it will attempt to decode the curious frontispiece miniature. Basic to this discussion is the splendid research of Anatole Claudin, the late nineteenth century bibliophile bookseller, who owned this manuscript at one time.[2]

1   See Manion, 'Juvenal, Sixteen Satires', Cat. 30, pp. 114–17, for a full technical description of this manuscript.

2   Claudin, *The first Paris Press*.

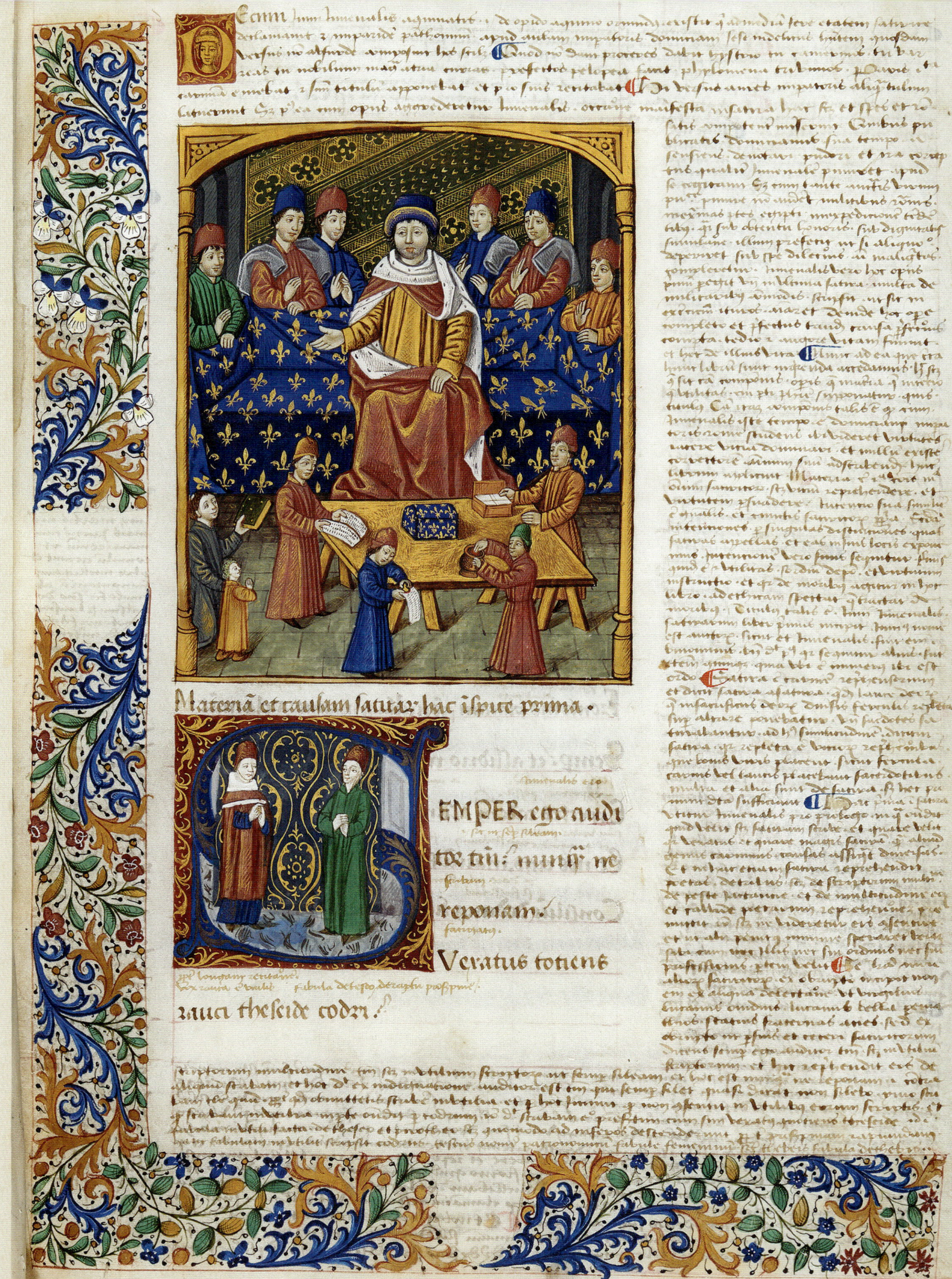
Materná et causam satuar hac ispue prima.
SEMPER ego audi
tor tantū: nunq̃ ne
reponam.
Veratus totiens
raua theseide codri.

The Sorbonne Press was established in 1470 by Johannes Heynlin, Prior of the Sorbonne and previously Rector of the University of Paris, and by Guillaume Fichet, who had also been Rector of the University of Paris, and was at the time Librarian of the Sorbonne. Both Heynlin and Fichet were early humanists, keen to obtain reliable texts of ancient classics and contemporary examples of Italian humanist thought, and they were attracted by the ability of the new movable-type printing press invented by Johannes Gutenberg in Germany to provide multiple correct copies free from scribal corruption.[3] To this end, Heynlin brought to Paris two German printers, Ulrich Gering and Martin Crantz, and a former fellow student, Michael Friburger, an academic experienced in printing.[4] Although the Press was housed in the library at the university and came to be called the Sorbonne Press, there is no evidence that the university made any financial contribution to it. During the approximately two and a half years of its existence, it printed twenty-two books, an astonishing number for such a small concern. The *Satires* of Juvenal was the seventeenth. The Sorbonne Press ceased production in its original form at the end of 1472, for political and health reasons of its principals. In 1473, it was taken over by the printers originally brought by Heynlin from Germany, who changed its character, scope, and the selection of books it published. Another figure, Erhard Windsberg, became more prominent, although

little is known about him; he may have been a friend of the German-born Heynlin as he briefly replaced him as the corrector of copy.

There is no indication that either Fichet or Heynlin was interested in the commercial possibilities of a printing press and its ability to produce very large numbers of books.[5] From the first they were lavish in their gifts of books to friends and supporters, with attached letters from Fichet or Heynlin expressing their excitement at the 'almost divine art' that made such copies possible. Funds were provided by Fichet, whose protector and mentor, Cardinal Jehan Rolin, Bishop of Autun, 'supplied him liberally with money'.[6] Indeed, when Cardinal Bessarion paid Fichet's messenger fifteen ducats to cover the expenses of printing Bessarion's *Orationes,* Fichet refused to accept it and instructed the messengers delivering copies to others that they 'were not to accept any money from any of them'.[7] Print runs were probably quite small, with the consequence that books from the Sorbonne Press are exceedingly rare. Printed copies of the Juvenal are now almost as rare as this manuscript copy.

The method of production was as careful as one might expect from these two scholars. Heynlin meticulously prepared the exemplars for the printers, using several different scribal versions of each text for the greatest possible accuracy. He also corrected each page when it was set, a task made as easy as possible for his poor eyesight by the large roman font they had chosen. This font, associated with Italian humanists, was a departure from the more familiar gothic font used by Gutenberg.[8] There was some resistance to this font and criticism of it

3   See Claudin, *The first Paris Press*, p. 72 for the text of a letter from Fichet to a former pupil, Robert Gaugin, which accompanied a gift of their second printed book. In it he states that 'the art of printing was first of all invented by Johannes Gutenberg'. Claudin says that 'this is the first authentic statement of the claim of Gutenberg to be the real inventor of printing ...', p. 5.

4   For discussion supplementary to Claudin, *The first Paris Press*, see McMurtrie, *Proofreading in the Fifteenth Century.*

5   Meserve, 'Patronage and Propaganda at the First Paris Press', pp. 521–88, particularly. p. 554n.

6   Claudin, *The first Paris Press*, p. 3.

7   Claudin, *The first Paris Press*, p. 44, n. 81.

8   Se Booton, 'Guillaume Fichet's Literary Gift to Duke François II of Brittany', pp. 121–130.

Figure 9.1: Tours, Frontispiece from Juvenal, *Sixteen Satires (with marginal and interlinear glosses).* Folio 4, *c.*1472. Parchment, 30cm × 20.7cm. Kerry Stokes Collection, Perth. LIB.2014.230.

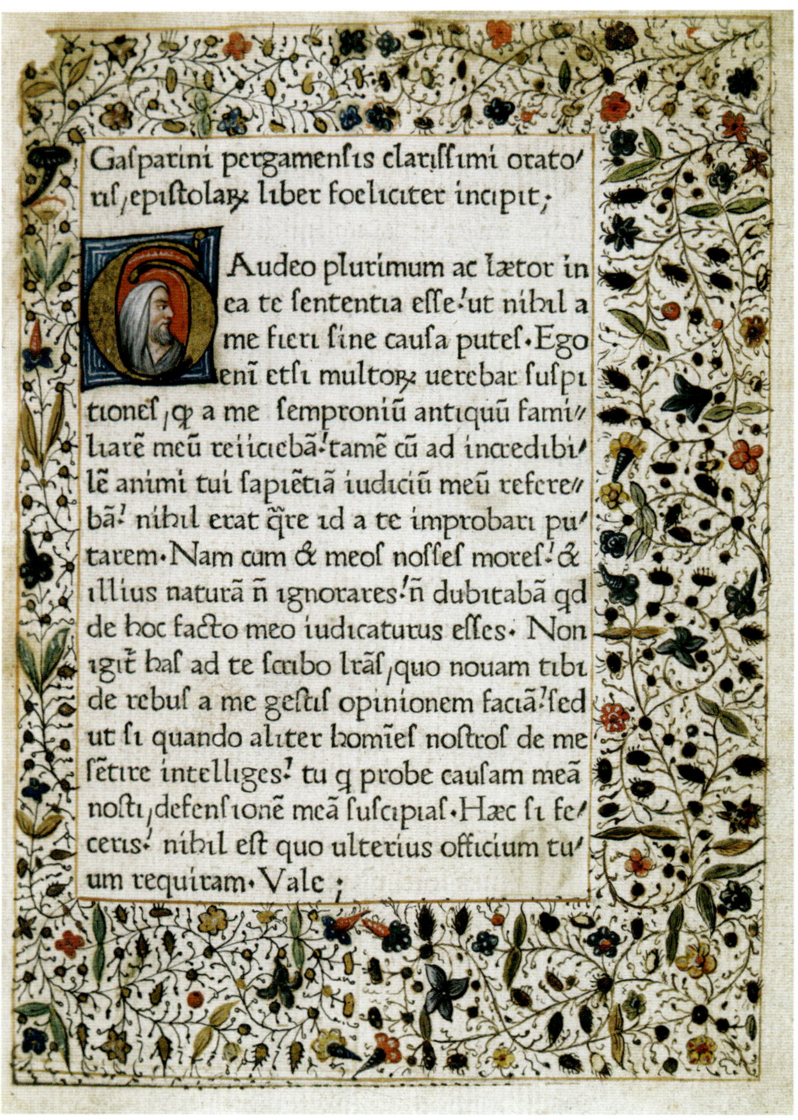

Figure 9.2: Gasparinus Barzizius, *Epistolae* (Paris: Ulrich Gering, Martin Crantz and Michael Friburger). Folio 2, 1470. Parchment. The John Rylands Library, The University of Manchester, UK. R4452.

lasted for a long time. In the eighteenth century, Thomas Frognall Dibdin, engaged in recording the early printed books in the library of the second Earl Spencer, still described the 'first, rude, large roman type' as 'repulsive'.[9] Nonetheless, it now presents as visually elegant and distinctive in the simplicity of the large, clear letters, evident in a decorated gift copy of the press's first book, a quarto, the *Epistolae* of Gasparinus Barzizius (Figure 9.2).

The main aim of the Sorbonne Press was to produce reliable and accurate texts of the classics for the founders for fellow academics and for students. A letter from Fichet to

9	Dibdin, *Aedes Althorpianae*, p. 144.

Heynlin contained in a copy of their first printed book, the *Epistolae* of the humanist Gasparino da Barziza of Bergamo, expresses Fichet's gratitude to Heynlin for his care in providing a sound text as an exemplar for the printers; until now, he says, the carelessness of scribes ('this plague') has kept Latin literature in 'the darkness of ignorance'.[10] The enthusiasm of Fichet, Heynlin, and later Erhard Windsberg for the printing press never waned, and continued to be expressed in cosmic metaphors: a printed copy of the Juvenal has a colophon in which Erhard speaks of 'the new and ingenious art' as 'a step towards the stars', that is, immortality.[11] In light of such excitement and enthusiasm, the very existence of a full *manuscript* copy of Juvenal's *Satires* is even more surprising.

There were however departures from the Sorbonne Press focus on classical and humanist texts. The fifth book printed, the *Orationes* of Cardinal Bessarion, shifted the focus from texts for learning. A scholar, diplomat, book collector, and Platonic philosopher, Bessarion was actively engaged in persuading the princes of Europe to mount a crusade against the Turks, to regain Constantinople and other Christian lands conquered by the Ottomans. To this end, he put together a collection of his letters and orations on the subject, and he sent it to Fichet, introduced to him by Cardinal Rolin, to be prepared for the press.[12] This would be an openly political book. The *Orationes* was thus perhaps the first ever printed propaganda

work.[13] A list of recipients was drawn up of people with power who might support Bessarion's cause, such as the King of England, the Duke of Burgundy, and the Duke of Savoy, and presentation copies were prepared.[14] Seven copies are known, although there may have been more. These were printed on parchment, and before the printed text in each copy a special miniature – painted on parchment – was bound in, which followed the form which had become traditional in luxury presentation manuscripts. Whether it was Fichet, Heynlin, or even Bessarion himself who thought of increasing the chance of success by inserting a hand-painted frontispiece miniature into each printed book, is not known. Some copies also had special letters of dedication inserted, either printed or in manuscript.

A brief glance at the formal purpose of presentation miniatures, and the first use the Sorbonne Press made of them, demonstrates the very unusual nature of the Juvenal miniature. The presentation frontispiece has its forebears in ancient literature, but with the growth in private ownership of secular manuscripts in the late medieval period, it acquired a special importance.[15] Typically, the miniature depicts an elaborate and formal court ritual, in which an author kneels before a patron, offering the book that he or she has written, translated, or commissioned. The miniature's main purpose was to flatter the status, the wealth, and the cultural sophistication of the patron in the hope of attracting some favour or reward, necessary in a culture of patronage. The book is always

<hr>

10   'litterarum graviores iacturas ... ignoratio tenebris obumbravit ... hanc pestem'. The full text of this letter is printed in Claudin, *The first Paris Press*, p. 75.

11   Claudin, *The first Paris Press*, p. 26. '... arte nova impressus et ingenio ... Qui studia ornantes fortis in astra gradus'.

12   Whether it was Bessarion or Fichet who decided to print the *Orations* is discussed by Meserve in 'Patronage and Propaganda at the First Paris Press', who also suggests that the Orations were more like 'private memoranda' than publicly delivered speeches, pp. 521–60.

13   See Veyrin-Forrer, 'Hommage aux Premiers Imprimeurs de France, 1470 – 1970', p. 2. This point is also made by Meserve, 'Patronage and Propaganda at the First Paris Press', p. 525.

14   Claudin, *The first Paris Press*, p. 10.

15   See Inglis, 'A book in the hand: some late medieval accounts of manuscript presentations', pp. 57–97, for an interesting discussion of medieval book presentations.

central to the composition, opulently bound, and held like a precious object, as indeed it was. The patron always looks pleased to be receiving it. For the author, the miniature could be a means of self-advertisement, and perhaps lead to desirable commissions. A typical example is the frontispiece miniature in a copy of the *Traité sur l'oraison dominicale,* where the author, Jean Miélot, presents his manuscript to Philip the Good, Duke of Burgundy (Figure 9.3). Philip is surrounded by a populous, fashionably dressed court, and the room is elegant, with costly furnishings. Though centrally placed, Philip fades a little into the background in his black clothes; the kneeling author and his book are deliberately more strategically positioned in the foreground and attract the eye.

Despite their apparently specific context, scenes of presentation are, of course, entirely fictional: an event depicted as taking place cannot already be inside the bound book being presented. They are more a type of make-believe or wishful thinking, devised in the hope of attracting some 'gift' in return. Documented examples of an author being admitted to an audience with royalty or nobility, albeit to make a presentation, are extremely rare.[16] A book as a 'gift' would customarily have made its way through the hands of several courtiers before reaching a chamberlain, whose duty was 'to screen everything before it could be delivered to its final destination'.[17] Interestingly, one such account is contained in a letter written by Fichet to Bessarion. Fichet had personally presented a copy of Bessarion's *Orationes* to King Louis XI, much later than to the other recipients, and in a letter dated 21 March 1472, he

describes the king's receipt of it and the king's pleasure in its illustrations.[18]

Including a specially prepared presentation miniature in gift copies of Bessarion's *Orationes* was done for the customary reason of attracting the attention of the recipient and deriving consequent benefit: in this case, support for a crusade against the Turks. The presentation miniature inserted in a printed copy presented to Edward IV of England follows the traditional form described above, albeit with the interesting inclusion of Fichet, who was not the author, as the main presenter (Figure 9.4).[19] In a formal, ceremonial setting, Fichet, dressed in the costume of a Doctor of Theology of the Sorbonne, kneels before the King of England. Both are named in a rubric at the beginning of the text addressed to *Edwardo Anglie regi* from Fichet, *parisientis theologii doctor* (folio 4v).[20] Behind Fichet is Cardinal Bessarion, identifiable by his red cardinal's hat and staff. His hand touches Fichet's back in a proprietorial gesture, perhaps to make himself part of the presentation. Other lesser courtiers stand at a deferential distance from the king, who is looking towards the book and reaching out his hand to accept it.

16   Jean Froissart is a rare example. In his *Chroniques* he describes presenting a manuscript to Richard II, made possible by childhood associations. He was rewarded with a huge gift; enough, he says, to set him up for life.

17   Buettner, 'Past Presents: New Year's Gifts at the Valois Courts, ca. 1400', pp. 598–626, particularly p.613.

18   See Claudin, *The first Paris Press*, p. 28 for Fichet's letter to Bessarion describing the king's reception of the book: '*Gracioso quidem vultu librum tuum excepit, legitque parumper prefatiunculam quam operi tuo prescripsi. Revolutis dein membranis, picturas et imagines in marginibus sparsas cominus inspexit ...* ('Indeed he received your book with a gracious countenance, and read the brief preface which I had written in your work. Then, turning over the pages, he inspected each picture and the images in the borders'.)

19   Claudin, *The first Paris Press*, p. 28, notes that almost all who had received copies of Bessarion's work with accompanying letters offered sums of money as contributions to the crusade but 'he nobly declined their offer.' Presumably it was soldiers rather than money he wanted.

20   It is unclear as to why Fichet is depicted as the main presenter of the book. Although he had it prepared for the printing press, Bessarion was the author.

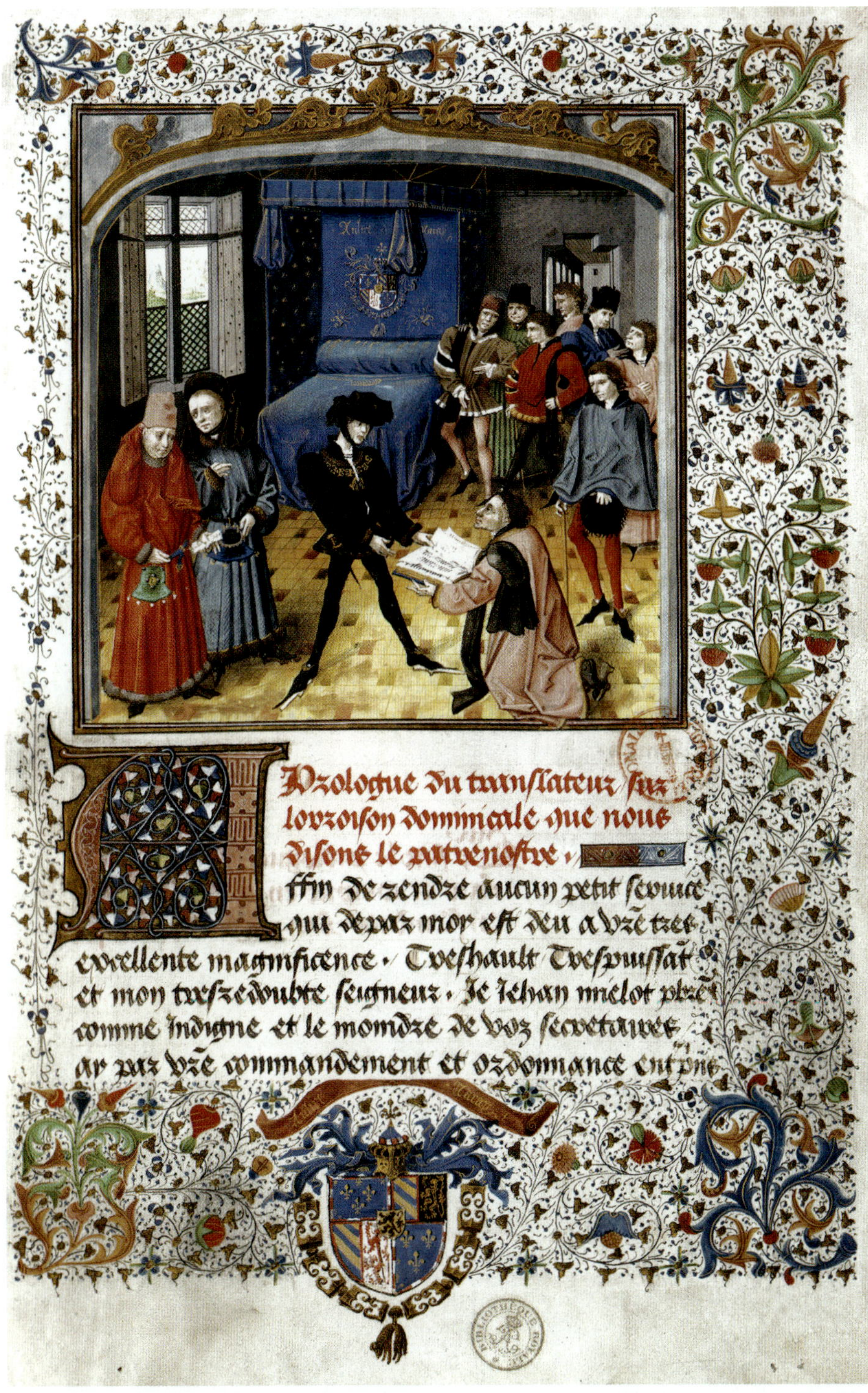

Figure 9.3: Jean Miélot, Presentation to Philip the Good from *Traité sur l'oraison dominicale*. Folio 1, after 1457. Parchment, 39.5cm × 28.5cm. Bibliothèque Royale, Brussels. MS 9092.

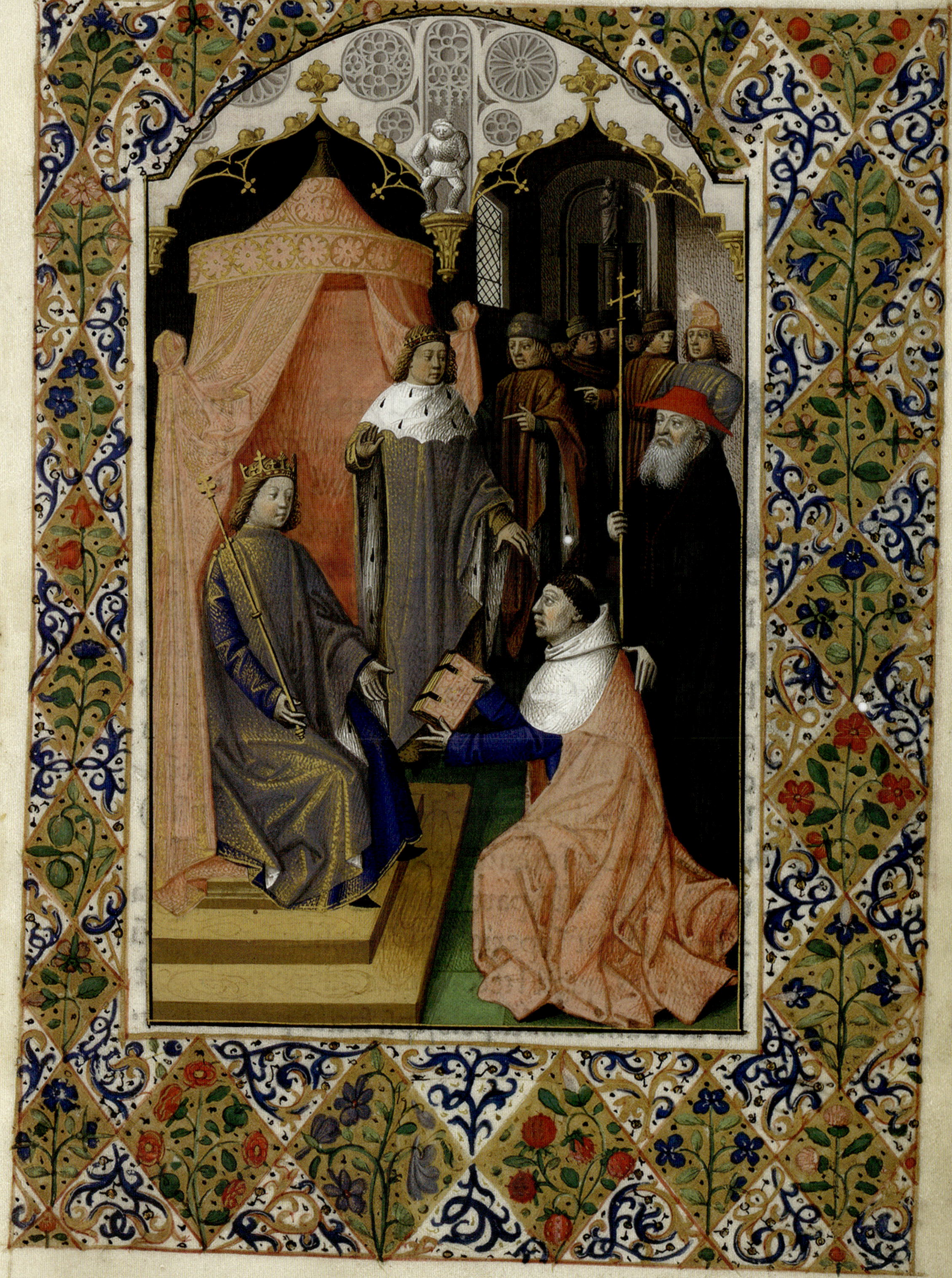

Until this point the Sorbonne Press had commissioned no manuscript copies of the books they printed.[21] With their next book, Fichet's own *Rhetorica,* for the first time at least four full manuscript presentation copies were prepared along with the printed copies. Both manuscripts and printed books included presentation miniatures. Claudin describes the procedure thus: 'As soon as a sheet was printed off, a transcript was made on vellum by a copyist and richly illuminated, following the division of the printed page exactly, line for line.'[22]

One of these manuscripts was presented to Princess Yolande of Savoy, the daughter of Charles VII of France and sister of the reigning king, Louis XI, to whom she had introduced the Savoyard Fichet.[23] The form of the presentation miniature follows that of the *Orationes* (Figure 9.5). Fichet in his doctoral robes kneels before Yolande, in a formal, courtly context. A rubric beneath the miniature states that *Guillaumus Fichetus parisiensis theologus doctor* (Guillaume Fichet, Doctor of Theology at Paris) is sending the book to *principem dominam Yolandem* (the princess Lady Yolande) Again, Fichet has a visual importance that at least matches that of Yolande. In both these presentation miniatures, the book is central to the composition.

Fichet's decision to commission full manuscript copies is interesting, considering his new enthusiasm for printing. He was, however, like Heynlin, also an admirer and collector of manuscripts.[24] Presentation manuscripts to more

conservative patrons might simply have been in deference to tradition, and perhaps a glance toward aristocratic bibliophiles, for whom manuscript remained the preferred mode.[25] All presentations, however, were made for clear reasons: as appreciation for enthusiasm and support in their new venture of printing; as an attempt to stir up interest in a crusade; or as thanks to high officials, including Louis XI, who had shown great interest in the new printing press: the king later waived normal procedures to grant citizenship to the three German printers.[26]

This brings us to the manuscript of Juvenal's *Satires* and its curious presentation miniature, which is like no other. As far as is known, it is the only presentation manuscript of Juvenal's *Satires* made for the Sorbonne Press, and there are no known printed copies with presentation miniatures inserted (Figure 9.6). This presentation frontispiece is such a departure from those discussed above, and without any exemplar (to my knowledge), that 'decoding' it will of necessity be substantially conjectural. The manuscript was presented to Pierre Doriole, who had been appointed Chancellor of France on 26 June 1472. The identity of the recipient is made clear in a dedicatory acrostic poem of thirty-three lines, the first letter of each line spelling his name and title, PIERRE DORIOLLE CHANCELIER DE FRANCE (folio 2v). This was an extremely prestigious appointment. By the time of Louis XI, the chancellor was second only to the Constable of France, and influenced justice, finance, and diplomacy through his administration of crown communications. His office was responsible for the

21   More than a year later, the special copy of Bessarion's *Orationes* prepared for Louis XI, was an illuminated manuscript.

22   Claudin, *The first Paris Press*, p. 11. This is not quite accurate. A printed page of Juvenal has 32 lines, the manuscript 17.

23   Hirsch, 'Printing in France and Humanism, 1470–1480', pp. 111–123, particularly p.114.

24   See Halporn, 'The Carthusian Library at Basel', pp. 226, 241. Much of Heynlin's large collection of manuscripts

is now housed in Basel at the Öffentliche Bibliothek der Universität.

25   Carlson, 'The Latin Writings of John Skelton', pp. 13, 14, for an interesting discussion of this point.

26   Hirsch, 'Printing in France and Humanism, 1470–1480', p. 114.

◄ Figure 9.4: *Presentation* from Iohannes Bessarion, *Orationes*. Folio 4, 1470. Parchment, 13cm × 8.5cm. Biblioteca Apostolica Vaticana, Rome. Vat. lat. 3586 human 15 JH. 08.

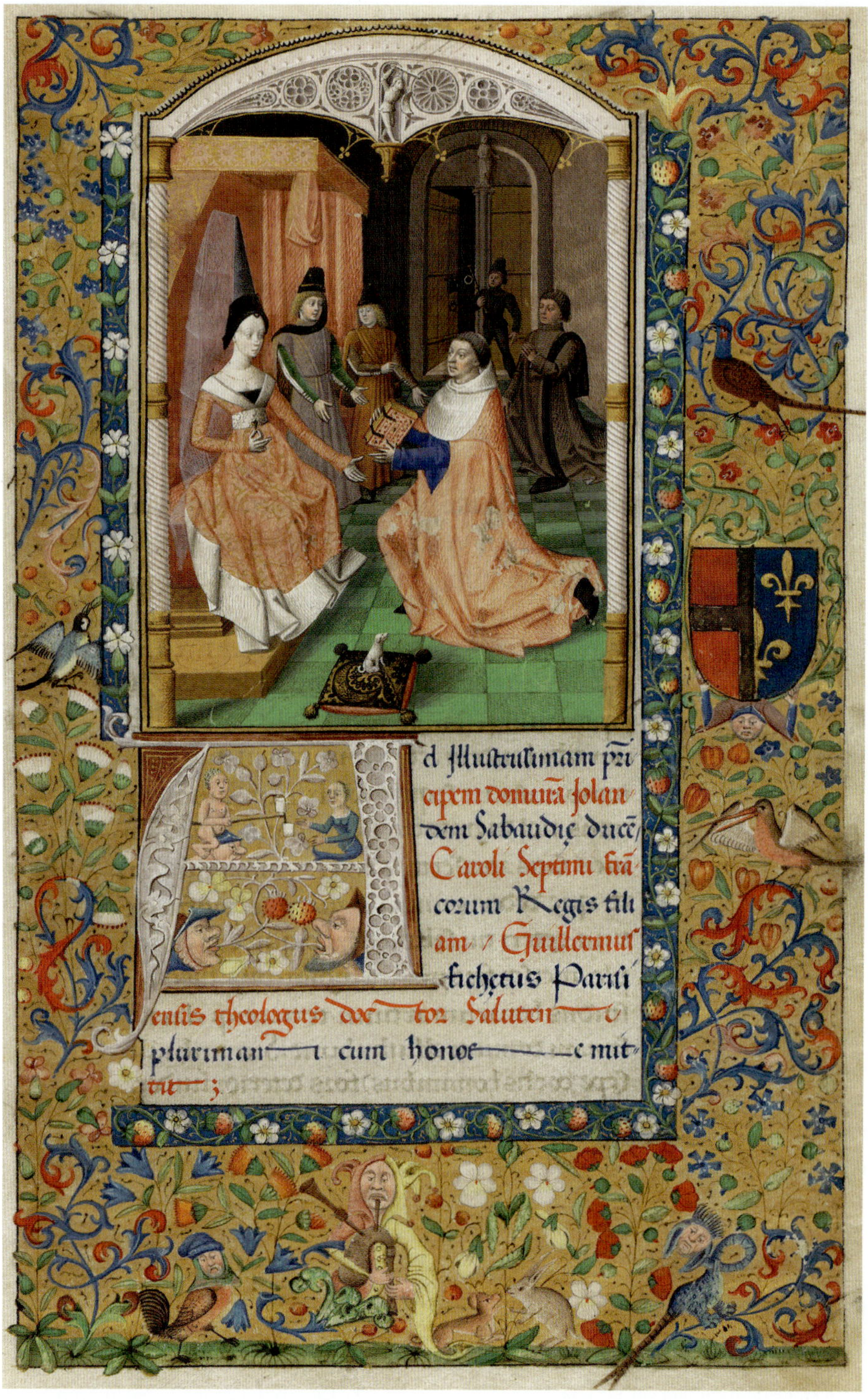

Figure 9.5: Guillaume Fiche, Presentation from *Rhetorica*. Folio 1, 1471. Parchment, 29cm × 27.5cm. Fondation Martin Bodmer, Cologny, Switzerland. MS Cod. Bodmer 176.

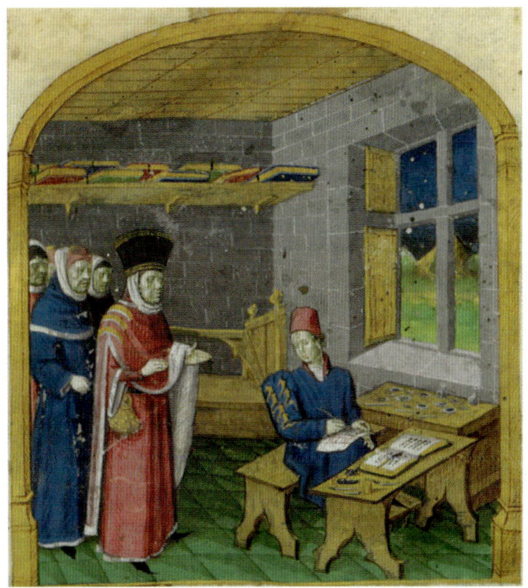

Figure 9.6: The chancellor orders a book from Giovanni Colonna, *Mare historiarum*. Folio 1, *c.*1455. Parchment. Bibliothèque Nationale de France, Paris. BnF MS lat. 4915.

preparation, publication and presentation of royal documents; his clerks drafted, edited, and verified diplomas and letters patent, and they sealed them with appropriate ribbons and waxes to ensure their authenticity.[27] The prestige of the appointment is basic to the content of the acrostic poem, evidently written by Erhard Windsberg, who had assumed the editorial functions of Heynlin; he is known to have contributed verses in other, unrelated manuscripts.[28] The poem is mainly a pastiche of Virgil's *Eclogues*, especially *Eclogue* 1, particularly appropriate for a chancellor in its references

to legal concerns. It is frankly laudatory, full of allusions to great office and the privileged role of the writer in praising Doriole, who now 'alone deservedly holds the throne of justice'.[29] The choice of Juvenal compliments Doriole as a learned admirer of the Roman classics, but also has an appropriateness for one who has been elevated to high administrative office, as broadly speaking the *Satires* examine and criticize Roman contemporary power structures and social institutions. The manuscript was presented to Doriole shortly after he entered upon his duties, 'something like six weeks or two months later', Claudin suggests, so that preparation of it must have begun as soon as his appointment was made known.[30]

O mnia nunc rident. grandis tibi cedit amintas.
R ectus o felixque tuis: sic insere nunc nunc
I nsere, pascentem servabit titirus hedum.
O mnibus hic erit unus bonos quod ipsa minerva
L udera (qua velit) calamo permittit agresti.
L ittera carmentis pascit nunc: littera prisci
E t maronis opus, philos tis undique cernit.
C ernit habunde satis: nam pressi copia lactis
H ic in umbra lentus pascentem imbuit illum
A ssidue precor hinc sint nobis mitia poma.
N unc frondent silve, nunc omnis parturit arbos.
C antabis mecum stabis sic magnus apollo.
E t luctum et curam efugies: et tempora vite
L onga tibi post hec fato meliore dabuntur.
I usticieque tenax factis insignis et equus
E xpectatus multo tandem gallia cum te
R ectorem sumpsit. Gentes et dans frenare superbas
D ignus iusticie solium tu solus habere:
E t recte populi dubias discernere causas
F rancorum decet. He voces ad sydera iactant
R upes. hoc montes feri silveque loquuntur
A lcius. atque cadunt summotis nubibus ymbres.
N unc ad te et tua, magne pater consulta revertor
C armina suscipias. vivas cum Iove beatus.
E urus stat. pupis currens ad littora venit:
Vale vale inquit yolla.'

27   Kibler (ed.), *Medieval France: an Encyclopedia*, pp. 194, 195.

28   Claudin, *The first Paris Press*, p. 28. It reads:
P astores hedera crescentem ornate poetam
I liades. ut hic valeam tua dicere fata.
E stuat illa dies, totum mihi ferre per orbem
R ivos tis laudis. unde totus fluit aer
R ecte de te laudes. usque ad sydera notus.
E rgo alacris cape. que mitto tibi corde benigo,
D ans nam corde bono. memor et sis illius ergo.

29   '... *dignus justicie solium tu solus habere*'

30   Claudin, *The first Paris Press*, p. 26, argues, as evidence for 'six weeks or two months,' that the printed book of the Juvenal was issued after the manuscript copy, with the text of Persius's *Satires* added, and this was towards the end

In the traditionally structured presentation scene examples discussed above, the focus of the composition is shared by the patron, the presenter, and the book. Here, there is no shared importance: the focus of the scene is the large figure of Doriole alone. He is an august presence in the full ceremonial dress worn by the chancellor only on extraordinary state occasions, or ceremonies including the king: 'a cloak lined with ermine or miniver, a robe of cloth of gold, and a hat of black velvet, with a broad gold binding and band'.[31] That it was dress confined to special occasions is supported in a manuscript of *Mare historiarum*, by Giovanni Colonna, in which Chancellor Guillaume Jouvenel des Ursins, Doriole's immediate predecessor, is depicted ordering a book (Figure 9.6).[32] The Chancellor's clothes in this miniature are less elaborate and formal than those the artist has given to Doriole, and were presumably for wear on non-ceremonial occasions.

Yet the event depicted in the Juvenal frontispiece is clearly not a state occasion. The setting is more like a workroom than a court. The elegant green tiles which cover the floor in all other Sorbonne Press presentation miniatures are here replaced by pale stone flags appropriate to a place of work. There are some luxurious touches, such as the cover of fleur-de-lys which defines the shape of Doriole's strange, sofa-like seat, and the woven brocade hanging behind him. Yet Doriole seems overdressed in what is essentially a working space, as though

he has been or is going somewhere else and has dropped in on the way. The seat itself is loosely covered with the cloth and sags at the back and on the sides, where the standing figures lean in a slightly casual fashion. It is, of course, far too large for one person, no matter how august. It suggests, again, a place of work in which a gesture is being made to the presence of the new chancellor with a royally patterned fabric, hastily draped over something like a work bench.

In a line behind Doriole are four large men and two slightly smaller ones, presumably his assistants, the slight sense of crowding perhaps a reference to Louis XI's decision to increase the staff of the Chancellery, and hence its importance.[33] All are looking at Doriole. They are dressed in a version of the once-fashionable *houppelande*, although with narrow sleeves more appropriate to secretaries or clerks than the huge originals, and all are wearing the high-crowned hat that was modish in the second half of the fifteenth century.[34] These are men of some status, judging by their dress and their proximity to the chancellor. An interesting detail is the thick rolls of cloth on the shoulders of the four largest of them. Wearing a clothing accessory slung over the shoulder was high fashion at this time: this could be a hood, draped to hang almost to the ground, or a long scarf, sometimes even with a hat hanging at the end of it.[35] The drab, uniform colour of these rolls, however, and the fact that they are clearly rectangular, suggests that they are more to do with occupation than with fashion. These assistants to the chancellor would likely be the highly skilled clerks who actually did the preparation,

---

of August. Considering the time necessary to set up each page of the printed copy, if this was issued *after* the written copy then work must have begun on the written copy immediately after Doriole's appointment. Also Booton, 'Guillaume Fichet's Literary Gift', p. 124: '... by late 1472, Fichet and Heynlin had departed Paris leaving the printing press to their typographers'.

31   *The History of Paris*, p. 93.

32   See Lewis, 'The Chancellor's Two Bodies', p.263.

33   See Kibler, *Medieval France*, pp. 194, 185.

34   For a comprehensive study of medieval fashion, see Van Buren, *Illuminating Fashion*.

35   For a depiction of fashionable courtiers in 1470, see, for instance, BnF MS fr. 22547, folio 1. Bruges, 1470.

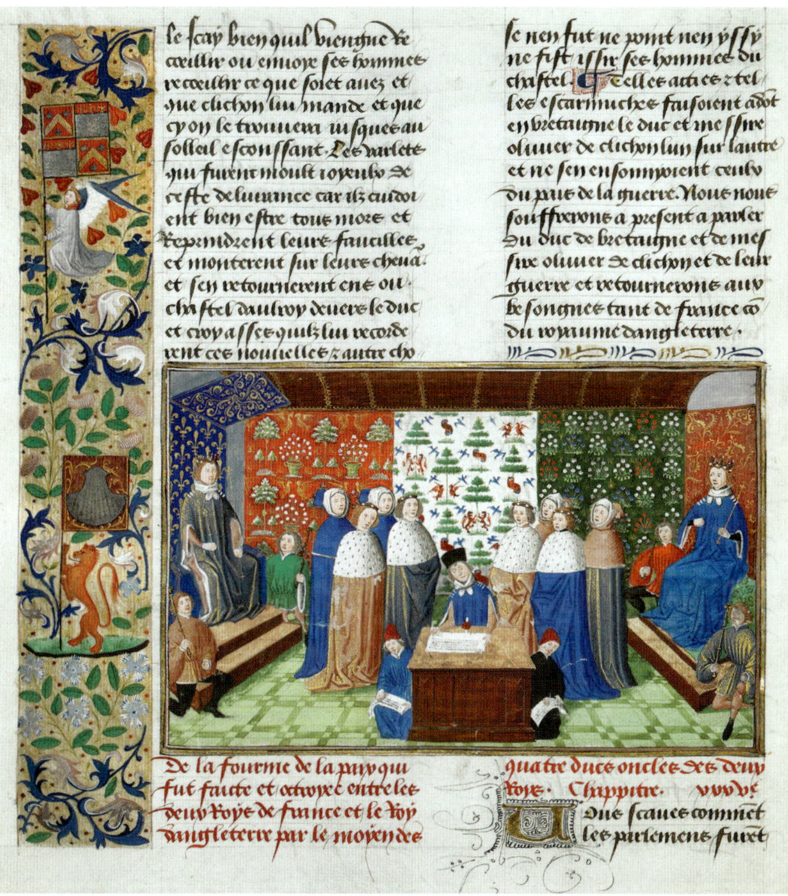

Figure 9.7: Treaty from Jean Froissart, *Chroniques*. Folio 10v, *c.*1471. Parchment, 42cm × 31.5cm. The British Library, London. Harley MS 4380.

publication, and presentation of royal documents described above. If so, what would the cloths be used for? Evidence from contemporary miniatures of administrative court proceedings might offer a clue (Figure 9.7). The scene depicted in this miniature is of a treaty being drawn up between two kings, a matter of the highest importance. Two clerks, dressed in a manner similar to those in the Doriole miniature, sit either side of the central table, writing on parchment resting on their knee.[36] These are not scribes, who sit at desks, but more like court officials recording statements as they are made. Would the cloths held over the shoulders of the four senior staff members in the Juvenal miniature perhaps be used to support the parchment which curled over their knees as they write? Or could they even be used to kneel on?

In front of Chancellor Doriole is a table where four smaller, less important clerks are busy carrying on with their work of applying

36   Other images of parchment being written on by clerks while supported on an upraised knee are to be found in the

British Library, BL Royal MS 17 E VII, folio 99; BL Harley MS 4379, folio 142v; and BL Harley MS 4380, folio 148; and in the Bibliothèque nationale de France MS fr, 606, folio 15.

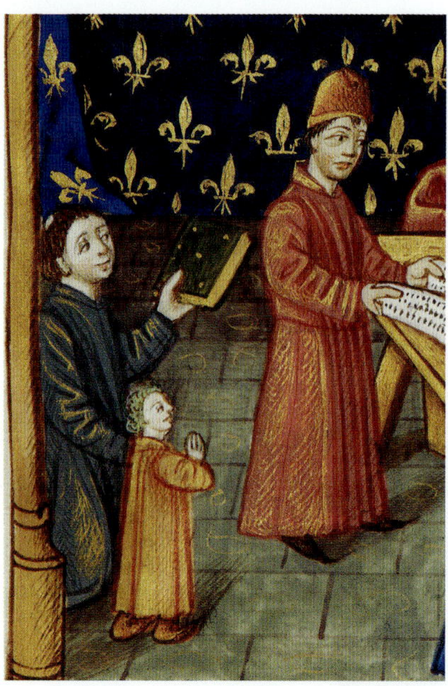

Figure 9.8: Two figures (detail) from Juvenal, *Sixteen Satires*. Folio 4, *c.*1472. Parchment, 30cm × 20.7cm. Kerry Stokes Collection, Perth. LIB.2014.230.

wax seals to documents: one is folding the document; one is applying the seal; one is mixing the wax; and one is packing the documents into a box.[37] The royal nature of the seal is indicated in the small, opulently covered chest and gold-covered box containing completed documents, details drawn from actual practice: in important ceremonies: 'the seals were carried in a coffer of silver gilt, covered with a napkin of cloth of gold, fastened with cords of violet silk and gold'.[38] At odds with the resplendent appearance of the chancellor, there is a kind of informality in the way the humble members of his staff carry on with their work in front of him and those on either side move their hands as if to speak.

Though there is a book presenter, which perhaps allows this miniature to be classified as

a 'presentation miniature', he is a small, insignificant figure clutching a small, insignificant book. He is wearing an unassuming, beltless gown and no hat, and he is a far cry from Fichet in full academic dress in the other Sorbonne presentation scenes (Figure 9.8). Placed in the bottom left hand corner of the composition, he almost escapes notice. If he is covered up, no difference is made to the scene as a whole. This would be impossible in the presentation images discussed above, where the coherence of the image would be entirely lost if one of the three main elements were removed. Although this person is holding out a book towards him, Doriole is not looking at him: his outstretched hand is not reaching for the book, but making a gesture which seems to encompass the whole room filled with his new staff, busy at their tasks.

Unusual and even puzzling is the very small figure standing beside the book presenter. So far, I have suggested that this miniature is depicting the personnel of the Chancellery in their workplace, carefully graded in size to suggest degrees of importance, and with the attributes of their particular roles. If this is correct, perhaps the very small figure is also an employee. He is surely no arbitrary inclusion. He may be the humblest of all the employees, perhaps a kind of errand boy, and hence by far the smallest. He, too, is holding something up to the chancellor. Though it is too small to be absolutely clear, it seems to be a container with holes in the top. It might be a pounce box: this was a container filled with a fine sand-like powder ('pounce') used to blot ink and to prepare parchment for writing.[39] A child could have been employed to shake the pounce over the parchment, when required, as well as to carry out other simple tasks. If this boy is also

<hr>

37   See Barbiche, 'Diplomatics of Modern Official Documents', p. 423.
38   *The History of Paris*, p. 93.

39   See Brown, *Understanding Illuminated Manuscripts*, p. 99 for a description of 'pounce' and its use.

a member of the new chancellor's staff, then the depiction of the group becomes one of commemoration and congratulation, in much the manner of a modern photograph of a new cabinet surrounding a prime minister.

This intriguing and arresting miniature is clearly the work of a highly skilled artist. The whole manuscript is illuminated 'in the best traditions of the royal court at Tours', that is, in the manner of Jean Fouquet, court painter to Louis XI and based in Tours.[40] While it is no argument for the hand of Jean Fouquet himself, it is interesting to note that Fouquet's paintings include a portrait of Chancellor Guillaume Jouvenel des Ursins, who immediately preceded Pierre Doriole in this office. There is evidence in the Juvenal frontispiece miniature of Jean Fouquet's characteristic style, whether by his hand or another's, in the gold highlights which model the folds in garments; in the dark shadows which define jaw lines; and in the manoeuvring of fabric patterns, particularly *fleur de lys*, to create shape as well as perspective. The form of the Chancellor's sofa-like chair is largely created by a manipulation of the fabric which covers it: the fleur de lys on the seat and on the side arms point in different directions.[41]

The Juvenal manuscript as a whole has a very fine yet understated program of illustration supporting the large presentation miniature. Each satire is preceded by a historiated initial in which two figures converse, one of them consistent throughout and therefore probably intended to be Juvenal. The other is appropriate to the subject of the particular satire. In the initial that begins Satire 11, which is about the misuse of wealth and possessions, Juvenal seems to be admonishing a man who is clutching a bag of gold (Figure 9.9). No two

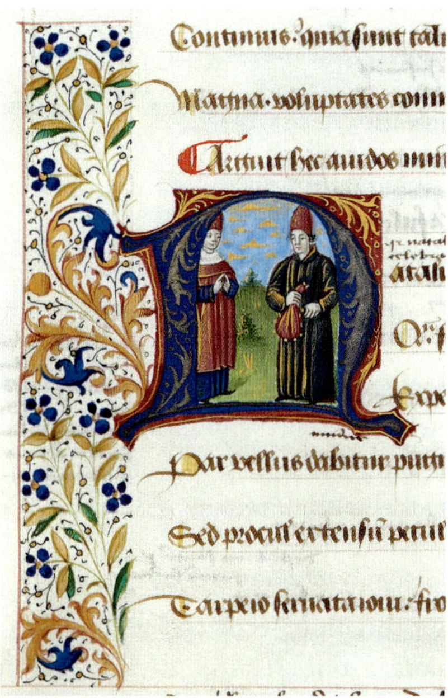

Figure 9.9: Initial, Satire 11, from Juvenal, *Sixteen Satires*. Folio 84, *c*.1472. Parchment, 30cm × 20.7cm. Kerry Stokes Collection, Perth. LIB.2014.230.

initials are the same. The disposition of the two figures against different backgrounds within the initials, their facial expressions, and the 'speaking' positions of their hands are varied throughout, and gently emphasize the dramatic nature of Juvenal's lines. The initials are enhanced by partial borders of flowers, leaves, and curling vines, appropriate to their positions on the page, and finely wrought. The scribal work is beautiful; each folio has seventeen lines only, and the consequent abundance of space gives the whole an air of sumptuous luxury. These refined yet conservative illuminations are strikingly at odds with the eccentricities of the presentation miniature. Can it even be described as a presentation miniature? The presenter and his book have no visual importance. He is scarcely noticed in the busy office-like context in which he is placed. Yet without him there would be no connection at all between the miniature

40   Manion, 'Juvenal, Sixteen Satires', p. 116.

41   Jean Fouquet's use of this technique is particularly striking in, for example, BnF MS fr. 6465, folio 301v, folio 332.

and the manuscript, and the miniature would seem quite arbitrary.

I would suggest that the Juvenal *Satires* was intended as a 'gift' in the best sense, in which the self-effacing nature of the miniature honours and congratulates Doriole in his new appointment as Chancellor of France, and is not deflected in any way towards the giver or the gift, with the expectation of reward or favour in return. Unlike traditional presentation miniatures in which the presenter, the book, and the patron have virtually equal importance, this one is all about the recipient, Doriole. We see his impressive new staff, his clerks at work with the official seals, and Doriole himself as a large figure, centrally placed, resplendent in his new ceremonial robes. The speed with which the manuscript was prepared and presented to him after he began his duties, as suggested above, means that his appointment would still have had the gloss of newness, and congratulations would still have been relevant. The near-adulatory acrostic poem intensifies the tone of congratulation.

In the absence of a visually identifiable presenter, a clarifying rubric, or an inserted letter, it is difficult to discover which of the Sorbonne principals commissioned this manuscript. Fichet's time and energies in late 1472 were concentrated on supporting his friend Cardinal Bessarion in his attempts to raise a new crusade.[42] In any case, as we have seen, Fichet clearly liked to be depicted as a presenter of the Press's books, and in full academic dress. There is no evidence of Heynlin's presence. Erhard Windsberg is the author of the colophon inserted on folio 118v, and he is probably the author of the acrostic

discussed above.[43] Claudin thinks he is also responsible for the interlinear and marginal commentaries in the manuscript.[44] Was he also responsible for the unconventional, even eccentric, design of the frontispiece miniature? In the absence of Fichet and Heynlin, he may have felt free from the usual practice of the Sorbonne Press regarding presentation miniatures, particularly if he had a special interest in this manuscript. There is a slight, very slight, hint of playful familiarity in the manner of the frontispiece miniature: in its extremely specific nature, and in the faintly humorous inclusion of the very junior staff member. Of these principals, Erhard is therefore the most likely candidate. But what if any was his connection with Doriole? My suggestion that it was a gift to congratulate Doriole and celebrate his prestigious new appointment, from one who knew him, implies some personal association. Unfortunately, a connection between Doriole and Windsberg – or indeed with either of the other principals – remains elusive. In the *Ciceronis Tusculanae Quæstiones*, of uncertain date, there are some verses by Windsberg printed at the end of the text. Otherwise, his name does not appear on the few remaining books produced by the Sorbonne Press. He is next recorded in Germany, where he later became a doctor of medicine.[45]

Claudin observes that after the departure of Fichet and with Heynlin permanently absent, the printers of the Sorbonne Press seem to have been left to go their own way. Their books were

---

42   Claudin, *The first Paris Press*, pp. 29, 30. Fichet 'had sworn never to leave (Bessarion).' Bessarion died on 14 November and Fichet remained in Rome, never to return to Paris.

43   See Claudin, *The first Paris Press*, p. 25, for the colophon. The text of the distich naming Erhard reads: *'ERHARDUS D. J. JUVENALIS CULTORI F[ELICITATEM] OPTAT Ecce parens Satyrarum princeps Eliconis et auctor In pravos mittens tela severa notae.'* ('To the lovers of Juvenal Erhard wishes happiness, See the father of Satire, a chief writer of Helicon, hurling upon the wicked the piercing darts of ignominy').

44   Claudin, *The first Paris Press*, p. 26.

45   Claudin, *The first Paris Press*, p. 23.

printed in a careless manner, 'unlike the high literary standard of the former editors and correctors.'[46] When they moved the press from the Sorbonne and set up on their own account, the characteristic roman type was changed to the more generally used gothic, and the emphasis was more commercial, with large numbers of books rapidly printed. These changes marked the end of the high-minded ideals which had created the press, a private press for the benefit of scholars.

About the author

Jan Fox holds a doctorate on medieval illuminated manuscripts and has presented her work at the State Library of Victoria's 2008 conference, Imagination, Books and Community in Medieval Europe. She has a background in literature, and has also published literary articles, co-edited two books of literary essays, and written several scripts for educational television. janfox@bigpond.com

Works cited

Bernard Barbiche, 'Diplomatics of Modern Official Documents (Sixteenth- Eighteenth Centuries): Evaluation and Perspectives', *The American Archivist*, 59/4 (1996), pp. 422–436.

Diane Booton, 'Guillaume Fichet's Literary Gift to Duke François II of Brittany', *Nottingham Medieval Studies*, 53 (2009), pp. 121–130.

Michelle P. Brown, *Understanding Illuminated Manuscripts. A Guide to Technical Terms* (London: The British Library, 1994).

Brigitte Buettner, 'Past Presents: New Year's Gifts at the Valois Courts, c.1400', *The Art Bulletin*, 83 (2001), pp. 598–626.

David R. Carlson, 'The Latin Writings of John Skelton', *Studies in Philology*, 88/4 (1991), pp. 1–125.

A. Claudin, *The first Paris Press. An Account of the Books Printed for G. Fichet and J. Heynlin in the Sorbonne 1470–1472* (London: Printed for the Bibliographical Society at the Chiswick Press, February 1898 for 1899).

Thomas Frognall Dibdin, *Aedes Althorpianae* (London: W. Nicol, Shakspeare [sic] Press, 1822).

Barbara Halporn, 'The Carthusian Library at Basel', *The Library Quarterly* 54/3 (1984) pp. 226, 241.

Rudolf Hirsch, 'Printing in France and Humanism, 1470–1480', *The Library Quarterly*, 30/2, (1960), pp. 111–123.

The History of Paris from the Earliest Period to the Present Day, 3 vols. (London and Paris: Geo. B. Whittaker and A. and W. Galignani, 1827).

Erik Inglis, 'A book in the hand: some late medieval accounts of manuscript presentations', *Journal of the Early Book Society*, 5 (2002), pp. 57–97.

William W Kibler, ed., *Medieval France: an Encyclopedia* (New York: Garland Publishing, 1995).

P.S. Lewis, 'The Chancellor's Two Bodies: Note on a Miniature in BnF lat. 4915', *Journal of the Warburg and Courtauld Institutes*, 55 (1992), pp. 263–65.

Margaret M. Manion, *An Illumination. The Rothschild Prayer Book & other works from the Kerry Stokes Collection c.1289–1685* (West Perth: Australian Capital Equity, 2015), pp. 114–17.

Douglas C. McMurtrie, *Proofreading in the Fifteenth Century. An examination of the evidence relating to correctors of the press at work in Paris prior to 1500* (Greenwich: Conde Nast Press, 1921).

Margaret Meserve, 'Patronage and Propaganda at the First Paris Press: Guillaume Fichet and the First Edition of Bessarion's *Orations against the Turks*', *The Papers of the Bibliographical Society of America*, 97/4, (2003), 521–588.

Anne H. Van Buren and Roger S. Wieck, *Illuminating Fashion. Dress in the Art of Medieval France and the Netherlands. 1325–1515* (New York: Giles and The Morgan Library and Museum, 2011).

Jeanne Veyrin-Forrer, 'Hommage aux Premiers Imprimeurs de France, 1470–1970', *Bulletin des bibliothèques de France* [en ligne], 2 (1971) accessed 9 April 2017 at http://bbf.enssib.fr/consulter/bbf-1971-02-0065-001.

46   Claudin, *The first Paris Press*, p. 31.

10. Thielman Kerver's Book of Hours of 10 September 1522 in the Kerry Stokes Collection

Hilary Maddocks

Dunlop, Anne (ed.), *Antipodean Early Modern. European Art in Australian Collections, c. 1200–1600*, Amsterdam University Press, 2018

DOI: 10.5117/9789462985209/CH10

Abstract

In the decades around 1500, hundreds of editions of printed Books of Hours issued from Parisian presses. Thielman Kerver published at least 124 editions of Books of Hours, including his last and finest example of 10 September 1522. This imprint, which is decorated with a complex program of metalcut and woodcut illustration, is extant in fourteen known copies. This article examines a previously uncatalogued copy of Kerver's last Book of Hours, now in the Kerry Stokes Collection. The particular copy and its program of illustration are described in the context of materiality, patronage and use.

Keywords: Printed Books of Hours; Thielman Kerver; Kerry Stokes Collection; Materiality; Metalcut; Woodcut

In 2015 the Kerry Stokes Collection acquired a printed Book of Hours (LIB.2015.051).[1] The book, which belongs to an edition of fourteen known extant copies, was printed on vellum in Paris by Thielman Kerver on 10 September 1522.[2]

Kerver died in October or November of that year, probably from the plague, and this was his final imprint. His last Book of Hours was also his finest, issued in a large quarto size and illustrated with numerous printed images and borders throughout the 136 folios. The edition is well known and has been fully described, most recently by Tenschert and

1   The book was purchased from the Sotheby's sale, *Livres et manuscrits*, Paris, 25 June 2015, lot 34. It was previously sold in the Allienne sale, Hôtel Drouot, 15 November 1985, lot 54. The ex-libris of Lucien Allienne appears on the front flyleaf. On the front pastedown is an unidentified ex-libris M.G. with a crown and identifying number H.15. This copy measures 22.5cm x 14.8cm and is bound in modern brown morocco.

2   In addition to the Stokes copy, thirteen others have been recorded. They include Antiquariat Bibermühle no. 118; Venice, Biblioteca Nazionale Marciana, ANT 37807, Membr. 0048; The Hague, Koninklijke Bibliotheek, KW 1084 C2; London, British Library C.41.e.5; Manchester, John Rylands Library, Special Collections R4548; San Marino, Huntingdon Library, Rare Books no. 108775; Oxford, Bodleian Library BB 179; Morlanwelz, Bibliothèque du Musée Royal de Mariemont, LA035964-001, Rel. 002; University of California, Berkeley University Library, Bancroft TYP AA52 C3 B6 1522, Poitiers, Bibliothèque Municipale, réserve CR50 and Paris, Bibliothèque de l'Institut de France, Paris. A fully illuminated copy was sold at Christie's sale 4035, *Maurice Burrus* on 15 December 2015. Another copy is recorded as having been sold by Henry Sotheran and Co., *Bibliotheca Pretiosa*, in London in 1907.

Nettekoven, but the Stokes example has not previously been listed among extant copies.[3]

As a product of the printing press, the Stokes Collection book is essentially the same as the other copies in the edition. However, this particular example has been individualised by the inclusion of numerous hand-painted initials and ten large painted illustrations. The purpose of this brief discussion is to characterize the Stokes Collection Book of Hours in the context of both Parisian printed Books of Hours and Kerver's career, and to describe aspects of its program of illustration.

Books of Hours in manuscript and print

Books of Hours were small prayer books owned largely by the laity in the late Middle Ages.[4] Conveniently small and portable, they could be used at home and in church. As treasured items they were often passed down in families and many contain genealogical inscriptions and other records and mementos of ownership. Manuscript Books of Hours were perhaps the most commonly owned type of book in the later Middle Ages and they were even more popular in print.[5] The first Book of Hours to be printed in France was issued in 1485, and from this time until the mid-sixteenth century, Books of Hours

were a staple of many printers and publishers.[6] Paris was the epicentre of production for printed Books of Hours and numerous editions were issued for French and export markets. Manuscript Books of Hours continued to be produced during this period, but in nowhere near the huge numbers of their printed equivalents.

Many hundreds of fifteenth- and sixteenth-century printed Books of Hours exist today in public and private collections. It is not known how many editions were issued, but the total was certainly in the thousands. Estimates based on extant copies are conservative, as many editions must have disappeared altogether over the years. Even so, Hans Bohatta's inventory of Books of Hours published in France suggests a staggering 1585 editions between the 1470s and 1599, including 1399 printed in Paris alone.[7] Based on extant copies in inventories at the Bibliothèque Nationale de France, Reinburg estimates about 625 editions were issued between 1501 and 1540.[8] It is impossible to know for certain how many copies comprised an edition. Lucien Febvre and Henri-Jean Martin suggest an average print run of between 1000 and 1500 for all types of books.[9] Reinburg suggests that editions of liturgical books were considerably smaller – more like 300 to 600 copies, as they were often made in limited numbers for specific dioceses.[10] Of course, Books of Hours were not strictly liturgical

---

3   Tenschert and Nettekoven, *Horae B.M.V*, III, no. 118, pp. 977–85. Other references to this edition are provided on p. 985.

4   Useful general references for Books of Hours include Wieck, *Painted Prayers* and also his *The Book of Hours*. Also see Reinburg, *French Books of Hours*; and Duffy, *Marking the Hours*.

5   In his study of will inventories in Amiens, Labarre, *Le livre dans la vie*, pp. 164–77, found that of 2687 identifiable books, 764 were Books of Hours. In addition, in 228 inventories the only books listed were Books of Hours.

6   For example, in 1528 the bookseller Loys Roger had 98,529 copies of Books of Hours in his shop out of a total of 101,860 books, and in 1545 Guillaume Godard possessed a stock of 263,696 books of which 148,919 were Books of Hours. Chartier, *The Cultural Uses Print*, p. 150. See also Labarre, *Le livre dans la vie*, pp. 166–71 for Amiens.

7   Bohatta, *Bibliographie der Livres d'Heures (Horae B.M.V.)*

8   Reinburg, *Books of Hours*, pp. 37–40

9   Febvre and Martin, *The Coming of the Book*, p. 218.

10   Reinburg, *Books of Hours*, p. 38. She refers to Parent, *Les métiers du livre à Paris*, pp. 136–37, 141.

books, and most were made for the general use of Rome rather than regional dioceses, but it is likely that they were not printed in editions as large as those suggested by Febvre and Martin. We can speculate that it may have been commercially prudent for a bookseller to produce these books in small, varied editions only at the rate they could be sold, thus avoiding the potentially high cost of a single large, uniform print run that might not appeal to the market. It is true that most surviving editions of Books of Hours are represented by only a few copies, although this is probably the case with early imprints in general.[11]

The demand for printed Hours appears to have been driven by a new aspirational clientele comprised of the bourgeoisie and the professional classes, including lawyers, doctors, apothecaries, artisans and merchants, all attracted to the lower prices afforded by the printing press. A Book of Hours printed on paper and without any additional hand decoration or fine binding was relatively inexpensive and affordable to many unable to purchase manuscript Books of Hours adorned with illuminations. However, not all printed Books of Hours were cheap, and many, like the Stokes example, which is printed on vellum and decorated by hand, were fashioned for wealthier buyers. From the very inexpensive to the luxurious and costly, there was a printed Book of Hours to suit almost any client.[12]

The contents and structure of printed and manuscript Books of Hours are very similar. All Books of Hours included a core devotional text, the Hours of the Virgin, designed to be recited or read at certain times (or hours) from early morning until late at night: the canonical hours of Matins, Lauds, Prime, Terce, Sext, None, Vespers and Compline. Typically, a Book of Hours might begin with a calendar, followed by readings from the Gospels, prayers to the Virgin (*Obsecro te* ('I beseech you') and *O intemerata* ('Oh, immaculate Virgin')), the Hours of the Virgin, Hours of the Cross, Hours of the Holy Spirit, Penitential Psalms, Litany and Office of the Dead, followed by Suffrages of the Saints. There was some variation in these set contents, but all Books of Hours, both manuscript and printed, are more similar than different. Images play an essential role in Books of Hours. They mark divisions in the text and provide a

11   Determining the size of editions is complicated by the special nature of Books of Hours. As treasured objects, particularly if they were made of sturdy vellum and enjoyed the status of family heirlooms, they may have been more likely to survive than other types of books. Of 145 printed Books of Hours listed by Tenschert and Nettekoven, *Horae B.M.V.* vol. III, pp. 1322–25, 40 are extant in only one copy (*unicum*), 27 in four or fewer copies (*rarissimum*) and 78 in nineteen or fewer copies (*rarum*). The 365 extant copies listed in Nettekoven, Tenschert and Zöhl, *Horae B.M.V.*, vol. IX, pp. 4344–57 survive in different proportions – 92 (*unicum*), 186 (*rarissimum*) and 87 (*rarum*) – but no edition is represented today by more than nineteen copies.

12   Ownership of printed Books of Hours was not limited to the bourgeoisie. Finely bound and painted copies appear alongside illuminated manuscript hours in aristocratic and royal inventories; Anne of Brittany owned a copy printed by Gillet Hardouyn, and Claude de France owned two by Simon Vostre, all finely bound and painted. See Quentin-Bauchart, *Les femmes bibliophiles* p. 378 and p. 384. Over a third of the Books of Hours in Nettekoven, Tenschert and Zöhl's 2014 catalogues include painted images. Many of these were owned by high-ranking aristocracy, including a copy of Kerver's 27 May 1522 edition, which may have belonged to Queen Claude of France (*Horae B.M.V*, VII, no. 117.3, pp. 3143–62). Labarre, *Le livre dans la vie*, pp. 172–77, found that the 491 Books of Hours listed in post-mortem inventories in Amiens ranged widely in price, from the cheapest, at under three sous (42 copies) to moderate, from three to eighteen sous (167 copies) to high at 20 to 70 sous (204 copies) and the most luxurious, at four to 20 livres (78 copies). He noted that inventories do not often differentiate between manuscripts and printed books, but the more expensive books were finely bound, painted, and made of parchment or vellum. Value seems to have been determined by what the book was made of, rather than whether it was printed or not.

focus for religious devotion, but also inform, entertain and enhance the overall attractiveness of the volume.

Because the basic contents of printed Books of Hours did not vary a great deal, in order to appeal to a broad market publishers and printers issued them in a range of sizes and formats, the most common being octavo and quarto (but also duodecimo and sextidecimo); on different supports (parchment, finer vellum, or cheaper paper) and with different text fonts. Books also included passages in the vernacular, which presumably were more accessible than Latin to a general audience. For example, the Stokes book includes the seven Penitential Psalms in French as well as in Latin. There was also some variation in how the hours were organised. The Stokes book is an example of a 'mixed Hours', where the Hours of the Virgin, Hours of the Cross, and Hours of the Holy Spirit are not separate, but grouped together according to hour, with Lauds in the Hours of the Virgin followed by Lauds in the Hours of the Cross, Lauds in the Hours of the Holy Spirit, and so on. But above all, publishers differentiated the multitude of editions of Books of Hours by adorning them with a range of different metalcut (a relief print from a copper plate) and woodcut illustrations and richly decorated borders.

Thielman Kerver, *Imprimeur-libraire*

Thielman Kerver leaves no doubt as to his primary role in the production of the 10 September 1522 Book of Hours. On the opening folio we see his printer's mark, comprising his name and initials in an escutcheon supported by two unicorns, above a brief description of the book's contents (Figure 10.1). At some stage Kerver also had a metalcut plate made that incorporated his initials in a coat of arms, together with an image of Vanitas in the form

of a naked woman with a skull head, and this appears in four lateral borders throughout the book (folios B8, I4, P1, R8v). His name is also recorded in the colophon, (folio R8v) where it is stated that the books were *nouvellement i(m) primees a Paris par Thielman Kerver Imprimeur & libraire iure de luniversite de Paris* ('newly printed in Paris by Thielman Kerver, printer & bookseller sworn under oath by the University of Paris'); Kerver is also listed here as residing in the rue Saint-Jacques at the sign of the unicorn, and the date given as 10 September 1522.

At the time, Thielman Kerver's publishing house was among the largest and most successful in Paris.[13] His name points to a German origin, and in an edition he printed in 1500 he calls himself *Confluentinus*, suggesting he came from Koblenz in central Germany. Kerver started his career in Paris as a bookseller and publisher who subcontracted printers. His name first appears in editions of Books of Hours dated 1497 that Kerver sub-contracted to the printer Jean Philippe, who was also of German origin. These books were issued with Kerver's mark and they record that he was established on the Pont Saint-Michel at the sign of the unicorn.[14] In 1498, after amassing his own punches, matrices, and metalcut and woodcut plates, Kerver also started operating his own press, becoming an *imprimeur-libraire*, or printer-publisher.[15] Kerver's rapid rise was sealed by his appointment, in 1501, to the position of *libraire-juré* at the University of Paris. He was one of only twenty-four booksellers so honoured, and

13   The most extensive study of Kerver is Claerr, 'Imprimerie et réussite sociale à Paris'. See also his 'L'édition d'Heures du 21 avril 1505', pp. 409–17.

14   These include the edition printed by Jean Philippe for Kerver on 20 December 1497.

15   The various roles of the publisher, printer, punch cutter, and bookseller often overlapped. For the different occupations in the sixteenth-century book trade see Parent, *Les métiers du livre à Paris*.

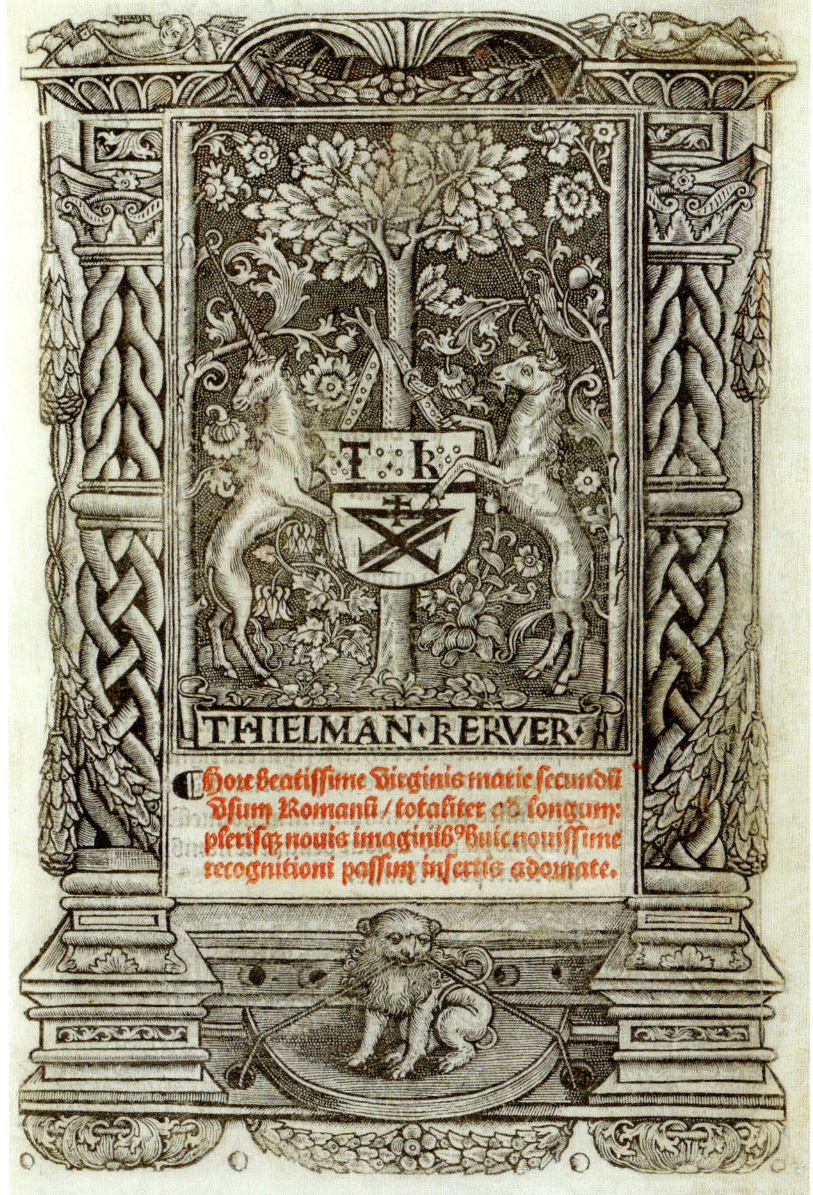

Figure 10.1: Thielman Kerver. *Book of Hours, Use of Rome*, Paris. 1522. Parchment, 22.5cm × 14.8cm. Kerry Stokes Collection, Perth. LIB.2015.051.

the title exempted him from certain taxes in exchange for publishing books for the university. As his prosperity increased he purchased additional properties, including, in 1519, premises in the rue Saint-Jacques, also identified by his sign of the unicorn, which was where the 10 September 1522 Book of Hours was printed. Kerver's position among the powerful elite of the Paris publishing world was further secured by his marriage to Yolande Bonhomme, sometime between 1508 and 1510. Scion of one of the city's oldest publishing families, Bonhomme succeeded Kerver at the rue Saint-Jacques address, where she continued the trade after her husband's death, publishing books under both their names then her own.

Thierry Claerr has identified 315 editions, including variants of editions, published by Kerver throughout his career. They included classical and humanist texts, legal works for the university such as the *Corpus juris canonici et civilis*, liturgical missals, breviaries, and Books of Hours. Kerver issued at least 124 editions of Books of Hours, either printed by himself or subcontracted to other printers. Over a third of his total output comprised Books of Hours and this was not atypical for Paris booksellers. There was such a demand for Books of Hours that some publishers, such as the Hardouyn brothers, published almost nothing else.

Kerver's Book of Hours in the Stokes Collection

The Book of Hours in the Stokes collection is complete and in exceptionally good condition. It is printed in black and red ink on quality vellum in a large quarto size, with generous margins that accommodate ornate printed illustration on all four borders of every page. The volume is decorated with fifty-eight large and numerous small metalcut illustrations on religious and secular themes. It has been further embellished with hand decoration. Overall, it is a high-quality production, as are most of the remaining copies in the edition.[16]

The hand decoration on this copy includes the addition of painted two and three-line initials with floral infill and gold leaf. These have been applied selectively over printed red initials on folios B7 to K8v. In addition, ten of the fifty-eight, full-page metalcut images and borders have been painted. These include St John on Patmos from the Gospel readings (fol. B6v), all eight illustrations for the Hours of the Virgin (folios C6, D5, E4, E8v, F4v, F8v, G4v, H1v) and also David and Bathsheba, the first illustration in the Penitential Psalms (folio I2v). Several painted borders include the initials IC and IT, so far unidentified and probably added at the request of the first owner at additional cost.[17] This type of added adornment is common in printed Books of Hours. A modern aesthetic might prefer the classical 'purity' of the unadorned print, but for the sixteenth-century owner, added pigment and gold enriched the value of the book both as a precious devotional object and as an *objet de luxe* or *bijou*.[18] The degree of painted intervention in printed Books of Hours can vary from light colour washes to heavy painting that completely covers the print, sometimes with a completely different composition. The artist of the Stokes copy has painted over the

---

16   Online library catalogue entries do not always record details, but as far as can be determined, all fourteen extant copies, except for the one in the Huntingdon Library, San Marino, appear to be printed on vellum rather than the cheaper paper. In addition, several are richly embellished with additional decoration, some including owners' coats of arms. According to Claerr, *Imprimerie et réussite sociale à Paris*, Kerver often printed on paper, particularly towards

the end of his career; however, he does not seem to have economised with this edition. It is hazardous to make generalisations based on so few remaining copies, but the 10 September edition was possibly produced as an expensive, luxury imprint. Some editions of Kerver's Books of Hours, such as that for Sarum use printed for William Bretton in 1510, survive mostly on cheaper paper. Others, such as Kerver's 29 April 1522 and 27 May 1522 imprints, were printed without any decoration in the borders, which may have made them cheaper than the 22 September edition.

17   The painting and binding almost certainly took place after purchase, at the request and expense of the purchaser. Binders were sometimes also illuminators. See the example of Jean Leclerc, a sworn illuminator and binder discussed in Rouse & Rouse, 'Post-Mortem Inventories', pp. 469–78.

18   Labarre, *Le livre dans la vie*, p. 173, notes that precious Books of Hours were sometimes listed in inventories as *bijoux* and *objets de luxe* rather than books.

printed image, and even though he has followed the basic outlines, he often ignores the fine details. For example, comparing his treatment of the Flight into Egypt (folio G4v) with the unpainted version, we can see that the angels and palm trees of Egypt have been painted over with a scene resembling the French countryside (Figures 10.2 and 10.3).

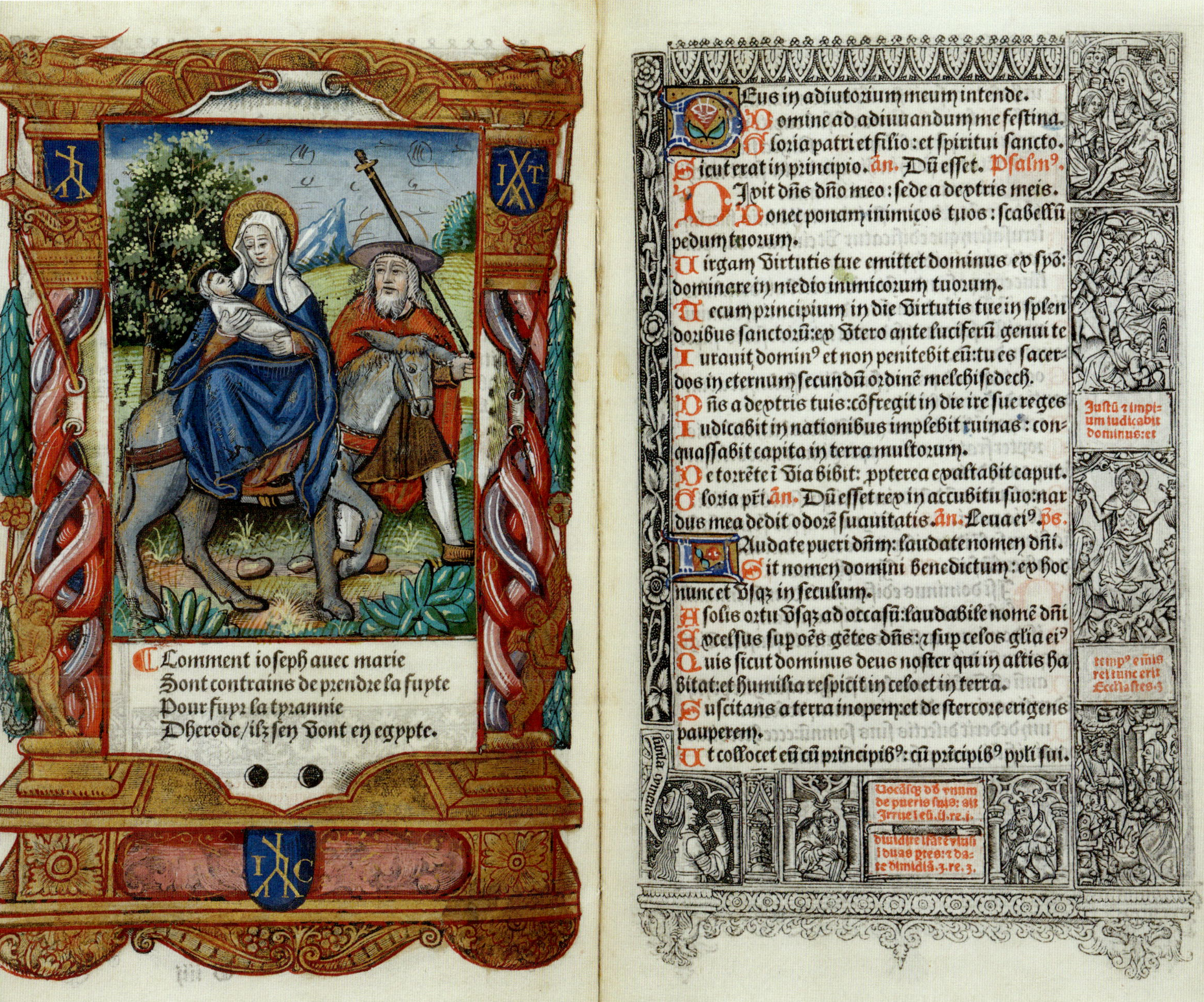

Figure 10.2: Thielman Kerver. Flight into Egypt from *Book of Hours*. Folios G4v–G5, 1522. Parchment, 22.5cm × 14.8cm. Kerry Stokes Collection, Perth. LIB.2015.051.

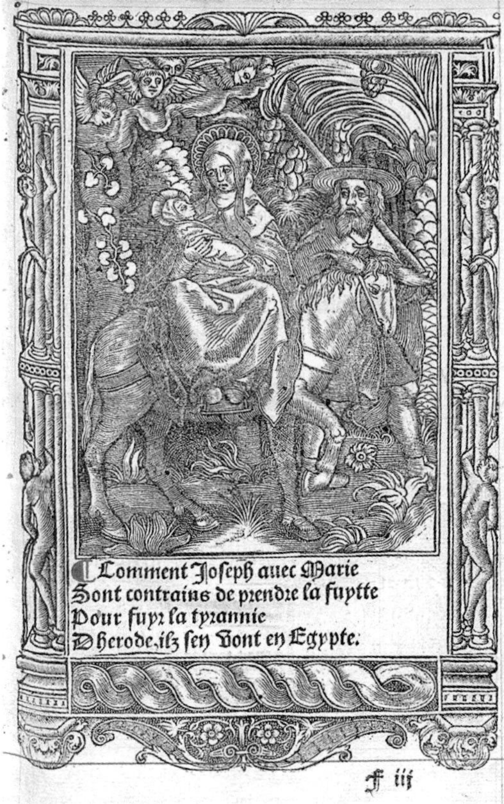

Figure 10.3: Thielman Kerver (printed by Yolande Bonhomme), *Hor(a)e beat(a)e Marie virginis ad vsum fratrum predicatorum, ordinis sancti dominici*. Folio 3, 1542. Staatsbibliothek, Berlin. DV 7260.

The publishers of printed Books of Hours were well aware of the importance of illustration for their clients and they frequently promoted it on the opening page. Kerver's last edition is described as *'Hore beatissime virginis marie secundu(m) usum Romanu(m) totaliter ad longum plerisq(ue) nouis imaginib(us) huic nouissime recognitioni passim insertis adornate'*. ('Hours of the Blessed Virgin Mary according to the Use of Rome, complete and without abbreviation, with many new images inserted everywhere for this most recent decorated edition').[19] The colophon at the end of the book repeats

the promise of new illustrations, but in French: *'avecques plusieures belles hystoires nouvelles'* ('with several beautiful new images') (folio R8v).

This enticement to prospective clients is followed by unusually profuse illustration for a Book of Hours. Most Books of Hours preface each hour in the Hours of the Virgin with a series of large illustrations on standard subjects, and this edition is no exception.[20] However, the seven large illustrations for each of the Penitential Psalms, the eleven for the Office of the Dead and the seven-plate cycles for the Hours of the Cross and Hours of the Holy Spirit are not so commonly included. More usually these Offices are represented by only one or two illustrations. In addition, many Books of Hours illustrate the calendar, but usually with the Labours of the Months or the signs or the zodiac; here we see the rare subject of the Twelve Ages of Man, one illustration for each month. Every page of this book has also been printed with detailed figurative or decorative borders on all four sides. The subjects include a Creation cycle (in the borders of the Gospel Readings), typological sets of three images (in the mixed Offices up to Vespers), the Apocalypse (Vespers and Compline of the mixed Offices), Fifteen Signs before Doomsday (Penitential Psalms), as well as narrative excerpts from the Prodigal Son and Life of Susanna from the Old Testament Book of Daniel. In addition to these subjects from biblical history, the popular theme of the Dance of Death appears in the lateral borders of the Office of the Dead. Secular border imagery includes figures from classical mythology, bucolic hunting and rural

---

19   Thanks to Stephen Kennedy for the translation from the Latin.

20   The Hours of the Virgin in the Stokes Hours follows the conventional subjects: Annunciation (Matins), Visitation (Lauds), Nativity (Prime), Annunciation to the Shepherds (Terce), Adoration of the Magi (Sext), Presentation in the Temple (None), Flight into Egypt (Vespers) and Coronation of the Virgin (Compline). See Wieck, *Painted Prayers* and *The Book of Hours* for conventions of illustration in Books of Hours.

scenes, grotesques, Renaissance-inspired putti, and decorative and intertwining vegetation. Also of note are the ornate tabernacle frames around all large illustrations. These extravagant structures incorporate interlace or panelled columns, architraves and capitals, laurel swags and tassels, decorative corners, putti and lions. Many of the large metalcut illustrations appear

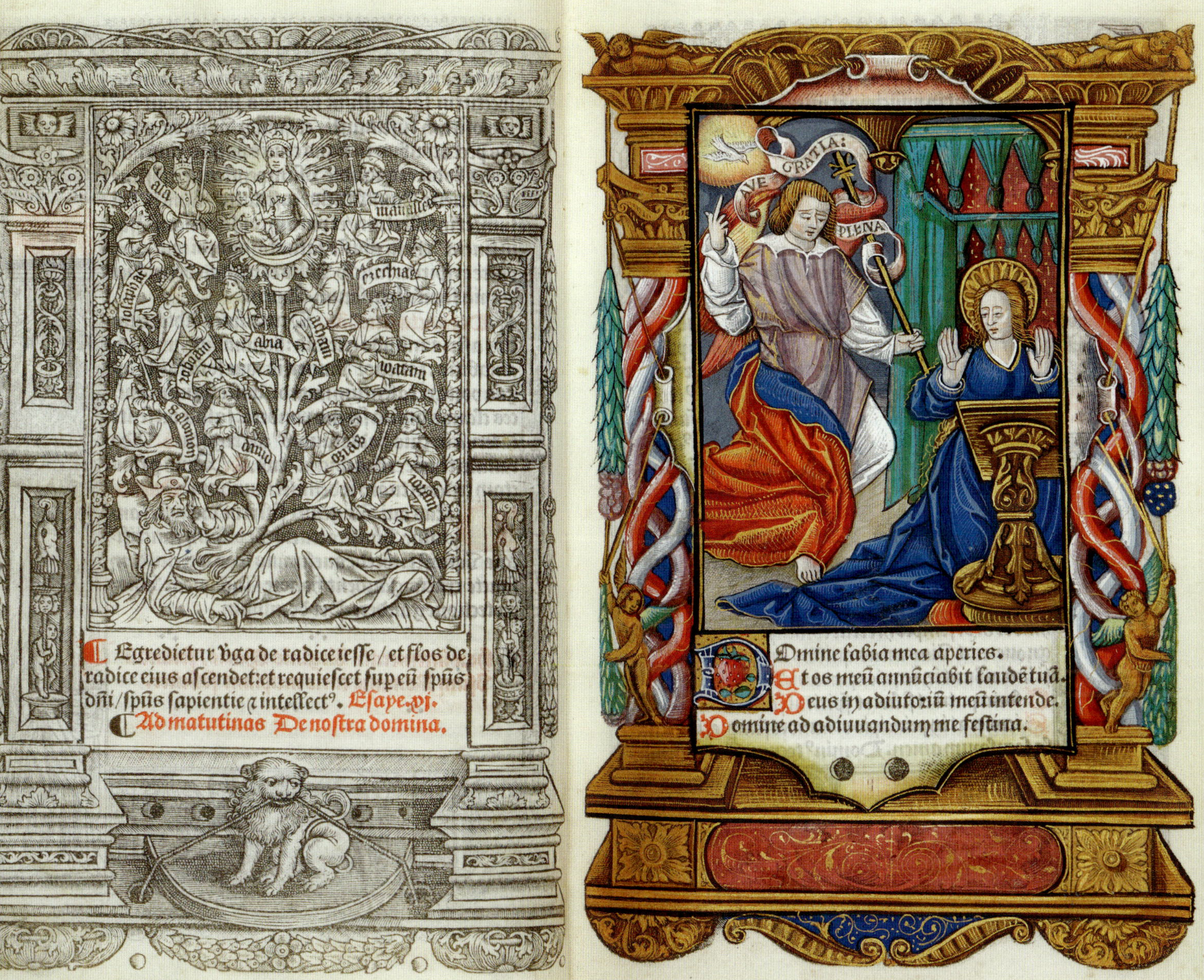

Figure 10.4: Thielman Kerver. Tree of Jesse and Annuciation from *Book of Hours*. Folios C5v–C6, 1522. Parchment, 22.5cm × 14.8cm. Kerry Stokes Collection, Perth. LIB.2015.051.

as illusionistic pages, possibly even animal skins in reference to the book's composition, unfurled and secured by ropes held by putti or in the mouth of a crouching lion (Figure 10.4).

Thanks to the remarkable publications of Tenschert, Nettekoven and Zöhl on the printed Books of Hours in the Antiquariat Bibermühle collection, the artists responsible for the designs in Kerver's last Book of Hours have been described and identified.[21] Over the years Kerver successively used three principal designers: the Master of the Apocalypse Rose of the Sainte-Chapelle, Jean Pichore, and a third one strongly influenced by Dürer and other German artists. The designs of all these artists are represented in this imprint. The earliest artist was active in Paris from around 1480 to 1510 and not only illuminated manuscripts but provided designs for other media including tapestries and stained glass, in addition to printed Hours by several printers and stationers, including Anthoine Vérard, Philippe Pigouchet and Simon Vostre, Jean Petit, Jean Du Pré as well as Kerver himself.[22] This artist is known, confusingly, by three different names after his three major works in different media: the Master of the Cloisters Unicorn (*Maître de la Chasse à la Licorne*), the Master of Anne de Bretagne (*Maître des Très Petites Heures d'Anne de Bretagne*) and the Master of the Apocalypse Rose of the Sainte-Chapelle.[23]

This style of the artist we will call the Master of the Apocalypse Rose is often characterised as 'gothic' because of the elegance of his clear, careful line work, minimal shading and concern with pictorial depth, and his pleasingly

even distribution of forms across the picture plane. Kerver included this artist's designs in Books of Hours throughout his career, and four large illustrations in the Stokes Hours were based in his designs: the Tree of Jesse (fol. C5v) (Figure 10.4), the Virgin of the Immaculate Conception (folio N6v), the Trinity (folio O1v) and the *Arma Christi* (folio Q3v), all from an octavo set commissioned by Kerver between 1498 and 1502 and based on designs originally commissioned by another eminent Parisian publisher, Simon Vostre, around 1495.[24] Also designed by the Apocalypse Rose Master were Kerver's printer's mark (this version dating from *c*.1507), the Anatomical Man (a guide to good health according to the zodiac) (folio A2) and several smaller illustrations (folios B8, B8v, C3v, C4, C4v, P1v, P3, Q4v, R5, R7).

Kerver also employed border designs designed by the Master of the Apocalypse Rose. According to Tenschert et al., some of these were directly commissioned from the artist by Kerver, while others were copied from existing designs originally made by the artist for Vostre.[25] The master's designs include the five standing sibyls (folio O5v) who foretold the birth of Christ, placed in the lateral border of the prayer to the Virgin, *O Intemerata*, and the half-length sibyls appearing in the corners of borders throughout the book. The Master's twenty-one-plate Apocalypse cycle comprising forty-two scenes, which first appears in Kerver's Hours around 1505, is seen here in its entirety and in sequential order in the lateral

21   Tenschert and Nettekoven, *Horae B.M.V.*, III, no. 118, pp. 977–85, list all the subjects of the illustrations in this book and identify the various artists.

22   For a full discussion of the work of the Master of the Apocalypse Rose see Nettekoven, *Der Meister der Apokalysenrose*.

23   For a summary of the nomenclature of this artist see Claerr, 'L'édition des heures du 21 Avril 1505', p. 414.

24   These metalcuts are described by Ina Nettekoven in Tenschert and Nettekoven, *Horae B.M.V.*, I, pp. 229–32. See also Nettekoven, Tenschert and Zöhl, *Horae B.M.V.*, IX, pp. 3975–78 and Nettekoven, *Der Meister der Apokalysenrose*, pp. 91–4, 122, figures 178–95. For Vostre's designs of 1495–8 see Nettekoven, Tenschert and Zöhl, *Horae B.M.V.*, IX, pp. 3964–71.

25   The Master of the Apocalypse Rose's border designs for Kerver are discussed in Tenschert and Nettekoven, *Horae B.M.V.*, I, pp. 229–32 and III, p. 985. See also Nettekoven, Tenschert and Zöhl, *Horae B.M.V.*, IX, pp. 4190–97 and Nettekoven, *Der Meister der Apokalysenrose*, pp. 98, 124, figures 235–8.

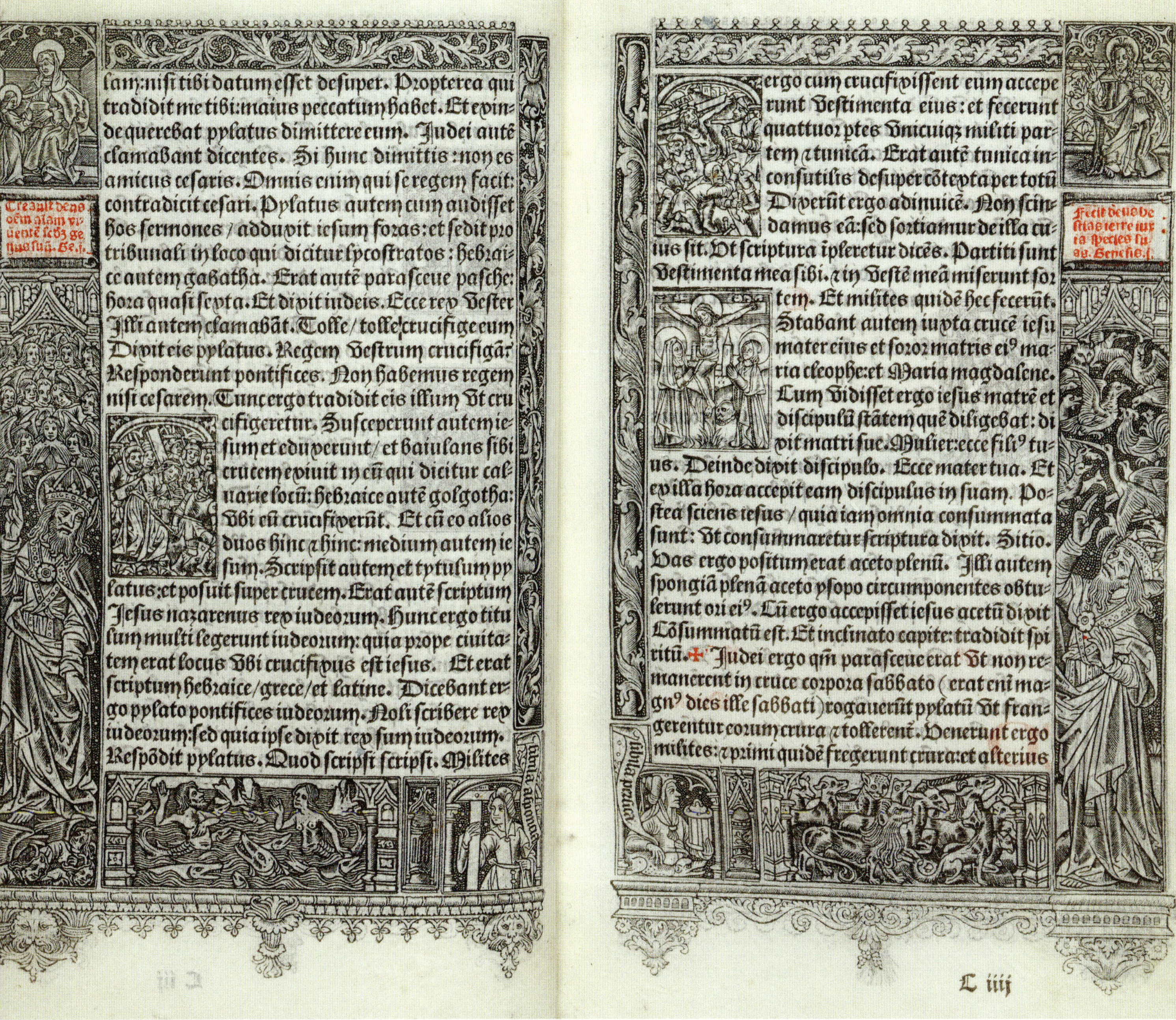

Figure 10.5: Thielman Kerver. Creation scenes in the borders, Gospel readings from *Book of Hours*. Folios C3v–C4, 1522. Parchment, 22.5cm × 14.8cm. Kerry Stokes Collection, Perth. LIB.2015.051.

borders from half-way through the mixed hours to the beginning of the Penitential Psalms (folios G6–I3). Each scene is captioned with the appropriate biblical text in Latin in red print. The Master has also contributed a ten-plate Creation cycle, first used by Kerver in 1497 and employed here in the lower and lateral borders of the Gospel readings (folios C3–C5) (Figure 10.5). All the ten plates have been used in this book; however, whoever set the images has made a mistake. On the lower border of folio C3v we see the third sign from the Master's 1497 Fifteen Signs before Doomsday, the 'great fish surface and roar', instead of the Creation scene of the Fall of the Rebel Angels, which is used out of sequence on folio N5v. This is the only plate from the Fifteen Signs cycle used in the book; a different set of images by another artist on the same theme appears in the borders of the Penitential Psalms (folios I5v–I8).[26]

Other border material by the Master of the Apocalypse Rose is used in a piecemeal way, possibly because many of the old plates had worn out after years of use. For example, around 1497 this master devised forty-six plates (each comprising three scenes) representing typological scenes based on the *Biblia Pauperum*. Only three of these plates are re-employed here, the central New Testament subjects being Mary's Betrothal (folio C7), the Massacre of the Innocents (folio D3v), and the Mocking of Christ (folio E5v) The other forty-one typological borders in the Stokes book were printed from plates designed by a different artist working in a Germanic style.[27] Other metalcuts by the Apocalypse Rose Master in the book are

best described as 'fillers' rather than contributions to planned narrative cycles. These include fragments of two sequences of Susanna and the Elders (folio O2v) and the Prodigal Son (folio O8v) and three small plates from the New Testament in the lateral border of folio O6.

The second principal designer for images in early sixteenth-century printed Books of Hours was Jean Pichore, who was active in Paris from 1502 to 1521, in the generation after the Master of the Apocalypse Rose.[28] His style was strongly influenced by the French and Italian Renaissance and can be seen in Books of Hours by all the major publishers and printers, including Vostre, the Hardouyn brothers, Vérard, Kerver and others. Kerver commissioned several sets of plates from him, including a single border cycle of the Dance of Death, which is the only design by Pichore used in the 10 September 1522 imprint. It shows figures from all levels of society being courted by Death in the form of a cadaver or skeleton. Its purpose is to remind readers of the fragility of life and the futility of earthly vanities, and perhaps it offers them a diversion from the devotions of the main text in which it appears, the Office of the Dead. The theme first appeared in the late fifteenth century and was soon adopted for the borders of printed Hours, including by Jean du Pré around 1488 and Simon Vostre in 1496. Pichore's design for the Dance of Death was the only border cycle he completed for Kerver, and it first appears in a Book of Hours published on 23 June 1507.[29] Thirty-three plates comprise sixty-six figures

---

26   For the Fifteen Signs before Doomsday see Driver, 'Picturing the Apocalypse'.

27   This anonymous artist with German stylistic influences was responsible for most of the typological borders, which first appeared in Kerver's Books of Hours in 1511, and also the Fifteen Signs before Doomsday, first used in 1515, which appears in the borders of the Penitential Psalms. See Tenschert and Nettekoven, *Horae B.M.V.*, II, p. 985 and

Nettekoven, Tenschert and Zöhl, *Horae B.M.V.*, IX, pp. 4131, 4152, 4208, 4215–17.

28   Jean Pichore's contribution to Kerver's Books of Hours is discussed in Tenschert and Nettekoven, *Horae B.M.V.*, II, p. 449–53 and Nettekoven, Tenschert and Zöhl, *Horae B.M.V.*, IX, pp. 3999–4003. See also Zöhl, *Jean Pichore*, pp. 137–8, 155.

29   Zöhl, *Jean Pichore*, p. 155, fig. 236; Nettekoven, Tenschert and Zöhl, *Horae B.M.V.*, IX, pp. 4204, 4207.

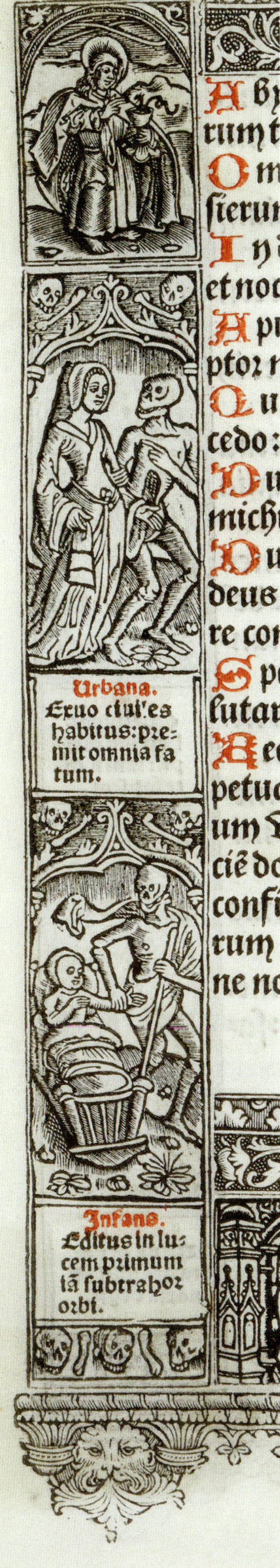

including thirty-one men, thirty-four women and one baby: the complete cycle appears in the Stokes book (Figure 10.6).

So far, these are not the 'new images inserted everywhere' promoted by Kerver on the first page of the book. All had been previously published in Kerver's Books of Hours, and in 1522 the most recent were seven years old. However, the great majority of the other illustrations in the book were new, including the Twelve Ages of Man images in the calendar, two for the Gospel Readings, eight for the Hours of the Virgin, six for thc Hours of the Cross (there are seven illustrations but the Arrest of Christ is repeated from the Gospel Readings), seven for the Hours of the Holy Spirit, seven for the Penitential Psalms, and eleven for the Office of the Dead. Kerver commissioned these metalcuts between 1519 and 1522 and their first appearance together is in an octavo edition Kerver published on 29 April 1522, less than five months before the Stokes imprint.[30] This small-format edition was printed without the extraordinarily rich borders of the 10 September edition or any additional hand decoration, and it may have been offered as a cheaper version.

The subjects of some of these fifty-three new metalcuts are rarely represented. These include the Ages of Man, an allegory that compares every six years of life to the months of the year, from childhood in January to death in December (Figure 10.7); the story of David in the Penitential Psalms (Figure 10.8); and the highly original cycle for the Office of the Dead.[31]

30 This imprint has been described by Nettekoven, Tenschert and Zöhl, *Horae B.M.V*, VII, no. 117.2, pp. 3131–42. I thank Caroline Zöhl for kindly sending me this catalogue entry. The entire set of fifty-three metalcuts is listed and illustrated in Nettekoven, Tenschert and Zöhl, *Horae B.M.V.*, IX, pp. 4060–9.

31 These illustrations are described in detail by Zöhl in 'A Phenomenon of Parallel Reading'.

◄ Figure 10.6: Thielman Kerver. Dance of Death (townswoman and infant) border images, Office of the Dead from *Book of Hours*. Folio M6v, 1522. Parchment, 22.5cm × 14.8cm. Kerry Stokes Collection, Perth. LIB.2015.051.

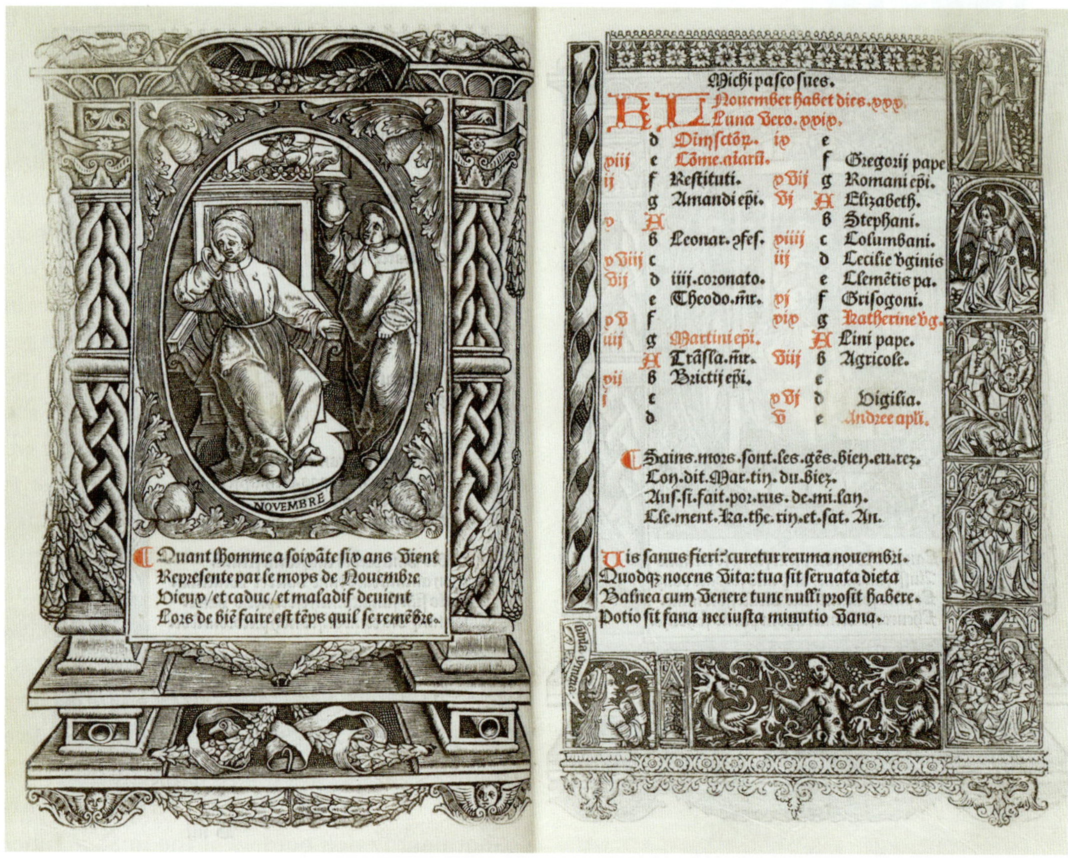

Figure 10.7: Thielman Kerver, Paris. Month of November, age of 66, Calendar from *Book of Hours*. Folios B4v–B5, 1522. Parchment, 22.5cm × 14.8cm. Kerry Stokes Collection, Perth. LIB.2015.051.

It has been shown that all these illustrations were derived from a program of metalcuts by Jean Pichore first published in a Book of Hours issued by Jean Barbier and Guillaume le Rouge on 22 August 1509.[32] Although the

subjects were based Pichore's metalcuts, for the most part the anonymous artist chose not to imitate his style or composition. Rather, the well-modelled, robust, and expressive figures are indebted to the traditions of German printmaking, specifically Dürer, Cranach, and Holbein. For example, the figures from Adam and Eve in the Expulsion from the first reading at Matins in the Office of the Dead (folio L5v) are clearly based on the *Expulsion* woodcut from Dürer's *Small Passion* of *c*.1510. The prostrate figure in the foreground of Cranach's *Christ Crowned with Thorns* from the Passion series of *c*.1509 (Figure 10.9) appears in reverse as a shepherd in the *Annunciation to the Shepherds* illustrating Terce in the Hours of the Virgin

32   These metalcuts from the Barbier and le Rouge edition of 1509 are discussed and reproduced in Nettekoven, Tenschert and Zöhl, *Horae B.M.V.*, IX, pp. 4030–40. After Kerver's death these subjects were used in Books of Hours published by his widow, Yolande Bonhomme, first employing Kerver's plates and then a new set in a different style. Publishers François Regnault and Germain Hardouyn also used these subjects in their Books of Hours. While different from each other, both these sets share elements of style and composition with Bonhomme's second series. Around 1532, the Master of François de Rohan executed illuminations on the themes based on these printed models. See Sutton, 'Sources and the Sarum Hours'.

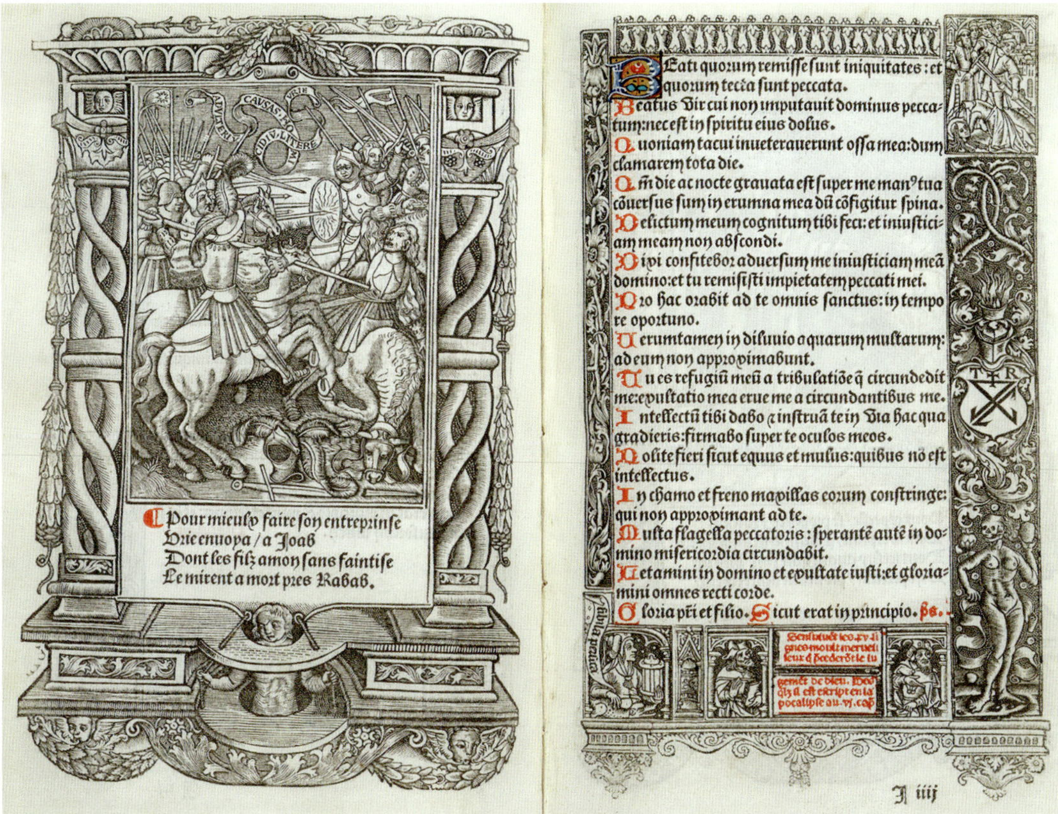

Figure 10.8: Thielman Kerver. Death of Uriah, Penitential Psalms from *Book of Hours*. Folios I3v–I4, 1522. Parchment, 22.5cm × 14.8cm. Kerry Stokes Collection, Perth. LIB.2015.051.

(Figure 10.10, folio E8v). Tenschert and Nettekoven have noted these and many other German quotations, such as the figure balanced on one leg to the right of Christ in the Arrest (folio E2 and folio C1), which compares with the same subject by Hans Schäufelein in Pinder's *Speculum passionis* of 1507.[33]

This artist's familiarity with German printmaking might indicate that he was of German origin or that he was influenced by contemporary German prints circulating in France. Regardless of his background, he skilfully synthesised his influences into coherent, successful compositions. Kerver's claim on the first page is surely justified by

the richness and abundance of this artist's program of illustration. His metalcut designs, together with those by the other artists, made this edition a tour de force of invention, skill, and coordination. Kerver's final imprint was one of the most accomplished and beautiful editions of printed Books of Hours of the sixteenth century, and the hitherto unknown copy in the Stokes collection is one of its best examples.

About the author

Hilary Maddocks is an Honorary Fellow in Art History at the University of Melbourne. Recent publications include articles on medieval

---

33 Tenschert and Nettekoven, *Horae B.M.V.*, III, pp. 961–66.

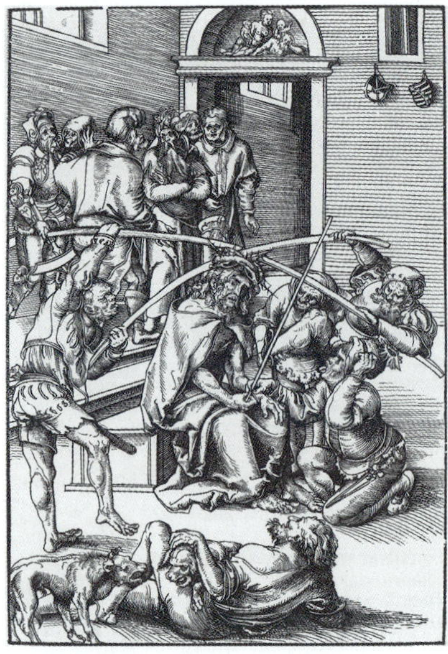

◀ Figure 10.9: Lucas Cranach the Elder, *Christ Crowned with Thorns*, *c*.1509. Woodcut print, 25cm × 17cm. National Gallery of Art, Washington, Accession Number 1949.14.9.

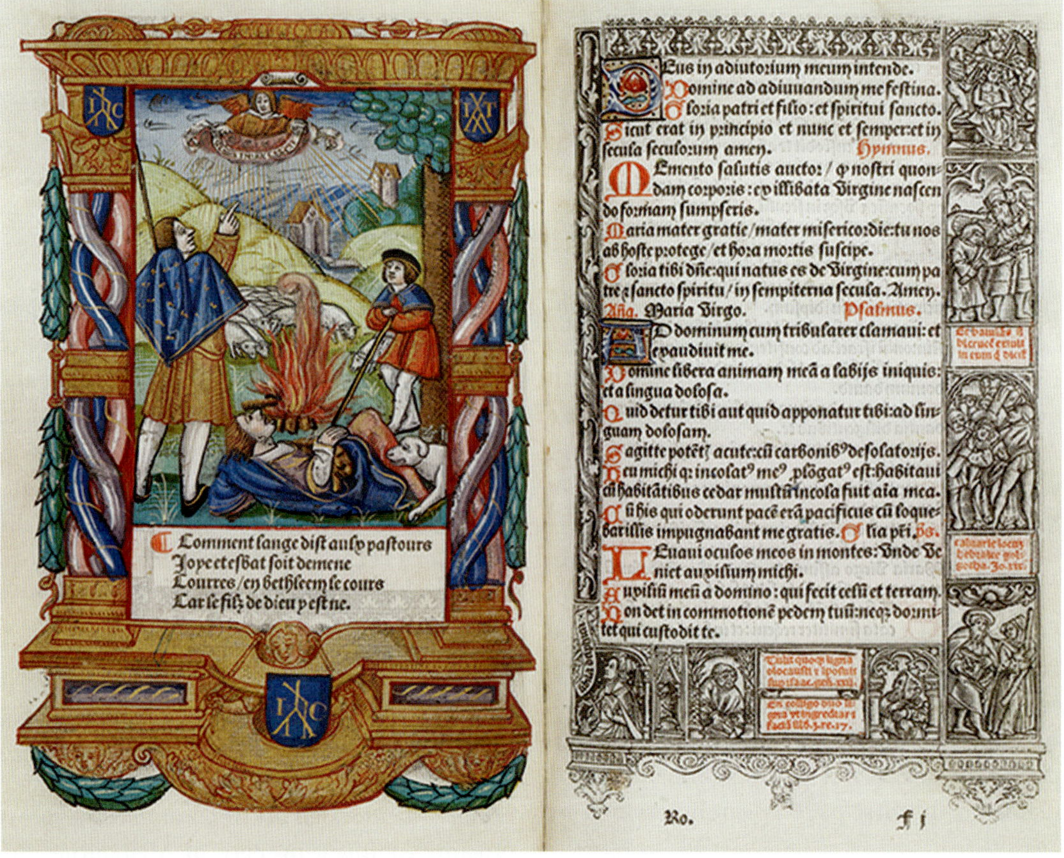

Figure 10.10: Thielman Kerver. Annunciation to the Shepherds, Hours of the Virgin from *Book of Hours*. Folios E8v–F1, 1522. Parchment, 23.7cm × 16cm. Kerry Stokes Collection, Perth. LIB.2015.051.

manuscript illumination and early printed book illustration, and the monograph *Hertha Kluge-Pott: Printmaker* (2015). h.maddocks@unimelb.edu.au

Works cited

Hans Bohatta, *Bibliographie der Livres d'Heures (Horae B.M.V.) Officia, Hortuli Animae, Coronae B.M.V, Rosaria und Cursus B.M.V. des XV und XVI Jahrhundert* (Vienna: Verlag Von Gilhofer and Ranschburg, 1924).

Roger Chartier, *The Cultural Uses of Print in Early Modern France* (Princeton: Princeton University Press, 1987).

Christie's, *Maurice Burrus (1882–1959): La Bibliothèque d'un Homme de Goût, Sale 4035, Paris, 15 December 2015*, lot 99, accessed 15 July 2015 at http://www.christies.com/Maurice-Burrus-1882-1959-la-25794.aspx.

Thierry Claerr, 'Imprimerie et réussite sociale à Paris à la fin du Moyen Âge: Thielman Kerver, imprimeur-libraire de 1497 à 1522', thesis, Diplôme de conservateur de bibliothèque, Ecole Nationale Supérieure des Sciences de l'Information et des Bibliothèques, 2000.

Thierry Claerr, 'L'édition d'Heures du 21 avril 1505, une œuvre charnière dans la production de Thielman Kerver?' in *Books of Hours Reconsidered*, ed. by Sandra Hindman and James H. Marrow (London: Harvey Miller Publishers, 2013), pp. 409–17.

Martha W. Driver, 'Picturing the Apocalypse in the Printed Book of Hours', in *Prophecy, Apocalypse and the Day of Doom*, ed. by Nigel Morgan (Donnington: Shaun Tyas, 2004), pp. 52–67, pls. 3–17.

Drouot, *Livres Anciens, Première Partie, Bibliothèque Lucien Allienne, Manuscrits, Incunables, Livres d'heures, Livres Illustrés du XVIII Siècle, Littérature, Voyage, Les Métamorphoses d'Ovide, Hôtel Drouot, 15 November, 1985* (Paris: Drouot, 1985).

Eamon Duffy, *Marking the Hours: English People and their Prayers 1240–1570* (New Haven, London: Yale University Press, 2006).

Lucien Febvre and Henri-Jean Martin, *The Coming of the Book: The Impact of Printing 1450–1800* (London: Verso, 1997).

Albert Labarre, *Le livre dans la vie amiénoise du seizième siècle* (Paris: Nauwelaerts, 1971).

Ina Nettekoven, *Der Meister der Apokalypsenrose der Sainte Chapelle und die Pariser Buchkunst um 1500* (Turnhout: Brepols, 2004).

Ina Nettekoven, Heribert Tenschert and Caroline Zöhl, *Horae B.M.V.: 365 gedruckte Stundenbücher aus der Sammlung Bibermühle, 1487–1586*, 6 vols (Ramsen, Switzerland: Heribert Tenschert, 2014).

Annie Parent, *Les métiers du livre à Paris au XVIe siècle (1535–1560)* (Geneva: Droz, 1974).

Ernest Quentin-Bauchart, *Les femmes bibliophiles de France: XVIe, XVIIe et XVIII siècles* (Paris: Damascène Morgand, 1886).

Virginia Reinburg, *French Books of Hours: Making an Archive of Prayer c.1400–1600* (Cambridge and New York: Cambridge University Press, 2012).

Mary and Richard Rouse, 'Post-Mortem Inventories as a Source for the Production of Manuscripts and Printed Books of Hours', in *Books of Hours Reconsidered*, ed. by Sandra Hindman and James H. Marrow (London: Harvey Miller Publishers, 2013), pp. 469–78.

Sotheby's, *Livres et manuscrits, Sale PF1503, Paris, 25 June 2015*, lot 34, accessed 15 July 2016 at http://www.sothebys.com/fr/auctions/2015/livres-manuscrits-pf1503.html.

Henry Sotheran and Co., *Bibliotheca Pretiosa: Being an Unusually Choice Collection of Books and Manuscripts in Exceptionally Fine Condition* (London 1907) no. 265, accessed 15 July 2016 at https://archive.org/details/bibliothecapretioolonduoft.

Kay Sutton, 'Sources and the Sarum Hours illuminated by the Master of François de Rohan', in *Quand la peinture était dans les livres. Mélanges en l'honneur de François Avril*, ed. by Mara Hoffman and Caroline Zöhl (Turnhout: Brepols and Bibliothèque nationale de France, 2007), pp. 331–43.

Heribert Tenschert and Ina Nettekoven, *Horae B.M.V.: 158 Stundenbuchdrucke der Sammlung Bibermühle, 1490–1550*, 3 vols (Ramsen, Switzerland: Heribert Tenschert, 2003).

Roger S. Wieck, *The Book of Hours in Medieval Art and Life* (London: Sotheby's Publications, 1988).

Roger S Wieck, *Painted Prayers: The Book of Hours in Medieval and Renaissance Art* (New York: George Braziller and Pierpont Morgan Library, 1997).

Caroline Zöhl, *Jean Pichore: Buchmaler, Graphiker und Verleger in Paris um 1500* (Turnhout: Brepols, 2004).

Caroline Zöhl, 'A phenomenon of parallel reading in the Office of the Dead', in *Mixed metaphors: The Dance Macabre in medieval and early modern Europe*, ed. by Sophie Oosterwijk and Stefanie Knll (Newcastle upon Tyne: Cambridge Scholars, 2011), pp. 325–60.

11. An accessory of intellect: a Renaissance writing casket from the Kerry Stokes Collection

Miya Tokumitsu

Dunlop, Anne (ed.), *Antipodean Early Modern. European Art in Australian Collections, c. 1200–1600*, Amsterdam University Press, 2018

DOI: 10.5117/9789462985209/CH11

Abstract

This essay discusses a Northern Italian bronze writing casket from *c*.1500, once owned by Cardinal Francesco Todeschini Piccolomini, later Pope Pius III (1439–1503). The casket emerged from a thriving industry of bronze manufacture around Padua and the Veneto specialising in sophisticated, small-scale objects typically destined for *studioli* and other private domestic spaces. Looking beyond the casket's site of production, the essay also discusses its social roles as a medium for posterity and family honour, as well as its ability to help constitute the *studiolo* as an environment for learned pursuits and the construction of a modern, Renaissance individuality.

Keywords: Bronze; *Studiolo*; Italy; Collecting; Humanism; Miniature

In her book, *On Longing,* Susan Stewart writes, 'The collection's space must move between the public and the private, between display and hiding. Thus the miniature is suitable as an item of collection because it is sized for individual consumption at the same time that its surplus detail connotes infinity and distance'.[1] A fifteenth-century bronze writing casket in the Kerry Stokes collection (Figure 11.1) is an object that encapsulates the dyadic qualities of individual fascination and infinite possibility that Stewart ascribes to the collectible object. The casket is rendered in the format of a miniature ancient sarcophagus, and is precisely the kind of object once found alongside other small-scale precious items in a private *studiolo,* or study. These rooms and the objects in them

held a special place in Italian Renaissance society; they helped constitute individual and familial honour, both essential for self-fashioning and preserving memory.[2] The Stokes casket was at once a deeply intimate possession and an important tool for defining the public face of its owner and his family.

Although attribution has been wide-ranging and contested, current scholarship coalesces around the idea that the Stokes casket and related variants emerged from the workshop of Paduan sculptor Severo da Ravenna (active *c*.1496–1543), who specialized in finely worked small-scale bronzes for élite collectors.[3]

[1]   Stewart, *On Longing,* p. 155.

[2]   Thornton, *Scholar in His Study,* pp. 4–7; Hendrix, 'Italian Humanists at Home', p. 25.

[3]   Reid and Vaughan, 'Writing Casket', cat. No. 52. See Radcliffe, 'Writing Casket', cat. no. 31, Pope-Hennessy, *Renaissance Bronzes,* and Scholten, *Robert Lehman Collection,* cat. nos. 134–136 for discussion of attribution history.

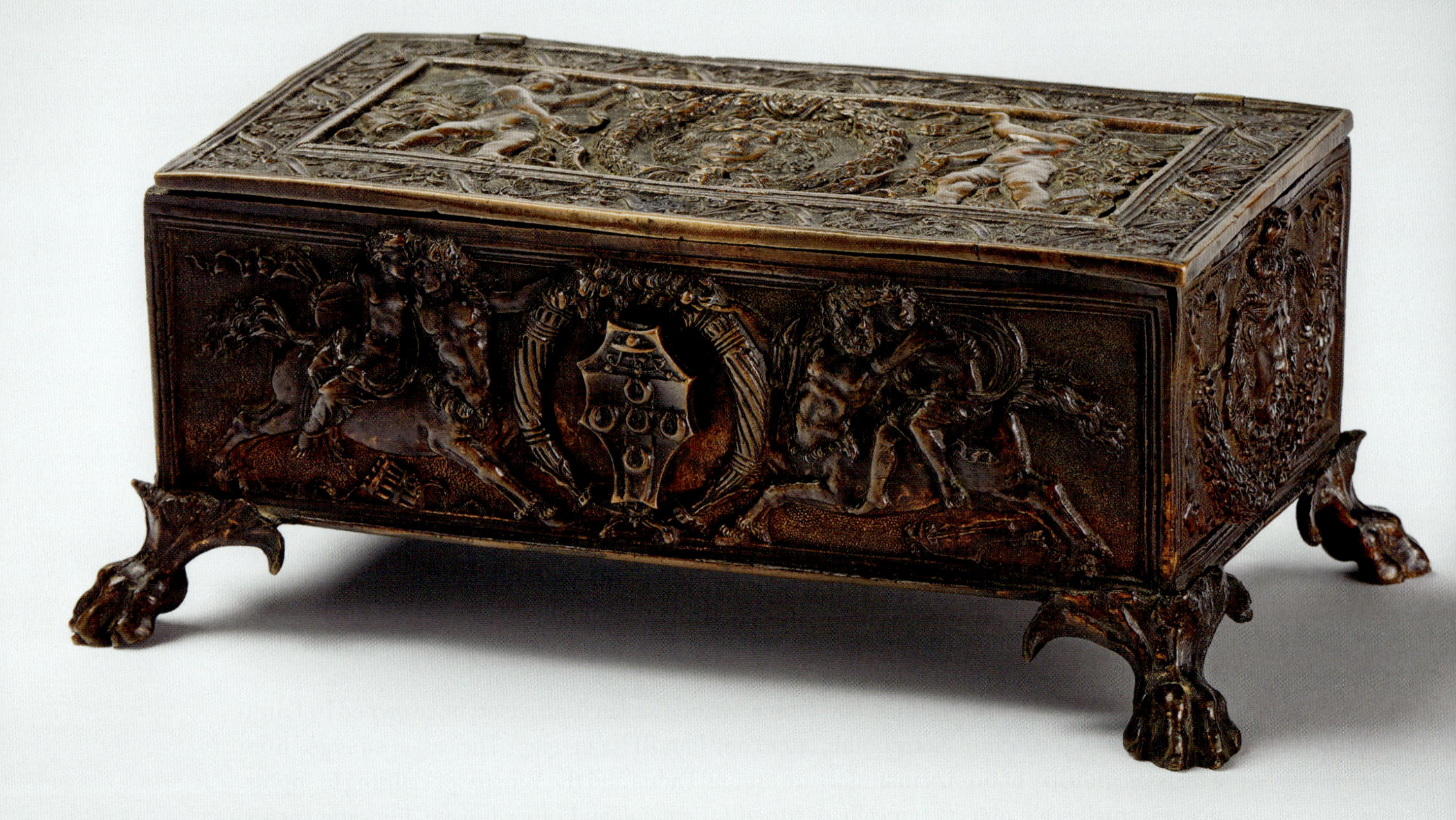

Figure 11.1: Paduan(?), *Writing Casket*, *c.*1500. Bronze, 9.3cm × 23cm × 13.5cm. Kerry Stokes Collection, Perth.

The casket is decorated with a diverse array of classical motifs. On the lid are two putti flanking a garland-encircled mask. The front panel features a family coat of arms in the centre surrounded by two cornucopias and centaurs bearing nymphs. The short sides of the rectangular casket bear winged Medusa masks nested in ribboned garlands. The casket itself sits upon four feet shaped like lion paws. Together with this complex iconography, the basic physical facts of this casket are significant: it is a box, that is, a utilitarian *thing,* as much as it is a work of art, and it is small (9.3cm x 23cm x 13.5cm). The captivating power of the miniature is that it demands physical proximity and interaction. The Stokes casket was an object meant to be handled and used as well as admired visually. The miniaturization of a larger-scale antique work evident in the Stokes casket was a common feature of *studiolo* objects. The small but thriving industry of bronze casters in northern Italy specialized in producing precious miniature objects specifically for *studioli,*

and sculptors like Severo and Pier Jacopo Bonacolsi (also known as 'Antico') translated famous antique – often large-scale – sculpture into bronze miniatures for the wealthy collectors of the late fifteenth and early sixteenth centuries.

We may begin by asking *who* handled and used this casket, and for what purpose. The first question can be answered straightforwardly, thanks to the coat of arms. They are those of Cardinal Francesco Todeschini Piccolomini (1439–1503), who briefly became Pope Pius III in 1503 (he died a within a month of his election).[4] The presence of Piccolomini's arms indicates that the casket was a personal household item, or else a diplomatic gift, as the Cardinal often represented his uncle, Pope Pius II, on diplomatic missions.[5]

The arms are a personalized element central to yet another aspect of the casket – the history of its production. The casket is in fact

4   Reid and Vaughan, 'Writing Casket', cat. no. 52.
5   Reid and Vaughan, 'Writing Casket', cat. no. 52.

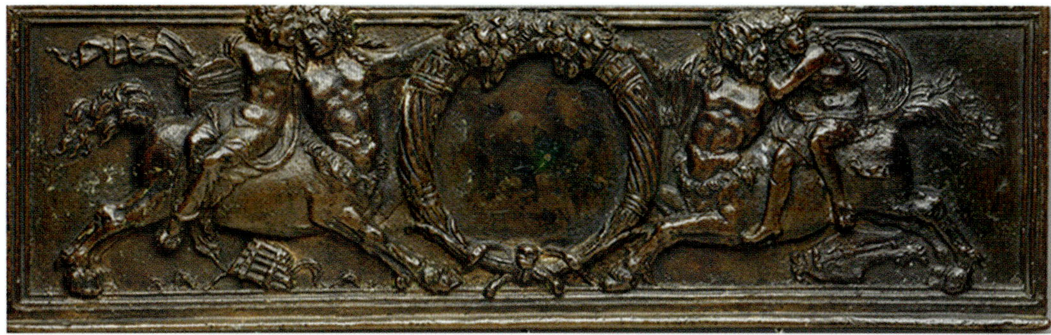

Figure 11.2: Model attributed to Severo Calzetta da Ravenna, *Front panel of a writing box decorated with centaurs and nymphs*, sixteenth century. Copper alloy, 6.5cm × 20.5cm. Lehman Collection, Metropolitan Museum of Art, New York.

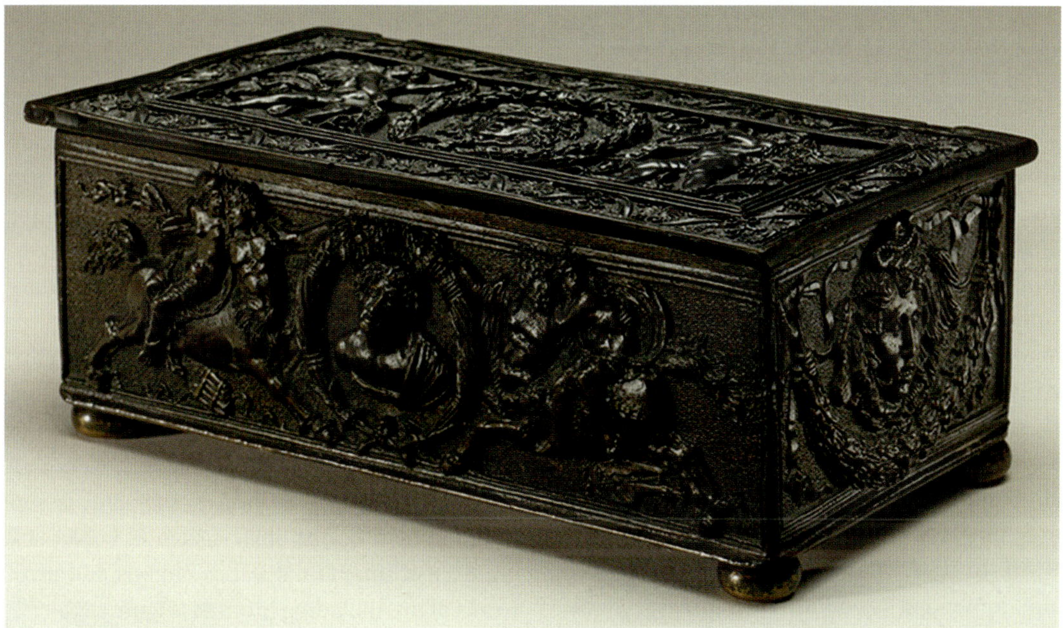

Figure 11.3: Paduan, *Writing Casket*, *c*.1500. Bronze, 7.8cm × 20.3cm × 12cm, National Gallery of Art, Washington.

a variant of a type that exists in numerous versions with many formulations.[6] A version of the Stokes casket's front panel is in the Metropolitan Museum, New York (Figure 11.2); in this work there is a blank space between the cornucopias, presumably to allow for customization with personal or favoured motifs such as coats of arms.[7] Other variants of the casket are

---

6   Pope-Hennessy, *Renaissance Bronzes*, cat. no. 491; Radcliffe, 'Writing Casket', cat. no. 31. An isolated front panel with a bust of a young man is in the National Gallery of Art, Washington, accession no. 1942.9159.b.

7   See Scholten, *Robert Lehman Collection*, cat. no. 134. The Metropolitan Museum also houses two Medusa panels similar to the side panels on the Stokes casket: accession nos. 1975.1.1333 and 1975.1.1334.

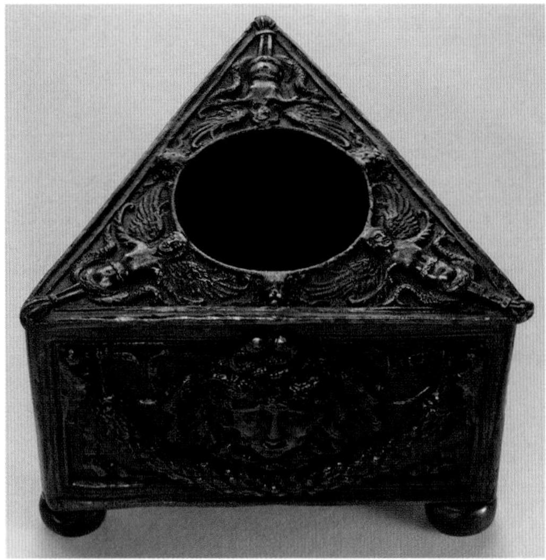

Figure 11.4: Paduan, *Sand Box, c.*1500. Bronze/Black lacquer over medium brown bronze, 8cm × 10.6cm × 9.4cm. National Gallery of Art, Washington.

housed in the National Gallery of Art, Washington (Figure 11.3), and the Thyssen-Bornemisza Museum in Madrid; in both these cases there are busts of young men between the cornucopias (although the busts themselves are not identical).[8] The Washington casket most closely resembles the Stokes one, having the same lid, sides, and front panel but differing in the decoration inside the front panel's cornucopias and resting on depressed ball feet rather than on lion's paws.

All of the related caskets' panels, feet, and appended decorative flourishes were cast separately as individual elements and then either soldered or pinned together. This piecemeal production allowed craftsmen and patrons to 'mix and match' the elements to create bespoke works that were personal tokens of self-presentation or of relationships between individuals or families in the case of gifts. Piecemeal production also allowed workshops the flexibility to experiment rapidly with

different formulations of cast elements as they responded to 'market feedback.' Not only is the Stokes casket part of a series of variants, individual elements similar or identical to those of the Stokes casket were reformulated and circulated as other vessels and isolated plaquettes.[9] For instance, a triangular sand box comprised of three Medusa mask panels akin to the side panels on the Stokes casket is in the National Gallery in Washington (Figure 11.4).[10]

These themes of customization and personal intimacy are critical to understanding how the Stokes casket originally functioned and where it circulated. Such a casket might have held inkpots or sand for blotting, but to its owner, it was no mere container. It was a luxurious tool for manifesting intellectual labour, namely writing, and therefore an extension of the owner's body and mind.[11] Despite their seeming quotidian functionality, *studiolo* objects served as a physical medium for family posterity. Families tried strenuously to keep their *studiolo* items out of the secondary market.[12]

Objects like the Stokes casket helped constitute the private study as an environment. In Vittore Carpaccio's famous painting of St Augustine at work in a modern Venetian oratory outfitted as a *studiolo,* the saint is surrounded by precious objects such as books, scientific instruments, natural specimens, and small works of art, including bronzes (Figure 11.5).

Although the theme of the scholar in his study seems to have been a particular preoccupation for Carpaccio (he returned to it time and again in drawings), he was hardly alone in his interest. The image of the scholar-saint tucked into his study, surrounded by books,

8   Radcliffe, 'Writing Casket', cat. no. 31.
9   Pope-Hennessy, *Renaissance Bronzes,* cat. nos. 491–93.
10   Pope-Hennessy, *Renaissance Bronzes,* cat. no. 493.
11   Campbell, *The Cabinet of Eros,* p. 31.
12   Thornton, *Scholar in His Study*, p. 113.

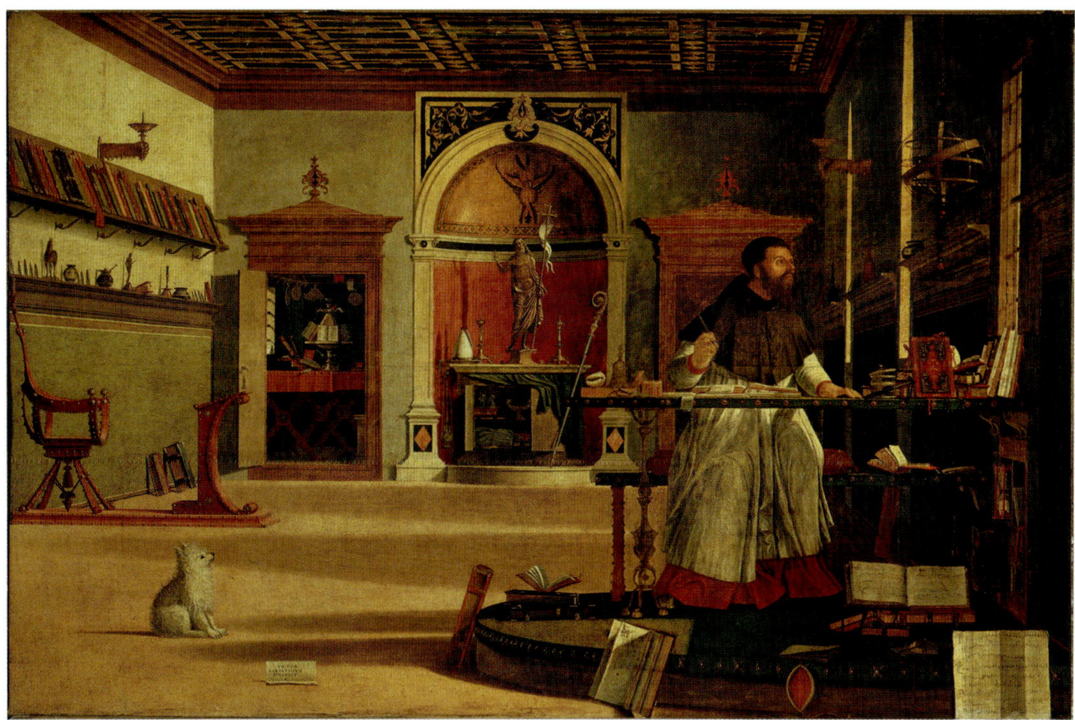

Figure 11.5: Vittore Carpaccio, *Vision of St. Augustine/St Augustine in His Study*, 1502. Tempera on canvas, 141cm × 210cm. Scuola di San Giorgio degli Schiavoni, Venice.

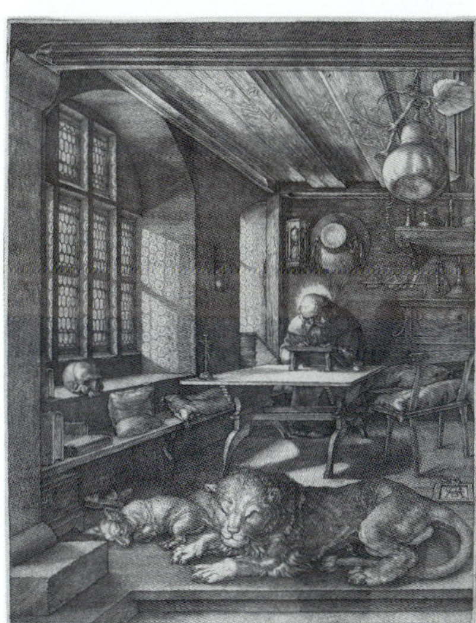

Figure 11.6: Albrecht Dürer, *St Jerome in His Study*, 1514. Engraving, 25.4cm × 19cm. National Gallery of Art, Washington.

scrolls, and other scholarly supplies, was conventionalized in Italian art during the first half of the fifteenth century, probably in emulation of Netherlandish painters who developed the theme and whose works were popular with élite Italian collectors.[13] Carpaccio's northern contemporary, Albrecht Dürer, situated another scholar saint (and Augustine's epistolary interlocutor) Jerome in a cozy, if humbler space than that of Carpaccio's Augustine (Figure 11.6). Despite the fantastical elements in Dürer's engraving – Jerome's halo, the sleeping lion and lamb, and the curious hanging gourd[14] – this is a room that looks lived in and lovingly used, evinced by a panoply of engaging details: rumpled pillows, books strewn on the bench, documents pinned to the wall, shucked-off slippers, and especially, the cracked plaster on the wall behind St Jerome.

These works give us a perspective on the lived environment of the Stokes casket.

13   Stapleford, 'Intellect and Intuition', p. 69.

14   For an analysis of the gourd's role in this picture, see Parshall, 'Albrecht Dürer's St. Jerome', pp. 303–305.

Carpaccio and Dürer show the saints at work, responding to spiritual stimulus that fuels their intellectual endeavours. Carpaccio's Augustine has momentarily ceased writing – something has dawned upon him. In fact, Carpaccio has shown Augustine at the moment when he receives in Hippo a miraculous visitation from St Jerome, which occurred upon the moment of Jerome's death in faraway Jerusalem. The account of the visitation circulated via a forged letter by Augustine to St Cyril of Jerusalem. In the letter, 'Augustine' recounts sitting down at compline to pen a letter containing some theological questions to Jerome. 'Suddenly an indescribable light, not seen in our times, and hardly to be described in our poor language, entered the cell in which I was, with an ineffable and unknown fragrance....'[15] It is a moment of disjointed awareness – Augustine knows viscerally that something momentous has occurred, and is only on the cusp of understanding what it is – the revelation is not yet complete. In Carpaccio's painting, the practical and aesthetic elements of Augustine's environment play an important role in priming him (and the viewer) to receive this inspired knowledge. The well-lit space, writing tools at hand, and other accessories of intellect, including natural specimens, miniature bronzes, and an armillary sphere, establish Carpaccio's figure as paradigmatic of an ideal scholar or sage.[16] Augustine receives the visitation while in the process of philosophical writing, an activity that requires a sufficiently illuminated, secluded space stocked with necessary implements and intellectually stimulating décor, all features of a functional Renaissance *studiolo*.

Writing tools and enclosed nooks appear in depictions of scholar-saints even when they are shown in the wilderness, as in Giovanni Bellini's *St Francis in Ecstasy* of *c*.1476–1478, now in the Frick Collection. Even if the actual enclosure is rudimentary, the accessories of intellectual work define both the person and the space as scholarly. The wilderness, like the study, is a retreat, but it is through the presence of *things* – a desk, a book, a bench – that we understand St Francis to be a writer as well as a mystic. The fact that scholar saints are consistently shown with the utilitarian and aesthetic accoutrements of scholarship indicates that these objects helped define the ideal conditions for intellectual work, and indeed what constituted a scholar. Scholarship required seclusion, quiet, and privacy; these conditions could be ensured by the proper space, whether a simple, closed-off nook or a wilderness retreat. In fact, pictures of scholar saints served as visual *exemplaria* within libraries and *studioli*. In his mid-fifteenth-century tract, *De politia litteraria*, Angelo Decembrio writes, '[In the library] we often see, too, some pleasant picture of St. Jerome at his writing in the wilderness, by which we direct the mind to the library's privacy and quiet and the application necessary to study and literary composition'.[17] The 'privacy and quiet' required for intellectual production are not mere matters of space and acoustics, but also formed by visual stimuli such as 'decent pictures or sculptures representing gods and heroes'.[18]

If depictions of scholar-saints in their studies provide images of the ideal occupants and occupations of the *studiolo*, other sources shed light on how these spaces actually functioned

---

15   Stapleford, 'Intellect and Intuition', pp. 71–72; Roberts, 'St. Augustine in "St. Jerome's Study"', p. 292. The letter explicitly states compline at the hour of St. Augustine's visitation, though this is incongruous with the apparent daylight in Carpaccio's painting.

16   Stapleford, 'Intellect and Intuition', p. 71.

17   Angelo Decembrio, translated and quoted in Baxandall, 'Guarino, Pisanello and Manuel Chrysoloras,' p. 196. See also Campbell, *Cabinet of Eros*, p. 32.

18   Decembrio, quoted and translated in Baxandall, 'Guarino, Pisanello and Manuel Chrysoloras,' p. 169.

in the private home or court. While most fifteenth- and sixteenth-century *studiolo* owners were not busy penning theological tracts, they nevertheless drew upon visual and literary tropes of scholars and scholarly life to dignify their *studiolo* activities. Leon Battista Alberti's *Della famiglia* provides some insight into what occurred in these spaces:

> It pleased me to keep only my books and papers, and those of my ancestors, shut up then and for always in such a way that the woman [i.e. his wife] should never see them. I never kept my papers in the sleeves of my clothes, but always locked up in their allocated place in my study, almost as if they were sacred or religious things. I never gave my wife permission to enter my study either with me or alone and furthermore I command her that if she ever came across any paper of mine, she should hand it over to me immediately.[19]

This passage, though brief, illuminates several aspects of intellectual and domestic life in the fifteenth century. Alberti emphasizes the cloistered nature of the study – it is a space both private and personal. It is a place in which one generates and maintains patriarchal identity; indeed it is where the papers of one's ancestors are kept under the (male) owner's complete control, where he builds and maintains family dignity. Both of these interests, the personal and the familial, are embodied by the Stokes casket. The appended coat of arms on the front panel personalizes it and renders it a representative object of the Piccolomini family. In the context of the study as a space for identity and lineage formation, the coat of arms is an apt adornment to fill the space between the cornucopias. Furthermore, bronze, as the

material of ancient monuments, carried the connotations of memorialization, posterity, and durability. Although Cardinal Piccolomini was not married, he still represented the family name in a prominent public office. The Stokes casket indicates that he did so on the model of St. Jerome and other contemporary scholars who were deeply engaged in male-to-male intellectual exchange.

Scholarship on the *studiolo* emphasizes that these spaces and the objects therein were not only critical to manifesting dynastic heritage but also to constituting a sense of selfhood on the part of the owner, although of course dynastic heritage played a part in this.[20] The exhibition of sophisticated personal taste was essential to this project, and the *studiolo* was a venue in which to display 'small works of fine craftsmanship associated with literacy and learning'.[21] Especially prized were aesthetic objects that also bore an exemplary or utilitarian character, such as miniature artworks, especially those with classical, erudite themes, and finely crafted writing and reading tools, such as inkwells, sand boxes, and seal-dies. Similarly, utilitarian objects of élite, sophisticated pursuits such as musical and scientific instruments often bore, and were displayed for, their formal aesthetic appeal.[22] In the *De politia litteraria*, Decembrio mentions that lutes are appropriate library objects, even if present solely for the aesthetic and intellectual richness they add to a space: 'it makes no noise unless you want it to'.[23] In this instance, the lute is valued less for its utilitarian possibility than for the role it plays in constituting a physical environment and aura of sophisticated taste.

19   Alberti, *I Libri de familigia* [1427] translated and quoted in Thornton, *Scholar in His Study,* p. 90.

20   See especially the classic studies: Liebenwein, *Studiolo* and Thornton, *Scholar in His Study.*

21   Thornton, *Scholar in His Study,* p. 142.

22   Campbell, *Cabinet of Eros*, p. 32.

23   Decembrio, translated and quoted in Baxandall, 'Guarino, Pisanello and Manuel Chrysoloras', p. 196.

What, exactly, was the 'self' that the *studiolo* was meant to fashion? Stephen Campbell notes a subtle but important distinction between what he terms 'the humanist and the socio-historical' readings of how the *studiolo* reflected a distinctly modern sense of self in the fifteenth and sixteenth centuries.[24] He notes that for scholars like Wolfgang Liebenwein, who give a humanist account of the *studiolo,* it is fundamentally an extension of a model of contemplation among the social élite based on Petrarchian self-isolation.[25] Modern individuality according to Petrarch was accomplished partly through reading and contemplation undertaken in deliberate isolation as described in his letters and tracts like *De vita solitaria* (1360).[26] The self-formed therein hews closely to Jacob Burckhardt's Renaissance 'individual,' a figure made modern through his introspection: 'These people were forced to know all the inward resources of their own nature…'.[27] More recent accounts of the *studiolo* by writers such as Dora Thornton and Paula Findlen cast the modernity of the Renaissance self as marked instead by refined consumerism as a practice of sophistication.[28] In contrast to Liebenwein who focuses on the *studiolo* dweller as a reader, Thornton and Findlen emphasize him as a commissioner and consumer of objects.[29] These interpretations are not at odds with one another, but reflect the dual possibilities of the *studiolo* as a space for private contemplation as well as a venue for display. Objects within the *studiolo* would ideally accommodate these diverse functions of the space by stimulating introspective reflection

and demonstrating the owner's good taste. Luxury writing accessories such as the Stokes casket were designed to meet these criteria.

The manifestation of these accessories in precious metals like silver and bronze speaks plainly to the owner's enactment of knowledgeable connoisseurship and a discerning taste for rarity. Their diminutive size does likewise in spectacular ways. Many of these writing accessories, bronze inkwells and sand boxes in particular, make playful references to antiquity by scaling down famous large or even colossal works into tabletop objects. The Stokes casket, for instance, resembles a Roman sarcophagus in miniature, not only in its horizontal rectangular format, but also in its antique decorative motifs of centaurs, winged genii figures, and the Medusa mask, all common sarcophagus embellishments.[30] A brief comparison with an opulent second-century Roman sarcophagus in the Walters Museum in Baltimore (Figure 11.7) reveals a number of reformulations of common sarcophagus features on the part of the artisan who made the Stokes casket.[31] On the lid of the Stokes casket are two winged genii, or putti, flanking a central disembodied head, just as on the sarcophagus. On the short ends of both the casket and the sarcophagus are masks placed above a single garland.

Although intimate, *studioli* could serve as social spaces for an individual's close circle of (usually male) friends and family. In these spaces, one would be expected to engage in erudite conversation.[32] *Studioli* objects served as conversation pieces; owners and their guests would be invited to comment upon their fine craftsmanship as well as their iconography. The Stokes casket might foster conversation

24   Campbell, *Cabinet of Eros*, p. 39.

25   Campbell, *Cabinet of Eros*, p. 39; Liebenwein, *Studiolo*.

26   Campbell, *Cabinet of Eros,* p. 39.

27   Burckhardt, *Civilization of the Renaissance in Italy,* p. 107.

28   Campbell, *Cabinet of Eros*, p. 40.

29   Campbell, *Cabinet of Eros*, Chapter 1, note 35.

30   Reid and Vaughan, 'Writing Casket', cat. no. 52.

31   On the Baltimore sarcophagus, see Gerry, 'Garland Sarcophagus', cat. no. 1.

32   Thornton, *Scholar in His Study*, pp. 119–20.

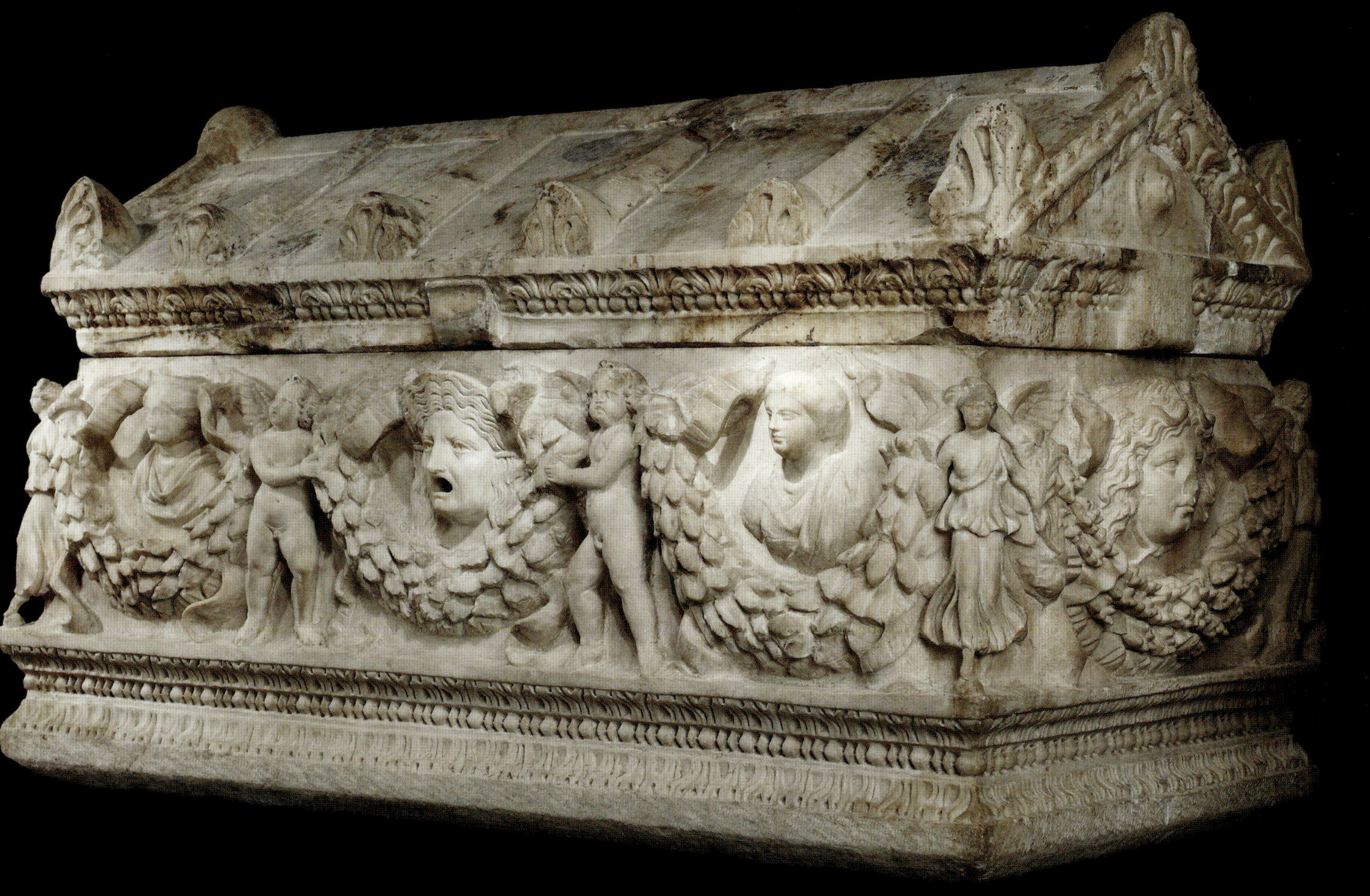

Figure 11.7: Asia Minor, *Garland sarcophagus*, *c.*150–80. Dokimeion marble, 83.5cm × 143.35cm × 69.85cm. Walters Art Museum, Baltimore.

about classical literature featuring figures such as centaurs and Medusa. Beholders might also show off their knowledge of Roman sarcophagus motifs as well as the contemporary art in which these motifs reappeared. They might comment on the ingenuity of the bronze caster in 'translating' a large-scale classical work into a bronze miniature.

Indeed the careers of turn-of-the-sixteenth-century small bronze casters coincided with an important development in Italian letters, namely classically trained writers combining the principles of ancient rhetoric, poetics, and philosophy with literary subject matter appealing to a cultivated but non-specialist audience. For instance, Pomponio Gaurico, in his 1504 treatise, *De sculptura,* delineated principles for craftsmen as well as their learned audiences, demonstrating the affinity of sculpture with other kinds of knowledge, including poetry, natural philosophy, geometry, and optics.[33] Gaurico in fact cautioned against the excessive creative license he saw in contemporary Paduan bronze casters, condemning them for making 'little satyrs, hydras, and monsters the likes of which no one has ever seen…', when instead they should be directing their attention to the ideal human form.[34] Such miniature works could therefore offer a transgressive frisson, perhaps evoking friendly conviviality in the privacy of a *studiolo.*

33   Campbell, 'Antico and Mantegna,' pp. 28–29.
34   Campbell, *Cabinet of Eros*, pp. 160–61.

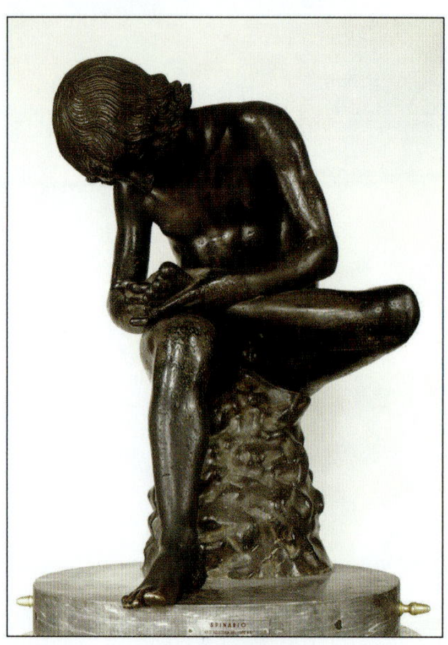

Figure 11.8: Roman, *Spinario*, first century BCE.
Bronze, 73cm. Musei Capitolini, Rome.

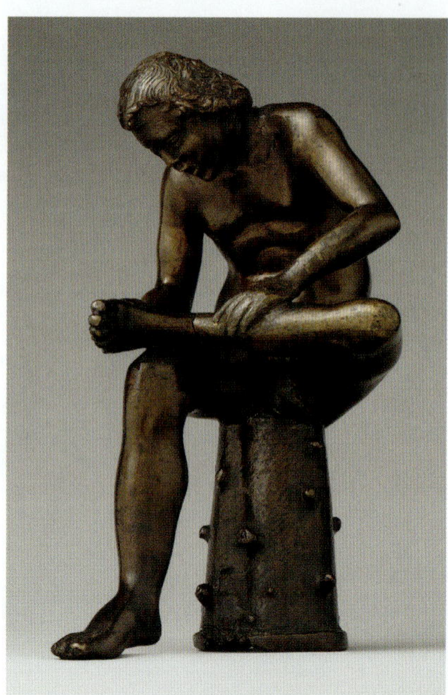

Figure 11.9: Workshop of Severo Calzetta da
Ravenna(?), *Spinario*, mid-sixteenth century. Bronze,
16.2cm × 8.6cm × 11.7cm. Metropolitan Museum of Art,
New York.

Monuments of antiquity were especially popular as modern miniatures, partly because there were few known around 1500. One of the most famous Roman sculptures among Renaissance artists and connoisseurs was the so-called '*Spinario*', or 'thorn puller' (Figure 11.8). The original Roman bronze is 73cm high, but miniature bronze versions of the *Spinario* proved popular among collectors; one version, about 15cm high, is thought to come from Severo's workshop (Figure 11.9). Occasionally, these modern bronze miniatures were incorporated into inkwells or other utilitarian objects.

However, around 1500 Severo would have been drawing on an already long-established tradition of copying and translating the *Spinario*. Sculptors and other artisans throughout the Renaissance referenced this work – one of the most famous reformulations was Filippo Brunelleschi's *Sacrifice of Isaac* panel (almost 100 years before Severo), submitted as a contest entry piece in his (unsuccessful) attempt to win the commission to create a new set of bronze doors for the Florence Baptistery.

At the dawn of the sixteenth century then, *Spinario* figurines and inkwells invoked not only the wisdom and beauty of the ancient world, but also the achievements of artists of Italy's more recent past.

Antico, another bronze sculptor active in northern Italy, made even more drastic reductions.[35] Both the colossal *Marcus Aurelius* bronze (over 4 metres high) and the large *Apollo Belvedere* (224cm) were reduced and rendered in gilded bronze for a discerning and free-spending clientele who, in all likelihood, would have kept these objects in their *studioli*.[36]

35   Antico also enlarged small-scale figures on Roman coins in modern relief sculpture. Luciano, 'Antico', pp. 5–6.
36   In 1500 Isabella d'Este specifically requested that Antico produce something for the door of her *camerino*. Although Antico did not fulfill this initial request, he produced numerous statuettes for her in the ensuing years. Luciano, 'Antico', pp. 8–9.

In these cases of extreme manipulation of scale, the particular pleasure that miniaturization provides is the transcendent position it gives the viewer by presenting a diminutive and manipulable version of known objects beyond the spectator's physical control.[37] For a fifteenth- or sixteenth-century spectator, such monumental works drastically reduced in size but also finely rendered would have been spectacular novelties as well as achievements of craftsmanship.

Eventually *studiolo* owners began to require specific display apparatuses to house their collections of writing accessories and miniature artworks.[38] In fact, some *studioli* seem to have been conceived as display spaces as much if not more than as work spaces.[39] In 1566, Gerolamo Garimberto, an 'archeological advisor', advised his patron, Cardinal Alessandro Farnese, to build a study to 'house all your small objects, such as medals, cameos, inkstands and clocks'.[40] *Studiolo* owners often amassed objects in numbers that belied their ostensible utilitarian functions. Note that Cardinal Farnese had inkstands and clocks in plural. By 1509 Isabella d'Este had at least two precious silver inkstands.[41] As Mieke Bal points out, the threshold between procurement for functional purposes and collecting is obscure; it is not always clear when a group of objects tips from an assemblage of necessities into being a proper collection.[42] Indeed, the *studiolo* context seems to muddle distinctions between tool and collectible; although Renaissance patrons might keep commissioning things like writing caskets, clocks, and seals in multiple, they might also simultaneously claim a real need for these items.

This acquisitiveness, and especially the pretensions to gentility and learning that it bore, naturally attracted satirists.[43] Fra Sabba di Castiglione mocked collectors who spent large sums on miniatures of antique statues or statuettes of horses, the latter of which could cost five times the real thing:

> What can we say about the vanity of the man who spends five hundred or a thousand ducats on a statue of metal or marble which serves him nothing, yet this man cannot serve himself in any way, and does not dare buy a living and true servant for twenty-five ducats, by whom he could have been served in many things? And what can one say about the man who goes on foot so as not to spend ten ducats on a horse, and then spends five hundred ducats on a silly little antique horse of bronze only a palm high, which not only cannot carry him, but is a load to carry?[44]

Of the Stokes casket, Fra Sabba might have pointed out that one could purchase a much larger wooden crate, which can hold a great deal more, for significantly less.

Erasmus of Rotterdam also turned his satirical eye on those over-invested in the study as a vehicle for self-fashioning. In his dialogue *The Ciceronian,* he mocks the stylized Latin and scholarly pomposity of those who claim to require such enclosures:

---

37   Stewart, *On Longing*, p. 69.

38   Thornton, *Scholar in His Study*, pp. 69–75.

39   Findlen traces the development of the private *studiolo* into, in some cases, venues explicitly designed to display collections over the sixteenth century: Findlen, *Possessing Nature*, pp. 109–29.

40   Thornton, *Scholar in His Study*, p. 69, p. 105. Robertson, *'Il Gran Cardinale'*, doc. 49, p. 299, p. 50.

41   Thornton, *Scholar in His Study*, p. 148.

42   Bal, 'Telling Objects', pp. 97–115.

43   According to Thornton, such satire was 'part of the literature of collecting'. See Thornton, *Scholar in His Study*, pp. 116–20; and Fenton, 'A Room of One's Own.'

44   Sabba, *Ricordi*, quoted in Thornton, *Scholar in His Study*, p. 117; Fenton, 'A Room of One's Own'.

Nosoponus: ...If, as I was saying the soul of man has anything divine it comes out in this most profound silence.

Bulephorous: I have noticed that the seclusion of which you speak is seized upon by the most able men whenever they attempt anything worthy of immortality.

Nosoponus: I have a library in the innermost part of my house with thick walls, double doors and windows, and all the cracks stopped carefully with pitch and plaster, so that by day scarcely a ray of light can break through or a sound unless it is unusually loud such as that of women's quarrels or of workmen's hammers.[45]

In trying to one-up Bulephorous's comment on the intellectual need for seclusion, Nosoponus undermines his own claim to understanding the *studiolo*'s purpose. Nosoponus replies that his library is so hermetically sealed off, that 'by day, scarcely a ray of light can break through'. As we have seen, proper illumination is essential for receiving inspiration and writing, yet Nosoponus presents a figure sitting in the dark. A *studiolo,* apparently, does not make a scholar. If a person is frivolous, Erasmus implies, a *studiolo* will not render him a substantial thinker. Rather, it can only be a showcase for the essential qualities of each person, whether they are flattering or not.

To return to the Stokes casket, it is a happy circumstance that today it sits in a collection dedicated in large part to precious books. It is precisely the kind of object that a fifteenth- or sixteenth-century person would have deemed a desirable, or even necessary, part of their reading and writing environment, which facilitated so much more than merely the absorption or production of text, but indeed created an aesthetic world conducive to these endeavours.

45   Desiderius Erasmus, *Ciceronianus*, p. 28.

About the author

Miya Tokumitsu is Lecturer in Art History at the University of Melbourne She has recently published the essay 'The Currencies of Naturalism in Dutch Pronk Still Life Painting: Luxury, Craft, Envisioned Affluence' (in *RACAR: Revue d'art canadienne / Canadian Art Review* 2016). She is currently working on a book on the affinities of prints, sculpture, and applied art in medieval and early modern Germany. miya. tokumitsu@unimelb.edu.au

Works cited

Mieke Bal, 'Telling Objects: A Narrative Perspective on Collecting,' in *Cultures of Collecting*, ed. by John Elsner and Roger Cardinal (London: Reaktion, 1994), pp. 97–115.

Michael Baxandall, 'Guarino, Pisanello and Manuel Chrysoloras', *Journal of the Warburg and Courtauld Institutes*, 28 (1965), pp. 183–204.

Jacob Burckhardt, *The Civilization of the Renaissance in Italy*, trans. by S.G.C. Middlemore (Kitchener: Bartoche Books, 2001).

Stephen Campbell, *The Cabinet of Eros: Renaissance Mythological Painting and the Studiolo of Isabella d'Este* (New Haven: Yale University Press, 2004).

Stephen Campbell, 'Antico and Mantegna: Humanist Art and the Fortune of the Art Object,' in *Antico: The Golden Age of Renaissance Bronzes*, ed. by Eleonora Luciano (Washington: National Gallery of Art, 2011), pp. 27–44.

Desiderius Erasmus, *Ciceronianus: Or a Dialogue on the Best Style of Speaking*, trans. by Izora Scott (New York: Teachers College, Columbia University, 1908).

James Fenton, 'A Room of One's Own,' review of *The Scholar in His Study: Ownership and Experience in Renaissance Italy* by Dora Thornton, *The New York Review of Books*, accessed 31 October 2017 at http://www.nybooks.com/articles/1998/08/13/a-room-of-ones-own.

Paula Findlen, *Possessing Nature: Museums, Collecting, and Scientific Culture in Early Modern Italy* (Berkeley, CA: University of California Press, 1994).

Kathryn B. Gerry, 'Garland Sarcophagus', in *Treasures of Heaven: Saints, Relics, and Devotion in Medieval Europe*, ed. by Martina Bagnoli et al. (New Haven: Yale University Press, 2011), cat. no. 1.

Harald Hendrix, 'Italian Humanists at Home: Villas, Libraries and Collections', in *Les labryinthes de l'esprit:*

collections et bibliothèques à la Renaissance, ed. by Rosanna Gorris Camos and Alexandre Vanautgaerden (Geneva: Librairie Droz, 2015), pp. 24–42.

Wolfgang Liebenwein, *Studiolo: die Entstehung eines Raumtypus und seine Entwicklung bis zum 1600* (Berlin: Gebr. Mann, 1977).

Eleonora Luciano, 'Antico: Pier Jacopo Alari Bonacolsi (*c.*1544–1528)', in *Antico: The Golden Age of Renaissance Bronzes*, ed. by Eleonora Luciano (Washington: National Gallery of Art, 2011), pp. 1–14.

Peter Parshall, 'Albrecht Dürer's *St. Jerome in His Study:* A Philological Reference', *The Art Bulletin*, 53/3 (1971), pp. 303–305.

John Pope-Hennessy, *Renaissance Bronzes from the Samuel H. Kress Collection: Reliefs, Plaquettes, Statuettes, Utensils and Mortars* (London: Phaidon Press, 1965).

Anthony Radcliffe, 'Writing Casket,' in *The Thyssen-Bornemisza Collection: Renaissance and Later Sculpture with Works of Art in Bronze*, ed. by Anthony Radcliffe, Malcolm Baker, and Michael Maek-Gérard (London: Philip Wilson Publishers, 1992), cat. no. 31.

Callum Reid and Gerard Vaughan, 'Writing Casket', in *An Illumination: The Rothschild Prayer Book and Other Works from the Kerry Stokes Collection c.1280–1685*, ed. by Margaret M. Manion (West Perth: Australian Capital Equity, 2015), cat. no. 52.

Helen I. Roberts, 'St. Augustine in "St. Jerome's Study": Carpaccio's Painting and its Legendary Source', *The Art Bulletin*, 41/3 (1959), pp. 283–297.

Clare Robertson, *'Il Gran Cardinale': Alessandro Farnese, Patron of the Arts* (New Haven: Yale University Press, 1992).

Frits Scholten, 'Bronze: The Mythology of a Metal,' in *Bronze: The Power of Life and Death*, ed. by Martina Droth and Penelope Curtis (London: The Henry Moore Institute, 2005), pp. 20–35.

Frits Scholten, *The Robert Lehman Collection at the Metropolitan Museum of Art, Volume XII: European Sculpture and Metalwork* (Princeton: Princeton University Press, 2012).

Richard Stapleford, 'Intellect and Intuition in Botticelli's *Saint Augustine*', *The Art Bulletin*, 76/1 (1994), pp. 69–80.

Susan Stewart, *On Longing: Narratives of the Miniature, the Gigantic, the Souvenir, the Collection* (Baltimore: The Johns Hopkins University Press, 1984).

Dora Thornton, *The Scholar in His Study: Ownership and Experience in Renaissance Italy* (New Haven: Yale University Press, 1997).

12. 'A Very Rich Adornment': a discussion of the Stokes *Cassone*

Callum Reid

Dunlop, Anne (ed.), *Antipodean Early Modern. European Art in Australian Collections, c. 1200–1600*, Amsterdam University Press, 2018

DOI: 10.5117/9789462985209/CH12

Abstract

Set upon dolphin-form feet, and carved with swirling mythological figures, a sixteenth-century wedding chest, or *cassone,* in the Kerry Stokes Collection can be examined through various lenses. Serving ceremonial, utilitarian and decorative functions within their lifetime, *cassoni* are unique historic artefacts and important documents for the history of taste and collecting. This essay positions the Kerry Stokes *cassone* within a history of this object type, reflecting on its various functions and analysing its decoration. New details are also brought to light regarding its original owners along with its relationship to a nearly identical chest in Kiev.

Keywords: *Cassone*; Italian Renaissance Art; Furniture; Mannerism; Taste and collecting

In 2015, visitors to the exhibition *An Illumination: the Rothschild Prayer Book & other works from the Kerry Stokes Collection c.1280–1685* encountered, among the paintings and sculptures, a sarcophagus-form Italian *cassone* (Figure 12.1), richly carved, painted and gilded.[1] Raised on a plinth directly beneath a seventeenth-century painting, this chest was the only object of furniture in the room, with a context long forgotten as twenty-first-century viewers examined its carved relief panels. Seen and collected primarily as *objets d'art* today, the rich history and changing functions of *cassoni* allow us to examine them from various angles. Here, we will look at the Stokes *cassone* within these different contexts (ceremonial, utilitarian, decorative) and more broadly discuss its position within the history of taste. This chapter will also bring the chest together with its counterpart, currently in Kiev, while identifying the family who ordered their construction.

The *cassone,* also referred to as *forziere* or *cassa,* had existed for some time in several forms, but came into greatest prominence from the fourteenth century. In very basic terms it is a marriage chest, tied into the wedding celebrations of important Italian families.[2]

---

1   On the Stokes *cassone*, see Reid, 'Cassone', pp. 192–3.

2   On the history of the *cassone*, see in particular Musacchio, *Art, Marriage, & Family*, pp. 136–189. The last twenty years have seen a significant new literature emerge on the *cassone,* in particular those with painted panels, while the early texts by Schubring (*Truhen und Truhenbilder*) and Schottmüller (*Furniture and interior decoration*

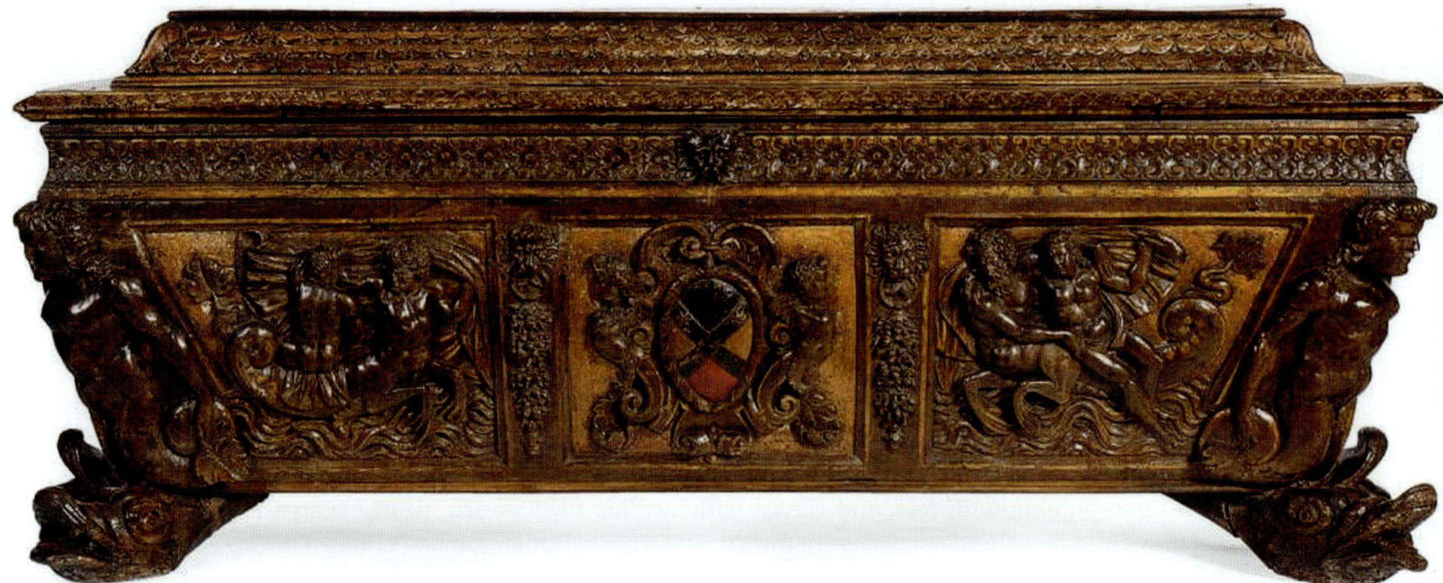

Figure 12.1: Italian, *Cassone*, late sixteenth century. Walnut, 71cm × 183.5cm × 58cm. Kerry Stokes Collection, Perth.

Throughout the fifteenth and sixteenth centuries, *cassoni* were of relatively standardised dimensions, as they would often serve the same task. The majority of known sixteenth-century examples are, like that from the *Illumination* exhibition, around 180cm in length and 60cm to 70cm high and deep. There are of course exceptions to this rule, but generally *cassoni* would be quite similar in shape and size, dictated in part by their function as wedding chests, usually filled with the bride's *trousseau,* the portion of the dowry customarily consisting of clothes and linens.

Tied to marriage, *cassoni* were often created within a discrete period: between the

public agreement of the terms of marriage and the ring ceremony. Created in pairs, they would usually be garnished with the coat of arms of one or both of the betrothed families.[3] In eminent Renaissance weddings, the bride would be led along a public procession from her family home to that of the bridegroom, while both *cassoni*, filled with the *trousseau,* would generally be carried along within the procession.[4] The highly decorative nature of

---

of the Italian Renaissance, pp. XVIII–XXI), were standards for twentieth-century discussion of these objects. For more recent work see Campbell, *Love and marriage in Renaissance Florence*; Baskins, *Cassone painting*; Hughes, *Renaissance cassoni*; and Krohn, 'Rites of Passage'.

3   Krohn, 'Rites of Passage', p. 64.

4   In some cases, *cassoni* became too cumbersome to carry as they developed in style into heavier and more deeply-carved objects. Others also had a painted back panel or *spalliera* that made carrying difficult. In these instances (and also in situations where the *cassoni* were not completed in time), the *trousseau* was carried in baskets while the *cassoni* were installed in the homes of the newly betrothed. See Musacchio, *Art, Marriage, & Family*, pp. 136–7.

these chests emerged as a result of this very ceremonial, very public performance. Having the money to commission wedding chests was a luxury only enjoyed by Italy's wealthier families, and marriage provided one avenue by which to display this prosperity. It is for this reason that the coat of arms was made so conspicuous, generally placed in the centre of the front panel.

Once it found its way to the newlyweds' home, the *cassone* would operate in much the same way as a regular linen or object chest, sometimes locked with a key if it contained material of high value. In mid-sixteenth-century Florence, Eleonora of Toledo, Duchess and future Grand Duchess of Tuscany, had several *cassoni* listed, many of them locked, amongst the possessions in her Palazzo Vecchio.[5] Along with the inventories, some letters in the *Archivio di Stato di Firenze* give an idea of the value she placed on objects retained in these chests, as on several occasions she sent orders from the road for certain items to be moved. In 1544, while at the court of Figline, about thirty-five kilometres outside of Florence, she sent a key back with instructions to open her *cassone* and send several terracotta jars and flasks of cosmetics to her.[6] In March 1545, she ordered a black velvet dress stored in a *cassone* in the Palazzo Vecchio be sent to the Palazzo Medici in Pisa, while in July of the same year, she requested that a gold medallion with a rock

crystal portrait be sent to the Medici villa Poggio a Caiano.[7]

Before reaching the form that we will discuss in the present example, the *cassone* spent several centuries evolving. Originally quite rudimentary in decoration, the style of the *cassone* developed through the fourteenth century, as the addition of polychromy, gilding and storiated adornments in *pastiglia* became fashionable.[8] The fifteenth century saw the emergence of *cassoni* painted with complex narrative scenes. Amidst early Renaissance developments in painting, household furniture and objects like bed panels, *cassoni* and birth trays became domestic canvases to fill the home with the new Albertian *istoria*.[9] Many of the leading exponents of *quattrocento* narrative painting produced panels for *cassoni*, with extant examples attributed to artists such as Paolo Uccello and Jacopo del Sellaio.[10]

Within the history of these objects, one of the most important early sources can be found in Giorgio Vasari's *Lives of the Artists*,

---

5   Conti, *La prima reggia*. Conti transcribes the 1553 inventory of the Palazzo Vecchio, (Archivio di Stato di Firenze, Guardaroba Medicea, 28) and in particular there are several *cassoni serrati* (locked *cassoni*) listed in the section of the palace reserved for the Duchess, the 'Quartiere della Duchessa' (see pp. 56–69).

6   Archivio di Stato di Firenze (ASF), Mediceo del Principato (MdP) 1171, insert 3, f. 124, Letter from Lorenzo Pagni, Secretary to the Grand Duchess to Pier Francesco Riccio, 14 September 1544. This and the documents in note 7 were accessed through the online platform for the Medici Archive Project on 25 September 2015 (bia.medici.org).

7   ASF, MdP 1171, insert 7, f. 302, Letter from Lorenzo Pagni to Pier Francesco Riccio, 27 March 1545; ASF, MdP 1171, insert 9, f. 423, Letter from Vincenzo Ferrini (Poggio a Caiano) to Pier Francesco Riccio, 5 July 1545.

8   One striking early example from around 1350 is today held at the Victoria and Albert Museum, (Inv. n. 317–1894). See Wilk, *Western furniture*, pp. 26–7.

9   A particularly notable example of a painted birth-tray, or *desco da parto*, is Pontormo's *Birth of St John the Baptist*, held in the Galleria degli Uffizi, Florence (1890 Inv. n. 1532). For more discussion of this object type, see Hughes, *Renaissance Cassoni*, pp. 113–121; Pope-Hennessy and Christiansen, *Secular painting in 15th-century Tuscany*.

10   Paolo Uccello's *Hunt in the Forest* (c.1470) from the Ashmolean Museum (Acc. no. WA1850.31) is believed to be from the back panel or *spalliera* of one of these fifteenth century *cassoni*. The most famous example to which Jacopo del Sellaio contributed, is the pair of Morelli-Nerli *cassoni*, 1472, Courtauld Gallery, London (Acc. nos. F.1947.LF.4 and F.1947.LF.5). With only several nineteenth-century interventions, the Morelli-Nerli chests are among the nearest examples of *cassoni* in their complete original state. See Barraclough, 'Technical Notes', pp. 78–9.

specifically in his *Life of Dello Delli*.[11] Identifying Dello (*c.*1403–*c.*1470) as a specialist in *cassone* painting, Vasari goes on to discuss the object type and its fashion in the fifteenth century:

> [Dello] soon acquired a good mastery in colouring, as many pictures that he made in his own city demonstrate, and above all those with little figures, wherein he showed better grace than in the large. And this ability served him in good stead, because the citizens of those times used to have in their apartments great sarcophagus-form *cassoni*, with the covers shaped in various fashions, and there were none that did not have said chests painted. And for many years this fashion was so much in use that even the most excellent painters exercised themselves in such labours, without being ashamed, as many would be today, to paint and gild such things.[12]

Presumably because of this passage, there have been a number of *cassoni* historically attributed to Dello Delli, in most cases erroneously. Indeed, nineteenth-century scholars or dealers would most often ascribe an unknown fifteenth-century *cassone* painting with small figures to this artist.[13]

Vasari's passage also highlights the important role that these chests would play not only as art objects, but as documents demonstrating the rising status of the artist in Renaissance Florence. Where painters were once willing to collaborate on these household items, this readiness would lessen in the sixteenth

century. As definitions of the Renaissance artisan and artist continued to diverge, Vasari's 'most excellent painters' would try to restrict themselves to traditional, two-dimensional wall paintings, while chest-decoration was left to smaller provincial painters.[14]

Vasari's life of Dello Delli continued by bringing discussion of the *cassone* into the sixteenth century, as he identified what had at that point become the contemporary style:

> …it was not long before the refinement of men's intellects led them from that first method of working to the making of richer ornaments and of carvings in walnut-wood overlaid with gold, which indeed produce a very rich adornment.[15]

The Stokes *cassone* falls into this category of carved and gilded chests, created in the second half of the sixteenth century around the time of the publication of the second edition of Vasari's *Vite* in 1568.[16] The movement towards this carved form of *cassone* was abrupt, and thereafter few if any painted examples were made again as the chests embraced mannerist ornament, with figures in elongated poses carved in high relief. Alongside these new principles of flowing inventiveness, deference to the classical past was maintained, and as a result, the types of *cassoni* that emerged in the second half of the century were a unique synthesis of classicism and mannerism.

The present example has a distinctive shape, the edges sloping inwardly. The decoration is distinctly classicising, with the theme of water

---

11   Vasari, *Le Vite*, 1568, Volume I, pp. 256–8.

12   Vasari, *Vite*, 1568, pp. 256–7.

13   For example, Marco del Buono Giamberti and Apollonio di Giovanni di Tomaso's *Story of Esther* (New York, Metropolitan Museum of Art) was attributed to Dello in the nineteenth century. See Bayer, *Art and Love in Renaissance Italy*, p. 64: 'this panel was, like several other *cassone* panels, then attributed to Dello Delli'.

14   Campbell, *Love and Marriage*, p. 26.

15   Vasari, *Vite*, 1568, p. 257.

16   The discussion of *cassoni* was brought in for the second edition of the *Vite* in 1568; the text may be compared against the 1550 first edition (Giorgio Vasari, *Le Vite de' più eccellenti pittori, scultori, e architettori da Cimabue insino a' tempi nostri*, Florence: Torrentino, 1550)

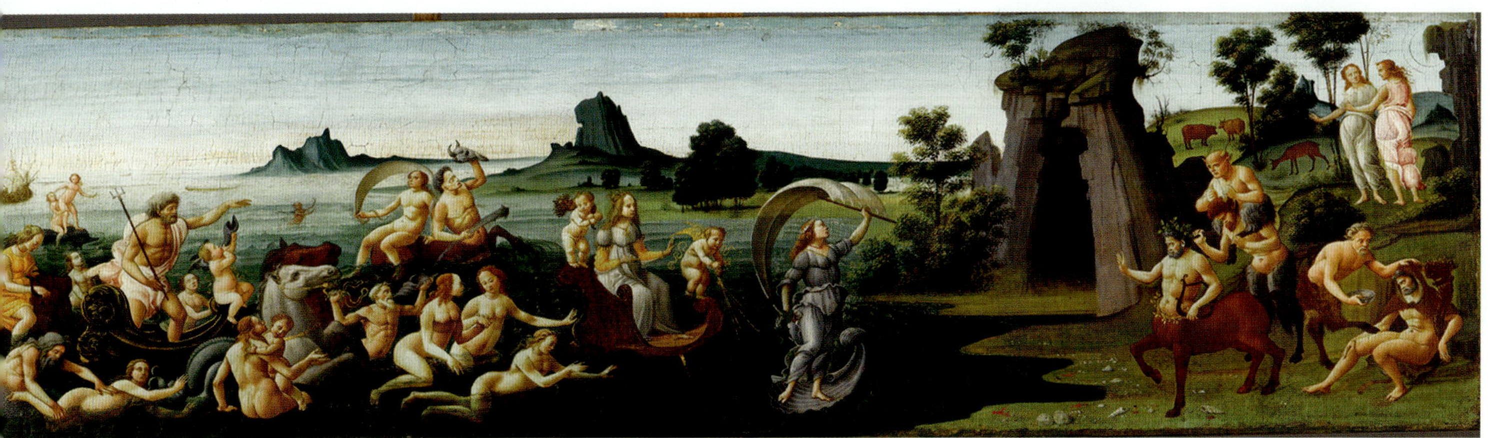

Figure 12.2: Bartolomeo di Giovanni, *Procession of Thetis, c.*1490–1500. Tempera on wood, 42cm × 150cm. Musée du Louvre, Paris.

spread across each side. Hybrid sea creatures swim on the lateral panels, dolphin-form feet support the chest, while Tritons and Nereids surge towards the centre of the front panel. After Hesiod in *Theogony* (*c.*700 BCE) wrote of an individual called 'Triton,' son of Poseidon and Amphitrite and the messenger of the sea, the figure would come to be pluralised in the later Roman period to refer more broadly to groups of hybrid sea spirits.[17] Nereids, also mentioned in *Theogony*, were nymphs of the ocean, who together with the Tritons made up the entourage of Neptune. Nereids were often represented in human form, riding on the backs of the hybrid Tritons, who had the tails of fish and the upper bodies of men. Works of art with these figures enjoyed a particular vogue during the Renaissance, with the mythological sea creatures prevalent in classicising *cassoni*, caskets and paintings adding dramatic movement to Raphael's *Triumph of Galatea*, or taking centre stage in Piero di Cosimo's battling *Tritons and Nereids*.[18]

The incorporation of these figures into wedding furniture may be a reference to the mythological marriage of the mortal Peleus to the immortal Nereid Thetis, a popular story of love in unusual circumstances recounted by Homer and Ovid among others. A pair of *cassone* panels, painted by Bartolomeo di Giovanni in the final decade of the fifteenth century, represent the *Wedding of Thetis* and the *Procession of Thetis*.[19] One of these panels (Figure 12.2) shows a group of Tritons and Nereids making up the wedding procession, following in the wake of the bride. In the second half of the sixteenth century, the twisting forms of these hybrid beasts suited the new trend for deeply carved mannerist *cassoni*, with examples including that in the Metropolitan Museum of Art (Figure 12.3) and the Nasher Museum of Art in North Carolina, whose panel depict Neptune presiding over the Tritons and Nereids.[20]

Along with the shape of the Stokes *cassone*, the decoration calls to mind the reliefs of an

17   Hesiod, *Theogony*, verses 930–3. Pluralized by the second century, Tritons are discussed in Aelian: 'Concerning Tritons, while fishermen assert that they have no clear account or positive proof of their existence, yet there is a report very widely circulated of certain monsters in the sea, of human shape from the head down to the waist', Vol. 3, Book 13, p. 119.

18   Raffaello Sanzio, *Triumph of Galatea*, fresco, *c.*1514, Rome, Villa Farnesina; Piero di Cosimo, *Tritons and Nereids*, oil on panel, *c.*1500, Milan, Altomani Collection. For these works, see Dussler, *Raphael*, pp. 99–100, 188; Geronimus, *Piero di Cosimo*, pp. 104–5.

19   Bartolomeo di Giovanni, *The Wedding of Thetis and Peleus*, tempera on wood, *c.*1490–1500, Inv. no. RF 1347, Musée du Louvre; Bartolomeo di Giovanni, *Procession of Thetis*, tempera on wood, *c.*1490–1500, Inv. no. RF 1346, Musée du Louvre.

20   The Nasher Museum *cassone* is fragmentary, with only the frieze on the front panel extant. Florentine artist, Cassone *panel with Neptune presiding over a wedding*, *c.*1560, carved walnut with gilding, 55.3cm x 172cm. For the chest in the Metropolitan Museum, see Koeppe, *The Robert Lehman Collection*, pp. 200–2.

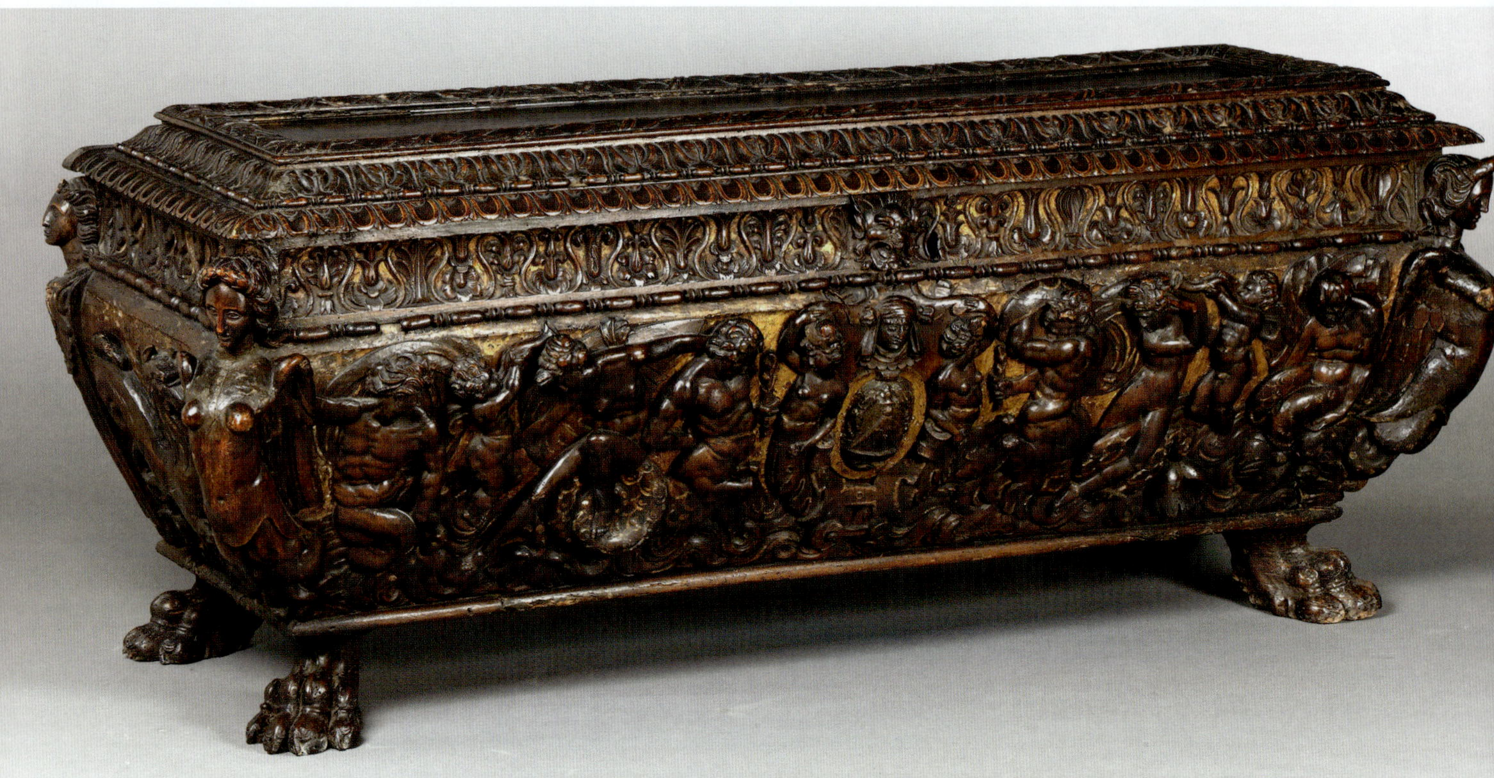

Figure 12.3: Italian (Tuscany or Rome?), *Cassone*, c.1550–80 (rebuilt, with later additions). Walnut, carved and partially gilded, 70.5cm × 149.8cm × 45.7cm. Lehman Collection, Metropolitan Museum of Art, New York.

ancient sarcophagus. The poses used for the two Triton/Nereid groups were a popular motif, as seen in several Roman examples. The *Sarcophagus of Quinta Flavia Severina* from the third century (Figure 12.4) for example, exhibits these two groupings on the right side of its front panel: one Nereid with her back to the viewer, alongside another facing forward, her arm raised. A similar sarcophagus must have provided the prototype for the Stokes *cassone*; however instead of an equivalent frieze stretched across the front of the chest, the workshop has divided the front into three discrete panels, two with a pair of figures, flanking a central panel with the traditional coat of arms. The classical sarcophagus appears particularly tranquil, the figures suspended neatly across the front plan, a stillness highlighted in

comparison to the Stokes *cassone*, which emphasises the movement of the ocean and torsion of figures. The figures placed on each corner of the chest contribute to the overall sense of movement as they cause the edges to swell out, giving it an appearance of plasticity. This is a popular feature of carved *cassoni* from this period, also seen in the previous example from the Metropolitan Museum of Art (Figure 12.3).

Hybrid creatures with the head of a griffin or eagle and the tail of a sea serpent adorn each end of the Stokes *cassone* (Figure 12.5). It is a motif found in several other chests from the same period. A similar example can be found in the Metropolitan Museum *cassone* mentioned above (Figure 12.6) and there is a slightly different variant in the Frick collection, on a pair of *cassoni* decorated with scenes from the

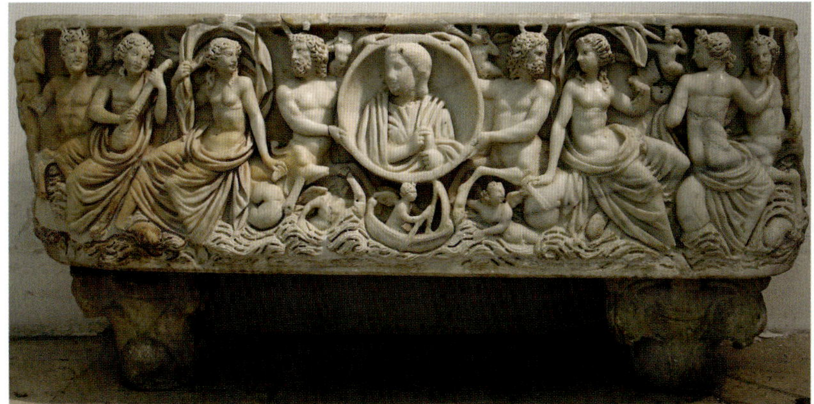

Figure 12.4: Roman, *Sarcophagus of Quinta Flavia Severina. relief with Nereid and Triton*, third century. Musei Capitolini, Rome.

life of Caesar.[21] This creature appears possibly for the first time in Giulio Romano's design of *Scipio meeting Hannibal*, here reproduced in a later engraving from around 1540 (Figure 12.7).[22] Artists such as Andrea Mantegna and Giulio Romano have been cited as possible sources of inspiration for the figural compositions of carved *cassoni* and this mythological creature may well be one of the inventions borrowed by the carvers of the *cassoni* in the Metropolitan Museum and in the Stokes collection.[23]

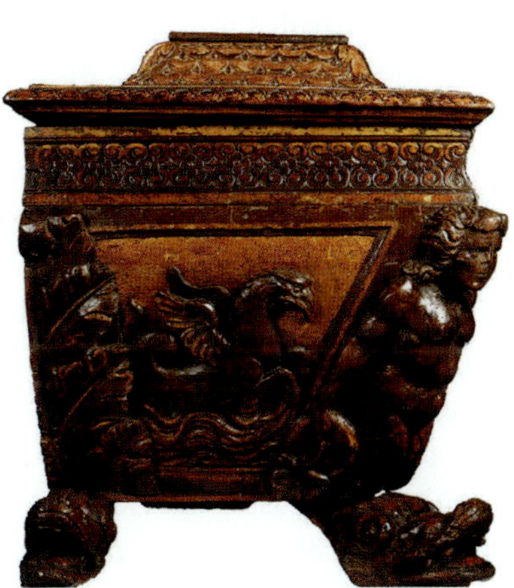

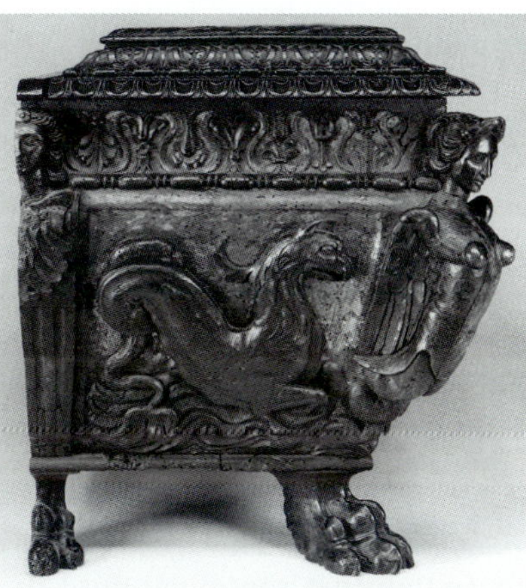

Figure 12.5: Italy, *Cassone*, detail of end panel, late sixteenth century. Walnut, overall 71cm × 183.5cm × 58cm. Kerry Stokes Collection, Perth.

Figure 12.6: Italy (Tuscany or Rome?), *Cassone with Tritons and Nereids*, detail of end panel. Walnut, carved and partially gilded, *c.*1550-80 with later additions, overall 70.5cm × 149.8cm × 45.7cm. Lehman Collection, Metropolitan Museum of Art, New York.

Framed by a swirling cartouche, the polychrome coat of arms at the centre of the *cassone* represents the Valenti family from Trevi

21   For the Frick examples (Inv. nos. 18.5.78 and 18.5.79) see Dubon, 'Renaissance Furniture. Sixteenth Century', pp. 34–44 (the creature is illustrated on p. 39).

22   Koeppe, *The Robert Lehman Collection*, p. 201. For the original work, see Massari, *Giulio Romano*, pp. 42–44.

23   Koeppe, *The Robert Lehman Collection*, p. 201.

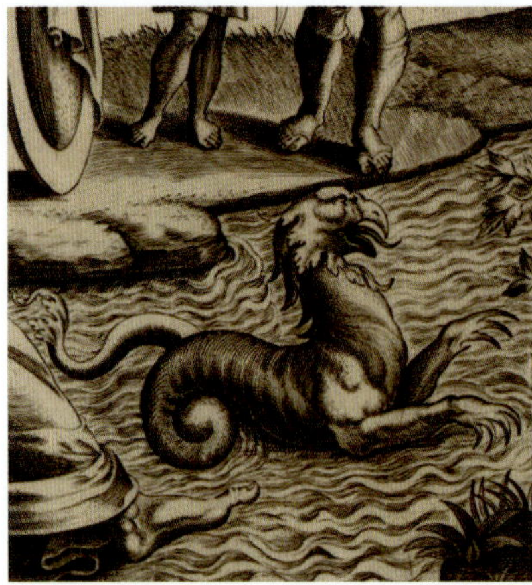

Figure 12.7: Antonio Salamanca (publisher), *Scipio et Hannibal coloquuntur* ('The meeting of Scipio and Hannibal'), detail, 1541. Engraving, 39.3cm × 55.7cm. British Museum, London.

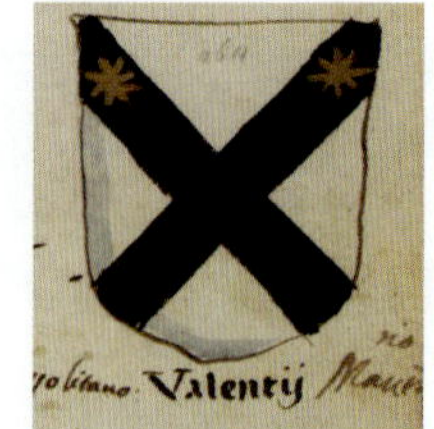

Figure 12.8: Valenti family coat of arms from Angelo Maria da Bologna, *Araldo nel quale si vedono delineate e colorite le armi de' potentati e sovrani d'Europa*. Folio 67, c.1715 or early eighteenth century. Drawing with body colour. Biblioteca Estense universitaria, Modena. Inventory number: gamma.i.2.23 = cam.766Su.

in Umbria. The gilding and colouring is a later intervention, one that sought to make this element a focal point on the chest.[24] The traditional *stemma* of the Valenti family would be represented by a black St Andrews cross with silver six-point stars (Figure 12.8), but was likely left uncoloured here, perhaps with the exception of some original gilding. The identification of the coat of arms suggests that the Stokes *cassone* was commissioned for a member of the Valenti family to commemorate their marriage.[25] Whether this family member was the new bride or groom is not definite. The earliest *cassoni* were traditionally commissioned by the bride's family, a convention that continued until the mid-fifteenth century, after which the husband

would generally provide the bedroom furnishings for the family. Thus on most occasions, later *cassoni* would come from his family.[26] With this in mind, the groom's family (Valenti) would likely have commissioned this *cassone*.

Like most *cassoni,* the Stokes chest is one of a pair. What is almost certainly the second of this couple can be found in the Bohdan and Varvara Khanenko Museum of Arts, Kiev, Ukraine (Figure 12.9), and it provides a little more information about the Stokes example.[27] At first glance, the two chests are identical in their carving, the conspicuous difference being that the Kiev example is unpainted. It takes a second inspection to notice that the panels of these *cassoni* are in fact mirror images of one another, keeping each of them unique. While their early provenance is unknown, the Kiev *cassone* can be traced to the collection of Roman artist and antiquarian Augusto Alberici (1846–c.1904). It was sold in his 1891 sale, at which

24   I am particularly grateful here for the help of Franco Spellani from Associazione Pro Trevi, who confirmed my attribution to the Valenti family of Trevi and who pointed me in the direction of several other important sources.

25   The precise family member and their spouse remain unknown, and are a potential subject for further research. Historical members of the Valenti family are discussed in Natalucci, *Historia Universale*. Further thanks to Franco Spellani for providing this reference.

26   Musacchio, *Art, Marriage, & Family,* p. 136. She identifies exceptions to this rule, with *cassoni* commissioned for Piero de Medici's daughter in 1466 and Tommaso Spinelli's daughter in the same year.

27   For this chest, see Lymar, '*Cassone* with figures of mythological sea-creatures', pls. 68–72. Regarding this *cassone*, I am very grateful for the assistance of Olesya Lyahovec from the Bohdan and Varvara Khanenko Museum of Art.

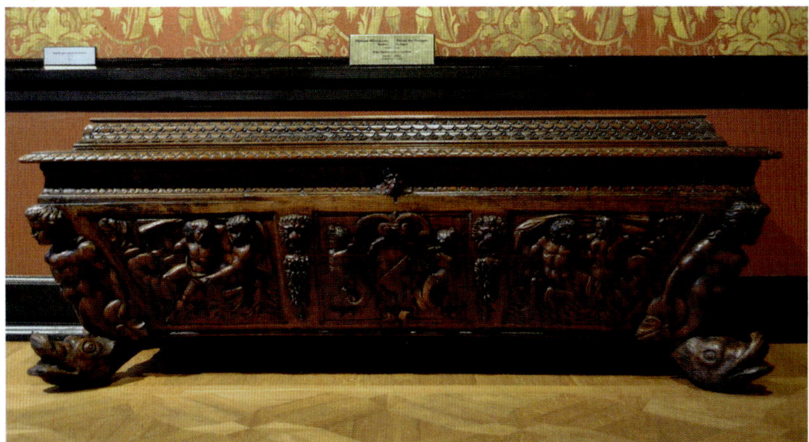

Figure 12.9: Italian, *Cassone*, second half of sixteenth century. Walnut, 67cm × 172cm × 55cm. Bohdan and Varvara Khanenko Museum of Art, Kiev.

point it was purchased for the Bohdan and Varvara Khanenko collection.[28] The lack of paint on the Kiev chest either indicates that it was cleaned, or that the Stokes *cassone* has been repainted at some point in its history after the pair were separated. Evidence points toward a combination of both of these factors. Later filling in the keyhole features gilding consistent with the adjacent sections of the chest. The colour and gilding on the Stoke *cassone* is also inconsistent with the heraldic colours of the Valenti, and is likely to be a creative interpretation applied at a later date. Museum staff

at the Bohdan and Varvara Khanenko Museum of Arts have identified traces of pigments in the Kiev *cassone*, present in the decoration just above and below the lid, as well as in the coat of arms.[29] The likelihood is that both *cassoni* were gilded in a manner similar to the later intervention, with the figures left uncoloured in original walnut and set against a gold background such that they appear in even higher relief.

Alongside these two *cassoni*, there is a third, distantly related object. The Hermitage Museum holds a contemporary walnut *cassapanca*, a type of *cassone* with a backrest and arms added to create a carved bench or day bed.[30] At its centre is a combination of the Valenti and Tempestivi coats-of-arms, which represent the wedding of Perpetua Valenti with Girolamo Tempestivi. Silvestro Nessi notes that the Kiev *cassone* is of the same period and offers the possibility that it may have been created for Perpetua Valenti, but notes that this is entirely

28   Sold in Rome 5 March 1891. See Alberici, *Catalogue des objets d'art antiques du Moyen-Age*, p. 43, Lot 367; *'Beau Coffre de Mariage en noyer sculpté. XVIe siècle. Sur la façade, frise de trois compartiments. Dans celui du milieu armoiries entre deux chimères; dans les autres, sujets de Tritons et de Néréides. Mascarons et cariatides formant les angles. Pieds en forme de dauphins. Long. M. 1.72. Haut m. 0.68'* ('Beautiful carved walnut wedding chest. XVIth century. On the front face, a frieze of three compartments. In the middle one, a coat of arms between two chimeras; in the others, subjects of Tritons and Nereids. Masks and caryatids at the corners. Feet in the form of dolphins. Length. 1.72. Height m. 0.68'). Lymar, *'Cassone'*, 1983 (here erroneously identified as lot no. 1048 in the Alberici sale, with thanks to Olesya Lyahovec for the correction); Nessi, 'I Tempestivi', p. 25.

29   With thanks once again to Olesya Lyahovec, who reported the traces of pigment present on the *cassone* under ultraviolet light.

30   *Cassapanca Nuziale*, walnut, 1564, 115cm x 208cm x 40cm, Inv. no. 1775 (accessioned 1925), Leningrad: Hermitage Museum. See Lymar, *'Cassone* with figures of mythological sea-creatures', pls. 75–80; Nessi, 'I Tempestivi', p. 25.

speculative.[31] That the Hermitage *cassapanca* holds a composite coat of arms in comparison to the *cassoni*'s exclusive Valenti heraldry would indicate two different types of commission and reaffirm that these objects were created for different people.

The final function that the *cassone* has adopted since the nineteenth century returns us to the beginning of this essay, and to its place within the museum and the sustained taste for these objects beyond their initial function. Unsurprisingly, examples of intact painted *cassoni* are rare, as many were pulled apart in the nineteenth and twentieth centuries, the panels highly prized artworks in their own right. The paintings by Bartolomeo di Giovanni referenced earlier are two such examples. While these and many similar fifteenth- and early sixteenth-century *cassoni* were dismantled and reframed as two-dimensional panel paintings, intact chests were used to bring together wall displays in public galleries and private residences. Placing a *cassone* directly under a painting from a similar period created a mini-installation, allowing the viewers to experience the work on the wall, the *cassone* underneath, and the conversation between the two objects. Private collectors exploited the depth of these chests: placing them beneath their more precious paintings not only served an aesthetic function, it also prevented viewers from getting too close to the art on the walls.[32]

During his time as director of the National Gallery of Victoria in Melbourne (1942–55) Daryl Lindsay acquired two carved sixteenth-century *cassoni*, with the intention of placing them beneath the Gallery's best Renaissance works.[33] Lindsay had argued that the acquisition of *cassoni* would benefit the gallery's holdings, with paintings by Veronese and the Master of the Stories of Helen (then attributed to Pisanello) identified as works that they would combine with to great decorative effect.[34] Informing the acquisition, Lindsay received an account of some *cassoni* in London by A.J.L. McDonnell, an international advisor to the Felton Bequests Committee.[35] McDonnell observed that the 'chests have stood for many years in the octagonal room at the National Gallery here, under the four Veronese, where they combine with the pictures to make a very handsome effect'.[36]

As more *cassone* were incorporated into museums and collections, their utilitarian function disappeared almost entirely. Tellingly, the sculptural qualities of the Kiev *cassone* saw it listed in the Alberici sale not under furniture, but rather *sculptures en bois* – wooden sculptures. Today the Kiev *cassone* is pleasingly displayed beneath Palma il Giovane's *St John in the Desert*, whose posture echoes the twisting figures on the face of the chest below.[37] It is hoped

31　Nessi, 'I Tempestivi', p. 25 (42).

32　Koeppe, *The Robert Lehman Collection*, p. 201. Koeppe observes that, 'when placed under a sizable painting, a *cassone* emulated the noble displays in Italian Renaissance palazzi, but its proportions and depth also suited a New York mansion by providing a protective barrier between visitors and artwork'.

33　For this pair of *cassoni*, their purchase, decoration and provenance, see Drummond, 'Marriage and Murder', pp. 8–19.

34　Drummond, 'Marriage and Murder', p. 10.

35　The Felton Bequest was a large philanthropic trust established in the will of Alfred Felton in 1904. It supported the continued acquisition of artworks for the National Gallery of Victoria among other cultural projects. For the bequest and its advisors, see Poynter, *Mr Felton's Bequests*, and the introductory chapter to the present volume by Anne Dunlop.

36　A.J.L. McDonnell, letter to the Secretary of the Felton Bequests Committee, 4 July 1955, cited in Drummond, 'Marriage and Murder,' p. 10.

37　Palma il Giovane, *St John the Baptist in the Desert*, oil on canvas, 1602–10, Kiev: Bohdan and Varvara Khanenko Museum of Arts. See also Rinaldi, *Palma il Giovane*, p. 88, n. 122.

that down in the southern hemisphere the Stokes *cassone* stays displayed in a similar fashion, beneath a contemporary work, preserving the dialogue between two important historical objects and maintaining public interest in an historically rich art form.

About the author

Callum Reid has recently completed his PhD on display in the Uffizi in the Gran Ducal Era. callum.reid@unimelb.edu.au

Works cited

Archivio di Stato di Firenze (ASF), Florence

Mediceo del Principato (MdP) 1171, insert 3, f. 124, Letter from Lorenzo Pagni, Secretary to the Grand Duchess to Pier Francesco Riccio, 14 September 1544.

Mediceo del Principato (MdP) 1171, insert 7, f. 302, Letter from Lorenzo Pagni to Pier Francesco Riccio, 27 March 1545.

Mediceo del Principato (MdP) 1171, insert 9, f. 423, Letter from Vincenzo Ferrini (Poggio a Caiano) to Pier Francesco Riccio, 5 July 1545.

Other works

Aelian, *On the Characteristics of Animals,* trans. by A.F. Scholfield, 3 vols (Cambridge: Harvard University Press, 2014).

Augusto Alberici, *Catalogue des objets d'art antiques du Moyen-Age, de la Renaissance et des temps modernes, appartenant à un illustre personnage romain, de la collection de M. Auguste Alberici et des objets collectionnés par feu le comte Charles des Dorides, Rome 5 March 1891* (Rome: Imprimerie editrice romana, 1891).

Graham Barraclough, 'Technical Notes', in *Love and Marriage in Renaissance Florence: The Courtauld Weddings Chests,* ed. by Caroline Campbell (London: The Courtauld Gallery in associated with Paul Holberton Publishing, 2009), pp. 78–9.

Cristelle Louise Baskins, *Cassone painting, humanism, and gender in early modern Italy,* (Cambridge and New York: Cambridge University Press, 1998).

Andrea Bayer, *Art and Love in Renaissance Italy* (New York: Metropolitan Museum of Art, 2008).

Caroline Campbell, *Love and Marriage in Renaissance Florence: the Courtauld Wedding Chests* (London: Courtauld Gallery in association with Paul Holberton Publishing, 2009).

Cosimo Conti, *La prima reggia. Cosimo I de' Medici nel Palazzo gia della Signoria di Firenze, descritta ed illustrata* (Florence: Giuseppe Pellas, 1893).

Anna Drummond, 'Marriage and Murder: Two wedding chests with representations of Judith,' *Art Journal of the National Gallery of Victoria,* 53 (2014), pp. 8–19.

David Dubon, 'Renaissance Furniture. Sixteenth Century', in *The Frick Collection: An illustrated catalogue, Vol. 5, Furniture,* ed. by Joseph Focarino (New York: The Frick Collection, 1992), pp. 3–182.

Luitpold Dussler, *Raphael: A Critical Catalogue of his Pictures, Wall-Paintings & Tapestries* (London and New York: Phaidon, 1971).

Dennis Geronimus, *Piero di Cosimo: Visions Beautiful and Strange* (New Haven: Yale University Press, 2006).

Hesiod, *Hesiod,* ed. and trans. by Glenn W. Most (Cambridge: Harvard Univesity Press, 2006).

Graham Hughes, *Renaissance cassoni: masterpieces of early Italian art. Painted marriage chests 1400–1550* (London: Art Books International, 1997).

Wolfram Koeppe, *The Robert Lehman Collection. Decorative Arts* (New York: Metropolitan Museum of Art in association with Princeton University Press, 2012).

Deborah L. Krohn, 'Rites of Passage: Art Objects to Celebrate Betrothal, Marriage, and the Family' in *Art and Love in Renaissance Italy,* ed. by Andrea Bayer (New York: Metropolitan Museum of Art, 2008), pp. 60–67.

Tatyana Lymar, 'Cassone with figures of mythological sea-creatures', in *Italian Cassoni from the Art Collections of Soviet Museums,* ed. by Luibov Faenson (Leningrad: Aurora Art Publishers, 1983), unpaginated.

Stefania Massari, *Giulio Romano pinxit et delineavit, catalogo della mostra di Mantova* (Rome: Palombi, 1993), pp. 42–44.

Jacqueline Marie Musacchio, *Art, Marriage, & Family in the Florentine Renaissance Palace* (New Haven and London: Yale University Press, 2008).

Durastante Natalucci, *Historia Universale dello stato temporale ed eclesiastico di Trevi,* ed. by Carlo Zenobi (Foligno: Edizioni dell'Arquata, 1985).

Silvestro Nessi, 'I Tempestivi da Montepennino a Montefalco a Spoleto,' in *Montefalco: Periodo dell'Accademia di Montefalco,* 23/1 (2009).

John Pope-Hennessy and Keith Christiansen, *Secular painting in 15th-century Tuscany: birth trays, cassone panels and portraits* (New York: Metropolitan Museum of Art, 1980).

John Poynter, *Mr Felton's Bequests* (Melbourne: Miegunyah Press, 2008).

Callum Reid, 'Cassone', in *An Illumination, the Rothschild Prayer Book and other works from the Kerry Stokes Collection c.1280–1685*, ed. by Margaret M. Manion (West Perth: Australian Capital Equity, 2015), pp. 192–3.

Stefania Mason Rinaldi, *Palma il Giovane: L'opera completa* (Milan: Electa, 1984).

Frida Schottmüller, *Furniture and interior decoration of the Italian Renaissance* (New York: Brentano's, 1921).

Paul Schubring, *Truhen und Truhenbilder der italienischen frührenaissance*, 2 vols (Leipzig: Hiersemann, 1915, supplement, 1923).

Giorgio Vasari, *Le Vite de' più eccellenti pittori, scultori, e architettori da Cimabue insino a'tempi nostri* (Florence: Giunti, 1568).

Giorgio Vasari, *Le Vite de' più eccellenti pittori, scultori, e architettori da Cimabue insino a' tempi nostri* (Florence: Torrentino, 1550).

Christopher Wilk, *Western furniture: 1350 to the present day in The Victoria and Albert Museum* (London: Philip Wilson Publishers in association with The Victoria and Albert Museum, 1996).

13. *The Dormition of the Virgin* altarpiece from the Kerry Stokes Collection

Ursula Betka

Dunlop, Anne (ed.), *Antipodean Early Modern. European Art in Australian Collections, c. 1200–1600*, Amsterdam University Press, 2018

DOI: 10.5117/9789462985209/CH13

Abstract

The paper aims to elucidate the significance of this Spanish altarpiece in relation to the imagery of the *Dormition of the Virgin* along with its distinctive inscription and crowning crest. Based on the large size of the painting and the recent conservators' report, the work is interpreted as a single-panelled altarpiece in which the composition also refers to the Virgin's Assumption and Glorification as one of the Seven Joys – a prevalent theme for altarpiece dedication in the Catalonia region.

Keywords: Catalonia; Spanish art; Spanish altarpieces; Dormition of the Virgin; Seven Joys of the Virgin; Mateu Ortoneda

The remarkable Spanish painting of *The Dormition of the Virgin* (hereafter the Stokes *Dormition*) was purchased from Christie's in New York on 29 January 2014 (Figure 13.1). It takes the form of a horizontal rectangle with a trapezoidal top. A gilded timber structure frames the work, which includes an inscription across the full width of the base. At its apex is the distinctive feature of a raised red lozenge with the crest of a silver goat, flanked by a representation of two figures robed in white and kneeling in shallow tombs.[1] The altarpiece's 2013 attribution by Rene Millet to an anonymous Catalonian painter known as the Master of Cabassers, with a date of 1410–1415, was based on comparison to an unsigned altarpiece of *The Seven Joys of the Mother of God* in the church of the Nativity in Cabassers or Cabacés (Priorat), Tarragona, which gives the master his name (Figure 13.2).[2] In the same year, however, the Catalonian art historian Francesc Ruiz i Quesada convincingly argued for an identification of the anonymous master and the attribution of the Stokes panel to Mateu Ortoneda and his family workshop. He also suggested a possible origin of the commission in the Catalonian town of Cabra, now Cabra del Camp, near Tarragona, proposing the reconstruction of a monumental altarpiece in which the Stokes *Dormition* formed the

---

This paper is dedicated to my husband, Chris Haymes, who passed away on 23 November 2015.

1   Vaughan and Reid, 'The Dormition of the Virgin', p. 157. Lot 148, Christie's, New York, 29 January 2014.

2   Noted in the catalogue entry for the sale of the Master of Cabassers' panel on 19 June 2013 at the Hotel Drouot, Paris (Anonymous sale; lot 1). See Ruiz i Quesada, 'Revisió del catàleg,' p. 4 note 6, and p. 3.

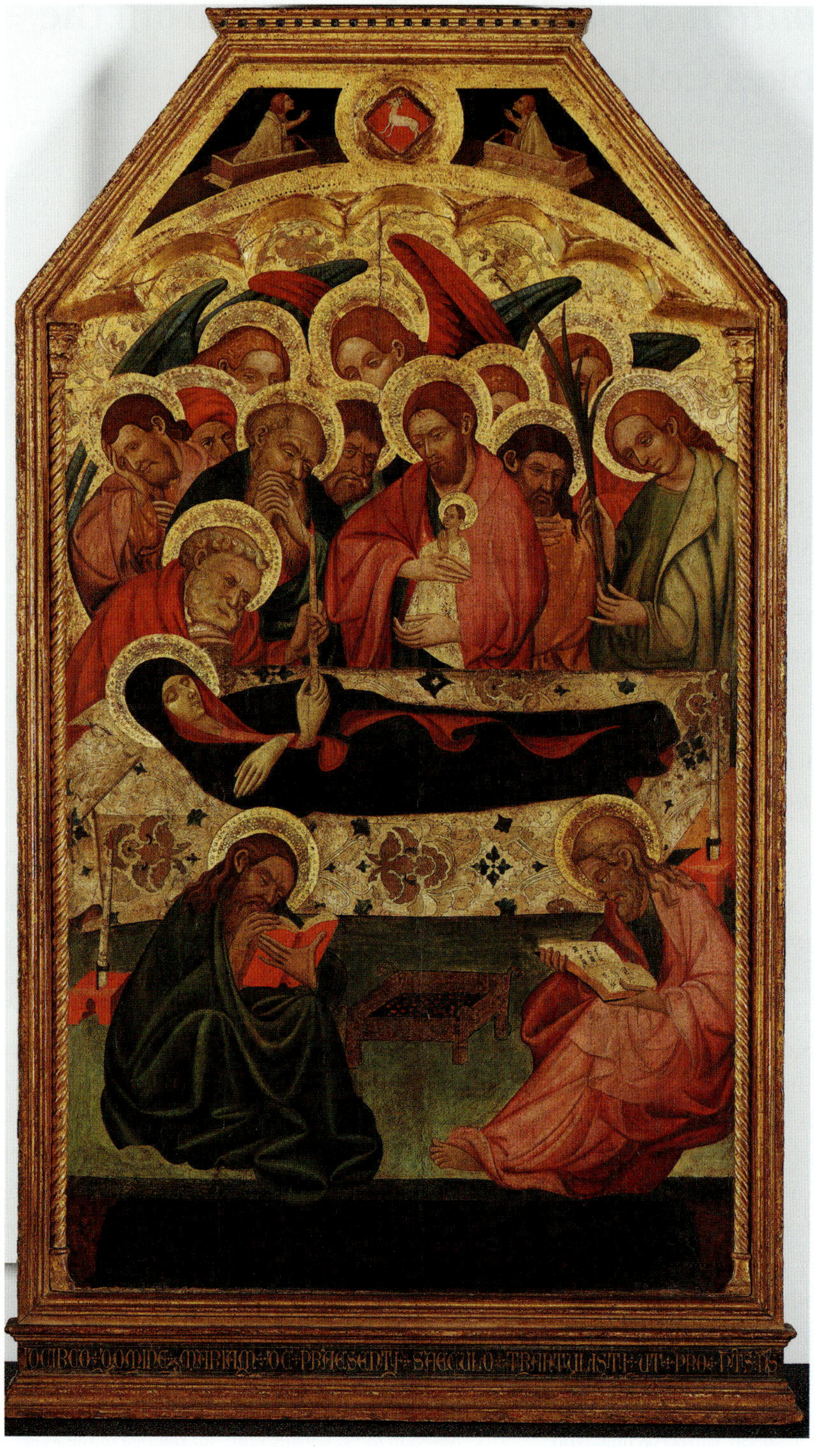

Figure 13.1: Master of Cabassers or Mateu Ortoneda, *The Dormition of the Virgin*, 1410–1415. Tempera and gold on wood panel, 170.8cm × 97cm. Kerry Stokes Collection, Perth.

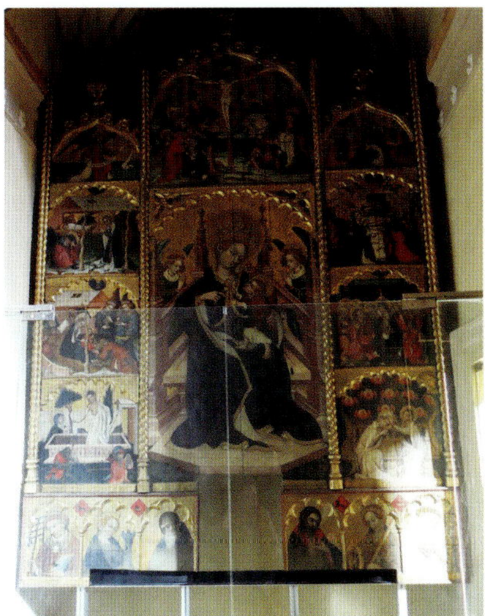

Figure 13.2: Master of Cabassers or Workshop of Mateu Ortoneda, *Altarpiece of the Seven Joys of the Mother of God*, c.1415. Tempera and gold on wood panel. Church of the Nativity, Cabassers (Priorat), Tarragona, Spain.

central panel, capped by an image of the *Deesis* (or 'entreaty') with the Resurrection of the Dead.[3] However, the most recent conservators' report confirms that the Stokes *Dormition* was a stand-alone panel rather than part of a larger construction (Figure 13.3).[4] Given this new information, this essay aims to elucidate the significance of the Stokes altarpiece within Catalonian art. It will examine the imagery of the *Dormition of the Virgin* along with its inscription and crowning crest, and it will propose a new possible patron and original setting.

The iconography of the Dormition is linked to the oldest aspects of the Marian cult, and more particularly to the feast of the Virgin's Assumption, celebrated as the Dormition in the Eastern Church. With the formal recognition of Mary as *Theotokos* – Mother of God – at the Council of Ephesus in 431, the feast came to be observed throughout the Byzantine world in particular.[5] The representation of the Virgin's Dormition, or passing from earthly life, became integrally linked to the idea of her bodily assumption and glorification in heaven. It was a key event in the visual narrative of her life because it stressed that her body was uniquely blessed among human creation. In Europe from the twelfth century, a vigorous discourse on the place of Mary in salvation history emerged, stressing her role in the incarnation of Christ.[6] The feast of the Assumption, celebrating her bodily elevation to Heaven at the moment of death, acclaims the Mother of God as the most powerful intercessor with Christ for the salvation of humanity.[7]

The composition of the Stokes *Dormition* draws on a long iconographic tradition, beginning with the early Byzantine type where the Greek title, *Koimesis*, parallels the Latin *Dormitio* in its reference to Mary 'falling asleep in death', and not suffering the indignities of mortal decay.[8] In these images, the adult Christ appears in the midst of the apostles by the

---

3   See Ruiz I Quesada, 'Revisió del catàleg', pp. 19–20 for a reconstruction diagram.

4   '...we have inspected the side and top and there is nothing visible that confirms it was part of a larger multi-panelled altarpiece.' Email to the author from Erica Persak (Executive Administrator of the Kerry Stokes Collection in Perth, Australia), 8 July 2016. On the construction of Spanish and Catalan altarpieces in this period, see Sobré, *Behind the Altar Table*.

5   Schiller, *Ikonographie*, p. 88; Graef, *Mary: A History*, p. 133.

6   See Schiller, *Ikonographie*, pp. 90–91; Verdier, *Le couronnement de la Vierge*, pp. 13–14; and Morgan, 'The Coronation of the Virgin', p. 234.

7   See, for example, Verdier, *Le couronnement de la Vierge*, pp. 9–16; Graef, *Mary: A History*, p. 138; Schiller, *Ikonographie*, pp. 83–92; and Rahner, *Our Lady and the Church*, especially p. 45 and p. 125.

8   See Schiller, *Ikonographie*, p. 89. For the theological explanation of the iconography of the Dormition in the east, see Ouspensky and Lossky, *The Meaning of Icons*, pp. 213–214.

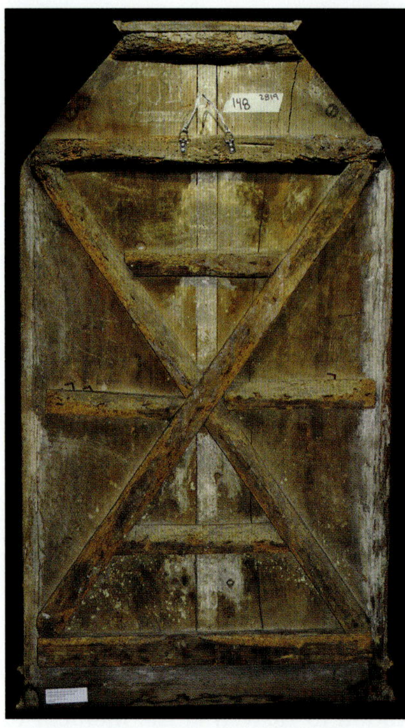

Figure 13.3: Master of Cabassers or Mateu Ortoneda, *The Dormition of the Virgin* (reverse), 1410–1415. Tempera and gold on wood panel, 170.8cm × 97cm. Kerry Stokes Collection, Perth.

compositional source, reflecting the strong links between the Veneto and the east. In contrast to the Stokes *Dormition*, Mary's swaddled soul is represented in the apex of the same painting as an ascent or assumption into the heavens.[9] In other important examples, Mary's final crowning in glory in paradise is highlighted as a distinct but related event, as it is shown in the Stokes *Dormition*. In particular in the apse mosaic of the *Dormition of the Virgin* by Jacopo Torriti in the Basilica of Santa Maria Maggiore in Rome, commissioned by Pope Nicholas IV in 1295 (Figure 13.4). The coronation, which culminates in Mary's glorification, is a new visual theme positioned directly above the Dormition scene.[10] This was clearly intended to assert the theological point that immediately following her death the Virgin was taken to heaven and glorified, with her pure soul and uncorrupted body united.[11] Christ welcomes his mother into the topmost sphere of heaven, with its numerous gold and silver stars. Both are robed in gold. As Christ honours Mary with a crown of glory, she turns to him with hands raised in the gesture of intercession. The book in Christ's left hand is inscribed with a direct quotation from the Office for the Feast of the Assumption.[12] As the major Marian basilica of Rome, built in formal recognition of Mary as *Theotokos,* Santa Maria Maggiore's monumental program with its new central theme of the coronation of the Virgin provided a doctrinal and devotional framework for the observance

bedside of his mother's mortal body, to embrace her soul or immortality. In the Byzantine tradition, the small figure held in the arms of Christ signifies the spirit of Mary or her enduring immortal essence. Many early visualisations of the Virgin's pure soul or spirit in both Eastern and Western traditions render this as a babe tightly swaddled in white binding cloth like a newborn child.

Whereas in Eastern icons the *Koimesis* itself symbolises the passage of the Virgin to Paradise, in the European West it was combined with an image of the Virgin's ascent. Thus a 1333 Italian altarpiece from Vicenza by Paolo Veneziano represents the *Dormition of the Virgin* on its central panel and employs a Byzantine

9   Now in the Civic Museum of Vicenza, inventory number A 157. The polyptych is the first documented work by Paolo Veneziano, signed and dated 1333. The other surviving panels of the polyptych depict St Francis of Assisi and St Anthony of Padua.

10   Henkel, 'Remarks on the late 13th-century Apse Decoration' pp. 128–149.

11   Tronzo, 'Apse Decoration', pp. 167–93, esp. p. 168.

12   Tronzo, 'Apse Decoration', p. 174.

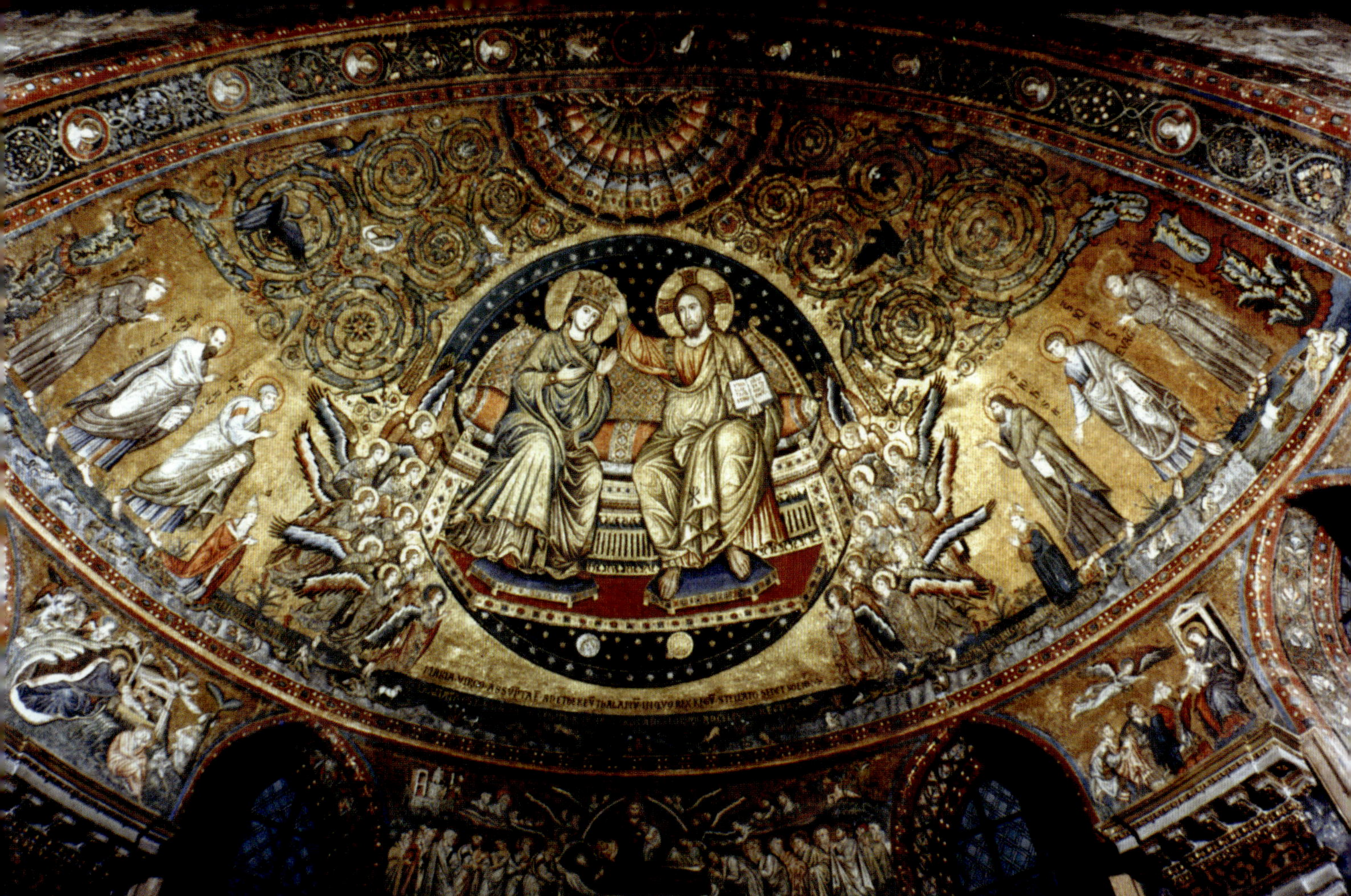

Figure 13.4: Jacopo Torriti, *Dormition of the Virgin*, 1295. Mosaic. Apse of the Basilica of Santa Maria Maggiore, Rome.

of the Assumption feast. The two lines of Latin text beneath the apse derive from the Office for the feast in the Breviary: 'The Virgin Mary is taken up to the ethereal bride-chamber, where the King of Kings sits on a starry throne. The Holy Mother of God is exalted to the heavenly realms above the choirs of angels.'[13] This presentation of Mary as bride could also found in the popular thirteenth-century text known as *The Golden Legend*. Its description of the Dormition and Assumption draws on the biblical Song of Solomon (4:8) for the words that Christ

sings in beckoning his bride and mother to heaven: 'And the chanter of chanters entuned more excellently above all others, saying, *Come from Lebanon, my spouse, come from Lebanon, come, thou shalt be crowned.*'[14]

Yet the Stokes *Dormition*, in the sheer scale of its altarpiece subject, is characteristic of fifteenth-century Spain. Millard Meiss observed that during this period in Spain the altarpiece itself, rather than murals, 'became the carrier of relatively large historical scenes.'[15] That the Virgin was celebrated as a spiritual queen and bride is amply attested in major polyptychs

13   'Maria Virgo assumpta est ad aethereum thalamum, in quo Rex regum stellato sedet solio. Exaltata est sancta Dei genitrix super choros angelorum ad celestia regna' in *Breviarium Romanum. Ex Degreto Sacrosancti Concilii Tredentini* restitutum.Venetiis, MDCCXCVI, p. 480. Also see Henkel, 'Remarks', p. 141 and footnote 38.

14   Jacobus de Voragine, *The Golden Legend*, 4, p. 238. 'Come with me from Lebanon, my bride, come with me from Lebanon' (Song of Solomon 4:8).

15   Meiss, 'Italian Style in Catalonia', p. 64.

from Catalonia and Valencia. These include: *The Seven Joys of the Virgin* in Cabassers, mentioned above (Figure 13.2), *The Virgin of Solivella* signed by Mateu Ortoneda (Figure 13.5),[16] *The Mother of God* attributed to Pere Nicolau and dated to 1390–1408 (Figure 13.6), the *Pentecost* by Pere Serra of *c.*1394,[17] and the altarpiece of *Santa Maria de Santes Creus* by Guerau Gener and Lluís Borrassà of 1407–1411. In each of these multi-panelled works the Coronation rather than the Dormition-Assumption narrative is featured or stressed. The Dormition is only included in the Pere Nicolau altarpiece, where the Coronation takes prominence as the upper central panel (Figure 13.6), and in the *Santes Creus* altarpiece, where it appears as one the Seven Joys of the Virgin in the side panels. In Spain, as elsewhere, the 'Joys of the Virgin' was a popular theme in medieval devotional painting and literature. In its earliest form it embraced five joys. The Annunciation and Nativity of Christ were presented as 'human joys' in contrast to the Resurrection, Ascension of Christ, and Assumption, which were seen in terms of final glorification or 'divine power'. Later the number was increased to seven, with the addition of the Adoration of the Magi and Pentecost.[18] These events or experiences also corresponded to major feasts of the liturgical year. Thus a polyptych with *Scenes from the Life of Christ, the Life of the Virgin, and Saints, c.*1350, by the workshop of Ferrer Bassa, presents the Dormition as the culminating seventh joy,[19] as does Pere Nicolau's portable polyptych of the

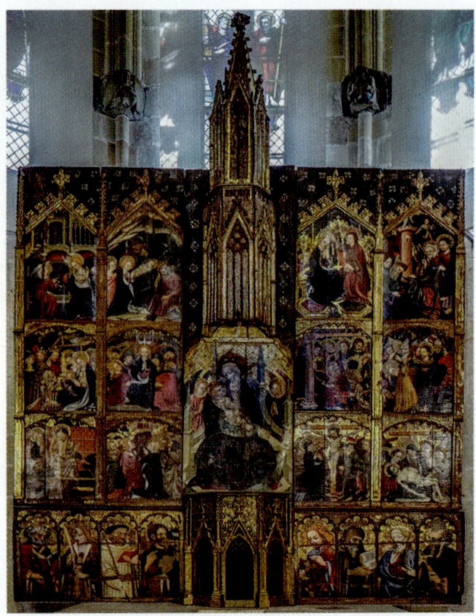

Figure 13.5: Mateu Ortoneda (signed), *Altarpiece of the Mother of God of Solivella* from the Chapel of Solivella Castle, *c.*1415. Museu Diocesà de Tarragona, Spain.

Seven Joys of the Virgin from Valldecrist,[20] and the early-fifteenth-century altarpiece with *Scenes from the Life of the Virgin* by the Gonzalo Perez workshop.[21] This suggests that the Virgin's dormition was also interpreted as her glorification in a number of major Spanish altarpieces from this period, and contextualizes the Dormition as one of the Virgin's Joys.

This is important for the interpretation of the Stokes *Dormition* because the panel invites a meditation on the role of Mary in the history of salvation and presents her as the most powerful mediator with her son for the souls of the living and dead.[22] The miniature effigy of the Virgin in

16   It is held in the Museu Diocesà de Tarragona.

17   Held in the Monastery of Santa Maria de l'Aurora, Manresa, Catalonia.

18   Still later the Joys numbered fifteen or sixteen. Alcoy, 'Gothic painting in the Catalan-speaking lands', p. 38. For lay confraternity devotion to the Joys of Mary in Europe see Meersseman, *Ordo Fraternitatis*, p. 40, n.2.

19   Workshop of Ferrer Bassa, Catalonia (MET, Pierpont Morgan collection),inventory number AZ071.

20   The *Dormition* pancl is now in the Philadelphia Museum of Art. See Ruiz i Quesada, 'Una obra documentada de Pere Nicolau', pp. 2–43; see p. 23 for a diagram of the theorized reconstruction.

21   Now in the Nelson-Atkins Museum of Art, Kansas City, Missouri, USA.

22   The status of Mary as mediator was enhanced by her glorification in both body and soul: beside her Son in Heaven, and her sharing in the mystery of his ascension. Schiller, *Ikonographie*, p. 91.

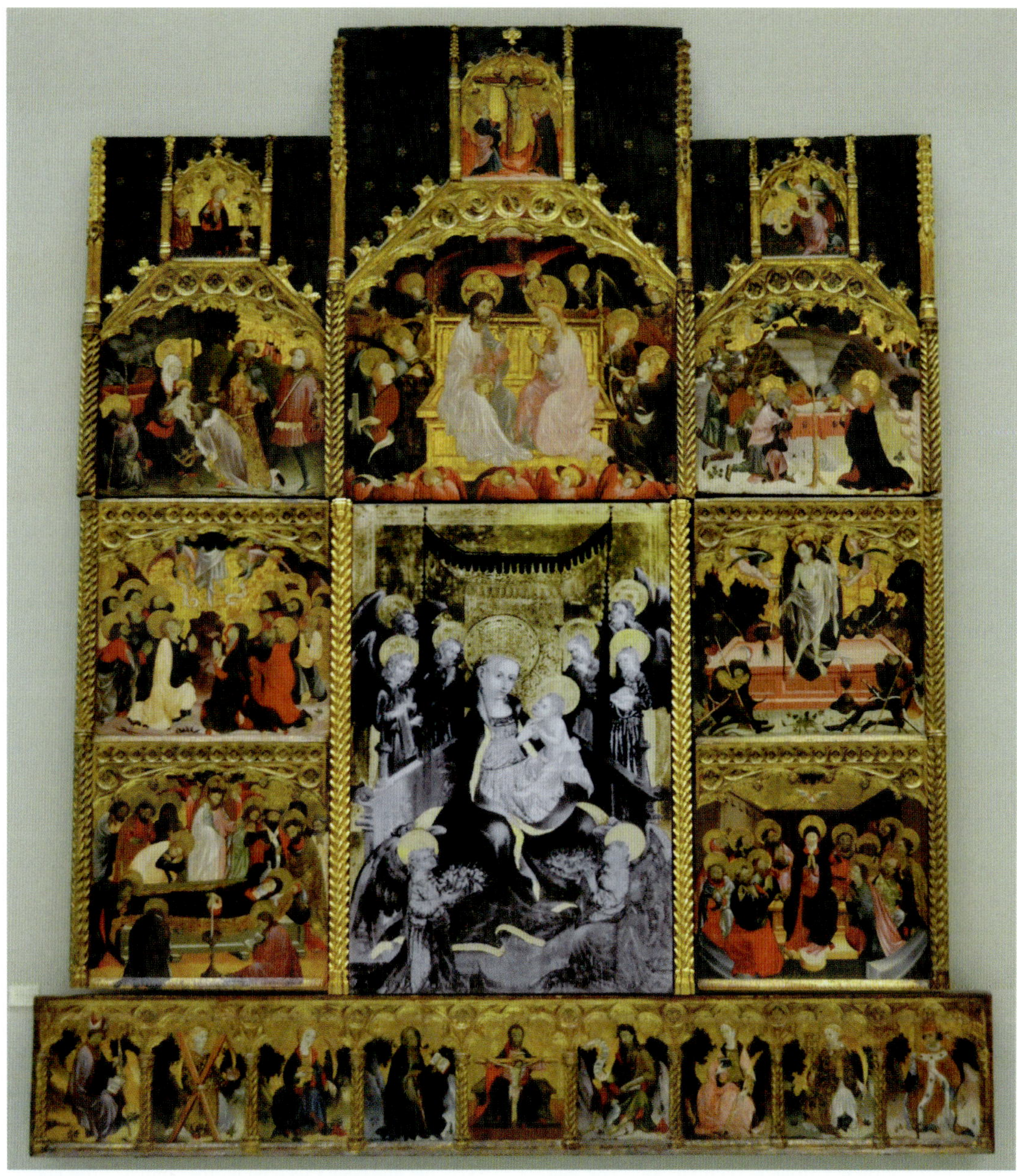

Figure 13.6: Pere Nicolau attributed, *The Mother of God*, 1390–1408. Oil on panel, 377cm × 309cm. Museu de Bellas Artes de Valencia, Spain.

Christ's arms implies her enduring immortal essence, as in the Byzantine tradition where the glorification is not shown. However, in contrast to both Byzantine and Italian renderings of her 'soul' or 'essence', here the effigy is gowned in white silk with a delicate pattern of gold brocade.[23] The choice of such elegant dress is typical in the Catalonian renderings cited above, surely stressing that this is the image of the 'Holy Mother of God… exalted to the heavenly realms above the choirs of angels', as the Breviary describes.

The crest of the silver goat upon a raised red lozenge at the summit of the Stokes altarpiece may reveal more about the ownership, location, and function of this unique work. As mentioned, in 2013, Ruiz i Quesada proposed a possible origin of the commission in the Catalonian town of Cabra, now Cabra del Camp, near Tarragona, and the attribution of the panel to Mateu Ortoneda and his family workshop.[24] The Ortoneda shop, and in particular Mateu and Pasqual Ortoneda, left a number of significant early-fifteenth-century Marian altarpieces, including the signed work by Mateu from the chapel of Solivella Castle of c.1415 (Figure 13.5).[25] Mateu was a prominent artist and citizen of Tarragona in this period, along with the acclaimed Ramon de Mur.[26] Ruiz i Quesada cites a document dating to 1424 that tenuously links Mateu Ortoneda and his workshop to an altarpiece commission for the parish church of Cabra del Camp, dedicated to Mary.[27] His argument for the origins of the commission in Cabra also depends on the inclusion of the crest of the silver goat; by 945, the crest of the town of Cabra was the *cabra* ('goat') through word association.[28]

There is however another possibility for the commission. Flanking the crest of the Stokes *Dormition* are two figures robed in white cloth who emerge from tombs in attitudes of prayer. The imagery strongly suggests the Resurrection of the Dead on Judgment Day. Indeed Ruiz i Quesada's theoretical reconstruction of a polyptych includes an image of the *Deesis* at the summit of the panel, based on an important precedent in Tarragona: Ramon de Mur's multi-panelled

---

23   In medieval plays in England a white cloth of gold edged with miniver was used to represent the soul, *Anima* 'dressed as a maid'. See Woolgar, *The Senses in Late Medieval England*, p. 169.

24   The paper was written shortly after the private sale of the panel in Paris, 2013. Ruiz i Quesada, 'Revisió del catàleg', p. 19.

25   It is signed on its central panel *Matheo Ortoneda pinxit me* ('Matthew Ortoneda painted me'.) The altarpiece is now in the Museu Diocesà de Tarragona, inventory numbers 1848 and 1856. Also see Alcoy, 'Gothic painting', p. 38; Ruiz i Quesada, 'Revisió del catàleg', p. 3; and Post, *A History of Spanish Painting*, Vol. 7, pt.1 p. 751, where the author states in relation to the Cabassers retable that 'internal evidence indisputably proves (it) to have been executed by Mateo Ortoneda' and that it 'closely resembles in style and makeup the signed example from Solivella'. Ruiz i Quesada, writing in 2013, concurred with this view.

26   See Ruiz i Quesada, 'Revisió del catàleg', p. 2.

27   Ruiz i Quesada, 'Revisió del catàleg', p. 18: '*Amb data 30 d'octubre de l'any 1424, Mateu Ortoneda ciustada de Tarragona, va atorgar poders al pintor Pere Huguet, oriund de Valls i oncle del tambe pintor Jaume Huguet, per cobrar dels jurats de Cabra el preu del retaule que havia executat per a l'esglesia d'aquest poble. Aquest temple parroquial era dedicate a Santa maria i el fet que la reclamacio fos cap als jurats d'aquesta poblacio ens porta a una obra sufragada pel poble i, molt probablement, al retaule major de la parroquial de la vila*' ('on 30 October of the year 1424, Mateu Ortoneda, citizen of Tarragona, granted power to the painter Pere Huguet, a native of Valls and uncle of the painter Jaume Huguet, to charge the jury of the price of the Cabra altarpiece that had been executed for the church of this village. This parish church was dedicated to Santa Maria and the fact that the request was to the juries of this village leads us to a work funded by the people, and, very probably, the altarpiece of the parish of the town'). See also Post, *A History of Spanish Painting*, vol. 6, p. 604; and vol. 7, p. 751.

28   Ruiz i Quesada, 'Revisió del catàleg', p. 19, also links the *Stokes Dormition* to the main altar of the parish church of Cabra del Camp based on a rather uncertain archaeological discovery in 1994 of the south wall of the romanesque foundation.

altarpiece from the parish church of Santa Maria in Guimerà (Alt Urgell, 1402–1412), has, as its central panel, a monumental *Deesis* that incorporates a narrative of the Resurrection of the Dead and the Last Judgment.[29] The upward gaze of the two figures praying from their tombs clearly references the Byzantine icon, which traditionally represents the enthroned Christ flanked by the glorified Mother of God and John the Baptist, who raise their hands in supplication before the Pantocrator.[30] The praying dead thereby invoke the Virgin's aid at the call to judgment, so that their souls may be re-united with their mortal bodies – reiterating the core tenets of the Apostles' Creed: the communion of saints, the forgiveness of sins, the resurrection of the body, and life everlasting.

The coat of arms on the Stokes panel may instead be a symbol of familial affiliation. The Catalonian nobility, which included barons and bishops, was composed of a small group of interrelated families. One prominent family of Catalonia during the early fifteenth century was that of the Viscounts of Cabrera. The Cabrera name is derived from the Spanish word *cabra*, meaning goat; and their coat of arms depicts a Pyrenean mountain goat.[31] The Cabrera

had a castle in the province of Girona, and in the fourteenth century they substantially financed the building of the adjoining gothic church of Santa Maria de Blanes. The town fountain in Blanes bears the Cabrera arms, a mountain goat within a framing lozenge.[32] At the time when the Stokes *Dormition* was created, the Viscount was Bernardo IV de Cabrera y Bas (1352–1423) who had succeeded as Viscount since 1373. Bernardo had two wives. With the first, Timbor de Prades (1385), he had five children. Her date of death is unknown. He married his second wife, Cecelia de Urgell, in 1409.[33]

Did the Cabrera nobility of Girona commission the Stokes painting of the *Dormition of the Virgin* for a family chapel in Santa Maria de Blanes? The prominent inclusion of the crest at the summit of the painting suggests an initial association. Circumstantial evidence also suggests that Mateu Ortoneda was contracted in 1428 for the altarpiece of the Chapel of St. Mary Magdalene of Girona, linking him to the Cabrera lands.[34] The rising dead flanking the crest, while generic figures, might also suggest that the Stokes *Dormition* was intended as a singular altarpiece for the intercessory prayers of family. If the panel was commissioned from the Ortoneda workshop between 1410 and 1415, as suggested by Ruiz i Quesada, it coincides with the period of Bernardo's marriage to his second wife, Cecelia de Urgell, in 1409, and perhaps commemorated the death of his first wife Timbor de Prades, on behalf of their five children; it could also have marked his eldest

29   The altarpiece was originally on the main altar of the parish church of Santa Maria in Guimerà (Alt Urgell). Ramon de Mur had his workshop established in Tarragona, taking altarpiece commissions in the region. The work is now preserved at the Museu Episcopal de Vic, in Barcelona. Also see Duch i Mas, 'Ramon de Mur', pp. 46–79. The *Deesis* image in this case presents the glorified Virgin and St John the evangelist accompanied by other saints, who collectively intercede on behalf of the rising dead.

30   In the Byzantine tradition the Virgin Mary and St John the Baptist are represented on either side of the Pantocrator on the iconastasis. Tradego, *Icons and Saints of the Eastern Orthodox Church*, pp. 248–251. Also see Kalavrezou, 'Images of the Mother', pp. 170–171; and Cormack, *Painting the Soul.* p. 40 and pp. 101–107.

31   See Sire, *King Arthur's European Realm*, p. 101. For the symbolism of goats in art see Werness, *The Continuum Encyclopedia of Animal Symbolism in Art*, pp. 196–198.

32   Homburg and Golder, *Costa Brava. Costa Dorada*, p. 40.

33   C. Señores de Cabrera, Vescomtes de Cabrera in Girona, Vescomtes de Girona 1050–1565. See also Francisco Ruanom and Joannes Ribades, *Casa da Cabrera en Cordoba*, pp. 94–109; pp. 123ff.

34   Riuz i Quesada, 'A l'entorn d'un patrimoni dispers i perdut', p. 87.

son's marriage to Violante de Prades sometime between 1409 and 1419.

Masses and prayers were traditionally offered daily for the souls of both the living and the dead, especially within the context of a private family chapel.[35] On the eve of a funeral, too, relatives gathered before the coffin, often in the choir of the church, for the recitation of the Office of the Dead by the clergy or friars.[36] Testaments also provided for alms to pay for anniversary masses to be celebrated in memory of the testator.[37] The choice of the Dormition of the Virgin as the main theme for an altarpiece is relatively unusual, as is the inclusion of the reference to the Resurrection of the Dead in the apex. In conjunction with the image of the two rising dead, Mary's role as mediator with God at the moment of death and judgment is clearly stressed. It is significant, then, that the little effigy of the Virgin in the arms of Christ depicts her with hands clasped in prayer as she directs her gaze towards the two figures in coffins beside the Cabra crest. In the foreground of the Stokes *Dormition*, the two apostles sitting before the Virgin's deathbed pray the obsequies of the dead using medieval prayer books. Their prominence at the edge of the picture, along with the open space between them, invites the

viewer to an intimate participation in these rites, as does the expression of mourning by the other apostles.[38]

Further, Mary's mortal body lies on a silken floral cloth of white, gold, and deep blue, richly woven or embroidered with a pattern of roses and lilies. Medieval paraliturgical associations amplify the significance of this cloth, particularly since the account of Mary's funeral in *The Golden Legend* was recited on the feast of the Assumption:

> Then said our Lord to the apostles: *Bear ye the body of this virgin, my mother, into the vale of Jehosaphat and lay ye her in a new sepulchre that ye shall find there, and abide me there three days till that return to you. And anon she was environed with flowers of roses, that was the company of martyrs, and with lilies of the valley, that was the company of angels, of confessors and virgins.*[39]

Popular belief, from the fourth century, considered that the Last Judgment would take place in the Valley of Jehosaphat.[40] This interpretation draws on the passage in the book of Joel 3:2:

> I will gather together all nations, and will bring them down into the valley of Jehosaphat: and I will plead with them there for my people, and for my inheritance Israel, whom they have scattered among the nations.

It would seem that the image of the Virgin in quiet repose on her lavish flower-strewn bed cloth could recall all the dead for those who

---

35   Betka, 'Marian images and *Laudesi* Devotion' especially pp. 175–183 for the role of private chapels in the funerary rites and commemorative prayers for the dead of lay confraternities, which parallels the privileges given to wealthy families.

36   The Office of the Dead evolved from the commemorative practices and prayers of monastic communities and came to form an integral part of its funeral rites. See Harthan, *Books of Hours and their Owners*, p. 17; and Wieck, *Time Sanctified*, pp. 124–136; Paxton, *Christianizing Death*, pp. 134–8, and Ottosen, *The Responsories and Versicles of the Latin Office of the Dead*.

37   'The third manner of suffrages is the oblation and offering of the holy sacrament of the altar...' along with the observation of 'the anniversary of them that be dead unto their profit and our devotion...'. Jacobus de Voragine, *The Golden Legend*, 'The Commemoration of All Souls', Vol. 6, p. 118 and p. 124.

38   See Daniell, *Death and Burial in Medieval England. 1066–1550*, pp. 27–28; on friends praying for the dying, p. 34; and for the presence of Christ at the last rights and the battle for the soul, pp. 35–36.

39   Jacobus de Voragine, *The Golden Legend*, Vol. 5, p. 238.

40   Abel, 'Valley of Josaphat'.

prayed before this altarpiece – Bernardo de Cabrera, his wife and children, and the family ancestors – those who lay entombed beneath the floor of the church in Girona, and in the biblical Valley of Jehosaphat awaiting the Last Judgment, and who also anticipated the 'company of martyrs' and 'angels, confessors and virgins' in paradise.

Further, in this context of a private altarpiece, the miniature figure of the Virgin's soul or essence might have given form to the hopes for eventual resurrection. Passages from *The Golden Legend* for the feast of the Assumption were read in conjunction with prayers of intercession for the faithful living and dead:

> Lady, remember thee of us. And then the company of saints that were abiding there – were awaked with the sound of the song… and saw their king bear in his arms the soul of a woman, and saw that this soul was joined to him…[41]

The moulding at the base of the Stokes *Dormition* displays a Latin inscription that spans the entire width of the painting and reinforces the link to intercession and the Assumption – O CIRCO[sic] / O DOMINE / MARIAM / DE /PRESENTI/ SAECULO/ TRANTULISTI/UT/ PRO / PTS /NS. It derives from the Vigil Mass of the Assumption feast: *Magna est, Domine, apud clementiam tuam Dei Genitraicis oratio, quam idcirco de praesenti saeculo transtulisti, ut pro peccatis nostris [apud te fiducialiter intercedat]* ('It is great, O Lord, Thy mercy for the prayer of the Mother of God, because of which, O Lord, you have taken Mary from this present world so that for our sins she might faithfully intercede'.)[42]

Within the context of the glorification of Mary, the exotic cloth on the deathbed and funerary bier can be further interpreted. The depiction of a cloth of honour, often made of expensive gold and silver brocade or richly coloured lampas silk and draped or hung behind the Virgin's throne, is a consistent element in European paintings of this theme from the early fourteenth century.[43] Fittingly, the cloth of honour parallels the use of actual luxury cloths in contemporary ecclesiastical, royal or courtly settings.[44] An altarpiece by Pere Serra from the Monastery of Sant Cugat del Vallès, Catalonia (*c*.1405), features a red silk velvet cloth behind the Mary's throne, while in Pere Nicolau's altarpiece of the *Mother of God,* four angels support an extended cloth made of red and gold brocaded silk (Figure 13.6).[45] The gilded backdrop of the Stokes *Dormition* scene too, in its bold patterning with scrolling vine-leaves, is suggestive of a luxury hanging cloth in the court of heaven. Close parallels are apparent in the *Mother of God* altarpiece in the church at Cabassers, mentioned above, where the punch-work of the gold ground reflects a very similar scrolling grapevine pattern, and is contextualised as a cloth of honour behind the throne of a crowned Mother of God. If Mateu Ortoneda is in fact the painter of both the anonymous Mother of God altarpiece at Cabassers – the Master of Cabassers – and the Stokes *Dormition*, he was probably using a stock pattern.

It has been argued that the compositional treatment of the Stokes *Dormition* refers to the Virgin's assumption and glorification in paradise beside Christ. Functioning as a single panel in a family chapel, the painting expressed

41   Jacobus de Voragine, *The Golden Legend*, Vol. IV, p. 238.
42   Ruiz i Quesada 'Revisió del catàleg', p. 16; see also Vaughan and Reid '*Dormition of the Virgin*', p. 157.

43   Woolgar, *The Senses in Late Medieval England*, p. 168.
44   Gantzhurn, *Oriental Carpets*, pp. 100–115, argues that many of these 'hangings' derive from carpet designs, or were in fact carpet hangings.
45   Museu de Belles arts de Valencia.

the ultimate joy of the Virgin and her role as intercessor. The abbreviated scene of the resurrection of the dead in the pediment, as well as the crest of the silver goat, affirm this reading. A final point can be made about the popularity of the Seven Joys theme with the laity. Many altarpieces were dedicated to it in Catalonia; and a well-established tradition, including in the province of Girona, expressed this popular devotion through vernacular song, dance and enactment.[46] A surviving manuscript from Girona written in fourteenth-century Catalan contains a large number of compositions that are couched as *laude* or vernacular songs of praise.[47] These narrate the joyful highlights of the life of the Virgin Mary. One such *lauda*, published in 2003 by Pep Vila, praises each of the seven joys in its respective verses. The honouring of the seventh joy, together with the final verse, acclaims the ascent of the Virgin's 'heart' in the 'heavens with Jesus', as the 'imperial queen' with the 'heavenly King … for all eternity':

> Humble Virgin of great suffering
>> I wish to pray you, in all humility, please
>> that in a fitting way you graciously listen to
> your seven joys
>> [...]
>> The seventh joy was fulfilled all goodness,
> all the others were together with it,
> when your heart, with greatest clarity,
>> was placed high up in the heavens with
> Jesus.[48]

The sentiments expressed in this *lauda* directly refer to the Marian altarpiece imagery of that province; the *Retable of the Joys of the Virgin* for example, attributed to the Master of Girona, was from the parish church of Púbol (la Pera), Girona.[49] Artists like Mateu Ortoneda and his workshop knew this well. In the painting of the Seven Joys in the church of the nativity in Cabassers, and the *Dormition of the Virgin* as the main theme for an altarpiece, the image of the rising dead is irrevocably fused with the Virgin's final joy – her Assumption and glorification in heaven – resounding the festal prayer inscribed at the base of the panel: 'because of which, O Lord, you have taken Mary from this present world so that for ours sins she might faithfully intercede'.

About the author

Ursula Betka is an active iconographer and co-editor of *Byzantine Narrative. Papers in Honour of Roger Scott* (2006). She teaches medieval tempera painting and gilding methods. Her work will be featured on the 2018 Australian Christmas stamp. ursulabetka@gmail.com

vostres vjj- goigs ojats. VIII. *Lo setè goig fo complit de tots béns, tots los altres foren ab est ensemps, quant vostre cors, ab molt gran claradat, fo alt als cels ab Jhesús col·locat.* I thank Dr. Paolo Baracchi (Italian Historical Society & Museo Italiano, Melbourne 28 February 2016) for his assistance in the translation. Vila, 'Els Set Goigs', p. 183.

49   The altarpiece has been missing since 1936 but is recorded in photographs. See Monllau, 'Quattrocento Calvary', pp, 47–83. Alcoy, 'Gothic painting', p. 38, dates this altarpiece to the late-fourteenth century, noting that some sections are conserved in the Museo de Bellas Artes of Bilbao. The close link between imagery and sung prayer, especially on the feast of the Assumption, also parallels the devotions of lay confraternities in Italy during this period, similarly expressed in the vernacular. See also: Riuz i Quesada, 'A l'entorn d'un patrimoni dispers i perdut', pp. 94–108, and Betka, 'Marian Images and *Laudesi* Devotion', pp. 12–34, and pp. 213–250.

---

46   Vila, 'Els Set Goigs' p. 180, where the author discusses the body of medieval religious literature in Latin, Provençal and Catalan related to the earthly joys of the Virgin.

47   El ms. Num. 91. Biblioteca de l'Arxiu Capitular de Girona, Catalonia (Vila, 'Els Set Goigs, p. 179).

48   IX. Per què-n vos prech, regina emperial, vullats preyar lo Rey celestial qu-en paradís puxam tuyt habitar e Ell e Vós en per tots temps loar. 1. *Humil Verge de gran dolsor, preyar-vos' vull, tot humilment, sius plats, que dignament*

Works cited

Félix Marie Abel, 'Valley of Josaphat', *The Catholic Encyclopedia*, 8 (New York: Robert Appleton Company, 1910), acccessed 25 July 2015 at http://www.newadvent.org/cathen/08503a.htm.

Rosa Alcoy, 'Gothic painting in the Catalan-speaking lands between the 14th and 15th centuries', *Catalan Historical Review*, 8 (2015), pp. 29–44.

Ursula Betka, 'Marian images and *Laudesi* Devotion in late medieval Italy, *c.*1260–1350', Ph.D. dissertation, University of Melbourne, 2001.

Christie's, *Old Master Paintings Part I, Sale 2817, 29 January 2014, New York, Rockefeller Center* (New York: Christie's, 2014).

Robin Cormack, *Painting the Soul. Icons, Death Masks and Shrouds* (London: Reaktion Books, 1997).

Christopher Daniell, *Death and Burial in Medieval England. 1066–1550* (London: Routledge, 1997).

Joan Duch i Mas, 'Ramon de Mur, autor del retaule de Guimerà (segle xv)', *Urtx, revista cultural de l'Urgell,* 22 (2008), pp. 46–79.

Volkmar Gantzhurn, *Oriental Carpets* (Cologne: Taschen 1998).

Hilda C. Graef, *Mary: A History of Doctrine and Devotion*, 2 vols. (New York: Sheed and Ward, 1963).

John Harthan, *Books of Hours and their Owners* (London: Thames and Hudson, 1977).

Herbert Henkel, 'Remarks on the late 13th-century Apse Decoration in S. Maria Maggiore, *Simiolus*, 4 (1971), pp. 128–149.

Elke Homburg and Marion Golder, *Costa Brava. Costa Dorada* (Munich: Nelles, 2001).

Jacobus de Voragine, *The Golden Legend* (London: J.M. Dent, 1973).

Ioli Kalavrezou, 'Images of the Mother: When the Virgin Mary Became *Meter Theou*', *Dunbarton Oaks Papers*, 44 (1990), pp. 165–72.

Gilles-Gérard Meersseman, *Ordo Fraternitatis. Confraternite e pietà dei laici nel Medioevo*, 3 vols. (Rome: Herder, 1977).

Millard Meiss, 'Italian Style in Catalonia and a Fourteenth Century Catalan Workshop', *The Journal of the Walters Art Gallery,* 4 (1941), pp. 45–87.

Cèsar Favà Monllau, 'The Quattrocento Calvary from Catalonia at the Bilbao Fine Arts Museum. An outline of the artistic context', *Buletina, Museo de Bellas Artes de Bilbao*, 8 (2014), pp. 47–83.

Nigel Morgan, 'The Coronation of the Virgin by the Trinity and Other Texts and Images of the Glorification of Mary in Fifteenth-Century England', in *England in the Fifteenth Century,*, ed. by Nicholas J. Rogers, (Stamford: Paul Watkins, 1994), pp. 223–41.

Knud Ottosen, *The Responsories and Versicles of the Latin Office of the Dead* (Aarhus: Aarhus University Press, 1993).

Léonide Ouspensky and Vladimir Ouspensky, *The Meaning of Icons* (Crestwood, New York: St. Vladimir's Seminary Press, 1999).

Frederick S. Paxton, *Christianizing Death. The Creation of a Ritual Process in Early Medieval Europe* (Ithaca and London: Cornell University Press, 1990).

Chandler Rathfon Post, *A History of Spanish Painting*, 14 vols. (Cambridge: Harvard University Press, 1930–1966).

Hugh Rahner, *Our Lady and the Church* (London: Darton, Longman and Todd, 1961).

Francisco Ruanom and Joannes Ribades, *Casa de Cabrera en Cordoba: obra genealogia historia, dedicada a el senor D. Fernando de Cabrera* (Cordoba: D. Juan Rodriguez, 1779).

Francesc Ruiz i Quesada, 'A l'entorn d'un patrimoni dispers i perdut. Els obradors pictòrics gironins del darrer gòtic', *Bernat Martorell. La tardor del gòtic català, Girona*, exh. cat., (2003), pp. 94–108.

Francesc Ruiz i Quesada, 'Revisió del catàleg artístic dels Ortoneda, a partir d'un retaule de Cabra', *Retrotabulum. Estudis d'art medieval*, 10 (2013), pp. 2–44, accessed 5 February 2016 at http://www.ruizquesada.com/index.php/ca/ retrotabulum/104-retrotabulum-10.

Francesc Ruiz i Quesada, 'Una obra documentada de Pere Nicolau per al rei Marti l'Huma. El poliptic dels set Giogs de la cartoixa de Valldecrist', *Retrotabulum*, 8 (Nov. 2013), pp. 2–43.

Francesc Ruiz i Quesada, 'A l'entorn d'un patrimoni dispers i perdut. Els obradors pictòrics gironins del darrer gòtic', *Bernat Martorell. La tardor del gòtic català, Girona* (2003), pp. 94–108, accessed 18 February 2016 at http://www.ruizquesada.com/index.php/es/ articulos-eses/179-a-lentorn-dun-patrimoni-dispers-i-perdut-els-obradors-pictorics-gironins-del-darrer-gotic

Gertrud Schiller, *Ikonographie der christlichen Kunst 4:2: Maria* (Gütersloh: Gerd Mohn, 1980).

Paul Sire, *King Arthur's European Realm: New Evidence from Monmouth's Primary Sources* (Jefferson, NC: McFarland and Company, 2014).

Judith Berg Sobré, *Behind the Altar Table: the Development of the Painted Retable in Spain, 1350–1500* (Columbia: University of Missouri Press, 1989).

Alfredo Tradego, *Icons and Saints of the Eastern Orthodox Church* (Los Angeles: J. Paul Getty Museum, 2006), pp. 248–251.

William Tronzo, 'Apse Decoration, the Liturgy and the Perception of Art in Medieval Rome: S. Maria in Trastevere and S. Maria Maggiore', in *Italian Church Decoration of the Middle Ages and Early Renaissance: functions, forms and regional traditions: ten contributions to a colloquium held at the Villa Spelman, Florence*, ed. by William Tronzo (Bologna: Nuova Alfa, 1989), pp. 167–93.

Gerard Vaughan and Callum Reid, 'The Dormition of the Virgin' in *An Illumination. The Rothschild Prayer Book and other works from the Kerry Stokes Collection c.1280–1685*, ed. by Margaret M. Manion (West Perth: Australian Capital Equity, 2015), pp. 155–157.

Phillipe Verdier, *Le couronnement de la Vierge: les origines et les premiers développements d'un thème iconographique* (Montréal and Paris: Institut d'études médiévales and Vrin, 1980).

Pep Vila, 'Els Set Goigs Terrenals de la Verge Maria de la Catedral de Girona', *Annals de l'Institut d'Estudis Gironins*, 44 (2003), pp. 179–184.

Hope Werness, *The Continuum Encyclopedia of Animal Symbolism in Art* (New York: Continuum, 2006).

Roger S. Wieck, *Time Sanctified. The Book of Hours in Medieval Art and Life* (New York: G. Braziller in association with the Walters Art Gallery, Baltimore 1988).

Christopher M. Woolgar, *The Senses in Late Medieval England* (New Haven: Yale University Press, 2006).

14.   Through the son: Pieter Brueghel the Younger's *Crucifixion*

Larry Silver

Dunlop, Anne (ed.), *Antipodean Early Modern. European Art in Australian Collections, c. 1200–1600*, Amsterdam University Press, 2018

DOI: 10.5117/9789462985209/CH14

Abstract

Not only is the large *Crucifixion* panel (1615) in the Kerry Stokes Collection signed by Pieter Brueghel the Younger, the finest version of that essential subject by its prolific painter, but it also provides the most reliable version of a presumed lost *Crucifixion* composition by his celebrated father Pieter Bruegel the Elder. The crowded composition shows vignettes of holy figures, tormentors, and ordinary onlookers, many of them in contemporary dress, characteristic of the Bruegel family heritage, all presented before a mountaintop setting of Golgotha and above the circular Temple of Jerusalem. The original painting likely stemmed from shortly after 1560, and it accords well with other Bruegel Calvary subjects by both father and son.

Keywords: Pieter Brueghel, Bruegel, Calvary, Crucifixion

Pieter Bruegel the Elder (*c.*1520/1525–1569) remains a most familiar and beloved painter, renowned for his images of peasant leisure and labour. But he also produced significant works of religious art, some of which surely disappeared in the iconoclastic cleansing of churches that began late in his life, first arising in August of 1566. How exciting, then, to rediscover a major religious work by Bruegel, a *Crucifixion*, carefully replicated in multiple copies by his painter son Pieter the Younger (1564–1637/1638), who frequently made use of both his father's designs and finished paintings throughout his productive career. As we shall see, echoes of the same lost work were adapted for the same subject by Bruegel's other painter son, Jan Brueghel (1568–1625). But the best version of this missing masterpiece can be found in the Kerry Stokes Collection, Perth.

Pieter Bruegel the Elder not only left a lasting artistic legacy in his forms and favorite themes, but also in the achievements of his two painter sons, Pieter the Younger (1564–1637/1638) and Jan Brueghel (1568–1625). Jan was celebrated as one of the most distinguished and well-rewarded painters of the early seventeenth century. He served as a court painter for the archdukes in Brussels and produced some of the most expensive paintings of the day, including sumptuous still life flower bouquets as well as finely wrought miniature landscapes, often crowded with tiny figures.[1]

Pieter Brueghel the Younger was born in 1564 (or early 1565; the year started in March then), and he died as late as 1638 around age 74.[2] He entered the Antwerp painters' guild in 1585 as a 'freemaster's son', and certainly could be called a 'second Bruegel', just as his father had been called a 'second Bosch' earlier. In fact, although he probably was apprenticed to a distinctive landscape specialist named Gillis van Coninxloo, Pieter the Younger made his entire career out of what are often dismissively considered 'slavish' copies after the compositions of his father, whether known from prints or from original drawings and paintings.[3] Yet he registered nine apprentices of his own over a long career. Indeed, his output, even of the same compositions, varies considerably in quality, so it is likely that from the 1590s onward Pieter the Younger freely utilized the assistants in his large workshop, which produced so many variants of basic compositions by Pieter the Elder. Pieter the Younger's likeness is one of the great portrait etchings in Anthony van Dyck's series, called the *Iconography*, which describes him accurately in Latin (ANTVERPIAE PICTOR RURALIUM PROSPECTUUM) as an 'Antwerp painter of rural views'.[4]

The large-scale *Crucifixion* panel by Pieter Brueghel the Younger in the Stokes Collection is therefore an important object (Figure 14.1). It displays an impressive multitude of figures against a vast panoramic landscape to convey its Gospel story. But in addition, as one of eight closely-related versions of this same subject in two variants by Pieter the Younger, it almost certainly points to a missing original by his celebrated father and namesake, Pieter Bruegel the Elder.[5] Whereas we might wish to see the Crucifixion as a distant narrative, Bruegel's composition recasts it into a living event for the sixteenth- (or seventeenth-) century beholder, and his son Pieter the Younger retains that same staging. As a result, the *Crucifixion*, with its distant, witnessing holy figures, becomes a work of the artist's present, like Bruegel the Elder's own composition of the *Massacre of the Innocents*, another of his works copied by Bruegel the Younger, which is also vividly punctuated with redcoats and

The author is deeply grateful to the Stokes Family and to Dr. Philip Gregory Kent of the Melbourne University Library for the invitation to present this paper in conjunction with the exhibition of the Stokes Collection at the Potter Gallery, Melbourne, in autumn 2015. Thanks are due as well to Prof. Charles Zika for his discussion of the picture in the Stokes catalogue as well as for both fruitful discussion and gracious hospitality in Melbourne.

1   Ertz and Nitze-Ertz, *Brueghel-Breughel*; for Jan Brueghel, see also Neumeister, *Breughel*; and Honig, *Jan Brueghel and the Senses of Scale*.

2   Ertz, *Pieter Brueghel der* Jüngere; Currie and Allart, *The Brueg[H]el Phenomenon*, esp. pp. 48–90.

3   Currie and Allart, *The Brueg[H]el Phenomenon*; see also van den Brink, *Bruegel Enterprises*.

4   For the Pieter Brueghel the Younger etching by van Dyck, see Depauw and Luijten, *Anthony van Dyck as a*

Printmaker, pp. 104–08, no. 7; on the *Iconography* more generally see Depauw and Luijten, *Anthony van Dyck as a Printmaker*, pp. 73–91; also Spicer, 'Anthony van Dycks Iconography', pp. 327–56.

5   Dimensions 99.9cm x 147.5cm. Signed P BRVEGHEL 1615. Currie and Allart, *The Brueg[H]el Phenomenon*, pp. 614–45, is now definitive; the Stokes version, then in the Coppée-le Hodey Collection, is illustrated as Figure 418. Its composition is replicated in another version in Antwerp, Koninklijk Museum. See also the definitive catalogue of works by Brueghel the Younger: Ertz, *Brueghel der Jüngere*. I, pp. 414–38, where the Stokes painting is 435, Figure 292, no. E414. Only the Stokes picture and the Budapest variant of 1617 are signed and dated. The core of eight Pieter the Younger versions are ascribed with confidence by Ertz along with thirteen other more uncertain attributions, known through photographs. A Philadelphia version, 69.2cm x 122.2cm is analysed in the catalogue by Sutton, *Northern European Paintings*, pp. 44–48, no. 15, with a list of copies and variant versions, where the Stokes panel is number one. Ertz, *Brueghel der Jüngere*, p. 436, no. E420, ascribes the fine background of the Philadelphia panel to Joos de Momper as well and considers it a variant of the Budapest picture.

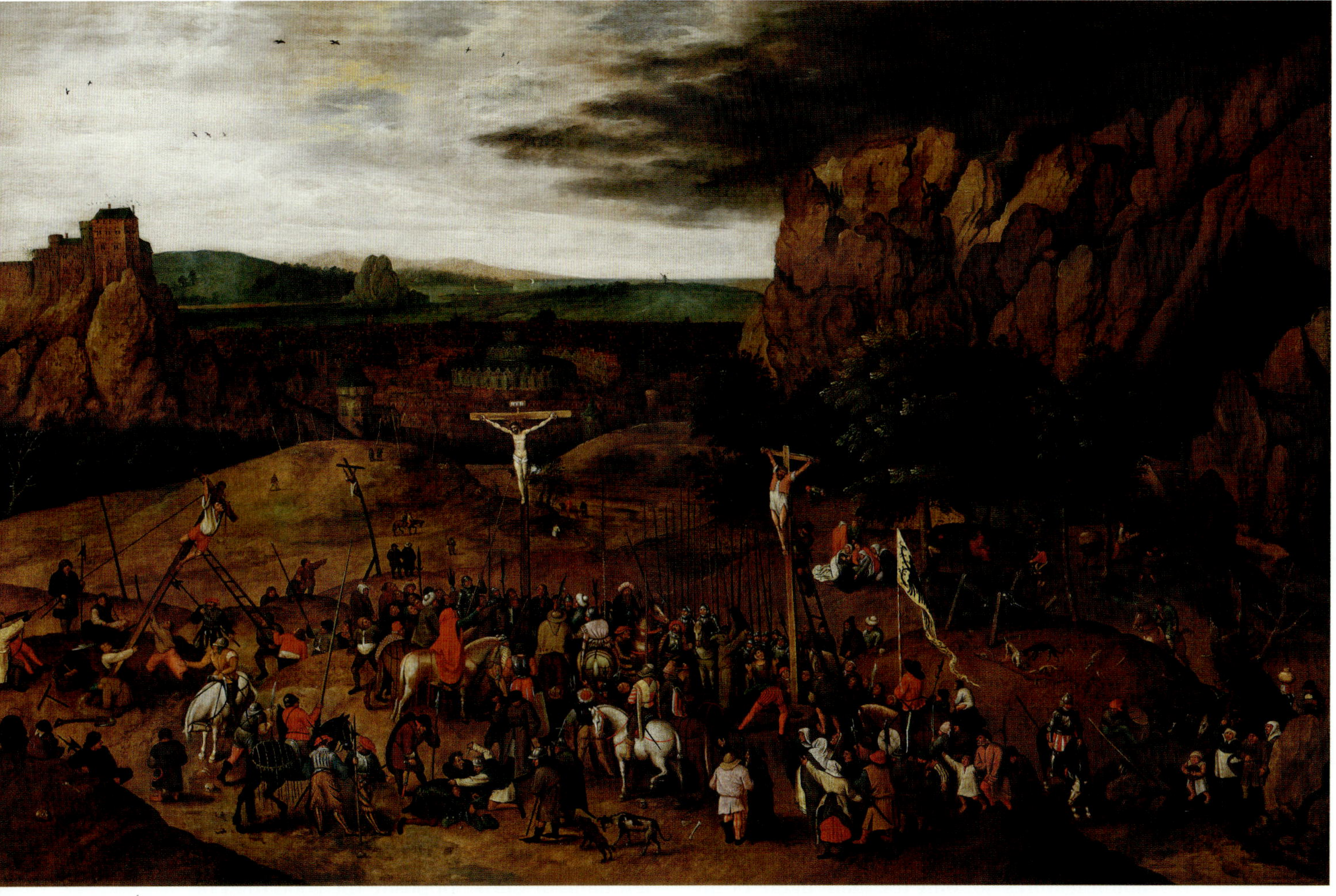

Figure 14.1: Pieter Brueghel the Younger, *Calvary* or *Crucifixion*, signed and dated 1615. Oil on oak panel, 99.9cm × 147cm. Kerry Stokes Collection, Perth.

grieving village peasants.[6] This sensibility of seeing Gospel events anachronistically as if in the present, therefore stems ultimately from the father, Pieter Bruegel the Elder.[7]

A survey of the events depicted in the Stokes panel reveals that this image presents a typical 'figure-rich' Crucifixion, a type popular in painting of the late Middle Ages, beginning in Germany with the Cologne School of the early fifteenth century but also adopted by Netherlandish artists, such as Dutch engraver Lucas van Leyden (Figure 14.2).[8] The Stokes

6   Ertz and Nitze-Ertz, *Brueghel-Breughel*, pp. 322–25, nos. 98–99, with variant composition, p. 328, no. 100. Fourteen versions are associated with Pieter the Younger.

7   On the re-experience of the Passion, particularly the torments of the Crucifixion, as spectacle, see Merback, *Thief, Cross and Wheel*, esp. pp. 41–68 and pp. 126–57.

8   Roth, *Der volkreiche Kalvarienberg*. For the Lucas engraving, see Jacobowitz and Stepanek, *The Prints of Lucas van Leyden and his Contemporaries*, pp. 161–63, nos. 56–58.

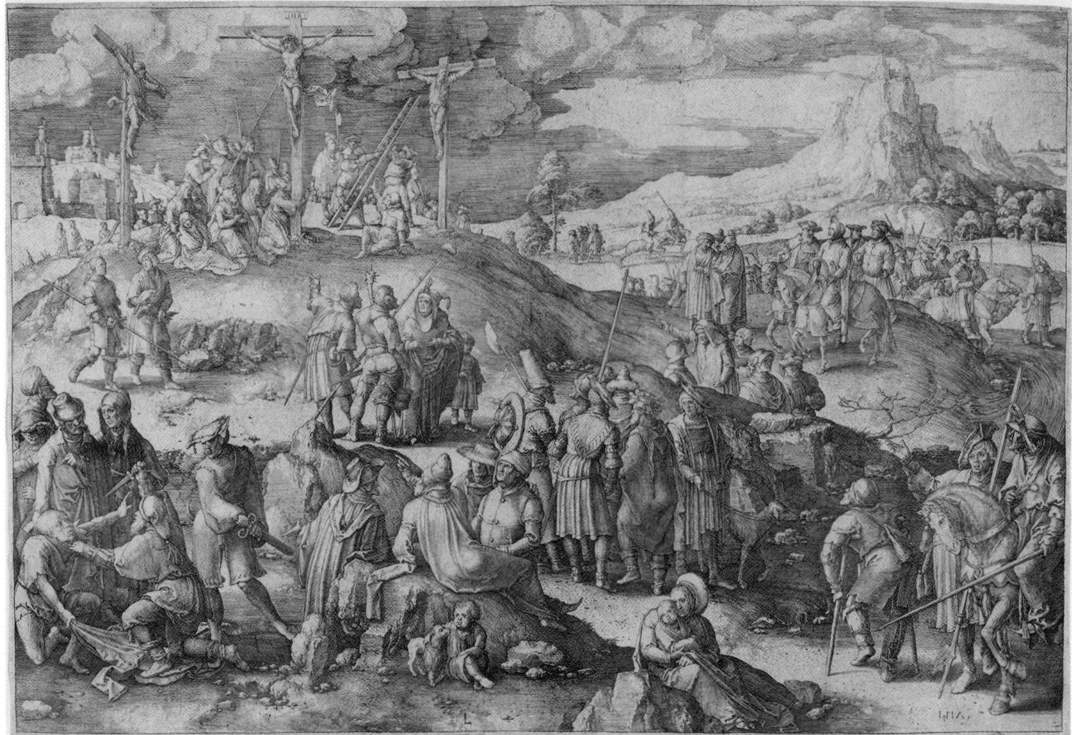

Figure 14.2: Lucas van Leyden, *Golgotha*, dated 1517. Engraving, 28.9cm × 41.3cm (trimmed within plate mark). National Gallery of Art, Washington.

Crucifixion panel recounts the full Gospel narrative. It includes crowds of small-scale figures throughout the elevated setting of Golgotha, and it features not only the main figure of the cross with Jesus but also the adjacent crosses with figures of the two thieves beside him (one of them is still being erected at viewer left). Below the crosses stands the persecuting crowd of Roman soldiers, with many figures mounted on horseback.

The entire scene accords with the Gospel of Luke (23:32-49). One specific torment of Jesus is prominently featured in the composition: a prominent, red-robed soldier on horseback beneath the central cross who applies a vinegar-soaked sponge to the wound of Jesus (John 19:28-29). Curiously, this setting is largely devoid of holy figures, except for the one cluster of holy women who appear under background

trees behind the figure of the thief at the left hand of Jesus. In many Crucifixion scenes the bad thief appears to the unfavorable, *sinister* left hand of Christ, opposite the good thief on the side of his blessing hand, but the composition here still retains considerable ambiguity about the two thieves' identities. In fact, a fourth cross stands in the middle ground, to the viewer left of the central axis formed by Christ; it is located between the Crucifix and the cross that is still being erected.

Many accessory vignettes are featured, such as the strife among Roman foot soldiers over the seamless cloak of Christ (John 19:23-24) in the immediate foreground – a fracas witnessed by two helmeted onlookers as well as by a pair of dogs. Two other dogs at the far right gnaw on the carcass of a dead horse, while diminutive figures in the contemporary

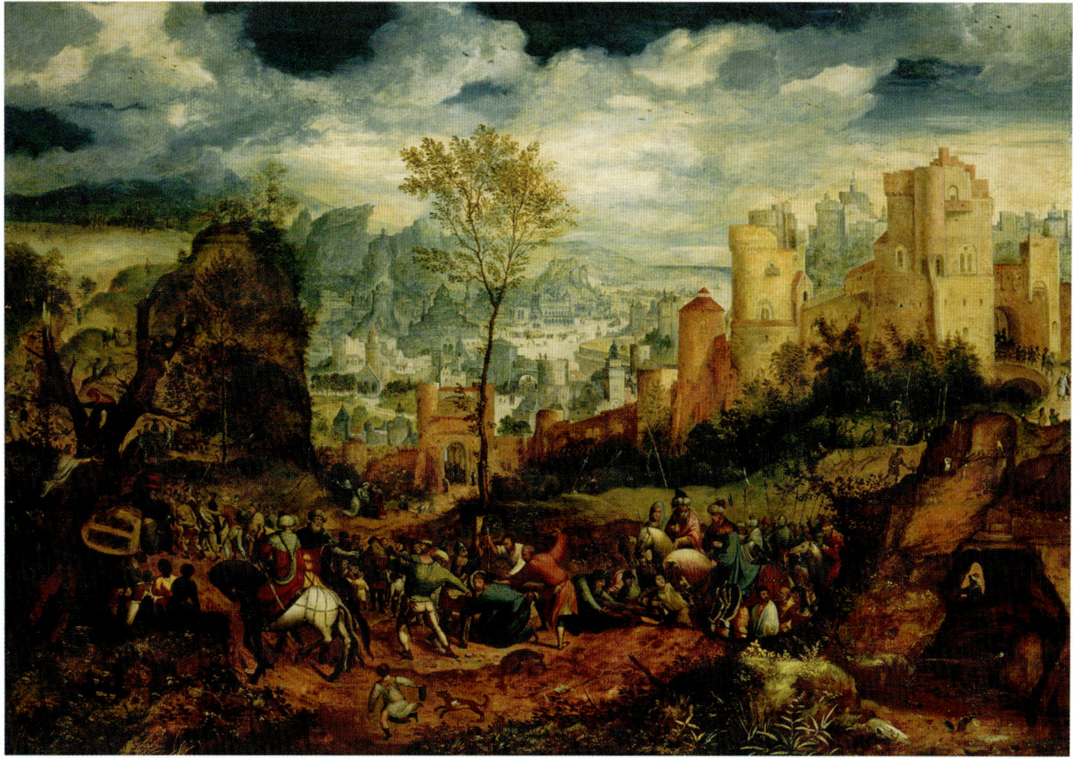

Figure 14.3: Herri met de Bles, *The Way to Calvary*, *c*.1535. Oil on wood panel, 82.2cm × 114.3cm. Princeton University Art Museum.

costumes of peasants and soldiers, many seen from behind, stand across the foreground as passive observers.

The background setting presents a richly elaborated landscape in a wide panorama across the horizontal format of the painting. In the sky above, darkness masses over Golgotha, as described in all four Gospels, in the form of a gathering storm cloud. In the central distance in a plain below the elevated foreground, appears a large domed building, the traditional representation in Flemish paintings of the sacred Temple of Herod, which marks the background city as Jerusalem itself.[9] Such a Temple building appears in earlier images of Christ

Carrying the Cross – for example, by Herri met de Bles in the generation previous to Pieter Bruegel the Elder (Figure 14.3).[10]

The numerous versions of this *Crucifixion* composition by Pieter the Younger demonstrate a consistent basic layout, though some versions contract the space at the right side. The larger version, exemplified by the Stokes panel, frames the scene within towering background cliffs and takes a slightly more

9   Krinsky, 'Representations of the Temple of Jerusalem before 1500,' pp. 1–19; Pinson, 'The Iconography of the

Temple in Northern Renaissance Art,' pp. 147–74; Rosenau, *Visions of the Temple*, esp. pp. 64–75.

10   The prototype for such representations of Christ Carrying the Cross is a lost Jan van Eyck, preserved in a copy in Budapest; see Urbach, *Early Netherlandish Paintings*, pp. 138–61, no. 11; Belting and Eichberger, *Jan van Eyck als Erzähler*, pp. 116–29. For the Princeton painting and related works, Muller, Rosasco and Marrow, *Herri met de Bles*.

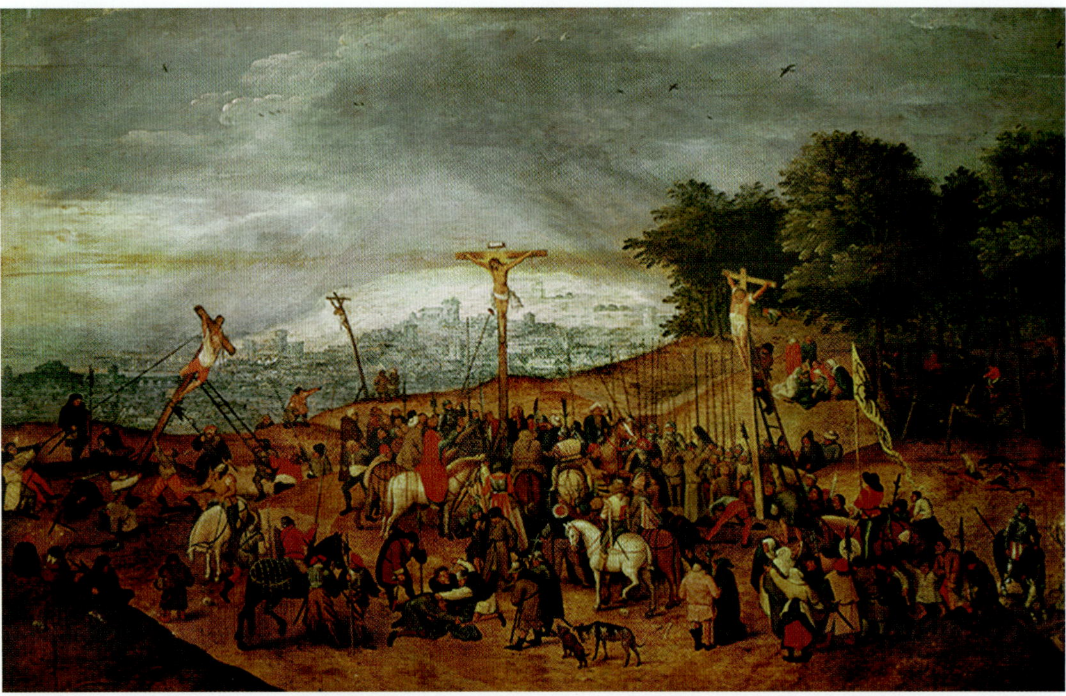

Figure 14.4: Pieter Brueghel the Younger, *Crucifixion*, *c.*1617. Oil on panel, 82 x 123cm. Museum of Fine Arts (Szépmüvészeti Muzeum), Budapest.

elevated bird's-eye view of the scene, with a high horizon. The woody copse above the holy figures backs up the main figural clusters at right. In a second version, exemplified by paintings in Philadelphia and Budapest (signed and dated 1617; Figure 14.4), the cliffs are absent, and the background city, suffused in loosely painted blue-green atmosphere, (attributed to a collaborator, landscape specialist Joos de Momper the Younger in the version in the Philadelphia Museum of Art), appears in a plane set close behind the figures from a lower viewpoint.[11] The Temple building remains indistinct, placed at the left edge of the composition, and sheltering trees end the scenery at right. What is common to all versions by Brueghel the Younger is their

identical layout of the figures, which clearly implies a common cartoon used in the artist's workshop.[12] This procedure is confirmed by detailed outline figural underdrawings, suggesting tracings, found in all versions of the image that have undergone technical examination to date, but not in the backgrounds or in certain fine details that were added from scratch.[13]

11   For the attribution, see Ertz, *Josse de Momper der Jüngere.*

12   Currie and Allart, *The Brueg[H]el Phenomenon*, pp. 632–34, showing traced overlays of the figures with precise alignments among Antwerp, Budapest, and Stokes compositions. However, the Budapest painting, as noted, was produced in collaboration with Joos de Momper the Younger, who painted the atmospheric landscape (de Momper also collaborated frequently with Jan Brueghel the Elder, the painter's brother).

13   Currie and Allart, *The Brueg[H]el Phenomenon*, p. 622, note that the Stokes painting has no landscape underdrawing, whereas light outlines of rock and fortress as well as the domed building in the Antwerp version suggest a

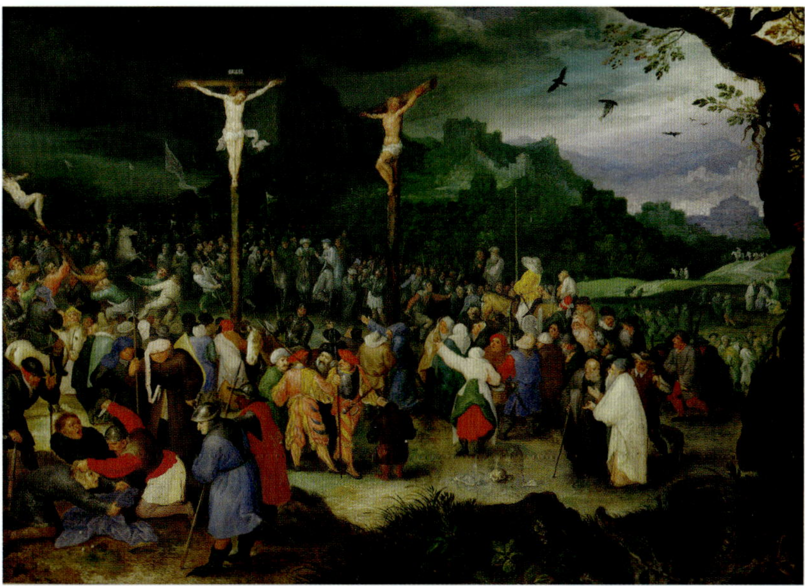

Figure 14.5: Jan Brueghel the Elder, *Crucifixion*, *c.*1595. Oil on copper, 26cm × 35cm. Kunsthistorisches Museum, Vienna.

As noted, no original prototype by Pieter Bruegel the Elder survives, nor any engraved or painted copies other than these works from the workshop of Pieter the Younger. However, his younger brother Jan Brueghel the Elder painted his own *Crucifixion* (Kunsthistorisches Museum, Vienna, Figure 14.5).[14] It completely

truncates the imagery at the left, and it shoves the disputing soldiers, now enlarged, to the foreground left corner. It also repeats the two colourful soldiers with slashed garments, moved to a new position between the crosses, as well as a group of conversing foreground witnesses, led by a pointing woman with a red skirt, common to both Jan and Pieter the Younger. At the same time, Jan relegates the domed building of the Temple of Jerusalem to the hazy blue distance of the right horizon, and he makes the holy figures almost disappear, miniatures in the distance at the far right side. The close overlap of conception and even of specific motifs, especially the nearly exact trio of battling soldiers, strongly suggests that, like his brother, Jan Brueghel also relied on an underlying prototype by Pieter Bruegel the Elder, but varied it more freely rather than relying on literal tracings.

Jan also produced his own smaller variant of Pieter Bruegel's lost figure-rich prototype, a copper *Crucifixion*, dated 1598 (Alte Pinakothek,

more direct copying of its prototype. Their assessment of the authorship of the Stokes painting, p. 626, clearly suggests that it stems from the 'confident, bold, yet accurate handling of form typical of Brueghel the Younger, whereas the [Antwerp] KMSKA version's more numerous yet feeble out-lines can be interpreted as the work of a workshop assistant or apprentice.'

14   Ertz and Nitze-Ertz, *Brueghel-Breughel*, pp. 104–05, no. 12, where Alexander Wied also argues for a lost Bruegel the Elder model for these figures; the Stokes composition in its Budapest version of 1617 appears in Ertz and Nitze-Ertz, *Brueghel-Breughel*, pp. 100–03, no. 11. Currie and Allart, *The Brueg[H]el Phenomenon*, summarize these arguments and show the Jan Brueghel Vienna painting (dated 'around 1595') as p. 636, Figure 436. They also summarize, p. 637, the extant documents that mention a *Crucifixion* by Bruegel the Elder: a 1595 inventory of Archduke Ernst as well as a bequest to the daughter of Pieter the Younger in 1627.

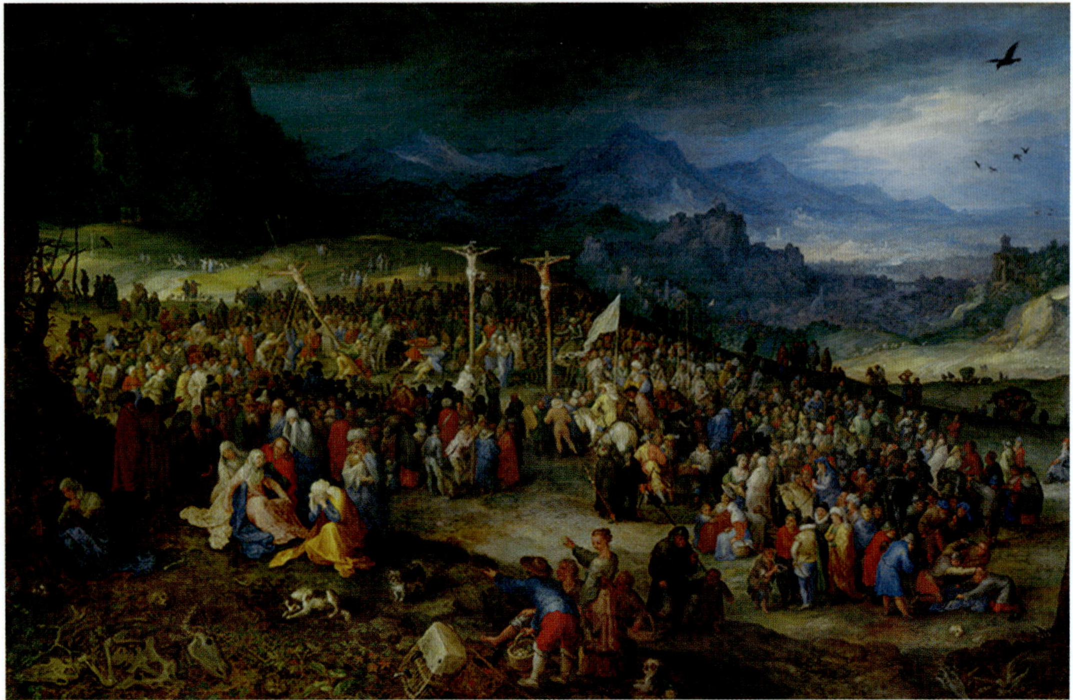

Figure 14.6: Jan Brueghel the Elder, *Crucifixion*, 1598. Oil on copper, 26.2cm × 55.4cm. Alte Pinakothek.

Munich, Figure 14.6).[15] Not a copy, it omits the fourth cross but retains the rising cross at the viewer left. The holy figures are more prominent in the left foreground (i.e. on the favorable right hand side of Jesus) ahead of the main execution scene, while the scuffling soldiers occupy the right foreground corner. At the very front and middle of the composition a genre scene shows market peasants with baskets of eggs and chickens; they stand and point to the holy figures, possibly mocking their unusual costumes. In characteristic Jan Brueghel fashion, the atmospheric blue distance extends out to the right horizon, with a diminutive Temple

building illuminated by a distant light in the valley downhill.

If we use Pieter the Younger's *Crucifixion* to try to recreate the lost prototype by Pieter the Elder, we find that the reconstruction would fit very well into his surviving oeuvre. The closest comparison for overall effect is also Bruegel's largest panel: his signed and dated 1564 *Way to Calvary* (Figure 14.7).[16] That painting also includes a welter of bystanders and observers as it almost completely submerges the figure of Jesus, fallen under the cross but located at the geometrical center of the composition. Here the holy figures are again isolated, but, as in the Stokes picture, they also feature prominently

15   Ertz and Nitze-Ertz, *Brueghel-Breughel*, p. 637, Figure 437; Figures 438 a-c; Neumeister, *Jan Brueghel*, no. 26, notes that some of Jan's figure groups also draw upon a model by Albrecht Dürer, replicated in his 1604 panel (Uffizi, Florence; Neumeister, *Jan Brueghel* pp. 204–05, no. 27). See also Larry Silver, 'Translating Dürer into Dutch,' pp. 208–23.

16   Recent discussion by Larry Silver, *Pieter Bruegel*, pp. 15–33; for the missing *Crucifixion* and for its place in Bruegel's *oeuvre*, see Larry Silver, *Pieter Bruegel*, pp. 260–61, dated there more loosely to the early 1560s rather than the *c.*1559 date assigned by Gibson, *'Mirror of the Earth.'*

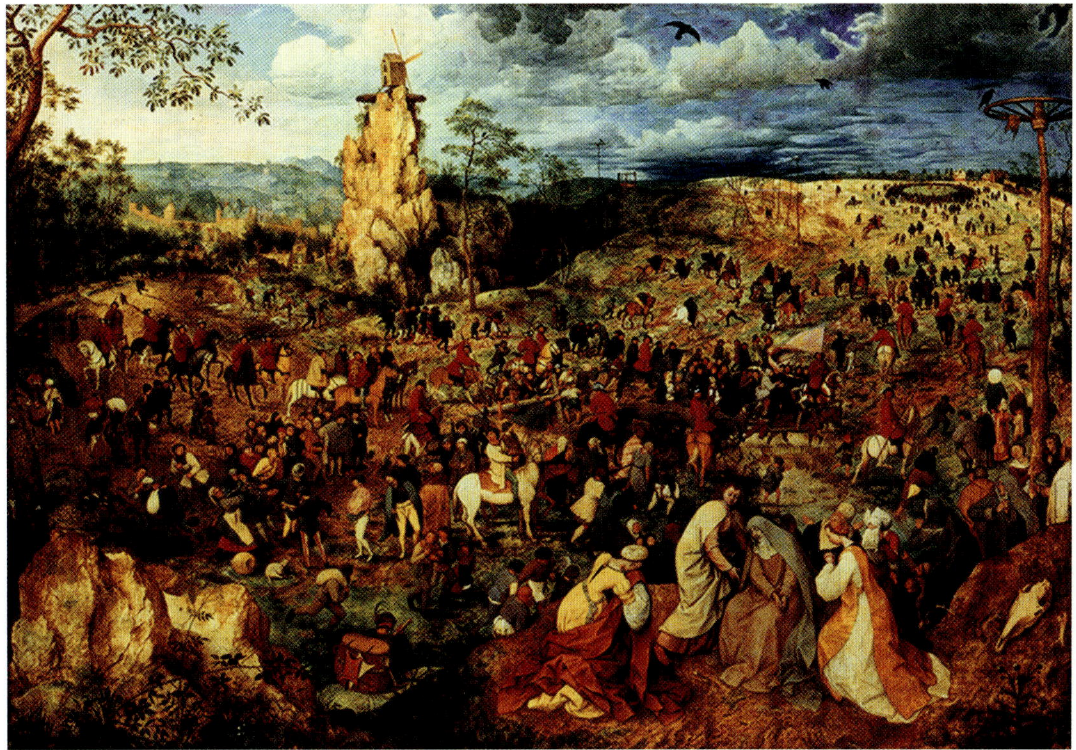

Figure 14.7: Pieter Bruegel the Elder, *The Way to Calvary*, 1564. Oil on oak panel, 124cm × 120cm. Kunsthistorisches Museum, Vienna.

on a ledge in the right foreground. Bruegel's Vienna *Way to Calvary* also features gathering storm clouds above a horizontal landscape expanse with gallows or crosses as well as the distant dome of the Jerusalem Temple, suffused in the blue haze of the left background. While its earlier moment in the Passion narrative precludes any direct overlap of figural motifs connected to the Crucifixion episode, such as the struggle for the seamless cloak, both paintings feature a crowd of peasant types as on-looking figures.

In the Vienna picture, the two thieves appear in a cart that crosses the stream behind the figures of John and the Virgin Mary; as they approach their execution, one of them holds a cross and is confessing to a Franciscan friar, while the other, pale and stricken, gazes

upward to heaven as he receives the prayers of a Dominican whose face is shrouded in his black robes. This confessional detail also returns us to the Stokes painting, where we note the unique figure of another hooded Franciscan beneath the cross of the bad thief. He holds up a panel, painted or inscribed – a final image for contemplation and consolation for the condemned man – to be used as a spur for the thief's ultimate repentance and salvation. The use of such images is chiefly known from contemporary Italian scenes of capital punishment, where they are called *confortari*.[17]

17   On the thieves as contrasting behaviours regarding the acceptance of faith and grace, Merback, *Thief, Cross and Wheel*, pp. 218–65, esp. p.148 and p. 264, noting that in Rome the spiritual care of prisoners was administered by a lay confraternity of San Giovanni Decollato, who visited

As more specific evidence for identifying Pieter Bruegel the Elder as the artist of the original composition, one can even point to individual figures, such as the men who raise the cross at left or the quarreling soldiers, who closely resemble active characters in Bruegel's celebrated 1559 *Netherlandish Proverbs* (Berlin). Based on such comparisons, Walter Gibson assigned a date of around 1559 for the missing original Bruegel composition.[18] This date also matches the recorded date of a lost *Crucifixion* in an early seventeenth-century publication, *Res Pictoriae*, by Arnoldus Buchelius (1583–1639) of Utrecht, although that work is described as partly painted in grey tones and on canvas, so it might refer to a different picture (we do not know whether Bruegel's original *Crucifixion* was in color).[19] Several other documentary references to a Bruegel *Crucifixion* stretch from the late sixteenth across the seventeenth century.

Pieter the Elder's *Way to Calvary* emphasized those quotidian activities that proceed uninterrupted even while the epochal sacrifice of Jesus is still underway. Indeed, one main point of his Vienna image is to force the viewer to discern the tiny figure of Jesus with his cross in the midst of so much activity, which

the condemned prisoner on his last night in his cell and encouraged him to identify with the good thief of the Crucifixion. See for consoling friars and priests, Edgerton, *Pictures and Punishment*, pp. 165–67. On the rise of similar confraternities in France, Silverman, *Tortured Subjects*, pp. 111–30. Charles Zika is preparing a fuller study of the *confortari* phenomenon.

18   Earlier literature summarized by Currie and Allart, *The Brueg[H]el Phenomenon*, pp. 635–36. Gibson, '*Mirror of the Earth*', p. 69, illustrates the version by Pieter the Younger in the Noordbrabants Museum, 's-Hertogenbosch, as Figure 5.23, but he dates the original composition as early as 1555.

19   Currie-Allart, *The Brueg[H]el Phenomenon*, p. 637, no. 39. For Buchelius, also cited by Sutton, *Northern Paintings*, p. 44, no. 4, see Hoogeweeff and Van Regteren Altena, *Arnoldus Buchelius*, p. 78.

threatens to overwhelm the significance of the event. Viewer attention across the composition is further distracted by the vivid red coats of mounted soldiers who punctuate the entire expanse of the panel. In the foreground, several peasants are even making their way to market in precisely the opposite direction as Christ carries the cross to his execution, so ordinary life fails to fall in with history-changing events.

Opposite, and equally quotidian is the ultimate destination of the Way to Calvary, the summit of Golgotha, identified in the Gospels as the 'place of the skull', where the Crucifixion will take place. For Bruegel, this place resembles contemporary sites of punishment and execution, as he illustrated them in his *Justice* drawing (Royal Library Albert I, Brussels) and his print of 1559 from a series of engravings of the Seven Virtues.[20] In both cases, crowds have massed under gathering storm clouds to behold the spectacle of painful death. This public event and its instruments of torture are underscored in the Vienna painting at the right edge, where a foreground wheel frames the background locale.[21] With a horse skull at its base and a rag fluttering from its rim, this wheel balances a leafy, living tree under sunshine at the left edge.

A particularly poignant moment occurs in the left foreground behind the rock, where an older couple engages in a struggle as a soldier in striped pants accosts the husband with the point of his halberd weapon. The older man continues to resist those pulls and he drags his feet as his wife also struggles to prevent his forced conscription. She is wearing an anachronistic rosary around her at her belt, but as scholars have long recognized, this scene depicts the moment in the story when Simon of

20   Orenstein, *Pieter Bruegel the Elder*, pp. 177–93, nos. 72–73.

21   Merback, *Thief, Cross and Wheel*, esp. pp. 158–72.

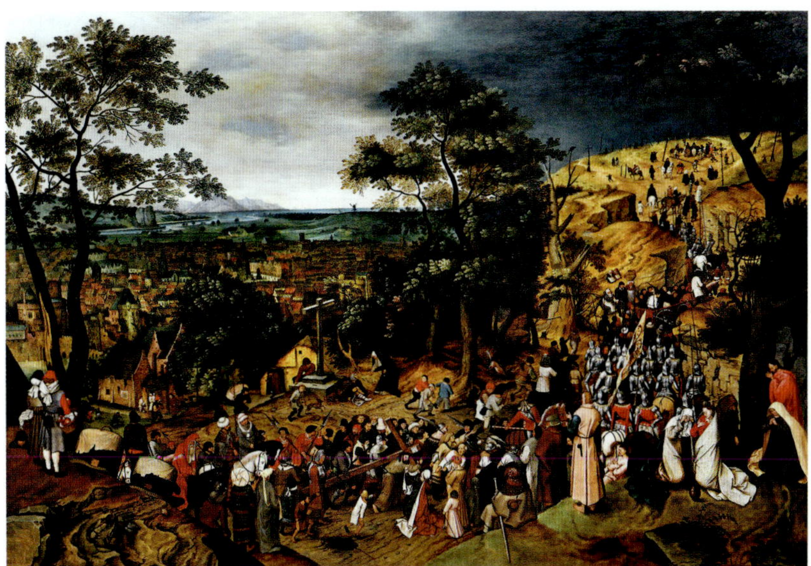

Figure 14.8: Pieter Brueghel the Younger, signed, *The Way to Calvary*, dated 1603. Oil on panel, 106.8cm × 161.5cm. Koninklijk Museum voor Schone Kunsten, Antwerp.

Cyrene, 'coming from the country' was 'compelled' to assist in carrying the cross along with Jesus (Luke 23:26; Mark 15:21; Matthew 27:32).[22] Thus Bruegel shows how very resistant and hypocritical was this self-centered couple, country folk who were drafted against their will to participate in the Passion events, despite the actual coercion and the moment of need when Jesus fell beneath the weight of the heavy cross. The irony is compounded when the viewer notices that Simon has dropped his own burden: a bound lamb – sacrificial symbol of Christ on the cross – as well as a jug of spilled milk. His resistance has also drawn a crowd of gaping onlookers even more attentive than those who look at the self-sacrificial figure of figure of Jesus.

From all this activity, the holy figures stand isolated but prominent on a ridge in the lower right of the composition. Their lanky bodies with tiny heads contrast utterly with the sturdy bodies of the peasants below, and their forms,

while characteristic of Bruegel's holy figures, derive from prototypes in Flemish painting from a century earlier, such as the mourning figures in Rogier van der Weyden's *Crucifixion* (Philadelphia; *c.*1460).

Whether in adaptation from his father or in his own original composition, Pieter Brueghel the Younger produced several versions of the same theme, *The Way to Calvary* (e.g. Koninklijk Museum, Antwerp, Figure 14.8).[23] Today's scholarly consensus holds that this composition is actually an original design by Pieter the Younger himself, though it revisits and reshapes his father's great Vienna precedent into an ascending, turning procession. Akin to the Vienna painting, the mourning holy figures hover on a ledge in the right

<hr>

22   For example, Gibson, *Bruegel*, p. 123, Figure 85; Falkenburg, 'Pieter Bruegels *Kruisdraging*', pp. 17–33.

23   Ertz and Nitze-Ertz, *Brueghel-Breughel*, pp. 95–97, no. 9; the version in the Koninklijk Museum, Antwerp, is signed and dated 1603; see also Ertz, *Pieter Brueghel der Jüngere*, pp. 396–408, with 21 versions. The two versions in Antwerp have considerably more detail in their landscape underdrawings, according to Currie and Allard, *The Brueg[H]el Phenomenon* p. 623.

corner at the pivot point of the composition, above the weary climb by Christ with the cross. John turns to watch from his elevated viewpoint, while the holy women turn their backs to the sorrowful scene. The procession is led by armored and mounted soldiers with the banner of the (Holy) Roman Empire and the open cart with the two thieves (without confessors this time, however). All are seen from the back. Jesus himself appears at the bottom center, carrying the heavy cross with the help of Simon of Cyrene and with the comfort of Saint Veronica and her veil. Pilate and the high priest follow on horseback before Jerusalem and its domed Temple, which appear below and behind the figures before a horizon with open water. At the upper right, the site of the crosses of Golgotha with its dark storm clouds clearly derives from the Vienna prototype, but near the center of the composition stands a cross shrine, akin to one included by Pieter the Elder in his late, non-religious village landscape of 1568, *The Magpie on the Gallows* (Hessische Landesmuseum, Darmstadt). Thus this *Way to Calvary* by Pieter the Younger added further components to the basic layout of his father's 1564 painting in Vienna, and thereby fashioned his own novel composite image.

Another reason to connect Pieter Bruegel the Elder with the multi-figure Stokes *Crucifixion* composition is its overall conception of the Passion scene, derived from works by a number of other layouts by artists prior to Bruegel himself. During the previous generation, several painters had focused on a figure-rich Way to Calvary, including for example Herri met de Bles, active in Antwerp between *c.*1535 and *c.*1550.[24] His

Way to Calvary (Figure 14.3) already shows the procession across a horizontal landscape with Jerusalem and the Temple behind the foreground centered figure of Christ, fallen under the cross. It winds in the opposite direction of Bruegel's 1564 Vienna painting, visually emerging out of the city walls at right, but it also culminates in the tiny figures at the execution place of Golgotha in the blue left distance. Thus it proleptically captures a series of Passion scenes from the Entry into Jerusalem to the Crucifixion, while featuring in its main focus the Carrying of the Cross.

Even closer to the formulation of Pieter Bruegel the Elder is the horizontal *Entry into Jerusalem* (Figure 14.9) by an anonymous painter, the Master of the Brunswick Monogram.[25] Here Jesus, uniquely dressed in a blue kaftan, descends on his donkey from the distant left mountain to cross the foreground expanse and proceed to the right horizon, where Jerusalem's walls and the Temple await him for the events of Passion week (Matthew 21:1-11; Mark 11:1-11; Luke 19:28–40; John 12:12–19). But this image presents a unified moment, not a series of scenes scattered across the landscape space. Here too, peasants in sixteenth-century clothing fill the setting and dominate viewer attention, especially the figures wearing bright yellow garments. The figures who have climbed trees in the center derive from medieval pictorial tradition. Even this peaceful moment does not pass without strife, however, as another trio is already fighting for a garment, which might have been extended as a sign of welcome during the advent of the Lord (as modeled by the figures just before Jesus and described in the Gospel of Matthew). Another man near the center kicks out at the ass

24   Most recently Weemans, *Herri met de Bles*; for the *Way to Calvary* in particular, Muller et al, *Herri met de Bles*, especially in its relation to other works by met de Bles of the Way to Calvary by Luc Serck, 'La Montée au Calvaire dans l'oeuvre d' Henri Bles', pp. 51–72; see also Falkenburg,

'Marginal Motifs in Early Flemish Landscape Paintings', pp. 153–69, where the Simon of Cyrene episode is noted, pp. 163–64.

25   Ubl, *Der Braunschweiger Monogrammist*, esp. pp. 125–37.

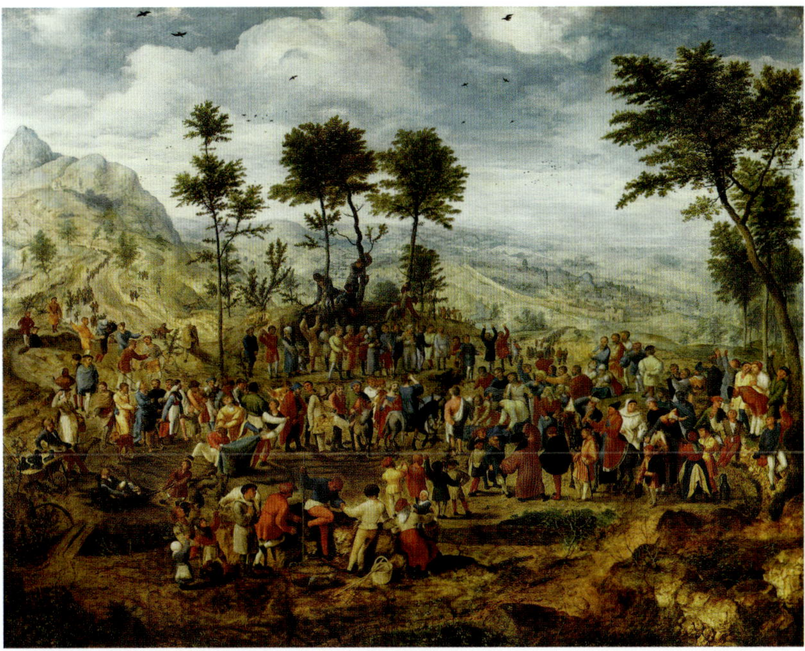

Figure 14.9: Master of the Brunswick Monogram, *Entry of Jesus into Jerusalem*, *c.*1535–40. Oil on panel, 83.3cm × 102.5cm. Staatsgalerie, Stuttgart.

behind Jesus. Close inspection reveals a man in yellow who picks the pocket of the woman in blue before him. In the left foreground a man on his way to market has already trussed up a lamb to carry on his shoulders, and the animal is approached by children with branches. But they call attention to the widespread presence of such branches, which anticipate the palm leaves that traditionally signal both the beginning of Holy Week (Matthew 21:8; John 12:13) as well as provide the symbol of martyrdom for Christian saints. On the right side of the panel, an equestrian group is clearly marked off as Jews because of the scripture placed on their foreheads (in accord with the dictates of Deuteronomy 6:8); they turn to face Jesus as he approaches and discuss the significance of his advent, as recounted by John about the Pharisees (12:19). This group even includes a black man looking on, perhaps to signal the eventual mission of the Church to the Gentiles and to the entire globe. Thus both

sacred and everyday profane elements surround the Entry into Jerusalem and suggest the unruly nature of humankind, even in relation to sacred events.

As noted, Pieter the Younger often followed closely some of his father's most celebrated large compositions, including the 1566 *Census at Bethlehem* (Brussels, Musées Royaux). For that work, his source was likely a lost compositional drawing by his father. Thirteen copies are known, and the three dated versions stem from 1604 to 1610. Even the measurements of Pieter the Younger's various *Census at Bethlehem* compositions closely correspond to Pieter the Elder's large panel in Brussels. Despite the existence of a prior model, Pieter the Younger proceeded like his father with careful underdrawings that outline the figures and buildings. By implication, he proceeded from a lost full-size cartoon that could be re-used for all other versions of the same composition that came from his atelier. In the case of the *Census at Bethlehem*, he changed the colors of costumes from version to version, so he likely did not work from the original Brussels panel of this father, but rather from the preparatory compositional drawings instead. According to conservator Christina Currie, the sizes and placements of figures match so exactly in the various versions that a cartoon is the only possible explanation for their commonalities.[26] There are other such cases. Brueghel the Younger as well as his brother Jan Brueghel also carefully copied their father's *Preaching of John the Baptist* (1566; Budapest), a biblical subject with the main figures buried amidst a massive crowd of listening congregants outdoors.[27]

But Pieter the Younger's favourite images also extended beyond biblical subjects to ordinary everyday rural subjects, as if excerpted from life in Flemish villages, whether summer grain harvests or winter skating scenes (in no fewer than 45 versions!). As we saw above in his own *Way to Calvary*, Pieter the Younger also produced several novel compositions of his own but in the spirit of his father. He even made some other small genre scenes after a contemporary of his father, Hans Bol, especially his design for a print, a scene of *Winter* to complement the print design by Bruegel the Elder of *Summer* (thirteen versions by Pieter

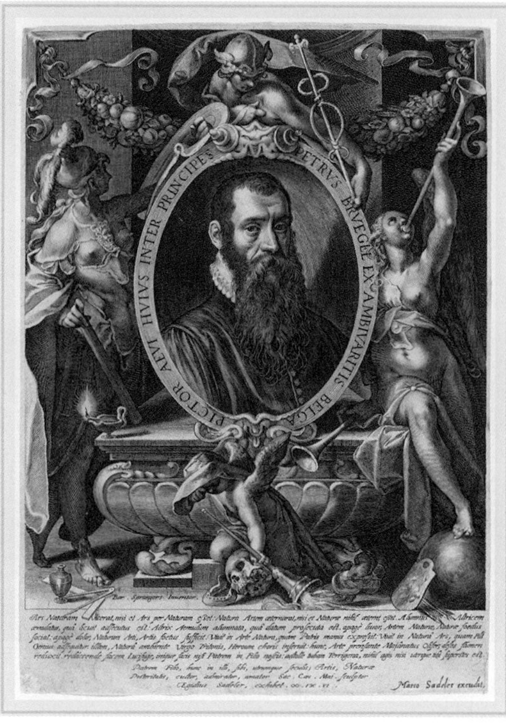

Figure 14.10: Aegidius Sadeler II after Bartholomeus Spranger, *Portrait of Pieter Bruegel the Younger*, 1606. Engraving, 30.6cm × 21.3cm.

the Younger, three dated and five more signed). Bruegel the Younger also invented a scene of a busy office of a *Peasant Lawyer* (24 versions, all but one of them signed).[28]

Ultimately, Pieter the Younger's significance stems largely from this continuation he made of his famous father's work. His contemporary renown (but also the sense that he continued his father's work rather than being a distinctive artist in his own right) is celebrated prior to van Dyck's etched portrait in an earlier seventeenth-century ambiguous portrait, which fuses the features of both father and son into a single oval likeness (Figure 14.10). That

26 Currie and Allart, 'Understanding the Father through the Son: Lost Secrets of Pieter Bruegel the Elder's Working Practice,' in *The Brueg*[H]*el Phenomenon*, pp. 877–98, esp. p. 879, where the *Crucifixion* is analyzed as based on 'two to four sheets divided vertically.' Currie, 'Demystifying the Process', pp. 80–124, based on study of ten of the 13 known copies. The Brussels panel is 115.3cm x 164.5cm, approximately four by six Antwerp feet. She notes, p. 84, that these dimensions are consistent for Pieter the Younger's larger-scale panel formats.

27 Currie and Allart, *The Brueg*[H]*el Phenomenon*, pp.143–82, pp. 446–83; Ertz and Nitze-Ertz, *Brueghel-Breughel*, pp. 88–90, no. 6.

28 Ertz and Nitze-Ertz, *Brueghel-Breughel*, pp. 378–80, pp. 404–05, nos. 122, 137.

print was engraved in Prague by Aegidius Sadeler, printmaker for the Holy Roman Emperor Rudolf II, an avid collector of Northern paintings.[29] The accompanying text fully underlines the father-son relationship: it presents the figure of Minerva with her lamp at left as the protector of the arts but also as someone who took the father away, only to have him returned by winged Mercury, god of eloquence, who appears above the portrait with his attributes of winged cap and caduceus staff. At the right, above a painter's palette, Fame blows her trumpet in triumph, since she has conquered Death in the form of a skull and a torch in danger of being extinguished. The Latin caption finishes with verses which read, 'You are being unjust if you do not recognize the father in the son. Sound your trumpet, Earth-daughter! You do your work in vain if you do not make them both survivors.' The caption ends with claims that the father lives on in the son, almost as a two-in-one portrait, with overlapping bearded identity and of course with the very same name. We can compare this face of 1606 to the older man in the van Dyck image, made around 1630, as well as to a prior portrait of Peter the Elder, published in 1572 in Antwerp as part of a series of famous painters of the Low Countries.[30]

A return to the Stokes *Crucifixion* to view it on its own terms reveals that this is the finest extant version of the same Bruegel the Younger composition, although technical examination reveals what we see on the surface, namely, that the figures and overall composition (except for the distant background landscape) are identical across all other versions. Two of these are signed and dated (Stokes and

Budapest), which provides additional support for their significance. Regarding the religious content of the imagery, we note anew the minimal presence of the holy figures during this ultimate Passion event, as briefly noted in Luke 23:49, 'And all his acquaintance, and the women that followed him from Galilee, stood afar off, beholding these things.' Thus the perpetrators of this sordid execution and its passive witnesses become the principals of the scene in this depiction.

Concerning dress and staging, only a few fashion elements of Orientalism appear to localize and to distance the events away from contemporary Flanders. Beneath Christ and next to the centurion in red, a prominent white turban head covering is worn by a mounted figure, and some other Levantine millinery appears on the opposite side. Thus, most of the costumes of the crowd remain contemporary to Bruegel's Flanders – especially the uniforms of foot soldiers, with striped pants, slashed leggings, and partial armour, body armour or helmets; a few cavalry soldiers wear full field armour. Their weapons – halberds, pikes, and spears – also stem from this same moment, when Europe was beginning to undergo widespread religious wars. Notably absent are the new gunpowder weapons, already widespread during Pieter the Younger's lifetime. Such handguns or arquebus muskets are depicted in paintings by Sebastian Vrancx (1573–1647), contemporary of both Pieter the Younger and Jan Brueghel; for example, in his representations of a devastated Flemish village or of the aftermath of a contemporary battle.

Pieter Bruegel the Elder therefore fashioned the original composition of all these figures, now replicated with exactitude by his painter-son, Pieter the Younger. Brueghel the Younger's background settings vary in two main formulations (the exceptional atmospheric

29   Currie and Allart, *The Brueg[H]el Phenomenon*, pp. 51–55; Bedaux and van Gool, 'Bruegel's Birthyear', pp. 133–56.
30   Melion, *Shaping the Netherlandish Canon*, pp. 143–44, p. 179.

background in the Budapest version was even added separately by the seventeenth-century landscape specialist Joos de Momper the Younger). But otherwise the composition, exemplified and best painted in the Stokes version, remains consistent throughout the copies. Furthermore, the absence of contemporary firearms and military costume fashions still points back to their original mid-sixteenth-century origin with Pieter the Elder. Unlike the larger figures and strikingly bright colors in the more personalized variants of the Crucifixion produced by Peter the Younger's painter-brother Jan Brueghel, these more literal replica figures truly convey the appearance of the original, lost masterwork by Pieter Bruegel the Elder.

Thus the Stokes panel holds great fascination in its own right as the finest version of the *Crucifixion* composition produced in the workshop of Pieter Brueghel the Younger. Its active crowded of figures continues to attract our attention within their expansive mountaintop landscape of Golgotha. But this painting holds added importance within the Bruegel heritage: it remains our finest indication of a long-missing masterpiece by Pieter Bruegel the Elder, a work that boldly mixes religious narrative with the emerging elements of both genre activity and landscape setting. Here we do truly come to the father only through the son.

About the author

Larry Silver is James and Nan Farquhar Professor of Art History at the University of Pennsylvania and author of the monograph *Peter Bruegel* (2011). lasilver@sas.upenn.edu

Works cited

J.B. Bedaux and A. van Gool, 'Bruegel's Birthyear, Motive of an Ars/Natura Transmutation', *Simiolus*, 7/3 (1974), pp. 133–56.

Hans Belting and Dagmar Eichberger, *Jan van Eyck als Erzähler* (Worms: Werner, 1983).

Peter van den Brink, ed., *Bruegel Enterprises* (Brussels: Musées des Beaux-Arts, 2001).

Christina Currie, 'Demystifying the Process: Pieter Bruegel the Younger's *The Census at Bethlehem*. A Technical Study,' in *Bruegel Enterprises*, ed. by van den Brink (Brussels: Musées des Beaux-Arts, 2001), pp. 80–124.

Christina Currie and Dominique Allart, *The Brueg[H]el Phenomenon. Paintings by Pieter Bruegel the Elder and Pieter Brueghel the Younger with a Special Focus on Technique and Copying Practice*, 3 vols. (Brussels: Royal Institute for Cultural Heritage, 2012).

Carl Depauw and Ger Luijten, eds., *Anthony van Dyck as a Printmaker* (New York: Rizzoli, 1999).

Samuel Edgerton, *Pictures and Punishment: Art and Criminal Prosecution during the Florentine Renaissance* (Ithaca: Cornell University Press, 1985).

Klaus Ertz, *Josse de Momper der Jüngere (1564–1635)* (Freren: Luca Verlag, 1986).

Klaus Ertz, *Pieter Brueghel der Jüngere. Die Gemälde* (Lingen: Luca Verlag, 1888/2000).

Klaus Ertz and Christa Nitze-Ertz, *Brueghel-Breughel* (Essen: Kulturstif-tung Ruhr, 1997).

Reindert Falkenburg, 'Pieter Bruegels *Kruisdraging*: Een proeve van "close reading"', *Oud Holland*, 107 (1993), pp. 17–33.

Reindert Falkenburg, 'Marginal Motifs in Early Flemish Landscape Paintings,' in *Herri met de Bles. Studies and Explorations of the World Landscape Tradition*, ed. by Norman Muller, Betsy Rosasco, and James Marrow, (Turnhout: Brepols, 1998), pp. 153–69.

Walter Gibson, *Bruegel* (New York: Oxford, 1977).

Walter Gibson, *'Mirror of the Earth.' The World Landscape in Sixteenth-Century Flemish Painting* (Princeton: Princeton University Press, 1989).

Elizabeth Honig, *Jan Brueghel and the Senses of Scale* (Pennsylvania The Pennsylvania State State University Press, 2016).

J.G. Hoogewerff and J.Q. Van Regteren Altena, eds., *Arnoldus Buchelius, 'Res Pictoria: Aantekeningen over Kunstenaars en Kunstwerken voorkomende in zijn Diarium* ('s-Gravenshage: Nijhoff, 1928).

Ellen Jacobowitz and Stephanie Stepanek, *The Prints of Lucas van Leyden and his Contemporaries* (Washington: National Gallery of Art, 1983).

Carol Krinsky, 'Representations of the Temple of Jerusalem before 1500,' *Journal of the Warburg and Courtauld Institutes,* 33 (1970), pp. 1–19.

Walter Melion, *Shaping the Netherlandish Canon. Karel van Mander's Schilder-Boeck* (Chicago: University of Chicago Press, 1991).

Mitchell Merback, *The Thief, the Cross and the Wheel: Pain and the Spectacle of Punishment in Medieval and Renaissance Europe* (Chicago: University of Chicago Press, 1999).

Norman Muller, Betsy Rosasco, and James Marrow, *Herri met de Bles. Studies and Explorations of the World Landscape Tradition* (Turnhout: Brepols, 1998).

Mirjam Neumeister, ed., *Brueghel. Gemälde von Jan Brueghel d. Älter.* (Munich: Hirmer, 2013).

Nadine Orenstein, ed., *Pieter Bruegel the Elder. Drawings and Prints* (New York: Metropolitan Museum of Art, 2001).

Yona Pinson, 'The Iconography of the Temple in Northern Renaissance Art,' *Assaph: Studies in Art History*, 2 (1996), pp. 147–74.

Helen Rosenau, *Visions of the Temple: The Image of the Temple in Judaism and Christianity* (London: Oresko, 1979).

Elisabeth Roth, *Der volkreiche Kalvarienberg in Literatur und Kunst des Spätmittel-alters* (Berlin: Schmidt, 1958).

Luc Serck, '*La Montée au Calvaire* dans l'oeuvre d' Henri Bles: Création et composition', in *Henri met de Bles: Studies and Explorations of the World Landscape Tradition,* ed. by Norman Muller, Betsy Rosasco, and James Marrow (Turnhout: Brepols, 1998), pp. 51–72.

Larry Silver, 'Translating Dürer into Dutch,' in *Invention: Northern Renaissance Studies in Honor of Molly Faries,* ed. by Julien Chapuis, (Turnhout: Brepols, 2008), pp. 208–23.

Larry Silver, *Pieter Bruegel* (New York: Abbeville, 2011).

Lisa Silverman, *Tortured Subjects. Pain, Truth, and the Body in Early Modern France* (Chicago: University of Chicago Press, 2001).

Joaneath Spicer, 'Anthony van Dyck's Iconography: An Overview of its Preparation,' in *Van Dyck 350*, ed. by Susan Barnes and Arthur Wheelock (Washington: National Gallery, 1994), pp. 327–56.

Peter Sutton, *Northern European Paintings in the Philadelphia Museum of Art* (Philadelphia: Philadelphia Museum of Art, 1990).

Matthias Ubl, *Der Braunschweiger Monogrammist* (Petersberg: Imhof, 2013).

Susan Urbach, *Early Netherlandish Paintings. Old Masters' Gallery Catalogues. Szépmüvészeti Múzeum Budapest* (London: Harvey Miller, 2015).

Michel Weemans, *Herri met de Bles. Les Ruses du paysage au temps de Bruegel et d'Erasme* (Paris: Hazan, 2013).

15. The Kerry Stokes *Schembart* book: festivity, fashion and family in the late medieval Nuremberg Carnival

Charles Zika

Dunlop, Anne (ed.), *Antipodean Early Modern. European Art in Australian Collections, c. 1200–1600*, Amsterdam University Press, 2018

DOI: 10.5117/9789462985209/CH15

Abstract

The richly illustrated Kerry Stokes *Schembart* book represents a very fine example of a genre that recorded the pre-Lenten carnival parades in the city of Nuremberg between 1449 and 1539. It depicts the flamboyant costumes of the Runners who danced their way through the city and the floats ritually destroyed in the city square. It testifies to the significance of carnival in the city's festive life, the use of fashion to display the wealth and status of its leading families, and the emotional investment of those families in ensuring the survival of their pride and honour in such visible form.

Keywords: Nuremberg; Carnival; Fashion; Family; Festivity; *Schembart*

The *Schembart* book purchased by Kerry Stokes in 2006 represents a graphic and beautifully illustrated record of the annual pre-Lenten carnival parade, called the *Schembart*, that took place in the city of Nuremberg on Shrove Tuesday between 1449 and 1539.[1] Shrovetide festivities were common throughout European cities in the late Middle Ages, as a time for physical pleasure, enjoyment, and excess before the rigours and fasting of Lent, which began on Ash Wednesday, the first of forty fasting days before Easter.[2] The pre-Lenten Shrovetide festivities in southwest Germany were called *Fastnacht* or *Fasching* and were strongly linked to the regional Swabian and Alemannic traditions of mumming, costumes and masks. The city of Nuremberg, located in the cultural region of Franconia, shared in these mumming traditions, and mounted one of most extravagant and well-known of such festivals, held sixty-three times between 1349 and 1524.

I thank Charlotte-Rose Millar and Julie Davies for assistance with this article. The research was supported by the Australian Research Council Centre of Excellence for the History of Emotions (project number CE110001011).

1   For the Nuremberg *Schembart*, see especially Sumberg, *The Nuremberg Schembart Carnival*; Roller, *Der Nürnberger Schembartlauf*; Kinser 'Presentation and Representation: Carnival at Nuremberg, 1450–1550,'; Küster, '*Spectaculum Vitiorum*'; Morgan and Panayotova, 'Fitzwilliam Museum MS 382. Schönbartbuch'.

2   For Carnival in fifteenth- and sixteenth-century Europe, see Scribner, 'Reformation, Carnival and the World Turned Upside-Down'; Burke, *Popular Culture in Early Modern Europe*; Moser, *Fastnacht, Fasching, Karneval*.

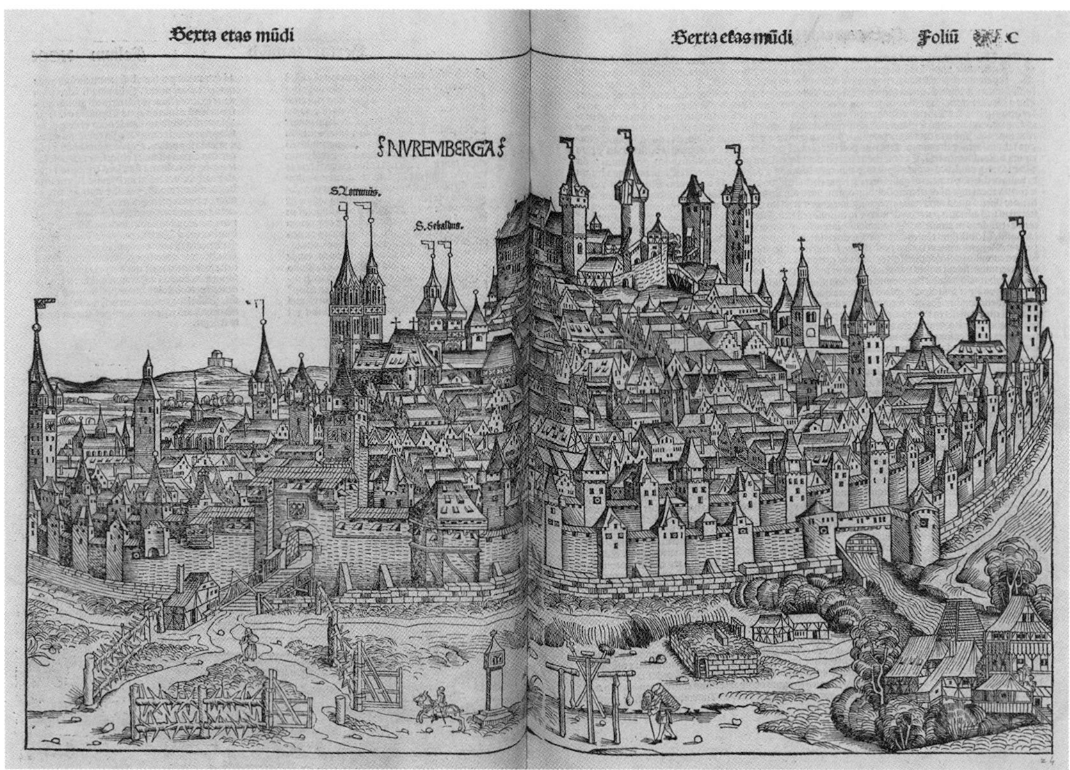

Figure 15.1: Nuremberg in Hartmann Schedel's *Liber Chronicarum*. Folios 99v–100, 1493. Woodcut, 48.3cm. Rare Books Collection, University of Melbourne. UniM Bail SpC/RB 62FF/1.

It was cancelled in some years because of plague and war, and was also suspended in the year the religious Reformation was introduced in the city in 1525; thereafter it was only held one more time in 1539 before being permanently banned. The extravagance and civic support of Nuremberg's *Schembart* had much to do with its strong link to the city's social and political history in this period, and its ongoing civic memory was a result of the numerous recordings of these events by different Nuremberg families in their *Schembart* books.

The fame of the Nuremberg carnival rested on the city's wealth and cultural prominence in the late Middle Ages.[3] Nuremberg was the third largest city after Cologne and Vienna in the so-called Holy Roman Empire, the federation of territories that included most of German- speaking Europe in the Middle Ages. It had a population of 40,000–50,000 within the city walls and another 60,000 in its substantial territories beyond the city itself (Figure 15.1). Its wealth and reputation as an economic and proto-industrial powerhouse in the centre of Europe rested on its metalworking and textile industries, as well as on the regional and long-distance trade run by its leading mercantile families. Patrician families controlled the social and political organs of a fundamentally

---

3   For Nuremberg in this period, see Strauss, *Nuremberg in the Sixteenth Century*; Smith, *Nuremberg, A Renaissance City, 1500–1618*; Zika, 'Nuremberg: the City and its Culture in the Early Sixteenth Century'.

oligarchic form of government. The French political philosopher Jean Bodin called Nuremberg 'the greatest, most famous and best ordered' of Germany's cities, while many commented on its beauty, wealth and creativity. It was also a prominent printing and cultural centre, supporting artists like Albrecht Dürer, Peter Vischer and Adam Kraft, and writers such as Willibald Pirckheimer, Conrad Celtis and Hans Sachs. As a result, Nuremberg was often the object of lavish praise and was referred to as the Venice or Florence of the North.

In the following essay, my intention is firstly to describe some of the most important physical features and content of the Stokes *Schembart*, in particular the nature of its different illustrations, and its relationship to other surviving examples of such books. Secondly, I aim to provide a brief history of the Nuremberg *Schembart*, the origins and development of this festive parade, in order to highlight and clarify some of the details of the book's illustrations, to explain the symbolic and social function of the different floats that were created in different years, and to demonstrate how the parade gradually became an opportunity for extravagant display on the part of the city's patrician families. Thirdly, I shall examine the broader social meanings of carnival in order to understand how it conflicted with the forces of the evangelical Reformation in the sixteenth century, which led to its permanent banning by the Nuremberg government in 1539, an act that nevertheless gave birth to the genre of the *Schembart* Carnival book created by many of the city's leading families.

Features and content of the Kerry Stokes *Schembart* book

The Stokes *Schembart* is one of over eighty full *Schembart* manuscripts and fragments in libraries and collections throughout the world.[4] It is comprised of 138 leaves, written on paper in German cursive script and by several hands, and includes a number of different documents: an account of the origins of the Carnival parade in 1349 and a list of significant events for the city between 1355 and 1440; a record of the sixty-three annual parades held between 1449 and 1539, with the names of the captains of the Runners for each year, as well as a list of some significant events in each of those years; and an account of some of the dances performed in specific years. The most striking features of this manuscript, however, are the very fine illustrations on seventy-five of its folios, executed in ink and coloured with wash and gouache with touches of silver and gold leaf.[5] All except possibly one of the more than eighty surviving *Schembart* books originate after 1539, when the city government permanently banned the carnival festivities, and they continued to be produced through to the eighteenth century. The Stokes *Schembart* would seem to be one of the very earliest of these manuscripts and can be dated to *c*.1540, based on a watermark of 1538.

4   Lists of the manuscripts and locations appear in Sumberg, *The Nuremberg Schembart Carnival*, p. 193–200, and these are supplemented in Roller, *Der Nürnberger Schembartlauf*, p. 230–236. For a range of the images found in different manuscripts for the parades of each year, see: https://commons.wikimedia.org/wiki/Schembartlauf/Synopse'. Individual manuscripts are also described in Morgan and Panayotova, 'Fitzwilliam Museum MS 382. Schönbartbuch'; Reed, 'Schempart Buech'; Reed, 'Fireworks and Fish Baskets'.

5   For details, see Manion and Zika, *Celebrating Word and Image 1250–1600*, p. 70; Manion, *An Illumination*, p. 141; Christie's: *The History of the Book: The Cornelius J. Hauck Collection, New York, 27–28 June 2006*, lot 135. Note that in these entries the number of illustrated folios is mistakenly given as sixty-four instead of eighty-six, and the illustrated Runners as fifty-four instead of sixty-three (plus the *Altvater* in 1492, when the *Schembart* was not held). This miscalculation seems to have been partly a result of the confusing modern numbering of folios in pencil, in which folios 20–29 appear twice.

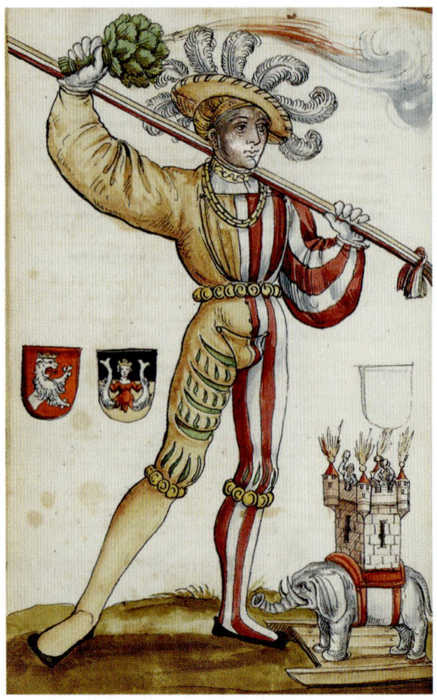

Figure 15.2: Runners' costume for 1524, with the arms of captains Paulus Grundherr, Hans Rietter and Endres Vocker; the 1524 float depicting an elephant and castle, in *Schembart Buch*. Folio 59v, *c*.1540. Paper, 32.8cm × 21cm. Kerry Stokes Collection, Perth. LIB.2006.088.

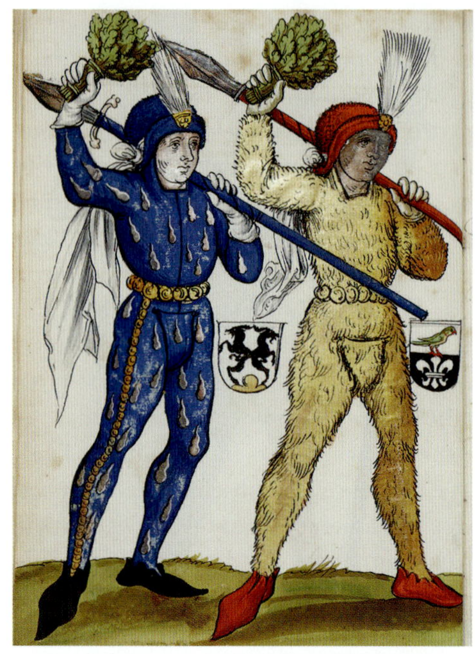

Figure 15.3: Runners' costumes for 1463, with the arms of captains Sebald Halbwachs and Michel Baumgartner, in *Schembart Buch*. Folio 16v, *c*.1540. Paper, 32.8cm × 21cm. Kerry Stokes Collection, Perth. LIB.2006.088.

This manuscript includes three of the five types of images commonly found in *Schembart* books. First and most prominent are the Runners or *Laüfer*, who constituted the main group in the Carnival parade. They are depicted for the sixty-three years the *Schembart* was held. The Runners would lead the parade, dancing their way through the city, and stopping off at different locations on their way to the denouement in the market place. The illustrations show the particular costumes of the Runners in each year, quite simple in the early period and very flamboyant in the later, depicting them with lances in one hand and the artichoke-like sheaves of greenery in the other. The latter were weapons containing concealed fireworks, which we see being fired in some illustrations,

as in that of the Runner of 1524 (Figure 15.2). All the Runners wear silver masks, executed in silver leaf, the wearing of which – the act of mumming – was a special privilege granted them by the city government for this occasion. Silver leaf is also used to accentuate the tips of the Runners' lances, while gold leaf is especially used on the bells and other metal ornaments that feature in their costumes. The Runners under captain Michel Baumgartner in 1463 are decked out in whole suits made of gold leaf (Figure 15.3). Also depicted are the family coats of arms of the captains of the Runners for each year. Chosen from the prominent families of the city, the captains were charged with organising the Runners and keeping their behaviour in check. The number of Runners increased from what was generally about twenty-four in

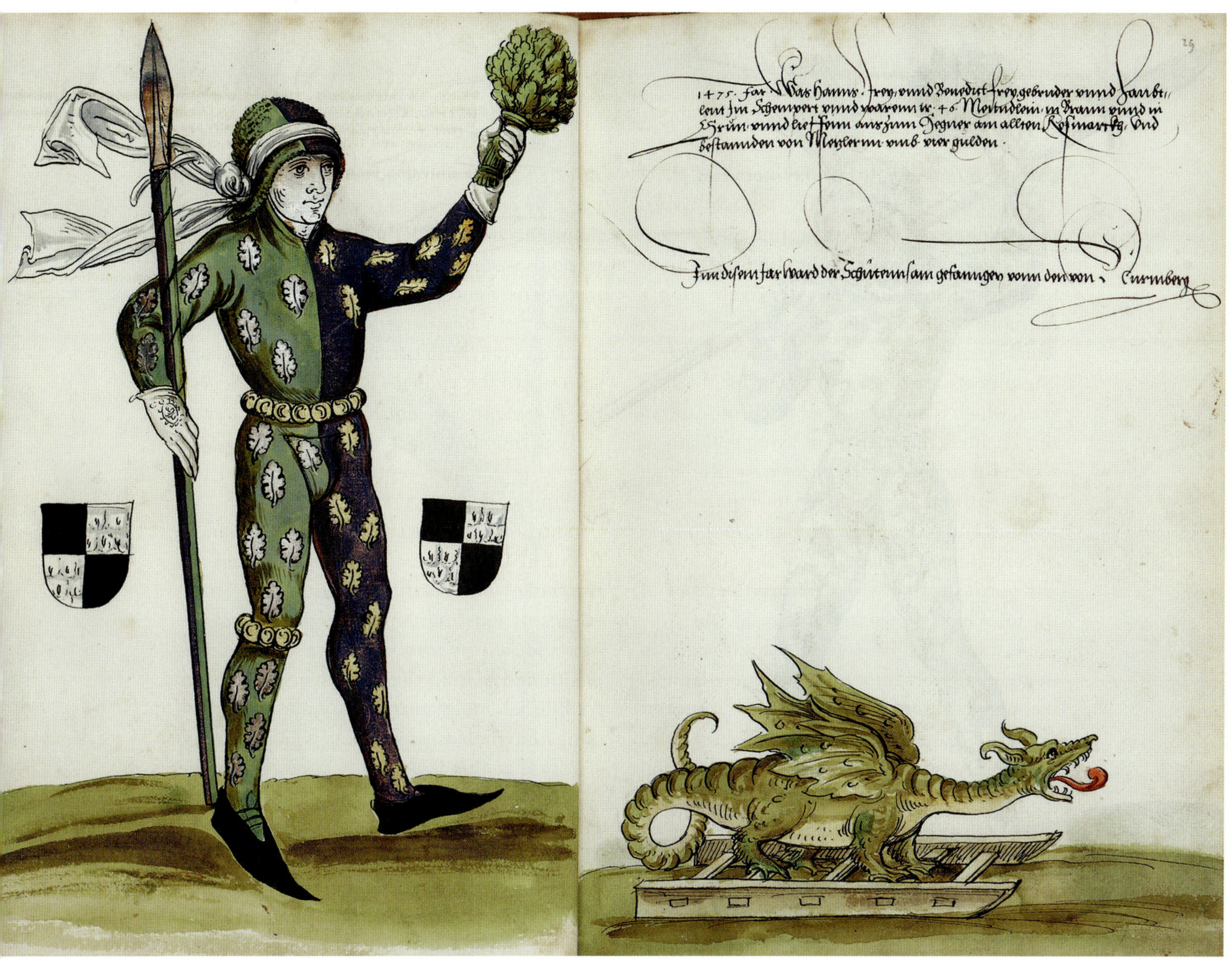

Figure 15.4: Runners' costume for 1475, with the arms of captains Hans and Benedict Frey; the 1475 dragon float, in *Schembart Buch*. Folios 28v–29, first series, *c.*1540. Paper, 32.8cm × 21cm. Kerry Stokes Collection, Perth. LIB.2006.088.

the early parades to ninety in 1518, and as many as 150 in 1539; and the number of captains also rose, from just one to as many as four.

The second type of image found in the Stokes *Schembart* is that of the Carnival floats called Hells or *Höllen*. These were introduced into the *Schembart* for the first time in 1475, and appeared again in 1493 and in 1503, after which they featured every year the *Schembart* was held except in 1509. Twenty-three floats are depicted in this manuscript, with half on the same leaf as the Runner and the others on the folio opposite. They represent fantastic and exotic subjects, most of them depicting monstrous creatures, castles, fools or other scenes involving destruction and violence. The first float of 1475, for instance, is a dragon, its wings spread and red tongue protruding (Figure 15.4).

The monstrous animal theme also appears in 1511, in a three-headed dragon with a Moor seated on its tail, and in 1507, with a giant basilisk. In 1508, a giant fool appears in a castle devouring child fools; and in a similar act of cannibalism, in 1516 a huge Satan figure devours human figures in the mouth of Hell.[6] The Hell float in 1518, by contrast, is a *Venusberg*, a mountain of love featuring the goddess Venus and her maidens feasting with their male paramours under a satyr figure atop a maypole; while in 1520 it is a summerhouse in which devils celebrate a wedding with witches. These floats are on sleds (except for the 1539 float, which is on wheels and discussed later in this chapter) many of them living tableaus in which theatrical performances were acted out. The floats were slowly pulled toward the city's political and economic centre, the *Hauptmarkt* or central market place, where they were ritually burnt or otherwise destroyed in front of the town hall (shown in Figure 15.13).

A third type of image that appears in many of the *Schembart* books but is almost completely absent from the Stokes manuscript is that of grotesques and other wild figures, who appeared in the parades from around the turn of the sixteenth century, and whose purpose was to follow the parade and harass onlookers. These included different kinds of demonic animal figures, the so-called Wild Men and Women, Amerindians and Moors, figures in costumes made up from chestnuts, mirrors, dice, cards, dolls, pine cones, and even indulgences.[7] The wild and demonic figures in particular were often shown with their own children, or with children they had kidnapped, in some cases carried in large baskets on their backs. Some of the figures brandished lances and sheaves like the Runners, and were even identified by family coats of arms. The only analogous figure to appear in the Stokes manuscript was the

Altvater ('Patriarch'), a term that is unclear, but may refer to a traditional older man who maintains order with the use of the whip that he holds instead of the Runners' lance (Figure 15.5).[8] The figure appears in the manuscript in 1492 as a bearded older man in a heavy cloak and hat, both trimmed with fur, in sharp contrast to the younger Runners. In that year the *Schembart* was not held, but the Council gave permission for a troupe of ninety-two people under four captains to dance in the costume of such an *Altvater*.[9]

The jousting tournament is another image found in some *Schembart* books and also in the Stokes manuscript (Figure 15.6).[10] Three scenes of jousting depict knights in full armour locked in combat. However, the fools positioned behind the horses, decked out in traditional fools' costumes with bells dangling from their asses' ears and wielding clubs, signify that this is a parody, a mock tournament. Fools were fundamental to the revelry, raucous festivity and especially the inversion of everyday morality during *Schembart*; and the armourers and members of various craft associations parodied the tournaments of the nobility, mimicking similar jousts performed by journeymen, the popular events called *Gesellenstechen*. In some *Schembart* mock tournaments the knights rode boxes on small wheels pulled along by ropes; others wore armour made of straw and rode barrels on sleds. In the Stokes manuscript the fools make clear the parody; on the four leaves preceding the

---

6   As well as Sumberg, *The Nuremberg Schembart Carnival* and Roller, *Der Nürnberger Schembartlauf*, see Münch, 'Wo seyd ihr Kinder, Wo?'.

7   Roller, *Der Nürnberger Schembartlauf*, pp. 56–98; Sumberg, *The Nuremberg Schembart Carnival*, pp. 97–13, pp. 218–221, figs. 16–31.

8   Sumberg, *The Nuremberg Schembart Carnival*, p. 125–126.

9   In 1485, the Council allowed two groups of thirty-two dancers and a captain each to dance in the costumes of peasants and Moors, in addition to the Runners.

10   For these tournaments in other *Schembart* manuscripts, see Sumberg, *The Nuremberg Schembart Carnival*, p. 13, p. 189; Roller, *Der Nürnberger Schembartlauf*, p 91, pp. 167–168.

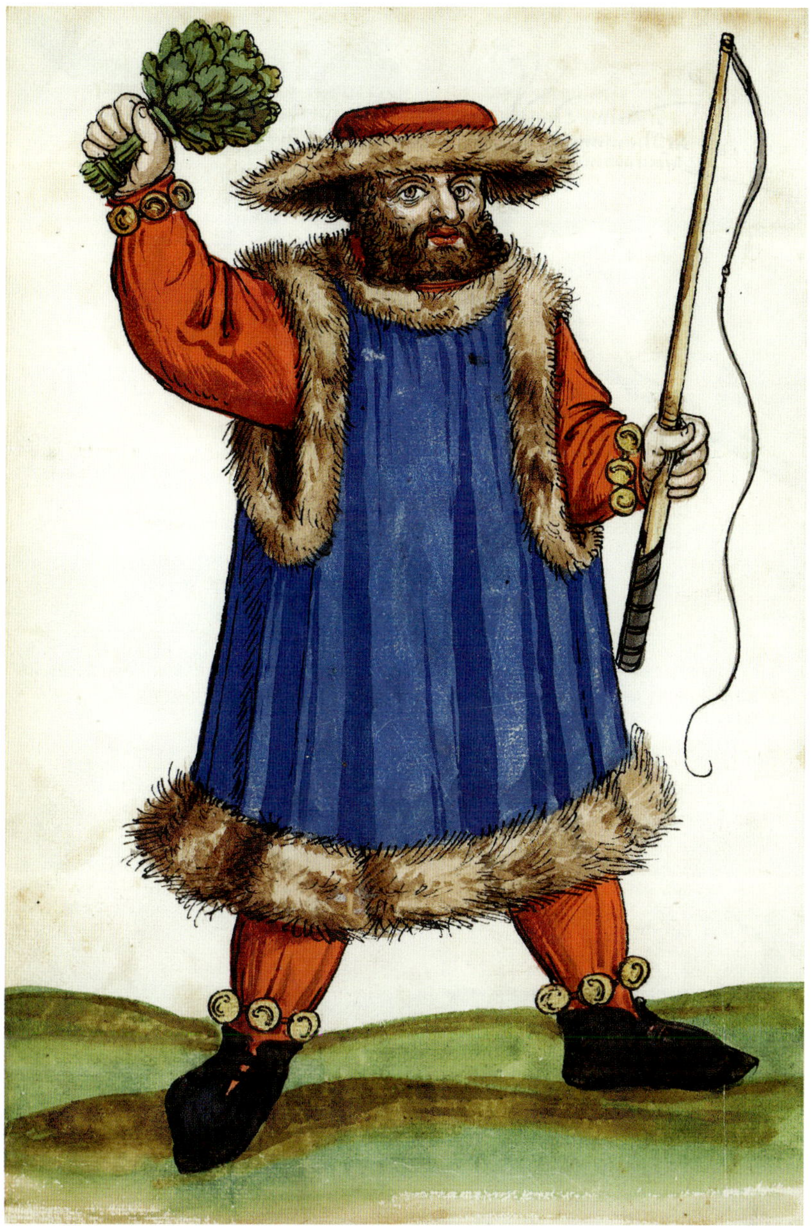

Figure 15.5: *Altvater* costume of 1492, in *Schembart Buch*. Folio 32v, *c.*1540. Paper, 32.8cm × 21cm. Kerry Stokes Collection, Perth. LIB.2006.088.

mock tournaments, buglers with the Nuremberg coat of arms and tournament 'officials' wearing sashes and staffs with the city's colours of red and white ride in on their horses, a piper and a drummer provide the musical accompaniment, and two fools parade with the knights' lances (folios 67v–69).

The Stokes manuscript does not include the images that illustrate the various dances performed by various artisans during the

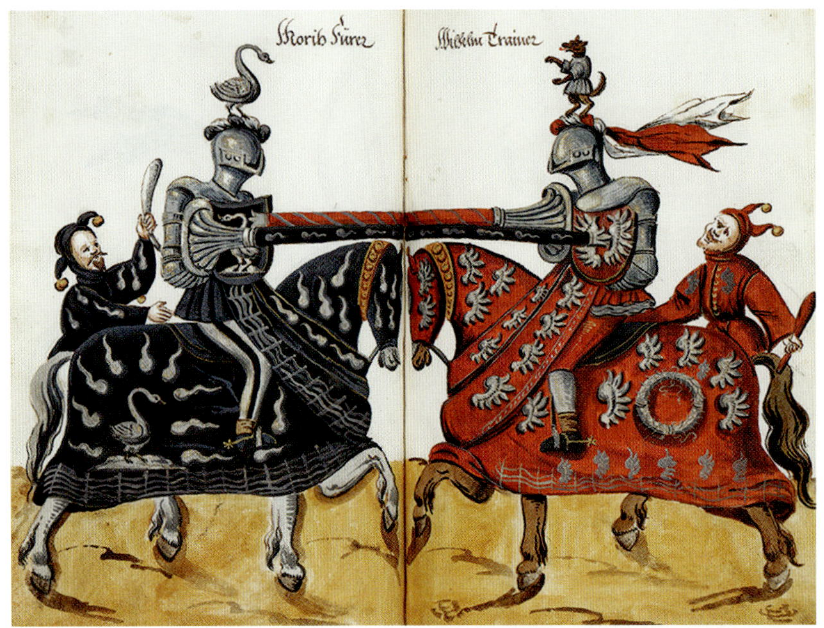

Figure 15.6: Moritz Fürer and Wilhelm Trainer as knights jousting in a mock tournament with fools as their assistants, in *Schembart Buch*. Folios 71v–72, *c.*1540. Paper, 32.8cm × 21cm. Kerry Stokes Collection, Perth. LIB.2006.088.

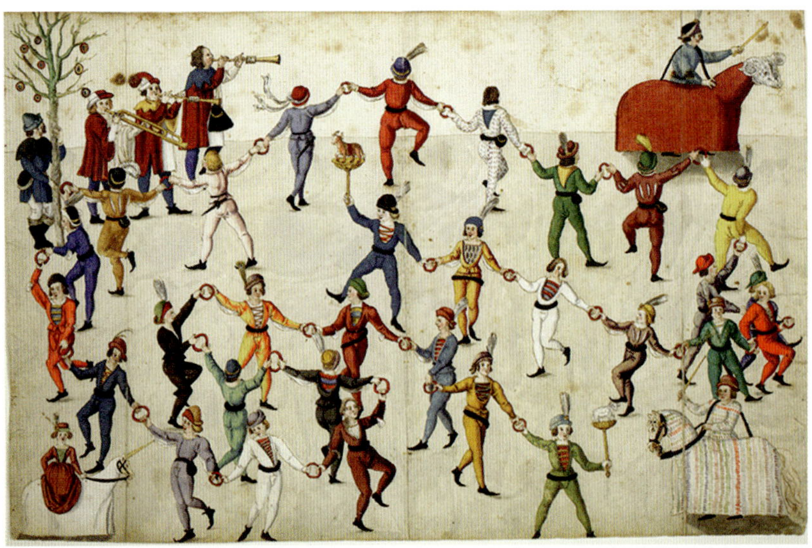

Figure 15.7: Butchers' Dance, in *Schempart Buech*. Folio I, mid-16th century. Stadtbibliothek, Nuremberg. Nor. K. 444.

Schembart – such as the Sword Dance (*Schwerttanz*) performed by the cutlers, the Carpenters' Dance (*Schreinertanz*), the Butchers' Dance, and the Garland Dance (*Reiftanz*) of the cloth-makers' apprentices.[11] The most important of these was the Butchers' Dance, with which the Carnival parade, the *Schembartlauf*, was said to have originated. The illustration of the Butchers' Dance in a Nuremberg City Library manuscript from the second half of the sixteenth century shows the masked butchers each holding a leather ring and dancing in the round, accompanied by three city pipers and led by two dancers holding maces decorated with a ram and an ox (Figure 15.7). The three figures dressed as hobby-horses also represent the butchers' right to wear full body 'masks', a privilege given them in 1349, along with the rights to have the city musicians playing, and for the dancers to wear masks as they made their way through the city.

Origins and historical development of the Nuremberg *Schembart*

To explain the significance of this association and its various privileges one needs to consider the supposed origins and historical development of the Nuremberg *Schembart*. The *Schembart* was linked to Nuremberg's oligarchic form of government that developed in the fourteenth and fifteenth centuries. The right to dance through the city and wear masks was described as a privilege specifically given to the butchers by the Holy Roman Emperor Charles IV in 1349, in return for their loyalty and protection during the so-called Craft Associations Revolt.[12]

In June 1348, a number of the craft associations had rebelled, dismissing the old city council for a council with power firmly based on a civic guild structure, and throwing their support behind the Wittelsbach party, Charles's enemy in the struggle for succession to the imperial throne following the death of the Wittelsbach Emperor Louis IV in the previous year. However, after Charles was elected Emperor Charles IV in 1349, he dismissed the short-lived council, declared all its legislation void, forbade the formation of guilds with political power, and granted the new council the right to punish the rebels by banning them from the city. Charles also granted the council the right to establish the *Hauptmarkt*, the main market place, on the site of the Jewish quarter that had been razed in a pogrom that led to the deaths of 562 Jews. These events of 1349 marked the beginning of a strong and close political link between the city and the Empire, and were instrumental in the city's growing economic power and prosperity.

Through the banning of the guilds found in most German cities and their replacement with sworn craft associations, the events of 1349 were also instrumental in concentrating power in the hands of Nuremberg's oldest and most powerful families. By 1521 this oligarchic form of government was formally ratified, ensuring that the key organs and most powerful offices of government were in the hands of the members of only forty-three Nuremberg families.[13] The privileges supposedly given to the butchers for their loyalty to the emperor and the city's powerful old families during the revolt of 1348–1349, now formalized in the *Schembartlauf*, were a visible reminder of those events, but also a way of legitimising the contemporary political and social order.

The precise meaning of the word *Schembart* remains unclear, but it may carry resonances of

---

11   For the various dances, see Sumberg, *The Nuremberg Schembart Carnival*, pp. 190–192; Roller, *Der Nürnberger Schembartlauf*, pp. 155–167.

12   For the following, see Sumberg, *The Nuremberg Schembart Carnival*, pp. 25–34; Pfeiffer, *Nürnberg – Geschichte einer europäischen Stadt*, pp. 73–75; Reicke, *Geschichte der Reichsstadt*, pp. 203–220.

13   Strauss, *Nuremberg*, p. 57–85.

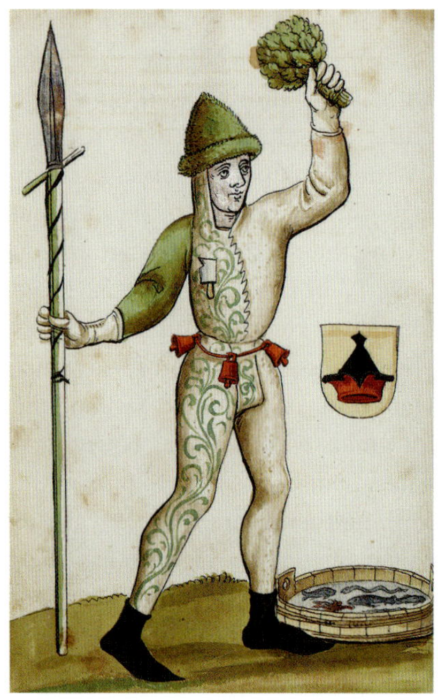

Figure 15.8: Runners' costume for 1449, with the arms of captain Cuntz Eschenloher; a tub of fish, in *Schembart Buch*. Folio 6v, *c.*1540. Paper, 32.8cm × 21cm. Kerry Stokes Collection, Perth. LIB.2006.088.

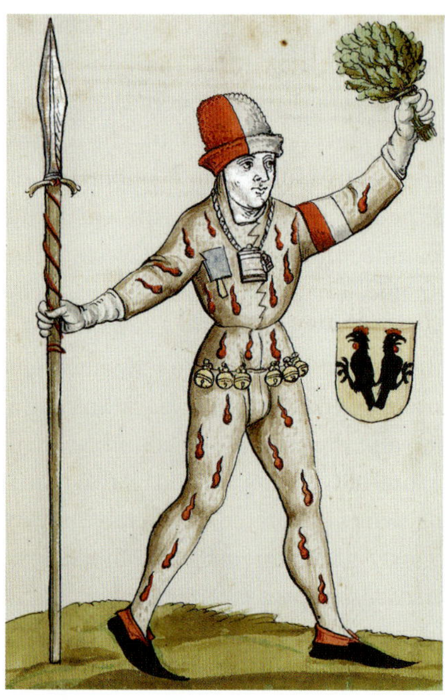

Figure 15.9: Runners' costume for 1458, with the arms of captain Hainrich Rumell, in *Schembart Buch*. Folio 11v, *c.*1540. Paper, 32.8cm × 21cm. Kerry Stokes Collection, Perth. LIB.2006.088.

these supposed origins. *Schem* means a mask, and linguistic variations of *Schembart* refer to demonic masks, or even demons and ghosts.[14] Some historians derive the word from *Schein-bart*, which refers to diabolical messengers who carry out their mischief before the serious time of Lent. Therefore, they argue, the *Schembart* Carnival represented a kind of morality play in which the deadly sins were able to run riot for the day, before they were ultimately subdued in the *Hauptmarkt* – similar to the way the craft associations ran riot in 1348–1349, before they were put down by the patrician government. In this way the *Schembart* represented the arche-typal origins of the Nuremberg polity.

As the oligarchic government of the city became more entrenched in the later fif-teenth century in response to growing popu-lation, wealth, and the expansion of the city's control over its hinterland, there was also a change in the appearance of the *Schembart* Runners.[15] Originally, the role of the Runners, captained by a member of the city's patri-cian families, was to protect the butchers in their dance. The butchers paid for this pro-tection. In the early years of the *Schembart*, the Runners appear in a simple and rough linen costume that covered them from head to foot, with large bells hung around the waist or around their shoulders, and a meat cleaver on their chest, signifying their role as

14   Maas, 'Schembart und Fasnacht: eine Rückkehr zu alten Deutungen'; Moser, *Fastnacht, Fasching, Karneval*, pp. 184–187; Moser, '"Schembart"-Scharmützel; Dietz-Rüdi-ger Moser antwortet auf Wolfgang Brückner: die "Höllen" werden Höllen bleiben'; Küster, 'Nürnberger Schembartlauf'.

15   In the Bavarian War of Succession in 1504, the city seized a large number of villages from the Upper Palatinate, thereby vastly expanding its territory and controlling a hin-terland larger than that of any other German city.

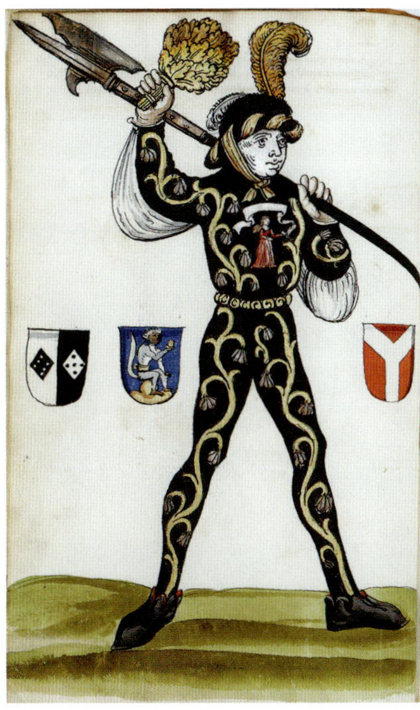

Figure 15.10: Runners' costume for 1489, with the arms of captains Jobst Dopler, Jörg Ketzel, and Sebald Tucher, in *Schembart Buch*. Folio 29v, second series, c.1540. Paper, 32.8cm × 21cm. Kerry Stokes Collection, Perth. LIB.2006.088.

protectors of the butchers (Figure 15.8). Being the day before Lent, (when eating meat was forbidden) they also collected fish from the onlookers. The 1449 Runner is shown with fish in a tub, while the fish are shown in a basket around the Runner's waist in 1451, hanging from a fishing rod in 1453, and poking out of a bag in 1456. The Runners soon replaced their collecting of fish with the far simpler collecting of cash – for which they now wore metal money boxes around their necks in 1457, 1458 and 1459 (Figure 15.9). However, by 1460, the meat cleaver, fish, and money boxes disappear, and the costumes of the Runners become more flamboyant, with the introduction of feathers on hats, mi-parti costumes and a variety of brightly coloured patterns.

The relationship between the butchers and the patricians completely changed in 1468.[16] Rather than the butchers paying the patricians to protect them in their dance through the city, the patricians now began to pay the butchers to take part in the festivities. The wealthier citizens from the patrician families began turning the *Schembart* into a patrician event, which placed emphasis on their costumes as a sign of wealth and extravagance. Gradually the Runners adopted hats festooned with feathers or ribbons, embroidered undershirts, fashionably slashed, padded and puffed costumes in wool and satin, gold neck chains and small gilded bells attached to their belts or knees. Their multi-coloured costumes were ornamented with decorative motifs such as foliage, roses, flames and clouds. Some now featured female figures on their chests (Figure 15.10); and on one occasion (1515), the bratwursts and herrings symbolic of the struggle between Carnival and Lent. By the early sixteenth century, the regular appearance of floats would have added to the spectacle; and so too the general increase in the number of Runners, rising to ninety in 1518 and 150 in 1539. The *Schembart* had truly become a spectacular parade, reflecting the wealth, fashion and privilege of a small group of patrician families who vied to be captains of the Runners and appropriated the festivities for their own ends.

But as well as this social and political dimension, Carnival was also a time when people ran riot – a time of pleasure, feasting, drinking, having sex, indulging the flesh before the onset of the rigours of fasting in Lent. This is a common trope in the Middle Ages: Carnival is a time when the world is turned upside down, when the fool is king, when the lower body is

16   For the significance of this change, see especially Kinser, 'Presentation and Representation'.

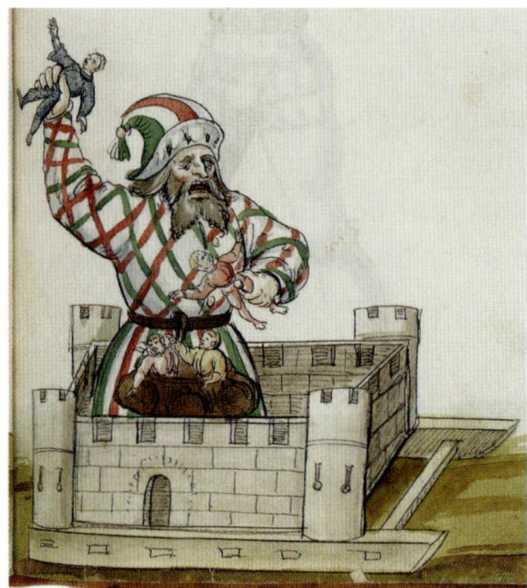

Figure 15.11a: Giant in a castle sticking fools in his pouch (detail), in *Schembart Buch*. Folio 44, second series, *c*.1540. Paper, 32.8cm × 21cm. Kerry Stokes Collection, Perth. LIB.2006.088.

allowed to rule over the upper.[17] Prior to the 1980s, Carnival was frequently interpreted as a kind of seasonal festival related to fertility and seasonal change, a remnant of pagan festivals celebrating the changes from winter to spring, to new light and new life.[18] Recent scholars have tended to see these changes more in Christian moral terms.[19] However we view the origins and symbolic resonances of Carnival, there is clearly a tension between its riotous and disruptive behaviour, the ubiquitous references to pleasure and folly, the violence frequently performed on the moving stages of the floats – significantly called Hells and featuring images of cannibalism (especially in 1508, 1516, and 1522) that appear very similar to contemporary images of the Mouth of Hell and the fact that at the end of the parade the floats are burnt or destroyed (Figure 15.11a and 15.11b).

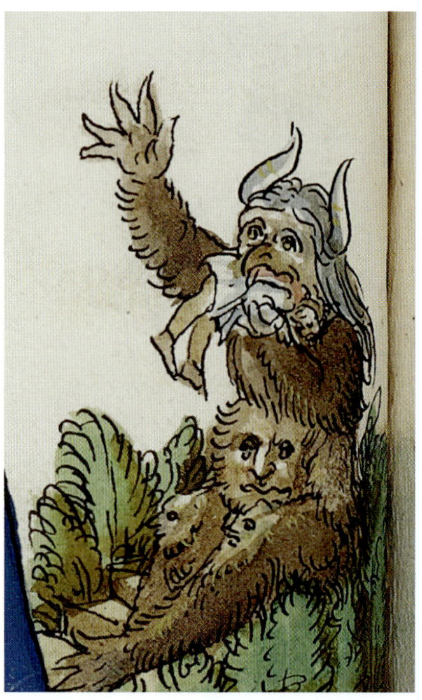

Figure 15.11b: The float of 1516, showing a horned devil devouring souls (detail), in *Schembart Buch*. Folio 51v, second series, *c*.1540. Paper, 32.8cm × 21cm. Kerry Stokes Collection, Perth. LIB.2006.088.

It seems clear that Carnival was not simply a case of extreme festivity. Contemporary literature about Carnival, and especially the Carnival plays that were performed at this time, testify to that.[20] Carnival works with deep moral tensions in the human condition; it draws on the different human passions, many of them considered sinful. These are represented in many of the *Schembart* floats, through the ubiquity of folly, through the dances of the so-called Runners, through their aggressive attacks on individuals whom they snatch from the crowd and symbolically entrap in baskets.[21] We know

17   See the many references in Scribner, 'Reformation, Carnival and the World Turned Upside-Down'.
18   See, for example, Sumberg, *The Nuremberg Schembart Carnival*.
19   Küster, '*Spectaculum Vitiorum*'; Küster, 'Nürnberger Schembartlauf.'

20   Kinser, 'Presentation and Representation'; Küster, '*Spectaculum Vitiorum*'.
21   The demon and an old woman with baskets on their back can be observed in *Schempart Buech*, UCLA Library, Coll. 170, MS. 351.

from several descriptions that the Nuremberg Runners themselves also acted as pranksters and revellers. Their meeting place in the morning was frequently a tavern or inn, where they had their first drink, and then they also often dropped into brothels for a dance as they advanced through the city.[22] But ultimately, as the floats were burned and the participants dispersed in the denouement on the market place, they were subdued and vanquished, and society moved symbolically into the sombre and serious time of Lenten penance.

The broader meaning of *Schembart* and survival in the *Schembart* books

Carnival probably had quite different meanings for individual participants and observers, and maybe even for the same individual at different stages of a three-day festival that culminated in the *Schembart* dance and parade on Shrove Tuesday. The literary and historical analysis, however, suggests the following as the most important aspects.

(i)   It was a celebration of the city's history and identity, linking it to the tumultuous events of 1348–1349 through the Butchers' Dance

(ii) It provided a justification and legitimisation of Nuremberg's tight oligarchical form of government, in which the most ancient 'honourable' families were thought to rightly maintain their control

(iii) It offered an opportunity for the butchers' guild, especially in the early years, to celebrate its sense of internal cohesion as a kind of brotherhood, at a time when there were strong challenges to the city's traditions by outsiders and immigrants

(iv) It was a time for communal festivity and celebration in line with changes in the seasons of nature and also in the church year

(v)   It represented an occasion to reflect, possibly in hindsight, on supernatural realities and deep moral tensions within the human condition, the push and pull of desire and its consequences

(vi) Finally, it provided a social safety valve, a moment in a society's life when social restrictions were relaxed, passions were given free reign, when riot, violence and sin were tolerated, when society was ritualistically and symbolically and temporarily overturned – until the proper social order was returned and re-enshrined.[23]

While we know Carnival usually worked as a safety valve, it could also at times encourage and facilitate social disturbance and disorder. During the conflicts that swept across many south and central German territories in 1524 and 1525 that we customarily call the Peasants' War, the beginnings of social unrest in some localities coincided with the period of Carnival. The Nuremberg patricians were well aware of this. From mid-1524, peasant revolts broke out on the northern border of Nuremberg's territory, and then for a short moment even penetrated the quarter of the city populated by many of its low-paid workers, precisely at a time when the city was having to control the protests and social upheavals associated with the movement for religious reform. The city government decided to close down the *Schembart* as dangerous to law and order: in March of 1525, after a debate in the Town Hall at which the city formally adopted the Lutheran brand of Church Reform throughout its territory, it also banned the *Schembart* for that year.

22   Sumberg, *The Nuremberg Schembart Carnival*, pp. 90–92.

23   See especially Scribner, 'Reformation, Carnival and the World Turned Upside-Down,' pp. 314–29; Davis, 'The Reasons of Misrule'.

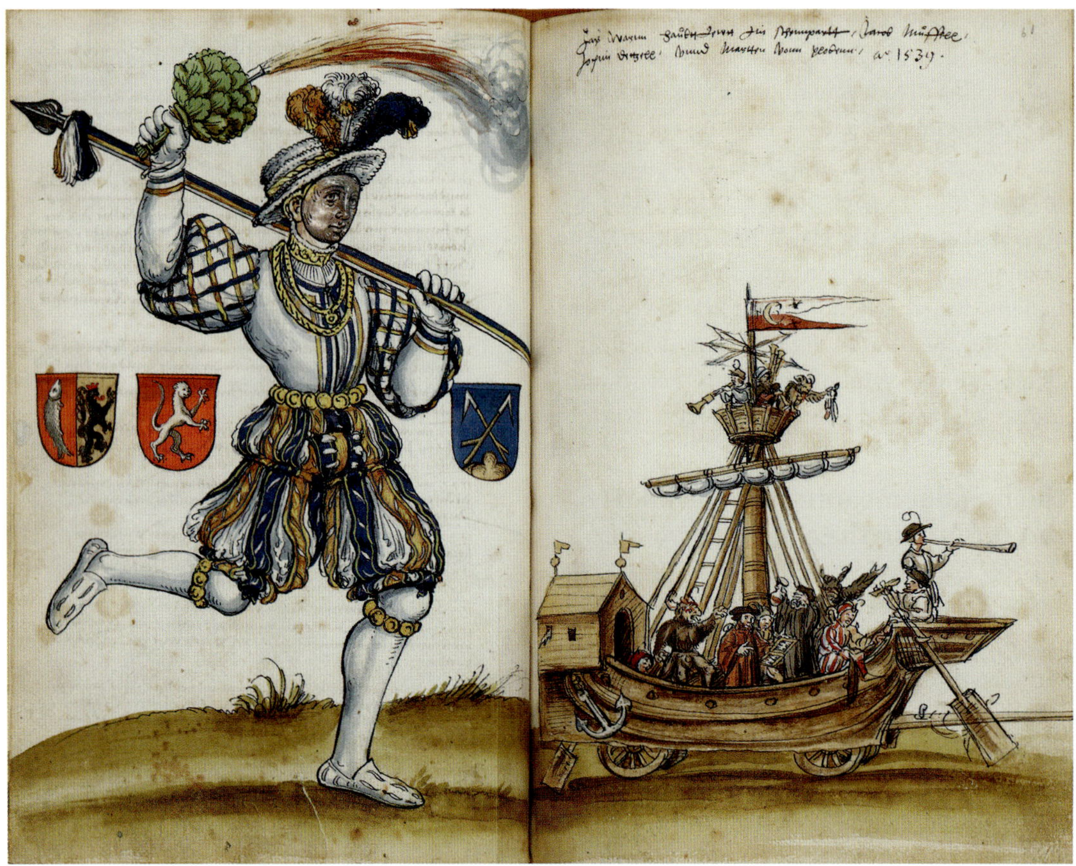

Figure 15.12: Runners' costume for 1539, with the arms of captains Jacob Muffel, Joachim Tetzel and Martin von Plowen; the float for 1539, a ship of fools with Pastor Andreas Osiander, in *Schembart Buch*. Folios 60v–61, *c.*1540. Paper, 32.8cm × 21cm. Kerry Stokes Collection, Perth. LIB.2006.088.

In fact, it turned out that the ban remained in place not only for that year, but for the next fourteen years. After much pleading from some Nuremberg citizens, the city fathers permitted the *Schembart* to take place again in 1539.[24] But the captains for that year – Jacob Muffel, Joachim Tetzel, and Martin von Plowen – used the event to attack the city's leading Lutheran preacher, Andreas Osiander, one of the key figures who had introduced the Reformation in the city in 1525 (Figure 15.12). On the deck of the ship of fools they placed a figure of Osiander holding a backgammon board, a reference to the gaming pleasures he had condemned in recent sermons. Surrounding him were fools, devils and a physician with a urine glass – parodying Osiander's claim in a sermon that faith rather than medicine would save Christians from the plague. In some of the *Schembart* manuscripts Osiander is also shown holding a key, a reference to his claims about the rights of the Lutheran clergy to absolve from sin and also excommunicate. In the Kerry Stokes *Schembart* Book, the keys are being dropped by a devil in the crow's nest.[25] The

24   For the following, Sumberg, *The Nuremberg Schembart Carnival*, pp. 176–183.

25   The keys are very clear in a Bodleian *Schembart* Book of *c.*1590–1640: MS Douce 346, folio 258.

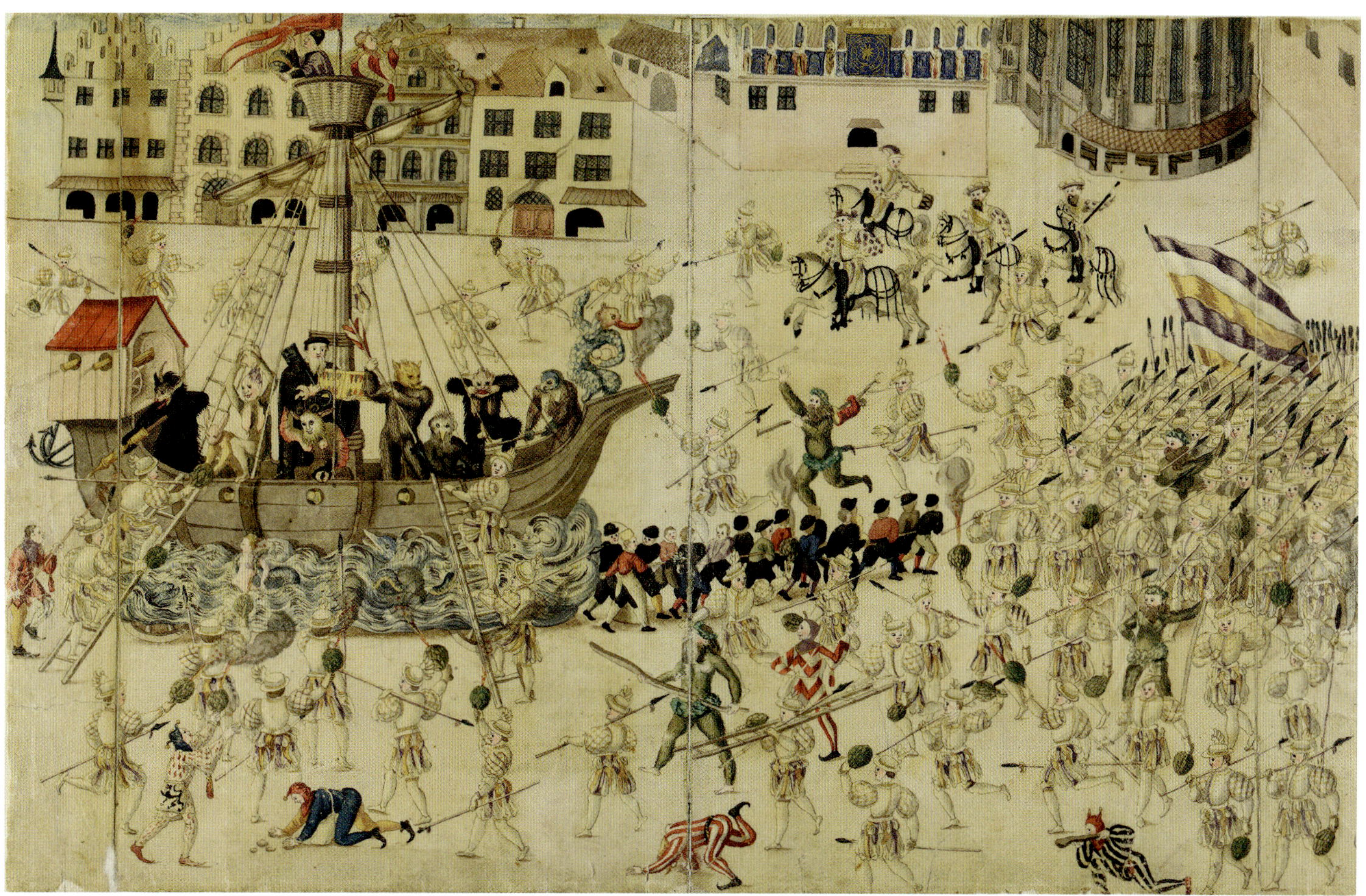

Figure 15.13: The storming of the 1539 float, a ship of fools in the Nuremberg market place, in *Schempart Buech*. Folio II, mid-sixteenth century. Stadtbibliothek, Nuremberg. Nor. K. 444.

crescent and star on the pennant would have identified this as a Turkish ship, the traditional enemy of Christianity – especially in the 1530s, when the Hapsburg Emperors were at war with the Ottomans, who less than a decade earlier in 1529 had advanced as far as the walls of Vienna.

This must have truly been a magnificent float and it is found in many of the *Schembart* books. In some cases the illustration offers a panoramic view of the market place (Figure 15.13), depicting the patrician houses with their shops below, at top left; and from top right, the town hall, the large east choir of the main parish church of St Sebald with its row of shops facing the square, and then the *Alte Schau*, the institution in which the quality of gold, silver, precious metals, lead, pearls and coral were weighed, tested, melted and regulated, and fundamental in particular for the exchange of various types of international currency by merchants and traders. There the parody of the city preacher was continued until the float was ritually stormed and destroyed by the Runners and attendant fools and other grotesque figures, bringing to an end the *Schembart* not only for 1539, but for all time. The mockery of Osiander, as well as the physical attacks on his house that occurred later in that evening, served to confirm for Osiander and his followers on the Council that the *Schembart* was nothing less than a pagan and also Catholic survival displeasing to God. He succeeded in having the city government ban it permanently. Carnival had become too dangerous;

society's safety valve was no longer safe, and the passions of the Nuremberg citizens had to be held in check.

One of the consequences of the government's decision, however, was that patrician families, now banned from their street celebration, began to celebrate the *Schembart* virtually – on paper. They clearly looked back on that period with considerable nostalgia, especially as the critical political and cultural position of Nuremberg in the Holy Roman Empire began to wane a little after the Peace of Augsburg in 1555, and even more so during the years of the Thirty Years War in the first half of the seventeenth century. But that combination – nostalgia for the past, pride in family honour, a tight oligarchical state, and a socially and morally cautious and paternalistic government that was ceding much of its power to the Duchy of Bavaria – came together to give us the *Schembart* Carnival on paper. From 1539 through to the eighteenth century Nuremberg families began to produce the manuscripts that re-lived and re-presented that combination of nostalgia, pride, honour and flamboyance in their *Schembart* books, which both give us pleasure and also offer quite unusual insights into the social and cultural life of Nuremberg and other European societies in the late Middle Ages. The Stokes *Schembart* Book is one of the very fine examples of this genre.

About the author

Charles Zika is Professorial Fellow in History at the University of Melbourne, and Chief Investigator in the Australian Research Council Centre of Excellence for the History of Emotions. His recent books include *The Appearance of Witchcraft: Print and Visual Culture in Sixteenth-Century Europe* (2007); *Celebrating Word and Image 1250–1600* (with Margaret Manion, 2013);

and *Disaster, Death and the Emotions in the Shadow of the Apocalypse, 1400–1700* (edited with Jenny Spinks, 2016). c.zika@unimelb.edu.au

Works cited

Peter Burke, *Popular Culture in Early Modern Europe* (London: Temple Smith, 1978).

Christie's, *The History of the Book: The Cornelius J. Hauck Collection, New York, 27–28 June 2006* (New York: Christie's, 2006).

Natalie Zemon Davis, 'The Reasons of Misrule: Youth Groups and Charivaris in Sixteenth-century France', *Past and Present*, 50 (1971), pp. 41–75.

Samuel Kinser 'Presentation and Representation: Carnival at Nuremberg, 1450–1550', *Representations*, 13 (1986), pp. 1–41.

Jürgen Küster, *'Spectaculum Vitiorum': Studien zur Intentionalität und Geschichte des Nürnberger Schembartlaufes* (Remscheid: Ute Kierdorf, 1983).

Jürgen Küster, 'Nürnberger Schembartlauf', *Historisches Lexikon Bayerns*, 2012, accessed 16 July 2017 at http://www.historisches-lexikon-bayerns.de/artikel/artikel_45244.

Herbert Maas, 'Schembart und Fasnacht: eine Rückkehr zu alten Deutungen,' *Mitteilungen des Vereins für Geschichte der Stadt Nürnberg*, 80 (1993), pp. 147–59.

Margaret M. Manion, ed., *An Illumination: The Rothschild Prayer Book and other works from the Kerry Stokes Collection, c.1280–1685* (West Perth: Australian Capital Equity, 2015).

Margaret M. Manion and Charles Zika, *Celebrating Word and Image 1250–1600. Illuminated Manuscripts from the Kerry Stokes Collection* (Perth: Australian Capital Equity and Fremantle Press, 2013).

Nigel Morgan and Stella Panayotova, 'Fitzwilliam Museum MS 382. Schönbartbuch,' in *A Catalogue of Western Book Illumination in the Fitzwilliam Museum and the Cambridge Colleges, Illuminated Manuscripts in Cambridge*, Vol. 1, ed. by Nigel Morgan and Stella Panayotova (London & Turnhout: Harvey Miller Publishers, 2009), pp. 232–36.

Dietz-Rüdiger Moser, *Fastnacht, Fasching, Karneval: das Fest der 'verkehrten Welt'* (Graz: Kaleidoskop im Verlag Styria, 1986).

Dietz-Rüdiger Moser, '"Schembart"-Scharmützel; Dietz-Rüdiger Moser antwortet auf Wolfgang Brückner: die "Höllen" werden Höllen bleiben,' *Literatur in Bayern*, 47 (1997), pp. 28–35.

Birgit Münch, 'Wo seyd ihr Kinder, Wo? Spielarten des Kinderfresser-Motivs zwischen Mythologie, schwarzer Pädagogik und unerfüllter Mutterschaft,' in *Monster:*

Fantastische Bilderwelten zwischen Grauen und Komik, ed. by Peggy Große et al. (Nuremberg: Germanisches Nationalmuseum, 2015), pp. 291–295.

Gerhard Pfeiffer, ed., *Nürnberg – Geschichte einer europäischen Stadt* (Munich: Beck, 1971).

Marcia Reed, 'Schempart Buech,' in *The World from Here: Treasures of the Great Libraries of Los Angeles*, ed. by Cynthia Burlingham and Bruce Whiteman (Los Angeles: Getty Publications, 2001), pp. 158–59.

Marcia Reed, 'Fireworks and Fish Baskets: The Schembart Festival in Nuremberg,' *Getty Research Journal*, 4 (2012), pp. 145–52.

Emil Reicke, *Geschichte der Reichsstadt* (Nuremberg: Raw, 1896).

Hans Ulrich Roller, *Der Nürnberger Schembartlauf: Studien zum Fest- und Maskenwesen des späten Mittelalters* (Tübingen: Tübinger Vereinigung für Volkskunde, 1965).

Robert Scribner, 'Reformation, Carnival and the World Turned Upside-Down,' *Social History* 3 (1978), pp. 303–329.

Jeffrey Chipps Smith, *Nuremberg, A Renaissance City, 1500–1618* (Austin: University of Texas Press, 1983).

Gerald Strauss, *Nuremberg in the Sixteenth Century: City Politics and Life between Middle Ages and Modern Times* (Bloomington: Indiana University Press, 1976).

Samuel Leslie Sumberg, *The Nuremberg Schembart Carnival: With Sixty Reproductions from a Manuscript in the Nuremberg Stadtbibliothek, Ms Nor. K. 444*, 2nd ed. (New York: AMS Press, 1966).

Charles Zika, 'Nuremberg: the City and its Culture in the Early Sixteenth Century,' in *Dürer in the National Gallery of Victoria*, ed. by Irena Zdanowicz (Melbourne: National Gallery of Victoria, 1994), pp. 28–44.

Index